MASTERING THE **SAS** SYSTEM

MASTERING THE SAS SYSTEM

Second Edition

Jay A. Jaffe, Ph.D.

INTERNATIONAL THOMSON COMPUTER PRESS

I(T)P™ An International Thomson Publishing Company

London • Bonn • Boston • Johannesburg • Madrid • Melbourne • Mexico City • New York • Paris
Singapore • Tokyo • Toronto • Albany, NY • Belmont, CA • Cincinnati, OH • Detroit, MI

Library of Congress Cataloging-in-Publication Data
Jaffe, Jay.
    Mastering the SAS system / Jay A. Jaffe.—2nd ed.
        p. cm.
    Includes index.
    1. SAS (Computer file) 2. Mathematical statistics—Data processing. I. Title.
QA276.4.J34   1993
519.5'0285'53—dc20

93-12397
CIP

Contents

Preface   **ix**

Part I: Fundamentals   1

Chapter 1. The SAS System   3
    What Is "The SAS System?"   4
    SAS Datasets and SAS Files   6
    The Course of a SAS Job   11

Chapter 2. The ABCs of SAS Programming   14
    SAS Statements   14
    Writing Readable SAS Code   24
    SAS Errors   28

Chapter 3. Creating SAS Datasets   30
    The DATA Statement   30
    Referring to External Input Files   33
    Reading Raw Data: The INPUT Statement   36
    Data Step Iteration   47
    Record Selection   48
    Variable Selection   53
    The Assignment Statement   55
    INPUT: Repeated Execution   57
    Variable Attributes   60

Chapter 4. Rebuilding SAS Datasets   66
Data Step Processes and the Program Data Vector   67
Rebuilding a Single Dataset   70
Working with More Than One Dataset   78
Sorting and Rebuilding by Subgroups   86

Chapter 5. SAS Procedures   93
Common PROC Step Statements   95
Common Descriptive and Display Procedures   98
Using WHERE Conditions to Select Observations   119

Chapter 6. The SAS Job Log   124
Overview of the SAS Log   124
SAS Log Components   126
Writing Notes to the SAS Log   130

Part II: Constructing SAS Datasets   135

Chapter 7. Missing Values   137
Assigning Missing Values   138
Missing Values and SAS Procedures   139
Special Missing Values   141
Comparison of Missing Values   142
Missing Values Generated by the Data Step Compiler   143
Character Missing Values   144

Chapter 8. Input Tailoring   146
INFILE Statement Options   146
The INPUT Statement: Additional Features   153
More SAS Informats   157
Date/Time Informats   160
User-Defined Informats   161

Chapter 9. Selecting and Summarizing Observations   166
WHERE Processing in the Data Step   167
Direct Access to Observations   168
Summarizing Data in the Data Step   174
The SUMMARY Procedure   176

Chapter 10. Combining, Dividing, and Updating Observations   188
Dividing Observations   188
Combining Observations: Merge Statement Variations   189
Combining Observations: Multiple SET Statements   208

Updating Observations   214
Modifying Datasets in Place   217

Chapter 11. SAS Formats   226
Standard Numeric Formats   227
Character Formats   231
Date/Time Formats   233
User-Defined Formats   237

Part III: Base SAS Procedures   257

Chapter 12. Procedures for Describing Data   259
The CORR Procedure   259
The UNIVARIATE Procedure   262
The TABULATE Procedure   265

Chapter 13. Procedures for Displaying Data   279
The Chart Procedure   279
The TIMEPLOT Procedure   294
The REPORT Procedure   300

Chapter 14. Utility Procedures   315
SAS Library Management   316
SAS Catalog Management   329
Appending SAS Data Files   332
Data Verification Using PROC COMPARE   333
Printing Special Forms   335
An Introduction to the *SQL* Procedure   337
Transposing Dataset Observations   348

Part IV: More DATA Step Programming   353

Chapter 15. SAS Functions   355
Function Terms   355
Numeric Functions   356
Character Functions   360
Date/Time Functions   369
Formatting Functions   372

Chapter 16. Flow of Control   375
Conditional Choice of Action   375
Repeated Action   379
Transfer of Control   398

Chapter 17. Custom Output   406
The FILE Statement   406
Writing External Files   408
Custom Reports   416

Chapter 18. A SAS-Based Business System   425
Designing Our SAS-Based System   425
System Implementation   428

Part V: The SAS Macro Language   449

Chapter 19. SAS Macros: Basic Concepts and Methods   451
Macros: Reasons Why   451
The SAS Macro Facility   455
Macro Programming   466
Macro Errors; Macros and the SAS Log   490

Chapter 20. More Macro Processing Features   501
Macro Variable Resolution   501
Macro Variable Reference Environments   506
Automatic "System" Macro Variables   511
Macro Quoting and Quoting Functions   511
Information Exchange with the Data Step   522

Part VI: Using the SAS System   535

Chapter 21. Base SAS Features   537
SAS System Options   538
Configuring the SAS System   544
Data Step Views   546
Compressed Data Files   547
Indexed Datasets   548
Precompilation   549

Chapter 22. SAS User Resources   553
SAS Software Documentation   553
Getting Help with the SAS System   557
SAS "Add-On" Program Products   558

Index   563

Preface

The user new to the SAS System often despairs of the weight of its documentation manuals. In their encyclopedic endeavor, the manuals can confound and confuse novice SAS users. *Mastering the SAS System* is offered as an antidote to that confusion. The user who has already become familiar with the SAS System by determined effort may gain new insights from *Mastering the SAS System,* insights into what s/he's been doing and, perhaps, how to do it a little better. The SAS System really *does* make sense: There is pattern in it.

The SAS System is exciting to write about precisely because it is so often misunderstood. It is a challenge to organize and present SAS software step-by-step, that others may learn about it. This book, if its serves its purpose, will illuminate and elucidate. It is meant not to replace the SAS manuals, but to get the reader off the ground and on the fast track in using the Base SAS software.

In the three years that have passed since the publication of the first edition of this book, which was based on SAS Version 5, the SAS System has undergone some far-reaching changes. Surely (thought I), I would have to serve up a revised work when SAS Version 6 was finally ripe. Van Nostrand Reinhold had plenty of faith in the title: the first edition had held strong in sales, despite the fact that after its publication a surge of competition followed. Some of that competition had more provocative titles on more eyecatching covers, some of it was published or pushed by SAS Institute in its direct mail; still, we held our own.

There were no two ways about it, and with the release of SAS 6.07, Version 6 could at last be considered mature. The time to write the second edition of *Mastering the SAS System* had finally come.

So here you are.

This edition has been updated in its entirety to reflect the new standard, through Versions 6.07 and 6.08. Since the text is designed for all SAS users, and since at this point in history I assume most users have moved at least to Version 6.07—and I urge you Version 5 *and 6.06* stragglers to do so right away—I have not attempted to distinguish new features from old but have integrated the new features in seamlessly as co-equal parts of "The SAS System" as it is today. Within the Base SAS software Version 6.08 adds very little over Version 6.07, which is and will remain the touchstone Version 6 standard. Indeed, the Base SAS changes between 6.07 and 6.08 are so minor that none needed elaboration in the scope of this book, and the reader may remain confident that our material holds for 6.07 as well as for subsequent Version 6 releases.

It was tempting to write about some of the interesting aspects of the SAS System under OS/MVS. But again, this text is designed for all SAS users. Therefore, with rare exceptions, I have not delved into features that are specific to any particular operating system, but have limited discussion to those software features that apply to all operating editions of the SAS System. Program samples used in this book were written to the 6.07 standard and the source code will operate across platforms, if with occasional small differences in the appearance of the output. The actual program output listings used in this book were produced, with a few exceptions, under SAS Release 6.08 TS402 (Developer's Beta) for the Windows 3.1 operating system running on a 486-class personal computer.

I welcome your comments. Write me:

> Jay A. Jaffe
> POB 31652
> Walnut Creek, CA 94598

part I

FUNDAMENTALS

1

The SAS System

According to the introduction to one of the SAS software manuals: "The SAS System is a software system for data analysis. The goal of SAS Institute [the company that publishes the SAS System] is to provide data analysts one system to meet all their computing needs." Indeed, from modest beginnings twenty years ago the SAS System is now serving business, government, and educational institutions at thousands of locations worldwide. Viable on many computer systems from desktops up to the most powerful mainframe, the SAS System is used to enter, manipulate, and manage data of all kinds; to provide not only printouts but plots, charts, and technical graphs; to undertake complex statistical analysis; even to monitor the performance of computer systems themselves. While the day has not arrived that the SAS System is perceived by all data analysts as "one system to meet all their computing needs," the SAS software line has some prominent strengths that account for its popularity across a wide range of applications.

This chapter provides a quick tour of the SAS System and the SAS approach to data management and programming. It is a very quick tour indeed, and you may find it thick or overly theoretical. If so, simply jump right ahead to Chapter 2, where we begin the practical study of SAS programming. But if you do so, be sure to come back to this chapter at some time, so you can understand your practice in proper context.

WHAT IS "THE SAS SYSTEM?"

The SAS System is a set of interrelated software products that contains a full-featured language translator, strong data management utilities, powerful statistical applications programs, and the ability to communicate across operating systems and even to non-SAS application systems. It is, of course, the statistical, "stat-pack" functionality that gained the SAS System its early fame. But accounting for its wider success is the performance of its programming language and data-handling features.

At the heart of the SAS System is the *Base SAS software,* which contains the *SAS supervisor* (the control program which works closely with the computer's operating system to manage hardware and software resources during the course of a SAS job), the DATA Step Language compiler, input/output access methods ("engines"), a number of SAS *procedures* (subprograms that easily take care of complex computing or data processing tasks), and other services required or desirable for SAS data processing.

Many specialized features can be added to the Base SAS software, licensed in various "SAS program products" which generally consist of collections of related procedures. There are procedures for full-screen data entry, terminal/plotter graphics, advanced statistics, specialized statistics (e.g., econometrics, operations research), communication with other software systems, and other purposes. Those products which your company licences and to which you have computer access along with the Base software, together comprise the *your* own "SAS System." Chapter 22 includes a short description of many of the SAS program products, and tells you how to find out which may be already available at your site.

The Base SAS Software

The Base SAS software (informally herein, the "Base software") provides the central facilities of the SAS System. The Display Manager interface is one of these. Other services of the Base software are introduced below, and we will be concerned with the Base SAS software through the remainder of this book.

The SAS Supervisor

The SAS supervisor is the name by which the control program that handles a SAS interactive session or noninteractive program is known. The supervisor takes control from the computer operating system, whereafter as far as your session or program is concerned, the SAS supervisor *is* the operating system. SAS applications are directed by and extract services from the supervisor. The supervisor handles abnormal error conditions that may not be the responsibility of any one SAS System component, controls what is written to the SAS log (printable output that serves to document the course of a SAS job; we'll study the SAS log in Chapter 6), and keeps tabs on the state of global or "system" options that the installation or the user may specify.

The SAS user need not be concerned with the internal workings of the SAS supervisor. However, it can be helpful to understanding the concepts of SAS data processing to reflect on the fact that the operation of various components of the SAS System is coordinated and managed as a logical whole.

Data Access Engines

The Base software provides several access mechanisms with which to deal with physical data. The impressive phrase *multiple engine architecture* is sometimes used to denote the fact that SAS software is designed to handle SAS data in a standard fashion (from the user's point of view), regardless of the underlying methods it uses to wrestle with this or that computer or operating system.

There is nothing you, the user, must actually do in your programs with respect to SAS data access engines. The emphasis on engines and on multiple engine architecture (MEA) seen in SAS documentation has little practical implication for the average SAS user. It simply means that SAS data models, and SAS program code, can be expected to behave in the same way from one computer system to another.*

The DATA Step Language Compiler

As will be explained later in this chapter, SAS programs are often divided into several segments or "steps", each of which is either a "DATA step" or a "PROC step". A DATA step is written in a computer language, which we will call the SAS DATA Step Language.† The Base SAS software includes a compiler which takes what you have written in the DATA Step Language and turns it into a sequence of instructions the computer can execute.

The DATA Step Language is a full-featured, high-level computer language, with especially powerful data-reading, -selecting, and -combining abilities. The number one learning priority for the user wishing to master the SAS System— and therefore, the major emphasis of this book—has to be DATA Step Language programming.

Base Software Procedures

SAS procedures are subprograms that may be invoked within a larger SAS program by the user's encoding of a PROC step. Each procedure has a well-defined task or set of related tasks.

---

*The user documentation appears to reflect, perhaps unconsciously, the central importance of MEA to the software designers and engineers who developed Version 6 and who continue to refine and revise the SAS System. To these individuals, MEA is key to the transportability not only of SAS programs, but of the SAS System itself, between various computers and operating systems.

†SAS documentation tends to use the more general term "SAS language" to refer to the DATA Step Language, but SAS programs may include source code logically outside the DATA Step Language.

The procedures shipped with the Base SAS software are used to print data in a variety of forms, to enact data summaries and statistical analyses, and to do numerous tasks useful for the management and care of programs and data. Base SAS procedures are the topic of Chapter 5 and Part III of this book.

The Macro Facility

Like some other computer programming systems, the SAS System includes a *preprocessor* that takes a look at a program's source code and may alter it (in effect) before the underlying language syntax parsers kick in. The SAS preprocessor is known as the SAS *Macro Facility*.

As preprocessors go, the SAS Macro Facility is very well-developed and versatile. Besides allowing the user's program to include code segments from other sources and to convert symbolic to explicit code, its *Macro Language* can be used to emit detailed code as specified by the user or by existing program conditions, when and where the situation warrants. The Macro Facility and Macro Language programming are explored in depth in Part V of this book.

SAS DATASETS AND SAS FILES

SAS Datasets

A SAS dataset is a data model, that is, a consistent logical description of information layout that is independent of the particular ways the data may physically be stored. As a SAS user, you need not know how the SAS access engines actually store and retrieve information from physical media, any more than you need to know exactly how programs and data are held in the computer as your program runs. You *do* need to know how to make your program communicate to the SAS System about data manipulation, and to do so you must understand the SAS dataset model.

A SAS dataset represents the information contained in a given collection of data thought of as an abstract rectangular grid (see Figure 1.1). The columns of the grid represent *variables*, or categories of information,* while the rows represent a set of variables' values (instances of information), each set called an *observation*. In a SAS dataset, each observation row contains a particular value for every variable associated with the dataset.† As an example, your own checkbook could be entered into a SAS dataset with the variables date, payee, amount, and (possibly) memo, each observation representing one check. As another example,

---

*A SAS variable is of one of two basic storage types: numeric or character. Numeric variables represent numbers (of course), while character variables represent strings of one or more letters, numerals, or punctuation.

†Users familiar with the relational database model will appreciate the analogy between a SAS dataset and a database table.

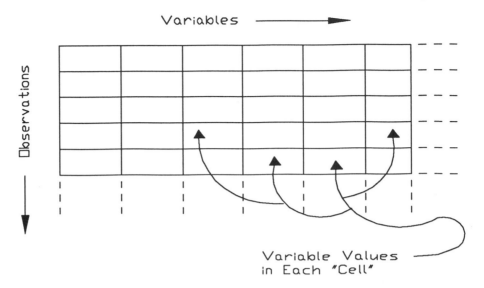

Figure 1.1. A SAS dataset, as if a rectangle of observations (rows) and variables (columns). All rows have the same cells; in each resides a particular value of a variable.

information giving name, address, birthdate, height, weight, and hair color, as might appear on a driver's license, might be entered into a SAS dataset with variables for each information category (name, address, etc.), each observation representing one license.

A SAS dataset is implemented as a computer file* in one of several storage models. The standard storage model is the *SAS data file*. A SAS data file contains actual data values, as laid out for a particular access method, and a header or *descriptor* area which contains information the SAS System needs in order to "understand" how to deal with the dataset and its component observations. Data in a *native SAS data file* are formatted by some version of the SAS System, and take the form thought best by the system designers and accessed with one of the native SAS data engines. Figure 1.2 gives an abstract view of a native SAS data file. Data in an *interface data file* are formatted by another software system that SAS Institute has chosen to support by building an access engine that can handle the data directly without conversion to native SAS form.

The actual data values comprising a SAS dataset may be stored in one or more physical files dissociated from the dataset descriptor information. In this case the storage model is that of the *SAS data view*. When accessing a dataset as a SAS data view, the SAS System uses information in the view descriptor to locate and

---

*In computer jargon, a "file" generally connotes a collection of information organized in some specified manner and stored on computer-readable medium such as magnetic disk or tape. A SAS file is a file that is created and used by the SAS System.

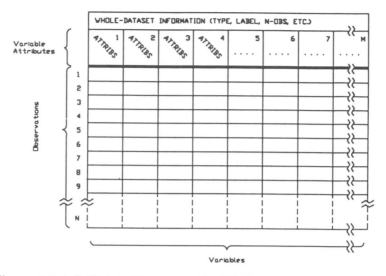

Figure 1.2 A SAS data file, as a grid of N observations of M variables' values: each "cell" contains a value of one variable in one observation. General information about the variables (name, type, other attributes) and about the dataset as a whole (name, optional label, type, creation history) are also stored. The data-value part of a SAS data file is "rectangular" in that each observation is identically laid out to every other, with the same variables in the same order; the values, of course, may differ.

put together the actual data that comprise the logical dataset.* Various non-SAS databases may be accessible to SAS programs via *interface data views* created by SAS/Access software. The SQL procedure, which we overview briefly in Chapter 14, produces *native SAS data views* that mimic the result of SQL queries with respect to one or more other SAS datasets (files or views). The DATA Step Language, which is often used to create native SAS files, can also be used to define a type of native view called a *DATA Step view*. DATA Step views can be of significant benefit to users interested in conserving computing resources, as explained in Chapter 21.

Besides descriptor information and data values, SAS datasets created by one of the Version 6 native engines may be associated with one or more dataset *indexes* that can improve efficiency in accessing the data. Dataset indexes are also discussed in Chapter 21.

Again, whether it is represented as a native file, an interface file, or some type of view, because the SAS System access engines take care of the details, a SAS program can obtain and use the information in a SAS dataset with little or no

---

*You can imagine a SAS data view as the top portion of the illustration in Figure 1.2, above the heavy line. Note that a data view is still a SAS "file" in that it is stored on computer medium in an organized way; it just does not contain the data that it describes.

regard for how it is actually stored. The logical model remains consistent, and only in a very few places in this book—and in your practice of SAS programming —will it be necessary to distinguish between the true forms of SAS datasets.

Other SAS Files

In discussing SAS datasets, we have introduced two of the most important types of SAS file: the SAS data file and the SAS view. The SAS System makes use of a few other types of files as well. Those that are in use as of Version 6.07 are listed below, for your general information, after which we will have little more to say about any of them during the course of this book. Your study of SAS programming will revolve around the SAS dataset model as far as data representation is concerned.

Access descriptors are SAS files created by SAS/Access software. They contain data that the interface engine may use to implement an access view. Discussion of access descriptors would go beyond the scope of this book.

Stored programs are another kind of SAS file. These contain compiled code produced by a DATA Step program. As we will see in Chapter 21, stored programs can make SAS data processing more efficient in some circumstances.

SAS catalogs are a kind of SAS file that may contain within them one or many components. A component of a SAS catalog is called a catalog entry, and there are many different types of possible entries. SAS catalog architecture allows the SAS System to handle a wide variety of data structures in collections that are manageable by standard access methods. Some kinds of catalog entries are created and used by the Base SAS software or its procedures; other kinds serve the purposes of add-on products or their procedures. A type designation, which becomes part of each entry's name,* identifies the entry type; for example, a type of SOURCE identifies an entry that contains stored program source code.

Most kinds of SAS catalog entries can be moved about by the user, using methods such as the CATALOG procedure (Chapter 14). Some SAS catalog entry types, such as source code or program output, are created at the direction of the user; most are created by the SAS System or a SAS procedure for its own purposes. Some entire catalogs are used for special purposes, and may be subject to certain usage restrictions. Base SAS examples include user profile catalogs, format catalogs, and catalogs containing compiled macros. Sometimes, these catalogs are required to have certain special names (such as SASMACR for compiled macros).

SAS Libraries

SAS files (including data files and views) are stored in SAS *libraries*, each of which may include one or more files, of one or more types. This organization offers both greater convenience and, in most cases, greater efficiency than if there were no way to aggregate SAS files. The library data model does not depend on a

---

*File names are discussed more fully below.

particular operating system; the user need not, under normal circumstances, be concerned with the true physical methods the SAS System uses to collect and arrange files.

Member files in SAS libraries have unique names to distinguish them from other members of the same library. Each file also has a member type designation, e.g., DATA (SAS data files), VIEW (SAS data views), PGM (stored programs), and CATALOG.

A name called a library name or (in SAS jargon) a *libname* may be associated with a SAS library, either prior to SAS invocation or dynamically during the SAS program or session using the SAS LIBNAME statement (as we will see later on in this book). The libref is not a fixed, "real" name like a file name, but only an alias that is associated with the library for the purpose of the SAS session or program. But once a library is identified to the SAS program, files within the library may then be referred to by a "two-level" name, one part being the libref and the other the actual file name.* We will talk more about file names—particularly, SAS dataset names—in Chapter 3.

Certain SAS library names are (or should be) reserved to designate special libraries. The libname WORK, for example, normally refers to the library where SAS data files created for use during the present program only reside, and not stored permanently.

In Chapter 14, we will discuss ways to manage the contents of SAS libraries, in case you need to do so. Normally, however, you can study SAS data processing, and do most of your actual SAS work, with little attention to library organization.

SAS Execution Environments

SAS programs can be run interactively either in "line mode" or by using the full-screen SAS user interface (called the SAS *Display Manager System* (DMS), or, informally, the Display Manager). Nowadays, with the almost universal deployment of full-screen display devices and the advent of the Display Manager, line-mode interactive SAS is obsolescent.

Operating systems that support "batch" execution give users the choice of running their SAS programs alone or in batch. It is also generally possible to run a SAS program non-interactively but "in the foreground," having it run to completion while other work in the computer session is suspended. On mainframe systems, batch execution is generally more appropriate than foreground execution for large computing tasks. During program development and early testing, however, it is sometimes more productive to use the Display Manager environment.

---

*For example, under MVS a libname may be preassigned in batch using a DDNAME or with a TSO ALLOC FI() statement.

†Strictly speaking, the "full name" includes the file type as a third level, although the SAS System can usually pick this up from the context in which the two-level name is used. A SAS catalog entry has four levels in its full name: the libref, the file name, the entry name, and the entry type (the type can often be picked up by context).

DMS can be supplemented with programmer-written full-screen systems created within windowing techniques provided by DMS itself or by even more powerful user-interface development tools included in the SAS/FSP and SAS/AF products.*

THE COURSE OF A SAS JOB

In SAS jargon we refer to a SAS program from beginning to end as a SAS *job*, which is normally divided into one or more job *steps*.† Macro definitions, and a small number of SAS statements containing general directives, might be found outside step boundaries, but you should always think of SAS jobs as a series of steps. Each SAS job step is run to completion before the next one is begun.

There are two types of SAS job step: DATA steps, where data are read, stored, rearranged, and written in any way the user may specify using the SAS DATA Step Language, and PROC steps, which call upon the services of one of the SAS procedures. There is no minimum nor maximum number of DATA or PROC steps required in a SAS program, nor is there any special order: a program may have three DATA steps in a row, then a couple of PROC steps. Some programs may have but a single DATA step, others just a couple of PROC steps, and so on.

Without explaining it, for construction of SAS source code will be discussed in depth in the next chapter, we provide in Listing 1.1 the code for a simple SAS job. The listing contains comments by the author that were hand-edited in; in this book, author's comments within a listing appear in triple angle brackets (<<<comment>>>) so they will not be confused with actual computer-printed lines.

The example program is divided into three steps (one DATA, two PROC). It creates a SAS dataset in the DATA step (SAS datasets may also be created by PROC steps), and produces printed output from its two PROC steps (PROC steps may at times produce no output at all, and a DATA step may produce printed output). Listing 1.2 presents the printed results of the example program: a listing of the dataset, and some statistics describing the data.

---

*Programming the user interface goes beyond the scope of this book. Unfortunately, so too does a discussion of the Display Manager, even in general. Armed with your understanding of SAS programming provided with this book, however, you will be in an excellent position to "log on" to the Display Manager yourself and just have at it. Keep your *SAS Language* guide at hand; the primary documentation for the Display Manager is found therein. DMS also has a pretty extensive online help system that not only explains its own commands and windows but also provides a quick reference to various DATA Step statements and SAS procedures.

†Certain computer operating systems, such as MVS, also divide work into "jobs" and "steps." Do not get confused by the analogous terminology. A SAS job executes as a single MVS job step, and the SAS job steps within it have no meaning to MVS but only to the SAS supervisor.

```
<<< Sometimes your author will write a note >>>
<<< to say something about the program listings. >>>
<<< Anything in triple angle brackets is such ...>>>
<<< It was not printed by the computer, but typed in for this book. >>>



<<< PROGRAM SOURCE CODE FOLLOWS >>>

***** A SAS PROGRAM *****;
* THIS IS A COMMENT ON THE PROGRAM;
* IT IS PRECEDED BY AN ASTERISK,
   AND LIKE ALL SAS STATEMENTS, ENDS WITH A SEMICOLON;
************************;
DATA A; INPUT NAME $ HEIGHT WEIGHT AGE; CARDS;
JOEY 62 189 23
FRANNIE 54 121 30
BOBBY 59 172 19
JOY 51 108 17
RUN;
* NOW LET US PRINT IT;
PROC PRINT DATA=A; TITLE 'A Printout of our Data'; RUN;
* AND LET US FIND THE AVERAGES;
PROC MEANS DATA=A; TITLE 'Averages of our Data'; RUN;
```

Listing 1.1. Example of SAS source code

```
                    A Printout of our Data

        OBS     NAME        HEIGHT      WEIGHT      AGE

          1     JOEY          62          189        23
          2     FRANNIE       54          121        30
          3     BOBBY         59          172        19
          4     JOY           51          108        17

                    Averages of our Data
```

Variable	N	Mean	Std Dev	Minimum	Maximum
HEIGHT	4	56.5000000	4.9328829	51.0000000	62.0000000
WEIGHT	4	147.5000000	39.0939040	108.0000000	189.0000000
AGE	4	22.2500000	5.7373048	17.0000000	30.0000000

Listing 1.2. Example of SAS job output

Impressive results, for so simple a computer program! And of course, there's a lot more a SAS programmer can do, with techniques that are, really, only extensions of this simplicity. Perhaps the SAS System will become *your* "one system to meet all [your] computing needs."

2

The ABCs of
SAS Programming

SAS program source code is composed of SAS *statements*. There are many different kinds of SAS statements, some for the PROC step, some for the DATA step, some used in either step, and some whose effects transcend step boundaries. A SAS statement either commands a SAS program to take some action, modifies another action-oriented statement, or directs the SAS supervisor to impose some condition upon the program as it executes or upon the datasets that are being created or used.

In this chapter, we will look at how SAS statements are properly constructed. We will also examine SAS coding style: how statements are arranged to form an orderly program. Readers entirely inexperienced with SAS, and who do not program in another language, may find this concise presentation difficult. For now, just take an overview: There will be plenty of SAS code explained throughout this book.

SAS STATEMENTS

Though SAS statements differ widely in what they do, they all are constructed in accordance with certain well-specified rules. Some of these rules apply to all or most SAS statements. Other rules may be unique to one or a few statements.

SAS statements all end with the universal statement delimiter, a semicolon (;), and most SAS statements begin with a SAS statement identifier, a "name" that identifies the statement to the system. Here are some examples of SAS statements:

```
PROC FREQ DATA=GROUP1;

DATA SALES;

INFILE RAWSCORE END=EOF;

TABLES COST*CATEGORY / NOROW NOCOL;

NEWVALUE=PUT(TODAY,MMDDYY8.) || ': ' || PUT(VALUE,NEWVALF.);
```

The last one illustrated is an Assignment statement, beginning with a variable name (NEWVALUE). The others are named statements, and in discussions about the SAS System we refer to the statements by their names: we have just illustrated a "PROC statement," and a DATA, INFILE, and TABLES statement. The last one is an exception to the rule: it is called an Assignment statement (the givaway is the equals sign), and the word NEWVALUE is the name of a SAS dataset variable, not of a SAS statement.

In the program examples in this book we will generally use all uppercase to help distinguish program from text, and we will also show SAS names and other SAS keywords (special words that have meaning in statement syntax) in capitals when mentioned in text. But in your programs, SAS statements can be written in any combination of uppercase and lowercase letters, for SAS language parsers disregard alphabetic case when interpreting source code.

The SAS System also cares little about spacing within and between statements. SAS statements can begin anywhere on a data line, cut across several data lines, appear with other statements on the same line, have plenty of extra spaces, etc. Thus the following two segments of SAS code contain the same five statements and are exactly equivalent:

```
(1)     DATA FIRST;
            SET PRELIM;
            BY ITEM1 NOTSORTED;
            ITEM2 = ITEM1 + ROUND(COST) / (TIMEVAL * TIMEWGT);
        RUN;

(2)     DATA FIRST;SET PRELIM;BY ITEM1 NOTSORTED;
        ITEM2=ITEM1+ROUND(COST)
        /(TIMEVAL*TIMEWGT);RUN;
```

In this book, we will describe the syntax requirements of SAS statements using a standard, generalized form of illustration, a form similar (though not identical) to that used in the SAS manuals: Uppercase signifies words that should be used exactly as shown (remember that in "real" programs, you don't have to use uppercase if you don't want to), lowercase indicates the user must supply required information of a certain kind, items in square brackets ([ ]) are optional, items followed by an ellipsis (. . .) may be repeated more than once, and items separated by a vertical bar (|) are mutually exclusive alternatives. To eliminate ambiguity, when the ellipsis or vertical bar are used, the item(s) to which they refer will be enclosed in angle brackets (<>).* Symbols other than those just discussed should be coded exactly as shown. As an example,

```
XYZ <variable> | <ALL>;
```

means the statement being described consists of the exact word XYZ followed either by a variable name or the exact word ALL, and then a semicolon. Another example:

```
STMNT <variable>... [/ <NOOUT> | <OUT=datasetname>];
```

indicates that the "STMNT" statement begins with word STMNT, names at least one variable but may name more, and may be (but need not be) suffixed with a slash and then either NOOUT or else OUT= and some SAS dataset name. When it is easier to read and thus understand, we will use a plural word instead of an ellipsis to indicate one or more items of a certain kind, e.g., "variables" means one or more variable names (the same as "<variable>..."). For example, in Chapter 3, the DATA statement is generally described as

```
DATA [<datasetname[(datasetoptions)]>...];
```

which means it begins with the exact word DATA, ends with a semicolon, and may or may not have one or more dataset names, each of which may or may not have one or more dataset options named within a following set of parentheses. Occasionally, a SAS statement will require that repeated items be separated by commas, instead of the usual blanks. In such cases, an ellipsis will be used with a preceding comma (", ...").

Sometimes generalized elements will be used as pseudocode in SAS code examples, as well as in statement syntax descriptions. In such cases, the generalized elements will be written in lowercase. For example,

```
IF condition THEN DO;
```

means that in real SAS code, "condition" is not actually written, but something else; the text will provide an explanation of what that something called a "condition" is supposed to be.

---

*Besides their use as operators in expressions, which will never appear in a generalized statement description, angle brackets have only one very small place in the SAS language: as denominator enclosures in a TABLE statement under PROC TABULATE. In this book, their use in generalized statements should not mislead you.

Executable and Nonexecutable Statements

A distinction between "executable" and "nonexecutable" statements is important in understanding how SAS programs work. The majority of DATA step statements are *executable*: they demand the compiler to prepare code for an immediate action. *Nonexecutable* statements provide information to the SAS System but are not associated with a specific demand for immediate computational action. These include statements such as DROP, KEEP, LABEL, and TITLE. The information given in nonexecutable statements can alter the way the SAS System constructs datasets, prepares printouts, or otherwise takes care of business.

No syntactic difference distinguishes executable from nonexecutable statements; each statement must be studied and understood in its own right. You will, of course, learn many SAS statements as you study this book, and we will mention if a statement is nonexecutable.

Statement Domain

Also to be learned as you study individual SAS statements is where they may be used in your program code. Some SAS statements, such as SET, MERGE, INFILE, and many others, are meaningful only inside a DATA step. Others are meaningful only inside a specific PROC step; actually, a same-named statement in two different PROC steps may lead to very different actions. A few statements, such as FORMAT or LABEL, may be used in either DATA or PROC steps, and several, which we call *global* statements, can even be coded between steps. Global statements, such as TITLE, LIBNAME, and OPTIONS, normally continue in effect throughout the remainder of the program unless countermanded by another statement.

SAS Statement Elements

Besides an identifying name and the ubiquitous terminal semicolon, most SAS statements contain some combination of other statement elements, such as *statement modifiers*, *names*, *format identifiers*, *literals*, *labels*, *operators*, *function terms*, and *expressions*.

Statement Modifiers

SAS statement modifiers are words that, when used in certain contexts, signal the SAS system to make specific refinements to the way it carries out the instructions in the statement. To explain by example, consider the following SAS statements:

```
(1a) TABLES COUNT;

(1b) TABLES COUNT / NOPERCENT;

(2a) INFILE FILE1;

(2b) INFILE FILE1 END=EOF;
```

Statement 1a or 1b might appear in a FREQ procedure step (see Chapter 5). In 1b, the TABLES statement has been modified by the keyword NOPERCENT (some statements require modifiers to be placed after a slash). Similarly, Statement 2b contains the INFILE statement modifier END= bound to a variable name EOF. Statement modifiers do not, as a rule, have meaning for each and every statement. Again, it is only by studying each statement in its own right that you will come to learn its particular syntax and the meaning of any modifiers it may accept.

Most SAS statement modifiers are better known as statement *options*, because they instruct SAS to proceed with its work in a manner optionally chosen by the user. In this book, and in the SAS manuals, you will see phrases such as "the END= option of the INFILE statement" or "the NOPERCENT option of the TABLES statement."

Names

Anything in a SAS statement that is not a number, a special symbol, a literal (see below), a statement name, or a statement modifier, is likely to be a SAS *name*. SAS uses names to refer to SAS variables or datasets, informats and formats, arrays, and other things your program may need to identify individually. Some names, such as those associated with SAS-supplied formats, are provided for your use by the SAS System. Others, such as those associated with SAS variables and datasets, are chosen by the SAS user.

Most SAS names can be up to eight characters long, the first character being an underscore (_) or a letter, the remaining characters any combination of letters (case irrelevant: ABC=abc=AbC), underscores, and numerals. Names of SAS formats (see Chapter 11) have additional restrictions. No spaces are allowed within names, and no nonalphanumeric characters other than the underscore are allowed. The following are all valid SAS names: VAR1, PRUNES, X___32_, VALUE, THIS_ONE. The following are invalid:

PREDICTVAL	(too long, 10 chars: 8 is max)
12JAN86	(may not begin with numeral
THIS.ONE	(unallowed character: .)
THAT ONE	(embedded space)

Certain special variable and dataset names are reserved by the SAS System, which is to say they have a specific pre-defined meaning and cannot be chosen by you to mean something else. These names are few in number, and all begin and end with an underscore, for example _N_, _ERROR_, _NULL_. Never name a variable or dataset with a beginning and ending underscore, and you won't run into any reserved names by mistake.*

---

*Compared with other computer languages SAS is very tolerant of your using most anything for names, so long as the syntax of the statement renders your meaning exact. Thus the statement "INPUT INPUT;" would be perfectly valid: the first INPUT signifies the INPUT statement, and the second is a variable name.

Variable lists. Often, SAS statements contain lists of variables:

```
TABLES APPLE ORANGE PEAR LEMON;
```

SAS variable lists normally consist of variable names separated by blanks. As a convenience to the user, with a few exceptions the SAS System generally allows the list to be abbreviated, in one of the following ways.

1. If a set of variables is named with a constant character portion followed by an incrementing digit portion, you can abbreviate the list by connecting the first and the last of the variables with a single hyphen. For example, the statements

```
VAR DIR1 DIR2 DIR3 DIR4 DIR5 DIR6 DIR7;
```

and

```
VAR DIR1-DIR7;
```

are equivalent. In a DATA step, this abbreviation may be used whether or not the variables have yet been created, i.e., whether they have ever been named before; if not, they are created on the spot.

2. If a series of variables physically follow one another within a SAS dataset or DATA step program data vector (see Chapter 4), you can use a double hyphen abbreviation. Thus if the variables WEIGHT, HEIGHT, AGE, SEX, RACE, SCORE, and DETAIL are stored in a SAS dataset in that same order and with none in between (other variables may precede WEIGHT or follow DETAIL), then the statements

```
KEEP WEIGHT HEIGHT AGE SEX RACE SCORE DETAIL;
```

and

```
KEEP WEIGHT -- DETAIL;
```

are equivalent.

3. Refer only to variables of numeric type that lie physically between two variables by variation on the double hyphen, as follows:

```
KEEP WEIGHT-NUMERIC-DETAIL;
```

and similarly, refer to intervening character variables only with −CHARACTER−.

4. Refer to *all* variables in the program data vector with __ALL__, all numeric variables with __NUMERIC__, and all character variables with __CHARACTER__. For example, to drop all character type variables:

```
DROP _CHARACTER_;
```

Format Identifiers

The SAS System allows the values of variables to be output in different ways. For example, the number 1327.6 could be printed as $1,327.60. To do so, you invoke a SAS *format* by coding its *format identifier*, a special keyword that refers to a particular format.

Format identifiers are similar to SAS names, except they cannot end in a numeric digit, and they begin with a dollar sign if they refer to a character (not numeric) format. In use, they are immediately followed either by a single period, or by a number containing a decimal point. SAS formats are discussed in Chapter 11, where examples of format identifiers will be found.

Literals

A literal is a specific value appearing right in the program. When you write TEETH=27, 27 is a literal, TEETH a variable. Literals are also called *constants*. In SAS there are two fundamental types of constants, numeric and character, just as there are numeric and character variables.

A numeric literal is usually coded with a numeral, e.g., 1, 3, 38.2, 1927 (special case exceptions are hexadecimal numerics, and the date/time constants discussed elsewhere in this book). A character literal is usually a series of letters, digits, symbols, or a combination thereof, enclosed in single or double quotes. Character literals are usually used to assign values to character (string) variables, or to assign labels, titles, or footnotes for use in SAS output. Character literals, and the values of character variables, are not parsed by the SAS compiler or any procedure module (e.g., you could write A='PROC PRINT;' to get the string PROC PRINT; assigned to the character variable A). Lowercase letters are kept different from uppercase within literals, and spacing is exactly preserved.

Statement Labels

A statement label is a name, followed by a colon, that precedes a statement, as in

```
THIS: INPUT X Y Z;
```

Like a statement name, a statement label appears as the first non-blank element after a statement boundary (i.e., a semicolon); SAS identifies it as a statement label, not a statement name, because of the postfixed colon.

Statement labels allow the user to refer to specific points in the program source code. They are used in DATA Step programming statements to transfer control within the program, as from a LINK or GOTO statement (see Chapter 16).

Operators

SAS operators are special symbols that demand certain operations—arithmetic calculation, string manipulation, comparison, logical combination, or value assignment. A few SAS operators precede a single operand upon which action is to take place (*prefix* operators); most must be placed between two operands to be related by the operation (*infix* operators).* One operator, IN, takes a syntax uniquely its own.

Numeric operators include the arithmetic operators + (addition if infix, positivity if prefix), − (subtraction if infix, negation if prefix), * (multiplication), ** (exponentiation), and / (division). Maximum (<>) and minimum (><) are two other numeric operators: 3<>10 is equal to 10, 12><10 is also equal to 10.

Comparison operators include EQ (=)† for "is equal to" and various inequalities: NE (^=) not equal to, LT (<) less than, GT (>) greater than, GE (>=) greater than or equal to, LE (<=) less than or equal to. A colon (:) can be used as an "operator modifier" to facilitate certain special comparisons of character values: For purposes of the comparison, the longer value is compared with the shorter one only up through the length of the shorter one. Thus, " 'A'='ABC' " is false, but 'A'=:'ABC' is true. Any of the comparison operators can be modified by a colon, e.g., 'JONES'<:'K' is valid (and true).

Another convenience for value comparison is the IN operator, which can be used to compare an expression (character or numeric) with a list of values enclosed in parentheses, the comparison being "true" if the expression is equivalent to any one of the listed values. Thus

```
IF 'APPLE' IN('BANANA','PEAR','MANGO')
```

is false, but

```
IF 'APPLE' IN('BANANA','APPLE','MANGO')
```

is true. The expression to be compared can include variables and constants, but the values in parentheses must all be constants (quoted for character comparsion, unquoted for numeric comparison).

Logical operators include AND (&), OR (|), and NOT (^), and are most often used to combine comparison operations (e.g.,"A=1 AND B=2"). NOT is a prefix, the others infix operators. Logical and comparison operators result in the value 0 if the operation is "false," 1 if "true."‡ Thus the value of "3>5" is 0.

The basic string operator is || (concatenation), entered from the keyboard as two adjacent vertical bars. 'ABC'||'123' yields 'ABC123'. The assignment operator is

---

*Though we use constants in our simple examples, anything that can be evaluated—constants, variables, function terms, parenthesized expressions—can be imposed as an operand on either side of an infix operator.

†Comparison and logical operators have both alphamnemonic and special-character forms, either of which may be used at your pleasure.

‡While the SAS compiler *creates* only the values "1" and "0" based on true/false conditions, it *tests* true/false values based on the following:

Value missing or zero: "false"

Value nonmissing and nonzero: "true"

Thus if X=3, the phrase "IF X" is true; if X is zero or missing, the phrase is false. IF statements are discussed beginning in Chapter 3; missing values are discussed in Chapter 7.

TABLE 2.1. SAS DATA STEP LANGUAGE OPERATORS

SYM	ALT[a]	Definition	P[b]	Example	Result
NUMERIC OPERATORS					
+		(prefix) Makes value positive	1	+2	2
−		(prefix) Makes value negative	1	−17	−17
**		Exponentiation	1	3**3	27
*		Multiplication	2	5*10	50
/		Division	2	5/10	.5
+		Addition	3	3 + 4	7
−		Subtraction	3	3 − 4	−1
<>		Maximum	1	5 <> 10	10
><		Minimum	1	5 >< 10	5
STRING OPERATORS					
I		Concatenation[c]	4	'ABC'I'XYZ'	'ABCXYZ'
COMPARISON OPERATORS					
=	EQ	Equal	5	3 + 4 = 7	1 (true)
=	NE	Not equal[c]	5	3 + 4 = 7	0 (false)
<	LT	Less than	5	3 + 4 < 7	0
>	GT	Greater than	5	3 + 4 > 7	0
<=	LE	Less than or equal	5	3 + 4<= 7	1
>=	GE	Greater than or equal	5	3 + 4 >= 7	1
(none)	IN	List membership	5	3 + IN (6,7,8)	1
LOGICAL OPERATORS					
∧	NOT	(Prefix) negation[c]	1	(5 − 3 = 2)	0 (false)
&	AND	Conjunction	6	1 = 1 & 2 = 2	1 (true)
I	OR	Disjunction[c]	7	3 > 7 I 7 < 10	1

[a]SYM = symbol, ALT = alphabetic alternative.

[b]Priority in evaluation; see "Expressions" in text.

[c]Different symbols for the "not" and "bar" characters may be used by different computer or terminal systems. (Note that the concatenation operator is coded by two consecutive vertical bars.) IBM-connected terminals often have a right angle symbol, which will be used instead of the caret, and both a solid and a broken vertical bar, and if so, the solid bar should be used. Where a terminal does not have either character, alternatives may be available with the CHARCODE system option.

the equal sign (=): A=3 says "let the value 3 be assigned to the variable A." The DATA Step compiler distinguishes assignment from equality comparison by syntactic context.

Table 2.1 shows examples of the SAS operators in action.

Function Terms

A *function* is a prescribed operation not easily represented by standard operators. Programming languages usually provide a number of functions (for powers and roots, trigonometric calculations, etc.), and may allow the user to define still other

TABLE 2.2. SOME SAS DATA STEP LANGUAGE FUNCTIONS

Purpose	Example	Result
NUMERIC FUNCTIONS		
Round to the nearest specified unit	ROUND(27.3,.5)	27.5
Closest lower integer	FLOOR(18.9)	18
Absolute value	ABS(−83)	83
Modular remainder	MOD(16,3)	1
Summation	SUM(1,2,3,4,5)	15
Average	MEAN(1,2,3,4,5)	3
Maximum	MAX(1,2,3,4,5)	5
CHARACTER FUNCTIONS		
Locate character	INDEXC('HELLO,'L')	3
Locate string	INDEX('HELLO','LO')	4
Find *n*th word	SCAN('HELLO THERE',2)	THERE
Find substring	SUBSTR('ABCDE',2,3)	BCD
Uppercase	UPPER('Pqrst')	PQRST

Note: There are many more SAS functions than illustrated here. See Chapter 16.

functions by specifying them with more basic operations. The SAS Data Step Language does not permit user definition of functions as such, although it is easy to simulate this effect. It does provide a large set of ready-to-use numeric and character functions.

SAS functions are invoked with function terms. A function term is a SAS function name followed by one or more function *arguments* in parentheses. If a function is like an operation, its arguments are like operands. An example of a function term is

```
ROUND(387.26,.1)
```

which equals 387.3: The function ROUND is defined as the value of the first argument rounded to the nearest second argument.

Some examples of SAS functions are shown in Table 2.2. The more generally useful of the SAS functions are discussed in Chapter 16.

Expressions

A SAS expression is a sequence of operands and operators which may be resolved into a single value. The operands may be constants, variables, function terms, or other expressions. When operands are other expressions, parentheses are used as special grouping symbols. Expressions are evaluated as follows:

- Subexpressions within parentheses are evaluated first.
- After parentheses are taken into account, the order of evaluation is as follows:
  - Function terms are resolved

- The following operations are performed, right to left: **, + (prefix), − (prefix), NOT, <>, ><
- The following are performed left to right: *, /
- The following are performed left to right: + (infix), − (infix)
- The following is performed left to right: ||
- The following are performed left to right: comparisons
- The following is performed left to right: AND
- The following is performed left to right: OR

So, for example, the expression

```
A + SQRT(B) ** 1 <> R
```

is evaluated

```
(A + ((SQRT(B)) ** (1 <> R))
```

If A=2.5, B=16, and R=2, the expression will be resolved to the numeric value 18.5.

Always exercise caution before mixing numeric variables with character operators or vice versa in the same expression. Numeric/character conversion, discussed elsewhere in this book, can occur at unexpected times if you are not careful about this.

WRITING READABLE SAS CODE

In order to create programs that are easily understood by others (or by yourself some weeks later), some stylistic guidelines are called for. The rules we will follow in this book include:

- Use levels of indentation to reflect logical structure.
- Use spaces to improve legibility of expressions.
- Generally, no more than one statement per line of program code.
- Use extra indentation and regular spacing for multi-line statements.
- Use statement-style comments (see below) for instream documentation.
- Show dataset names in all SET statements and in PROC calls, even if using the last dataset created.
- End all program steps with the RUN statement.

These style rules make no difference to the SAS System, but they can help make for source code that human beings, as well as computers, can understand.

Spacing and Indentation

Let's look again at some SAS code presented earlier:

```
(1)  DATA FIRST;
     SET PRELIM;
     BY ITEM1 NOTSORTED;
     ITEM2 = ITEM1 + ROUND(COST) / (TIMEVAL * TIMEWGT);
     RUN;

(2)  DATA FIRST;SET PRELIM;BY ITEM1 NOTSORTED;
     ITEM2=ITEM1+ROUND(COST)/(TIMEVAL*TIMEWGT);RUN;
```

Forget about what it means; which of the examples is easier to read? If there were dozens or more lines of code, which style would be *much* easier to read?

Levels of Indentation

This simple SAS program illustrates the principle of indenting a group of statements within logical bounds. The DATA step is a group beginning with a DATA statement. The statements logically within the DATA step are indented relatively, by a couple of spaces. The RUN statement serves to indicate the end of the DATA step, and I like to place it at the same level as the DATA statement so the group stands out easily to the eye.

Besides program steps, logical groups deserving of indentation include mainly control structures: "IF" constructions, "DO groups," and the like.

Spacing for Legibility

Look at the two "ITEM2" statements above. The expression is less clear in example 2 because the variables, constants, and operators are all run together. When they are separated by spaces, it is easier on the eye. If a space improves readability within a line, use it, even if it is not strictly required (as it is not between words operators).

One Statement per Line

It is easier to read SAS code that is not all run together. Just as spaces are used to separate statement elements, a new line should be used to separate statements, and for the same, simple reason—it's easier to read.

In some cases, it is acceptable to bend this rule. In the example above, the BY statement following the SET statement on the same line would be acceptable. As another example, the SORT procedure, which always requires a BY statement to follow the SORT statement, might be written in one line, especially if the SORT and BY statements are short. The line

```
PROC SORT; BY DATE; RUN;
```

communicates quite elegantly.

Multiline Statements

Some SAS statements will have so many modifiers or variables to specify that they will have to extend over to a second line, or even to many lines. If this happens, choose an appropriate place and break the line, indenting the second and subsequent lines a moderate amount relative to the first (length of the keyword plus two spaces looks nice). For example, write

```
DATA ARK;
   INPUT CATS DOGS TURKEYS FISH ELEPHNTS PORPSES BEARS WOLVES
         SLAMNDRS OCELOTS PUFFINS ...
         ... ;
   [more step statements];
RUN;
```

SAS Comments

Like most computer languages, SAS allows the user to document code internally by the use of comments. Two kinds of comment may be used. A statement-style comment or *comment statement* is a SAS statement that starts with the symbol "*" (asterisk) and ends with the usual semicolon. Any text (except unquoted semicolons and certain other unquoted symbols) may intervene, and the comment statement may be of any length.

A *delimited comment* is any text bounded by the special delimiter "/*" (slash-asterisk) at the start and "*/" at the end.* Special symbols, including semicolons, may be included within the bounds of a delimited comment, which may be of any length.

```
* THIS IS A STATEMENT-STYLE COMMENT;
/* WHILE THIS IS A DELIMITED COMMENT; YES, IT IS! */
```

Unfortunately, SAS in its present versions does not allow nesting of delimited comments, e.g., the following is NOT allowed:

```
/* THIS IS A /*AND HERE IS ONE IN BETWEEN*/ COMMENT */
```

In this case, the compiler will interpret the first "*/" as the end of a comment beginning with the first "/*" (the second "/*" being bypassed as part of the first comment), and the compiler will attempt to parse the text "COMMENT */" as SAS code, resulting in a compiler error. Neither does the SAS System provide a second kind of comment delimiter to effect nesting of comment text as one can with literal

---

Users writing batch programs with IBM JCL should avoid coding "/" as the first two columns of a physical line.

text by using single and double quotes alternately. Perhaps future SAS versions will implement nested comments, which can be very useful during program development.

For the present, it is best whenever practical to save delimited comments for bypassing chunks of code during development, and to *use comment statements* for instream documentation. Stylistically, comments associated with a particular section of code would well precede that section, and on the same indentation level. Brief comments incidental to one or two statements might be placed on the same line as a short statement. Comments of great importance can be accentuated by multiple asterisks.

Naming Datasets on Statements

SAS "remembers" the name of the most recent dataset created in a program. A subsequent step can use the most recent dataset by leaving out an input SAS dataset name where one would normally be expected. For example, the statement SET (see Chapter 4), when written thus without a dataset name:

```
SET;
```

requests the last dataset created in a prior job step. Similarly, PROCs that take SAS datasets as input can be written with or without the procedure modifying keyword DATA= on the PROC statement:

```
PROC FREQ DATA=MYDATA;
```

and

```
PROC FREQ;
```

are equivalent if, and only if, MYDATA was the last dataset created in the present job prior to the PROC FREQ statement. The DATA statement itself can be written without a dataset name, in which case the compiler assigns one (first "DATA1," then "DATA2," etc.).

Although these may seem convenient shortcuts, you can get in trouble as you change and rerun program code to correct errors, make improvements, or adapt to a new situation; it is easy to forget that the last dataset this time is different from the last dataset last time. Therefore, it is recommended you always *name datasets explicitly* in statements even when referring to the last-created dataset.

Using the RUN Statement

The simplest SAS statement, in form and function, is

```
RUN [CANCEL];
```

which simply indicates that the step source is complete and the step should be executed. Since the next DATA or PROC step (or the end of the source code) marks the end of the preceding step and causes it to be executed, why is RUN needed? It is *not* "needed," at least in batch jobs, but it is nice. It makes the end of the step easier to perceive visually. The SAS log, where the supervisor documents job compilation and execution (see Chapter 6), will also be improved, and certain subtle errors, such as associating TITLEs with the wrong procedures, will be eliminated. Furthermore, in interactive SAS, RUN causes the step to execute; without it, the last job step would not execute unless a superfluous PROC or DATA statement were coded. RUN says "execute this step" explicitly.

In interactive SAS, the CANCEL option can be used to abort a step if a coding error has been made. "RUN CANCEL;" ends the step code but the step does not execute. With respect to the DATA Step and most SAS procedures, this feature is obsolescent with the SAS Display Manager user interface; interactive program step code now can, and should, be proofed in its entirety before submission.

RUN Groups

A few SAS procedures do not actually execute to completion upon presentation of a RUN statement in an interactive environment. These procedures (e.g., PLOT and CATALOG) do complete certain execution actions after RUN, but remain active afterward awaiting further instructions or until a DATA or PROC statement is encountered (these procedures may also accept the statement "QUIT;" as a proper way to tell them you are done).

SAS ERRORS

There are basically three kinds of SAS errors (exluding data errors and errors in programming logic, which though they may be important to the user are not really the SAS System's concern). "Compile-time" errors are errors which make a step impossible to compile; these are usually errors of syntax. "Run-time" errors are usually nonsyntactic programming errors, or else errors in data that are closely bound to program execution. For example, an array subscript out of bounds (arrays are discussed in Chapter 16) can cause a DATA step to halt. The third class of errors are Macro Language errors; we'll defray that discussion to Part V.

If a SAS dataset is being created at the time an error is made, SAS will normally enter "syntax check mode," by setting the system option OBS to zero and proceeding (setting OBS=0 causes the compiler to check SAS statements but not actually execute steps; see Chapter 21). If there is an error in a procedure that does not create a new dataset, SAS may continue with subsequent steps normally (i.e., without setting OBS=0).

Compile-time errors

Some compile-time errors are due to misunderstanding (or simply mistyping) SAS statements: The compiler detects a problem with syntax and cannot go on. An unknown keyword might cause this kind of error, as may a misplaced operator. Such errors are, accordingly, called *syntax errors*. Related problems occur when a statement is coded out of proper context, such as a TABLES statement with a PROC that doesn't use TABLES, or when a required statement is missing, e.g., PROC SORT without BY.

Most compile-time errors are noted with the offending code fragment underlined in the SAS job log and an error number printed near it. Errors will usually be explained briefly within the SAS log, at the end of the step.

Due to interdependencies between the statements in any SAS step, a single omission may cause a kind of propagation of compiler errors. For example, a missed semicolon can wreak havoc. Therefore, you should not be alarmed if many errors appear in the SAS log; there may only be one or two real culprits.

Run-time errors. Under certain conditions, SAS cannot continue with a step that compiled successfully because the data are incompatible with the demands of the step beyond mere invalidity. The array-out-of-bounds error can be a run-time error, if the array subscript is read from data lines, or a procedure uses a VAR statement that names a variable not on the input dataset. SAS Basics calls such run-time errors *programming errors*, though this term is perhaps too general. They too will be noted in the SAS log.

Logic errors. These are a kind of programming error not reported as such on the SAS log. They cannot be, because they cannot be recognized as errors by the compiler. They are the user's misapplications of the computer language, the intention to tell the computer one thing while actually telling it another. Some errors are obvious: When the computer reports the average salary of an employee in Department XYZ to be $983,255, a reasonably alert employee, before putting in for a transfer, would first check to see if what was actually programmed produced the sum when the mean was required.

More serious are programs whose results are not so obviously in error, but are in error nevertheless. Suppose an algorithm for finding the arithmetic mean "SUM VALUES, COUNT VALUES, DIVIDE SUM BY COUNT" was accidentally misimplemented such that the computer was not made to count the last value, and thus the sum of the values was divided by one less than the count of the values. If Department ABC has 10 employees, with a true average salary of $25,000, but the sum was divided by 9 and not 10, the average would be output as $27,778. A reasonable result, but wrong. The less extreme the error, the longer it may take to discover.

Since the SAS system cannot determine, and the log cannot report, when a result makes sense or not, it is up to you, the user, to find ways to verify or test the results. Because it is so easy to get the SAS System to produce *some* kind of important-looking results, it is imperative that for all but the simplest applications you *test your programs well* before relying on them. Don't just look through your code. Create test datasets, using simple cases to cover many variations. The more powerful the SAS tools you use, the more important it is for you to understand exactly what you are doing.

3

Creating SAS Datasets

Making SAS data out of non-SAS data is one of the primary uses of the DATA step. In this chapter, you will learn how to get the DATA step to do exactly that.

THE DATA STATEMENT

A SAS DATA step begins with a DATA statement:

```
DATA [<datasetname[(datasetoptions)]>...];
```

The simplest DATA statement is

```
DATA;
```

which tells the SAS system to create a dataset and assign it the current default name, "DATAn", where *n* starts as "1" and is incremented through the program when default naming occurs. That is to say, the first dataset created in a given SAS program to which the user has not given a name (either by omitting a name on the DATA statement or for some other reason, such as omitting the OUT= option from certain procedures that produce output datasets) will be named DATA1, the next DATA2, and so on. But it is better practice, as advised in Chapter 2, always to give SAS datasets explicit names, so there will be no doubt which is meant when referred to later in the program. Try to choose dataset names that have at least some intuitive meaning or connection. Here are some more DATA statements:

```
DATA GRADES;

DATA DAILY MONTHLY YEARLY; * CREATES THREE DIFFERENT DATASETS;

DATA EMPLOYEE(KEEP=DEPARTMENT SALARY AGE);
```

The last one shows the use of a *dataset option* (discussed in Chapter 4), in this case the KEEP= option.

Designating a SAS Library

If your dataset is to be stored "permanently"—that is, to survive in a SAS library after your job or session is completed—you usually must give it a two-level name, which is written as two SAS names separated by a period (e.g., SALESDPT.EM-PLOYEE). The first level is not actually part of the dataset name proper, but a reference to a SAS library (in SAS jargon, a *libref*) that your operating system associates with a disk or tape storage location for that library; review Chapter 1. So for example,

```
DATA SALES.EMPLOYEE;
```

refers to a SAS dataset EMPLOYEE that is to be stored in the dataset library referred to by SALES. The first level name is an operating system file reference; EMPLOYEE is the true SAS dataset name.

More than one SAS dataset may be stored in a dataset library; e.g.,

```
DATA SALES.REVENUE;
```

will create a separate SAS dataset in the operating system file referred to by SALES; the SAS library now has two datasets. Just as only the SAS System can read and write SAS datasets, only it can build or take apart a SAS library. As far as the operating system is concerned, the SAS library is one file, but the SAS System data access methods recognize the separate entities within it.

If a one-level name is used, referring to a temporary dataset, the SAS system provides a default libref anyway. Unless the SAS installation or current SAS job specifies otherwise, SAS uses the name WORK. So the statements

```
DATA CARS;
```

and

```
DATA WORK.CARS;
```

are exactly equivalent under normal circumstances. They both refer to a SAS dataset in a library that is allocated temporarily and erased after the job has completed its run.

The SAS system option WORK= can be used at job initialization (i.e., when the SAS System is invoked) to override the SAS System's creation of a temporary storage file, and in fact can be used to "fool" SAS into storing one-level-named datasets into a single library of the user's choice, which may be a permanent library. Generally more proper in these situations is the USER= option, which also allows one-level dataset names to be associated with the specified, which (unlike WORK=) can be (re-)specified in OPTIONS statements. But actually, in most cases it will be clearer and less error-prone to use two-level names to refer to permanent SAS datasets, making the libref explicit. It is also the case that many SAS programs use transitional datasets, many of which are a means to an end and of no interest in themselves; these should stay in WORK, and an explicit library used for permanent datasets.*

A LIBNAME statement,

```
LIBNAME libref [engine] name [options];
```

can be used to assign a libref to a named storage location that contains (or will contain) a SAS library. The form of the storage name, which should be enquoted, depends on the operating system in quesion. For example, under MVS and similar systems it is an OS dataset name, normally fully qualified, as in

```
LIBNAME INVENTRY 'GROUP1.DEPT.INVENTORY';
```

that associates the libref INVENTRY with the OS dataset GROUP1.DEPT. INVENTORY.

In rare circumstances when creating a new library, you may need explicitly to specify an access engine; normally you can let the SAS System figure it out. Options on the LIBNAME statement are very much dependent on the host operating system in question; consult the SAS documentation for your operating system for details.

Librefs can also, under some operating systems, be assigned before your program is begun. For example, under MVS a DDname can be used, assigned in batch JCL or via a TSO ALLOC FI( ) statement.†

---

*If you absolutely insist, you could use USER=libref and later re-associate one-level names back to the work library with USER=WORK.

†Your author recommends external allocation for batch job execution under MVS, if there is any chance of file contention, so JES can handle the contention before execution of the SAS step commences. However, using LIBNAME in TSO sessions may be more convenient, since the SAS System will automatically free the files when you end your SAS session. I should mention that under MVS a LIBNAME option allows you to specify an allocation disposition.

When you are done using a SAS library that was allocated with a LIBNAME statement, you may free its association with your program or session and unassign the libref, with another form of the LIBNAME statement,

```
LIBNAME <libref> | <_ALL_> CLEAR;
```

After this statement is executed, references to the named libref will not be recognized by your SAS program.

You may list the attributes of a libref (or __ALL__ librefs) by using a LIBNAME statement with the LIST keyword:

```
LIBNAME <libref> | <_ALL_> LIST;
```

The attributes that will be listed (in the SAS log), and their meanings, depend on your operating system.

REFERRING TO EXTERNAL INPUT FILES

Input to a SAS dataset may come from other SAS datasets (see Chapter 4) or from SAS procedures (Chapter 5). Input data may also come from non-SAS sources. Non-SAS data may include that obtained using SAS/Access views (of a database system or other "special" file structure), about which we will have no more to say in this book. However, much computer data are stored in forms which have no special organization but merely lay sequentially within a data file, as readable characters, perhaps, or in some other less readable but nevertheless straightforward representation (e.g., hexadecimal, "packed" form, etc.). We may call this kind of data "raw" data, and the SAS System can handle most any kind of it.

Designating In-Stream Data with the CARDS Statement

External data can originate from one of two places: non-SAS data files, and the input stream of the SAS job code itself (whether entered from the terminal or in batch job source), where it can be called in-stream data. The DATA Step compiler provides the CARDS statement to indicate that data follow immediately in-stream. The statement takes the simple form

```
CARDS;
```

If the word CARDS seems archaic* and bothers you, you can use the synonym

---

*Once upon a time, stacks of cardstock paper rectangles ("cards") with little holes punched in them were used as one of the more popular ways to feed programs as well as data to computers. To this day, data lines entered from terminals are often called "card-image," because most punched cards had space for 80 characters, just as most terminal lines still do.

```
<<< PROGRAM SOURCE CODE FOLLOWS >>>

TITLE 'A Simple SAS DATA Step';
DATA SIMPLE;
  INPUT A B C;
    CARDS;
123 456 789
111 222 333
9876 5432 10
RUN;
PROC PRINT; RUN;

<<< SAS JOB OUTPUT FOLLOWS >>>

  A Simple SAS DATA Step

OBS       A       B       C

  1      123     456     789
  2      111     222     333
  3     9876    5432      10
```

Listing 3.1. Example of a DATA Step.

DATALINES instead. When the compiler comes across the statement "CARDS;" (or "DATALINES;"), it reads subsequent lines as data instead of as source code until it encounters a semicolon. (The line with the semicolon, as well as lines following, are interpreted as source code once again.)

Only one CARDS statement and data group may be used in a DATA step. CARDS and its data immediatly following must be the last lines entered in a DATA step, except perhaps for a terminating RUN statement. For example:

```
DATA SAMPLE;
[ more SAS statements ]
CARDS;
1 2 34 587
22 33 298 5
[ more data lines ]
RUN;
```

An explicit example is shown in Listing 3.1. You can terminate the data with a null statement (a lone semicolon) if you like, so long as it appears on its own line or with the next PROC, DATA, or global statement, although as pointed out in Chapter 2 the RUN statement is a more proper way to conclude most SAS job steps.

If your data contain semicolons, there is in fact a way to pass them in-stream, and that is by using the CARDS4 statement instead of the CARDS statement. When you code

```
CARDS4;
```

then the compiler will treat as data all lines following until a line is found with four semicolons in columns 1-4. So long as your data doesn't have to have semicolons as the first four characters on any "card," you're in.

Designating External Files with the INFILE Statement

Most of the time, raw data you wish to analyze is not included within your job source code, but resides in a preexisting non-SAS (external) file on tape or disk. To refer to a non-SAS input file, which can be called an external file, you normally use a file reference or *fileref* (the term "libref" connotes a SAS library, "fileref" a non-SAS file). A fileref can be assigned with a FILENAME statement, which operates more or less exactly the same as the LIBNAME statement as far as most users need be concerned, or by an allocation preceding the SAS session (see our discussion of the LIBNAME statement earlier). As with librefs allocated by LIBNAME statements,

```
FILENAME <fileref> | <_ALL_> CLEAR;
```

can disassociate the name and free the file.

Once a fileref is assigned, it can be used in the INFILE statement to point to the desired external file. The INFILE statement has the form

```
INFILE file_specifier [options];
```

The file specifier may be a fileref as defined prior to your SAS job or with a FILENAME statement. Or, the literal name of the storage location as your operating system knows it, enclosed in quotes, can be used in lieu of a fileref.

An INFILE statement says to the SAS supervisor, "Your data to execute subsequent input tasks will be found in the specified file [and take note of the options you are to use when reading the input]." INFILE is an executable statement and

---

I do not recommend this practice. A fileref, designated externally in JCL, should be used where practical in MVS batch jobs if there is any chance of contention; see our discussion of LIBNAME earlier. It is also better in most interactive work to use a fileref, rather than an explicit name, as an INFILE filespec, because control over allocation disposition (and over freeing the file, if it was allocated with FILENAME) can be achieved. Note that a fileref can be made to point to a member of an aggreate storage location under certain operating systems (including MVS) by enclosing the member name in parentheses after the fileref, i.e.,

```
INFILE 'MY.PDS(MEM1)';
```
and
```
FILENAME MP 'MY.PDS'; INFILE MP(MEM1);
```
are equivalent.

must in fact execute before you "do" anything with the data using an INPUT statement (discussed below); an INPUT statement gets its data from the file referenced in the most recently preceding INFILE statement (or if none, from the CARDS in-stream file). INFILE is required in any DATA step that will use an INPUT statement, except when data follow in-stream after CARDS or CARDS4.*

Options on the INFILE statement are used for many purposes, all in the service of making your data acceptable to the SAS System no matter how it may arrive. Two INFILE options, DELIMITER= and DSD, will be described later in this chapter. In Chapter 7, we will look at some other INFILE options.

READING RAW DATA: THE INPUT STATEMENT

An INPUT statement, generally

```
INPUT [<specification>...] [ <@> | <@@>] ;
```

consists of the name INPUT followed by zero or more *input specifications* (and, occasionally, a "trailing @" or "@@"). Input specifications tell the system where to look for a data element, or how to read the data it finds. The INPUT statement is powerfully expressive; very intricate data-reading can be accomplished with a single INPUT statement correctly constructed.

Column Input†

Imagine a collection of raw data on company employees giving surname, title, sex, age, and monthly salary. The cards or card-images are prepared from written coding forms, on which the data items were arranged in their own "fields," as in the following, where for example "name" is placed in columns 1–14 (card columns are shown in the first two lines, for our illustration only; they are not part of the data):

---

*While no INFILE statement is required to read data from CARDS, one *may* be coded using the word CARDS in place of a fileref (you should never use the word CARDS *as* a fileref). The only reasons you may need to do this is if you need to apply one or more INFILE statement options to data following in-stream after a CARDS (or CARDS4) statement, or if you want to read data from an external file at one point in the step and from the in-stream CARDS elsewhere in the step.

†There are several ways to indicate where and how data is to be read, and in SAS jargon we casually reify these into "kinds" of input; thus, for example, when we speak of "column input" we are really just talking about an INPUT statement's column-type specification, and not something intrinsic to the data or the way the SAS System stores and uses it after INPUT. This holds, too, when we discuss formatted input, list input, etc.

```
                1            2            3            4            5            6            7
       12345678901234567890123456789012345678901234567890123456789012345678901234567890
       JONES          SECRETARY       M341050.00
       BLATHERER      BOSS            M624880.50
       MEEKLEY        BOOKKEEPER      F531290.33
       DUMPSTER       GOFER           M19 920.10
       JANSSEN        ADMIN ASST      F442945.00
       [ more cards ...]
```

Problem: Read this external data into a SAS dataset.
Solution: This INPUT statement will work:

```
DATA EMPLOYEE;
   INFILE EMPLOYEE;   * NOT NECESSARY, BUT OK, TO USE SAME NAME HERE;
   INPUT EMPLOYEE $ 1-14 TITLE $ 15-30 SEX $ 31 AGE 32-33 SALARY 34-40;
RUN;
```

This is an example of *column input:* Each SAS variable is followed by an explicit indication of the input "columns"—the position in each input record—in which it may be found. See Figure 3.1, where (as in some other illustrations to follow) the column positions are emphasized by drawing a line of data as if its characters are encased in a series of contiguous boxes.

By default, variables first named in INPUT and read with column input are considered numeric. That is to say, unless the SAS compiler is told otherwise, when it comes across a new variable name it will treat it as a number. To declare a variable to be character type in an INPUT statement, a dollar sign can be placed after the variable name but before the column specification. So in our example, SAS will make EMPLOYEE, TITLE, and SEX character variables and the other variables numeric.

Note that an item does not have to take up all the spaces in its allowed field; with column input, valid data can be placed anywhere within the field specified by the columns; SAS does *not* automatically consider blanks to be zeroes. Character values are in effect left-justified, i.e., the first nonblank column is where the value will be considered to start. Blanks *within* a character value (i.e., between nonblanks) are preserved, however.

Decimal points in numeric values can be implied with a numeral, prefixed with

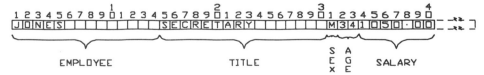

Figure 3.1. The input buffer as the first line of data in the "column input" example (see text) is processed. The fields defined by the INPUT statement are shown.

a decimal point, following the column indicator. If in the example above SALARY were read with "2" following the column specifier, i.e., "SALARY 35-41 .2, Janssen's salary could have been entered as 294500 and SAS would have assumed the last two digits were to the right of an implied decimal point. However, an explicit decimal point in the data field overrides the decimal specification.

It is perfectly permissible to "reuse" columns. In the statement

```
INPUT A 6-10 B 11-15 ALLCHAR $ 3-17;
```

one numeric variable is taken from columns 5–10 and another from 11–16, and finally, a character variable is taken from columns 3–17! If this INPUT statement were to read the line

```
12345678900987654321
```

the value of A would be 67890, the value of B would be 9876 (the leading zero won't count), and ALLCHAR would be '345678900987654.'

List Input

In some cases, raw data might have been entered one item after another without restrictions on column location. The SAS compiler accomodates this by requiring only that each value be separated with one or more blanks. If an INPUT specification includes no column numbers or informats (see below), but just a variable name, SAS will read the variable's value starting at the next nonblank column from where it was, and stopping when it encounters the next blank after that. When data is read in this manner it is called list input (presumably because variable name is simply "listed" on the INPUT statement). List input helps make casual data entry easy. For example, you may have a brief list of data and wish to type it in at the terminal quickly after CARDS; list input is easiest because items need not be lined up neatly in columns. You still must use "$" after the name to declare a variable to be of character type. Single embedded blanks are allowed if "&" is also placed after a character variable name; in this case, be sure that at least *two* blanks separate the value from the next one.

The following sequence illustrates the use of list input:

```
DATA INFORM;
  INPUT NAME $ & AGE HEIGHT WEIGHT SEX $;
  CARDS;
J. JONES   23 46  189 F
   W. O. OZ  18  60     128 M
G. ZEEBO   84  68 138 M
  ;
```

Note how each variable is separated from the others by at least one blank (values of NAME may contain single blanks, and must be followed by at least two blanks),

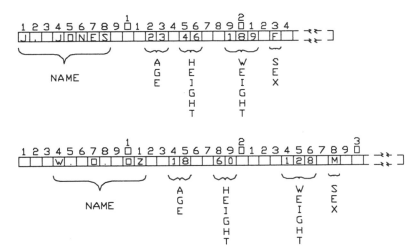

Figure 3.2. The input buffer as the first and then the second lines of the "list input" example are processed. The data themselves determine the fields under list input.

but that otherwise the position of the variables on the "cards" matters little, as long as they are in the *same relative order* as their names appear in the INPUT statement. INPUT scans along to determine where the data elements begin and end, based on the position of nonblanks between blanks; see Figure 3.2. List input is sometimes called *free-format* input to emphasize the fact that data values are not constrained to reside in a particular column location.

While specific columns may not be important, the relative position *and occurrence* of each variable value is vital with list input. The missing value indicator, a single period, *must* be used as a "placeholder" when data are missing.* Refer to the example above; if G. Zeebo's height and age were unknown, the appropriate data line would read

    G. ZEEBO . . 138 M

If

    G. ZEEBO 138 M

were used instead, SAS would record Zeebo's AGE as 138, but see "M" where HEIGHT should be, report an illegal numeric value and set HEIGHT to missing, and worse, might seek WEIGHT and SEX on the *next* data card (see Chapter 7), effectively destroying that observation as well. A solitary period anywhere in an

---

*A *missing value* occurs when SAS does not have an item of information (i.e., a variable value) for a given observation. Missing numeric values are usually excluded from statistical analyses. See Chapter 7 for a complete discussion of SAS missing values.

input field may be used to indicate a missing numeric value with column input, too, but if a column input field is simply left all blank, that will be enough.

A default length of 8 is assigned to character variables first named on the INPUT statement, if no directions to the contrary are given, such as a LENGTH statement. It is possible to read values in excess of eight characters with "modified" list input, using format modifiers (discussed shortly below; LENGTH and related statements are treated later in this chapter).

Altering the Field Delimiter

Our discussion of list input has thus far assumed that input fields are separated by one or more blanks. In many cases, however, this is not so. For example, data may be entered with slashes (/) as the intended separators. It may even be that more than one field separator is possible, for example both the blank *and* the slash.

The SAS System provides a method to handle this situation: the DELIMITER= option on the INFILE statement. The DELIMITER= option is followed by an enquoted character constant which specified each character that is to be treated as a delimiter. For example,

```
INFILE MYDATA DELIMITER='/';
```

sets up the slash as the list input field delimiter, and allows you to read data lines such as

```
123/456/33/44/55
```

with a statement such as

```
INPUT V1-V5;
```

Consecutive delimiters function as one:

```
123///456//33////44/55
```

produces the same result. But with the INFILE statement just shown

```
123 456 33 44 55
```

or

```
123/ 456/ 33/ 44/ 55
```

would be in error. Why? Because when DELIMITER= is specified, the blank is not presumed also to be a delimiter. To read these lines correctly, the blank would have to be explicitly encoded in the delimiter string, e.g.,

```
INFILE MYDATA DELIMITER=' /';
```

In other words, the blank is the default list input field delimiter if and only if DELIMITER= is not specified.

The DSD Option

The INFILE statement option DSD is specialized to read the kind of comma-delimited input that is common to certain file transfer protocols. It changes several of the ways list input handles input lines. In the first place, if DSD is specified and DELIMITER= is not, then the comma, not the blank, is the default field delimiter. Secondly, under DSD each delimiter is treated as a separator; without DSD, consecutive delimiters are treated as one separator. Thus, for example,

```
INFILE MYDATA DSD; INPUT FIRST $ MIDDLE $ LAST;
```

could read

```
JOHN,PAUL,JONES
HARRY,S,TRUMAN
JOE,,KENNEDY
```

and correctly pick up the fact that MIDDLE should be missing for the last observation. If these lines were instead read with

```
INFILE MYDATA DELIMITER=','; INPUT FIRST $ MIDDLE $ LAST;
```

then the last observation would not be read correctly: the two commas would be treated as one separator and KENNEDY would be read as the value of MIDDLE. Finally, DSD allows values to be quoted and, if so, to contain delimiters. Thus, given

```
INFILE X DSD; INPUT A $ B $;
```

the line

```
ALPHA,"HI,THERE"
```

would be read to contain variables A and B valued at 'ALPHA' and 'HI,THERE' respectively. The DSD option causes the quotes (single or double) to be stripped off the value after they serve their purpose of "passing through" the delimiter as part of the character value. Used this way, the DSD option is especially powerful when used along with the colon format modifier on the INPUT statement. Should you need to keep the quotes as part of the value when DSD is specified, the tilde format modifier can be used. Format modifiers are described later in this chapter.

Formatted Input

A SAS *informat* is a special name used to designate the form of incoming data values. Syntactically, an informat is represented by a format identifier and decimal specification, just like a format is (recall Chapter 2). An informat is so called because it is used to read, rather than to write, an external value.

SAS informats are used for three primary purposes: to handle numeric data arriving in unusual form (e.g., dates, hexadecimal values); to allow character values more than eight bytes in length or which contain leading or trailing blanks to be read without column specifications; and generally to set input field width specifications in lieu of column specifications.

This INPUT statement illustrates all three uses just mentioned:

```
INPUT CONTCODE 1. CNAME $ 20. POPMILS 4.1 PRCAPGNP COMMA7.;
```

This statement might be used to read a continent code of one digit length, a country's name beginning in the next column and as long as 20 letters, its population in millions immediately following the 20-space field, four spaces wide and with one implied decimal point, and per capita gross national product, entered with dollar signs and commas. The statement as coded could handle data such as the following (the first two lines are column numbers for our illustration, not actual data lines):

```
         1         2         3         4         5         6         7
12345678901234567890123456789012345678901234567890123456789012345678901234567890
1UNITED STATES       2298$12,820
4USSR                2650$ 4,155
3UNITED ARAB EMIRATES  11$24,660
```

The INPUT statement is parsed as follows: CONTCODE is an integer of one digit length (1.), CNAME is a character variable ($) that may be up to 20 spaces in length (20.), POPMILS follows with up to 4 digits, the last of which is assumed to be in the tenths place (4.1), and the next 7 spaces are devoted to PRCAPGNP, which is to be interpreted as a number after disregarding extraneous spaces, dollar signs, and commas (COMMAw. and some other common informats are reviewed in Chapter 7).

Remember always to use a decimal point with a width specification. It is a common SAS error to forget this (or simply to type it incorrectly). INPUT VAR 3.; means "get a value for variable VAR beginning in the current position and allowing three places with no decimal fraction." INPUT VAR 3; is interpreted as column input meaning "get a value for variable VAR which is found in column 3 (and implicitly, is one digit long)."

Format Modifiers

There are instances when it would be most convenient to use list input because of the way data were entered, and yet specify informats on the INPUT statement.

There are three specification elements called *format modifiers* that handle this. One of these is the colon (:). Followed by a format, it asks that the formatted value be taken starting at the next nonblank column. In other words, while

```
INPUT A B $5.;
```

expects the value of B to begin one space after the value of A ends,

```
INPUT A B : $5.;
```

begins to *look* for B one column after A; B is taken from the next nonblank column, until the next blank column or the end of the input line or until five characters have been read, whichever occurs first. We call this modified list input, because while it causes the INPUT to apply a format specification when reading the value, it uses the "scanning" behavior of list input to determine the location of the value.

Another format modifier, the ampersand (&), was introduced earlier as a way of reading character values that might contain embedded blanks with list input. The ampersand may be used as a format modifier, in contexts where a colon could be used, such as in

```
INPUT A B & $5.;
```

which causes INPUT to scan along from the next nonblank character until two consecutive blanks (not just one) are encountered, or until five characters are read, whichever occurs first.

The other format modifier is the tilde (~), which has an effect only if the DSD option was specified on the INFILE statement and causes quote marks to be treated as a valid part of the input value (they still serve to enquote delimiters), e.g.,

```
INFILE INF DSD; INPUT AUTHOR & $15. TITLE ~ $25.;
```

reading

```
T. CAPOTE,"OTHER VOICES, OTHER ROOMS"
```

leaves the title in quotes.

Column and Line Pointers

When INPUT executes, the first thing that usually happens is that one or more lines of raw data are taken from INFILE (or CARDS) and copied into a temporary in-memory data structure called the *input buffer*. The compiler can then work with the input lines very freely, because it doesn't have to perform physical I/O at every point in the INPUT statement, but only has to look at what is in memory.

When I illustrate a line of input as if it were a row of characters in little boxes, I really mean to connote the input buffer and not the data "as it is" in the external file.

Because the input buffer is an in-memory structure, it is easy for INPUT to move freely about a data record. As INPUT processes the information in the input buffer, it keeps track of where it is with two special variables called the *column pointer* and the *line pointer*.

The Column Pointer

The column pointer contains the value of a logical "position" in a row of input data. This is how the pointer is set:

- It starts with a value of "1," meaning column 1.
- After reading a column input value, it becomes the column immediately following; e.g., after reading a value in columns 23-27, the pointer is set at 28.
- The pointer is also set to the column immediately following the last column of the field of a variable read with an informat; e.g., if a variable of informat 5. is read beginning in column 9, the pointer winds up at column 14 afterwards.
- The pointer is set to the column one space after a variable read with list input; e.g., if a variable read with list input actually ends in column 27, due to a space in 28, the column pointer will rest at 29. However, the pointer is set to the column *two* spaces after a character value read with "&."
- The pointer may be set by the user with a *pointer control expression*, as we will presently discuss.

Caution: Because of the way the SAS compiler does its free-format scanning, although a character value may be given a specific length using a format modifier, when modified list input is used the position of the column pointer will be as if list input were used. If the card

```
123 ABCDEFGHIJKLMN
```

were read with the ": 5." INPUT statement shown above, the value of B would be ABCDE, but the pointer would be placed one blank past the N.

Be especially careful if using the format modifiers to read *numeric* values. The results might not be what you expect. Not only will the pointer behave as it does with character variables, but the input format will *not* restrict the number of columns taken for the value, as it does with character variables. Thus the statement

```
INPUT Z : 5.;
```

reading the line

```
12345678
```

will result in Z having a value of 12345678, *not* 12345!

Column pointer control. There are two column pointer control operators that are used in the INPUT statement. @ is the absolute pointer control operator, which demands the pointer to be placed at the column indicated. + is the relative pointer control operator, which demands the pointer be placed a certain number of columns after its current position. A positive integer constant, a variable name that at the time of INPUT execution contains a positive integer, or an expression in parentheses that yields a positive integer value, must follow an @ operator. A positive constant, or a variable or parenthesized expression with a positive or negative integer value, must follow a + operator.

Pointer control is a powerful way to gain access to input data in almost any form.

Problem: Data on countries' population and income come in a similar form as in the example above, but more liberally spaced, thus:

```
         1         2         3         4         5         6         7
1234567890123456789012345678901234567890123456789012345678901234567890
1   UNITED STATES          2298      $12,820
4   USSR                   2650      $ 4,155
3   UNITED ARAB EMIRATES     11      $24,660
```

Solution: An INPUT statement to read this data could be

```
INPUT CONTCODE 1. +2 CNAME $ 20. @28 POPMILS 4.1 @38 PRCAPGNP COMMA7.;
```

which says to the SAS compiler, "read CONTCODE as a one-digit integer, then skip two spaces and find CNAME, a character variable up to 20 characters in length, go to column 28 to find POPMILS in up to four columns (decimal point implied before the rightmost digit), and finally go to column 38, there to pick up a number PRCAPGNP, which you will discover after removing extraneous dollar signs, commas, and spaces." This is illustrated in Figure 3.3. Note that in this example, "@4" could have been used instead of "+2".

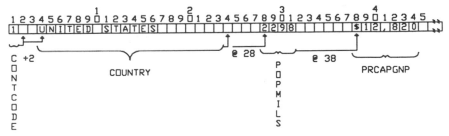

Figure 3.3. Column pointer control. Pointer positioning is shown by arrows, using the first line of the example data (see text).

The column pointer gives the ability to jump around the input buffer. The following INPUT statements have equivalent results:

```
INPUT CONTCODE 1. +2 CNAME $ 20. @38 PRCAPGNP COMMA7. @28 POPMILS 4.1;
INPUT @38 PRCAPGNP COMMA7. @28 POPMILS 4.1 @4 CNAME $ 20. @1 CONTCODE 1.;
```

The Line Pointer

One logical data record may arrive on more than one card or card-image record, useful when there is a lot of data to carry for each observation. INPUT maintains a *current line pointer* for these cases. The line pointer may be set absolutely with the operator # followed by a positive integer, a variable with a positive integer value, or an expression in parentheses that yields a positive integer. The line pointer may be set relatively with / (which says "go to the next line"). In either case, when the pointer is first moved to a new line, it rests at column 1. So the statement

```
INPUT VAR1 3. @20 VAR2 2. / @10 VAR3 3.2 #3 VAR4 $ 5.;
```

requests VAR2 beginning column 20, VAR3 beginning column 10 of the next (second) card, and VAR4, a character variable, beginning column 1 of card 3. See Figure 3.4.

Backward as well as forward placement is allowed with the line pointer as with the column pointers, because the entire logical input record—which may consist of more than one physical input line—is read into the input buffer. In fact, the dimensions implied by pointer controls in the INPUT statements of a DATA step help determine the dimensions of the input buffer SAS allocates to execute the step.

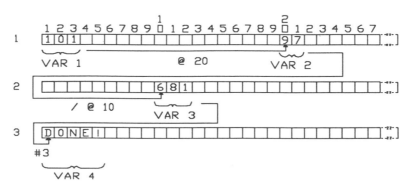

Figure 3.4. Line pointer control, shown for a line read by the statement: INPUT VAR1 3. @20 VAR2 2./@10 VAR3 3.2 #3 VAR4 $5.

Mixing INPUT Modes

The INPUT statement is parsed specification by specification, and the compiler doesn't care how INPUT is laid out so long as each specification is syntactically correct. The upshot is that SAS allows the user great freedom in mixing input modes on the INPUT statement. For example, the statement

```
INPUT A $ B $3. C 23-42 @60 D 5.3 @70 E;
```

can be used to request a character variable with list input, a three-byte character variable starting after the end of the last one, a numeric variable within columns 23–42, a numeric variable within columns 60–64 whose last three digits are to the right of an implied decimal point, and a numeric variable beginning at or after column 70, list input again.

We will return to INPUT in Chapter 7, and see what more can be done with input specifications.

DATA STEP ITERATION

Before going on to study other statements that help create SAS datasets, let's take a moment to discuss a concept that seems at once so natural (at least, once you've programmed a little using the SAS System) and yet is very important. This is the concept of DATA step iteration.

Most SAS DATA steps will have one or more statements that obtain data from sources outside the step. These steps include INPUT, which obtains raw data from non-SAS sources and which we have just examined, and SET, MERGE, and UPDATE, which obtain data from pre-existing SAS datasets and which we will soon study.

When a SAS DATA step containing any of these statements executes, the SAS System determines whether there are more records it is supposed to read by looking ahead (as it were) in the input file or dataset. If it gets to the end of the step code but more records remain to be read, it happily starts to execute the step code again. For example, the step

```
DATA MINE;
INPUT A B;
CARDS;
123 456
15 20
RUN;
```

executes twice: the first time through, A=123 and B=456, the next time, A=15 and B=20. Dataset MINE winds up with two observations, one for each of these executions.

Each run-through of a DATA step is called an *iteration* of the step, and some of the problems many people new to SAS have in understanding program execution flow (especially programmers who are used to other languages that may not take care of business so automatically) can be traced back to a misunderstanding of this concept. It's really very simple: generally speaking, when a DATA Step containing INPUT, SET, MERGE, or UPDATE gets "to the bottom" and there is more input remaining, it goes back "to the top" and starts again, ready to read the next input and write the next observation.

The SAS programmer has, to be sure, ways to alter the iterative process: to stop the iteration before all its code executes, to stop the DATA step entirely, to execute desired code segments more than once per iteration, etc. You will learn these techniques and their applications in the course of this book.

RECORD SELECTION

Three SAS DATA Step Langauge statements are designed strictly to control the selection of observations for the dataset being created in a DATA step. They are IF (subsetting), DELETE, and OUTPUT.

The IF Statement (Subsetting)

Problem: Given the following raw data (columns illustrated):

```
          1         2         3         4         5         6         7
1234567890123456789012345678901234567890123456789012345678901234567890
JOHNNY   8   A-
MARY     9   B
JOEY     8   B+
JAN     11   D+
. . .
```

create a SAS dataset, STUDENTS, containing observations from students with grades "B or better" (B− up through A+).

Solution: Calling the variables NAME, AGE, GRADE, write the simple INPUT statement:

```
INPUT NAME $ AGE @14 GR $1. @14 GRADE $2.;
```

Notice that GRADE contains the precise grade, and that a new variable GR contains the single-letter portion of the grade. This may now be used to test "B or better" with the following statement:

```
IF GR = 'A' OR GR = 'B';
```

This is the subsetting IF statement, so called to distinguish it form the normal IF-THEN statement (see below). It has the form

```
IF logical_expression;
```

The subsetting IF statement demands that if the logical expression evaluates "false," the current observation should be excluded from the SAS dataset being created, and processing return for the next iteration of the DATA step. Johnny's grade is A−, so GR=A and the expression is true; in this instance processing of the observation continues, likewise for the observations representing Mary and Joey. What happens to Frank? As far as the SAS dataset being built is concerned—nothing. The record is read but rejected ("GR='A' OR GR='B' " is false): no more work is done with it, and its information is not added to the new dataset. The flow of a DATA step with a subsetting IF is shown in Figure 3.5.

IF-THEN Statements; DELETE and OUTPUT Statements

The subsetting IF statement is a special case of the IF-THEN statement, which has the form

```
IF logical_expression THEN [statement];
```

where "statement" is any executable statement (without its semicolon: the IF-THEN's semicolon serves the purpose). The IF-THEN statement, in general, tells SAS to execute the statement following THEN only if the logical_expression is "true." (If no statement appears, it tells SAS to do nothing; this has applications in certain IF-THEN-ELSE situations.) The subsetting IF statement

```
IF logical_expression;
```

is equivalent to the IF-THEN statement

```
IF NOT(logical_expression) THEN DELETE;
```

and is provided by SAS as a shorthand method of giving this common command.* The DELETE statement, which takes only the form

```
DELETE;
```

causes SAS to stop processing the current observation. The current observation is not added to the dataset, and no further program statements are performed upon it.

The OUTPUT statement, with the form

---

*There is a small difference: An ELSE statement may not follow a subsetting IF.

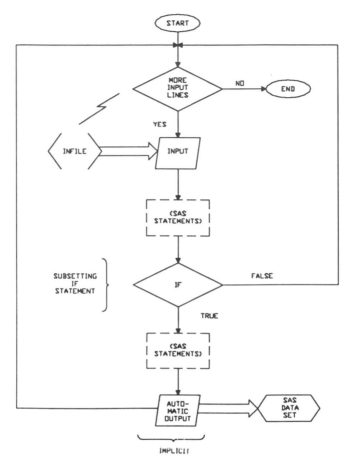

Figure 3.5. Flow of control, subsetting IF statement. Shown is a DATA step in abstract, with boxes in dotted outline indicating there may or may not be statements at that point. If the IF expression is false, the observation is immediately deleted. The "more input line?" choice and the output at the end (*if* no explicit OUTPUT statement is coded), are automatic services provided by SAS. Double line arrows show data flows.

```
OUTPUT [<datasetname>...];
```

says "add the current observation to the SAS dataset(s) named, or if none are named then to all datasets named on the DATA statement." Datasets named on an OUTPUT statement *must* also be named on the DATA statement.

OUTPUT is an executable statement. An observation is added to the dataset when and if OUTPUT is encountered, *except*: if *no* OUTPUT statement appears anywhere in the DATA step, "OUTPUT;" is implied as the last executable statement of the step. That is, if no OUTPUT statement appears, observations are written to the SAS dataset as the program's last action prior to returning to the beginning of the DATA step for the next iteration (look again at Figure 3.5). The

OUTPUT statement is often not used in the DATA step because it is implied at the end of the step; if that's the only time an observation is to be written, and only one dataset is being built, then there is no need for OUTPUT. Thus the statement

```
IF X=3 THEN OUTPUT;
```

if written as the last executable statement of a DATA step, is the same as

```
IF X=3 ;
```

written in the same position.

But if it is not the last executable statement, these two results would be different. Many beginning SAS users make the mistake of thinking that once OUTPUT is executed, the step begins again; this is not so. For unlike the subsetting IF or the DELETE statement, OUTPUT does *not* cause a return "to the top" of the DATA step. In other words, the current iteration continues.

The OUTPUT statement helps you create two or more SAS datasets in a single DATA step, to create more than one observation from a single line of raw input, and to combine more than one line of input into a single observation of the new dataset. We'll discuss creating more than one SAS dataset in this chapter, and other OUTPUT applications later on.

Creating Two SAS Datasets

Consider the raw data presented earlier containing students' names, ages, and grades. To keep only observations for students in the A or B range,

```
DATA STUDENTS;
  INPUT NAME $ AGE @14 GR $1. @14 GRADE $2.;
  IF GR = 'A' OR GR = 'B';
RUN;
```

was written. But suppose we have an additional requirement:

Problem: Also keep the grades of students not attaining "B or better" in a separate dataset.

Solution: Write the DATA statement with two SAS dataset names, setting the stage for creation of more than two SAS datasets in the same DATA step. Then use OUTPUT to refer explicitly to one or more dataset names. The following program creates one dataset containing observations of students with "B or better," and another containing other students (given: the external data are in a file called GRADES):

```
DATA STDNT_AB STDNT_CF;
  INFILE GRADES;
  INPUT NAME $ AGE @14 GR $1. @14 GRADE $2.;
  IF GR = 'A' OR GR = 'B' THEN OUTPUT STDNT_AB;
  ELSE OUTPUT STDNT_CF;
RUN;
```

IF-THEN-ELSE

This program also illustrates the IF-THEN-ELSE construct. The ELSE statement is a special statement that can only appear after an IF-THEN statement (or a DO group conditioned on an IF-THEN statement; DO groups will be covered in Chapter 16, as will SELECT groups, an alternative to IF-THEN-ELSE); it should in fact be considered an extension of the IF statement. It tells SAS that "If the logical expression in the immediately preceding IF statement was false, execute *this* statement instead of the statement following THEN." (See Figure 3.6.) Any executable SAS statement, including another IF statement, can follow ELSE.

There are many possible applications for this behavior. Here is a program that creates three SAS datasets, one containing A-B students, one all other students, and one all the students:

```
DATA STUDENTS STDNT_AB STDNT_CF;
  INFILE GRADES;
  INPUT NAME $ AGE @14 GR $1. @14 GRADE $2.;
  OUTPUT STUDENTS;
  IF GR = 'A' OR GR = 'B' THEN OUTPUT STDNT_AB;
  ELSE OUTPUT STDNT_CF;
RUN;
```

Note, by the way, that the OUTPUT STUDENTS line could have been placed after the IF-THEN-ELSE group with no difference in effect. The one thing has nothing to do with the other. OUTPUT STUDENTS is not within the IF-THEN-ELSE group, nor has any other program statement intervened to alter the data.

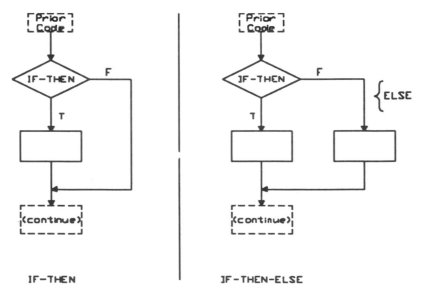

Figure 3.6. Flow of control, IF-THEN and IF-THEN-ELSE groups. With IF-THEN, it's something or nothing; with IF-THEN-ELSE, it's this or that.

But to transpose the order of the IF- THEN-ELSE and the OUTPUT statements in the following program, which keeps all the students together in the STUDENTS dataset but "hides" their grades therein, would be wrong, because intervening program statements change the data after they are output to STDNT_AB or STDNT_CF:

```
DATA STUDENTS STDNT_AB STDNT_CF;
   INFILE GRADES;
   INPUT NAME $ AGE @14 GR $1. @14 GRADE $2.;
   IF GR = 'A' OR GR = 'B' THEN OUTPUT STDNT_AB;
   ELSE OUTPUT STDNT_CF;
   GR='?'; GRADE='??';
   OUTPUT STUDENTS;
RUN;
```

The differences in the datasets produced by these programs is illustrated in Listing 3.2.

VARIABLE SELECTION

DROP and KEEP Statements

Any variable name used in a DATA statement may become a variable in the SAS dataset(s) being built. Variables are created not only by INPUT, but by any other statement that uses a given name for the first time; we will return to this point in Chapter 4. Sometimes, variables are created only to do a DATA step task, not because they are themselves of interest. In the SAS datasets created by the "grades" example above, there is an "unnecessary" variable, GR. It is redundant with GRADE, and was created only for the purpose of assigning observations to datasets.

To control what variables will finally get written to the SAS dataset(s) being created, the DROP or KEEP statements may be used. They have the forms

```
DROP variables;
```

```
KEEP variables;
```

If in the DATA step that created the three student datasets the statement

```
DROP GR;
```

had been included, GR would not have been added to any of the datasets created in the step. Alternatively, in this program

```
KEEP NAME AGE GRADE;
```

```
FIRST WAY: Grades are shown in All Datasets
           DATASET: STUDENTS

     OBS    NAME      AGE    GR    GRADE

      1     JOHNNY     8     A     A-
      2     MARY       9     B     B
      3     JOEY       8     B     B+
      4     JAN       11     D     D+
      5     ALICE     11     A     A
      6     BOBBY      8     B     B-
      7     LINDSAY   10     C     C+


FIRST WAY: Grades are shown in All Datasets
           DATASET: STDNT_AB

     OBS    NAME      AGE    GR    GRADE

      1     JOHNNY     8     A     A-
      2     MARY       9     B     B
      3     JOEY       8     B     B+
      4     ALICE     11     A     A
      5     BOBBY      8     B     B-


FIRST WAY: Grades are shown in All Datasets
           DATASET: STDNT_CF

     OBS    NAME      AGE    GR    GRADE

      1     JAN       11     D     D+
      2     LINDSAY   10     C     C+


SECOND WAY: Hide student grades in dataset "STUDENTS"
            DATASET: STUDENTS

     OBS    NAME      AGE    GR    GRADE

      1     JOHNNY     8     ?     ??
      2     MARY       9     ?     ??
      3     JOEY       8     ?     ??
      4     JAN       11     ?     ??
      5     ALICE     11     ?     ??
      6     BOBBY      8     ?     ??
      7     LINDSAY   10     ?     ??
```

Listing 3.2. Output, Students' Grades example

Continued

```
SECOND WAY: Hide student grades in dataset "STUDENTS"
                 DATASET: STDNT_AB

        OBS     NAME     AGE    GR    GRADE

         1      JOHNNY    8     A     A-
         2      MARY      9     B     B
         3      JOEY      8     B     B+
         4      ALICE    11     A     A
         5      BOBBY     8     B     B-


SECOND WAY: Hide student grades in dataset "STUDENTS"
                 DATASET: STDNT_CF

        OBS     NAME     AGE    GR    GRADE

         1      JAN      11     D     D+
         2      LINDSAY  10     C     C+
```

Listing 3.2. *Continued*

would achieve the same result.

Variables created during the DATA step are available for the purposes of the step whether or not they are added to the datasets being created. In the present example, whether or not the KEEP or the DROP statement is used, GR is available to serve its purpose. The DROP and KEEP statements are concerned only with whether variables listed will remain in the SAS dataset(s) created; see Figure 3.7). DROP and KEEP are exact opposites; SAS provides both for convenience, as in some cases it will be easier to write the list of variables to keep, while in other cases only a few variables will be dropped and that list easier to write.

DROP and KEEP are nonexecutable statements, and may appear anywhere within the DATA step statements (except between an IF-THEN and its ELSE, or the statements of a SELECT group [Chapter 16], which must stay together). More than one DROP or KEEP statement may appear, but you should avoid using both DROP and KEEP statements in the same DATA step.

THE ASSIGNMENT STATEMENT

One way SAS assigns values to variables is with INPUT statements. There is also another way of specifying variable values. It is through use of the *Assignment statement*, which has the form

```
variable = expression ;
```

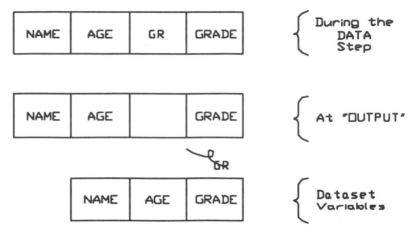

Figure 3.7.   KEEP or DROP statements affect only the SAS dataset being built, not the DATA step as it runs. (Illustration based on "grades" example in text.)

The Assignment statement doesn't have a syntactic name, it just begins with the name of some dataset variable, followed by the assignment operator "=" and a valid SAS expression. An example:

```
DATA BOTMLINE;
   INFILE SALES;
   INPUT PROJECTD ACTUAL;
   ACT_DIFF = ACTUAL - PROJECTD;
   IF ACT_DIFF > 0 THEN BOTMLINE = 'GOOD';
   ELSE BOTMLINE = 'BAD!';
RUN;
```

Here the variable ACT_DIFF is created by assignment, taking on the numeric value of an arithmetic difference. The variable BOTMLINE is also created by an Assignment statement, which follows the logical expression of an IF statement. BOTMLINE will be a character variable, because it is set equal to one or the other character constant "GOOD" or "BAD!."

In this example, ACT_DIFF and BOTMLINE were originally created by Assignment statements, but preexisting variables, not just new ones, can be affected by assignment. Here is an example of a variable created by INPUT, but changed by assignment:

```
DATA COMEDY;
   INFILE COMICS;
   INPUT NAME & $20. AGE;
   IF NAME='JACK BENNY' THEN AGE = 39;
RUN;
```

Whatever Jack's age in COMICS, his age in COMEDY will always be 39.

INPUT: REPEATED EXECUTION

The INPUT statement is an executable statement, and there is no reason why INPUT cannot be coded more than once in a DATA step. For example, given a lengthy set of input information, spanning several input data lines, you can use the relative linepointer operator /:

```
INPUT NAME $25. ADDRESS $55. / HEIGHT WEIGHT AGE ETC ;
```

But, alternatively and equivalently, you can code:

```
INPUT NAME $25. ADDRESS $55.;
INPUT HEIGHT WEIGHT AGE ETC;
```

This works as intended because in general, when INPUT is executed, it's first action is to retrieve a fresh record from the external data set referenced by the most recent INFILE statement (or from CARDS). The first INPUT statement in this example reads NAME and ADDRESS, and the second one takes the *next* line of input to look for HEIGHT and the rest.

But SAS is also capable of "holding" a data line for subsequent executions of INPUT, and does not *have* to get a new data line each time. SAS provides two special INPUT specifiers, @ and @@, for this purpose. These may be used only at the end of an INPUT statement, i.e., as the last items before ";", and each serves a different purpose.

Holding a Record for More INPUT

The single trailing @* can be used to allow INPUT statements later in the DATA step to operate upon the same input data record. What the trailing @ commands SAS to do is keep hold of the present input record for the next INPUT statement; the line and column pointers hold at the place they stopped, i.e., on the current line number and at the first or second position after the last value read (or at the place specified by a pointer operator if one immediately precedes the trailing @). The first subsequent INPUT statement in the DATA step that does not have a trailing @ releases the line so any subsequent INPUT statements will use a fresh input record. The line is released when the DATA step begins the next execution, i.e., at the end of the step statements or after a DELETE.

This comes in very handy when input data contain different kinds of records. Let's take as an example a lengthy questionnaire about health habits, which upon

---

*Do not confuse this with the absolute column pointer specifier, which uses the same symbol placed before a column number. The "trailing" @ is so called because it must be the last element in an INPUT statement before the terminating semicolon.

data entry must be broken into several 80-column records to handle the amount of information required. With a large volume of data so broken into separate records, it is customary to reserve one column (usually the first or the last) for a "card" number: if it is card 1 certain variables appear, if 2 there are others, and so on. [Card 1 might have a name, address, and phone number; card 2 demographic information (such as age, sex, marital status, education); card 3 smoking information; etc.] It is also customary to assign each respondent an identification number, which is included on each card.

Now for purposes of this example, suppose it takes eight card-image lines to contain all possible questionnaire information, but that not all respondents will generate each kind of record: In some cases, a whole series of follow-up questions, which would not apply to nonsmokers, is asked only if a respondent says "Yes" to a smoking question (what brand, how many packs/day, etc.). Therefore, not all subjects will have all cards 1 through 8.

This sort of input data is a good candidate for a single trailing @ operator, used as follows:

```
DATA SURVEY;
   INPUT ID 1-5 @80 CARDNUM @ ;
   IF CARDNUM = 1 THEN
      INPUT LNAME $15. FNAME $15. ADDRESS $40.;
   ELSE IF CARDNUM = 2 THEN
      INPUT AGE 2. +1 SEX $1. +1 MSTATUS $1. +1 EDUCLVL 2.;
[conditions 3 through 7 ...]
   ELSE IF CARDNUM = 8 THEN
      INPUT CIGBRAND $15. PACKSDAY 2. DEADYET $1.;
```

Shown is just a portion of the code. In the actual program, there would be a total of nine INPUT statements: the first one with the trailing @ and eight following the IF and ELSE IF statements.*

More than one INPUT statement can have a trailing @. Suppose we have our ID numbers coded such that the 90000 series represents special cases that are to be ignored for the data analysis. We could write:

---

*As mentioned earlier, an IF statement can follow ELSE just like any other executable statement. Note that each ELSE still refers to the IF immediately preceding. The example programs could have been written the same way without the ELSE keyword, i.e., with all IF statements rather than one IF and the rest ELSE IF. However, while achieving the same result, this would be more costly in execution time: the logical expression following each IF would be executed for all observations, while with the ELSE IF construction, the logical expressions need to be evaluated only until one is found "true." Multiple IF-THEN statements (as opposed to multiple ELSE-IF-THEN statements) should be used when the choices are not mutually exclusive, i.e., when there may be cases where more than one of the clauses following an IF may be "true" and be important for purposes of your program.

```
DATA SURVEY;
   INPUT ID 1-5 @80 CARDNUM @ ;
   IF ID >= 90000 THEN DELETE;
   IF CARDNUM = 1 THEN
      INPUT LNAME $15. FNAME $15. ADDRESS $40.;
   ELSE IF CARDNUM = 2 THEN
      INPUT AGE 2. +1 SEX $1. +1 MSTATUS $1. +1 EDUCLVL 2.;
[etc ...]
```

But the following would also work:

```
DATA SURVEY;
   INPUT ID 1-5 @;
   IF ID >= 90000 THEN DELETE;
   INPUT @80 CARDNUM @;
   IF CARDNUM = 1 THEN
      INPUT LNAME $15. FNAME $15. ADDRESS $40.;
   ELSE IF CARDNUM - 2 THEN
      INPUT AGE 2. +1 SEX $1. +1 MSTATUS $1. +1 EDUCLVL 2.;
[etc ...]
```

Holding an Input Record Indefinitely

It sometimes happens that input data lines contain more than one logical observation. For example, if the number of variables is small, it may have been convenient to enter data values one right after another. An informal listing of names and ages might be an example. Data might be entered thus:

```
FRED 24  JANE  16  ALISON 12  HUMPHREY 43  RONNIE 77
BOB 39 ALVIN 22
```

This data can be read with the statement

```
INPUT NAME $ AGE @@;
```

which says to SAS, "get the name (from the next character value, up to 10 characters long) and then the age, and then stay right where you are, even after the present DATA step iteration is complete." The double trailing @@ is a separate and distinct operator from @ and must not be written with embedded spaces (@ @ is invalid).

Unlike the trailing @, under which a new input line will be obtained if the DATA statement begins executing again "from the top," the input buffer is held even for subsequent DATA statement iterations when INPUT is terminated with @@. Thus the same INPUT statement can process one line again and again. With the trailing @@, SAS goes to the next input line when it is necessary: A new input line is brought in when an attempt is made to read past the end of the current line.

Thus after finding no input after "RONNIE 77" on the first line, the next time through the INPUT statement the next line is retrieved and "BOB 39" read.

As with @, you can force SAS to release the current line and pick up the next INPUT from a fresh data line if you include a subsequent INPUT statement without @@. You may use an INPUT statement with neither @@ nor @ to release the line immediately, or an input statement with a trailing @ to release the line at the end of the current DATA step iteration.

Releasing a Held Line Unconditionally

Sometimes, you may wish to release an input line within the DATA step, but have no additional variables to read with an INPUT statement. You can use a "null" input statement

```
INPUT;
```

to accomplish this. (It is, after all, an INPUT statement without a trailing @ or @@.) This technique works for lines that were held by a prior INPUT statement that used either @ or @@.

VARIABLE ATTRIBUTES

Every SAS variable must have a name. In addition, all SAS variables have associated with them several other items of information, the variable *attributes*. SAS variable attributes include *type*, *length*, *label*, *format*, and *informat*. Each variable has at all times a defined type and length; label, format, and informat may or may not be defined for a given variable.

Variable Type

The SAS System considers all variables to be of one of two types: numeric or character. Default type for new variables is numeric; as we have seen, to declare a character type with INPUT requires the $ specifier. Valid numeric input values may contain only numerals, a leading plus or minus sign, a decimal point, and if the user wants to use scientific notation, the "E" exponent indicator. Attempts to use any other characters will cause an input error, unless an appropriate informat has been specified.

Character values on input can include any characters that can be represented by the physical machine, including numerals, letters, spaces, punctuation, and special characters.

Type Conversion

It is very common for the SAS System to decide to change a numeric value to a character value or vice versa.* You would be wise to know when this might come about.

SAS execution will automatically convert a numeric value to character in two cases:

1. If a character variable is set equal to a numeric value in an Assignment statement, the character representation of the number is given to the character variable.
2. If a numeric variable is used in an expression using a character operator (the concatenation operator ||, entered from the keyboard as two consecutive vertical bars), the character numeral is used in the operation.

SAS execution will automatically convert a character variable to a numeric representation in two cases:

1. If a numeric variable is set equal to a character variable containing only numeric-valid characters (i.e., numerals, perhaps a decimal point or leading sign), the numeric value of the character numeral is assigned.
2. If a character variable is used in an expression using a numeric operator, such as +, or a logical comparison operator, such as <, *and* the character variable contains only numeric-valid characters, the numeric representation of the number is used in the operation.

While numeric-to-character translation always succeeds (at least as far as the SAS System is concerned—but is the logic of your program correct?), character-to-numeric translation may result in an error, because the character variable may not contain characters other than sign, numeral, decimal point, and possibly the exponent specifier E. In the case of numeric-invalid characters, an error will be noted in the SAS log (see Chapter 6) and the resulting numeric variable set to the system missing value. To warn about automatic type conversions, the log will note when any type conversions have taken place, even if no error resulted.

Variable Length

SAS data files require storage space for each variable, for each observation; for uncompressed datasets† the space allocated is the same for a given variable across all observations. The SAS System allows the programmer direct control over vari-

---

*The type of a variable itself does not actually change by automatic type conversion. What changes is the value of the variable as used in the assignment or expression causing type conversion.

†Data compression is discussed in Chapter 21. Length conservation as discussed here is beneficial in all cases, whether or not data compression is planned.

able storage length, which can be an important space conservation measure when SAS data files with large numbers of observations are constructed.

Variable lengths are expressed in bytes of storage. The length of a character variable is set the first time the variable is named in the creating DATA step. If the variable name first appears in an INPUT statement, the length will be set to that implied in the statement: Column specification "11–15" sets the length of the subject variable to five bytes, informat specification "$15." sets the length to 15 bytes, etc. Character variables mentioned first on INPUT using list style input are set by default to 8 bytes. Character variables created by assignment of the value of another character variable take the length of that variable, while character variables created by assignment of the value of a character expression take the length of the result of that expression. The maximum character variable length in any case is 200 bytes.

Caution: If a character variable is first mentioned in an Assignment statement and assigned to a constant, the length of the constant will prevail and there is a danger of truncation, i.e., cutting off the tail end of a value. Thus the statements

```
IF A = 1 THEN B = 'NO';
ELSE IF A = 2 THEN B = 'YES';
```

will produce unwanted results if the first line is the first mention of B in the DATA step. That assignment sets the length of B to 2 bytes; if a record contains a value of 2 for A, B will be "YE," not "YES."

By default, numeric variables are allocated 8 bytes, the maximum numeric length, which can represent values up to 16 significant digits and therefore is sufficient even for exacting scientific calculations.

The LENGTH Statement

You can gain precise control over variables' storage lengths by using the LENGTH statement, with the form:

```
LENGTH [<variables [$] length_specifier>...] [DEFAULT=n];
```

The LENGTH statement must appear early in the DATA step for it to apply to new character variables, the lengths of which are governed by their first mention in the step. The optional parameter DEFAULT can be used to change the default length of *numeric* variables from the normal eight bytes. Here are two examples:

    1. Variables A and B are numeric variables with a length of four bytes, C a character variable with a length of ten:

```
LENGTH A B 4 C $ 10;
```

    2. Variables V1 through V10 are numeric variables with a length of eight bytes, R and S character variables each with a length of 25 bytes, T a numeric variable with a length of 2 bytes, and the default length for all new numeric variables created in the DATA step is set to 3 bytes:

```
LENGTH V1-V10 8 R S $ 25 T 2 DEFAULT=3;
```

Notice that in the LENGTH statement no period is needed after the number signifying the length.

For numeric variables, eight bytes are sufficient in all cases, but oftentimes, especially for integers whose maximum expected value can be known, shorter storage lengths may suffice. The SAS documentation for your operating system will tell you just what storage lengths are required for numeric variables to guarantee sufficient precision. A potential problem with nonintegral numeric variables of lengths less than eight bytes is that fractional values may not compare as expected. For example, if the value 1/3 (computed to 0.333 . . .) is assigned to variable V which has been given a length of less than eight, the comparison in a statement such as "IF V=1/3 THEN . . ." will be *false*, because the constant on the right will have the full eight-byte representation; full precision is always used in arithmetic computations, regardless of variable storage length.

Note that all new numeric variables, even those assigned to others with specific lengths, take the default numeric length unless explicitly altered with a LENGTH statement. For example, in a dataset created by

```
DATA SAMPLE;
  LENGTH A 4 B $ 5;
  A2=A; B2=B;
  ...
RUN;
```

variable B2 will be a character variable of length 5, but A2 a numeric variable of length 8, not 4.

Variable Labels

Many SAS procedures allow the use of up to 40 characters as output variable labels. That is, many procedures will print a variable's label, rather than its name, if a label has been defined. Given:

```
LABEL AGE='AGE AT DATE OF POLICY INCEPTION';
```

the variable name remains AGE. AGE is used in all program statements that are intended to refer to the variable, but "AGE AT DATE OF POLICY INCEPTION" is printed by certain procedures which otherwise would print only "AGE," the variable name.

A variable label may be defined with a LABEL statement, the general form of which is

```
LABEL <variable = 'label'>...;
```

Any number of "variable='label'" specifications may follow LABEL, and any number of LABEL statements may be used in a DATA step.

Variable Formats and Informats

We have already encountered informats in our discussion of the INPUT statement. An informat tells the SAS DATA step compiler about the nature of raw input data. The informat "$12." in an INPUT statement (for example; this and other SAS informats will be reviewed in Chapter 7) lets the compiler know that there is a 12-byte character value coming.

In some applications, it may be useful to describe the informats of certain variables prior to INPUT. This can be done with an INFORMAT statement:

```
INFORMAT <variables [informat]>... ;
```

This can allow the user to write an INPUT statement more easily, using list-style input but still having the data item read with an implied informat.

SAS formats are, in a sense, the reverse of informats: while an informat tells SAS how to change incoming raw data to a SAS variable, a format tells SAS how to change a SAS variable to an output value, for printing or for storing in a non-SAS dataset. The SAS format MMDDYY8. (for example; this and other SAS formats will be reviewed in Chapter 11) tells SAS to produce from a SAS date value a character sequence in the form MM/DD/YY (e.g., "11/29/85").

SAS formats can be specified in the FORMAT statement:

```
FORMAT <variables [format]>... ;
```

for example,

```
FORMAT A 8.4 B1-B5 MONYY5. C D E DOLLAR15.2;
```

requests A be written with format 8.4, B1 through B5 with MONYY5., and C, D, and E with format DOLLAR15.2. These and other standard SAS formats will be reviewed in Chapter 11, where we also discuss how to create user-defined formats.

SAS informats or formats, if specified in the DATA step, are permanently associated with the variables in the SAS data set(s) created. It is also possible to associate an output format temporarily with a SAS variable, by use of the FORMAT statement in a PROC step. This is often preferable, as it allows maximum flexibility in using the data for different purposes.

The ATTRIB Statement

SAS provides the ATTRIB statement as an alternative for specifying variable attributes. Using ATTRIB is often convenient when several of the attributes type, length, format, informat, or label need to be specified. It has the form:

```
ATTRIB < <variable>... [FORMAT=format]
[INFORMAT=informat]
[LABEL='label'] [LENGTH=[$]length] >...;
```

The statement

```
ATTRIB MYVAR LABEL='THIS IS MY VARIABLE' LENGTH=$20;
```

is equivalent to the statements

```
LABEL MYVAR 'THIS IS MY VARIABLE'; LENGTH MYVAR $20;
```

Attributes at DATA Step Compilation

The various attribute-setting statements (ATTRIB, FORMAT, INFORMAT, and LENGTH) are nonexecutable statements; their effects are taken at DATA Step compile-time, not during step execution.

It is, nevertheless, true that even at compile-time the order of nonexecutable statements may make a difference. This is the case when variable names are coded. The SAS compiler makes allowances for two variable attributes—type and length—at the time it first encounters their names in passing through the program code.* It is a good idea if you want to set a variable's length explicitly to declare the variables up front with a LENGTH (or ATTRIB) statement, to make your wishes known explicitly before the compiler takes it upon itself to decide on storage length.

---

*The reason it must do this is so it can set up the program data vector, which we discuss in the next chapter.

4

Rebuilding SAS Datasets

We have seen that with the appropriate program statements, a SAS user can change or augment data originally read from external files with INPUT. In this chapter, we will see that after data has been stored in SAS datasets, the data can be used to create other SAS datasets with altered structure or content. If using INPUT to process external data can be called "building" SAS datasets (and I think that is appropriate), then this chapter is about rebuilding SAS datasets: changing SAS datasets around. More details and techniques for building and rebuilding SAS data will be revealed in Part II.

There are many reasons to rebuild SAS datasets. The user may have overlooked something when writing the original DATA step; a large SAS data file may have been built on tape but only a small subset of records or variables is needed online for a certain series of analyses; or additional variables may have to be created for special purposes (for example, a variable AGE, based upon today's date and a birthdate stored in the original dataset). Furthermore, so that SAS procedures can have the datasets they need to give back the results desired, the user may have to combine datasets by adding observations from two or more datasets to a new dataset, combine observations by adding variables from two or more datasets to a dataset with a new variable structure, or create subsets of data.

A simple yet important fact should be mentioned before proceeding further: *An existing SAS dataset is not itself changed by the methods described below; rebuilding is accomplished by creating one or more new, different SAS datasets*. The new datasets share information with their "parent"; the parent remains unchanged. DATA steps create new SAS datasets, they do not alter existing ones. (There is one noteworthy exception to this rule, and that is when data is rebuilt using the MODIFY statement. We will discuss MODIFY processing in Chapter 10.)

DATA STEP PROCESSES AND THE PROGRAM DATA VECTOR

While at work on a DATA step, the SAS System maintains a temporary data structure in computer memory called the program data vector, or PDV. The program data vector represents one "row" of data, and can be drawn for illustration as a linear set of boxes in which values of SAS variables can be contained (as in Figure 4.1; compare this with our illustrations of datasets in Chapter 1, and contrast with our drawing of the input buffer as a linear set of characters). If you want to understand DATA Step processing, you must understand how the DATA Step compiler creates the PDV, and how DATA step execution affects its contents dynamically.

To construct the PDV is one of the DATA step compiler's first jobs on its first pass through DATA step source code. All the SAS statements in the step's source are scanned for variable names and dataset names, and the PDV is constructed with space for each variable in the order encounered in the code (or in the input SAS datasets; see "The SET Statement", below); see Figure 4.1a. The attributes of PDV variables, and their order, then remain constant throughout the step, though values within the PDV can change; see Figure 4.1b.

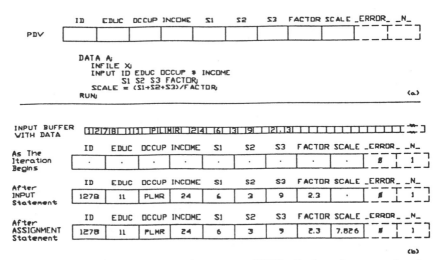

Figure 4.1. The SAS program data vector (PDV), displayed as an ordered series of boxes, each representing a variable. Automatic DATA step variables are depicted in dotted outline. (a) The PDV created by a specific DATA step: ID is the first variable named in the step, EDUC the second, etc. Names are shown on top, leaving the boxes to contain values. (b) At execution of the DATA step, with a line in the input buffer being processed.

Automatic Variables

There are a couple of variables the SAS System keeps track of at each iteration, besides those variables declared in your program or in preexisting datasets. These are called "automatic" variables because they are generated automatically (as it were) by the SAS System's DATA step execution process. Two of these, _N_ and _ERROR_, always come into existence and can be used by your program. They can be thought of as part of the PDV, although they do not become part of the dataset being rebuilt (they appear in Figures 4.1 and 4.2, but in dashed borders as a reminder that they are not part of the data vector proper). _N_ contains a count of how many times the DATA step has begun iterating "from the top," and _ERROR_ is set to 1 (true) when a data error occurs (see Chapter 6) or when an ERROR statement is executed.

Note that other automatic variables may come into existence as a result of using BY statements and certain other statements or statement options; we will study some of these variables later in this chapter. Like _N_ and _ERROR_, the other automatic variables are available for use in your program and change dynamically with each step iteration, and can be informally thought of as part of the program data vector even though they don't become part of the rebuilt dataset.

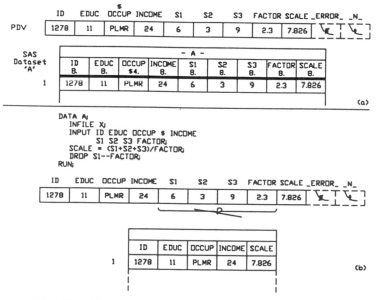

Figure 4.2. The PDV and the dataset observation. (a) At output, automatic variables such as __N__ and __ERROR__ are dropped. (b) Should a DROP or KEEP be present, declared variables (variables named in the step) may also be dropped from the dataset. Illustrated is a DROP statement using the double-hyphen variable list abbreviation, signifying the variables S1, FACTOR, and any in between.

The PDV During Step Iteration

Each time the executing DATA step begins another iteration, the values of variables to be created by INPUT or by assignment in the PDV are initialized to missing (unless a RETAIN or Sum statement has been used; see below), __N__ is incremented, and __ERROR__ is set to zero. Variables created by SET or MERGE (also discussed below) may retain their values from the prior observation. As the step executes, the values of the variables in the PDV may be changed as a result of INPUT or other SAS statements. When output (with OUTPUT, or at the end of the DATA step statements), the observation is written to the SAS dataset(s) with the current values of the PDV, excluding the automatic system variables and any DROPped (or not KEEP't) variables; see Figure 4.2. When the DATA step "returns to the top" for the next iteration, the PDV is reinitialized and the process repeats.

As illustrated, the order of the variables in the PDV is determined by the order in which they are first named in the DATA step. This will also be the order in which the variables are logically stored in the SAS dataset being created. (The order must be known if "the double-hyphen variable list" abbreviation is later to be used.)

The RETAIN and Sum Statements

By default, variables in the PDV that are named with assignment or with INPUT statements are initialized to missing each time the DATA step begins a new iteration. The RETAIN statement,

```
RETAIN [<variables [value]>...];
```

causes the named variables not to be initialized, i.e., to keep their values from the previous iteration when the next one starts. They can still be changed if INPUT reads a new observation, or when an assignment statement (including the Sum statement, below) is executed. If a constant value is specified after the variable list, the variable starts with that value before the first iteration; otherwise, numeric variables start with a value of zero. See Figure 4.3.

The Sum statement is a special type of assignment statement, provided as a convenience for incrementing variables during the DATA step. A statement of the form

```
A + expression;
```

is identical in action to the statements

```
RETAIN A; A = A + expression;
```

In other words, a Sum statement implies both a RETAIN of a certain variable and an assignment to that variable of its present value incremented by the value of an expression.

```
DATA NEW;
    INFILE IN;
    RETAIN GROUP 1;
    INPUT X Y Z;
    IF_N_=100 THEN GROUP = 2;
RUN;
```

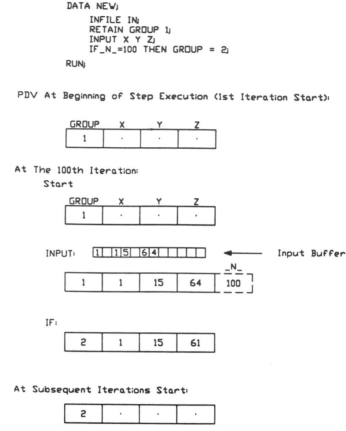

Figure 4.3. PDV with RETAIN. Variables except GROUP are initialized to missing at the beginning of each iteration. GROUP starts the step with a value of 1; in subsequent iterations, it begins with whatever value it had at the end of the prior iteration.

REBUILDING A SINGLE DATASET

The SET Statement

Before any action can be taken to rebuild SAS data, the SAS System must be told from where to retrieve preexisting SAS datasets. This is accomplished with the SET statement.

As INFILE (or CARDS) refers to an existing external dataset, so the SET statement refers to an existing SAS dataset. The SET statement takes the form

```
SET [<dataset_name[(dataset_options)]>...] [set_options];
```

The dataset name must refer to an already existing SAS dataset, temporary or permanent; a two-level name can be used to refer to a permanent SAS dataset (created earlier in the present job, or before it). If no dataset name is given (though as we have discussed, it is always good practice to name datasets explicitly), SET uses the dataset most recently created in the present program, i.e., as a result of a preceding DATA or PROC step. Certain *dataset options* may be placed in parentheses after a dataset name, and certain SET statement options may appear at the end of the statement. No INPUT-like specifications are necessary, since the existing data is already in SAS format.

Basically, SET asks that an observation be retrieved from a named dataset, and its variables' values placed into the program data vector. The PDV was constructed by taking into account the existing dataset data vector, and at SET execution the variables' existing attributes are used, and they are entered in the dataset in order. Consider the simple DATA step

```
DATA DSCOPY;
  SET DS1;
RUN;
```

The SAS dataset DSCOPY will be observation for observation and variable for variable identical to the (pre-existing) dataset DS1. With nothing but DS1's dataset vector to account for, the compiler builds a PDV with the same variables in the same order. As execution begins, the first observation in DS1 is brought in, and when RUN is encountered, it is written to DSCOPY. Each time this SET statement is executed, the next observation in DS1 is retrieved. Execution stops after the last observation in DS1 has been read and written.

Adding Variables

Suppose that a dataset contains several variables, among them GROSS and NET, and from this a new dataset is to be created that contains these and also a variable MARGIN, being the difference between GROSS and NET. This is done very simply as follows:

```
DATA SECOND;
  SET FIRST;
  MARGIN = GROSS - NET;
RUN;
```

When the DATA step runs, the dataset SECOND contains six variables: the five originally from FIRST and the new variable MARGIN created by assignment. SECOND has the same number of observations as FIRST, but an additional variable for each observation. Figure 4.4 illustrates how the PDV was constructed to contain a variable not found in the input dataset.

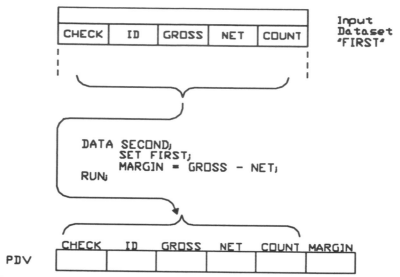

Figure 4.4. The PDV with SET. As SET is encountered, the PDV grows by the variables from the input dataset, taken in the order they are in the dataset.

Changing Variable Values

Not only may new variables be assigned and take their places in the output dataset, but new values may be assigned to an existing variable coming in from an input dataset.

Problem: A permanent SAS dataset, MYDATA.MONEY, contains among other variables one called BALANCE. BALANCE may be zero, positive, or negative. For certain purposes, you wish to produce a new dataset containing BALANCE, but without any negative figures; rather, when BALANCE is negative, it should be treated as zero.

Solution: Create a working dataset (here called ASSETS) as follows:

```
DATA ASSETS;
  SET MYDATA.MONEY;
  IF BALANCE < 0 THEN BALANCE = 0;
RUN;
```

The working dataset ASSETS is observation for observation identical to MONEY, except that when the BALANCE showing in MONEY is less than zero, the correponding BALANCE in ASSETS is zero. (At the beginning of iteration the location of BALANCE in the PDV is refreshed by a value from the input dataset. However, if that value happens to be less than zero the value in the PDV at this location is again changed, this time by the IF-THEN. The observation is output, remember, at the end of the iteration [there was no OUTPUT statement elsewhere], taking the values as they are in the PDV *at that time*.)

Selecting Observations or Variables; Renaming Variables

Keeping Only Some Observations

Selecting observations for a rebuilt dataset can be done with subsetting IF statements. Here a dataset is created with information on company employees from Department 1:

```
DATA DEPT1.EMPLOYEE;
  SET PERSONNL.EMPLOYEE;
  IF DEPT = 1;
RUN;
```

It is of course permissible to use "IF . . . THEN- OUTPUT" constructions, helpful if more than one dataset is being created, but remember that this is not exactly the same: the subsetting IF performs a DELETE when its expression is not satisfied, but IF...THEN goes on to the rest of the step code (if any; results are the same in the simple example just given).

Keeping Only Some Variables

DROP or KEEP statements may be placed among the DATA step program statements to create a SAS dataset containing subsets of the variables in another dataset. Here we obtain only the variables needed for a mailing list from a personnel file that contains these and (presumably) others:

```
DATA MAILDATA;
  SET PERSONNL.EMPLOYEE;
  KEEP LNAME FNAME MI ADDRESS1 ADDRESS2 CITY STATE ZIP;
RUN;
```

KEEP and DROP statements apply to the new dataset when it is written; as observations are being processed, even variables that will "disappear" are available for use, because KEEP and DROP statements do not change the PDV. So to get only names of California personnel from the MAILDATA dataset, you could write:

```
DATA CANAMES;
  SET MAILDATA; * FROM ACROSS THE NATION;
  DROP ADDRESS1 ADDRESS2 CITY STATE ZIP;
  IF STATE = 'CA';
RUN;
```

Notice that the values of STATE are used in the program, even though they are not written to the output dataset. The PDV contains all the variables from MAILDATA; the DROP statement only causes them to be ignored when the output observation is written.

Renaming Variables

The RENAME statement can be used to have variables of the same content as in an old dataset take different names in a new dataset. The RENAME statement has the form

```
RENAME <oldname=newname>...;
```

and is used as in the following:

```
DATA NEW;
   SET OLD;
   Z = X + Y;
   RENAME X=OLDX Y=OLDY;
RUN;
```

Dataset OLD contains variables X and Y; dataset NEW contains OLDX, OLDY, and Z. This example is portrayed in Listing 4.1.

Note that RENAME, like DROP or KEEP, is a nonexecutable statement that can appear anywhere within the step. However, you must use the *old* name anywhere else in the DATA step that the variables might be needed, as in the example just shown (i.e., "Z=OLDX+OLDY;" would be incorrect here). This is because a RENAME statement, like DROP or KEEP, takes its effect as the data are written to the new dataset, not while an observation is being processed; see Figure 4.5. (Of course, in any subsequent job step calling upon dataset NEW, the new names must be used.)

SAS Dataset Options

When a SAS dataset name is mentioned in a SAS program, certain information or directions concerning how that dataset is to be processed can be included by coding SAS dataset options. SAS dataset options are specified within parentheses after a dataset name. There are a number of different dataset options, some of which can be stated in PROC steps, some only in DATA steps, and some are allowed only in certain statements. Dataset options apply only to the dataset named before their parentheses, and not to any others that may be named in the DATA step.

The following example shows the use of the dataset options DROP= and RENAME=:

```
DATA NEW;
   SET OLD(DROP=A B C RENAME=(D=X));
RUN;
```

The new dataset contains variables from the old one, except for A, B, and C, and old D is renamed X in the new dataset; see Listing 4.2. Note the second set of parentheses that must be used with RENAME= because of its "old=new" construction.

```
<<< PROGRAM SOURCE CODE FOLLOWS >>>

DATA OLD;
   INPUT X Y;
   CARDS;
123 456.7
8910 11121.3
987 654.32
RUN;
DATA NEW;
   SET OLD;
   Z=X+Y;
   RENAME X=OLDX Y=OLDY;
RUN;
PROC PRINT DATA=OLD; TITLE 'OLD Dataset'; RUN;
PROC PRINT DATA=NEW; TITLE 'NEW Dataset'; RUN;

<<< SAS JOB OUTPUT FOLLOWS >>>

              OLD Dataset

       OBS      X         Y

        1      123      456.70
        2     8910    11121.30
        3      987      654.32

              NEW Dataset

 OBS    OLDX       OLDY           Z

  1      123      456.70       579.70
  2     8910    11121.30     20031.30
  3      987      654.32      1641.32
```

Listing 4.1. The RENAME statement

The KEEP=, DROP=, and RENAME= dataset options, which may be used with some other statements as well as with SET, are analogous to the programming statements of the same names, with one big difference: When used as dataset options in a SET statement, action takes place immediately, not at the end of the step (see Figure 4.6). Variables lost with DROP= or KEEP= are *not* available for other programming statements, and the *new* names must be used to refer to variables affected by RENAME=.

But note that when these dataset options are used on a DATA statement, in contrast to their use on SET (or MERGE, see below), the effect is as if they were used as separate statements. That is, you must refer to the old variable names even if there is a RENAME, may use DROPped variables in the step, and so on. This is because when named on the DATA statement, the dataset options are

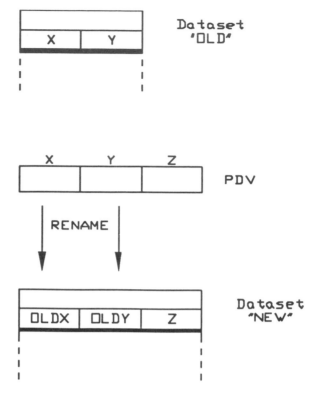

Figure 4.5. The RENAME statement has its effect not on the PDV, but only as the new dataset is written (see text for program example).

applied at the time of output, just as if separate KEEP/DROP or RENAME statements had been used. As discussed later on, dataset options on the DATA step are generally used when more than one dataset is being built, to restrict their application to one of the datasets; used as statements in the body of the step, RENAME, DROP, and KEEP apply to all datasets named on the DATA statement.*

Changing Variable Attributes; Reordering Variables

A dataset is rebuilt with new variable attributes by including new attribute statements. For example, variable labels can be changed. Suppose in a preexisting

---

*One dataset option can be used *only* on the DATA step. This is LABEL='label', which associates a label of up to 40 characters with the dataset. The label will be printed when PROC CONTENTS is executed, and it may be accessed with an option when PROC QPRINT is executed.

```
<<< PROGRAM SOURCE CODE FOLLOWS >>>

DATA OLD;
  INPUT A B C D;
  CARDS;
11 22 33 44
99 88 77 66
RUN;
DATA NEW;
  SET OLD (DROP= A B C  RENAME=(D=X));
RUN;
PROC PRINT DATA=OLD; TITLE 'OLD Dataset'; RUN;
PROC PRINT DATA=NEW; TITLE 'NEW Dataset'; RUN;


<<< SAS JOB OUTPUT FOLLOWS >>>

        OLD Dataset

OBS    A    B    C    D

 1    11   22   33   44
 2    99   88   77   66

      NEW Dataset

     OBS    X

      1    44
      2    66
```

Listing 4.2. Dataset options on a SET statement

dataset, STUFF, there is a variable TOTAL, labeled "TOTAL THIS YEAR" in the DATA step that originally created it. Now, it's next year, so write:

```
DATA MYDATA.NEWYEAR;
  SET MYDATA.STUFF;
  LABEL TOTAL='TOTAL LAST YEAR';
  [other programming statements]
RUN;
```

or remove the label entirely by using a "null" LABEL statement instead; i.e., "LABEL TOTAL=;".

Note that in this example it is appropriate to place the LABEL statement after the SET statement. This way, other attributes from the original dataset are preserved. If, however, you wanted to change the length or type of the variable, the statement (e.g., LENGTH) would have to come before the SET, because the PDV storage length is fixed at compilation in the order variables are encountered.

```
DATA LATTER;
    SET FORMER (DROP = THE SILLY
        RENAME= (STRANGE = QUICK BEAR = FOX
                 AWAY = OVER FAST = LAZYDOG))j
RUNj
```

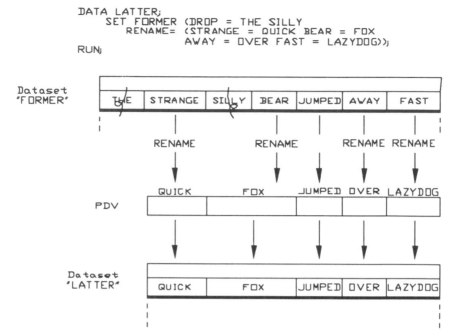

Figure 4.6. Dataset options on a SET statement do affect the program data vector. Were there more executable statements in the step after SET, they would have to refer to the variable FOX, not BEAR, and would not be able to refer to SILLY at all. If BEAR or SILLY were mentioned, these would become new variables, with missing values, at the end of the PDV.

Since the order of variables in the PDV depends on the order variables and existing datasets are named in the DATA step, including the variables in SET datasets, to change the variable order in the PDV—and hence, the output dataset—just name the variables in the order desired *before* the SET statement. Attribute statements can serve this purpose, but be careful to specify the correct type and length.

WORKING WITH MORE THAN ONE DATASET

Concatenating SAS Datasets with SET

Problem: A company has employee records in separate SAS datasets by department, but for a certain cost analysis a user needs a dataset with all employees from Sales (SAS dataset SALES), Marketing (MKTNG), and Customer Service (CUSTSRVC).

Solution: All the user need do is write the simple DATA step:

```
DATA COSTANLS;
  SET CORP.SALES CORP.MKTNG CORP.CUSTSRVC;
RUN;
```

Now COSTANLS contains the observations in SALES, followed by those in MK-TNG, followed by those in CUSTSRVC.

This is called dataset *concatenation*. In the example, when SET is first executed, the first observation of the first dataset contributes the first values of the PDV, which are immediately written to COSTANLS. After the last observation of SALES has been used, processing continues with the first observation of the next dataset (MKTNG), and so on, until it is exhausted, whereupon the observations from CUSTSRVC are used.

When multiple datasets are named on SET, as the compiler retrieves attribute information from each named dataset in turn, so it constructs the PDV. The datasets can have the same or different variables; if there are different variables, then the variables unique to certain datasets will have missing values in observations taken from other datasets (see Figure 4.7 for illustration).

The IN= Dataset Option

When the IN= dataset option is specified within a SET statement, a temporary variable is created that takes the value 1 (logical true) if the dataset contributed values to the current PDV and 0 (logical false) otherwise. That is to say, given the statement

```
SET A (IN=INA) B;
```

an automatic variable, INA, will exist during the DATA step (but will not be added to the dataset being created). The value of the variable will be 1 (true) if the SET statement has just obtained an observation from A, 0 (false) if SET has just retrieved an observation from any other dataset (in this instance, from B). IN= allows selective data processing based on the dataset membership.

IN= may be used with SET to make a record of the file from which an observation came.

Problem: A user needs a DATA step to combine three departments' data into the SAS dataset COSTANLS, as shown above, but wishes also to keep track of the department from which each record came.

Solution: In this variation on the previous example, a new variable DEPT contains the department name:*

---

*Note that the phrase "IF SAL" means "if SAL is nonmissing and nonzero." "IF NOT SAL" would be shorthand for "if SAL is missing or zero." In an IF statement, the expression following the IF keyword is considered "false" if its value is zero or missing, and "true" otherwise, and a solitary variable can serve as the IF expression.

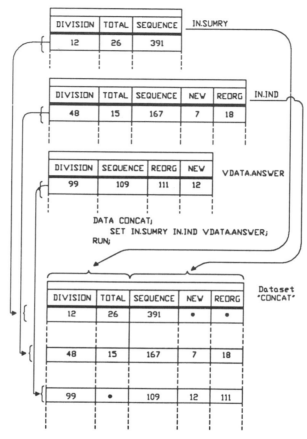

Figure 4.7. Rebuilding with SET. The PDV is based both on variables named in source code and on variables in preexisting SET datasets. The variable order in the new dataset is based on the order as processing proceeds: Up to down and left to right. Values of the observations built with SET are taken in from the observations of the datasets named on SET.

```
DATA ALLEMPL;
  SET CORP.SALES(IN=SAL) CORP.MKTNG(IN=MKTG) CORP.CUSTSRVC;
  LENGTH DEPT $ 5;
  IF SAL THEN DEPT='SALES';
  ELSE IF MKTG THEN DEPT='MKTNG';
  ELSE DEPT='CSERV';
RUN;
```

Because automatic variables created by IN= are not written to the rebuilt dataset, if you wish to have them in there you must create another variable by assignment, e.g., coding "INSALES=SAL" in the example above would make a variable INSALES on the output dataset that has the value 1 if its data came from CORP.SALES, 0 otherwise.

Always choose variable names for IN= variables that do not conflict with variable names anyplace else in the DATA step or its input datasets, for although these temporary variables are not themselves output to the new dataset, there cannot be more than one variable with the same name in the PDV.

Combining Observations with MERGE

SET combines datasets by taking observations one after the other. The MERGE statement is used to combine observations from more than one dataset by taking one observation's variable values from one dataset after another and using these to build a single observation for the new dataset. The MERGE statement has a form similar to SET:

```
MERGE <dataset_name[(dataset_options)]>...[merge_options];
```

and at least two dataset names should be coded. When a MERGE statement is encountered, the new dataset's PDV is built up corresponding to the variables in the several datasets, in the order named. So far, this is like SET. But as MERGE executes, variable values are brought in to the PDV from the next observation of each dataset. Figure 4.8 illustrates these actions.

Suppose there are several datasets in a library called STATES. Each dataset contains 50 observations, arranged alphabetically by state name (variable STATE). One dataset, STATES.GEOG, contains information about land size, elevation, and topography. Another, STATES.POP, has information about population size and demographics. Still another, STATES.TRIVIA, reveals the official state flower, the official state bird, the state's nickname, and the date it entered the Union.

Problem: A student wishes to create a new combined dataset that has all the information contained in the three input datasets; i.e., 50 observations with geographic, population, and trivial information.

Solution:

```
DATA STATES;
   MERGE STATES.GEOG STATES.POP STATES.TRIVIA;
RUN;
```

Observations in STATES will contain the variables in the three input datasets.

If the same variable appears in more than one dataset, the value from the rightmost dataset named on MERGE will be used, for the PDV is overwritten as MERGE proceeds. If the datasets named on a MERGE statement have unequal numbers of observations, the new dataset will have observations equal in number to that of the largest dataset. As the smaller datasets are exhausted in MERGE

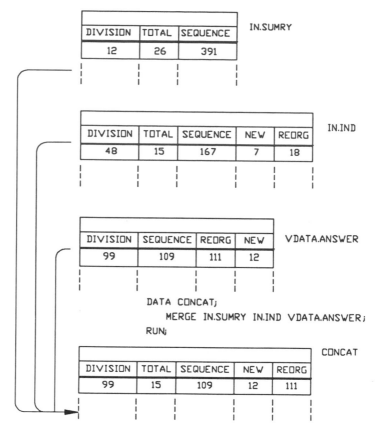

Figure 4.8. Rebuilding with MERGE. Values from rightward datasets' variables on MERGE replace values of variables of the same name that may exist in the PDV.

processing, values of their variables are set to missing in the new dataset, unless the PDV already contains a value from another dataset "to the left"; see Listing 4.3.

DROP or KEEP statements or DROP= or KEEP= dataset options can be used to tailor the new dataset structure. Two ways to have STATES contain only certain variables from each dataset are:

```
MERGE STATES.GEOG(KEEP=STATE AREA)
      STATES.POP(KEEP=STATE MALES FEMALES)
      STATES.TRIVIA(KEEP=STATE NICKNAME);
```

and

```
<<< PROGRAM SOURCE CODE FOLLOWS >>>

DATA FIRST;
  INPUT VAR1-VAR3;
CARDS;
1 1 1
2 2 2
3 3 3
4 4 4
RUN;
DATA SECOND;
  INPUT VAR3-VAR4;
CARDS;
11 11
22 22
RUN;
DATA THIRD;
  MERGE FIRST SECOND; * KEEP AN EYE ON VAR3;
RUN;
PROC PRINT DATA=FIRST; TITLE 'FIRST Dataset'; RUN;
PROC PRINT DATA=SECOND; TITLE 'SECOND Dataset'; RUN;
PROC PRINT DATA=THIRD; TITLE 'THIRD Dataset'; RUN;

<<< SAS JOB OUTPUT FOLLOWS >>>
```

```
                 FIRST Dataset

     OBS     VAR1     VAR2     VAR3

      1        1        1        1
      2        2        2        2
      3        3        3        3
      4        4        4        4

                SECOND Dataset

         OBS     VAR3     VAR4

          1       11       11
          2       22       22

                 THIRD Dataset

     OBS     VAR1     VAR2     VAR3     VAR4

      1        1        1       11       11
      2        2        2       22       22
      3        3        3        3        .
      4        4        4        4        .
```

Listing 4.3. A simple MERGE

```
MERGE STATES.GEOG STATES.POP STATES.TRIVIA;
KEEP STATE AREA MALES FEMALES NICKNAME;
```

In this example, the two methods achieve the same result. If, however, the datasets have variable names in common, then the two usually will be different.

IN= and MERGE

The IN= dataset option may be associated with a dataset named on the MERGE
statement. The meaning is the same: If a dataset contributed values to the state of
the PDV during this iteration, then the IN= variable equals 1; otherwise, it
equals 0. Yet, many SAS users make serious mistakes using IN= with MERGE
because they don't understand this simple fact. Pay close attention to this topic
when we turn to it in Chapter 10.

Creating Two or More Datasets

As described earlier, an IF construction may be used following SET in a way
similar to its use after INPUT. The only difference is that values in the PDV come
from SAS datasets rather than from crude data via INPUT. The effect can be to
subset one existing dataset; for example,

```
DATA SUBSET1;
  SET SOMEDATA;
  IF SOMEVAR = 1;
[more programming statements]
RUN;
```

As may be inferred from earlier discussion, several dataset subsets can be combined, as in

```
DATA SUBDATA;
  SET SOMEDATA MOREDATA STILMORE;
  IF SOMEVAR = 1;
[more programming statements]
RUN;
```

In this case, observations from the three datasets in the SET statement are
included in SUBDATA, provided SOMEVAR=1.

If you combine a multiname DATA statement with these SAS features, your
data processing options increase even more. Multiple SAS datasets can be created
based on values in a single SAS dataset, akin to something shown in Chapter 3
with INPUT data:

```
DATA SUBONE SUBTWO;
  SET SOMEDATA;
[more programming statements]
  IF SOMEVAR = 1 THEN OUTPUT SUBONE;
  ELSE IF SOMEVAR = 2 THEN OUTPUT SUBTWO;
RUN;
```

This can be extended to cover several preexisting SAS datasets:

```
DATA ALLDATA SUBONE SUBTWO;
  SET SOMEDATA MOREDATA STILMORE;
[more programming statements]
  IF SOMEVAR = 1 THEN OUTPUT SUBONE;
  ELSE IF SOMEVAR = 2 THEN OUTPUT SUBTWO;
  OUTPUT ALLDATA;
RUN;
```

which creates a dataset containing all observations concatenated from the three input datasets, and two subsets of the concatenated input datasets.

Subsetting may be done after a MERGE statement; whether INPUT, SET, or MERGE is used, selection logic is the same. So, for example, using the STATES data library exemplified earlier,

```
DATA STATES;
  MERGE STATES.GEOG STATES.POP STATES.TRIVIA;
  IF STATE = 'NEVADA';
[more programming statements]
RUN;
```

creates a data set with a single observation, containing geographic, population, and trivial information about Nevada. Analogously, to create two datasets, one covering west coast states and one covering all other states:

```
DATA WESTSTS OTHRSTS;
  MERGE STATES.GEOG STATES.POP STATES.TRIVIA;
[more programming statements]
  IF STATE = 'CALIFORNIA' OR STATE='OREGON' OR STATE='WASHINGTON'
              THEN OUTPUT WESTSTS;
  ELSE OUTPUT OTHRSTS;
RUN;
```

When more than one dataset is being created, dataset options on the DATA step provide the only way to differentially control what variables are to be kept. For example, if dataset A has variables A1, A2, A3, and dataset B has variables B1, B2, B3, the DATA step:

```
DATA C1(KEEP=A1 B1) C2(KEEP=A2 B2);
  MERGE A B;
RUN;
```

results in dataset C1 having only variables A1 and B1, and C2 having only variables A2 and B2. This example is drawn out in Listing 4.4.

SORTING AND REBUILDING BY SUBGROUPS

PROC SORT and the BY Statement

PROC SORT is one of the most important yet easiest to use of the SAS procedures. SORT's basic mission is to create a new dataset with observations of a preexisting dataset reordered with respect to one or more of its variables. That is to say, SORT rebuilds SAS data by shuffling observations around until they are in some kind of sorted order. SORT can also oblige the user by discarding duplicate observations as it sorts, if that is desired.

PROC SORT is always followed by one and only one statement, the BY statement, which tells SORT what variables sort BY. For example,

```
PROC SORT DATA=SCHOOL.STUDENTS OUT=AGEORDER;
  BY AGE;
RUN;
```

asks for an output dataset, AGEORDER, to be rebuilt from SCHOOL.STUDENTS with observations sorted by values of AGE.

The PROC SORT statement keyword OUT= specifies the output dataset; if left off, then a temporary name is assigned and, if the step completes successfully, the original input dataset is erased and the sorted dataset takes its name (this is still a rebuild process, but the effect from the user's point of view is as if the input dataset was itself sorted).

PROC SORT may be required when you plan to do something with the dataset that involves a BY statement. If the data were entered in sorted order, or if the dataset was previously sorted, PROC SORT does not have to be reinvoked. Indeed, PROC SORT will mark a dataset as sorted and by what variables (there is a place in the dataset header for this), and if it discovers a dataset is so marked then, to save computer resources, it will not go and re-sort it the same way again, but simply copy the input dataset over to the output dataset.* If an input dataset

---

*If this bothers you, you can make the procedure go ahead and sort, unconditionally, with the FORCE option on the PROC SORT statement. On the other hand, you can assert a sort order and mark the dataset as sorted in a certain way if you know that to be the case, with the SORTEDBY= dataset option coded during a DATA step or with PROC DATA-SETS. The SORTEDBY= option, which names one or more variables by which the data are known to be sorted, is normally used on the DATA statement to mark the dataset header so that PROC SORT will not perform the same sort.

```
<<< PROGRAM SOURCE CODE FOLLOWS >>>

DATA A;
  INPUT A1-A3;
CARDS;
1 2 3
RUN;
DATA B;
  INPUT B1-B3;
CARDS;
11 22 33
RUN;
DATA C1 (KEEP=A1 B1)  C2 (KEEP=A2 B2);
  MERGE A B;
CARDS;
PROC PRINT DATA=A; TITLE 'Dataset "A"'; RUN;
PROC PRINT DATA=B; TITLE 'Dataset "B"'; RUN;
PROC PRINT DATA=C1; TITLE 'Dataset "C1"'; RUN;
PROC PRINT DATA=C2; TITLE 'Dataset "C2"'; RUN;


<<< SAS JOB OUTPUT FOLLOWS >>>

        Dataset "A"

OBS    A1    A2    A3

 1      1     2     3

        Dataset "B"

OBS    B1    B2    B3

 1     11    22    33

        Dataset "C1"

  OBS     A1    B1

   1       1    11

        Dataset "C2"

  OBS     A2    B2

   1       2    22
```

Listing 4.4. Dataset options on the DATA statement

is not sorted (or indexed; see Chapter 21) and you use BY, you risk runtime error.*

More than one BY variable may be mentioned in a BY statement; the effect is to call for a two- (three-, four-) way grouping. The grouping is governed by the order variables are coded. If AGE contains persons' ages and SEX their sexes (as character values 'M' or 'F'), then

```
PROC SORT; BY SEX AGE;
```

builds a dataset with all females first, in order of age youngest to eldest, then all males, in order of age. The order of sort is ascending (numeric or character: M before F, small numbers before large), unless psecified otherwise with the DESCENDING keyword on the BY statement. DESCENDING must be coded after each variable name to which it is meant to apply. If PARTY is REPBLICN or DEMOCRAT, SEX is M or F, and AGE is chronological age, then

```
PROC SORT; BY DESCENDING SEX PARTY DESCENDING AGE;
```

produces a dataset with male Democrats in order from eldest to youngest, followed by eldest to youngest male Republicans, followed by female Democrats and female Republicans each from eldest to youngest.

We will return to PROC SORT in Chapter 5, when the PROC step BY statement is introduced. For now, let's begin to see how PROC SORT and BY are relevant to rebuilding SAS datasets, a topic we will return to, in depth, in Chapter 10.

Interleaving Datasets with SET-BY

Suppose there exist not one but several customer datasets (perhaps representing different sales regions). *If* each had been sorted (or indexed) BY SEX, the step

```
DATA ALLBYSX;
  SET OUR.CUSTMRXA OUR.CUSTMRXB OUR.CUSTMRXC;
  BY SEX;
RUN;
```

would result in a dataset with observations in this order: women (SEX='F') from CUSTMRXA, women from CUSTMRXB, and women from CUSTMRXC, followed by men from CUSTMRXA, men from CUSTMRXB, and men from CUSTMRXC. This is called *interleaving* the data. Example results are shown in Listing 4.5.

---

*There *are* some exceptions to this rule that have to do with the NOTSORTED keyword on the BY statement, but even if NOTSORTED is coded, observations with the same BY values must still be grouped together. NOTSORTED asserts that observations with the same BY values come together after one another, although their BY values and those of the next group of observations may have no orderly relationship.

```
            OUR.CUSTMRXA

    OBS      NAME        SEX

     1     BELLAMY        F
     2     JONES          F
     3     BENNETT        M
     4     MEIR           M
     5     MYERSON        M
     6     REAGAN         M


            OUR.CUSTMRXB

   OBS      NAME         SEX

     1    FRIEDMAN        F
     2    GONZO           F
     3    SCHWARTZ        F
     4    SCHWEITZER      F
     5    TWELVETREES     F
     6    BOZYMSKI        M
     7    FIREMAN         M
     8    HIATT           M
     9    NIXON           M
    10    SMITH           M
    11    TURMAN          M


            OUR.CUSTMRXC

   OBS       NAME        SEX

     1    GOODNIGHT       F
     2    LATTIMORE       F
     3    OZECHOVSKI      F
     4    THACKER         F
     5    TRIMBLE         M
     6    WINDSOR         M


ALLBYSX: Interleaved "BY SEX"

   OBS    NAME          SEX

     1   BELLAMY         F
     2   JONES           F
     3   FRIEDMAN        F
     4   GONZO           F
```

Listing 4.5. Interleaving datasets with SET and BY

Continued

```
  5     SCHWARTZ        F
  6     SCHWEITZER      F
  7     TWELVETREES     F
  8     GOODNIGHT       F
  9     LATTIMORE       F
 10     OZECHOVSKI      F
 11     THACKER         F
 12     BENNETT         M
 13     MEIR            M
 14     MYERSON         M
 15     REAGAN          M
 16     BOZYMSKI        M
 17     FIREMAN         M
 18     HIATT           M
 19     NIXON           M
 20     SMITH           M
 21     TURMAN          M
 22     TRIMBLE         M
 23     WINDSOR         M
```

Listing 4.5. *Continued*

If more than one BY variable is used, then the datasets are interleaved accordingly: The BY groups from each dataset follow one another in the new dataset. If non-BY variables are not present in all datasets, they will just go missing in the new dataset, as happens with simple concatenation. But the BY variable(s) *must* appear on *each* dataset, or the step will halt in error.

Identifying Key Observations with MERGE-BY and the IN= Option

Problem: Build a dataset that will contain the sex of selected customers. As input, there are the desired names in a list, and the sex-sorted ALLBYSX dataset from the previous example.

Solution: The following SAS program creates the new dataset:

```
DATA NAMES;
    INPUT NAME $CHAR20;
    CARDS;
[data lines, one with each name on the list]
  RUN;
  PROC SORT DATA=NAMES; * OVERWRITES ORIG. DATASET WITH SORTED;
    BY NAME;
  RUN;
  PROC SORT DATA=ALLBYSX OUT=ALLNAMES;
    BY NAME;
  RUN;
  DATA OUT.SELECTSX;
    MERGE NAMES(IN=INN) ALLNAMES;
    BY NAME;
    IF INN; * SELECT ONLY NAMES IN 'NAMES';
  RUN;
```

List of names (dataset NAMES), sorted by NAME

OBS	NAME
1	BELLAMY
2	BOZYMSKI
3	FIREMAN
4	JONES
5	MEIR
6	OZECHOVSKI
7	REAGAN
8	TURMAN
9	TWELVETREES

ALLNAMES (being same as ALLBYSX but sorted by NAME)

OBS	NAME	SEX
1	BELLAMY	F
2	BENNETT	M
3	BOZYMSKI	M
4	FIREMAN	M
5	FRIEDMAN	F
6	GONZO	F
7	GOODNIGHT	F
8	HIATT	M
9	JONES	F
10	LATTIMORE	F
11	MEIR	M
12	MYERSON	M
13	NIXON	M
14	OZECHOVSKI	F
15	REAGAN	M
16	SCHWARTZ	F
17	SCHWEITZER	F
18	SMITH	M
19	THACKER	F
20	TRIMBLE	M
21	TURMAN	M
22	TWELVETREES	F
23	WINDSOR	M

Listing 4.6. Selecting MERGE observations with the IN= dataset option

Continued

Listing 4.6 shows the results.

Multiple BY variables can be used, in which case observations will be merged if they share the same combination of BY values. Any BY variable(s) must, of course, be present on all the datasets named in the MERGE statement.

```
Merge of NAMES with ALLNAMES, if in NAMES

OBS     NAME            SEX

1      BELLAMY          F
2      BOZYMSKI         M
3      FIREMAN          M
4      JONES            F
5      MEIR             M
6      OZECHOVSKI       F
7      REAGAN           M
8      TURMAN           M
9      TWELVETREES      F
```

Listing 4.6. *Continued*

Placement of BY Statements in the DATA Step

In the DATA Step, a BY statement should be placed immediately following the SET, MERGE, UPDATE, or MODIFY statement with which it is associated. Even if a DATA step contains more than one such statement, a BY statement applies only to the preceding statement. It is possible to write a DATA step that contains several SET or MERGE statements, each with its own BY statement.

5

SAS Procedures

SAS procedures are routines that perform highly specialized and often complicated data processing tasks. With a few lines of code, a SAS user can produce with
a procedure what otherwise might take hundreds of lines of DATA Step code—and
the DATA Step Language is not even capable of some of the tricks some procedures can perform.* In the context of this chapter, we will review several com-
monly used procedures. Elsewhere in the book, particularly in Part III, we will
review a number of other base SAS procedures.

Procedures often result in printable output that can be used as a solution to
some data processing problem. However, many procedures can create other SAS
datasets instead of or in addition to producing printed output. These datasets can
be used, in turn, as input to other DATA or PROC steps. With a few special
exceptions, procedures do not alter preexisting SAS datasets.

Some SAS procedures incorporate a surprising breadth of power and functionality. The SQL procedure, for example, includes its own programming language and
data management techniques. The REPORT procedure incorporates a set of statements that approach a programming language as well as a unique user interface
for interactive report development.

Even procedures more modest in scope still give the user a number of choices,
accepting user directions in the form of procedure-modifying statements and

---

*But most SAS procedures take input from SAS datasets. This is a major reason why it is
so essential to understand SAS datasets and the SAS DATA step. Without appropriately
constructed and arranged input datasets, procedure output can be severely incorrect or
misleading. "Garbage in, garbage out," as the saying goes.

options. Some of the allowed statements and options will have the same name in a number of different procedures. However, you cannot always assume that they work the same way from one procedure to another. (For instance, the ID statement has profoundly different purposes in PROCs PRINT, MEANS, and TRANSPOSE.) Many SAS procedures also have statements and options uniquely their own. As we discuss specific procedures in the course of this book, we will cover in context many of the various statements and options that can be used to work with them.

Consider the following example program:

```
DATA EXAMPLE;
  INPUT A B C;
  CARDS;
1 2 3
4 5 6
7 8 9
RUN;
PROC PRINT;
  TITLE 'Example of PROC PRINT';
  FOOTNOTE '(Simple, isn't it?)';
RUN;
```

Output from the PRINT procedure is shown in Listing 5.1. Notice at the top the title, the date and time of execution, and the page number "1". The footnote appears at the bottom. If there were more pages, each would be numbered sequentially, but the title and the date and time would be the same. If no TITLE statement were active, the default title "The SAS System" would be used. If no footnote were active there would be nothing; there is no default footnote.

Note how the output is centered on the page. This is generally the default, but you can choose to have the output left-justified with the SAS system option NOCENTER, in which case the titles and footnotes will print flush left, and the

```
                Example of PROC PRINT

                OBS    A    B    C

                 1     1    2    3
                 2     4    5    6
                 3     7    8    9
```

```
                (Simple, isn't it?)
```

Listing 5.1. Procedure output from PROC PRINT

body of the output will also start at the left. Pagination and date notation are likewise but general defaults: the page number can be suppressed, as can the date and time of the run, with SAS system options (discussed in Chapter 21). For most examples in this book of timeless value, the date and time have been suppressed. The title itself can be suppressed by using a null title statement, i.e.,

```
TITLE;
```

More about titles and footnotes below.

COMMON PROC STEP STATEMENTS

The PROC Statement

A SAS procedure is invoked with a PROC statement. The PROC statement commands the SAS supervisor to retrieve a certain procedure module and give it control of step execution. The PROC statement takes the form:

```
PROC procname [options];
```

where "procname" is a keyword naming the procedure module. The statement

```
PROC SORT;
```

that we saw in Chapter 4 instructs the supervisor to invoke the SORT procedure.

Options allowed on the PROC statement depend entirely upon which particular procedure is invoked. The DATA= option is very common, specifying a SAS dataset from which the procedure is to take input. When DATA= is used, the dataset options KEEP= or DROP= can usually be applied. For example,

```
PROC PRINT DATA=FLEET.TRUCKS(DROP=MODEL YEAR);
```

requests the PRINT procedure to use as its input an existing SAS dataset named TRUCKS (stored in a library with libref FLEET), but without TRUCKS variables MODEL and YEAR.

If DATA= is not specified, a procedure requiring an input dataset takes on the SAS dataset most recently created in the present job. As we have said before, however, it is good practice always to name the datasets being used in each SAS step, to avoid any possible confusion.

The VAR Statement

Of all the statements that may follow PROC, perhaps the most often used is the one that selects variables for analysis from a SAS dataset that may contain many more variables. The VARIABLES statement is usually signified by the the abbreviated name VAR. It specifies one or more SAS variable names, which must exist in the input data used by the procedure. An example:

```
PROC PRINT DATA=FRUIT; VAR APPLE ORANGE PEAR; RUN;
```

Abbreviated variable lists (e.g., using "-" or "--") are allowed.

Only one VAR statement may appear within a PROC step. There are no options to the VAR statement, just its name followed by one or more variable names or variable lists.

Titles and Footnotes

Printed procedure output may be annotated with up to ten title lines at the top, and up to ten footnote lines at the bottom. Titles are specified by TITLE statements, of the form

```
TITLEn ['text'];
```

where "n" is either blank or a number from 1 to 10. TITLE3 refers to the third title, TITLE7 to the seventh; TITLE and TITLE1 are equivalent, i.e., TITLE can be used instead of TITLE1. 'text' is any text, which can be as long as the line length of your output device. It forms the actual title material, and must be enclosed in single or double quotes. Here are some valid TITLE statements:

```
TITLE 'ACME Widget and Thingmajig Co., Inc.';

TITLE2 'SALES SUMMARY, Western Region';

TITLE3 'THIRD QUARTER, 1988';
```

The rules governing FOOTNOTE are the same, except the lines produced by FOOTNOTE statements appear at the bottom of each output page rather than at the top. FOOTNOTE (or FOOTNOTE1) refers to the first footnote, FOOTNOTE2 to the second, etc.

TITLE and FOOTNOTE are two of a class of "global" SAS statements whose effects transcend step boundaries. These statements take effect at the point in the SAS job they appear, and continue in effect until canceled or overridden later in the source code. TITLE and FOOTNOTE statements written between steps (i.e., at the beginning of the source code, or between RUN and the next PROC or DATA statement) apply to the subsequent steps until overridden. TITLE and FOOTNOTE statements written within a step apply to the step within which they occur as well as to subsequent steps. A TITLEn statement replaces the title specified in any former TITLEn statement, and cancels any titles defined in TITLEn statements with higher *n*s. To clear all titles, code the null title statement

```
TITLE;
```

and, similarly, clear footnotes with a null FOOTNOTE statement.

To explain by example (considering titles; the same thing applies to FOOT-NOTEs): In the following job:

```
DATA ...;
  ...
RUN;
TITLE 'EXPERIMENT 1';
PROC PLOT ...;
  ...
  TITLE2 'HEIGHT AND WEIGHT';
  TITLE3 'PLOT OF VALUES';
RUN;
PROC CORR ...;
  ...
  TITLE3 'CORRELATIONS';
RUN;
PROC PRINT ...;
  ...
TITLE2 'LIST OF CASES'
RUN;
```

the output from all procedures has the top title "EXPERIMENT 1," the output of the PLOT and CORR procedures have an additional, second title "HEIGHT AND WEIGHT," the PLOT procedure has a third title "PLOT OF VALUES," the CORR procedure has a different third title "CORRELATIONS," and the PRINT procedure has a different second title "LIST OF CASES" and no third title.

We will see more illustrations of titles, and some of footnotes, throughout this book.

Attribute Statements in the PROC Step

The forms of the attribute statements used in the PROC step are the same as those used in the DATA step. FORMAT, and to a lesser degree LABEL, are frequently used in PROC steps. As described in Chapter 3, FORMAT associates an output format with a SAS variable, while LABEL associates a variable with a descriptive phrase which may be printed with some procedures.

Attributes should be used in a PROC step rather than a DATA step when it is deemed undesirable to associate the attribute permanently with a variable stored in a SAS dataset. Unwanted variable attributes set in a DATA step cannot be eliminated easily without rebuilding the SAS dataset.

The OUTPUT Statement

As used by several procedures, the OUTPUT statement has the general form

```
OUTPUT OUT=dataset [<keyword=variable>...];
```

Procedures that accept an OUTPUT statement use it to name an output dataset, and perhaps to name one or more keywords referring to procedure output elements that are to be stored as variables in the output dataset. For example, the MEANS procedure can contain a statement

```
OUTPUT OUT=MEANOUT MEAN=MEANVAL N=NUMBER;
```

causing an output dataset MEANOUT to be created, which will have two variables, MEANVAL and NUMBER, representing the arithmetic mean and n of cases, respectively.

Some procedures do not use an OUTPUT statement, but can still create an output dataset, usually by an OUT= option on the PROC statement. Generally, the SAS procedures that take this approach produce output datasets in some kind of standard form without user modification, and therefore do not require a separate statement with its own set of keyword options.

The OUTPUT statement, the OUT= option, and output datasets generally will be covered as necessary in our discussions of various SAS procedures later in this book.

COMMON DESCRIPTIVE AND DISPLAY PROCEDURES

Perhaps there is no better way to illustrate SAS procedures and procedure output than to show some of the more popular descriptive and display procedures, useful for so many data processing tasks. Let's take a look at four of these. PRINT lists variables as they exist in SAS datasets, PLOT displays the values of selected variables graphically, FREQ accumulates counts and percentages of variables depending on the values they take, and MEANS provides sample descriptive statistics.

The PRINT Procedure: An Introduction

In the most general case, for each observation in a SAS dataset, PRINT lists the values of the variables. Assume MY.DATA has the five variables HEIGHT, WEIGHT, AGE, RACE, and SEX (M or F), stored in that order. For our example, MY.DATA has ten observations. The statement

```
PROC PRINT DATA=MY.DATA;
```

then produces results like those shown in Listing 5.2a. Should we have written a VAR statement after PROC,

```
VAR WEIGHT HEIGHT;
```

<<< A >>>

```
          Physical Features of Sample Members

    OBS     HEIGHT    WEIGHT    RACE    AGE    SEX

     1        60       197       1      40      F
     2        68       154       3      35      M
     3        67       152       3      36      F
     4        61       127       1      54      M
     5        65       141       3      40      M
     6        67       163       3      46      F
     7        66       150       1      53      F
     8        61       139       2      48      F
     9        60       187       3      53      F
    10        64       104       2      45      M
```

<<< B >>>

```
        Weight and Height of Sample Members

         OBS     WEIGHT    HEIGHT

          1       197       60
          2       154       68
          3       152       67
          4       127       61
          5       141       65
          6       163       67
          7       150       66
          8       139       61
          9       187       60
         10       104       64
```

Listing 5.2. The VAR statement with PROC PRINT

we might see results as in Listing 5.2b. Note how WEIGHT is printed before HEIGHT. The VAR statement, used in PROC PRINT, determines not only what variables will be printed but in what order, even if this differs from the dataset vector. This gives the user a great deal of control with a single statement. Appropriate TITLEs enhance the output. Remember that the variables are not reordered in the input dataset, they are only *printed* in a different sequence.

The column "OBS" gives the observation number, the ordinal position of the record in the output. The NOOBS option on the PRINT statement can be used to suppress printing this column; use of an ID statement also prevents printing the

```
<<< A >>>

Printout with "ID AGE;"

    AGE     HEIGHT     WEIGHT     RACE     SEX

     40       60        197        1        F
     35       68        154        3        M
     36       67        152        3        F
     54       61        127        1        M
     40       65        141        3        M
     46       67        163        3        F
     53       66        150        1        F
     48       61        139        2        F
     53       60        187        3        F
     45       64        104        2        M



<<< B >>>

AGE, SEX, and RACE

    AGE     SEX     RACE

     40      F        1
     35      M        3
     36      F        3
     54      M        1
     40      M        3
     46      F        3
     53      F        1
     48      F        2
     53      F        3
     45      M        2
```

Listing 5.3. The ID statement with PROC PRINT

OBS column. ID identifies one or more variables with which to "name" the observation for the purpose of printout. These are shifted to appear as the leftmost columns of the printout. Listing 5.3a shows the results of PROC PRINT followed by ID AGE. ID and VAR often occur in combination. The following job produces the output shown in Listing 5.3b:

```
PROC PRINT;
   TITLE 'AGE, SEX, and RACE';
   ID AGE;
   VAR SEX RACE;
RUN;
```

In practice, ID would typically be used to list a true identifying variable—a name, perhaps, or a social security number—to the left of each physical line printed for an observation.

Accumulating Totals

The SUM statement of the PRINT procedure names one or more numeric variables that the user desires be totaled. If a SUM statement appears, then at the end of the printout the sum total follows beneath the last value in the column(s) of the named numeric variable(s).

General Layout

Several PROC PRINT statement options allow you to control certain general output layout features. The DOUBLE option requests that the output be double-spaced. The UNIFORM option is used to ensure that all pages of the printout have the same layout. If UNIFORM is not used, then depending on the the lengths of variable values (especially character values that can vary greatly in length) the column layout may vary between pages.

The ROUND option rounds numeric variables to the number of decimal places specified in a FORMAT statement or, if no format is declared for a variable, to two decimal places.

The LABEL option on the PROC PRINT statement can be used to ask that variables' labels, not their names, be used as column headings. The SPLIT= option specifies a character (quoted, e.g., "SPLIT='*' ") to serve as the "split" character for breaking up labels that may be too lengthy to print contiguously. For example, if the split character is '*' then the label "This*is a new*label" will print in three parts on separate lines: "This", "is a new", and "label." The split character itself is not printed; you can therefore trick the procedure into printing a blank heading for certain variables by defining the variable label as the split character, e.g.,

```
PROC PRINT DATA=D SPLIT='*';
  LABEL MYVAR = '*';
  . . .
```

The PLOT Procedure

The PLOT procedure can produce "x by y" graphs showing the relationship of one variable to another, useful for a visual presentation of two-variable relationships. While more potent graphic displays may be created with SAS/GRAPH software and a plotter, PROC PLOT provides an easy way to make pictures on an ordinary line printer. Again using MY.DATA as input, we can examine the relationship of weight to height with a two-way plot:

```
PROC PLOT DATA=MY.DATA;
  PLOT HEIGHT*WEIGHT;
  TITLE 'HEIGHT and WEIGHT';
RUN; QUIT;
```

or to reverse the axes (the first-named variable is displayed along the vertical), use

```
PLOT WEIGHT*HEIGHT;
```

producing output shown in Listing 5.4a and b.

Notice the required PLOT statement, which gives the variables to be used in the plot. Together, HEIGHT*WEIGHT is called a *plot request*. In fact, more than one PLOT statement may appear, or alternatively, more than one plot request can appear in one PLOT statement. Most options on the PLOT statement are placed after all plot requests, and a slash precedes the options. Using PLOT statement options, we can specify coordinate dimensions (rather than letting the procedure decide; see Listing 5.5), use a third variable for the plot character (thus achieving a three-variable display; see Listing 5.6), overlay plots one upon another, and even produce surface or contour plots—two-dimensional areas with degrees of shading to illustrate a third variable.

The PROC PLOT statement itself may take a couple of special options (coded without a preceding slash). UNIFORM requests the procedure to decide axis scaling, but keep it the same for each requested plot so they may more easily be visually compared. NOLEGEND keeps the list of variable names (the plot legend) from printing at the top of each output page.

PLOT is one of the SAS procedures that can be executed as separate RUN groups. The procedure executes statements in a RUN group, each of which can have one or more PLOT statements, and remains ready to execute some more. A QUIT statement (or a DATA or PROC statement) terminates the procedure with finality.

The FREQ Procedure

The FREQ procedure counts the numbers (frequencies) of observations falling into categories defined by variable values. In MY.DATA, SEX takes one of two values, M or F, and the step

```
PROC FREQ; TABLES SEX; RUN;
```

produces the output shown in Listing 5.7. Observe that percentages are shown in addition to raw frequency counts. A TABLES statement defines the variables to appear in the frequency listings. If several variables are listed as in

```
TABLES SEX RACE;
```

then two separate tables will be printed. But if the variables are joined by an asterisk:

```
TABLES SEX*RACE;
```

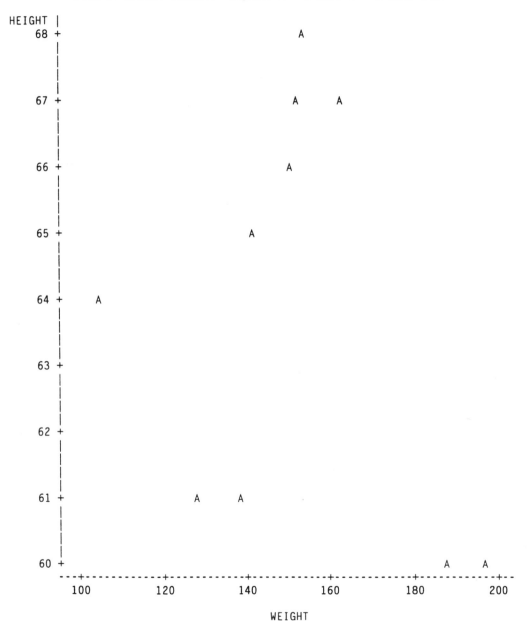

Listing 5.4. Procedure output from PROC PLOT

Continued

<<< B >>>

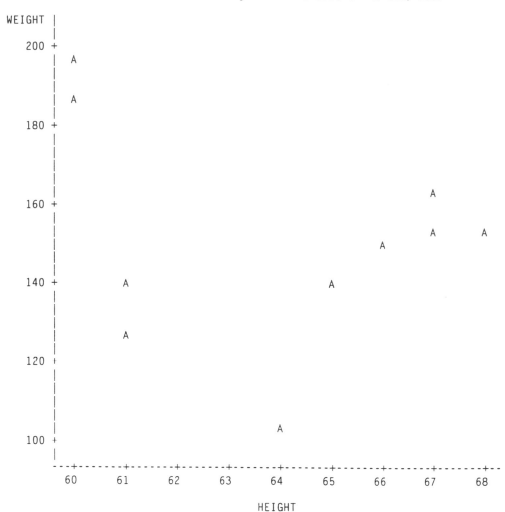

Listing 5.4. *Continued*

then a single, two-way cross tabulation will be produced (see Listing 5.8a). Values of the first-named variable are shown down the side; if RACE*SEX had been specified in this example, the table would be transposed.

The three percentage values given with the cross tabulation are the percent each "cell" (one box in the table, the crosspoint of a row and a column) is of the grand total of all cells, of its column (column percent), and of its row (row percent). Marginal totals also appear, along the right side and the bottom.

```
<<< PROGRAM SOURCE CODE FOLLOWS >>>
TITLE 'HEIGHT and WEIGHT';
PROC PLOT DATA=MY.DATA;
  PLOT HEIGHT*WEIGHT / VAXIS=55 TO 75  HAXIS=90 TO 240 BY 10;
RUN;

<<< SAS JOB OUTPUT FOLLOWS >>>
```

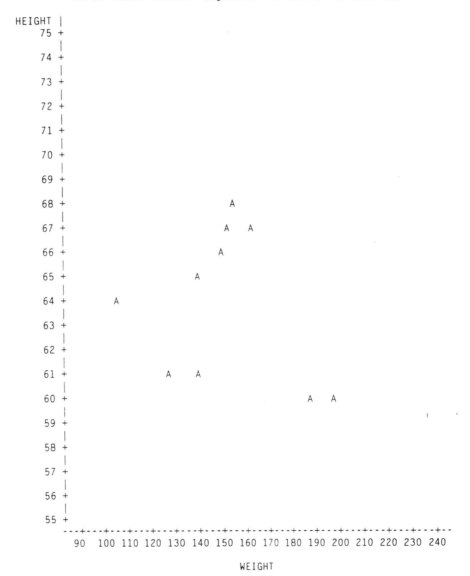

Listing 5.5. Specifying axes with PROC PLOT

```
<<< PROGRAM SOURCE CODE FOLLOWS >>>

TITLE 'HEIGHT and WEIGHT';
PROC PLOT DATA=MY.DATA;
  PLOT HEIGHT*WEIGHT=SEX / VAXIS=55 TO 75  HAXIS=90 TO 240 BY 10;
RUN;

<<< SAS JOB OUTPUT FOLLOWS >>>
```

                            HEIGHT and WEIGHT

              Plot of HEIGHT*WEIGHT. Symbol is value of SEX.

```
HEIGHT |
    75 +
       |
    74 +
       |
    73 +
       |
    72 +
       |
    71 +
       |
    70 +
       |
    69 +
       |
    68 +                                    M
       |
    67 +                                 F     F
       |
    66 +                                 F
       |
    65 +                          M
       |
    64 +              M
       |
    63 +
       |
    62 +
       |
    61 +                   M     F
       |
    60 +                                             F     F
       |
    59 +
       |
    58 +
       |
    57 +
       |
    56 +
       |
    55 +
       ---+---+---+---+---+---+---+---+---+---+---+---+---+---+---+--
          90  100 110 120 130 140 150 160 170 180 190 200 210 220 230 240

                                  WEIGHT
```

Listing 5.6. PROC PLOT: Using a third variable for the plot points

SEX	Frequency	Percent	Cumulative Frequency	Cumulative Percent
F	6	60.0	6	60.0
M	4	40.0	10	100.0

Listing 5.7. Procedure output from PROC FREQ with one variable

Certain options on the TABLES statement, which are coded following a slash,* can be used to suppress printing percentages in table cells. Not uncommonly, the lem. The NOPERCENT option suppresses cell percents, NOROW the row percents, NOCOL the column percents. The statement cell percentages and either the row or column percents are irrelevant to a prob

```
TABLES SEX*RACE / NOPERCENT NOROW NOCOL;
```

produces the output shown in Listing 5.8b, from which the cell, row, and column percents have been purged, leaving only the raw frequencies. It is possible to suppress the frequencies themselves, leaving only desired percentages, with the NOFREQ option. The NOPRINT option suppresses all printouts; it is used when the only reason FREQ is run is to obtain an output dataset (discussed below).

The MISSING and MISSPRINT options provide the user a way to include missing values in the procedure output. Normally, missing values are completely excluded from both frequency counts and other statistics (such as percentages). The MISSING option requests that the procedure treat missing values as valid variable levels for all purposes. The MISSPRINT option requests that frequencies be reported for missing values, but that no other statistics should count them.

More than one table request can be made. One could write, for example,

```
TABLES A*B A*C;
```

to request two tables. Multiple table requests may be grouped in parentheses, as a shorthand method of coding. The result is interpreted distributively, so that

```
TABLES A*(B C);
```

gets the same two tables A*B and A*C.

---

*Statement options on many statements require the preceding slash, because many statements accept one or more non-optional elements that follow the statement name and the SAS compiler needs a syntactic way to decide when the option list begins. TABLES is one of these statements, since a series of tables specifications may be coded; the slash tells the compiler that the list of specifications is finished and whatever else follows should be interpreted as TABLES statement options. On the other hand, for example, the PROC statement does not require a slash because everything after the name of the procedure has to be a procedure option to be an option.

<<< A >>>

TABLE OF SEX BY RACE

SEX   RACE

```
Frequency|
Percent  |
Row Pct  |
Col Pct  |         1|        2|        3| Total
---------+--------+--------+--------+
F        |       2 |      1 |      3 |      6
         |   20.00 |  10.00 |  30.00 |  60.00
         |   33.33 |  16.67 |  50.00 |
         |   66.67 |  50.00 |  60.00 |
---------+--------+--------+--------+
M        |       1 |      1 |      2 |      4
         |   10.00 |  10.00 |  20.00 |  40.00
         |   25.00 |  25.00 |  50.00 |
         |   33.33 |  50.00 |  40.00 |
---------+--------+--------+--------+
Total            3        2        5      10
             30.00    20.00    50.00  100.00
```

<<< B >>>

TABLE OF SEX BY RACE

SEX   RACE

```
Frequency|        1|        2|        3| Total
---------+--------+--------+--------+
F        |       2 |      1 |      3 |      6
---------+--------+--------+--------+
M        |       1 |      1 |      2 |      4
---------+--------+--------+--------+
Total            3        2        5      10
```

Listing 5.8. PROC FREQ with two variables

Multiway cross tabulations can be specified, but these really result in two-way frequencies, one for each level or combination of levels of other variables; FREQ can produce no "three-way" printouts on a single page. Thus, for example, the statement

```
TABLES A*B*C;
```

results in a B*C table for each level of A. If we write

```
TABLES SEX*HEIGHT*WEIGHT;
```

we get two tables: HEIGHT by WEIGHT for males (SEX=1), and the same for females. If there are five values for RACE, requesting

```
TABLES SEX*RACE*HEIGHT*WEIGHT;
```

would generate *ten* tables: a HEIGHT by WEIGHT table for each combination of SEX and RACE. Therefore, be careful with crossed table requests, or consider using PROC TABULATE (see Chapter 12) in such cases. You might also consider using the TABLES option LIST, which will cause multi-way tables to print out in listwise fashion, rather than as cross tabulations.

The PROC FREQ statement can specify the order in which variable levels are printed with the ORDER= option.

```
PROC FREQ ORDER=FREQ;
```

for example, will result in a table printed in order by frequency size (descending). ORDER=FORMATTED uses the values as formatted (see Chapter 11) to determine printout order. The default ordering, i.e., that which is used if ORDER= is not specified, is ORDER=INTERNAL, meaning that the ascending order of actual values of the table variables determines the order of printout, as may be observed in our examples.

PROC FREQ can produce a variety of simple statistics, such as chi-square, to test the associations displayed in the frequency table. The various statistics available with FREQ are discussed in the *SAS Procedures* guide.

For special applications, it is possible to cause each observation to be counted more than once to inflate the reported frequencies. This is done by the WEIGHT statement, taking the form

```
WEIGHT weightvar;
```

where "weightvar" is a variable telling how many times to count the present observation. For example, to count how many "person-years" per sex and race are represented in the data, weight a SEX*RACE table by AGE, as follows:

```
PROC FREQ; TABLES SEX*RACE; WEIGHT AGE; RUN;
```

The results tell us the "total age" of white males, black females, etc. in our sample. (AGE, of course, must be variable in the dataset.) Why one would want to know this is a good question, but the WEIGHT statement has more realistic uses. For example, stockholders' votes may be tallied proportional to their ownership by weighting each member's vote by a variable showing their total shares. A weight-

```
        PROC PRINT of dataset "MY.FREQDATA"

    OBS    SEX    RACE    COUNT    PERCENT

     1      F      1       2         20
     2      F      2       1         10
     3      F      3       3         30
     4      M      1       1         10
     5      M      2       1         10
     6      M      3       2         20
```

Listing 5.9. An output dataset produced by PROC FREQ

ing variable may have noninteger (fractional) values, but they must be positive; zero or negative weights are not allowed.

Output Datasets

The FREQuency procedure can create output datasets. This is done with a TABLES statement option, OUT=, giving a SAS dataset name, e.g.,

```
TABLES SEX*RACE / OUT=MY.FREQDATA;
```

The output dataset can have one observation for each combination of values of the variable in the table request or, in other words, one observation per table cell. If there are "empty" cells (frequency=0), there will be no observation: Only *value*value* combinations that actually exist in the data are represented in the output dataset. In our example, MY.FREQDATA has six observations (for there is at least one member of each sex/race combination), shown (thanks to PROC PRINT) in Listing 5.9. The variable COUNT is the variable frequency, PERCENT the percent, and SEX and RACE show the variable levels. SEX and RACE come, of course, from the input dataset. COUNT and PERCENT are created by PROC FREQ whenever an output dataset is built. Only one output dataset can be produced per TABLES statement; if more than one table is requested on a TABLES statement with OUT=, the *last* table that would be printed contributes the output dataset. The order of observations depends on the occurrence of values and the ORDER= option on the PROC statement.

Output datasets from PROC FREQ are one of the ways you can use the SAS System to get summary statistics based on one dataset into another dataset. The OUT= dataset is no different from any other SAS dataset: It may be selectively printed, sorted, used as input to other DATA or PROC steps, etc. Using OUT= gives you that much more power to design additional analyses, or to print FREQ table output in a layout of your own design.

The MEANS Procedure

There are several SAS procedures that give some simple statistics (the arithmetic average, standard deviation, and so on), or count and report the number of miss-

The MEANS Procedure (default statistics)

Variable	N	Mean	Std Dev	Minimum	Maximum
HEIGHT	10	63.9000000	3.1428932	60.0000000	68.0000000
WEIGHT	10	151.4000000	27.0686370	104.0000000	197.0000000
RACE	10	2.2000000	0.9189366	1.0000000	3.0000000
AGE	10	45.0000000	7.0710678	35.0000000	54.0000000

Listing 5.10. Procedure output from PROC MEANS

ing observations, the outer values (high and low) of the valid observations, etc. One of these is PROC MEANS.* By default, the simple job

```
PROC MEANS DATA=MY.DATA; RUN;
```

produces a printout showing the name of the variable and the statistics N (number of nonmissing observations), MEAN (of the nonmissing observations), STD (standard deviation), MIN (minimum value), and MAX (maximum value). Applied to the example data, the output appears in Listing 5.10. A VAR statement can be used with PROC MEANS to select or re-order variables to be reported. Note that only numeric variables are processed in any case (even RACE, yielding an "average race" of 2.2; RACE should have been DROPped with a dataset option or deselected with VAR).

Any of the default statistics can be suppressed, or others requested, by indicating specific statistic keywords on the PROC MEANS statement. For example,

```
PROC MEANS N MEAN SUM STD STDERR;
```

requests a printout with the statistics N, MEAN, the SUM of the values, STD, and STDERR. MIN and MAX will be suppressed, SUM and STDERR included. Other statistics available through PROC MEANS include NMISS (N's complement, i.e.,

---

*A word about MEANS and SUMMARY is in order here: Prior to SAS Version 6, the MEANS and SUMMARY procedures used to differ in capability, even though they performed many of the same calculations. Now the procedures are virtually identical, with the exception of one or two defaults. For example, PROC MEANS produces printed output unless NOPRINT is specified, whereas the PRINT option would have to be made explicit to get printed output from SUMMARY. This has an historical basis: Prior to Version 6, SUMMARY did not produce printed output at all, only an output dataset. In this book we look at the printed output of the procedure in this chapter, and study the output dataset in detail in Chapter 9. Also in deference to history, then, we will refer to PROC MEANS in this chapter but speak of PROC SUMMARY in Chapter 9. Just remember that the options and statements discussed in both chapters can be used in either case, i.e., whether it is "MEANS" or "SUMMARY" you've written on the PROC statement, and with the same effect.

Goodold Junior High

OBS	GRADE	SECTION	NSTDNTS	CLASSAVG
1	6	A	26	85.5
2	6	B	28	88.9
3	6	C	27	85.4
4	6	D	20	89.8
5	7	A	26	90.0
6	7	B	21	88.6
7	7	C	27	80.1
8	8	A	22	84.6
9	8	B	19	83.5
10	8	C	25	84.0
11	9	A	22	81.9
12	9	B	22	83.1

Listing 5.11. An input dataset used in upcoming examples

the number of missing values), VARiance, T (Student's t testing H0: mean=0), PRT (significance of T: probability of a greater absolute value of Student's t), the RANGE (=MAX-MIN), moments about the mean SKEWNESS and KURTOSIS, and sums of squares (corrected, CSS, and uncorrected, USS).

As with PROC FREQ, a WEIGHT statement can be used to specify a numeric variable in the input dataset which will be used to weight each observation. But here is a perfect example of the fact that many procedure-modifying statements have different actions in different procedures, and that you must study each procedure to use them effectively: In PROC FREQ, the WEIGHT statement named a variable representing the number of times the observation should be counted. In PROC MEANS, the WEIGHT statement specifies a variable that is used to calculate weighted means and variances, not for observation counting. That is, WEIGHT has no effect on the output N or NMISS. It takes another statement, the FREQ statement, to specify how many true observations each sample observation is to represent. If NUMOBS is a variable telling how many observations each sample record represents, the statement

FREQ NUMOBS;

used in a PROC MEANS step will, for example, add NUMOBS to the N count if the variable is not missing.

Problem: The principal wants to know the overall school results of a certain achievement test taken by students at Goodold Junior High. Each class has already taken the test, and the class average results were reported. That is, at hand are the average test scores of each class at Goodold. The number of students in each of 12 classes is also known. Let the facts be as PRINTed in Listing 5.11.

Goodold Junior High: Average Achievement Test Scores

Analysis Variable : CLASSAVG

```
                  N          Mean
       ---------------------------
                285    85.4561404
       ---------------------------
```

Listing 5.12. The VAR and FREQ statement with PROC MEANS

Solution: The school mean can be obtained from this data by treating each student as if he or she had the class mean as score, e.g., each student in grade 6 section B is given 87.2, and is then reaveraged. Therefore, the following program produces the correct statistics:

```
PROC MEANS DATA=GOODOLD.CLASSCOR N MEAN;
   VAR CLASSAVG;
   FREQ NSTDNTS;
   TITLE 'Goodold Junior High: Average Achievement Test Scores';
RUN;
```

The output is shown in Listing 5.12.

In this case, using "WEIGHT NSTDNTS" instead of FREQ would have given the same mean, but the N would show as 12, and had variance estimates been requested they would be different. Use WEIGHT with PROC MEANS only when you really want weighted estimates.

If appropriate, both FREQ and WEIGHT statements may appear in the same PROC MEANS step. Neither variable should take a negative value, but if a weighting variable does turn up negative it is treated as zero, and the observation contributes nothing to the reported statistics. WEIGHT variables may be fractional; however, FREQ variables are to be integers, and if not, only the integer portion is used (e.g., 3.7 is treated as 3).

An output dataset can be produced by the MEANS procedure and its virtually identical twin PROC SUMMARY. This output dataset can contain a great wealth of information about the original input data. Let's postpone the discussion of MEANS output datasets to Chapter 9, where we examine the SUMMARY procedure in detail.

BY GROUP PROCESSING

Many SAS procedures are able to do their work on subsets of input data defined by BY group values. (You will recall that if BY is used, the input dataset must be sorted or grouped according to the BY variables, or else indexed appropriately for access to the variables in the correct BY order.) When printed output is produced and a BY statement is used,* the SAS System provides several ways for the printout to show the values of the BY variables. For illustrative purposes, let's use the dataset from the junior high school grades example, shown earlier in Listing 5.11, which was produced by a simple PROC PRINT with no options or statements.

If we add a BY statement somewhere in the PROC code, thus

```
TITLE 'Goodold: PRINT "BY GRADE"';
PROC PRINT DATA=GOODOLD.CLASSCOR;
  BY GRADE;
RUN;
```

we get output shown in Listing 5.13. Notice that values of GRADE no longer show up as columns in the printout, because GRADE was used as a BY variable. BY variables generally do not take part in the "body" of an analysis, because they are used instead for the purpose of separating data into analysis subgroups.

We do see the values of GRADE in this printout, appearing in special separator lines between BY groups. These lines can be eliminated by using the SAS system option NOBYLINE; in this case, each BY group output will begin on a separate page,† as shown in Listing 5.14.

As you see in Listing 5.14, the value of the BY variable is lost. It is possible to use the values of BY variables in TITLE statements by using special keywords in the TITLE string. These keywords are #BYLINE, #BYVAR, and #BYVAL. These title elements can be used in any procedure that prints output according to BY statement subgroups, though we illustrate them here only with the PRINT procedure.

#BYLINE produces a string that corresponds to the BY group notation that would by default (i.e., without NOBYLINE) appear in the separator line; see Listing 5.15. This solves the problem of the "lost" BY line.

The #BYVAR and #BYVAL keywords refer to the name and the value, respectively, of a single BY variable, and to identify *which* BY variable, the keywords are used in one of two ways: Either the name of the variable is placed in parentheses after the keyword, or an integer is suffixed to the keyword that indicates the ordinal position of the desired BY variable in the BY statement. For example, given the BY statement

```
BY RED BLUE GREEN;
```

---

*Certain interactive procedures and procedures that use RUN groups can have more than one BY statement (one per RUN group). The most recently executed BY statement is the one that is in effect for that portion of the procedure.

†Many procedures will begin a new page for each BY group anyway, but PRINT, MEANS, and a couple of others will use separator lines unless you force separate pages with the NOBYLINE option.

```
                  Goodold: PRINT "BY GRADE"

-------------------------- GRADE=6 -------------------------

        OBS      SECTION      NSTDNTS      CLASSAVG

         1          A           26          85.5
         2          B           28          88.9
         3          C           27          85.4
         4          D           20          89.8


-------------------------- GRADE=7 -------------------------

        OBS      SECTION      NSTDNTS      CLASSAVG

         5          A           26          90.0
         6          B           21          88.6
         7          C           27          80.1


-------------------------- GRADE=8 -------------------------

        OBS      SECTION      NSTDNTS      CLASSAVG

         8          A           22          84.6
         9          B           19          83.5
        10          C           25          84.0


-------------------------- GRADE=9 -------------------------

        OBS      SECTION      NSTDNTS      CLASSAVG

        11          A           22          81.9
        12          B           22          83.1
```

Listing 5.13. PROC PRINT with a BY statement

the fragments "#BYVAL(BLUE)" and "#BYVAL2" are equivalent. When used in a TITLE statement, a BY variable name (or else its label, if it has a defined label) becomes substituted for a #BYVARn specification, and the current value of a BY variable is substituted for a #BYVALn specification. Listing 5.16 provides an example.

PRINT Procedure Variations

The PRINT procedure provides a few additional features for handling printed output when a BY statement is used. The PRINT procedure's PAGEBY statement

```
Goodold: PRINT "BY GRADE" (w/NOBYLINE)

OBS      SECTION      NSTDNTS      CLASSAVG

 1          A            26           85.5
 2          B            28           88.9
 3          C            27           85.4
 4          D            20           89.8
```

<<< PAGE BREAK WOULD BE HERE >>>

```
Goodold: PRINT "BY GRADE" (w/NOBYLINE)

OBS      SECTION      NSTDNTS      CLASSAVG

 5          A            26           90.0
 6          B            21           88.6
 7          C            27           80.1
```

<<< PAGE BREAK WOULD BE HERE >>>

```
Goodold: PRINT "BY GRADE" (w/NOBYLINE)

OBS      SECTION      NSTDNTS      CLASSAVG

 8          A            22           84.6
 9          B            19           83.5
10          C            25           84.0
```

<<< PAGE BREAK WOULD BE HERE >>>

```
Goodold: PRINT "BY GRADE" (w/NOBYLINE)

OBS      SECTION      NSTDNTS      CLASSAVG

11          A            22           81.9
12          B            22           83.1
```

Listing 5.14. Printing with a BY statement under the NOBYLINE system option

causes each BY group to print beginning on a new page. This could be achieved with the NOBYLINE system option, but PAGEBY does not eliminate the separator line. Furthermore, PAGEBY is more flexible when the BY statement names more than one variable. Suppose you have a dataset of census information with several observations per county per state. Printing "BY STATE COUNTY" you could have each state listing begin a new page with

```
PAGEBY STATE;
```

```
<<< PROGRAM SOURCE CODE FOLLOWS >>>

* Note: SAS system option NOBYLINE is in effect for this example;
PROC PRINT DATA=GOODOLD.CLASSCOR;
BY GRADE;
TITLE 'Goodold: #BYLINE';
RUN;


<<< SAS JOB OUTPUT FOLLOWS >>>

              Goodold: GRADE=6

OBS      SECTION      NSTDNTS      CLASSAVG

 1          A            26          85.5
 2          B            28          88.9
 3          C            27          85.4
 4          D            20          89.8

<<< PAGE BREAK WOULD BE HERE >>>

              Goodold: GRADE=7

OBS      SECTION      NSTDNTS      CLASSAVG

 5          A            26          90.0
 6          B            21          88.6
 7          C            27          80.1


<<< PAGE BREAK WOULD BE HERE >>>

              Goodold: GRADE=8

OBS      SECTION      NSTDNTS      CLASSAVG

 8          A            22          84.6
 9          B            19          83.5
10          C            25          84.0


<<< PAGE BREAK WOULD BE HERE >>>

              Goodold: GRADE=9

OBS      SECTION      NSTDNTS      CLASSAVG

11          A            22          81.9
12          B            22          83.1
```

Listing 5.15. Printing with a BY statement and the #BYLINE title keyword

```
        <<< PROGRAM SOURCE CODE FOLLOWS >>>

* Note: SAS system option NOBYLINE is in effect for this example;
PROC PRINT DATA=GOODOLD.CLASSCOR; BY GRADE;
TITLE 'Goodold: Subgrouped by #BYVAR1 (current value: #BYVAL1)';
RUN;

        <<< SAS JOB OUTPUT FOLLOWS >>>

Goodold: Subgrouped by GRADE (current value: 6)

        OBS     SECTION     NSTDNTS     CLASSAVG

         1         A          26         85.5
         2         B          28         88.9
         3         C          27         85.4
         4         D          20         89.8

    <<< PAGE BREAK WOULD BE HERE >>>

Goodold: Subgrouped by GRADE (current value: 7)

        OBS     SECTION     NSTDNTS     CLASSAVG

         5         A          26         90.0
         6         B          21         88.6
         7         C          27         80.1

    <<< PAGE BREAK WOULD BE HERE >>>

Goodold: Subgrouped by GRADE (current value: 8)

        OBS     SECTION     NSTDNTS     CLASSAVG

         8         A          22         84.6
         9         B          19         83.5
        10         C          25         84.0

    <<< PAGE BREAK WOULD BE HERE >>>

Goodold: Subgrouped by GRADE (current value: 9)

        OBS     SECTION     NSTDNTS     CLASSAVG

        11         A          22         81.9
        12         B          22         83.1
```

Listing 5.16. Printing with a BY statement and the #BYVAR and #BYVAL title keyword while having the counties appear on BY separator lines, with several counties' data possibly printing on each page.

The SUMBY statement in the PRINT procedure names a BY variable level within which totals are to be aggregated. If SUMBY is used, a SUM statement should also appear (unless you want each and every numeric variable to be totalled). The total will print out after the last observation. When BY groups are used and SUM is specified, normally a subtotal will print out for each subgroup defined by the BY statement as well as a grand total at the end of all BY groups. If SUMBY is used, then the subtotals are printed only when the value of the named BY variable changes.

Listing 5.17 shows the use of the PAGEBY and SUM statements. In this case, SUMBY is redundant: SUMBY is always redudant with SUM if only one BY variable is used. Refer to your *SAS Procedures* for illustrative examples of the SUM and SUMBY statements when more than one BY variable is used.

USING *WHERE* CONDITIONS TO SELECT OBSERVATIONS

The SAS System provides a way for you to intercept observations on their way for use in a procedure (or in a DATA Step, see Chapter 9) and determine whether they should be input to the procedure. You can, in effect, process datasets selectively as if you had first rebuilt the dataset with a DATA Step to eliminated unwanted observations prior to calling the desired procedure.

Problem: Compare the average achievement test results for Goodold Junior High to those of certain other districts whose junior high school does not contain a ninth grade class, get the average score for the school but do not take the ninth grade into account.

Solution: Instead of going through a DATA Step with "IF GRADE<9;" or something equivalent, proceed directly:

```
PROC MEANS DATA=GOODOLD.CLASSCOR N MEAN;
   WHERE GRADE < 9;
   VAR CLASSAVG;
   FREQ NSTDNTS;
   TITLE 'Goodold Junior High: Average Achievement Test Scores';
   TITLE2 '(Note: Data excludes Grade 9)';
RUN;
```

The output is shown in Listing 5.18. Compare this with the output in Listing 5.12. You don't have to calculate the means by hand to compare them, just look at the N column: 241 versus 285; cf. Listing 5.17, where it was shown there are 44 ninth graders.

WHERE= can also be specified as a dataset option, with its selection expression placed in parentheses. In the example above, the WHERE statement could have been left off and the PROC statement coded as

```
<<< PROGRAM SOURCE CODE FOLLOWS >>>

TITLE 'Once again presenting Goodold Junior High';
PROC PRINT DATA=GOODOLD.CLASSCOR;
  BY GRADE;
  PAGEBY GRADE;
  SUM NSTDNTS;
  SUMBY GRADE;
RUN;

<<< SAS JOB OUTPUT FOLLOWS: >>>
<<< Note that BYLINE system option has been turned on again; >>>
<<<   the page breaks are due to the PAGEBY statement in the PRINT procedure. >>>
```

Once again presenting Goodold Junior High

-------------------------- GRADE=6 --------------------------

OBS	SECTION	NSTDNTS	CLASSAVG
1	A	26	85.5
2	B	28	88.9
3	C	27	85.4
4	D	20	89.8

GRADE		101	

```
<<< PAGE BREAK WOULD BE HERE >>>
```

Once again presenting Goodold Junior High

-------------------------- GRADE=7 --------------------------

OBS	SECTION	NSTDNTS	CLASSAVG
5	A	26	90.0
6	B	21	88.6
7	C	27	80.1

GRADE		74	

```
<<< PAGE BREAK WOULD BE HERE >>>
```

Listing 5.17. PROC PRINT statements to produce summary totals

Continued

Once again presenting Goodold Junior High

```
-------------------------- GRADE=8 --------------------------

         OBS     SECTION     NSTDNTS     CLASSAVG

          8         A           22         84.6
          9         B           19         83.5
         10         C           25         84.0
                                ------
       GRADE                      66
```

<<< PAGE BREAK WOULD BE HERE >>>

Once again presenting Goodold Junior High

```
-------------------------- GRADE=9 --------------------------

         OBS     SECTION     NSTDNTS     CLASSAVG

         11         A           22         81.9
         12         B           22         83.1
                                ------
       GRADE                      44
                                ======
                                 285
```

Listing 5.17. *Continued*

```
Goodold Junior High: Average Achievement Test Scores
          (Note: Data excludes Grade 9)

         Analysis Variable : CLASSAVG

              N           Mean
        --------------------------
             241       85.9958506
        --------------------------
```

Listing 5.18. Using a WHERE statement to subselect observations for processing

```
PROC MEANS DATA=GOODOLD.CLASSCOR(WHERE=(GRADE<9)) N MEAN;
```

As you can imagine, WHERE can save a lot of computer resources because it allows observation selection "on the fly" without need for an intervening DATA step. Among SAS System statements, WHERE is also unique, almost peculiar, in two ways. In the first place, it takes effect even before a dataset observation is read into the program data vector. But also, there are some special SAS operators that can be used only in WHERE expressions and no place else! A couple of these are simply synonyms for expression-segments that can be used in any SAS expression (including WHERE expressions). The IS NULL (alternatively IS MISSING) operator is an example, and can be used for numeric or for character variables to test if they are missing.* For character variables,

```
WHERE X IS NULL;
```

is the same as

```
WHERE X = ' ';
```

and for numeric variables,

```
WHERE N IS NULL;
```

is the same as

```
WHERE N <= .Z;
```

NOT can be inserted to negate the expression, e.g.,

```
WHERE X IS NOT NULL;
```

is the same as

```
WHERE X NE ' ';
```

The BETWEEN-AND operator is an alternative way to specify an inclusive selection range, e.g.

```
WHERE A BETWEEN 100 AND 200;
```

is the same as

```
WHERE 100 <= A <= 200;
```

The '?' operator (which may also be spelled out as CONTAINS) is one of the WHERE operators that has no easy equivalence in non-WHERE expressions. Used only with character variables, it asks whether a certain character string is contained somewhere in another string. For example,

```
WHERE OBJECT ? 'BAT';
```

---

*See Chapter 7 for a general explanation of missing values.

would select observations where the value of the variable OBJECT was 'BATCH', 'BASEBALL BAT', 'BATTER', and so on. Even more versatile is the LIKE operator, which works on character variables looking for values that match certain "regular" expressions wherein two special symbols can be used to stand for any single character (_) and zero or more of any characters (%). For example,

```
WHERE SESAME LIKE '_R%';
```

would select observations with values of SESAME 'ERNIE' and 'GROVER', but not 'BERT': ERNIE and GROVER both have one character, then an R, then zero or more other characters. The *SAS Language Guide* gives some more examples. Note that NOT can precede LIKE to call for all observations where the value of the specified variable does *not* fit the regular expression.

The "sounds-like" operator "=*" can be used in WHERE expressions to compare one character value to another using the standard Soundex algorithm. As the *SAS Language Guide* observes,

```
WHERE LASTNAME =* 'SMITH';
```

selects Messrs. Smith, Smyth, Smythe, etc.

The SAME AND operator has a very special purpose: It adds on to an existing WHERE expression another WHERE expression, which from that point on must also be satisfied. It is used only when more than one WHERE statement is used, and that makes sense in limited circumstances, such as in certain procedures run in an interactive environment, or in procedures that are composed of consecutive RUN groups. For example,

```
SQZ = PROC PLOT DATA=MYDATA;
   WHERE expr1;
   plot specifications;
RUNS;
   WHERE SAME AND (expr2);
   plot specifications;
RUN;
```

selects only those observations for the second plot that satisfy both "expr1" and "expr2". "SAME" refers to the selection in effect when it executes, so if yet a third RUN group in this example were to use WHERE SAME AND, all three WHEREs would have to be satisfied for an observation to be selected during the third RUN.

6

The SAS Job Log

The SAS System provides a dutiful recordskeeper in the form of an output file called the SAS *log*. The log is printable, and usually prints by default, just like the standard procedure output file, when SAS executes in batch.* The SAS log provides documentation for your SAS program and the datasets it creates and uses. It is a most intimate form of documentation, being the SAS System's own record of what transpired to produce the results of your program.

In this chapter, we will discuss the standard and optional items that can appear in the SAS log, including SAS error messages and notes, and how to use the SAS log to take your own notes as well. The examples shown were produced using SAS Version 6.08 on a Windows system; the precise form of the log, as well as the contents of certain log elements (e.g., system notes), can vary between operating systems, so what you see in your own jobs may be slightly different from the illustrations in this chapter.

OVERVIEW OF THE SAS LOG

The log of a simple SAS job is shown in Listing 6.1. The log header typically shows a copyright notice, and licensing/site information (here replaced with the ficti-

---

*In the Display Manager, the SAS log has a window all its own, distinct from the OUTPUT window but also printable.

```
NOTE: Copyright(c) 1989 by SAS Institute Inc., Cary, NC USA.
NOTE: SAS (r) Proprietary Software Release 6.08  TS402
      Licensed to AKROYD ADVERTISING, Site 0000000000.


NOTE: AUTOEXEC processing beginning; file is C:\SAS\AUTOEXEC.SAS.

      The SAS System for Windows: Developer's Release

NOTE: AUTOEXEC processing completed.

1     DATA SAMPLE;
2        INPUT X Y Z;
3     CARDS;

NOTE: The data set WORK.SAMPLE has 140 observations and 3 variables.
NOTE: The DATA statement used 1.27 seconds.


144   RUN;
145   PROC PRINT DATA=SAMPLE;
146      TITLE 'Sample Data';
147   RUN;

NOTE: The PROCEDURE PRINT used 0.77 seconds.


148   PROC MEANS DATA=SAMPLE;
149      VAR X Y;
150      OUTPUT OUT=SAMPMEAN MEAN=MEANX MEANY STD=STDX STDY;
151   RUN;

NOTE: The data set WORK.SAMPMEAN has 1 observations and 6 variables.
NOTE: The PROCEDURE MEANS used 0.5 seconds.

NOTE: SAS Institute Inc., SAS Campus Drive, Cary, NC USA 27513-2414
```

Listing 6.1. Log of a simple SAS job

tious "Akroyd Advertising"), and may show other information as well, depending on the operating system and on certain SAS invocation options (such as the VERBOSE system option described in Chapter 21). A SAS installation may specify a dataset that contains "news" text of local interest; unless the NONEWS system option is in effect, this news, if any, appears after the header and before the list of SAS options.

Source code is normally printed along the log, as each statement is compiled. Each statement is given a line number for reference. Input data lines read by INPUT may optionally be printed (see below; if they follow CARDS, then whether or not they print, they count toward line numbers; hence you might see an apparent gap in the numbering of the source lines if the CARDS are not printed).

As each step is executed, SAS prepares standard information notes which are printed after the step runs. (If a RUN statement is not used after each step, the notes will show up *after* the *next* DATA or PROC statement in the source lines.) When datasets are built, a note telling the number of observations and variables is written. When printed output is generated, a note gives the page numbers on which the output may be found. Finally, at the end of a batch job (if it completes normally), a trailer note shows the name and address of the SAS Institute.

In addition to standard notes, other notes may be printed, including perhaps errors and warnings. The SAS Macro Facility writes certain notes to the SAS log as well. The user can also write comments or other information to the log. Certain procedures even write comments to the SAS Log.

SAS LOG COMPONENTS

Source Code

The source lines that are read from the standard system input file (normally SYSIN under batch, or the PROGRAM screen of the Display Manager) are printed on the SAS log if the system option SOURCE is in effect (use the NOSOURCE option to suppress printing the source lines). The source lines are numbered for reference; the line numbers appear at the left of the page. Remember that CARDS data are counted toward the line numbers, even if the data are not printed.

It is possible to insert source code from another file as input to the system—and to the log. This additional file is named or referenced on an %INCLUDE statement. Lines from this additional file will also be shown on the job log, if the system option SOURCE2 is in effect (use NOSOURCE2 to suppress them from the log), but the log will let you know they were not from the primary source file; see Listing 6.2* (note the plus signs that signify an %INCLUDEd line).

Input Data

Although data lines read with INPUT, whether from INFILE or CARDS, they are not normally printed on the SAS log. They *can* be printed, however, in one of two ways. _INFILE_ is a special SAS variable that can be used with the PUT statement (which we will discuss later in this book). Coding

```
PUT _INFILE_;
```

---

*Beginning with this listing, to save space we'll dispense with illustrating the standard job opening and closing notes when showing the SAS log.

```
1    OPTIONS SOURCE2;
2    DATA NOTHING; * Just to show both direct and %INCLUDEd source ...;
3      X=0;
4    RUN;

NOTE: The data set WORK.NOTHING has 1 observations and 1 variables.
NOTE: The DATA statement used 1.04 seconds.


5    *NOW LET'S INCLUDE THE SOURCE THAT PRODUCED LISTING 6.1:;
6    %INCLUDE 'L06-1.SAS';
NOTE: %INCLUDE (level 1) file L06-1.SAS is file C:\SAS\MASAS2\L06-1.SAS.
7    +DATA SAMPLE;
8    +  INPUT X Y Z;
9    +CARDS;

NOTE: The data set WORK.SAMPLE has 140 observations and 3 variables.
NOTE: The DATA statement used 0.39 seconds.


150 +RUN;
151 +PROC PRINT DATA=SAMPLE;
152 +  TITLE 'Sample Data';
153 +RUN;

NOTE: The PROCEDURE PRINT used 0.7 seconds.


154 +PROC MEANS DATA=SAMPLE;
155 +  VAR X Y;
156 +  OUTPUT OUT=SAMPMEAN MEAN=MEANX MEANY STD=STDX STDY;
157 +RUN;

NOTE: The data set WORK.SAMPMEAN has 1 observations and 6 variables.
NOTE: The PROCEDURE MEANS used 0.48 seconds.


NOTE: %INCLUDE (level 1) ending.
158  *THAT'S ALL, FOLKS!;
```

Listing 6.2. Log with %INCLUDEd source code

within a DATA step containing INPUT will put the current input line to the log. What is written is the last record read from the input source; even if a multiline input statement was coded (i.e., with the / or # specifiers), only a single line is printed.

The LIST statement is a little different. PUT may be directed elsewhere than the log; LIST goes only to the log. PUT writes one record. LIST writes the entire input buffer: If there is more than one line according to the INPUT statement, all will be listed. LIST also places a "column ruler" on the log so a reader can more

```
1     DATA ONE;
2       INPUT A B C $;
3       PUT _INFILE_;
4       CARDS;

12 34 56 ALPHA

78 910 1112 BETA

1314 1516 1718 OMEGA

NOTE: The data set WORK.ONE has 3 observations and 3 variables.
NOTE: The DATA statement used 1.2 seconds.


8     RUN;
9     DATA TWO;  * Note: Data cards exactly the same for TWO as ONE;
10      INPUT A B C $;
11      LIST;
12      CARDS;

RULE:----+----1----+----2----+----3----+----4----+----5----+----6----+----7---
13   12 34 56 ALPHA
14   78 910 1112 BETA
15   1314 1516 1718 OMEGA
NOTE: The data set WORK.TWO has 3 observations and 3 variables.
NOTE: The DATA statement used 0.33 seconds.

16    RUN;
```

Listing 6.3. The SAS log: PUT __INFILE__ versus LIST

easily inspect the input data, and the line numbers are shown if data is from
CARDS. See Listing 6.3.

PUT __INFILE__ and LIST can be used to print suspicious input lines to aid in
finding input data errors. The technique involves conditioning either statement
on an IF.

Problem: From a list on magnetic medium of names and addresses that are all
supposed to be in the same three-digit ZIP code prefix, 946, extract a SAS dataset,
ensuring it has all 946 zips, and also report what the errors are, if any, in the input
data.

Solution:

```
DATA ZIP946;
  INFILE IN946;
  INPUT NAME $ 1-25 ADDRESS $ 26-50 CITY $ 51-60 STATE $ 61-62
        ZIP 63-67 ZIPPRE 63-65;
  DROP ZIPPRE;
  IF ZIPPRE = 946 THEN OUTPUT;
  ELSE LIST;
RUN;
```

System Notes

Unless the system option NONOTES is in effect, the SAS System provides a good deal of information in log lines that begin with "NOTE:".

Standard Notes

As illustrated earlier, and as you can see in your own SAS jobs, one or more notes are printed for each job step. DATA step notes indicate the numbers of observations and variables in datasets created, and may contain other information, such as the size of the observations on disk storage. PROC step notes give the pages in the print dataset at which the PROC output can be found. Step notes may contain information about computer resources used to run the step; several system options (see Chapter 21) are available to control how much of this information is printed.

Other Information And Warnings

There are certain conditions that SAS treats as errors, which we will review shortly, and then there are those conditions that SAS feels the user should know or be warned about even though they are not treated as errors by the SAS System.

Invalid data and related warnings. Mistakes in input data are flagged by warnings if the data do not conform with what SAS expects or requires. Data errors include invalid data, that is, input data that do not conform to their input format (usually, alphabetic characters where a numeric field is expected), illegal function calls due to unsound argument (e.g., trying to take the logarithm of zero), and attempted division by zero. Data errors cause the value of the offending variable to be set missing in the observation where error occurs. SAS does not normally terminate the step in the face of invalid data, though the user can force this with an option (see Chapter 8), but it may print the offending data line as well as list the SAS variable values for the questionable observation.

Actions taken by the compiler in the face of incompatible data are reported on the SAS log. For example, the log notes where and how often missing values were created as a result of an operation on missing values (i.e., missing value propagation; see Chapter 7), or as a result of an impossible mathematical request implied by a data error, such as division by zero. It also notes when numeric variables have been converted to character or vice versa (which may be intended, not necessarily a mistake).

Other notes and warnings. There are several other messages that may be found on the SAS log. They do not necessarily indicate a problem, but they may. For example, SAS will print a message when the INPUT statement goes to a new line for a variable to be read with list (free-format) input. (It is possible to get SAS to treat such an occurrence as an error, not a mere warning; see Chapter 8.) Another example of this kind of warning occurs when a variable is used in a DATA step without having been initialized.

Error Notes

SAS errors besides data errors (and excluding errors in program logic, which only the analyst, and not the SAS System, can detect) are printed in the SAS log. Generally, the erroneous code fragment is flagged with an error number as the source code is printed, and when the step code finishes printing the errors are listed by number.

Sometimes, a single true error, perhaps an innocuous "typo", can give rise to a host of apparent errors. In Listing 6.4, the second DATA step produces an alarming list of problems, but the only real offense is the omission of the semicolon on the SET statement.

Procedure Output

Certain procedures write output to the SAS log. PROC DATASETS (Chapter 14), for example, reports its findings (except those produced by the CONTENTS statement) to the log. PROC OPTIONS (Chapter 21) is another example.

Macro Expansions and Errors

The SAS Macro Language is a preprocessor that prepares SAS source code for compilation. As the code is prepared, it may or may not be displayed on the SAS log, and if displayed, it may take several forms. Macro Language errors are also noted in the SAS log. We will return to the SAS log in Part V, where we investigate the Macro Language.

WRITING NOTES TO THE SAS LOG

The SAS user can cause notations on the SAS log, in order to count certain events, examine questionable input data, or simply augment the natural program/dataset documentation that the log provides.

Writing Log Notes with the PUT Statement

The PUT statement is the SAS DATA Step Language's way of allowing control over non-SAS-format output. It is more or less the reverse of INPUT and provides much of the flexibility for output that INPUT does for reading raw data. The output destination of a PUT statement may be the print output file, or an external file. We will study such PUT statement applications in Chapter 17.

PUT statement output can also be destined to the SAS log. In fact, by default (i.e., unless otherwise specified), PUT output will go to the log. We've seen PUT _INFILE_ above. Let's look at some ways PUT may be used to annotate the SAS log.

```
1      DATA CRIME;
2         INPUT CRIME $;
3         CARDS;
```

NOTE: The data set WORK.CRIME has 8 observations and 1 variables.
NOTE: The DATA statement used 1.1 seconds.

```
12     RUN;
13     DATA CRIMINAL;
14        SET CRIME
15        IF CRIME='MURDER' THEN SEVERITY='MAJOR';
                         -        ----
                        73        202
                       200
                       --------
                       200
```
ERROR: File WORK.IF.DATA does not exist.
```
16        ELSE SEVERITY='MINOR';
```
ERROR: No matching IF-THEN clause.
```
17     RUN;
```

ERROR 73-322: Expecting an ;.

ERROR 202-322: The option or parameter is not recognized.

ERROR 200-322: The symbol is not recognized.

NOTE: The SAS System stopped processing this step because of errors.
WARNING: The data set WORK.CRIMINAL may be incomplete. When this step was
         stopped there were 0 observations and 2 variables.
NOTE: The DATA statement used 0.76 seconds.

```
18    PROC PRINT; TITLE 'Crimes Do Not Pay!'; RUN;
```

NOTE: No observations in data set WORK.CRIMINAL.
NOTE: The PROCEDURE PRINT used 0.22 seconds.

Listing 6.4. A SAS log showing error markers and notes

Counting Events with Sum Statements

A Sum statement can be used to accumulate counts of specified events during the course of DATA Step execution.

```
IF expression THEN C+1;
```

for example, adds 1 to a variable if "expression" is true.

```
1    DATA CHILDREN;
2      INFILE CHEALTH END=FINISH;
3      INPUT IDNUMBR AGE SEX $ RACE $ HEIGHT WEIGHT
4            POLIMMUN RUBIMMUN HOSP;
5      IF SEX='M' THEN MALES + 1;
6      ELSE IF SEX='F' THEN FEMALES + 1;
7      DROP MALES FEMALES; * ONLY FOR COUNTING, NOT DATA;
8      IF FINISH THEN PUT  'COUNTS BY SEX: ' MALES= FEMALES= ;
9    RUN;

NOTE: The infile CHEALTH is:
      FILENAME=C:\SAS\MASAS2\CHEALTH.DAT,
      RECFM=V,LRECL=132

COUNTS BY SEX: MALES=51 FEMALES=37
NOTE: 88 records were read from the infile 'CHEALTH.DAT'.
      The minimum record length was 17.
      The maximum record length was 17.
NOTE: The data set WORK.CHILDREN has 88 observations and 9 variables.
NOTE: The DATA statement used 0.55 seconds.
```

Listing 6.5. Writing data to the SAS log

Problem: Create a SAS dataset from raw data that provides information on children of several ages and, as auxiliary file documentation, note how many children of each sex are represented in the data.

Solution: Without elaboration (it is a topic for Chapter 8) we must first note that if "INFILE filcref END=varname;" is coded, a special temporary variable named by "varname" will be created that has the value 1 (true) if the last statement in the input file is being processed, 0 otherwise. Now, using Sum and PUT statements:

```
DATA CHILDREN;
  INFILE CHEALTH END=FINISH;
  INPUT IDNUMBR AGE SEX $ RACE $ HEIGHT WEIGHT
        POLIMMUN RUBIMMUN HOSP;
  IF SEX='M' THEN MALES + 1;
  ELSE IF SEX='F' THEN FEMALES + 1;
  DROP MALES FEMALES; * ONLY FOR COUNTING, NOT DATA;
  IF FINISH THEN PUT  'COUNTS BY SEX: ' MALES= FEMALES= ;
RUN;
```

The log of this program step is shown in Listing 6.5. This PUT statement prints "COUNTS BY SEX:", and then the number of males and the number of females after the names MALES= and FEMALES= (Chapter 8 provides a full explanation of how PUT works). "IF FINISH" is true if FINISH is nonzero and not missing. Because FINISH is a variable created by the END= option of the SET statement, FINISH=0 except when the last record is read by SET, at which point

FINISH=1. Therefore, the PUT statement executes exactly once, after the last input record has been read.

Accumulating Totals

A similar mechanism can be used to summarize data as well as count instances of data. In the following example, a Sum statement is used to annotate the SAS log with the value of a total.

Problem: From a set of input data of bills due, containing creditor, due date, and amount, prepare a SAS dataset, and also indicate for information the total cost of paying all bills.

Solution:

```
DATA DEBTS.BILLS;
   INFILE INPUT.BILLS END=DONE;
   INPUT CREDITOR $CHAR20. DUE MMDDYY8. AMOUNT;
   TOTDUE + AMOUNT;
   DROP TOTDUE;
   IF DONE THEN PUT / 'TOTAL AMOUNT DUE: ' TOTDUE;
RUN;
```

Displaying Particular Events or Data

As shown earlier, the LIST statement, or else PUT _INFILE_, can be selected upon an IF condition in order to display a "problem" data item. You may display problem data in other ways as well. For example, the following program will display identifying information (observation number and identifying variable) for each observation that has a missing value for a certain variable:

```
DATA MYDATA;
   INFILE RAW;
   INPUT ID DATE MMDDYY6.;
   IF DATE = . THEN PUT _N_ 'MISSING DATE! ' ID=;
RUN;
```

Segmenting the Log with PAGE and SKIP

The PAGE statement consists of the keyword PAGE and a semicolon, nothing more, and its only function is to insert a page break in the log at the point it is coded. PAGE may come in handy if you are creating several datasets or producing several printouts in a job, and desire to file the documentation separately or perhaps to attach segments of the log separately to segments of output.

A related directive is the SKIP statement,

```
SKIP [n];
```

which skips *n* lines on the output; the default if *n* is not specified is to skip one line. SKIP can help make the log easier to read, or perhaps facilitate the inclusion of

```
1       /***
2     DATA SURVEY.ANALY1; * This is the first analytic dataset;
3       INFILE MYDATA(BETA);
4       INPUT VAR1-VAR6;
5       IF VAR1<VAR6 THEN CLASS=1;
6       ELSE CLASS=2;
7     RUN;
8       ***/
9     DATA ANALY2; * This is the second analytic dataset;
10      INFILE 'TEST1.SAS';
11      INPUT C1 C2 STATUS $;
12    RUN;

NOTE: The infile NEWDATA is:
      FILENAME=C:\SAS\MASAS2\NEWDATA.DAT,
      RECFM=V,LRECL=132

NOTE: 92 records were read from the infile 'TEST1.SAS'.
      The minimum record length was 16.
      The maximum record length was 24.
NOTE: The data set WORK.ANALY2 has 92 observations and 3 variables.
NOTE: The DATA statement used 1.6 seconds.
```

Listing 6.6. Two types of SAS source comment

anticipated notes or attachments. Because of their special function, "PAGE;" and "SKIP;" never literally appear in the log even if the SOURCE option is on.

Comments as Notes

Program documentation should begin with the program itself: A clear, well-written program, with an appropriate indentation style, datasets named wherever used, meaningful dataset and variable names, and sensibly informative TITLEs all contribute to a clear understanding of the program later on.

In addition, the judicious use of comments within the program provides a method of program annotation to help a future reader—who may be yourself 6 months down the line—understand the meaning behind what was done. I recommend using statement-style comments for this purpose, and reserving delimited comments for the task of "masking off" portions of code during program testing or for running a program in stages. Listing 6.6 shows both styles of comments. The delimited comment encloses a set of code that had been run before. This is a good way of keeping documentation together for programs that "bombed" due to error after completing some of their earlier steps, or whose steps for some other reason, while closely related, must be run at different times. Whatever the reason, in this example the second part only has been run, and yet the source code—and through the source code, the SAS log—contains a complete history of the originally intended program. (Of course, no system notes are generated for statements within blocked comments, because they cause no compiler activity.)

part II

CONSTRUCTING SAS DATASETS

7

Missing Values

In data analysis, a "missing value" is an instance of a variable that can be assigned no known real value. Suppose that you are taking a class and, during the course of the semester, you miss an examination. What is your score for that examination? Your instructor could assign a grade, perhaps a zero, but this would not be a "real" test score; it's not as if you took the test and got everything wrong. You have no true score for the test; or in other words, your score is *missing*. The instructor has other alternatives, of course, than to pretend the score is zero: s/he might simply not count that test toward the computation of your grade, or, if you miss too many tests, s/he might conclude that you cannot be assigned a course grade and hand you an incomplete.

In your SAS programming practice, you will inevitably be confronted with missing values. This respondent does not answer a question, that division does not return its budget report. Like our course instructor, you will have choices to make about missing values. Sometimes you might indeed want to assign zero—or some other value entirely—to missing data. At other times, you will want simply to ignore missing values. Perhaps you will want to delete from your dataset any observations that have missing values for certain variables; perhaps also, you want to proceed with data analysis only if you have sufficient numbers of observations remaining with nonmissing analysis variables. Maybe you'll want to classify missing values and print a summary report about them, but not use them in any "real" computations.

Because the SAS System is equipped to handle missing values, it allows you to make all these choices and take any of these actions. The SAS System lets you read missing values from input. It allows you to assign missing values to variables. You might, for example, assign a missing value to a variable when its input data is out of valid range. For classificatory purposes, you can even assign nominally different numeric missing values in different instances. The value of any variable defined in the PDV is either missing or nonmissing at any point in a SAS DATA step. In datasets, too, a variable has either a missing or nonmissing value stored for every observation.

Both character and numeric missing values are recognized. The character missing value is equivalent to a blank character, and is normally stored as such in the computer. There's nothing else you need particularly to know about character missing values, except how to read and to assign them. We will treat that in the final section of this chapter.

Numeric missing values are a different story, and are what this chapter is about. There are certain behaviors to be expected of SAS procedures where numeric missing values are concerned. And there are times when the SAS System will take it upon itself to create them. Therefore, you *must* know about SAS missing values* in order to use the SAS System correctly. It is fitting to begin this part of the book—our deeper look at how SAS datasets are constructed—with a complete explanation of how the SAS System creates and deals with missing values.

ASSIGNING MISSING VALUES

Missing Values in Input Data

Missing values can be represented in input data by a single period. If the statement

```
INPUT A 1 B 2 C 3;
```

were to read the line

```
5.7
```

then the value of B would be missing. If the input specification calls for more than one column, the period may be placed anywhere in the field. For example, the statement

```
INPUT VAR 10. COUNT 11-15;
```

will assign a value of missing to VAR if a single period appears anywhere within columns 1 through 10, and to COUNT if a period appears in any column 11

---

*Henceforward for purposes of this chapter, except in the final section, the term "missing value" will be used to mean *numeric* missing value.

through 15. More than one period, or a period and another value, will be treated as an invalid data error (the result of which will be a missing value anyway; see below).

All blanks in a field in which a value is expected is another way to represent a missing value, character or numeric. If the INPUT statement just discussed were to encounter a line with all blanks in columns 1 through 10, VAR would be assigned a missing value. Of course, if you are using list input, a period *must* be used, because no field boundaries are specified.

Missing by Assignment

The usual numeric missing value, called the *system missing value* to distinguish it from "special" missing values, is represented in programming statements, as well, by a single period. To code

```
A = .;
```

is to assign the variable A the system missing value. The period is the numeric missing value constant (though in the computer, it is not stored as a character period but as a special value the SAS System recognizes as "missing"). Like any constant, it may be assigned to a variable which then takes on the missing value. In other words, like any constant, if

```
VAR=.; VAR2=VAR;
```

then VAR2 as well as VAR has the value ".", missing.

MISSING VALUES AND SAS PROCEDURES

If numeric missing values are printed (by PRINT or another procedure), they print as a period (system missing value), or a letter or underscore (special missing values; see below). It is possible to respecify the character SAS should use to print the numeric system missing value with the MISSING system option (see Chapter 21).

Other than for straightforward printing, many procedures discard missing values, and often the observations that contain them. Some procedures allow you to specify by option that missing values should be treated as valid data for certain purposes, such as classification grouping. What is done with missing values varies from procedure to procedure. Consider a dataset SAMPLE that has some missing values for the variable V. The procedure

```
TITLE 'Missing values and PROC FREQ';
TITLE2 '(Missing values excluded from computations (default))';
PROC FREQ DATA=SAMPLE;
  TABLES V;
RUN;
```

<<< A >>>

Missing values and PROC FREQ
(Missing values excluded from computations (default))

V	Frequency	Percent	Cumulative Frequency	Cumulative Percent
0	7	7.4	7	7.4
1	13	13.8	20	21.3
2	9	9.6	29	30.9
3	6	6.4	35	37.2
4	8	8.5	43	45.7
5	7	7.4	50	53.2
6	7	7.4	57	60.6
7	11	11.7	68	72.3
8	10	10.6	78	83.0
9	16	17.0	94	100.0

Frequency Missing = 6

<<< B >>>

Missing values and PROC FREQ
(Missing values included as "valid" levels)

V	Frequency	Percent	Cumulative Frequency	Cumulative Percent
.	6	6.0	6	6.0
0	7	7.0	13	13.0
1	13	13.0	26	26.0
2	9	9.0	35	35.0
3	6	6.0	41	41.0
4	8	8.0	49	49.0
5	7	7.0	56	56.0
6	7	7.0	63	63.0
7	11	11.0	74	74.0
8	10	10.0	84	84.0
9	16	16.0	100	100.0

Listing 7-1. Missing values and PROC FREQ

might produce the output shown in Listing 7.1a. Note that the number of missing values is shown, but that this number does not enter into the calculation of cumulative totals or percents. Yet FREQ allows the user the MISSING option on the TABLES statement, for counting missings in percent and cumulative scores. The procedure

```
TITLE 'Missing values and PROC FREQ';
TITLE2 '(Missing values included as "valid" levels';
PROC FREQ DATA=SAMPLE;
  TABLES V / MISSING;
RUN;
```

produces the output shown in Listing 7.1b.

By and large, missing values are automatically excluded from statistical analyses, and with good reason. A missing number is not a zero, nor a missing answer a "no." You can't average your missing test score in with the others.

SPECIAL MISSING VALUES

Although missing values are usually excluded from analysis, when they are included—for purposes of counting, say, or of classification—it can be helpful to evaluate different *types* of missing value. Suppose a critical but sensitive question, Q23, is asked in a survey of attitudes. If respondents do not answer the question their responses cannot be included in most statistical analyses, but suppose the reasons they do not answer are considered important in their own right and should at least be tabulated. The survey designers therefore included a subsequent item, Q23NOANS, for the interviewer to fill out if no answer is obtained. The item is coded 1 if the respondent did not know the answer, 2 if they refused to say, 3 if the reason they were not answering was itself unclear.

Problem: How should this data be analyzed? The straightforward solution is to produce a frequency distribution of Q23NOANS. This may be perfectly acceptable, but it could also make it a little harder to deal with the results: Two different tables will have to be reviewed (i.e., Q23 and Q23NOANS). The situation gets worse if there are dozens of such questions.

Solution: Recode Q23 on the basis of Q23NOANS, as follows:

```
DATA SURVEY;
  [set or input, as may be the case]
  IF Q23NOANS=1 THEN Q23=.N;
  ELSE IF Q23NOANS=2 THEN Q23=.R;
  ELSE IF Q23NOANS=3 THEN Q23=.X;
RUN;
```

The values .N, .R, and .X represent special numeric missing values. As far as most statistical analyses go, these values of Q23 will be ignored. However, if a procedure such as PRINT or FREQ is used to process the data, the letters N, R, or X may appear as a value of Q23. Thus, one frequency table can show counts of both the actual values of the variable and also of the special missing values representing different reasons for a missing Q23.

There are 27 possible special missing values, representable in code as the constants .A through .Z and also .__ (period-underscore). When printed, they show up without the period (and even though they are numeric) as A through Z or an underscore.

Special Missing Values on Input

Consider the missing Q23 example, above. If the SAS programmer/analyst were consulted before data entry commenced, time and effort could be saved. Instead of entering the response for Q23NOANS in the first place, the data could be prepared such that right in the data lines, if Q23 was not answered on the questionnaire, there would appear in its place the letter N, R, or X. The MISSING statement is the SAS System's way to allow special missing data to come directly from raw input. The MISSING statement takes the form

```
MISSING values;
```

where the values are a list of valid special missing characters (i.e., letters A through Z or the underscore).

Thus in the present example the user would code

```
MISSING N R X;
```

in order to INPUT the data just described. If MISSING were not used, then invalid data errors would be generated when any of these letters were encountered, since N, R, and X are not valid numeric values. The value of Q23 in such instances would become the usual system missing value, and any distinction between classes of missing value would be lost.

Although usually used inside a DATA step, MISSING is a global statement and, once declared, holds true for the current and subsequent DATA steps unless another MISSING statement intervenes.

COMPARISON OF MISSING VALUES

In logical operations, missing values are, like zero, "false."

In arithmetic comparisons, any missing value is less than any nonmissing value, even negative values. Numeric missing values have relative magnitude, for the purpose of comparison operations among themselves. The largest missing value is .Z, then .Y, down to .A, then the system missing value ".", then the missing value "._". That is, $.Z > .Y > ... > .A > . > ._$.

Because of this, if there is any possibility that special missing values might occur, the standard "If variable is missing then ..." should be written not as

```
IF var = . THEN statement;
```

but as

```
IF var <= .Z THEN statement;
```

MISSING VALUES GENERATED BY THE DATA STEP COMPILER

We have seen how missing data may be defined by assignment or at INPUT. The SAS System may also create missing values: Each variable in each observation of a SAS dataset must have *some* value, and the occasions SAS generates a missing value are those when it cannot generate a valid nonmissing value. In so doing, it always uses the system missing value (hence the name "system" missing value) if the variable is numeric.

It is a serious thing for SAS to make missing values on its own, but it is not necessarily a bad thing. The point is to know when this occurs and what, if anything, to do about it. To help, a message is written to the SAS log to warn that missing values have been generated, or alert that events that automatically generate missing values have occurred (see Chapter 6). Always scan the SAS log for messages each time you run a job.

Missing values are automatically generated under the following specific circumstances.

Invalid Data

As discussed earlier, when invalid numeric data appear in an input field, the corresponding variable is given the system missing value. An invalid data warning, along with the offending input line, will usually (i.e., if not suppressed by system option) appear on the SAS log.

No Data

If a variable is defined in a DATA step but never gets assigned any value, it is assigned the system missing value. A warning that the variable was uninitialized will usually appear on the SAS log.

Impossible Operations

When an operation cannot return a valid value, a missing value is substituted. There are basically two ways this can happen. First, an undefined arithmetic operation may be attempted. An example of this is attempted division by zero; any value divided by zero is undefined. If

```
A=B/C;
```

is coded, then if C is zero at execution then A will be missing. Usually, the SAS log will note "division by zero."

Second, an impossible character-to-numeric conversion may be attempted. Character-to-numeric conversion is carried out by the compiler, you may recall, if a character variable is used in a numeric context. For example, if the character variable CHAR has the value '3' then

```
VAL = 5 * CHAR;
```

results in a value of 15 for VAL, which will be a numeric variable if not declared otherwise. But if CHAR has the value 'THREE', then the same assignment will result in a missing value for VAL: the conversion of 'THREE' to numeric for purposes of the operation fails, the value of CHAR *in the expression* (not in the dataset) is missing, and 5*missing is itself missing, for reasons to which we now turn.

Operations on Missing Values

If a numeric missing value is used in an expression, the result of the expression is invariably missing. There is no other alternative: "5 * missing" equals neither 5 nor not-5; it has to be missing. If in our previous example we innocently believed CHAR would be a numeral and it was not, then VAL would be missing. If we then used VAL in another assignment expression, the result of the expression would be missing and the new variable would also be missing. This is called *propagation of missing values*.

Look out for program errors arising from this cause. Whenever an operation is attempted upon missing values, a warning is given on the SAS log that a missing value was generated as a result of an operation on missing values, i.e., that missing values have propagated. The log will show the number of times this event occurred, and at what location in the source (i.e., which statements); see the example in Listing 7.2. This little note can be very important, because a small error may give rise to many instances of missing value when there should have been none.

CHARACTER MISSING VALUES

There is one character missing value, and it is the blank; when we speak of character missing values, we simply mean a blank field.

You can represent character missing values in your input data in one of two ways. If reading with list input, you can use the single period to indicate a missing value. That is, when a character variable is read with list input, a single period is stored not as a period, but as a blank. When other forms of INPUT specification are used (an informat, or a column location), periods are periods and missing character values are represented by blanks.

The missing character constant is, likewise, the blank (enquoted, of course):

```
MISSVAL=' ';
```

When printed, missing character values print blank, of course.

```
   <<< SAS JOB LOG FOLLOWS >>>

1    DATA D;
2      INFILE INDATA;
3      INPUT GROUP SYS CODE;
4      C1=CODE*GROUP; C2=CODE*SYS;
6    RUN;

NOTE: The infile INDATA is:
      FILENAME=C:\SAS\MASAS2\L07-2.DAT,
      RECFM=V,LRECL=132

NOTE: 283 records were read from the infile INDATA.
      The minimum record length was 5.
      The maximum record length was 5.
NOTE: Missing values were generated as a result of performing an operation on
      missing values.
      Each place is given by: (Number of times) at (Line):(Column).
      47 at 101:10   35 at 101:25
NOTE: The data set WORK.D has 283 observations and 5 variables.
NOTE: The DATA statement used 0.5 seconds.


103   PROC MEANS N NMISS DATA=D; TITLE 'INDATA'; RUN;

NOTE: The PROCEDURE MEANS used 0.39 seconds.


   <<< SAS JOB OUTPUT FOLLOWS >>>
```

INDATA

Variable	N	Nmiss
GROUP	265	18
SYS	277	6
CODE	254	29
C1	236	47
C2	248	35

Listing 7.2. Propagation of missing values

8

Input Tailoring

INFILE and INPUT were introduced in Chapter 3. Now, you will see how to handle multiple input source files, how to act upon end-of-file conditions, how to use SAS informats, and how still other features of INFILE and INPUT can enhance a SAS programming project.

Also in this chapter are examined the concepts of SAS dates, times, and date-times values, which make it easy to read, write, and calculate using measures of calendar and clock.

INFILE STATEMENT OPTIONS

Never underestimate the role of the INFILE statement in the SAS DATA Step Language. With INFILE statement options, a SAS user can handle input data in practically any form it may come.

A couple of important INFILE statement options were introduced in Chapter 3. Below, we cover several other generally useful INFILE options, options that let you select a subset of input records for processing, handle missing input data correctly, take appropriate action at the end of a file or of one of a series of concatenated files, or use more than one input file at a time.

Selecting Records

Sometimes, you may wish to process only a selected portion of an input file, not the whole thing. One application for this arises when you are writing a new SAS program. Especially when input files are large, computer resources can be saved during program development by running program tests on a small subset of the data.

SAS provides the INFILE statement options OBS= and FIRSTOBS= to handle this demand. OBS= specifies the ordinal number of the last record to be processed; all records following this one in the input file are ignored. FIRSTOBS= specifies the first record to be processed; all records prior to this one are skipped over. If you decide that 5,000 subscriber records would do nicely as a certain program is being tested and debugged (and that for some reason, which coincidentally lets us illustrate two options at once, you wish to select the *second* 5,000 records in the input file), then the statement

```
INFILE fileref FIRSTOBS=5001 OBS=10000;
```

does nicely: it limits processing to the second 5,000 records of the external input file. The SAS dataset created from this file will have a maximum of 5,000 observations. These numbers are absolute: if the input file has less than 10,000 records, SAS will process less than 5,000 observations; if the input file has less than 5,000 records, SAS will read none of it, and the SAS dataset will be empty of observations.

OBS= can be used without FIRSTOBS=, in which case processing will begin with the first input record and go until the OBSth record, and FIRSTOBS= can be used without OBS=, in whch case processing will begin with the record number specified with FIRSTOBS= and continue to the end of the input file.

OBS= and FIRSTOBS= also name SAS dataset options that could be used in a statement such as

```
SET dataset (OBS=1000);
```

which requests only the first 1,000 observations from "dataset" be used. OBS= and FIRSTOBS= are also SAS system options that can be specified on an OPTIONS statement (see Chapter 21.) Used as INFILE statement options, OBS= and FIRSTOBS= override the currently set system options* for purposes of processing the input file.

Limiting Input Line Size

Occasionally, it is necessary to avoid processing some columns at the end of an input record.

Problem: Data lines may contain sequence numbers in columns 73–80. Ensure that SAS never mistakes this for data.

---

*Be cautioned that it is easy to forget to reset SAS system options. It is generally better to use OBS= or FIRSTOBS= as INFILE statement options, rather than system options, making it explicit.

Solution:

```
INFILE fileref LINESIZE=72;
```

LINESIZE=72 ensures that SAS will consider column 72 to be the end of each input record. Anything in an input record past the LINESIZE column is completely ignored.

LINESIZE= may be abbreviated LS=. When specified on the INFILE statement, it overrides the system option of the same name.

End-of-File Processing

SAS provides three INFILE statement options with which you may control events when the end of raw input data is reached. END= names a variable to be set "true" when the last record in the input file is read in. EOV= sets a variable "true" when the last record in one of a set of a concatenated input files are read. EOF= creates a reference to a control label where execution is to continue if there are no more records in the input file.

True End-of-File: The END= Option

The END= option on the INFILE statement names a numeric variable that at the start of execution has a value of 0, but takes the value 1 when INPUT reads the last record in the file. Like the automatic system variables, the variable named by END= is available for use during the DATA step but is not added to any output dataset.

One use of this feature is to accumulate descriptive data about the input file as it is being processed, as illustrated in Chapter 6. A variation on the problem resolved in Listing 6.5 might go as follows:

Problem: Create a SAS dataset from records that include (among other data) the sex and age of each person, and also help document the file by noting the numbers of men, women, and children in the input file, and the number of persons of unknown age or adult sex.

Solution: The log in Listing 8.1 shows how this problem may be resolved with retained Sum variables* and the END= option of the INFILE statement. The IF-THEN statement checks ALLDONE, which is 1 (true) only when SAS is processing the last observation in the input file. When this occurs, the PUT statement writes to the log the special variables created for just this purpose. The automatic variable _N_, being the number of times the step has begun iterating, provides the total count, used to compute the number of adults with no sex given.

---

*Because a Sum statement implies a RETAIN of the variable involved, the RETAIN in this example is redundant (all the variables on the RETAIN statement appear in Sum statements). However, declaring these variables explicitly makes the program easier to understand.

```
1              DATA STUDY;
2                RETAIN MCOUNT FCOUNT CCOUNT NOAGE 0;
3                INFILE STDY1 END=ALLDONE;
4                INPUT ID 1-6 AGE 2. SEX $1. VAR1-VAR6;
5                IF AGE=. THEN NOAGE + 1;
6                ELSE DO;
7                  IF AGE<18 THEN CCOUNT+1;
8                  ELSE IF SEX='M' THEN MCOUNT+1;
9                  ELSE IF SEX='F' THEN FCOUNT+1;
10               END;
11               IF ALLDONE THEN DO;
12                 NOSEX=_N_-NOAGE-CCOUNT-MCOUNT-FCOUNT;
13                 PUT // 'SAMPLE KNOWN ADULT MALE=' MCOUNT
14                     /  '      KNOWN ADULT FEMALE=' FCOUNT
15                     /  '#CHILDREN OF EITHER SEX=' CCOUNT
16                     // '   # ADULTS UNKNOWN SEX=' NOSEX
17                     /  '   # SAMPLE UNKNOWN AGE=' NOAGE ;
18               END;
19               KEEP ID AGE SEX VAR1-VAR6;
20             RUN;
```

```
NOTE: The infile STDY1 is:
      FILENAME=C:\SAS\MASAS2\STDY1.DAT,
      RECFM=V,LRECL=90


SAMPLE KNOWN ADULT MALE=91
     KNOWN ADULT FEMALE=232
#CHILDREN OF EITHER SEX=243

   # ADULTS UNKNOWN SEX=14
   # SAMPLE UNKNOWN AGE=11
NOTE: 591 records were read from the infile  STDY1.
      The minimum record length was 84.
      The maximum record length was 84.
NOTE: The data set WORK.STUDY has 591 observations and 9 variables.
NOTE: The DATA statement used 0.8 seconds.
```

Listing 8.1. Using INFILE with END= to make a process decision

Detecting the End of a Concatenated Input Dataset

The INFILE statement option EOV= (for "end-of-volume," sometimes a misnomer) can be used to create a logical variable that starts as 0 (false) but is set 1 (true) when the last record of an input file that is part of a concatenated fileref* has just been read.

---

*A "concatenated" input file is one that consists of a series of physical files that are read in sequence and treated as one logical file. Implementation varies between operating systems.

Problem: Raw data from a survey that has been repeated in each of several successive years are available in separate files, one covering each year. The record formats are the same for each of the several files, but no variable within the data tells what year the file covers. A single SAS dataset must be created, with a variable distinguishing each of the original files.

Solution: Using a method appropriate to your operating system, concatenate the several files, in order by year, under a single fileref (let's call it SURVEY). Then, write something like this:

```
DATA SURVEY;
  RETAIN YEAR 1;
  INFILE SURVEY EOV=LAST;
  DROP LAST;
  INPUT variables;
[more SAS statements]
OUTPUT;
IF LAST THEN DO;
  YEAR + 1;
  LAST = 0;
END;
RUN;
```

The variable YEAR will have the value 1 at the outset: retain that value until the last record of the current volume of concatenated files is reached. When the end is reached, LAST=1 and the DO group is executed. YEAR is incremented for the next and subsequent iterations, and LAST is set back to zero for the next iteration.

The EOV=variable is set as soon as INFILE executes to read the last observation; this is why we have to OUTPUT *before* the DO group in this example; otherwise, the last observation in a given volume would have the wrong (one-too-large) YEAR value. Also note that EOV= sets its reference variable to 1 and *leaves* it at 1. In effect, LAST is retained, and the program must explicitly reset it.

Controlling Execution at End-of-File

There are occasions when it would be appropriate upon reaching the end of an input file to transfer control within the DATA step, i.e., to go to another statement elsewhere in the step. This action can be implemented with the EOF= option on the INFILE statement. EOF= *does not create a variable*, but rather names a statement label.

You might use EOF=, for example, when two or more files have similar data but different formats, or have slightly dissimilar data but one SAS dataset must be made from them.

Problem: Medical history data on men are contained in one file, data on women in another. The data are mostly the same (things such as age, race, diet, history of disease), but there are a few items that are different for men and for women. For example, women answer questions about birth control pills but men don't. Read this data into a single SAS dataset.

Solution:

```
DATA MEDHSTRY;
   INFILE WOMEN EOF=MEN_NOW;
   INPUT variables for women;
   SEX='F';
   GOTO MORE;
MEN_NOW:
   INFILE MEN;
   INPUT variables for men;
   SEX='M';
MORE:
   [more SAS statements if required]
RUN;
```

This works as follows: After each record is retrieved from the file referred to by WOMEN, the step proceeds as written. However, after the last record of WOMEN has been read, control is transferred straight from the first INFILE statement immediately to the label "MEN_NOW:"; this holds true for *each iteration after EOF= was first satisfied.*

Missing Input Data

In Chapter 3 it was stated that when raw data is read with list input, missing values must be represented with placeholder periods or else SAS not only will take the next value it finds to be the value of the variable that should have been missing, but may also seek subsequent variables on the next input record. In other words, if an INPUT statement attempts to read a value from the end of a record (i.e., from a point in a record where only blanks are contained until record's end), its default action will be to try to find the variable beginning at the first column on the *next* data card. As you can imagine, this action is to be avoided in most applications. There are several things you can do to handle "short" records.

Set Variables Missing

Not uncommonly, there may be up to a certain maximum number of data points for some but not for all observations.

Problem: Engineering data have been gathered that concern the temperatures created during a certain manufacturing process. Temperatures were measured at regular intervals during various replications of the process and may have been measured up to 12 times. Yet for different reasons, in many cases there were less than 12 measurements. Each input card line represents one replication, and the data look something like this:

```
958   996 912  955   1020   910  1060  1180  920

890 923 1022  1061   970  960  951  1032  882 898 950  1008

980  890  1103  976    1032  920  978

. . .
```

Create 12 variables, TEMP1-TEMP12, with data missing where there are less than 12 replicates. That is, TEMP10-TEMP12 should be set missing for the first observation, TEMP8-TEMP12 missing for the third, etc.

Solution: The irregular way the data were typed excludes column or formatted input, and list input seems the best way. SAS provides the MISSOVER option of the INFILE statement for just such occasions. The statement

```
INFILE fileref MISSOVER [other options];
```

causes the system to stop executing the INPUT statement when it would otherwise go to the next input line, and instead to assign the system missing value to the remaining variables.

Similar behavior can be elicited with the TRUNCOVER option. Like MISS-OVER, TRUNCOVER prevents the INPUT statement from reaching into the next input record if it comes up short. If part of a field is available before the end of the record occurs (that is, the record ends on an input field that is shorter than its INPUT specification), the variable will be missing if MISSOVER is coded. However, if TRUNCOVER is coded in the same situation, then the variable will contain whatever data was available in it even if it is "short." For example, reading

```
123JONES
```

with

```
INPUT ID 3. NAME $10.;
```

would fail if MISSOVER were used (name would be missing) but succeed if TRUNCOVER were used.

Set Error Condition

Now instead, suppose it is the case that all data had better be in place: If there are 12 variables, there must be 12 data points.

Problem: Halt program execution in case of missing data, so the data can be set right.

Solution: For these occasions, use the INFILE fileref STOPOVER. When SAS would otherwise go to the next line for a variable on INPUT, the system variable _ERROR_ is instead set to 1, the DATA step is immediately halted, and the offending input line will be printed on the SAS log.*

Back to Default: FLOWOVER

If MISSOVER, TRUNCOVER, or STOPOVER has been specified, the SAS System can be brought back to its default method of handling missing input data—going to the next line to look for it—by using the INFILE statement option FLOWOVER.

THE INPUT STATEMENT: ADDITIONAL FEATURES

"Recycling" Informats: Grouped INPUT Specifications

Within an INPUT statement, one informat can be made to control several preceding variables. If three values, in 6.2 informat, are found one after the other in columns 1-6, 7-12, 13-18, the statement

```
INPUT (BRTHDT ENROLLDT DRPOUTDT) (6.2);
```

will read them correctly. A set of parentheses placed around the consecutive variable names and followed immediately by an informat within parentheses, signifies "apply this informat repeatedly to the preceding list of names."

Using formatted input like this can save a lot of time over column input if a series of similar variables follow each other on the data cards. This short cut is actually a special case of the INPUT statement's ability to receive a parenthesized variable list followed by a parenthesized list of informats and pointer controls, and to reuse the informat list until the variables are exhausted, i.e., "apply this informat list repeatedly until all variables have been read." As an example, either of these two INPUT statements might be used to read data consisting of five variables in three-digit numeric fields separated from each other by five spaces:

---

*Note that this method will catch only the first of what may be a series of erroneous data cards. When rerun, the job may stop again at a later card. So an alternative technique, to find out *all* the data with missing observations, could be to do a test run with INFILE MISSOVER, using OUTPUT to write only those observations with the last variable (in this example, TEMP12) missing. Assign _N_ to another variable, and when the dataset is printed it may be discovered which observations, by record number, had missing values.

```
INPUT (V1-V5) (3. +5);
```

```
INPUT V1 3. +5 V2 3. +5 V3 3. +5 V4 3. +5 V5 3. +5;
```

Parenthesis syntax is also permitted in a complex INPUT statement such as

```
INPUT APPLE 1-10 ORANGE 5. (PEAR BANANA PLUM) (2. +1) MANGO;
```

Pointer and input buffer controls are allowed within an informat list, although in almost all cases the absolute pointer controls @n and #n would better be used outside the parentheses.

This all may seem a mere convenience, but there are situations where grouped format lists are very convenient indeed, as the following two problems will illustrate (imagine how tedious it would be to accomplish the same result without using groups specifications):

Problem: A dataset contains opinion research data, responses to 30 questions indicating agreement or disagreement and the strength of opinion. In this particular survey, for psychometric reasons first "agree/disagree" was asked, and then the strength of the conviction ("moderate/strong") was also asked: "Do you agree with . . ."; "How strongly do you feel?" For each of the 30 questions, then, there were actually two recorded responses: 0 = no opinion, 1 = disagree, and 2 = agree are valid values for the first, and 0 = don't know, 1 = moderate, 2 = strong are the second. The raw data were entered with the agree/disagree response followed by the strength-of-opinion response, each data record becoming 60 columns long, so that, for instance,

```
11201212 ...
```

would indicate question 1 moderately disagree, question 2 agree but not sure how strong, questions 3 and 4 strongly disagree, etc. Now, make a SAS dataset out of the information.

Solution: The following INPUT statement handles this easily:

```
INPUT (QUEST1-QUEST30) (1. +1) @2 (STRNTH1-STRNTH30) (1. +1);
```

Look carefully: QUEST1 is read at the beginning (column 1), one column (which will become STRNTH1) is skipped, and so on to read QUEST2–QUEST30 from columns 3, 5, 7, . . ., then return to column 2 and get STRNTH1, then skip one again, etc., until all STRNTHn values are read from the even-numbered columns.

Do not worry about the last "+1" in the sequence, the one that would appear to occur after STRNTH30 is read. After an INPUT statement exhausts all the values implied by its specifications, it ignores any remaining pointer definitions. At the end of the INPUT statement in this example, the pointer rests right after the column that held STRNTH30, not an additional space beyond. Similarly, at the end of either INPUT statement illustrated a little earlier with variables V1-V5, the last +5 is ignored; in either form, the pointer rests after V5's field.

Respecifying Single Informats

A special operator "*" can be used to reduplicate single informat items within a grouped list. For example, the INPUT statement

```
INPUT (VAR1-VAR10) (2.);
```

reads 10 variables with the informat "2." An identical effect is achieved using the INPUT statement

```
INPUT (VAR1-VAR10) (10*2.);
```

This is no improvement, but suppose the problem were as follows:

Problem: Continue to read variable GROUP1 from the four columns following VAR10, then read VAR11-VAR20 (two columns each again), then GROUP2 (four columns), . . . and so on through VAR60 and GROUP6.

Solution:

```
INPUT @21 (GROUP1-GROUP6) (4. +20) @1 (VAR1-VAR60) (10*2. +4);
```

Invalid Data on Input

An input value is invalid (as far as the SAS System is concerned) if it cannot be read with the input specification given, either because it requires an informat that is not available at execution time, or because it does not conform to a specified informat. By default, when invalid data are encountered in an input record, the SAS System sets the value of the corresponding SAS variable missing and the automatic variable __ERROR__ to 1. On the SAS log, the system generally prints an "invalid data" message, the input line and column number, and the input lines and SAS variable values for the observation.

The SAS System option ERRORS= can be set with an OPTIONS statement to limit the absolute number of complete error message sets that will be printed in a DATA step. The usual default is ERRORS=20. You can also control error handling by the special INPUT statement specifiers ? and ??, which are placed after the variable name but before its informat name, e.g.,

```
INPUT A ?? 5.;
```

"?" suppresses printing the "invalid data" message, but takes the other actions mentioned above. "??" suppresses the "invalid data" message, the setting of __ERROR__ to 1, and also the listing of the offending input lines. However, the variable value will still be missing.

Named Input

In some cases of data gathering, only a few of many possible variables will be entered. For example, a questionnaire may contain hundreds of questions, only a handful of which will be answered by any individual respondent. In some such cases, data entry might be expedited by the following device: Write the names of data items as well as their values on the same record, naming only the values that apply to that record. Consider a comprehensive opinion research survey, where one yes or no answer can lead to a cascade of other questions and answers branching out from it ("If 'yes,' also ask Question #s . . ."). Suppose there are 200 questions, and a place for sex and age as well. If the following record shows a 23-year-old male has answered just three of the 200 questions:

```
M 23 Q10=1 Q15=2 Q127=1
```

the statements

```
ARRAY X {*} Q1-Q200 ;
INPUT SEX $ AGE Q1= ;
```

will read this data. The variable with the "=" sets the stage for named input.

Not all the variables need be named on the INPUT statement, so long as at least one of them is (to toggle the compiler into "named input mode"). Any SAS variable names can be used with named input, not just those with consecutive numbers, so long as the name is declared (that is, appears somewhere in the step code). If a variable is not defined elsewhere in the program and yet appears in the data cards, a runtime error will occur, since the PDV is defined at compile time. (In the example, the ARRAY statement provides the variable list so the PDV will contain 200 variables Q1–Q200. Therefore, the step runs successfully.) You can declare a variable on the INPUT statement itself, and get the opportunity to specify informats if desired:

```
INPUT P Q R S A=12. B= C=MMDDYY6. D= S=$ N=$CHAR25.;
```

You cannot, however, go back to another INPUT style in the same INPUT statement, that is, any variables on the INPUT statement after the first one with an "=" should all have "=," and on the data cards as well the "var=value" entries should appear last.

If a data line cannot hold all the variables to be named (say a respondent answers 100 of the 200 questions in our example), data entry must simply append a forward slash (/) to any line that is continued. The slash has the effect it would on the INPUT statement itself: It gets the next line and continues. INPUT ends and the step continues when a data line without a terminating slash is encountered.

Variables defined in the source code but not named on the data line(s) of an observation simply keep their initial (missing or RETAINed) values after INPUT executes. The SAS record on the 23-year-old man of our example has 197 missing values.

The INFORMAT Statement

You can tease apart from the INPUT statement its formatting function with the INFORMAT statement, allowing variables to be expressed in list-style input in the INPUT statement. The statement group

```
INFORMAT X $ 6.;
INPUT X Y Z $;
```

reads Y and Z with their default informats (respectively, standard numeric and $), but X with the $6. informat.

INFORMAT can be used in any situation where you could use the ":" format modifier. The same precautions apply concerning the column pointer and the evaluation of numeric variables.

MORE SAS INFORMATS

Here is a brief overview of the more important SAS informats, excluding the date/time informats which we will introduce later.

Numeric Informats

Regular Numerics

In Chapter 3 was introduced the most common of the numeric informats, "w.d." w gives the field width in columns, and d the number of digits to the right of the decimal point (as a default if an actual decimal point does not appear in the data value). d is optional, but "w." must appear.

```
INPUT THIS 12.4 THAT 5.;
```

takes a value of THIS from the first 12 columns, treating the last four digits as a decimal fraction (unless a decimal point appears in the data value itself to override the informat), and takes THAT from the next five columns, treating it as an integer (but again, only if a decimal point does not appear in the data). Leading and trailing blanks are ignored; embedded blanks (blanks within a value) cause a runtime error.

A single decimal point in a data field is taken to be a missing value. All-blanks in a field also signify a missing value, but if desired, the user can have the compiler treat blanks as zeroes by using the BZw.d informat. For example, the statement

```
INPUT A 3. @1 B BZ3.;
```

reading the cards

```
123
 4
5 6
```

results in A values of 123, 4, and missing ("5 6," embedded blank, invalid data error, missing value), but B values of 123, 40, and 506.

An informat for scientific notation, Ew.d, is provided by SAS, but the ordinary w.d informat can read scientific notation and Ew.d is not really needed.

The PERCENTw. informat can be used to read data that may arrive with a percent sign. If a percent sign is indeed found in the input field, the number is, correctly, divided by 100. Parenthesized values are treated correctly as negative values. If the fields

```
12 4% (3) (2%)
```

are read with, say, PERCENT4., the values stored are 12, .04, -3, and $-.02$, respectively.

The w.d, BZw.d, Ew.d and PERCENTw. informats can take field widths (w values) as large as 32.

Data Conversion Informats

There are a number of ways input data values may arrive other than in numeric characters, especially if the data were created by another computer program. To read data in these unusual forms, the SAS compiler provides several informats.

RBw.d reads real (floating point) binary, IBw.d integer (fixed-point) binary, PIBw.d positive integer binary, PDw.d packed decimal, PKw.d unsigned (positive) packed decimal, and ZDw.d zoned decimal. You should have a good idea *why* you need these informats before using them (e.g., COBOL COMP-3 corresponds to PDw.d), and consult your SAS documentation for details about their implementation.

Hexadecimal values can be read with the HEXw.d informat; usually, the conversion is to fixed-point binary, but w can range up to 16, in which case the floating-point representation is used. Octal values can be read with OCTALw.d, where w can range up to 24, and even binary values can be read, with BINARYw.d, where w can range to 64.

For a special conversion task there is the special BITSw.d informat. The task is to extract particular bits from an input value. This can be useful when reading a field formatted by another program that packs information (such as several on/off flags) in each byte. w.d has an unusual interpretation with the BITSw.d informat: d is the zero-based offset, and w the number of bits to read. For example, "BITS3.2" asks that three bits be read from offset 3, being the fourth bit position (offset 0 is the first). The value stored is the result of the binary number formed by the extracted bits. If the three bits are 101, for example, the value stored is 5.

Financial Notation

Data that has been entered with dollar signs, commas, or parentheses (to represent negative values) can be read with the COMMAw.d informat. When read with COMMAw.d, dollar signs and commas are ignored, and thus do not generate invalid data errors. As with the PERCENTw. informat, parenthesized values are treated correctly as negative values, that is, "(1,230)" is taken to be -1230. w may range up to 32.

Character Informats

We have already seen the character informat $w., which accepts a value of up to w characters' length starting at the first nonblank column in the field. To read a character value including leading blanks, use the $CHARw. informat instead. For example, the statement

```
INPUT A $5. @1 B $CHAR5.;
```

reading the data line

```
bbXYZ
```

(where blanks are shown here as lowercase b), results in a value of "XYZ   " for A but "   XYZ" for B.

To encode nonprintable characters, write their hexadecimal equivalents in the data lines, and read them with the $HEXw. informat. You can also convert octal or binary values to their character equivalents, with $OCTALw. and $BINARYw.* For the special purpose of converting null (hex 00) bytes to blanks (EBCDIC hex 40), use the informat $CHARZBw.

The $VARYINGw. informat may be used in those cases where a character variable may come in a varying length. w in this instance represents a maximum length, and the actual length (determined by some means) must appear after the informat specification. See your *SAS Language* guide for usage details.

You can convert ASCII to EBCDIC and vice-versa with the $ASCIIw. and $EBCDICw. informats. The behavior of these informats depends on your computer system: if the computer system on which your SAS System is running is ASCII-based, $ASCIIw. performs no conversion, but values read with $EBCDICw. will be converted to ASCII. The reverse holds true if your system is EBCDIC-based.

The $UPCASEw. informat converts any lowercase letters found in the input to uppercase. The $QUOTEw. informat removes single or double quote marks arriving at the beginning or end of an input value (it leaves alone quote marks appearing inside the input value, that is, not in the first or last position). This format can be useful for reading comma-delimited data formatted by other software systems.

---

*Do you see the difference between these three informats and their "$-less" equivalents? These create character values.

For any of the character informats, the value of w may range as high as 200.

DATE/TIME INFORMATS

It is hard to do arithmetic with times and dates. Times are 60, 60, 24 and don't fit nicely into our usual calculation methods. Dates are worse: days fit 7 to the week, weeks 52 to the year, but the months have different numbers of days and then there's that business with leap year (and century and fourth-century adjustments, too).

So it can work on them arithmetically, the SAS System stores dates or times as ordinary numeric values. To do so, an arbitrary zero point must be assumed. For dates and datetimes, the SAS System uses January 1, 1960 as that point. A SAS data value is the number of days between January 1, 1960 and the date in question; dates prior to 1960 become negative numbers. A datetime value is the number of *seconds* between midnight, January 1, 1960, and the date and time in question. For time values not considering date, midnight is the zero point: a time value is the number of seconds between midnight and the time. You must always remember that these are three different things; do not confuse dates with datetimes or times, and don't write expressions mixing them.

While in their numeric forms, arithmetic calculations can be performed on the values.

Problem: Given birthdate and today's date in SAS date values, calculate the age of a person in years.

Solution:

```
AGE = (TODAYDT-BRTHDT)/365.25;
```

(We assume, of course, that TODAYDT is today's date, and BRTHDT the birthdate, both stored as SAS date values.)

Problem: Your little girl must know just how many days remain before her birthday.

Solution: This time, assign to BRTHDT this year's birthday, and code:

```
DAYS= BRTHDT-TODAYDT;
```

Date, Time, and Datetime Informats

The trick is to convert dates to numerics and back again, and the SAS System does it handily. Here, we consider reading data with date/time* informats. To get date/time values back out of the SAS System, there are the many date, time, and

---

*In this book, "datetime" means a SAS datetime, while "date/time" is used generally to mean "date, time, or datetime."

datetime formats, explained in Chapter 11. (Since many of the date/time informats are more or less the inverse of formats of the same name, you can turn to Chapter 11 to learn more about them.)

The TIMEw. informat reads time values, the DATEw. informat date values, and the DATETIMEw. informat datetime values. TIME expects values normally separated by colons (10:25:03 being 3 seconds after 10:25 a.m.; you could get down to hundredths of seconds with 10:25:03.29), DATE expects values in the form ddMMMyy or ddMMMyyyy, e.g., 4JUL1776, and DATETIME a combination, separated by a colon, e.g., 6:30 p.m. of June 12, 1955 could be represented in data by 12JUN55:18:30.

There are several alternative date informats. The three-part date informats, MMDDYYw., DDMMYYw., and YYMMDDw. read dates such as 02/15/87 (MMD-DYY). w can range from 6 to 32. The date can be compressed (021587), or blanks or other special characters can intervene (2 15 87, 2-15-87) and still be read correctly with the informat. The MONYYw. informat reads dates in the form MMMyy or MMMyyyy, e.g., JUL89 or JUL1989. The YYQw. informat reads dates in forms yyQq or yyyyQq as year/quarter, e.g., "79Q1" and "1979Q1" both refer to "first quarter 1979." A SAS date value created by YYQw. will actually represent the first date in the quarter (e.g., January 1, April 1).

Date/Time Functions

A series of special SAS functions exists to convert values to dates and back again, to calculate time intervals, even to obtain the current actual date and time. Please see Chapter 15 for descriptions.

Date, Time, and Datetime Constants

Another way to specify SAS date/time values is with special constants. Using date/time constants, a user can write a date, time, or datetime directly in SAS code but have the compiler treat and store it as a date/time value. The constants are written using the forms for the TIME, DATE, and DATETIME informats, enclosed in single quotes and suffixed with T, D, or DT. For example, February 4, 1972 is represented as '4FEB72'D, high noon as '12:00'T. A moment in date and time can be captured with a constant such as '30AUG62:13:28:06'DT.

USER-DEFINED INFORMATS

You, the SAS user, may specify your own precise methods for handling input data fields. These methods are given names, and in the context of your SAS programs, you use these names just as you would use SAS informats. Hence, they are called user-defined informats. There are, however, two very important differences between SAS informats and these user-defined informats:

1. Many of the SAS-supplied informats achieve their effects by special-ized behind-the-scenes algorithms. Imagine, for example, the kind of processing that must go on for BITSw., or even COMMAw.d, to work. The user-defined informats can't do anything like this; they are but simple *value-by-value replacement rules*.
2. User-defined informats can be (and often are) used to group values together in radical ways. For example, one could specify that all values less than 1000, or all values between 'AAA' and 'CCC', be converted to the same single value (whatever you choose) when read by INPUT. The SAS-supplied informats do not do this kind of value-grouping.

There are many potential uses for user-defined informats. The classic example is conversion of letter grades to numbers for calculating grade-point averages. Assume the existence of an informat, NGRADE., that translates 'A' to 4, 'B' to 3, 'C' to 2, 'D' to 1, 'F' to 0. Then an input file such as the following:

```
JOHNNIE   A
JOEY   C
MARY   B
KATHY   A
FREDDY   F
```

when read with the input statement

```
INPUT NAME $ GRADE NGRADE.;
```

would result in a dataset with a *numeric* variable GRADE, where Johnnie's grade would be 4, Joey's 3, etc.

User-defined informats, like SAS informats, are of one or the other type, "nu-meric" or "character." When discussing user-defined informats, a numeric infor-mat is one that results in a numeric value, whether or not the field it reads consists all of numerals. Thus the informat NGRADE in the example above is a numeric informat. Character informats create character values, whether or not the field it reads consists all of numerals. As with standard SAS informats, character informats are distinguished syntactically by a dollar sign preceding the name.

The FORMAT Procedure

The SAS System's way of letting you work this kind of magic is the FORMAT procedure. As we will see in Chapter 11, where the procedure is discussed in greater depth, the FORMAT procedure can be used to create user-defined formats, as well as informats, to store informats and formats in library catalogs for use in subsequent programs, to print the definitions of user-defined informats and for-mats, and to write or read special "control datasets" that contain information about user-defined informats and formats and which can be used to facilitate their creation and documentation.

To create user-defined informats (to which we limit the discussion in this chapter), the FORMAT procedure interprets INVALUE statements.

The INVALUE statement has the general form

```
INVALUE [$]infmtname [(options)]
<<<value>|<range>>,... = <invalue|informat>>...;
```

"Infmtname" is the name which you choose for the informat; do not choose the same name as an existing SAS informat. The name can be up to seven characters long, must begin with an underscore or a letter, and must not end in a numeral; thus the rules are slightly different than for SAS variable names, which may end in a numeral and be up to eight characters long. In the INVALUE statement, you do not place a period after the name in the INVALUE statement, although you *do* use a period after the name when you call upon the informat in use (e.g., in an INFORMAT or INPUT statement). The dollar sign *is* used, on the INVALUE statement as well as when the informat is called upon, to designate a character informat.

A "range" is two values separated by a either a hyphen or a "modified hyphen" form <-, -<, or <-<, except that the special keyword LOW may replace the value on the left, and the special keyword HIGH may replace the value on the right. "LOW- 15" means "from the lowest value up through 15," " 'XYX'-HIGH" means " '1000' to the highest value." The modified separators provide a means to exclude the endpoints from a range. For example, 10-20 means "10 through 20 inclusive," but 10-<20 means "from 10 up to but excluding 20," 10<-20 means "greater than 10 and up through 20," and "10<-<20" means "greater than 10 and less than 20."* You should take care not to use the same input values in more than one place in defining an informat and that ranges do not overlap other ranges or values.

The special keyword OTHER may be used in lieu of value or range, signifying that all other input values not named are to be assigned the label shown. When used in this special way, OTHER (and for that matter LOW and HIGH) are never enquoted.

---

*The results can be different, and you must choose what you want. For example, consider the statement

```
INVALUE A   1-10='A'  '2'-'20'='B';
```

The first range covers the values 1 through 10 *interpreted numerically*, but the second range is *interpreted as character* and includes any character values that may fall between the literals '2' and '20' in the collating sequence used by your computer system.

However, LOW never includes missing values: the "lowest" is the lowest non-missing value. To include missing values as well, they would have to be specified as another value, e.g., "VALUE x .__-.Z,LOW- 999=label".

Note that it is permitted to mix both quoted and unquoted values/ranges within the same INVALUE statement, provided that those that are unquoted are entirely numeric.

INVALUE statement options, if any, go in parentheses following the informat name. To left-justify input field character values before they are compared to the format value or range of values you use the JUST option. If this is not done, then character values with leading blanks will not compare equally to INVALUE values specified without leading blanks. The UPCASE option will convert input field values to uppercase before comparing them.

User-defined informats can be called with w. specifications (e.g., as in "INPUT V S5.;"), although in typical practice they are not. The option DEFAULT= may be used to alter the default width of the informat. If it does not appear, the default width of the informat is based on the lengthiest input value (and thus, the DEFAULT= option is rarely used). The related MAX= and MIN= options set, respectively, the maximum and minimum width of the informat.

Invalues

Following the specification of a value, range, or series of values and/or ranges separated by commas, there is an equal sign and either a constant input value or the name of another informat. If an input value is used, it must be a numeric constant for numeric informats, and should be an enquoted character constant for character informats, although the SAS System will supply the quotes for you if you code a numeral without quotes while defining a character informat. That is,

```
INVALUE $MYVAL 'A'='10' 'B'='20';
```

and

```
INVALUE $MYVAL 'A'=10 'B'=20;
```

are equivalent, and in both cases the *character* value '10' results when 'A' is read with the $MYVAL. informat.

In lieu of an invalue, another informat name may be used. If so, it must be *enclosed in square brackets* (the only place in SAS syntax where square brackets have meaning) or, if your terminal has trouble with this, with parentheses and vertical bars: "[FMT.]" and "(FMT.)" are equivalent. Note that the period *is* used. When an informat is used instead of an invalue, the effect is to apply that informat to the input value. This technique can be used when you "really" want to apply normal SAS informats to most input, but need to handle special cases in a different way.

Problem: Numeric responses to a survey question range from 1 through 5, but a value of 9 is encoded if the question was not answered. These values should be changed to zero.

Solution:

```
PROC FORMAT;
INVALUE S 1-5 = [1.] 9 = 0;
RUN;
DATA SURVEY; INFILE SURVEY.DATA;
INPUT QUESTION S.; ...
```

A response of 1 through 5 will be read into the SAS dataset as a numeric integer value using the 1. format, but an input value of 9 will be given the value 0 in the dataset.

Actually, in this example we could have used, instead of an informat, the special invalue _SAME_, which causes the input values in a range to stay, well, the same:

```
INVALUE S 1-5 = _SAME_  9 = 0;
```

There is one other special invalue, _ERROR_, which you can use to cause certain values or ranges of values to be treated as invalid data. For example, if we coded

```
INVALUE S 1-5 = _SAME_  9 = 0  OTHER = _ERROR_;
```

then any input value other than 1, 2, 3, 4, 5, or 9 would cause the automatic variable _ERROR_ to be set to 1 for the iteration, the value of QUESTION to be missing, and a warning to be generated to the SAS log, just as with any other invalid data.

9

Selecting and Summarizing Observations

As you will discover more and more in working with the SAS System, to maintain control over the form and contents of working datasets is exceedingly important: If you cannot get the right variables and observations into a SAS dataset, there is no point in running a procedure on it. In Chapter 4 you learned how to select and arrange observations and variables. In this chapter and the next, you will learn more ways and techniques of rebuilding SAS datasets.

As seen in Chapter 4, SAS datasets may be divided using the subsetting IF, with some records selected for the rebuilt dataset but others rejected. Here we illustrate the use of the WHERE statement to achieve similar results in a DATA step. We next look at a couple of ways to select observations nonsequentially, with special SET statement options specialized for the purpose.

The information in SAS datasets can be summarized and then written to a new dataset. For example, variable totals or averages can be obtained and assigned to new variables. This may be accomplished through the DATA Step, as we will see below. Data summarized by SAS procedures can (in some cases, depending on the procedure) be written to output datasets. For example, as we saw in Chapter 5, the FREQ procedure can be made to generate an output dataset that has an observation for each combination of TABLE specification values, giving summary frequencies for that combination. In this chapter, we will give detailed attention to the versatile SUMMARY procedure, that can produce output datasets with many kinds of information summarized in many different ways.

WHERE PROCESSING IN THE DATA STEP

WHERE statements, and WHERE= dataset options, can be used in the DATA step as well as in the PROC step. As you will recall from Chapter 5, WHERE selections can be used to filter out unwanted observations from a SAS dataset as it is passed to a procedure for execution. The construction of WHERE expressions and the special operators they may contain were explained in Chapter 5. WHERE selections have the same syntax in the DATA step as they do in the PROC step.

WHERE selections perform a similar function in the DATA step as they do in the PROC step: they determine which dataset observations will be subject to processing, even before the observation is selected into the program data vector. WHERE is used only for rebuilding SAS datasets, i.e., when data are obtained by SET, MERGE, UPDATE, or MODIFY statements. WHERE processing is inappropriate (and incorrect) when data come from INPUT.

WHERE differs from other SAS observation-selection statements since it peeks into an observation before it is actually read into the program data vector. When the DATA Step compiler recognizes that a WHERE statement appears in the step code, it ensures that the WHERE condition is applied before any other statements take effect, even if other statements appear to precede it in the program. This is one of the big differences between using a WHERE statement and a subsetting IF statement to select observations for dataset rebuilding. Listing 9.1 illustrates this behavior: note that statements preceding the subsetting IF execute even if the IF condition is false, but no statements (even those preceding WHERE) execute when the WHERE condition is false.

As you may see, WHERE selection can often be more efficient than subsetting IF selection. In both the illustrative DATA steps in Listing 9.1 the same observations were discarded from the input dataset, and the output datasets were the same. Yet a lot of wasted processing activity went on behind the scenes while IFDS was being produced. Even if no executable statements precede SET nor intervene between SET and a subsetting IF, the use of a WHERE statement will still be more efficient, because when IF is used the SET statement causes data to be read into the PDV.

The subsetting IF is still of value, for because of its special way of processing input observations WHERE cannot be used in all cases. A WHERE statement cannot be executed conditionally, that is, as the result of an IF-THEN or SELECT-WHEN. Because the input dataset must be examined outside the normal PDV process, you cannot use the SET statement options POINT= or KEY= (both discussed below) when applying a WHERE condition (statement or dataset option). Neither, when using WHERE conditions, can you enter or leave the input dataset at an arbitrary point: The FIRSTOBS= and OBS= system options (described in Chapter 21) must be at their normal defaults, FIRSTOBS=1 and OBS=MAX. The subsetting IF can, of course, be used with data read by INPUT, while the WHERE statement operates only on existing SAS datasets.

The WHERE= dataset option applies a WHERE condition only to the dataset with which it is associated. A WHERE statement applies its WHERE condition to all input datasets. If other dataset options appear on the SET (or MERGE, UP-

```
<<< SAS SOURCE CODE FOLLOWS >>>

TITLE '(The input dataset TEST)';
PROC PRINT DATA=TEST;RUN;
TITLE 'First, IF';
DATA IFTEST;
  SET TEST;
  A=A-1;
  IF A<4;
RUN;
PROC PRINT DATA=IFTEST; RUN;
TITLE 'Now, WHERE';
DATA WHTEST;
  SET TEST;
  A=A-1;
  WHERE A<4;
RUN;
PROC PRINT DATA=WHTEST; RUN;

<<< SAS PROGRAM OUTPUT FOLLOWS >>>
```

(The input dataset TEST)

OBS	A
1	1
2	2
3	3
4	4
5	5
6	4
7	3
8	2
9	1
10	2
11	3
12	4
13	5

Listing 9.1. WHERE Versus Subsetting IF
Continued

DATE, or MODIFY) statement, then they are applied before the WHERE condition is applied.

DIRECT ACCESS TO OBSERVATIONS

In computer jargon, the ability to go straight to a selected place in a collection of
data without going through all points in between is called *direct access,* or some-

First, IF

OBS	A
1	0
2	1
3	2
4	3
5	3
6	2
7	1
8	0
9	1
10	2
11	3

Now, WHERE

OBS	A
1	0
2	1
3	2
4	2
5	1
6	0
7	1
8	2

Listing 9.1. *Continued*

times random access. By way of analogy, a CD player is a direct access device, because the disk read head can be jumped to any location directly. An audiotape is a *sequential* device: even using fast-forward, you still must go through intermediate locations on the tape before getting to the desired selection; you cannot jump "sideways" to the cut you want.

SAS datasets are usually accessed sequentially—an observation is read, and then the next, and the next . . . but if a SAS dataset is known well enough that observations can be identified by their position in the dataset, a more efficient program may be written to access observations directly, using the POINT= option on the SET statement. The following code retrieves the 23rd observation from a dataset:

```
DATA ONLY_23;
  OBSNUM=23;
  SET ORIGINAL POINT=OBSNUM;
  OUTPUT;
  STOP;
RUN;
```

POINT= declares a special SAS variable. The POINT= variable contains an integer that is used to indicate—"point to"—an observation of the input dataset. The compiler uses the POINT= variable and the internal SAS data access methods to determine a physical location within the dataset and go directly to the observation desired.* The usual SET action of fetching the next observation in sequence is not activated when POINT= has been specified.

In the example above, we let OBSNUM=23, and then code a SET statement using OBSNUM as the point variable. The SAS compiler now knows not to add OBSNUM to dataset ONLY_23, but to use it to locate an observation in dataset ORIGINAL. The SET statement investigates the current value of the pointer variable,† in this case finding it to be 23, and reads the 23rd observation from ORIGINAL into the PDV.

Encountering the STOP statement, the DATA step in the example halts. Bear in mind in almost all cases where POINT= is used, a STOP statement must appear at the end of the step. This is because while a DATA step driven by sequential SET processing normally terminates after the last observation from the input dataset has been processed, using POINT= disrupts sequential processing. With POINT=, the SET statement's "last-obs-was-read" flag will never be automatically set. Therefore, without STOP, this DATA step would continue to run and run, never reaching the end of the step on its own, re-filling the PDV with the same values from the same input observation. Observe that an explicit OUTPUT is also necessary, because we have used a STOP statement. STOP will abruptly end the DATA step, before the implicit OUTPUT SAS provides in its iterative processing. We therefore must force output before the STOP, using an explicit OUTPUT statement.

---

*And for this reason, POINT= cannot be used to read compressed data files; POINT= access works by calculating an "offset" into a dataset based on a fixed record length, but compressed datasets (discussed in Chapter 21) have varying record lengths. Neither can POINT= (or NOBS=, see below) be used with datasets stored on tape, for the same reason that you must fast-forward through your audiotape but not your CD.

†Even though OBSNUM appears in the code prior to the SET statement, because it is named after POINT= the compiler sets things up so the SAS System knows that the variable was meant to be used as a pointer and not an ordinary SAS variable. Indeed, in most POINT= applications (including this example) the assignment *must* precede the SET statement so that the pointer will contain the correct value at the time SET executes.

A variation on the POINT= theme* allows selection of several observations, in this example numbers 23, 42, and 108:

```
DATA ONLYSOME;
  DO OBSNUM=23,42,108;
    SET ORIGINAL POINT=OBSNUM;
    OUTPUT;
  END;
  STOP;
RUN;
```

Note that the same effect could be achieved by using the automatic variable __N__, which always has as its value the current iteration number of the DATA step, that is, the number of times the DATA step has begun execution "from the top." In a DATA step where SET is executed once and only once per iteration, __N__ will correspond to the ordinal number of the input observation. Thus:

```
DATA ONLYSOME;
  SET ORIGINAL POINT=OBSNUM;
  IF _N_=23 OR _N_=42 OR _N_=108;
RUN;
```

While this looks simpler at first glance, imagine coding the IF statement to select 30, not 3, observations. Furthermore, the POINT= option is much more efficient in terms of computer time. Suppose there were 5,000 observations in the input dataset, or even 500,000. The complex IF statement, with its OR subparts, would need to be executed for each and every one. True, the statement

```
IF _N_ > 108 THEN STOP;
```

could follow the subsetting IF statement. Still, 108 iterations of the DATA step would be required—and what if the last observation wanted was not number 108,

---

*Though properly a topic of Chapter 17, the iterative DO group must be introduced here to continue the following examples. A DO group begins with some form of DO statement, and ends with an END statement. The iterative DO causes the statements between it and END to execute a variable number of times.

```
DO I=1 TO 10;
```

for example, causes statements following it, until END, to be executed ten times in a row; each time, I has a different value 1, 2, . . ., 10.

```
DO A=2 TO 10 BY 2;
```

causes five iterations of the statements in the group, with the variable A having the values 2, 4, 6, 8, and 10. And

```
DO X=1,3,27,9;
```

causes four iterations, with X having the first time a value of 1, next 3, next 27, and finally 9. See Chapter 17 for more details.

but instead far to the end of the huge dataset? With the POINT= form, the step runs much faster: only those records pointed to are ever retrieved in the first place.

Direct access using the POINT= SET statement option can be useful for creating sample subsets.

Problem: From a dataset of 200 questionnaire returns, select every fourth one for a one-fourth sample.

Solution:

```
DATA SAMPLE;
  DO TAKEIT = 4 TO 200 BY 4;
    SET SURVEY POINT=TAKEIT;
    OUTPUT;
  END;
  STOP;
RUN;
```

In this example, we needed to know how many observations were in the input dataset (200) in order to code the DO statement. Fortunately, there is a way around this: the NOBS= SET statement option. NOBS= may be used only if POINT= is also used. It creates a special variable that represents the number of observations in the input dataset.

Problem: Select every fourth record from a dataset with an unknown number of records.

Solution: Substitute the following lines for the DO and SET statements in the previous example:

```
DO TAKEIT = 4 TO LASTONE BY 4;
  SET SURVEY POINT=TAKEIT NOBS=LASTONE;
```

Here LASTONE is the name chosen to contain the number of records in SURVEY. Like the variable TAKEIT, LASTONE is available for DATA Step Language programming but is not added to the SAMPLE dataset, and, as with POINT=, it is all right that the SET statement declaring NOBS=LASTONE comes after the DO statement referencing LASTONE.

Random Selection

We have just examined a way to get a controlled sample by selecting every fourth record of a dataset. Other fractional samples can be requested by adjusting the BY clause of the DO statement (e.g., DO . . . BY 5 selects a one-fifth sample). In some applications, however, truly random selection may be required.

Problem: For an experimental study, select a random sample of about one-quarter the records in an input dataset.

Solution:

Using the RANUNI function, we code

```
DATA EXPER1;
  SET STUDYPOP;
  IF RANUNI(0) < .25;
RUN;
```

Since about one-fourth of the time RANUNI returns a value less than .25,* about one-quarter of the observations will be randomly selected.

If it doesn't matter if observations are selected more than once (i.e., when sampling with replacement) the POINT= option can be used as a more computationally efficient method than reading every observation in the input dataset:

```
DATA EXPER1;
  DO N = 1 TO TOT/4;
    GO = INT(RANUNI(0)*TOT) + 1;
    SET STUDYPOP POINT=GO NOBS=TOT;
    OUTPUT;
  END;
  DROP GO;
  STOP;
RUN;
```

To explain: the function INT returns the integer portion of a mixed number [e.g., INT(4.7)=4]. The DO statement uses an expression, TOT/4, as its stopping point. (It doesn't matter if TOT/4 yields a mixed number, for the DO statement can use a fractional value in a comparison.) TOT is the number of observations in STUDYPOP, obtained by the NOBS= option on the SET statement. Thus the DO group is to be iterated a number of times corresponding to one-quarter the number of observations in STUDYPOP. Now examine the assignment statement, evaluating the expression on the right. RANUNI(0) yields a number between 0 and 1. Multiply by TOT and a number between 0 and TOT is obtained. The integer portion must therefore fall between 0 and TOT-1, inclusive. Add 1 to it, and the result is a valid observation number since it is an an integer between 1 and TOT. Using POINT=GO on the SET statement, an observation from STUDYPOP is thus randomly selected. Note that this method ensures a sample of one-quarter (or whatever fraction desired) the observations of the input dataset, whereas using RANUNI with a subsetting IF only approximates this. However, with POINT= the same observation might be selected more than once; it would take some additional programming if sampling without replacement were required.

---

*RANUNI is a SAS function (SAS functions are explained in Chapter 15) that returns a random fraction between 0 and 1; that is to say, if A=RANUNI(0), A will have a random value between 0 and 1 after the assignment. Each time the RANUNI function executes during the course of a DATA step, it results in a new random value.

Indexed Data Selection

If your input SAS dataset is indexed* you can specify the KEY= option on the SET statement, giving as its value the name of an index to the dataset. When SET executes, the value(s) of the index's variable(s) are used to select the next observation for processing. That is, if

```
SET DD.INDS KEY=SSN;
```

then SSN must be an index defined for the dataset DD.INDS and when SET executes the current value(s) of the variable(s) contributing to the index SSN will be used to select an observation from DD.INDS. Suppose, for example, that SSN is a simple index on the variable SSN. Then if when SET executes SSN=123456789, an observation with the SSN value 123456789, if found, will be read into the PDV.

This technique is often applicable when observations are to be combined from two (or more) datasets at least one of which is indexed by the merge variables. In such cases, the technique of multiple SET statements with one (or more) using the KEY= option may be appropriate to select observations from the indexed dataset(s). We will study an example of this in Chapter 10, when we consider merging datasets with multiple SET statements.

You cannot use both KEY= and POINT= in the same SET statement; however, you can use NOBS= with KEY= if you find the need.

SUMMARIZING DATA IN THE DATA STEP

The END= option on the SET statement, like the END= option on INFILE, lets the running program know when it has come to the end of an input dataset. END= starts with a value of 0, but is set to 1 when the last observation in the input dataset has been read into the program data vector. Used with the RETAIN (or Sum) and OUTPUT statements, END= can help collect summary information for an output dataset.

Problem: Portions of a field are irrigated by central-pole mechanisms that water circular areas. A dataset is available that gives the lateral length of the watering mechanism, which is the radius of the watering area. Create a dataset containing only the total irrigated area.

Solution:

---

*Dataset indexing is described in Chapter 21. Basically, an indexed dataset is one that is associated with an index structure that has been created to associate the values of (a) selected "key" variable(s) with particular observations. The observations are indexed according to the keys so that an observation with a particular value for the key(s) can be directly identified.

```
DATA WHOLAREA;
  SET WTRGADGT END=FIN;
  AREA + 3.14159 * R * R;
  IF FIN THEN OUTPUT;
  KEEP AREA;
RUN;
```

The Sum statement creates a variable, AREA, which is retained and incremented throughout the step. OUTPUT executes only once, when the last observation from the input dataset WTRGADGT is being processed, because only then is FIN "true."

The special variables FIRST.byvarname and LAST.byvarname, made available whenever a BY statement is used in a DATA step,* can be used along with the RETAIN (or Sum) and OUTPUT statements to summarize data within BY group categories.

Problem: On a large farm, many different fields are irrigated in part by one or more central-pole mechanisms. An input dataset contains a record of the lateral length of each watering mechanism, and in addition a number identifying the field in which the mechanism is located. Create a dataset containing the total irrigated areas for each field.

Solution:

```
DATA FLDAREAS;
  SET FIELDS;
  BY FIELD; * (ASSUMES SORT OR INDEX BY FIELD);
  RETAIN AREA 0;
  IF FIRST.FIELD THEN AREA=0; * MUST RESET FOR EACH BY GROUP;
  AREA + 3.14159 * R * R;
  IF LAST.FIELD THEN OUTPUT;
  KEEP FIELD AREA;
RUN;
```

The output dataset, FLDAREAS, will have one observation for each of the BY levels of the input dataset, containing the field number and the total area of that field.

In Chapter 8, we used INFILE with END= to illustrate accumulation of totals with the goal of reporting to the SAS log, while here we accumulate totals in order to construct a "summary" SAS dataset. But we could as easily have constructed a dataset with data summarized from raw input using INFILE and INPUT, or produced a summary on the log based on an existing dataset processed with SET. The data management features of the SAS DATA Step Language are as versatile as they are powerful.

---

*These variables are fully explained in Chapter 10.

THE *SUMMARY* PROCEDURE

PROC SUMMARY, the identical twin to PROC MEANS,* proves time and again to be the most effective way to handle a variety of data summarizing tasks. SUMMARY can produce aggregate statistics by variable categories without BY-group processing, and can include all combinations of category variables in one sweep.

If the PRINT option is coded on the PROC SUMMARY statement, the procedure will produce the same printed output as will PROC MEANS. More interesting—and more important, for many data processing applications—is the output dataset that is produced whenever an OUTPUT statement accompanies the procedure. Like any SAS dataset, the SUMMARY output dataset can be rearranged in subsequent job steps to serve a variety of analytic and reporting needs. It is the structure of this output dataset that we will examine in this chapter.

A SUMMARY Example

Assume a sample of males and females is divided into four socio-economic status (SES) groups, for a total of eight (4*2) categories. A psychometric instrument is administered and three scores, Affinity, Empathy, and Flexibility, are derived for each sample member.

Using SUMMARY, we can collect the means and standard deviations for the test scores and be able to describe completely the results in terms of sex, SES, or both:

```
PROC SUMMARY DATA=SURVEY1;
  VAR AFFINITY EMPATHY FLEXIBL;
  CLASS SEX SES;
  OUTPUT OUT=S_SUMRY MEAN=AMEAN EMEAN FMEAN STD=ASTD HSTD WSTD;
RUN;
```

I have invented some sample data, run a SUMMARY step like that shown above, and used PROC PRINT to print the output dataset S_SUMRY. Results are shown in Listing 9.2.

There are a few things to notice immediately. First, each of the CLASS variables in S_SUMRY is represented in the output dataset, and each of the requested statistics appears under the names specified. But there are two additional variables: _TYPE_ and _FREQ_. And there are a number of additional observations besides the SEX*ETHNICGP breakdowns that appear here as observations 8-15. These additional observations provide marginal and grand total statistics. In this example, values of the first observation describe the sample as a whole, ignoring SEX and SES. Observations 2-5 provide breakdowns by SES only;

---

*Prior to SAS Version 6, PROC SUMMARY was used to output datasets in the manner described in this chapter, and MEANS could not do so. Today, you can use all the statements and options described in this chapter to get the same results with PROC MEANS as with PROC SUMMARY, including the same output datasets.

Dataset S_SUMRY

OBS	SEX	SES	_TYPE_	_FREQ_	AMEAN	EMEAN	FMEAN	ASTD	HSTD	WSTD
1		.	0	160	4.65375	3.75375	1.98375	2.56380	1.96504	0.97831
2		1	1	40	4.76000	3.61000	1.70000	2.97242	2.03807	0.96980
3		2	1	40	4.77000	4.29000	1.99000	2.73460	1.87422	0.83445
4		3	1	40	4.59500	3.24000	1.99000	1.87739	1.91790	0.94239
5		4	1	40	4.49000	3.87500	2.25500	2.62745	1.94827	1.10406
6	F	.	2	80	4.83750	4.25250	1.86000	2.67787	2.03650	0.96175
7	M	.	2	80	4.47000	3.25500	2.10750	2.44744	1.76649	0.98505
8	F	1	3	20	4.56000	3.84000	1.48000	3.26841	2.34866	0.90006
9	F	2	3	20	4.71000	4.87000	2.05000	2.73475	1.76459	0.77629
10	F	3	3	20	5.49000	3.88000	1.73000	1.57911	2.18839	0.79479
11	F	4	3	20	4.59000	4.42000	2.18000	2.92411	1.75187	1.21897
12	M	1	3	20	4.96000	3.38000	1.92000	2.71456	1.70251	1.00922
13	M	2	3	20	4.83000	3.71000	1.93000	2.80415	1.84074	0.90502
14	M	3	3	20	3.70000	2.60000	2.25000	1.74778	1.37802	1.02418
15	M	4	3	20	4.39000	3.33000	2.33000	2.36619	2.02409	1.00216

Listing 9.2. PROC SUMMARY Example

for example, the means and standard deviations shown in observation 3 are based on all sample members who fall under SES group #2, regardless of SEX. Observations 6-7 show breakdowns by SEX only; for example, means and standard deviations in observation 6 are based on all female sample members regardless of SES.

The __FREQ__ Variable

The __FREQ__ variable in the summary output dataset indicates how many input observations contributed to the summary statistics reported for the output observation. In the example we have been using, there were 160 observations in the original SURVEY1 dataset, 20 each in each of the eight possible categories. Knowing this, refer again to the listings and you will understand the __FREQ__ variable.

CLASS, __TYPE__, and the SUMMARY Dataset

The observation structure of the output dataset is controlled by the CLASS variable, if a CLASS statement is used, and nonzero values of the __TYPE__ variable are likewise based on the CLASS statement. To use the full power of the SUMMARY procedure to build and rebuild SAS datasets, you need to understand these relationships.

The CLASS Statement

The statement

```
CLASS variables;
```

SUMMARY example: No CLASS variable

OBS	_TYPE_	_FREQ_	AMEAN	EMEAN	FMEAN	ASTD	HSTD	WSTD
1	0	160	4.65375	3.75375	1.98375	2.56380	1.96504	0.97831

SUMMARY example: "CLASS SEX"

OBS	SEX	_TYPE_	_FREQ_	AMEAN	EMEAN	FMEAN	ASTD	HSTD	WSTD
1		0	160	4.65375	3.75375	1.98375	2.56380	1.96504	0.97831
2	F	1	80	4.83750	4.25250	1.86000	2.67787	2.03650	0.96175
3	M	1	80	4.47000	3.25500	2.10750	2.44744	1.76649	0.98505

SUMMARY example: "CLASS SES"

OBS	SES	_TYPE_	_FREQ_	AMEAN	EMEAN	FMEAN	ASTD	HSTD	WSTD
1	.	0	160	4.65375	3.75375	1.98375	2.56380	1.96504	0.97831
2	1	1	40	4.76000	3.61000	1.70000	2.97242	2.03807	0.96980
3	2	1	40	4.77000	4.29000	1.99000	2.73460	1.87422	0.83445
4	3	1	40	4.59500	3.24000	1.99000	1.87739	1.91790	0.94239
5	4	1	40	4.49000	3.87500	2.25500	2.62745	1.94827	1.10406

Listing 9.3. PROC SUMMARY Example: CLASS Statement variations

specifies one or more variables whose values are to be considered classificatory categories for purposes of producing statistics on the VAR variables. In the example just described, statistics were produced for various combinations of input observations based on their CLASS variable values. The CLASS variables appear in the output dataset, indicating the values on which each observation has been based. Refer back to Listing 9.2: Means and standard deviations shown in observation 12, for example, are based only on the group composed of males in SES category 1.

CLASS is optional with SUMMARY, that is, the SUMMARY procedure can be run without a CLASS statement at all. If we were to re-run the previous example without the CLASS statement but leave everything else the same, then the output dataset would consist of exactly one observation, and that observation would be exactly the same as the first observation in the dataset of Listing 9.2 except that the SEX and SES columns would not appear. If, instead, we were to use the CLASS statement but were to specify only one or the other, not both, of the variables SEX and SES, we would get less observations than in S_SUMRY, but the mean and standard deviation statistics would still correspond to certain observations in S_SUMRY.

Listing 9.3 shows three printouts based on variations of the PROC SUMMARY step illustrated earlier, the first with no class variable, the second with "CLASS

SEX;", the third with "CLASS SES;". It should now be very clear: If there is no CLASS statement, the single observation represents the "null" (no variables) CLASS summarization, covering all observations in the input dataset. If there is a CLASS statement with one variable, then there is created the null summarization observation, and then observations representing the summarization of each value level of the CLASS variable. If there are two CLASS variables, there is the null summarization, summarizations representing each level of *each* class variable, and summarizations representing each possible combination of levels of the CLASS variables.

This pattern continues for more than two CLASS variables. If an input dataset contains classificatory variables A, B, and C with 3, 2, and 4 levels respectively, a SUMMARY dataset with "CLASS A B C;" will have up to 1(null combination) + 3 + 2 + 4 + 3*2 + 3*4 + 2*4 + 3*2*4 = 60 observations.

CLASS and __TYPE__

The __TYPE__ variable identifies the unique variable combination a SUMMARY observation represents. __TYPE__=0 is the overall or grand summary: Statistics in this observation are based on the entire input dataset. The remaining variable combinations are given __TYPE__ values as shown in Table 9.1. In the table, YES indicates that the CLASS variable helps define the subgroup, NO indicates it does not. The cases of one, two, three, and four CLASS variables are shown.

As you can see in Listings 9.2 and 9.3, SUMMARY builds its output dataset in order by __TYPE__. Now look again at Listing 9.2. The two observations which correspond to the breakdown by SEX only are __TYPE__=2. Those corresponding to SES only are __TYPE__=1. The order of observations is: __TYPE__=0, the grand or overall statistics for the entire input dataset; __TYPE__=1, the SES summaries, one observation for each value of SES in ascending order; __TYPE__=2, the SEX summaries, one for each value of SEX; and finally __TYPE__=3, the SEX*SES summaries, one for each unique combination of SEX*SES values.

Observe that the order in which the variables are named on the CLASS statement is critical. Listing 9.4 is the PRINT of another twist on the program that produced Listing 9.2: the order of variables on the CLASS statement was reversed. Instead of

```
CLASS SEX SES;
```

I used

```
CLASS SES SEX;
```

As you can see in the listing, the same information is presented, but the observations come out in a different order than in Listing 9.2 because __TYPE__s 1 and 2 are reversed.

TABLE 9.1. PROC SUMMARY: RELATIONSHIP BETWEEN CLASS AND __TYPE

One CLASS Variable:	"CLASS C;"			
__TYPE__	C			
0	NO			
1	YES			

Two CLASS Variables:	"CLASS C1 C2;"			
__TYPE__	C1	C2		
0	NO	NO		
1	NO	YES		
2	YES	NO		
3	YES	YES		

Three CLASS Variables:	"CLASS C1 C2 C3;"			
__TYPE__	C1	C2	C3	
0	NO	NO	NO	
1	NO	NO	YES	
2	NO	YES	NO	
3	NO	YES	YES	
4	YES	NO	NO	
5	YES	NO	YES	
6	YES	YES	NO	
7	YES	YES	YES	

Four CLASS Variables:	"CLASS C1 C2 C3 C4;"			
__TYPE__	C1	C2	C3	C4
0	NO	NO	NO	NO
1	NO	NO	NO	YES
2	NO	NO	YES	NO
3	NO	NO	YES	YES
4	NO	YES	NO	NO
5	NO	YES	NO	YES
6	NO	YES	YES	NO
7	NO	YES	YES	YES
8	YES	NO	NO	NO
9	YES	NO	NO	YES
10	YES	NO	YES	NO
11	YES	NO	YES	YES
12	YES	YES	NO	NO
13	YES	YES	NO	YES
14	YES	YES	YES	NO
15	YES	YES	YES	YES

SUMMARY example: "CLASS SES SEX"

OBS	SES	SEX	_TYPE_	_FREQ_	AMEAN	EMEAN	FMEAN	ASTD	HSTD	WSTD
1	.		0	160	4.65375	3.75375	1.98375	2.56380	1.96504	0.97831
2	.	F	1	80	4.83750	4.25250	1.86000	2.67787	2.03650	0.96175
3	.	M	1	80	4.47000	3.25500	2.10750	2.44744	1.76649	0.98505
4	1		2	40	4.76000	3.61000	1.70000	2.97242	2.03807	0.96980
5	2		2	40	4.77000	4.29000	1.99000	2.73460	1.87422	0.83445
6	3		2	40	4.59500	3.24000	1.99000	1.87739	1.91790	0.94239
7	4		2	40	4.49000	3.87500	2.25500	2.62745	1.94827	1.10406
8	1	F	3	20	4.56000	3.84000	1.48000	3.26841	2.34866	0.90006
9	1	M	3	20	4.96000	3.38000	1.92000	2.71456	1.70251	1.00922
10	2	F	3	20	4.71000	4.87000	2.05000	2.73475	1.76459	0.77629
11	2	M	3	20	4.83000	3.71000	1.93000	2.80415	1.84074	0.90502
12	3	F	3	20	5.49000	3.88000	1.73000	1.57911	2.18839	0.79479
13	3	M	3	20	3.70000	2.60000	2.25000	1.74778	1.37802	1.02418
14	4	F	3	20	4.59000	4.42000	2.18000	2.92411	1.75187	1.21897
15	4	M	3	20	4.39000	3.33000	2.33000	2.36619	2.02409	1.00216

Listing 9.4. PROC SUMMARY Example: Another CLASS twist

As you may have observed in our listings thus far, when a CLASS variable does not differentiate an output observation, its value is set missing in the output dataset. The _TYPE_=0 observation has missing values for all CLASS variables, _TYPE_=1 observations have missing values for all but the rightmost-named variable on the CLASS statement, and so on.

Missing Values

As far as analysis variables are concerned, missing values in the input dataset simply do not contribute to the calculated statistics in the output dataset. When, however, any CLASS variable is missing in the input dataset, then the *entire input observation* is excluded from analysis.

If you wish, observations can be created in the output dataset that summarize input data where CLASS variables are missing. This is done by coding the MISSING option on the PROC SUMMARY statement. When MISSING is coded, then all input observations will contribute to the output dataset, whether or not their values for one or more CLASS variables are missing.

As you may have observed in our listings thus far, when a CLASS variable does not contribute to an output observation then its value appears as missing. Therefore, if you use the MISSING option, then the only way to tell whether a given observation represents a valid though missing CLASS level or a summary ignoring that CLASS variable is to interpret the _TYPE_ value.

Using the _TYPE_ Variable

When you understand exactly which _TYPE_ value will be assigned to any given combination of CLASS variables, you will be able to select any combination you desire for subsequent processing.

TABLE 9.2. FOUR CLASS VARIABLES SHOWN WITH BINARY
EQUIVALENTS OF __TYPE__

Four CLASS Variables:		"CLASS C1 C2 C3 C4;"			
__TYPE__	BINARY	C1	C2	C3	C4
0	0000	NO	NO	NO	NO
1	0001	NO	NO	NO	YES
2	0010	NO	NO	YES	NO
3	0011	NO	NO	YES	YES
4	0100	NO	YES	NO	NO
5	0101	NO	YES	NO	YES
6	0110	NO	YES	YES	NO
7	0111	NO	YES	YES	YES
8	1000	YES	NO	NO	NO
9	1001	YES	NO	NO	YES
10	1010	YES	NO	YES	NO
11	1011	YES	NO	YES	YES
12	1100	YES	YES	NO	NO
13	1101	YES	YES	NO	YES
14	1110	YES	YES	YES	NO
15	1111	YES	YES	YES	YES

Note: See text for explanation. Observe how the YES/NO pattern corresponds to
the 1/0 pattern of the binary expansion of __TYPE__.

The simple secret to understanding __TYPE__ is revealed, by example with four
CLASS variables, in Table 9.2. In the table, the __TYPE__ value is shown both as
a decimal and a binary numeral. Now imagine the CLASS variables as binary
digits that take the value 1 if the variable helped define a subgroup and 0 if not.
__TYPE__ corresponds exactly to the binary value that would be created by
treating answers to the question "Does this variable help define the subgroup
represented by this observation?" as 1 if 'YES', 0 if 'NO', taken in order the
variables originally appeared on the CLASS statement. For example, in the case
of four class variables (refer again to Table 9.2), you can always be sure that an
observation of __TYPE__=9 represents a subgroup defined by the first and the
fourth CLASS variables without regard to the second and third, because the
binary representation of 9 is 1001 (ones in the first and fourth positions, zeroes in
the second and third).

So, when working with a PROC SUMMARY output dataset, you can easily
limit processing to observations representing summarizations of your choosing.
For example, you can select those broken down only by the second-to-the-right-
most CLASS variable with

```
WHERE _TYPE_ = 2;
```

You can further subselect by paying heed not only to __TYPE__ but to the values
of the CLASS variables in the output dataset. Using our S__SUMRY example as

TABLE 9.3. "BIT TESTING" EXAMPLES

"IF __TYPE__ = bitmask;"	
BitMask	**__TYPE__ Selected**
'0 1 1 0 ' B	6
'1 1 1 0 ' B	14
'0 0 . 0 ' B	0, 2
'. 1 1 0 ' B	6, 14
'. . 0 0 ' B	0, 4, 8, 12
'. 0 0 0 ' B	0, 8
'1 . . . ' B	8, 9, 10, 11, 12, 13, 14, 15
'0 . . . ' B	0, 1, 2, 3, 4, 5, 6, 7

shown in Listing 9.2, you could examine only those summarizations that cut across all values of SEX and concern SES groups 2 and 4 only with

```
WHERE _TYPE_ = 1 AND SES IN(2,4);
```

Selecting __TYPE__ By "Bit-Test"

There is a little trick that can help you use the __TYPE__ variable effectively that takes advantage of a DATA Step Language feature we have not yet discussed, the so-called "bit-test" comparison.

As you know, a value is represented in the computer as a series of binary bits, 0's and 1's. "Bit-testing" checks the status of any of the bits in a data value. The SAS language makes this possible with a special comparison operation; as used in an IF statement:

```
IF expression=bitmask [THEN statement];
```

where "expression" is a numeric or character expression and "bitmask" is a sequence of zeroes, ones, or periods enclosed by single quotes and followed immediately by a B. When the DATA step bit-tests a value, it checks to see if the zeroes and ones in the bitmask match the zeroes and ones in the value; the periods are used as placeholders, in effect "matching" either a zero or a one. See Table 9.3 for some examples.

Because __TYPE__ variables' values correspond to the binary "yes/no" sequence of the CLASS variable list, bit-testing can be used as a sure way to select observations by __TYPE__. Consider a SUMMARY dataset that was created with six CLASS variables:

```
CLASS SEX AGEGROUP ETHNICGP INCOMGRP RELIGION PARTY;
```

To study the SEX by ETHNICGP breakdowns, you can create a working dataset with

```
SET dataset; IF _TYPE_='101000'B;
```

which selects those observations representing subgroups defined by the first and the third CLASS variables. "IF _TYPE_=40" would do, but using the bitmask frees you from having to calculate the decimal equivalent of the binary sequence.

Because of the way the SAS bit-testing feature handles literal periods, the relief it gives from binary-to-decimal calculation can be more than trivial. Suppose you decide somewhere down the line that religion and income group have no bearing on the survey results, and you wish to ignore RELIGION and INCOMGRP. You can create a smaller dataset with all the remaining information by

```
SET dataset; IF _TYPE_='...00.'B;
```

which selects every observation *except* those that are broken down by the fourth or the fifth variables.* If you wanted to do the same thing with "normal" code, you would require either a long series of OR expressions, or a lengthy IN() comparison that boils down to the same thing:

```
IF _TYPE_ IN(0,1,8,9,16,17,24,25,32,33,40,41,48,49,56,57);
```

Besides being a pain to the programmer, in the computer these IN (or OR) comparisons would take much more processing time than the single bit-test.

Requesting Summary Statistics: The OUTPUT Statement

The OUTPUT statement under PROC SUMMARY provides flexible ways to specify the variables and statistics to be placed in the output dataset. The programmer has no less than four different ways to associate statistics with variable names.

The first way to associate statistics with names is "statistic=names." (This was the method used in our S_SUMRY example.) The second way is to use the *original* variable name. To do so, use "statistic=." For example,

```
PROC SUMMARY; VAR RED BLUE; OUTPUT OUT=X MEAN=;
```

operates on an input dataset that has numeric variables RED and BLUE. In the output dataset, X, the variable names RED and BLUE also occur; but their values are the means of the input dataset values.

The third form of output request allows individual selection of output variables:

```
PROC SUMMARY; VAR THIS THAT;
  OUTPUT OUT=WHICH MEAN(THIS)=AVGTHIS SUM(THAT)=TOTLTHAT;
```

---

*The original _TYPE_ values would not be changed in the rebuilt dataset, so you would still have to base any subsequent selections on the original six-variable CLASS list.

creates two variables in the output dataset: AVGTHIS, containing the mean of values of THIS, and TOTLTHAT, containing the sum of values of THAT. More than one variable name may appear within the parentheses, in which case an equal number of new names should be specified.

The fourth way to specify output variables is like a combination of the second and the third: By not giving new names to the right of the request, the old variable names are used by default. Thus

```
OUTPUT OUT=WHICH MEAN(THIS)= SUM(THAT)=;
```

gives an output dataset with variables named THIS and THAT; the former contains the average value of its namesake in the input dataset, the latter the sum of the values of the namesake variable.

Omitting the Statistic Specifications

It is permissible to code an OUTPUT statement without any statistic specifications, e.g.,

```
OUTPUT OUT=OUTDATA;
```

If you do so, a special, semi-transposed kind of dataset will result. The variables in the dataset include the CLASS variables, _TYPE_, _FREQ_, _STAT_ (another special variable), and one or more variables named after the analysis variables in the VAR statement. These latter variables do not, however, contain the input value. Instead, they contain one of five statistics N, mean, maximum, minimum, and standard deviation.

You see, the so-called "_STATS_ dataset" contains five observations, not one, per CLASS combination. The value of the variable _STAT_ is 'N', 'MEAN', 'MIN', 'MAX', or 'STD'. Get the picture?

The BY Statement with PROC SUMMARY

A BY statement may accompany PROC summary (as always, assuming the input dataset is appropriately sorted/grouped or indexed), and if so, then the number of possible observations in the output dataset will be multiplied by the number of BY combinations.

Since CLASS can do it all, and since the interpretation of _TYPE_ does not account for BY groups, there is usually no good reason to use BY with this procedure.*

---

*Under past versions of the SAS System, SUMMARY would occasionally be unable to run when very large numbers of CLASS value interactions occurred; in these cases, BY group processing helped get things moving. Under Version 6 of the SAS System, it is doubtful that any realistic application could approach the maximum interaction limit.

Other SUMMARY Statements and Options

We discussed the MISSING option earlier: it causes missing CLASS variable values to be treated as legitimate levels. The ORDER= option can be used to determine how the observations will be sorted by CLASS variable value, within each __TYPE__; this usage is similar to the ORDER= option of PROC FREQ.

The DESCENDING option on the PROC statement can be used to reverse the default order in which observations are written to the output dataset. Normally the __TYPE__=0 observation is written first, then any other observations by ascending __TYPE__. With DESCENDING, observations of the highest __TYPE__ come first, and so on, the __TYPE__=0 observation being written last.

The NWAY option requests the procedure to write only the observations of the highest __TYPE__. That is,

```
PROC SUMMARY NWAY;
  CLASS P Q R S;
```

will result in a dataset that has observations only of __TYPE__=15 ('1111'B).* To view observations of lower __TYPE__ an output dataset has first to be produced and then to be printed by (say) PROC PRINT.

FREQ and WEIGHT statements may appear with PROC SUMMARY, as described in Chapter 5 when we discussed the procedure under the name PROC MEANS. FREQ identifies a numeric variable in the input dataset that tells how many "true" observations the record stands for, that is how many times it is to be counted. WEIGHT identifies a numeric variable whose value will be used to weight means and variances.

An ID statement may appear with the PROC SUMMARY statements. The variable(s) identified on the ID statement will be included in the output dataset. If ID names a numeric variable, the value appearing in an output dataset observation will be the maximum value the variable has in the input records that contributed to the observation. The IDMIN option coded on the PROC statement will cause the output ID values to take the minimum instead.

Two options (specified not on the PROC statement, but on the OUTPUT statement), MAXID and MINID, enable you to create variables that identify the maximum and minimum of chosen analysis variables. As an example, consider our well-worn SURVEY1 example, and suppose that the input dataset contained another variable, NAME, with values being the names of the persons filling out the form. Suppose further that the OUTPUT statement contained, along with its statistics requests, the element

```
MAXID(AGE(NAME))=OLDEST
```

---

*Printed output produced by SUMMARY/MEANS reflects, like NWAY, only the observations of highest __TYPE__.

In that case, a variable called OLDEST will appear in the summary output dataset, and its value will be the name of the individual with the greatest value of AGE in the input observations corresponding to the CLASS combination contributing to the ouptut observation. For example, given

```
CLASS SES SEX;
```

as in Listing 9.2, the name of the eldest responding female would be found under the variable OLDEST in the _TYPE_=2 observation where SEX='F', the name of the eldest male in SES group 3 in the _TYPE_=3 observation where SEX='M' and SES=3, etc.

MINID works similarly, except (of course) that the observation with lowest, and not the highest, value of the named input variable provides the value for the output dataset. You can specify more than one MAXID or MINID specification if you wish.

10

Combining, Dividing, and Updating Observations

In Chapter 9, we saw how the "vertical" structure of a SAS dataset—its ordered pattern of observations—can be manipulated to reorder, combine, divide, summarize, or otherwise transform the set of records found in one or more input datasets. Now, let's learn how to change the "horizontal" structure of a SAS dataset, its pattern of variables. KEEP and DROP, Assignment and Sum, and how to reorder values were described previously. In this chapter we cover some more ways to change the layout and alter the values of variables.

We delve again into the MERGE statement, introduced in Chapter 4. Study the MERGE statement well and you'll hold the key to one of the most powerful SAS data management capabilities. We also examine the use of more than one SET statement in a single DATA step in order to combine observations. Next, we introduce the UPDATE statement.

Finally, we take a look at the powerful MODIFY statement. In contrast to all other dataset-rebuilding techniques, MODIFY changes the actual input dataset itself, instead of building a new one, allowing selective replacement, deletion, and addition of observations.

DIVIDING OBSERVATIONS

To divide observations of an input dataset, rebuild it with KEEP= or DROP= dataset options. If multiple subsets are to be created, use the options on the DATA statement.

Problem: A dataset detailing the customers of a certain marketing company contains a great many variables. Create two shorter files, both containing social security number for identification, one containing address information, and one containing income information.

Solution: Specify the KEEP= dataset option on a DATA step naming both new datasets, then SET the master dataset:

```
DATA DD.ADDRESS(KEEP=SSN NAME ADDR CITY STATE ZIP)
     DD.FAMILY(KEEP=SSN JOBTYPE WAGE INDINCOM FAMINCOM);
  SET MAIN.MASTER;
RUN;
```

KEEP= on the DATA step does not have the same effect as it does when coded in the SET statement. It takes effect as the new observation is written, much as if a KEEP statement instead of a dataset option were used. But when KEEP= is used on the SET statement, or when a KEEP statement is used in the body of the step, it applies to all datasets being created.

Actually, the preferred method (when computer processing efficiency is a concern) is to code the DATA statement as shown, but use the KEEP= dataset option on the SET statement as well, keeping only the variables named in the DATA statement and elsewhere in the step. This prevents the SAS System from having to maintain all the variables from the input dataset, reading them into the PDV only to discard them again. You must ensure that all the variables named with all the KEEP= options in the DATA statement are kept with the SET statement.

KEEP and DROP strategies may be combined with other variable-limiting or observation-limiting methods. In the example above, had we wished to keep data for families of FAMSIZE > 3 only, the statement

```
WHERE FAMSIZE > 3;
```

might have been used after the SET statement to restrict records in both DD.FAMILY and DD.ADDRESS to families of size >3. You would have to take a different approach to restrict DD.FAMILY to families of size >3 yet still get addresses on all families regardless of size, for example:

```
DATA DD.ADDRESS(KEEP=SSN NAME ADDR CITY STATE ZIP)
DD.FAMILY(KEEP=SSN JOBTYPE WAGE INDINCOM FAMINCOM);
SET MAIN.MASTER(KEEP=SSN NAME ADDR CITY STATE ZIP
JOBTYPE WAGE INDINCOM FAMINCOM FAMSIZE);
OUTPUT DD.ADDRESS;
IF FAMSIZE > 3 THEN OUTPUT DD.FAMILY;
RUN;
```

COMBINING OBSERVATIONS: MERGE STATEMENT VARIATIONS

The MERGE statement, introduced in Chapter 4, allows the SAS user to combine observations from several datasets. MERGE, like SET, is an executable statement. Construction of the program data vector follows the general rule that variables are given positions in order as they are encountered in the DATA step, either by name or by input dataset after taking into account DROP=, KEEP=, and RENAME=. The values of the variables in each observation, and the number of observations in the output dataset, depend on other factors discussed below.

One-to-One Merge

When no BY statement appears after MERGE, variable values are selected by considering each observation from each input dataset in turn, according to the following general rules:

- If the variable is unique to one input dataset, the value of the variable in that dataset is chosen.
- If the variable is named in more than one input dataset, the value chosen is that of the rightmost dataset containing the variable named in the MERGE statement.
- If an input dataset runs out of observations while others still have observations, the system missing value is used for each variable named only in that dataset; processing stops and the output dataset is closed after the last observation of the largest dataset is processed. The number of observations in the new dataset thus becomes the number of observations in the largest input dataset.

Note that if more than one dataset has the same variable name(s), you must be careful of the order in which the datasets are mentioned in the MERGE statement.

Problem: The Tangled Web Computer Dating Service has no idea what makes people happy together, but if they pretend to know and just introduce anyone to anyone, they figure chances are fair that the customers will be satisfied. How can they do this?

Solution: They keep adding to two datasets (one females, the other males) the names, addresses, and telephone numbers of their clients, throw the remainder of the questionnaire away, and write the following program:

```
* PROGRAM TO PRODUCE MATCH LIST OF MEN AND WOMEN;
DATA MATCH;
  MERGE MEN (RENAME=(NAME=MNAME ADDRESS=MADDRESS PHONE=MPHONE))
        WOMEN (RENAME=(NAME=WNAME ADDRESS=WADDRESS PHONE=WPHONE));
RUN;
```

Now, they can print MATCH and send congratulatory letters to each man and women whose names/addresses are not missing, introducing them to their "match." If there are fewer women than men, a number of observations toward the end will show missing values for MNAME, MADDRESS, MPHONE; if more men than women, the other variables will be missing toward the end of the dataset. These customers can receive letters alerting them that due to their particularly fine (shall we say, matchless?) personal characteristics, no suitable match is available just now.

One-to-one merge is not often used in more serious applications. This is because under most circumstances, the user will wish to control what values get combined with others by some criterion other than the order within preexisting datasets. Furthermore, even if the data are in some logical co-order, there must be no missing records if the match is to proceed correctly, or else the merger will be "out of sync" (see Figure 10.1).

In conclusion, only if it is positively known that the data are in the right order and that no observations are missing might a one-to-one merge be justified, as in the example of STATES given in Chapter 4.

"NAMES1" FRSTNAME
GEORGE
ABRAHAM
WOODROW
FRANKLIN
JOHN
RONALD

LASTNAME "NAMES2"
WASHINGTON
LINCOLN
ROOSEVELT
KENNEDY
REAGAN

```
DATA PREZ;
    MERGE NAMES1 NAMES2;
RUN;
```

FRSTNAME	LASTNAME
GEORGE	WASHINGTON
ABRAHAM	LINCOLN
WOODROW	ROOSEVELT
FRANKLIN	KENNEDY
JOHN	REAGAN
RONALD	●

Figure 10.1. One-to-one MERGE "out of sync." MERGE can only take one value after another from the input datasets, and if an observation is missing or out of place, the result may be incorrect.

Match-Merge: MERGE with a BY Statement

If a BY statement is used after MERGE, the observations to be combined are controlled by the values of the BY variables. This is called a "match-merge": Observations are matched by certain identifying variables before their values are combined. Each BY variable mentioned in the BY statement must occur in each input dataset, and unless they are appropriately indexed the input datasets must be sorted in order of the BY variables. Most practical MERGE applications involve match-merging.

One BY Variable, One Observation per BY Group

The simplest case of match-merging resembles one-to-one merging. This is the case where there is only one BY variable, and one and only one observation per BY variable in each input dataset. In the STATES example (Chapter 4) we could have added

```
BY STATE;
```

after the MERGE statement and achieved the exact same effect as the one-to-one merge.

One BY Variable, Missing BY Observations

The similarity between match-merging and one-to-one merging quickly disappears as we get into other data situations. For example, what happens if one or more observations is missing is quite different. In one-to-one matching, the merge goes on "out of sync" to the end, and begins to add missing values when it exhausts the shorter dataset. In match-merging, when a BY group value occurs in at least one but not all datasets, missing values are generated just for that group; the merge then "restarts" at the next group. The case of one observation per BY group with some missing observations is illustrated in Listing 10.1.

One BY Variable, Several Observations per BY Group

If there are several observations per BY group, and some input dataset has more with a certain BY value than another, in the output dataset missing values will *not* "fill out" the BY group. A one-to-one merge, upon running out of observations in an input dataset, will cause missing values to be generated for that dataset's unique variables, until the last observation of the longest dataset is processed. With BY groups, however, the MERGE action is to retain values from the last observation of the shorter BY group, until the longest BY group is processed. For except when BY groups change, variables built with MERGE, SET, and UPDATE are *not* initialized to missing at each iteration (those built from external data, using INPUT, *are* initialized to missing prior to each iteration). This fact of SAS

Dataset ONE

OBS	BYVAR	A	B
1	1	1	1
2	2	2	2
3	3	3	3
4	4	4	4
5	7	7	7

Dataset TWO

OBS	BYVAR	B	C
1	1	11	11
2	2	22	22
3	4	44	44
4	6	66	66
5	7	77	77
6	8	88	88

Dataset THREE

OBS	BYVAR	C	D
1	2	222	222
2	3	333	333
3	4	444	444
4	5	555	555

MERGE ONE TWO; BY BYVAR;

OBS	BYVAR	A	B	C
1	1	1	11	11
2	2	2	22	22
3	3	3	3	.
4	4	4	44	44
5	6	.	66	66
6	7	7	77	77
7	8	.	88	88

MERGE ONE TWO THREE; BY BYVAR;

OBS	BYVAR	A	B	C	D
1	1	1	11	11	.
2	2	2	22	222	222
3	3	3	3	333	333
4	4	4	44	444	444
5	5	.	.	555	555
6	6	.	66	66	.
7	7	7	77	77	.
8	8	.	88	88	.

Listing 10.1. Match-MERGE, one BY variable, missing BY observations

MERGE processing is illustrated in Listing 10.2. (As can be seen in the listing, if a dataset has no observations at all for a certain BY value, missing values will still be generated.)

Problem: A meteorology student wishes to investigate the geographic patterns of rainfall across the country. A dataset is available from the weather service giving weekly rainfall, over a year, for all major metropolitan areas in the coun-

Dataset ONE

OBS	BYVAR	A	B
1	1	1	1
2	2	2	2
3	2	2	2
4	2	2	2
5	2	2	2
6	3	3	3
7	4	4	4
8	7	7	7
9	7	7	7
10	7	7	7

Dataset TWO

OBS	BYVAR	B	C
1	1	11	11
2	1	11	11
3	2	22	22
4	2	22	22
5	4	44	44
6	6	66	66
7	7	77	77
8	8	88	88

Dataset THREE

OBS	BYVAR	C	D
1	2	222	222
2	3	333	333
3	3	333	333
4	3	333	333
5	4	444	444
6	4	444	444
7	4	444	444
8	5	555	555

Listing 10.2. Match-MERGE, one BY variable, multiple BY observations

Continued

MERGE ONE TWO; BY BYVAR;

OBS	BYVAR	A	B	C
1	1	1	11	11
2	1	1	11	11
3	2	2	22	22
4	2	2	22	22
5	2	2	2	22
6	2	2	2	22
7	3	3	3	.
8	4	4	44	44
9	6	.	66	66
10	7	7	77	77
11	7	7	7	77
12	7	7	7	77
13	8	.	88	88

MERGE ONE TWO THREE; BY BYVAR;

OBS	BYVAR	A	B	C	D
1	1	1	11	11	.
2	1	1	11	11	.
3	2	2	22	222	222
4	2	2	22	22	222
5	2	2	2	22	222
6	2	2	2	22	222
7	3	3	3	333	333
8	3	3	3	333	333
9	3	3	3	333	333
10	4	4	44	444	444
11	4	4	44	444	444
12	4	4	44	444	444
13	5	.	.	555	555
14	6	.	66	66	.
15	7	7	77	77	.
16	7	7	7	77	.
17	7	7	7	77	.
18	8	.	88	88	.

Listing 10.2. *Continued*

try. The variables in the dataset are called CITY, RAIN, and WEEK. There are several thousands of observations in the dataset, 52 (weeks) for each city. To perform the statistical analyses the student requires, geographic position and elevation must be associated with rainfall. Therefore, a merge of the rainfall dataset with one showing city location is indicated.

Solution: The student first creates a separate dataset, GEOG, in the dataset library, including in it the same cities' (CITY) latitude (LAT), longitude (LONG), and elevation (ELEV). Using PROC SORT, she ensures that both datasets are in order BY CITY, and then writes:

```
DATA STUDY.MAINDATA;
  MERGE STUDY.GEOG WEATHER.RAINFALL;
  BY CITY;
RUN;
```

Values in the single observation per BY group in STUDY.GEOG are retained until the city's 52 observations taken from WEATHER.RAINFALL are used. There now exists a dataset, STUDY.MAINDATA, whose observations number as many as in WEATHER.RAINFALL but which have the classificatory variables LAT, LONG, and ELEV as well as RAIN and WEEK. The student is free to sort the data by any of these variables, if necessary, and analyze rainfall based on the geographic variables in whatever manner she chooses.

Propagation of retained values has other uses in SAS data processing. Because the SAS System works with rectangular observations-by-variables files, it is often essential that data be repeated across observations in this fashion.

Problem: An analyst for the sales division of a certain manufacturer must produce a report showing total sales dollars per customer. A dataset showing each sale value (variable name DOLLARS) includes and contains a unique customer ID number (variable ID). It is, therefore, natural to use

```
PROC MEANS SUM DATA=COMPANY.SALES;
  CLASS ID;
  VAR DOLLARS;
  TITLE 'TOTAL SALES PER CUSTOMER';
RUN;
```

However, the list is helpful to the sales manager only if the customers are presented by name. There is a dataset used for billing, COMPANY.CUSTOMER, that contains corporate name, address, and phone number for each ID.

Solution: Assume each dataset has been sorted or indexed BY ID (if not, the analyst would have to do so, perhaps directing the output to temporary datasets). Then the analyst codes the DATA step:

```
DATA SALES;
  MERGE COMPANY.SALES(KEEP=ID DOLLARS) COMPANY.CUSTOMER(KEEP=ID NAME);
  BY ID;
RUN;
```

and proceeds to run MEANS on the dataset SALES, using NAME as the CLASS variable.

Multiple BY values in more than one dataset. It was with a conscious decision that the designers of the SAS compiler specified that multiple BY values would cause variables to be retained, rather than be set to missing. We've seen how this feature can be useful indeed in cases where certain general identifying data must be associated with each record in a more specialized data set. The dataset from which this information is obtained normally contains one record per unit of analysis. Retention of unique variables' values allows this information to be combined with datasets that may have a variable number of records per unit of analysis.

This rule can cause trouble, however, if the user does not carefully visualize (and if necessary, test) how MERGE will behave in more complicated situations, such as when more than one dataset has duplicate BY values. If an input dataset is exhausted at the time MERGE executes, a retained value will remain the PDV, and when there is nothing else to intervene (such as a value from a dataset "to the right" in the MERGE statement), the retained value will be output to the dataset being created. The implication is that values in the output observations depend to a great extent upon the relative numbers of observations in the input datasets. Listing 10.3 makes this process explicit. Study it carefully.

Using the FIRST.by and LAST.by variables. As mentioned earlier, two temporary variables are created when a BY statement is used with SET, MERGE, or UPDATE. These are FIRST.byvariable and LAST.byvariable. That is, if the BY variable is called IDNUMBR, the special variables FIRST.IDNUMBR and LAST.IDNUMBR are created by the compiler for programming use, although they are not written to the output dataset.

Problem: The manufacturer in our previous example maintains another dataset which covers each debit/credit transaction with its customers. Observations in COMPANY.CUSTRANS contain and are sorted by the customer ID code and a variable AMOUNT which is negative if it is a customer debit and positive if a payment. An historical list of account balances must be produced for each customer, showing how their bottom-line credit due or debt owed has changed over the course of each transaction.

Solution: We need a printout of each transaction; a procedure such as PRINT might give the answer.* Listing 10.4 presents code and results (for the example, only six customers in all were used). The FIRST.by variable is used to reset the accumulator variable BALANCE whenever the BY variable changes.

The FIRST.by and LAST.by variables can help to produce a prettier list (Listing 10.5), or to produce a list showing only the "bottom line" after all transactions are accounted (Listing 10.6).

The IN= variable. One or more temporary variables may be created at the user's discretion if he or she associates the dataset option IN=varname with one or more dataset names on the MERGE statement (recall Chapter 4). While

---

*Similar results could be produced using PROC SQL, which we introduce in Chapter 14. Or, the post-MERGE report could be produced by PROC REPORT, reviewed in Chapter 13, which can produce effects including those illustrated in Listings 10.4 through 10.6. However, the examples here are meant to illustrate DATA step processing with BY variables, and using PROC PRINT lets us concentrate on that.

Dataset ONE

OBS	BYVAR	A	B
1	1	1	1
2	2	2	2
3	2	2	2
4	2	2	2
5	3	3	3
6	4	4	4
7	4	4	4
8	7	7	7

Dataset TWO

OBS	BYVAR	B	C
1	1	11	11
2	1	11	11
3	1	11	11
4	1	11	11
5	2	22	22
6	2	22	22
7	4	44	44
8	6	66	66
9	6	66	66
10	6	66	66
11	7	77	77
12	8	88	88

Dataset THREE

OBS	BYVAR	C	D
1	2	222	222
2	2	222	222
3	3	333	333
4	4	444	444
5	4	444	444
6	4	444	444
7	5	555	555
8	5	555	555

Listing 10.3. Match-MERGE, duplicate BY values in more than one dataset

Continued

MERGE ONE TWO; BY BYVAR;

OBS	BYVAR	A	B	C
1	1	1	11	11
2	1	1	11	11
3	1	1	11	11
4	1	1	11	11
5	2	2	22	22
6	2	2	22	22
7	2	2	2	22
8	3	3	3	.
9	4	4	44	44
10	4	4	4	44
11	6	.	66	66
12	6	.	66	66
13	6	.	66	66
14	7	7	77	77
15	8	.	88	88

MERGE TWO ONE; BY BYVAR;

OBS	BYVAR	B	C	A
1	1	1	11	1
2	1	11	11	1
3	1	11	11	1
4	1	11	11	1
5	2	2	22	2
6	2	2	22	2
7	2	2	22	2
8	3	3	.	3
9	4	4	44	4
10	4	4	44	4
11	6	66	66	.
12	6	66	66	.
13	6	66	66	.
14	7	7	77	7
15	8	88	88	.

Listing 10.3. *Continued*

```
MERGE ONE TWO THREE; BY BYVAR;
```

OBS	BYVAR	A	B	C	D
1	1	1	11	11	.
2	1	1	11	11	.
3	1	1	11	11	.
4	1	1	11	11	.
5	2	2	22	222	222
6	2	2	22	222	222
7	2	2	2	222	222
8	3	3	3	333	333
9	4	4	44	444	444
10	4	4	4	444	444
11	4	4	4	444	444
12	5	.	.	555	555
13	5	.	.	555	555
14	6	.	66	66	.
15	6	.	66	66	.
16	6	.	66	66	.
17	7	7	77	77	.
18	8	.	88	88	.

```
MERGE THREE TWO ONE; BY BYVAR;
```

OBS	BYVAR	C	D	B	A
1	1	11	.	1	1
2	1	11	.	11	1
3	1	11	.	11	1
4	1	11	.	11	1
5	2	22	222	2	2
6	2	22	222	2	2
7	2	22	222	2	2
8	3	333	333	3	3
9	4	44	444	4	4
10	4	444	444	4	4
11	4	444	444	4	4
12	5	555	555	.	.
13	5	555	555	.	.
14	6	66	.	66	.
15	6	66	.	66	.
16	6	66	.	66	.
17	7	77	.	7	7
18	8	88	.	88	.

Listing 10.3. *Continued*

```
<<< PROGRAM SOURCE CODE FOLLOWS >>>

TITLE 'Input dataset CUSTOMER';
PROC PRINT DATA=COMPANY.CUSTOMER;
RUN;
TITLE 'Input dataset CUSTRANS';
PROC PRINT DATA=COMPANY.CUSTRANS;
 FORMAT DATE MMDDYY8.;
RUN;
DATA BALANCE;
   MERGE COMPANY.CUSTOMER COMPANY.CUSTRANS;
   BY ID; IF FIRST.ID THEN BALANCE=0;
   BALANCE + AMOUNT;
   FORMAT BALANCE DOLLAR10.2 DATE MMDDYY8.;
RUN;
TITLE 'Running balance for company customers';
PROC PRINT DATA=BALANCE;
   ID ID;
   VAR LAST FIRST AMOUNT BALANCE DATE;
   TITLE2 'NOTE: Negative = due, Positive = credit';
RUN;


   <<< SAS JOB OUTPUT FOLLOWS >>>

                    Input dataset CUSTOMER


        OBS     ID    FIRST       LAST

         1       1    GERRY       RIVERA
         2      28    DANNY       RATHER
         3      55    HOWIE       COSELL
         4      82    DAVE        BRINKLEY
         5     109    MICKEY      WALLACE
         6     136    WALLY       CRONKITE
```

Listing 10.4. Example using FIRST.by and a retained accumulator

Continued

the IN= variable normally is true if the input observation makes a contribution to the PDV (see below), it may be reassigned true (1) or false (0) by the user. It can be used to select observations during a merge.

How the FIRST.by, LAST.by, and IN= variables operate. Many SAS users make mistakes designing problem solutions because they misconceive how these special variables operate. The key to correct understanding is that with MERGE, *FIRST.by, LAST.by, and IN= variables are controlled by the longest input BY group.* Listing 10.7 enlarges upon examples shown in Listing 10.3, revealing the

Input dataset CUSTRANS

OBS	ID	DATE	AMOUNT
1	1	02/18/93	-11.28
2	1	02/27/93	11.28
3	1	03/01/93	-113.13
4	1	03/02/93	-79.88
5	1	03/07/93	193.01
6	28	03/27/93	-125.26
7	55	03/18/93	-2.42
8	55	03/27/93	-113.98
9	55	03/28/93	116.40
10	82	02/19/93	-82.54
11	82	02/26/93	-145.33
12	82	03/02/93	-71.57
13	109	02/21/93	-149.46
14	109	03/10/93	-59.24
15	109	03/16/93	208.70
16	136	02/16/93	-137.83
17	136	02/17/93	105.00
18	136	03/08/93	-85.19
19	136	03/13/93	118.02

Running balance for company customers
NOTE: Negative = due, Positive = credit

ID	LAST	FIRST	AMOUNT	BALANCE	DATE
1	RIVERA	GERRY	-11.28	$-11.28	02/18/93
1	RIVERA	GERRY	11.28	$0.00	02/27/93
1	RIVERA	GERRY	-113.13	$-113.13	03/01/93
1	RIVERA	GERRY	-79.88	$-193.01	03/02/93
1	RIVERA	GERRY	193.01	$0.00	03/07/93
28	RATHER	DANNY	-125.26	$-125.26	03/27/93
55	COSELL	HOWIE	-2.42	$-2.42	03/18/93
55	COSELL	HOWIE	-113.98	$-116.40	03/27/93
55	COSELL	HOWIE	116.40	$0.00	03/28/93
82	BRINKLEY	DAVE	-82.54	$-82.54	02/19/93
82	BRINKLEY	DAVE	-145.33	$-227.87	02/26/93
82	BRINKLEY	DAVE	-71.57	$-299.44	03/02/93
109	WALLACE	MICKEY	-149.46	$-149.46	02/21/93
109	WALLACE	MICKEY	-59.24	$-208.70	03/10/93
109	WALLACE	MICKEY	208.70	$0.00	03/16/93
136	CRONKITE	WALLY	-137.83	$-137.83	02/16/93
136	CRONKITE	WALLY	105.00	$-32.83	02/17/93
136	CRONKITE	WALLY	-85.19	$-118.02	03/08/93
136	CRONKITE	WALLY	118.02	$0.00	03/13/93

Listing 10.4. *Continued*

```
    <<< PROGRAM SOURCE CODE FOLLOWS >>>

DATA BALANCE;
   MERGE COMPANY.CUSTOMER COMPANY.CUSTRANS;
   BY ID;
   IF FIRST.ID THEN BALANCE=0;
   ELSE DO; * If not the first, then "blank out" the identifiers;
     ID=.; LAST=' '; FIRST=' ';
   END;
   BALANCE+AMOUNT;
RUN;
OPTIONS MISSING=' ';

   <<< The MISSING system option is used to print system missing >>>
   <<< values with a character other than '.'; see Chapter 21. >>>

PROC PRINT DATA=BALANCE;
   ID ID;
   VAR LAST FIRST AMOUNT BALANCE DATE;
   FORMAT BALANCE DOLLAR10.2 DATE MMDDYY8.;
RUN;


    <<< SAS JOB OUTPUT FOLLOWS >>>
```

ID	LAST	FIRST	AMOUNT	BALANCE	DATE
1	RIVERA	GERRY	-11.28	$-11.28	02/18/93
			11.28	$0.00	02/27/93
			-113.13	$-113.13	03/01/93
			-79.88	$-193.01	03/02/93
			193.01	$0.00	03/07/93
28	RATHER	DANNY	-125.26	$-125.26	03/27/93
55	COSELL	HOWIE	-2.42	$-2.42	03/18/93
			-113.98	$-116.40	03/27/93
			116.40	$0.00	03/28/93
82	BRINKLEY	DAVE	-82.54	$-82.54	02/19/93
			-145.33	$-227.87	02/26/93
			-71.57	$-299.44	03/02/93
109	WALLACE	MICKEY	-149.46	$-149.46	02/21/93
			-59.24	$-208.70	03/10/93
			208.70	$0.00	03/16/93
136	CRONKITE	WALLY	-137.83	$-137.83	02/16/93
			105.00	$-32.83	02/17/93
			-85.19	$-118.02	03/08/93
			118.02	$0.00	03/13/93

Listing 10.5. Another use of FIRST.by

```
DATA BALANCE;
  MERGE COMPANY.CUSTOMER COMPANY.CUSTRANS;
  BY ID;
  IF FIRST.ID THEN BALANCE=0;
  BALANCE+AMOUNT;
  IF LAST.ID THEN OUTPUT;
RUN;
PROC PRINT DATA=BALANCE;
  ID ID;
  VAR LAST FIRST BALANCE DATE;
  FORMAT BALANCE DOLLAR10.2 DATE MMDDYY8.;
RUN;
```

ID	LAST	FIRST	BALANCE	DATE
1	RIVERA	GERRY	$0.00	03/07/93
28	RATHER	DANNY	$-125.26	03/27/93
55	COSELL	HOWIE	$0.00	03/28/93
82	BRINKLEY	DAVE	$-299.44	03/02/93
109	WALLACE	MICKEY	$0.00	03/16/93
136	CRONKITE	WALLY	$0.00	03/13/93

Listing 10.6. Using FIRST.by and LAST.by

values of the temporary variables.* Observe that the LAST.by variable is not 1 (true) until the last BY value in *all* datasets contributing to the PDV is being processed.

More difficult for many to remember, perhaps because it is counterintuitive, is the way the IN= variable operates. Inspect Listing 10.7 closely and note that IN= does not mean "the current BY observation was in the input dataset," but rather "the input dataset made a contribution to the current PDV." Whether this contribution was due to a fresh observation *or to value retention* does not matter. If a dataset has one or a few observations with a certain BY value, and is merged with a dataset having many observations for the BY value, an IN= variable will be 1 (true) for *each* output variable constructed in the PDV. Only when there is not a single instance of a certain BY variable in an input dataset will the dataset not contribute to the PDV. In this case, its unique variables take the system missing value, and its IN= variable takes the value 0 (false). As you can deduce, and confirm in the listings, the order of the datasets named on the MERGE statement has nothing to do with whether IN= or FIRST.by/LAST.by are true (i.e., "MERGE THREE TWO ONE" and "MERGE ONE TWO THREE" produce the same values for these variables).

While the SAS System has its own ideas about how to assign IN= variables, the SAS user can take control and assign the truth value of the IN= variable. This technique can be used to "refresh" the IN= variable so that it is true if and only if

---

*Variables IN1, IN2, FIRST, and LAST in Listing 10.7 were created by assignment from IN= variables, FIRST.by, and LAST.by.

Dataset ONE

OBS	BYVAR	A	B
1	1	1	1
2	2	2	2
3	2	2	2
4	2	2	2
5	3	3	3
6	4	4	4
7	4	4	4
8	7	7	7

Dataset TWO

OBS	BYVAR	B	C
1	1	11	11
2	1	11	11
3	1	11	11
4	1	11	11
5	2	22	22
6	2	22	22
7	4	44	44
8	6	66	66
9	6	66	66
10	6	66	66
11	7	77	77
12	8	88	88

Dataset THREE

OBS	BYVAR	C	D
1	2	222	222
2	2	222	222
3	3	333	333
4	4	444	444
5	4	444	444
6	4	444	444
7	5	555	555
8	5	555	555

Listing 10.7. The IN=, FIRST.by and LAST.by variables revealed

Continued

MERGE ONE TWO; BY BYVAR;

OBS	BYVAR	A	B	C	IN1	IN2	FIRST	LAST
1	1	1	11	11	1	1	1	0
2	1	1	11	11	1	1	0	0
3	1	1	11	11	1	1	0	0
4	1	1	11	11	1	1	0	1
5	2	2	22	22	1	1	1	0
6	2	2	22	22	1	1	0	0
7	2	2	2	22	1	1	0	1
8	3	3	3	.	1	0	1	1
9	4	4	44	44	1	1	1	0
10	4	4	4	44	1	1	0	1
11	6	.	66	66	0	1	1	0
12	6	.	66	66	0	1	0	0
13	6	.	66	66	0	1	0	1
14	7	7	77	77	1	1	1	1
15	8	.	88	88	0	1	1	1

MERGE TWO ONE; BY BYVAR;

OBS	BYVAR	B	C	A	IN1	IN2	FIRST	LAST
1	1	1	11	1	1	1	1	0
2	1	11	11	1	1	1	0	0
3	1	11	11	1	1	1	0	0
4	1	11	11	1	1	1	0	1
5	2	2	22	2	1	1	1	0
6	2	2	22	2	1	1	0	0
7	2	2	22	2	1	1	0	1
8	3	3	.	3	1	0	1	1
9	4	4	44	4	1	1	1	0
10	4	4	44	4	1	1	0	1
11	6	66	66	.	0	1	1	0
12	6	66	66	.	0	1	0	0
13	6	66	66	.	0	1	0	1
14	7	7	77	7	1	1	1	1
15	8	88	88	.	0	1	1	1

Listing 10.7. *Continued*

MERGE ONE TWO THREE; BY BYVAR;

OBS	BYVAR	A	B	C	D	IN1	IN2	IN3	FIRST	LAST
1	1	1	11	11	.	1	1	0	1	0
2	1	1	11	11	.	1	1	0	0	0
3	1	1	11	11	.	1	1	0	0	0
4	1	1	11	11	.	1	1	0	0	1
5	2	2	22	222	222	1	1	1	1	0
6	2	2	22	222	222	1	1	1	0	0
7	2	2	2	222	222	1	1	1	0	1
8	3	3	3	333	333	1	0	1	1	1
9	4	4	44	444	444	1	1	1	1	0
10	4	4	4	444	444	1	1	1	0	0
11	4	4	4	444	444	1	1	1	0	1
12	5	.	.	555	555	0	0	1	1	0
13	5	.	.	555	555	0	0	1	0	1
14	6	.	66	66	.	0	1	0	1	0
15	6	.	66	66	.	0	1	0	0	0
16	6	.	66	66	.	0	1	0	0	1
17	7	7	77	77	.	1	1	0	1	1
18	8	.	88	88	.	0	1	0	1	1

MERGE THREE TWO ONE; BY BYVAR;

OBS	BYVAR	C	D	B	A	IN1	IN2	IN3	FIRST	LAST
1	1	11	.	1	1	1	1	0	1	0
2	1	11	.	11	1	1	1	0	0	0
3	1	11	.	11	1	1	1	0	0	0
4	1	11	.	11	1	1	1	0	0	1
5	2	22	222	2	2	1	1	1	1	0
6	2	22	222	2	2	1	1	1	0	0
7	2	22	222	2	2	1	1	1	0	1
8	3	333	333	3	3	1	0	1	1	1
9	4	44	444	4	4	1	1	1	1	0
10	4	444	444	4	4	1	1	1	0	0
11	4	444	444	4	4	1	1	1	0	1
12	5	555	555	.	.	0	0	1	1	0
13	5	555	555	.	.	0	0	1	0	1
14	6	66	.	66	.	0	1	0	1	0
15	6	66	.	66	.	0	1	0	0	0
16	6	66	.	66	.	0	1	0	0	1
17	7	77	.	7	7	1	1	0	1	1
18	8	88	.	88	.	0	1	0	1	1

Listing 10.7. *Continued*

the *current* MERGE observation, not just its BY group partners, contributed to the dataset. In the following code fragment, "statement" is executed if and only if the observation retrieved from dataset B during the current iteration contributes a nonmissing value to the PDV:

```
DATA;
  INVAR=.; * ASSUME INVAR IS "FALSE" BEFORE THE MERGE;
  MERGE A B(IN=INVAR);
  BY MERGEVAR;
  IF INVAR THEN statement;
  ...
```

Now it doesn't matter if a BY group in B happens to have fewer observations than its companion BY group in A. Because the retained INVAR is explicitly set missing (zero could also have been used) before the MERGE, when B runs out of observations INVAR will remain missing, and "statement" will not execute for the remainder of the BY group being processed.

More Than One BY Variable

Generalization of the behavior of MERGE to more than one BY variable is straightforward. MERGE still operates on each distinct BY group. That is to say, whether an input dataset contributes nonmissing values to the PDV (and therefore will have an IN= value of 1) depends on whether the BY variable *value combination* exists in the input dataset.

Whenever the FIRST. or LAST. variable associated with one BY variable is 1 (true), the value of the FIRST. or LAST. variables associated with any BY variable appearing to the right of this BY variable is forced to 1. That is, if a more inclusive BY variable changes (and its FIRST. value becomes 1), even if the value of a subordinate BY variable stays the same, its FIRST. value also becomes 1. For example, given the following MERGE statement:

```
MERGE DATA1 DATA2; BY A B C D;
```

whenever B changes value, FIRST.B *and* FIRST.C *and* FIRST.D (but not necessarily FIRST.A) will be true whether or not C or D differ in value from the prior observation. This is reasonable, because the BY group as a whole has changed. Furthermore, and consistently with this fact, when a BY group changes the variables in the PDV are initialized to missing; values are retained only so long as the same BY group is being processed. Study carefully the example in Listing 10.8.

COMBINING OBSERVATIONS: MULTIPLE SET STATEMENTS

More than one SET statement may appear within a DATA step, and the way multiple SETs are implemented by the SAS compiler gives the user an alternative to MERGE that may help in certain cases.

Using multiple SET statements is quite different from using multiple dataset names in one SET statement. In either case, the program data vector is built from the variable names appearing in all datasets mentioned. But while one SET statement takes observations from the input datasets separately, rebuilding new observations out of each in turn, when rebuilding with multiple set statements each *single* new observation is filled out with data from several input datasets. This is consistent with the fact that each iteration of a DATA step is normally associated with one output observation, due to the "implied OUTPUT" at the end of the step (that is, if no explicit OUTPUT statements appear).

As you can see in Listing 10.9, multiple SET statements appear to act like a MERGE; in the example, "MERGE A B C;" would produce the same dataset as the three-SET method. But there is a major difference: When multiple SET statements are used, the output dataset stops being built when *any* of the input

Dataset ONE

OBS	BYV1	BYV2	A	B
1	1	1	1	1
2	2	1	2	2
3	2	1	2	2
4	2	2	2	2
5	2	2	2	2
6	2	3	2	2
7	3	1	3	3
8	4	1	4	4
9	4	2	4	4
10	7	2	7	7

Dataset TWO

OBS	BYV1	BYV2	B	C
1	1	1	11	11
2	1	2	11	11
3	1	2	11	11
4	1	3	11	11
5	2	1	22	22
6	2	1	22	22
7	4	1	44	44
8	4	1	44	44
9	4	2	44	44
10	6	1	66	66
11	6	1	66	66
12	6	3	66	66
13	7	1	77	77

Listing 10.8. Match-MERGE, more than one BY variable

Continued

MERGE ONE TWO; BY BYV1 BYV2;

OBS	BYV1	BYV2	A	B	C	IN1	IN2	FIRSTB1	FIRSTB2	LASTB1	LASTB2
1	1	1	1	11	11	1	1	1	1	0	1
2	1	2	.	11	11	0	1	0	1	0	0
3	1	2	.	11	11	0	1	0	0	0	1
4	1	3	.	11	11	0	1	0	1	1	1
5	2	1	2	22	22	1	1	1	1	0	0
6	2	1	2	22	22	1	1	0	0	0	1
7	2	2	2	2	.	1	0	0	1	0	0
8	2	2	2	2	.	1	0	0	0	0	1
9	2	3	2	2	.	1	0	0	1	1	1
10	3	1	3	3	.	1	0	1	1	1	1
11	4	1	4	44	44	1	1	1	1	0	0
12	4	1	4	44	44	1	1	0	0	0	1
13	4	2	4	44	44	1	1	0	1	1	1
14	6	1	.	66	66	0	1	1	1	0	0
15	6	1	.	66	66	0	1	0	0	0	1
16	6	3	.	66	66	0	1	0	1	1	1
17	7	1	.	77	77	0	1	1	1	0	1
18	7	2	7	7	.	1	0	0	1	1	1

MERGE TWO ONE; BY BYV1 BYV2;

OBS	BYV1	BYV2	B	C	A	IN1	IN2	FIRSTB1	FIRSTB2	LASTB1	LASTB2
1	1	1	1	11	1	1	1	1	1	0	1
2	1	2	11	11	.	0	1	0	1	0	0
3	1	2	11	11	.	0	1	0	0	0	1
4	1	3	11	11	.	0	1	0	1	1	1
5	2	1	2	22	2	1	1	1	1	0	0
6	2	1	2	22	2	1	1	0	0	0	1
7	2	2	2	.	2	1	0	0	1	0	0
8	2	2	2	.	2	1	0	0	0	0	1
9	2	3	2	.	2	1	0	0	1	1	1
10	3	1	3	.	3	1	0	1	1	1	1
11	4	1	4	44	4	1	1	1	1	0	0
12	4	1	44	44	4	1	1	0	0	0	1
13	4	2	4	44	4	1	1	0	1	1	1
14	6	1	66	66	.	0	1	1	1	0	0
15	6	1	66	66	.	0	1	0	0	0	1
16	6	3	66	66	.	0	1	0	1	1	1
17	7	1	77	77	.	0	1	1	1	0	1
18	7	2	7	.	7	1	0	0	1	1	1

Listing 10.8. *Continued*

Dataset A

OBS	A	B	C	X
1	1001	1002	1003	1004
2	2001	2002	2003	2004

Dataset B

OBS	A	B	C	Y
1	1011	1022	1033	1044
2	2011	2022	2033	2044

Dataset C

OBS	A	B	C	Z
1	1111	1222	1333	1444
2	2111	2222	2333	2444

SET A B C;

OBS	A	B	C	X	Y	Z
1	1001	1002	1003	1004	.	.
2	2001	2002	2003	2004	.	.
3	1011	1022	1033	.	1044	.
4	2011	2022	2033	.	2044	.
5	1111	1222	1333	.	.	1444
6	2111	2222	2333	.	.	2444

SET A; SET B; SET C;

OBS	A	B	C	X	Y	Z
1	1111	1222	1333	1004	1044	1444
2	2111	2222	2333	2004	2044	2444

Listing 10.9. Single versus multiple SET statements

datasets has run out of records when its SET attempts to execute. If each SET statement attempts to execute every time through the DATA step, the new dataset has a number of records equal to the number in the shortest input dataset. With MERGE, the number of records in the output dataset is equal to the number in the longest input dataset (see Listing 10.10).

SET, like MERGE, is an executable statement. Multiple SET statements can be used to spread out the merging operation: Computations and decisions can intervene between input datasets.

```
                            Dataset A

           OBS      A        B        C        X

            1      1001     1002     1003     1004
            2      2001     2002     2003     2004
            3      3001     3002     3003     3004
            4      4001     4002     4003     4004

                            Dataset B

           OBS      A        B        C        Y

            1      1011     1022     1033     1044
            2      2011     2022     2033     2044

                            Dataset C

           OBS      A        B        C        Z

            1      1111     1222     1333     1444
            2      2111     2222     2333     2444
            3      3111     3222     3333     3444

                        MERGE A B C;

     OBS     A       B       C       X       Y       Z

      1     1111    1222    1333    1004    1044    1444
      2     2111    2222    2333    2004    2044    2444
      3     3111    3222    3333    3004     .      3444
      4     4001    4002    4003    4004     .       .

                   SET A;  SET B;  SET C;

     OBS     A       B       C       X       Y       Z

      1     1111    1222    1333    1004    1044    1444
      2     2111    2222    2333    2004    2044    2444
```

Listing 10.10. MERGE versus multiple SET statements

Problem: From a dataset showing the observed height of a sample of trees, create another dataset which shows the deviation of this height from the sample mean (e.g., if the average is 100 feet and a certain tree is 85 feet tall, the deviation for that tree is -15).

Solution: The average is first found, and then used in calculating the deviation:

```
* FIND AVERAGE HEIGHT;
PROC SUMMARY DATA=TREES NOPRINT;
   OUTPUT OUT=AVGHITE MEAN=AVG;
   VAR HEIGHT;
RUN;
* NOW USE AVG TO COMPUTE DEVIATION IN NEW DATASET;
DATA TREES2;
   IF _N_=1 THEN SET AVGHITE;
   SET TREES;
   DEVIATN = HEIGHT - AVG;
   DROP AVG;
RUN;
```

How this job works is as follows: By the rules of the SUMMARY procedure, the output dataset in this case contains a single observation (there was no BY statement) with a single variable, AVG (no other statistics or IDs specified). In the DATA TREES2 group, SET AVGHITE is executed once, the first time through ($_N_=1$). The step does *not* terminate even though there is just one observation in AVGHITE, because SET AVGHITE does not attempt to execute a second time (if it did, there would be no more observations to get and the DATA step *would* terminate). Furthermore, AVG gets its value from the single observation in AVGHITE* and *keeps this value* throughout the step because, in the absence of BY group changes, variables created with SET, MERGE, or UPDATE are not initialized to missing at the beginning of the step.

If a dataset is indexed by the value of a certain variable or variables, then multiple SET statements can be used to find target observations in that dataset for merger with observations from another dataset. Suppose a manufacturing company produces hundreds of different products. It maintains a catalog database, PCAT, describing each product in terms of a number of characteristics. The dataset contains an identifying variable, CID, for each product. Suppose also that, for a certain marketing campaign, another dataset, MKT1, is prepared that contains observations that have the CID values for products that fall into a certain class. The observations in each dataset may not be in CID order, but it is known that PCAT has a simple index based on CID (indexes are explained in Chapter 21).

Problem: Create a dataset that contains the catalog entries only for those CIDs with observations in MKT1.

Solution: One straightforward approach would be as follows:

```
DATA M;
   SET MKT1; * GET OBS FROM TARGET DATASET, INCLDING CID VARIABLE;
   SET PCAT KEY=CID; * SEARCH FOR A CID MATCHING THAT IN MKT1;
   [other statments...]
RUN;
```

---

*We assume that TREES did not itself contain a variable called AVG.

In this example, the technique of multiple SETs works because CID is first read into the PDV from MKT1, and then the subsequent SET statement can use that value for its keyed search.

UPDATING OBSERVATIONS

We have seen how observations from datasets with different variables can be combined, using MERGE and the merging applications of SET, into another dataset whose observations combine variables from the several input sources. Another SAS statement has merging applications, but its application is usually more specialized: keeping data for the *same* variables up-to-date—maintaining correct addresses and phone numbers, for example. This matter is often handled as a transactions process: a batch of changes is applied to a dataset whose values may have gotten stale. The special DATA Step Language tool for this purpose is the UPDATE statement.

While more than two datasets may be MERGEd, two and only two datasets can be combined with UPDATE. The first is called the *master* dataset, and the second the *transaction* dataset. In records-keeping applications, the master dataset is either the single primary dataset, or in the case of larger systems, one of the datasets into which the data is partitioned. The transaction dataset is one in which incoming information has been stored, awaiting combination with the master dataset.

The UPDATE statement has the form

```
UPDATE master_data[(dataset_options)]
    trans_data[(dataset_options)] [END=variable];
```

Update must *always* be followed by a BY statement, and therefore the two input datasets must be arranged in order. In standard transaction-updating applications, the master dataset should have no more than one observation per BY value group,* although the transaction dataset may often have several observations per BY group.

If the transaction dataset happens to have one observation per BY variable, then the statements

```
UPDATE MASTER TRANSACTION; BY SSN;
```

and

---

*In Version 6 of the SAS System, a master dataset with more than one observation per BY group will not cause the DATA step to fail, but data errors will be generated (i.e., duplicate BY observations cause _ERROR_ to be set to 1 and an error message to be printed to the SAS log). An output dataset will be written, but with transactions applied only to the first observation in a BY value group; subsequent observations in the same BY group are written out unchanged.

Dataset A

OBS	ID	A	B	C	X
1	5	101	102	103	104
2	6	201	202	203	204
3	7	301	302	303	304
4	9	401	402	403	404

Dataset B

OBS	ID	A	B	C	Y
1	4	111	122	133	144
2	5	211	222	233	244
3	6	311	.	333	344
4	7	411	.	433	444

UPDATE A B; BY ID;

OBS	ID	A	B	C	X	Y
1	4	111	122	133	.	144
2	5	211	222	233	104	244
3	6	311	202	333	204	344
4	7	411	302	433	304	444
5	9	401	402	403	404	.

Listing 10.11. The UPDATE statement

MERGE MASTER TRANSACTION; BY SSN;

will be equivalent, with one big difference: System missing values in the transaction dataset do not overwrite nonmissing values in the master dataset with UPDATE (see Listing 10.11). With MERGE, any value (missing or not) in the rightmost dataset would be substituted over the value for the same variable in the leftmost dataset; new missing values can enter only if there is no matching BY value in the master. Thus UPDATE is valuable because unchanged variables left missing in transaction records will not destroy data in the master dataset.*

---

*Actually, it is only the system missing value that does not update the master. The special missing values do update a value in the master. Transaction dataset missing values .A through .Z update values in the master "as themselves," i.e., as do nonmissing values. UPDATE handles the missing value ._ (underscore) differently: When this value is found in the transaction dataset, the value in the master is updated not to "._" but to ".", the system-missing value. (This feature is provided because UPDATE does not use the system-missing value itself for updating; updating with ._ is a feature provided to give the programmer a way to update a value to system-missing when s/he really wants to.)

UPDATE is also distinguished from MERGE in a more important way: the way it handles multiple records per BY value group. MERGE will write an observation each time any of its input datasets contributes a fresh record. As shown earlier, the output dataset has as many observations per BY variable as in the input dataset with the most observations for that BY group. UPDATE, by contrast, applies the information in the several records in sequence to a single observation. It does this processing each input transaction in turn, but by waiting until all records with a given BY variable are processed before writing the PDV as an observation to the output dataset. The output dataset has only one observation per BY variable, reflecting all the changes implied by the transactions; see Listing 10.12. This feature both preserves the integrity of the master dataset and

Dataset A

OBS	ID	A	B	C	X
1	5	0101	0102	0103	0104
2	6	0201	0202	0203	0204
3	7	0301	0302	0303	0304
4	9	0401	0402	0403	0404

Dataset B

OBS	ID	A	B	C	Y
1	4	0111	0122	0133	0144
2	4	0211	.	0233	0244
3	4	0311	.	0333	0344
4	5	0411	0422	0433	0444
5	5	0511	.	0533	0544
6	5	0611	.	0633	0644
7	6	0711	.	0733	0744
8	6	0811	.	0833	0844
9	6	0911	.	0933	0944
10	7	1011	.	1033	1044
11	7	1011	.	1133	1144
12	7	1011	.	1233	1244

UPDATE A B; BY ID;

OBS	ID	A	B	C	X	Y
1	4	0311	0122	0333	.	0344
2	5	0611	0422	0633	0104	0644
3	6	0911	0202	0933	0204	0944
4	7	1011	0302	1233	0304	1244
5	9	0401	0402	0403	0404	.

Listing 10.12. UPDATE with multiple transactions per BY value

allows easy implementation of transaction processing in those cases where a transaction dataset may be augmented with various changes several times between processings.

MODIFYING DATASETS IN PLACE

Traditional SAS dataset rebuilding is accomplished by creating a new dataset. Even a DATA step such as

```
DATA ABC;
  SET ABC;
  [more statements]
RUN;
```

that uses the same dataset name for input and output, works behind the scenes by creating the new dataset with a system-determined temporary name, deleting the input dataset when the new one is successfully created, and finally renaming the newly created dataset using the program-defined name. Such a DATA step is perfectly valid, serving to create a new dataset that will be known by the same name as an old one departed.

The MODIFY statement, in contrast to SET, MERGE, or UPDATE, can *change the input dataset itself* without making a copy, and it provides other features that make it attractive in some situations.

MODIFY Processing In General

In syntax, the MODIFY statement appears similar to the SET statement. Like SET, it can take the statement options NOBS=, POINT= (or if the dataset is indexed, KEY=) for random access, and END= for determining whether the last observation of the dataset has been accessed. But unlike SET, which can name zero, one, or many datasets, MODIFY can name exactly one or two datasets (if two are named, then a BY statement is expected). Furthermore, one of the datasets named on the DATA statement must have the same name as the first dataset named on the MODIFY statement. As examples, while the following DATA statements may be correct:

```
DATA A; MODIFY A; [more statements]; RUN;
DATA A B C; MODIFY B; [more statements]; RUN;
DATA B; MODIFY B C; BY VAR; [more statements]; RUN;
```

the following are incorrect:

```
DATA A; MODIFY B; [more statements] RUN;
DATA B; MODIFY B C; (no BY statement) [more statements] RUN;
DATA B; MODIFY C B; BY VAR; [more statements] RUN;
```

```
Original Dataset "A"

OBS    N    NSQUARE

 1     1       1
 2     2       4
 3     3       9
 4     4      16
 5     5      25


Dataset "B": Like "A" but with NCUBE

OBS    N    NSQUARE    NCUBE

 1     1       1          1
 2     2       4          8
 3     3       9         27
 4     4      16         64
 5     5      25        125


Dataset "A", modified like "B"

OBS    N    NSQUARE

 1     1       1
 2     2       4
 3     3       9
 4     4      16
 5     5      25
```

Listing 10.13. MODIFY does not alter dataset variable layout

The reason the same dataset must be named on the DATA statement as well as the MODIFY statement is simple: MODIFY always works on an existing dataset,* yet in a DATA step, whenever you want an output dataset of a certain name, you put the name on the DATA statement.† Therefore, the SAS compiler will generate an error and refuse to continue if the name on MODIFY does not appear on DATA.

Because MODIFY works on existing datasets, it does not have the power to alter the order or attributes of variables in the dataset, nor to add or to remove any variables. Consider the following program, and its results as shown in Listing 10.13:

---

*Let's create some SAS jargon here that will serve us well below, and refer to the dataset being modified as the *modify dataset*.

†The designers of the SAS System could have written exceptions into the DATA Step Language such that in the presence of MODIFY the name on the DATA statement is implied, but it is less confusing, and therefore entirely proper, that the rules be as they are.

```
DATA A;
  DO N=1 TO 5;
    NSQARE=N*N;
    OUTPUT;
    END;
  RUN;
TITLE 'Original Dataset "A"'; PROC PRINT DATA=A; RUN;
DATA B;
  SET A;
  NCUBE=NSQUARE*N;
RUN;
TITLE 'Dataset "B": Like "A" but with NCUBE'; PROC PRINT DATA=B; RUN;
DATA A;
  MODIFY A;
  NCUBE=NSQARE*N;
RUN;
TITLE 'Dataset "A", modified like "B"'; PROC PRINT DATA=A; RUN;
```

It does not look like anything happened to dataset A as a result of the last DATA step, but in fact a lot happened: for each observation in A, the SAS System dutifully computed NCUBE—and then did nothing with the result! It cannot add NCUBE to the modified dataset, because the variable did not previously exist in it. But let's instead do something a little different in modifying dataset A:

```
DATA A;
  MODIFY A;
  N=1/N;
RUN;
TITLE 'Dataset "A", with the value of N replaced by its reciprocal';
PROC PRINT DATA=A; RUN;
```

Results of this step, shown in Listing 10.14, illustrate the fact that values of *existing* variables indeed may be changed. In fact, what happened in *both* MODIFY steps is that the observations of A were replaced; it's just that, in the first case, the replaced observations were the same as their replacements because none of their variables' values were changed.

Could we at least have renamed a variable with a RENAME statement? No. The step would not fail as far as the SAS System was concerned, but the RENAME would, in effect, be ignored. How about a dataset option:

```
DATA A;
  MODIFY A(RENAME=(N=NRECIP));
  NRECIP=1/NRECIP;
RUN;
```

This step would not fail, and in fact would work as intended—except that the variable in dataset A would *still* remain named N! That is to say, the reciprocal

```
Dataset "A", with the value of N replaced by its reciprocal

        OBS        N        NSQUARE

         1      1.00000         1
         2      0.50000         4
         3      0.33333         9
         4      0.25000        16
         5      0.20000        25
```

Listing 10.14. MODIFY may alter dataset variable values

would be calculated and assigned correctly during the course of each iteration, but in the output dataset the variable's name would come out unchanged.

These examples serve to show that even though a DATA step with MODIFY may alter the values of observations in an existing dataset, it simply cannot change their attributes.

As for what happens if more than one dataset is named on the DATA statement of a step containing MODIFY, let's return to that question later, when we discuss how observations may be explicitly written or removed.

Transaction-Based Updating: MODIFY with BY

As you know, SET with BY produces an interleaved output dataset. By contrast, MODIFY with BY behaves not like SET but very much like UPDATE. As with UPDATE, exactly two dataset names are expected on the MODIFY statement. And as with UPDATE, in SAS jargon we even call the first one the *master* dataset and the second the *transaction* dataset. But while a DATA step using UPDATE rebuilds a new dataset with information from the master and transaction datasets, with MODIFY the master dataset is also the modify dataset: it, not the transaction dataset, is named on the DATA statement, and it is modified "in place" based on information in the transaction dataset. Also differing from UPDATE and significantly, BY with MODIFY is implemented with dynamic WHERE processing, and *the datasets do not have to be in any particular sort or index order.**

If the master dataset has more than one observation with the same BY group values, then (as with UPDATE) transactions will be applied to the first such observation, and subsequent observations in the same BY group will be left alone. However, with MODIFY these situations are not considered data errors, and no

---

*If you are using a transaction dataset that is neither sorted nor indexed, however, the processing time involved with BY can be objectionably long. What happens during execution is that a WHERE expression is created from the BY value combination in the current master observation, and the transaction dataset is searched. Since this WHERE search takes place for *each* master observation, the amount of time saved if the transactions are sorted or indexed can be significant.

error message prints to the log nor is _ERROR_ set at 1. On the other hand, if any set of BY group values appears in an observation of the transaction dataset and the master does not have at least one observation with the same set of values, then this is considered an error, and the DATA step may halt, or its results become difficult to predict.* In similar circumstances when UPDATE is used, a new observation is simply created in the output dataset for each unique BY value group found in the transaction but not in the master dataset. But MODIFY cannot BY-replace observations that do not already exist in the dataset.

Since MODIFY does not alter the dataset descriptor or variable layout, variables from a transaction dataset that do not appear in the master still do not appear in the master after a MODIFY-BY update process. By contrast, UPDATE will add variables from the transaction dataset to the rebuilt master if they do not exist in the input master (unless, of course, variables are selected with DROP or KEEP), using missing values for those variables for BY groups in the master that have no equivalent in the transaction dataset.

Writing (Or Removing) Observations

There are two observation-writing statements that can be used with MODIFY: OUTPUT and REPLACE. As it does when a new dataset is being built or rebuilt, the OUTPUT statement causes a new observation to be written to the current end of a dataset being modified.

By contrast, the REPLACE statement causes a new observation to be written not to the end of the dataset being modified but to the same place in the dataset where the observation being worked on resides. (The REPLACE statement is never used with SET, or MERGE or UPDATE, since with these tools writing *always* takes place to a new observation at the current end of the dataset being rebuilt.)

Another statement, REMOVE, can also be used with MODIFY. The REMOVE statement deletes the observation from the dataset being modified. Depending on the access engine processing the dataset, the observation may be removed physically or only logically (an observation is "logically" removed by being marked as deleted without actually reclaiming its space).†

REMOVE and REPLACE cannot both execute in the same iteration. You can have both in the code, but only if they won't both execute (for example, if they are

---

*You may get greater control over the behavior of a MODIFY transaction, including BY group match failures, by basing code execution conditionally on the value of the automatic variable _IORC_ that is created in DATA steps where MODIFY (or SET with KEY=) is used. The _IORC_ variable, and the %SYSRC macro that interprets its values, can be used to determine "on the fly" when a data match has succeeded or failed. Such techniques, however, go beyond the scope of this book.

†If a dataset with logically- removed observations is subsequently rebuilt (e.g., with SET), the observations so marked will not be written to the new dataset, and the space thereby recovered within the new dataset.

coded as mutually exclusive objects of a SELECT group or IF...ELSE sequence). OUTPUT is not incompatible with either: it is acceptable to alter or get rid of the observation you are working on and still add a new observation to the end of the dataset. However, if OUTPUT is to be used in the same step as REPLACE or REMOVE (and more precisely, if the OUTPUT is to take place upon the modify dataset; see our discussion below of additional DATA statement datasets), OUTPUT must execute only after the REMOVE or REPLACE.

As explained in Chapter 3, when an explicit OUTPUT statement is not coded in a DATA step that builds (or rebuilds) a dataset, then iterations that reach the end of the code execute an implicit OUTPUT. By contrast, during dataset modification, if neither OUTPUT, REPLACE, nor REMOVE appear in the DATA step code, then an implicit REPLACE (not OUTPUT) is executed on the dataset being modified, as the last action of each iteration that goes to completion.

Additional DATA Statement Datasets

We may now return to the question raised earlier of what happens to additional datasets named on the DATA statement. In the simple case where neither OUTPUT, REPLACE, nor REMOVE appear in the code, then even as an implicit REPLACE is executed with respect the modify dataset, implicit OUTPUTs are executed with respect to the other datasets.

If more than one dataset was named on the DATA statement, desired datasets should be named on explicit output-writing statements. Like OUTPUT, REPLACE and REMOVE statements can include a dataset name if necessary.

Remember that REPLACE and REMOVE are operations not defined with respect to rebuilt (as opposed to modified) datasets. Thus the following code will work:

```
DATA P Q;
  MODIFY Q;
  [statements]
  IF [condition] THEN REMOVE Q;
  [more statements]
RUN;
```

but

```
DATA P Q;
  MODIFY Q;
  [statements]
  IF [condition] THEN REMOVE;
  [more statements]
RUN;
```

will not; the compiler will complain that REMOVE is not valid for the offending dataset P (because no dataset was named on the REMOVE statement, a REMOVE was attempted on all datasets named on the DATA statement).

The only exception to the rule (that when more than one dataset is named on the DATA statement a dataset should be explicitly named on an OUTPUT, REMOVE, or REPLACE statement) would be if you want all datasets, including the modify dataset, to have a new observation written at their end. OUTPUT is defined in all cases, and an OUTPUT statement that does not name any dataset can be written without error in a DATA step containing MODIFY. But, mind the cautionary notes below.

Because MODIFY changes the input dataset, then data loss can occur if the SAS System terminates abnormally, whether from a program error or a computer system failure. Depending on the conditions at the time, the dataset might be severely damaged and more will be lost than just the observation that was being handled at the time. If MODIFY is to be used on critical datasets that cannot readily be reconstructed, these datasets should first be backed up (perhaps with the COPY procedure).

To change a dataset's layout you must rebuild the dataset, e.g. by using SET. As described earlier, MODIFY cannot change the dataset descriptor nor its internal data vector: The orders and lengths of existing variables cannot be changed, nor can variables be added to or dropped from the dataset. A DATA step attempting such changes may in fact execute to completion, and the SAS log may not even produce a message to say something is wrong.

Using OUTPUT with MODIFY

Be mindful that dynamics of the OUTPUT statement when used in modifying datasets can be very different than when used in building or rebuilding datasets. In both cases, OUTPUT writes an observation to the dataset being built, and also in both cases, the observation is written to the end of the dataset. But since the MODIFY conception of the *current* observation is not the same as the *last* observation of the dataset, you can get into severe trouble if you use OUTPUT unless you explicitly stop the DATA step in some fashion, e.g. by executing a STOP statement. This is *not* a problem if REMOVE or REPLACE is also executed. But using the original (unmodified) dataset A from earlier examples, consider the innocent-looking program

```
DATA A;
  MODIFY A;
  N=2*N;
  OUTPUT;
RUN;
```

which has an OUTPUT but no REMOVE or REPLACE statement. This program will run *forever* (well, until the dataset runs out of space, or a program "timeout" occurs), happily adding a new observation to A for each existing observation *including those it has just added*. Listing 10.15 illustrates the results of such a

```
    <<< PROGRAM SOURCE CODE FOLLOWS >>>

DATA A;
  MODIFY A;
  N=2*N;
  OUTPUT;
  IF _N_ > 20 THEN STOP;
RUN;
TITLE 'Dataset "A", N replaced by 2*N, with explicit OUTPUT';
PROC PRINT DATA=A; RUN;

    <<< SAS JOB OUTPUT FOLLOWS >>>
```

        Dataset "A", N replaced by 2*N, with explicit OUTPUT

OBS	N	NSQUARE
1	1	1
2	2	4
3	3	9
4	4	16
5	5	25
6	2	1
7	4	4
8	6	9
9	8	16
10	10	25
11	4	1
12	8	4
13	12	9
14	16	16
15	20	25
16	8	1
17	16	4
18	24	9
19	32	16
20	40	25
21	16	1
22	32	4
23	48	9
24	64	16
25	80	25
26	32	1

Listing 10.15. An OUTPUT statement writes a completely new observation

program, where the original dataset is the one familiar from our previous examples, starting with file observations; a STOP statement has been included to break the DATA step out of its rut. There are occasions when you might want to extend a dataset in such a manner—just be sure a STOP will execute!

Why is this kind of thing always a problem? That is, why don't *all* MODIFY applications require a STOP? As we have indicated above, a DATA step using MODIFY may entail an implicit REPLACE (not an implicit OUTPUT) if REPLACE, REMOVE, or OUTPUT is *not* coded, and if REPLACE or REMOVE *is* coded *or* executed implicitly, then the DATA step *does* automatically stop after the iteration that processes the last observation. In other words, MODIFY "knows" it is at the last observation if and only if REPLACE or REMOVE executes.

11

SAS Formats

SAS formats are variable attributes that can be used to convert a SAS value to another form, usually for printing or for writing external files. Most often used with SAS procedures, formats can be put to several advantages in the DATA step as well, with PUT statments or with the PUT( ) function (Chapter 15).

Formats that convert numeric values are called numeric formats and those that convert character values are called character formats, but the converted (formatted) values are always character strings in either case. Similarly, formatted values of date/time variables are character strings, although date/time variables are stored numerically. *All formatted values are of type "character."* The terms "numeric format," "date/time format," and "character format" connote the type of the original, unformatted values.

Formats can be associated with variables with a FORMAT statement, which may be used either in a DATA or PROC step. When a FORMAT statement is used in a DATA step, the format becomes an attribute of the variable in the output dataset, and is said to be the "permanent" format for that variable. When used in a PROC step, the FORMAT statement associates a variable with a format only for purposes of executing the current procedure (if a permanent format has been defined for a variable, the PROC format temporarily overrides it).

Whether coded in a DATA or in a PROC step, the FORMAT statement looks the same: It specifies one or more variables and desired format identifiers. Format identifiers look like SAS names, but with a period, or a number containing a period, attached to the end, and perhaps a dollar sign up front. A couple of examples:

```
FORMAT VAR1-VAR6 HEX16. VAR7-VAR10 MMDDYY8.;

FORMAT A $12. B $CHAR35. C Z8.3 J JFORM.;
```

VAR1 through VAR6 are formatted with the HEX16. format, B with the $CHAR35. format, etc.

The Base SAS software provides many predefined formats ready to use in FORMAT statements. In this chapter are introduced many of the numeric, character, and date/time formats provided by the SAS System.

The SAS System also provides a way for the user to define pseudo formats for output variable grouping. This useful feature is often overlooked by SAS beginners. It is also often misunderstood, for user-defined formats are quite different entities than the SAS-provided formats, even though they are used in FORMAT statements the same way. We close this chapter with an in-depth discussion of "user-defined formats" and the FORMAT procedure that creates them.

STANDARD NUMERIC FORMATS

There are many different numeric formats, so we will group those discussed below by their general functionality. What we will call "regular" numeric formats provide alternative ways to write numeric values. Data-conversion formats let the user represent values in hexadecimal and other computer forms. Financial formats print dollar signs or commas within the numbers, or write numbers in words (for printing checks, etc.). And there are a few miscellaneous numeric formats that do not fit in these categories.

Refer to Listing 11.1 for illustrations of the formats discussed below. The following five test values were used for illustrative purposes: 126, 3.27, 2700, 33.5, and 0.72735. The PUT function, described in Chapter 15, was used to form the dataset used for this printout.

"Regular" Numeric Formats

The w.d Format. The so-called w.d format specifies a number of columns width, w, and a number of columns to the right of the decimal point, d. w should be large enough to hold the entire width, including d and the decimal point itself. d can be left off; it defaults to zero. That is to say,

```
FORMAT VAR1 7.0;
```

is equivalent to

```
FORMAT VAR1 7.;
```

Inspection of Listing 11.1, in which four different w.d specifications are shown (2., 5., 7.2, and 9.5), reveals some things about how SAS deals with inadequate format

The values 126,3.27,2700,33.5, and 0.72735, formatted
"Regular" Numeric Formats

2.	5.	7.2	9.5	Z9.5	BEST.	BEST5.
**	126	126.00	126.00000	126.00000	126	126
3	3	3.27	3.27000	003.27000	3.27	3.27
**	2700	2700.00	2700.0000	2700.0000	2700	2700
34	34	33.50	33.50000	033.50000	33.5	33.5
1	1	0.73	0.72735	000.72735	0.72735	0.727

E	FRACT.	PERCENT.	PERCENT10.
1.26000E+02	126	1E4%	12600%
3.27000E+00	3+27/100	327%	327%
2.70000E+03	2700	3E5%	270000%
3.35000E+01	33+1/2	3E3%	3350%
7.27350E-01	0.72735	73%	73%

The values 126,3.27,2700,33.5, and 0.72735, formatted
Data Converting Formats

HEX.	HEX16.	OCTAL.	BINARY.
0000007E	405F800000000000	176	01111110
00000003	400A28F5C28F5C29	003	00000011
00000A8C	40A5180000000000	214	10001100
00000021	4040C00000000000	041	00100001
00000000	3FE7467381D7DBF5	000	00000000

The values 126,3.27,2700,33.5, and 0.72735, formatted
Financial Formats

COMMA15.	DOLLAR15.	COMMA15.2	DOLLAR15.2	WORDS.
126	$126	126.00	$126.00	one hundr*
3	$3	3.27	$3.27	three and*
2,700	$2,700	2,700.00	$2,700.00	two thous*
34	$34	33.50	$33.50	thirty-th*
1	$1	0.73	$0.73	zero and *

WORDS60.	WORDF60.
one hundred twenty-six	one hundred twenty-six and 00/100
three and twenty-seven hundredths	three and 27/100
two thousand seven hundred	two thousand seven hundred and 00/100
thirty-three and fifty hundredths	thirty-three and 50/100
zero and seventy-two hundredths	zero and 72/100

Listing 11.1. Numeric formats

specifications. Look at the first column, the 2. format. With insufficient space for the integer portion of the value, SAS complains severely by printing asterisks for the length of the allowed field. In this case, the values that crash are 126 and 2700. If there is room at least for the integer portion, SAS will round the values. Thus if the format provides for no decimal places, 33.5 prints as 34, .72735 as 1. Rounding is also done if a decimals specification is provided, but is of insufficient width: with format=7.2, .72735 rounds to .73. Normally, if there is enough room, a single zero will be placed to the left of a value less than 1 (e.g., .72735 may print as 0.72735).

All the "regular" numeric formats, including w.d, write values right-aligned, that is, in the rightmost columns of the field alloted by the user. If the value '12345' is written with format 10., it appears in columns 6–10 of the ten-character-width field.

The Zw.d Format

The Zw.d format is similar to the w.d format, except that leading zeroes are used to fill the entire field to the left. Thus in the listing the value 3.27 prints as 3.27000 when format=9.5, but prints as 003.27000 with format=Z9.5. Zw.d is valuable for producing external files meant to be read by non-SAS programs that cannot tolerate blank columns. But note what happened to the value 2700, which was too small for its w specification (since d=5, only three spaces are available to the left of the decimal point). This shows another thing SAS does when space is inadequate: It may choose to represent the value in a BESTw. format (below). And it underscores how important it is to *make sure field width is sufficient for the largest value expected.*

The BESTw. Format

The BESTw. format is a way of allowing the SAS System to choose the "best" way of representing a value; this usually entails taking the least space. The user asks SAS to choose its best method by using BESTw. (or, as we just saw, SAS may itself decide to do so if the chosen format doesn't work). Decimal-columns specifications, e.g., BEST8.4, are not allowed, since the place for the decimal point is chosen by the format as best befits the value. Because decimal points are not forced into alignment when BESTw. is used, printouts will usually look nicer if you can determine both the maximum number of decimals needed and the maximum total field width needed, and code a w.d format identifier.

The Ew. Format

The Ew. format is used for scientific notation, which represents all numbers as a mixed number between 0.0 and 9.999 . . . and indicates the true decimal by power of 10 following an E. The results in the listing are based on the default width specification of 12 (w can range from 7 to 32).

The FRACTw. Format

This format prints the decimal portion of a mixed number as a proper fraction. As can be seen in the listing, FRACT. reduces fractions to the lowest common denominator. w can range from 4 to 32. The default, used in the listing, is 10. No rounding is attempted; FRACT. simply gives up and does not attempt a conversion when the result will exceed the field width. (Had we used a width of 11 or more, we would have found .72735 to be 14547/20000.)

The PERCENTw. Format

The PERCENTw.d format in effect multiplies values by 100, then tacks on a percent sign. Negative values are enclosed in parentheses. The width specification must allow for the parentheses (even if no negative values are anticipated) as well as for the percent sign.

Data Converting Formats

There are several formats besides Zw.d that convert values to representations more palatable to certain software systems. **HEXw.** writes hexadecimal values. w can range from 1 to 16. If it is under 16, the fixed-point binary representation of the value is converted, or from the human point of view, the integer portion. The default w value is 8, and Listing 11.1 shows that the fractions have been ignored (truncated). If $w = 16$, then the floating point representation is used.

Related to HEXw. are the **OCTALw.** and **BINARYw.** formats (not illustrated) which produce, respectively, the octal and binary representations of their numeric input values. Only the integer portion of the input value is used; that is, any fractional portion is ignored.

Other data conversion formats include integer binary (IBw.d) and positive integer binary (PIBw.d), real binary (RBw.d), packed decimal (PDw.d), and zoned decimal (ZDw.d). These formats can be useful when creating external files to be shared with other software systems. For implementation details, consult your *SAS Language* reference and the *SAS Companion* for your operating system.

Financial Formats

There are four formats that may be useful for financial reporting, and possibly for other applications. They are meant to handle dollars and cents values, and indeed, they will not treat fractions other than tenths or hundredths. With a couple of exceptions, the formatted values are written right-justified in their allotted output fields.

The COMMAw.d Format

The COMMAw.d format is used to print values with commas every three digits. d, if used, must be either 0 or 2. That is to say, only whole numbers, or numbers to two decimal places, may be printed with COMMAw.d. The default value of w is 6. Values will be rounded as required.

The DOLLARw.d Format

The DOLLARw.d format behaves exactly like the COMMAw.d format, except that a single leading dollar sign is printed. This format also can take only 0 or 2 as a value of d, and has a default w value of 6. It will round values if necessary. The variant DOLLARXw.d (not illustrated) reverses the role of the comma and the period, as is the usage in certain countries.

The WORDSw. Format

This format converts a numeric value to words. The default value of w is 12, which is often inadequate. As can be seen in the listing, too short a width causes an asterisk in the last position of the field and the result is useless. Note that the fractions are given all in hundredths; no reduction is attempted. As you might surmise, this format was designed to handle dollars and cents for automated check printing.

The WORDFw. Format

This format is exactly like the WORDSw. format, except the hundredths are written as a nonreduced fraction—another way to print checks. No rounding is done. WORDSw. and WORDFw. write formatted values *left*-justified in output fields.

Miscellaneous Numeric Formats

The SSNw. Format

The SSNw. format, not illustrated, prints values as social security numbers. The value of w can only be 11 (or left blank, in which case it defaults to 11). Give it a 9-digit integer, and it will place hyphens after digits 3 and 7 to form a social security number.

The ROMANw. Format

The SAS System has something for everyone, and someone might just need a few Roman numerals. Values are truncated to integer before conversion.

CHARACTER FORMATS

Because character variables are already stored in printable form, the character formats are few and simple. All but one of them exist only for the purpose of handling output field widths. The character formats all print left-aligned. They are indicated in format statements by the usual dollar sign, e.g.,

```
FORMAT CHARVAL $25.;
```

Character formats find their most important uses in conjunction with PUT statements for writing external files or customized reports; see Chapter 17.

Simple Field Width Control

The $w. Format

Character values will be padded to the right with blanks if w is longer than the variable length, or else the value will be truncated on the right if it is shorter. If $ without w. is coded, the length defaults to the length of the variable.

Multiple blanks are acceptable within character variables written with a $w. format. Blanks at the beginning of a character variable, however, are removed. That is, the first character printed, in the leftmost alignment, is the first non-blank character in the value.

The $CHARw. Format

This format is entirely equivalent to the $w. format except that leading blanks are *not* removed before printing; they are preserved.

The $VARYINGw. Format

$VARYINGw. is used for a special purpose and has a special form:

```
PUT variable $VARYINGw. lengthvar;
```

where "lengthvar" is a variable giving the actual length of "variable." w is used as the *maximum* allowable length. If w is not specified, SAS assigns a maximum length specification the same way it assigns character variable lengths: the length of "variable" is used if it is defined, or if not, then w = 8.

However, it is "lengthvar" that really determines the length of the formatted value. This variable *must* be named along with $VARYINGw. when the format is used on a PUT statement. If it is zero negative, or missing, nothing is written out.

The obvious use for $VARYINGw. is to avoid gaps in output written with PUT caused by trailing blanks. As you should realize (and as *SAS Basics* warns), this format is to be used only in the DATA step with PUT statements, not in the PROC step.

The **$UPCASEw.** format can be used to convert alphabetic character data that may arrive in mixed case to all-uppercase. The format is useful primarily to pass external data to printers or to other software programs that cannot handle lowercase.

The **$ASCIIw.** format converts character input to ASCII representation if the system on which the program is running does not already use ASCII as its native method of representation. Similarly, the **$EBCDICw.** format can be used to put values out in EBCDIC representation if the computer system used does not usually do so. If the native computer representation is already adequate (i.e.,

$EBCDICw. is used on an EBCDIC machine, or $ASCIIw. on an ASCII machine), then these formats just behave like the $CHARw. format.

The **$HEXw.** format converts a character value to its hexadecimal equivalent. This is sometimes useful for error diagnostics when "garbage" is printed out, or in other cases where normally nonprintable characters must be found out. The output values written by $HEXw. depend on the data storage format used by the computer operating system (e.g., ASCII, EBCDIC). In any case, each character of the original data will require *two* characters of formatted output, and this should be taken into account in specifying field width.

The related **$OCTALw.** and **$BINARYw.** formats convert character strings to, respectively, octal or binary representation. $OCTALw. will require an output field width three times the length of the input value, and $BINARYw. a width four times the input value length, to succeed in handling the entire value.

The **$QUOTEw.** format doesn't actually convert characters, but it does put double quotes around them. w should allow two extra spaces for the quote marks, in addition to the input value length.

DATE/TIME FORMATS

In order for SAS date and time values to regain their intuitive meaning after having been stored in their special numeric way (see Chapter 8), they must somehow be retranslated to normal dates or times. Date, time, and datetime formats are used to present the special numeric date, time, or datetime values in a manner more acceptable to the human reader. There are several different ways to do this using SAS functions (Chapter 15), and several ways using the SAS formats we will now discuss.

There are many SAS formats for putting out date values. For discussion, we can separate these into three-part dates, other numeric representations, and verbal dates. We will also discuss several formats to handle time values, and a couple designed for datetime values. The formats discussed in this section print *right*-aligned within their allotted fields.

Date formats should be used with date values, time formats with time values, datetime formats with datetime values. Because the internal numeric representations are generated according to different rules, *wildly incorrect results* arise if the wrong format is used. Indeed, where SAS date, time, and datetime values are concerned, it is recommended that formats be permanently associated with variables using FORMAT statements in the DATA step.

To illustrate the date/time formats, three different values were used: a date '14FEB27'D, a time '12:23:06.13'T, and the corresponding datetime '14FEB27:12:23:06.13'DT. Refer to Listing 11.2 as we continue our discussion below.

Three-Part Date Formats

These formats all print the two-digit representation of the month, day, and year together to form a date. These and the other date formats are illustrated with the date '14FEB27'D.

Date Formats

MMDDYY6. MMDDYY5. MMDDYY8. DDMMYY8. YYMMDD8. MONTH. YEAR. DAY. WEEKDAY.

021427   02/14   02/14/27 14/02/27 27-02-14   2   1927   14   2

YYQ.   MONYY.   MONYY7.   MONNAME.   DOWNAME.   WEEKDATE.

27Q1   FEB27   FEB1927   February   Monday   Monday, February 14, 1927

WORDDATE.   WORDDATE6.   WEEKDATX.   WORDDATX.

February 14, 1927   Feb   Monday, 14 February 1927   14 February 1927

Time Formats

TIME.   TIME12.2   HHMM.   HOUR.   MMSS.

12:23:06   12:23:06.13 12:23   12   743

Datetime Formats

DATETIME.   DATETIME7.   TOD.

14FEB27:12:23:06   14FEB27   12:23:06

Listing 11.2. Date/Time formats

The **MMDDYYw.** format produces data values like those used in many countries, including the United States, where we often write dates with the numeric month, day, and two-digit year separated by slashes. February 14, 1927 is written 2/14/27. The MMDDYYw. format behaves like this (more or less: it tends to use leading zeroes for each component, while we don't usually do this in handwriting). w can range from 2 through 8; the default value is 8, and normal values are 6 or 8. Leading zeroes are normally printed; thus, you see MMDDYY8. yields 02/14/27. When w = 6, the slashes are omitted; this may be of value when creating an external file.

The format will attempt to squeeze out as much as possible of the formatted value, and therefore MMDDYY4. or MMDDYY5. can be used to trick the format into writing the month and day, with or without a slash, but without the year. You can even use MMDDYY2. to get just the month printed, though the orthodox method is to use MONTHw. (see below).

The DDMMYYw. Format

In some countries, the date is normally written day/month/year. DDMMYYw. works exactly like MMDDYYw., except that the day comes first. Like MMDDYYw., short values of w obtain the first part or parts of the date.

The YYMMDDw. Format

Like MMDDYYw. and DDMMYYw., this format produces a three-part date. YYMMDD8. yields 27/02/14. You can trick this format like the others to get the year only (though the YEARw. format, below, is designed for this) or the year and the month.

Other Numeric Representations

The **MONTHw.** format produces the numeric value of the month of the input date value (or more precisely, a string of numerals representing this number: remember, formatted values are always of character type). Similarly, **YEARw.** writes the numeric year. **DAYw.** writes the numeric day of the month, and **WEEKDAYw.** the day of the week (Sunday=1, . . . Saturday=6).

The **YYQw.** format reveals the calendar quarter in which a date falls, useful for financial reporting. Valid values of w are 4 or 6, with 4 the default. The written value will be either the four-digit (YYQ6.) or two-digit (YYQ4.) year, followed by Q and a numeral from 1 to 4. February 14, 1927, as can be seen in the listing, lies within the first quarter of 1927.

Verbal Date Formats

The formats in this group prepare part or all of a date in words or abbreviations.

The **MONYYw.** format prints the three-letter abbreviation of the month, followed by a two-digit (MONYY5.) or four-digit (MONYY7.) year. w can be either 5 or 7, defaulting to 5.

The **DATEw.** format is like MONYYw., but the day of the month is tacked onto the front. w can range from 5 to 9. When w = 5 or w = 6, the format is tricked into producing the day and month only. When w is 7, DATEw. returns the same form of SAS date value that is used in specifying date constants.

MONNAMEw. writes out the name of the month, and **DOWNAMEw.** the name of the day of the week.

The **WEEKDATEw.** and **WORDDATEw.** formats are intended to present the full date in words. You can "trick" them with short w values, but you must test the results; these formats have their own ideas on how to abbreviate output values.

WEEKDATEw. presents the day of the week as a word, along with the calendar date and month as a word. As the space allotted to the format grows larger, more of the date can be printed. At 3 or values close to 3, the date will be represented only by the day of the week, in three-letter abbreviation. When w gets to around 9, the full day will be printed. When w gets to around 15, the full date (with the day abbreviated) will show. Finally, at large values of w, the full day and date are written.

WORDDATEw. is similar to WEEKDATEw., except the day of the week is not printed. w can range from 3 to 32. At 3 or close to 3, the three-letter month only is printed. At values around 9, the full month name shows. At values close to 12, the full date is abbreviated. At large values of w, the full date is written.

The **WEEKDATXw.** and **WORDDATXw.** formats behave, respectively, like the WEEKDATEw. and WORDDATEw. formats, except that the positions of the day and the month are reversed.

Time Formats

The TIMEw.d Format

This format writes the time in the form hh:mm:ss.ff, hh = hours, mm = minutes, ss = seconds, ff = fraction (100ths of seconds, if any). It is the form of time used in time constants. Printing of the fraction of seconds is done only if width permits *and* d = 2 (if coded, d may be 0 or 2). Like other time and date formats, the TIMEw.d format can be tricked into printing only hours, or only hours and minutes, with short values of w, which may range from 2 to 20 (default w = 8).

The HHMMw.d Format

This is similar to TIMEw.d, except that seconds do not print. If there are any seconds to be accounted for, they print as decimal fractions of minutes, or if d is not coded (or zero), they are used to round the value to the nearest minute. w can range from 2 to 20.

The HOURw.d Format

Continuing the logic of HHMMw.d, the HOURw.d format does not print seconds *or* minutes, but rather uses minutes and seconds either to compute a decimal fraction of an hour, or (if d is missing or zero) to round to the nearest hour. w can range from 2 to 20.

The MMSSw.d Format

This format may be used to convert a time value to minutes and seconds. As time values ultimately represent time since midnight, the MMSSw.d format gives the minutes and seconds since midnight. 3:20 a.m., for example, is 200:00 in MMSS format. If d = 0, the seconds will be rounded; otherwise decimal fractions of seconds (to the hundredth) can be printed.

Datetime Formats

The DATETIMEw.d Format

This format attempts to print a datetime value as ddMMMyy:hh:mm:ss.ff, that is, the day in two digits, the three-letter month abbreviation, the year in two (or four) digits, and hours, minutes, seconds, and fractions of seconds. The formatted values correspond to those used to write datetime constants. w can range from 7 to 40, with default w = 16. d may only be specified if w ≥ 18. d may be 1 if w = 18, and 1 or 2 if w > 18.

If w is short, then a portion of the datetime will be given, and the format may be tricked into releasing only the date, or the date and hour, etc., with this method. Only the date will print if 7 ≤ w ≤ 9, as if from a date value printed with a DATE. format with the same value of w.

The TODw. Format

Because the time portion of a datetime value usually appears "on the right," there is no comparable way to trick DATETIMEw. into producing only the time portion of a datetime value. The SAS System provides the **TODw.** format for this purpose. The value of w may range from 2 to 20. TODw. produces a formatted result from a datetime value that is identical to that which would be produced from an identical time value printed with TIMEw.

USER-DEFINED FORMATS

As you can define your own SAS informats (see Chapter 7), so also can you define your own SAS formats. SAS-supplied and user-defined formats are called upon using the same PUT, FORMAT, or PUT() function syntax. Like user-defined informats, however, there are deep differences between the user-defined formats and the SAS-supplied formats. The SAS formats achieve special effects by computational algorithms, while the user-defined formats simply replace values with other values (although PICTURE formats can produce special printing effects). And the user-defined formats can group values together in radical ways by assigning the same output value to many input values; the SAS-supplied formats don't do this kind of thing.

User-defined formats, like user-defined informats, are created with the FORMAT procedure. Before we take another look at the FORMAT procedure and the VALUE and PICTURE statements it interprets to create formats according to user specifications, let's consider some of the reasons why you might want to create and use your own formats.

Uses for User-Defined Formats

Printing Special Numbers

By "special" numbers, I mean numbers that must be enhanced in some way to convey a specific meaning, as does (for example) the SAS format DOLLARw.d.

Imagine a SAS dataset of customers' accounts contains account balances for the several months prior to the current collection cycle. MONTH1 is the balance for the most recent past month, MONTH2 the next, etc. Among other things stored on the dataset is customer phone number stored as a numeric value (10-digit integer, including area code). Each month, all accounts in arrears for the two most recent months in a row must be identified so they can be watched by account managers; balance in months 3 and 4 should also be printed. Of these, accounts in arrears more than $1,000 for the most recent month must be singled out for a friendly phone call.

Problem: Produce an easy-to-use printout containing the necessary information, in a format easy for the account managers to work with: phone numbers should look like phone numbers, and balances greater than $1,000 should stand out clearly.

Solution: Creating two user formats and using one SAS-supplied format, the implementation is as follows:

```
PROC PRINT DATA=ARREARS;
  ID NAME;
  VAR PHONE MONTH1-MONTH4;
  FORMAT PHONE PHONEF. MONTH1 FLAG1K. MONTH2-MONTH4 COMMA8.2;
  TITLE 'Four-Month Account Activity';
RUN;
```

Results for five hypothetical customers are shown in Listing 11.3a. For comparison, Listing 11.3b shows the same dataset printed without the FORMAT statement.

<<< A >>>

Four-Month Account Activity

NAME	PHONE	MONTH1	MONTH2	MONTH3	MONTH4
GRANT U	(415) 929-3876	1,025.77!!!!	267.74	55.79	0.00
EINSTEIN A	(415) 682-3964	68.89	22.71	0.00	0.00
PUCCINI G	(408) 428-3990	1,190.71!!!!	398.81	0.00	0.00
DE GAULLE C	(408) 428-5253	126.33	30.09	0.00	0.00
SIMMONS R	(415) 962-1109	2,025.80!!!!	1,260.41	355.00	290.84

<<< B >>>

Four-Month Account Activity
(without formats)

NAME	PHONE	MONTH1	MONTH2	MONTH3	MONTH4
GRANT U	4159293876	1025.77	267.74	55.79	0.00
EINSTEIN A	4156823964	68.89	22.71	0.00	0.00
PUCCINI G	4084283990	1190.71	398.81	0.00	0.00
DE GAULLE C	4084285253	126.33	30.09	0.00	0.00
SIMMONS R	4159621109	2025.80	1260.41	355.00	290.84

Listing 11.3. User-defined formats for "special" numbers

Labeling Values

As we have seen before, a LABEL (or ATTRIB) statement can be used to associate a character string with a variable. After a label is assigned to a variable, it can be used by most procedures as a substitute for the variable name.

But what about the *values* of variables? Sometimes a variable's values can be as obscure as its name; and it would be good to have labels for values, too. Happily, the SAS user can define formats that provide value labels.

Imagine now a survey research datafile contains variables representing sex (variable name SEX), income level (INCLVL), and education level (EDLVL), and answers to several survey questions, of which we are presently interested in Q28, "Do you plan to vote in the next election?" Results must be tabulated by the demographic items. All the variables have obscure numeric codes for values. The codes and their meanings are shown in Table 11.1.

Problem: Produce percentage distributions of Q28 within each of these categories that anyone can use without memorizing the code table.

Solution: Create four appropriate formats, and then code:

```
PROC FREQ DATA=OUR.SURVEY;
   TABLES Q28 * (SEX INCLVL EDLVL) / NOROW NOFREQ NOPERCENT;
   FORMAT Q28 Q28F. SEX SEXFMT. INCLVL INCLVL. EDLVL EDLVL.;
   LABEL INCLVL='Income Level' EDLVL='Education Level';
   TITLE 'QUESTION 28: Plan to Vote Next Election';
   TITLE2 'INITIAL BREAKDOWN: by single demographic variables';
RUN;
```

Results are shown in Listing 11.4.

TABLE 11.1. VALUE INTERPRETATIONS FOR PROC TABULATE "SURVEY" EXAMPLE

Variable	Value	Meaning
SEX	1	Male
	2	Female
INCLVL	1	Under $20,000 family income/year
	2	$20,000–$34,999
	3	$35,000–$49,999
	4	$50,000 and over
EDLVL	1	Did not complete high school
	2	High school graduate
	3	Some college courses
	4	College graduate
Q28	1	Yes
	2	Maybe
	3	No
	4	Refused to answer

Note: See text for explanation.

Observe in this example how a format can have the same name as a variable. SAS distinguishes variable names from format identifiers because they are used with a trailing period or w.d specification. EDLVL and EDLVL. are two entirely different things as far as SAS is concerned. (In fact, if a certain format is meant to be used only for one particular variable, it's not a bad idea at all to give it the same name as the variable.)

```
             QUESTION 28: Plan to Vote Next Election
         INITIAL BREAKDOWN: by single demographic variables


                      TABLE OF Q28 BY SEX

        Q28                SEX

        Col Pct       |MALE     |FEMALE  |  Total
        -------------+--------+--------+
        YES          |  27.03 |  25.40 |
        -------------+--------+--------+
        MAYBE        |  30.27 |  21.69 |
        -------------+--------+--------+
        NO           |  26.49 |  28.04 |
        -------------+--------+--------+
        REFUSED ANS  |  16.22 |  24.87 |
        -------------+--------+--------+
        Total              185      189       374




                     TABLE OF Q28 BY INCLVL

        Q28              INCLVL(Income Level)

        Col Pct      | < 20K  |20-34.9K|35-49.9K| >=50K  |  Total
        -------------+--------+--------+--------+--------+
        YES          |  22.77 |  25.51 |  25.56 |  31.76 |
        -------------+--------+--------+--------+--------+
        MAYBE        |  25.74 |  25.51 |  25.56 |  27.06 |
        -------------+--------+--------+--------+--------+
        NO           |  29.70 |  24.49 |  27.78 |  27.06 |
        -------------+--------+--------+--------+--------+
        REFUSED ANS  |  21.78 |  24.49 |  21.11 |  14.12 |
        -------------+--------+--------+--------+--------+
        Total             101       98       90       85       374
```

Listing 11.4. User-defined formats for value labelling

Continued

```
          QUESTION 28: Plan to Vote Next Election
       INITIAL BREAKDOWN: by single demographic variables

                     TABLE OF Q28 BY EDLVL

     Q28              EDLVL(Education Level)

     Col Pct     |NO HS   |HS GRAD |SOME COL|COL GRAD|  Total
     ------------+--------+--------+--------+--------+
     YES         |  22.83 |  27.00 |  28.57 |  26.37 |
     ------------+--------+--------+--------+--------+
     MAYBE       |  26.09 |  24.00 |  29.67 |  24.18 |
     ------------+--------+--------+--------+--------+
     NO          |  30.43 |  28.00 |  25.27 |  25.27 |
     ------------+--------+--------+--------+--------+
     REFUSED ANS |  20.65 |  21.00 |  16.48 |  24.18 |
     ------------+--------+--------+--------+--------+
     Total             92      100       91       91      374
```

Listing 11.4. *Continued*

Labeling Some Numbers, Printing Others Special

It is possible to combine the "special number printing" and value-labeling actions in a single format.

Problem: Print an account arrears list (see earlier example), but this time do not reveal the amount of credits in past months; all zero or negative past balances should just be listed as PAID.

Solution: Replace the format for MONTH2-MONTH4 in the format statement given in the earlier example with another, user-defined format:

```
FORMAT PHONE PHONEF. MONTH1 FLAG1K. MONTH2-MONTH4 PAID.;
```

Otherwise, let the program remain the same. Results are shown in Listing 11.5.

```
                   Four-Month Account Activity

NAME              PHONE               MONTH1      MONTH2      MONTH3      MONTH4

GRANT U         (415) 929-3876    1,025.77!!!!    267.74       55.79    **PAID**
EINSTEIN A      (415) 682-3964        68.89        22.71    **PAID**    **PAID**
PUCCINI G       (408) 428-3990    1,190.71!!!!    398.81    **PAID**    **PAID**
DE GAULLE C     (408) 428-5253       126.33        30.09    **PAID**    **PAID**
SIMMONS R       (415) 962-1109    2,025.80!!!!  1,260.41      355.00      290.84
```

Listing 11.5. Another example of user-defined formats

Value Grouping

Grouping values together is one of the most important applications of user-defined formats. Here is but one example.

The survey research datafile used in the "Q28" example above contains another demographic variable, AGE. AGE has not been pregrouped in the data as has INCLVL, and may range from 18 on up. Clearly, it would not do to report responses by each age 18, 19, 20, etc. Rather, a display by age *groups* would be desired.

Problem: It is decided that the voters be grouped in four age groups: 18–30, 31–50, 51–65, and over 65. Implement this program.

Now, you could go to the trouble and expense of rebuilding the dataset:

```
DATA TEMP;
SET OUR.SURVEY;
IF 18<=AGE<=30 THEN AGEGP=1;
ELSE IF AGE<=50 THEN AGEGP=2;
ELSE IF AGE<=65 THEN AGEGP=3;
ELSE IF AGE>65 THEN AGEGP=4;
RUN;
```

and create a value-labeling format for AGEGP. Or, you could even make AGEGP a character variable, and code

```
IF 18<=AGE<=30 THEN AGEGP='18-30';
```

etc. This would work, but it still requires a dataset rebuild where one is not really needed.

Solution: Create a format, AGES., that labels the ranges of values which must be distinguished. Certain procedures, including FREQ, will respond to format attributes if this is requested, automatically grouping values according to their format conversions. The step

```
PROC FREQ DATA=OUR.SURVEY;
  TABLES Q28*AGE / NOROW NOFREQ NOPERCENT;
  FORMAT Q28 Q28F. AGE AGES.;
  TITLE 'QUESTION 28: Plan to Vote Next Election';
  TITLE2 'Breakdown by age group';
RUN;
```

does the job well (see Listing 11.6). Had the format not been used, a great many columns (one for each age) would have been output.

The FORMAT Procedure: Once Again

User-defined formats are created with the FORMAT procedure. As FREQ interprets TABLES requests, so the mission of PROC FORMAT is to interpret IN-VALUE, VALUE, and PICTURE statements. The INVALUE statements define

```
            QUESTION 28: Plan to Vote Next Election
                     Breakdown by age group

                     TABLE OF Q28 BY AGE

    Q28              AGE

    Col Pct     |UNDER 26|26-35   |36-50   |OVER 50 |  Total
    ------------+--------+--------+--------+--------+
    YES         |  22.77 |  25.51 |  25.56 |  31.76 |
    ------------+--------+--------+--------+--------+
    MAYBE       |  25.74 |  25.51 |  25.56 |  27.06 |
    ------------+--------+--------+--------+--------+
    NO          |  29.70 |  24.49 |  27.78 |  27.06 |
    ------------+--------+--------+--------+--------+
    REFUSED ANS |  21.78 |  24.49 |  21.11 |  14.12 |
    ------------+--------+--------+--------+--------+
    Total            101       98       90       85      374
```

Listing 11.6. User-defined formats for value grouping

informats, as explained in Chapter 7. VALUE and PICTURE statements define two kinds of user-defined format. As many INVALUE, VALUE, and/or PICTURE statements as you may desire can be coded in a single PROC FORMAT step.*

Formats created by VALUE statements associate constant character strings with specific variable values. A format may specify that the same constant character string be linked to several different values or even to a wide range of values. VALUE-created formats may be character (that is, associate with input variables of character type) or numeric.

Formats created by PICTURE statements may also associate constant character strings to values or ranges of values. But in addition, these formats can specify how numeric values will be positioned in the output field, and whether constant characters will be inserted in the numbers (similar to the COMMAw.d, DOLLARw.d, and SSNw. formats). PICTURE-created formats are for numeric variables only.

In all cases, the statement

```
PROC FORMAT [options];
```

invokes the procedure. Options on the FORMAT statement control the behavior of the procedure as a whole. One option, LIBRARY=, is used to store the format(s)/informat(s) created by the FORMAT procedure in a permant SAS catalog, for later use by other programs. LIBRARY= specifies either a libref or a two-level

---

*It is possible to write a FORMAT procedure with none of these statements; the only reasons to do so would be to work with an existing format catalog, or to create a printed description of or an output control dataset based on formats in the catalog. See our discussion of the FMTLIB and CNTLOUT = options later in this chapter.

catalog name (i.e., "libref.catalog"). If the catalog name is specified in the LIBRARY= option, formats and informats created by the FORMAT procedure will be stored in that catalog. If only a libref is specified, the default catalog name FORMATS will be used. For example,

```
PROC FORMAT LIBRARY = MYSAS.FMTS1;
```

stores the format(s) created by the step in a catalog named FMTS1, in the library referenced by MYSAS, while

```
PROC FORMAT LIBRARY = ALPHA;
```

stores the format(s) created by the step in a catalog named FORMATS, in the library referenced by ALPHA. In either case, if the catalog does not exist in the named library when the FORMAT step executes, the SAS System will create it. If LIBRARY= is not coded, then the formats or informats created by PROC FOR-MAT will be stored in a catalog named FORMATS in the WORK library.

The NOREPLACE option on the PROC FORMAT statement can be used to ensure you do not overwrite an existing format by mistake. If you do *not* specify NOREPLACE, then formats and informats created by the procedure will be placed in the format catalog even if they have the same name as entries already existing in the catalog.

Several other options can appear on the PROC FORMAT statement. These have to do with printing the descriptions of stored formats, and with the creation and use of so-called format "control" datasets. We will describe these options below, when we discuss these topics.

Defining Formats with VALUE

The VALUE statement has the form

```
VALUE [$]fmtname [(options)]
<<<value>|<range>>,...=<'label'|format>>...;
```

"Fmtname" is the name of the format: a format identifier but without its trailing period or w.d specification; on the VALUE statement, coding the name with a period or width is an error. Format names may not end in a numeral on the VALUE statement, because in use they may be followed by a "w." width specification. Avoid choosing format names that are the same as SAS-supplied format names. The dollar sign is used if the format is to be a character format, i.e., to operate on character values as input. Otherwise, SAS assumes a numeric format is being created.

After the format name, there next appear one or more groups of values or value ranges with attributive labels. Values for numeric formats are numeric constants, those for character formats are character constants (enquoted, of course). The rules for specifying values and ranges are the same for the VALUE statement as for the INVALUE statement (review Chapter 8), except that quoted and non-quoted values/ranges may not be mixed: values for numeric formats are always unquoted, those for character formats are always quoted.

Labels must be enclosed in quotes, and may not exceed 200 characters in length.* The following are valid VALUE statements:

```
VALUE PDQ 1-10='ONE THROUGH TEN';

VALUE GRADES 'A'-'D'='PASS' 'F'='FAIL';

VALUE A 1,3,5,7='ODD' 2,4,6,8='EVEN' OTHER='UNKNOWN';

VALUE $EXOLANG 'BLEEP','BLOOP','GRELP'='MARTIAN' OTHER='VENUSIAN';

VALUE $FULLSEX 'M'='MALE' 'F'='FEMALE';

VALUE GOODRNGE LOW-<0='INVALID: NEGATIVE' 10001-HIGH='OUT OF RANGE';
```

(Because more than one value was specified per label, all of these examples except $FULLSEX. group values together as well as label them.) And these are VALUE statements to create some of the formats used in our earlier examples (under "Uses for User-Defined Formats"):

```
VALUE Q28F 0='(NO ANS)' 1='YES' 2='MAYBE' 3='NO'
4='REFUSED ANS';

VALUE SEXFMT 1='MALE' 2='FEMALE';

VALUE INCLVL   1=' < 20K'
2='20-34.9K' 3='35-49.9K' 4=' >=50K';

VALUE EDLVL   1='NO HS'
2='HS GRAD' 3='SOME COL' 4='COL GRAD';

VALUE AGES 18-25='UNDER 26' 26-35='26-35' 36-50='36-50'
51-HIGH='OVER 50';
```

In lieu of a label, a format specification enclosed in square brackets can be specified. This feature can come in handy when you want to use a SAS format in most instances,† but need to use special categories for other values.

---

*Bear in mind that some procedures will use only the first 8 or the first 16 characters of a value label.

†Actually, you can name a user-defined format here, but should not take this practice to extremes as it can downgrade the performance of your program.

Problem: Print out the retirement dates for all personnel who will retire by the end of 1995; for those who are not going to retire by then, print "Ineligible".
Solution:

```
PROC FORMAT;
  VALUE RETDATE LOW-'31DEC1995'D=[MMDDYY8.] OTHER='Ineligible';
RUN;
PROC PRINT DATA=PERSONNL.DATA;
  VAR NAME RETIRE; * 'RETIRE' IS A SAS DATE VALUE;
  FORMAT RETIRE RETDATE.;
RUN;
```

This program will print all values of RETIRE less than or equal to the date 31 December 1995 in MMDDYY8. format, and print the word "Ineligible" for all other values of RETIRE.

If a variable's value is covered by the VALUE statement that created it, the substitute formatted value will be used as appropriate in procedures and in lines written with PUT. If the particular value is not covered, then the original, unformatted value will be used. In the six examples of valid VALUE statements shown above, all values are covered only for formats A and $EXOLANG, because keyword was used. In the other examples, there are values that are not covered. Any value of PDQ not 1 through 10, for example, or any value of GOODRNGE between 1 and 10000 inclusive will print "as itself," that is, unformatted. (All format labels, which are character strings, print left-aligned, but if a numeric value prints as itself, it is right-aligned in its output field as numerics usually are.)

No value may be declared to have two different labels, e.g., the following VALUE statement will cause FORMAT to fail due to overlapping values:

```
VALUE BADVAL 1-10='A' 5-20='B';
```

It is all right, however, to have the last value of one and the first value of another range be the same: i.e.,

```
VALUE OKVAL 1-10='A' 10-20='B';
```

is not an error. In these cases, SAS treats the second format as if the range operator "<−" had been used. In this example, 10 would be formatted as A, 10.00001 as B.

VALUE formats are normally not called with a width specifier, although they may be. If so, the width specifier helps govern the size of the field that will be used. This may result in a label being truncated (chopped off) on the right. Formats may be called with w.d, but since the formatted labels are of type character, places after the decimal don't count. However, decimal specifications may be applied to numeric values that print as themselves.

VALUE Statement Options

Several options can appear on the VALUE statement, in parentheses after the name of the format is declared.

MIN=, MAX=, and DEFAULT= are the width-specifying options. None of them are used very frequently in practice because the width of a format can be left to the value labels themselves, which is usually adequate. DEFAULT=, if used, states the default width the format should take if it is called without a width specifier. DEFAULT itself defaults to the length of the longest label present in the VALUE statement. MIN= specifies a minimum width for the format; if not given, this too defaults to the length of the longest label in the VALUE statement. MAX= specifies a maximum width. MAX= can go up to 200, its default.

The VALUE statement option FUZZ=, applied to numeric formats only, can be used when inexact values are expected. It specifies a "fuzz factor," to be used to force a match when a number comes close to but does not exactly fall into a range. A typical value of FUZZ= is .5. This covers many situations where fractions are expected. For example, given

```
VALUE WUZZY (FUZZ=.5) 1-10='1ST GROUP' 11-20='2ND GROUP';
```

values from 0.5 through 10.5 would print as 1ST GROUP, values from greater than 10.5, through 20.5, would be 2ND GROUP. 10.5 is not a tie because in case of overlapping fuzzed values, the first one governs, as if $<-$ had been used. Indeed, if in this example we made FUZZ=1, then the value 11 would be formatted as 1ST GROUP: De-facto overlaps caused by FUZZ= are *not* overlapping value errors as far as PROC FORMAT is concerned.

FUZZ= has a default value, 1E-12 (i.e., .000000000001), that helps deal with the fact that computers can, when computing with fractions, be off from an integer by a tiny bit. If you are sure your values will all be integers, explicit specification of FUZZ=0 when creating permanent formats will cause them to take up less storage space.

The NOTSORTED option on the VALUE statement can be used to create a format that will operate more efficiently in practice, provided the relative probability of occurrence of the various input values is more or less known. For example, suppose the answers to a series of questions will take on values of 3, 1, and 2 in that order of probability (i.e., it is expected that most answers will be 3, next 1, least 2). Then the VALUE statement

```
VALUE MYVAL (NOTSORTED) 3='THREE' 1='ONE' 2='TWO';
```

will result in a more efficient format than will either

```
VALUE MYVAL 3='THREE' 1='ONE' 2='TWO';
```

or

```
VALUE MYVAL 1='ONE' 2='TWO' 3='THREE';
```

which will be identical in performance. The reason? When NOTSORTED is coded, the format ranges are stored in the order they are coded in the VALUE statement. If NOTSORTED is *not* coded, then they are stored in ascending sort order. Thus, both the second and third VALUE statement listed above are stored in the order 1, 2, 3. In use, formats are searched sequentially until a value/range match (if any) is found for the input value being formatted. Since in our example 3 is the most frequently-expected input value, then the first VALUE statement is most efficient because much of the time only one stored value will be tested before a match is found.

Defining Formats with PICTURE

PICTURE can create numeric formats only; input values must be numeric. The PICTURE statement takes the form:

```
PICTURE fmtname [(options)]
<<<range>|<value>>,...='picture' [(pic_options)]>...;
```

Format name, ranges, and values are specified just as in the VALUE statement, and the format's options, if any, are also coded in parentheses after the format name. Unlike the VALUE (and INVALUE) statements, certain *picture options* may be placed in parentheses following any or all range/value=picture groups.

A "picture," at first glance, looks like a label on a VALUE statement: It is a quoted character string. However, a picture is designed not just to produce labels, but also to print actual values—in a special way. Numeric characters in the picture string serve as placeholders for numerals from the actual value. Use "0" to suppress leading zeroes, and "9" to include them. The statement

```
PICTURE MYPICT 1-10='00000' 11-20='99999';
```

would have value 10 printed as " 10", but 11 as "00011". (Numeric values are right-aligned in their fields whether or not leading zeroes are printed.)

Nonnumeric characters print just as they appear. The picture format

```
PICTURE MYPICT1-10='00' OTHER ='000000: NOT IN RANGE!';
```

prints the value 1 as " 1", 10 as "10", and 45632 as " 45632: NOT IN RANGE!"

A picture must begin with a numeric character. If a nonnumeric character is to fill in the blanks or to precede a number, use one of the picture options described below. To make all possible values print with the same picture format, use just one picture specification with the OTHER keyword, e.g.,

```
PICTURE ALLOFEM OTHER='000009.99';
```

If SAS finds something that looks like a decimal point with digits following it in a picture, it will assume that this *is* to be a decimal point and will treat input values accordingly: It attempts to put the fractional value to the right of the decimal point and the integer portion to the left. If more than one period is placed within numeral placeholders, the first one is considered the decimal point.

The user must allow enough places for all potential values in picture definitions; serious consequences can result if not, including truncation *on the left*. Do not come up short on the left side! If a decimal point is included, enough places to either side of the decimal are required, although to force truncation on the right you may wish to give a short field to the right of the point.

As you can see, pictures are not as easy to grasp as value labels, and therefore not as predictable. Experiment to make sure your picture formats give what you want before relying on them. Be aware of how picture formats handle decimal points. Be especially careful of left-truncation; as a safeguard, have unexpectedly large values print an error message, e.g., the format

```
PICTURE EXAMPLE 0<-<10000='00009' OTHER='INVALID!';
```

causes values not between 0 and 10,000 exclusive to be printed as "INVALID!" (This is an example of "labeling some values, printing others.") If printing fractions, the least significant digit may sometimes appear to have been rounded downward, unexpectedly (see our discussion below of the MULT= picture option).

As examples, these PICTURE statements could produce some of the formats illustrated earlier under "Uses for User-Defined Formats":

```
PICTURE PHONEF OTHER=' 000) 000-0000' (PREFIX='(');

PICTURE FLAG1K 1000<-HIGH='00,009.99!!!!' LOW-1000='00,009.99    ';

PICTURE PAID 0<-HIGH='00,009.99' 0='**PAID**';
```

The first one shows the use of a picture option (PREFIX=).

PICTURE Statement Options

Certain options can be placed on the PICTURE statement, in parentheses after the name of the format, to alter the way the format as a whole is processed.

DEFAULT=, MIN=, and MAX= concern the length of the formatted values, and have the same effect as they do in the VALUE statement. FUZZ= specifies a "fuzz factor" for matching values and ranges, and also is like the option of the same name in the VALUE statement.

The PICTURE statement can also take the ROUND option. If ROUND is specified, values affected by a multiplier will not be truncated, but rounded to the nearest integer before being formatted. (Multipliers and truncation/rounding will be explained below as we discuss the MULT= picture option.)

Picture Options

Besides the formats that may be specified for the PICTURE statement as a whole, each picture within it can be defined with certain options of its own. The possible options are FILL=, PREFIX=, MULT=, and NOEDIT.

FILL= and PREFIX= have to do with characters that may appear to the left of the printed value. Recall that the first character in a picture must be a numeral, and that either blanks or zeroes fill any unused spaces if the number of numerals in the picture is greater than the length of the value. FILL= and PREFIX= provide a limited way to specify characters to appear to the left of the value. PREFIX= specifies one or two characters to appear immediately prior to the value (a dollar sign, for example). FILL= specifies a single character to fill in the spaces to the left of the value (or of the prefix, if any) instead of blanks or spaces (use FILL= with 0s in the picture). For example, to print checks, you might want to fill the left with asterisks. The format created by

```
PICTURE CHECKS OTHER='000,000. DOLLARS 00 CTS' (FILL='*');
```

produces output values such as these:

Input	Output
298	****298. DOLLARS 00 CTS
12698	*12,698. DOLLARS 00 CTS
24.95	*****24. DOLLARS 95 CTS
28683.2965	*28,683. DOLLARS 29 CTS
0.38	****************38 CTS
14638928	638,928. DOLLARS 00 CTS

Notice what happens with the value .038. Also, observe the consequences of a picture that is too short (value 14638928): the two *most* significant digits are lopped off. Implement an error check with something like

```
PICTURE CHECKS LOW-0='NEGATIVE!'
1000000-HIGH='>>OVERFLOW!<<'
OTHER='000,000. DOLLARS 00 CTS' (FILL='*');
```

to cause 14638928 to print ">>OVERFLOW!<<" instead of a valid-looking but profoundly incorrect amount.

The MULT= option provides a way to move the decimal point of a value for purposes of printing. To understand the MULT= option, let's consider how a picture format with decimals actually works: Whenever there is a decimal point in a picture specification, a picture format first multiplies input values by $10^{**}n$, where n is the number of digits following the decimal point in the specification. Next it throws away the fractional portion, which is why downward rounding may appear to have occurred when fractional values with many digits are processed; however, if the format option ROUND is specified (see "PICTURE Statement Options," above), fractions $>= .5$ will be rounded upward. Finally, the format fits the value into the specified places, where (since the multiplier has adjusted it) it comes out arranged correctly around the picture's decimal point.

Consider the example of the CHECKS format, illustrated above. It takes the "." following 000,000 as the decimal point. It multiplies each value by 100 ($=10^{**}2$) because there are two digit places within the picture after the decimal point. Thus, it converts 298 to 29800, 24.95 to 2495, 28683.2965 to 2868329 (after discarding the new fractional portion), etc. Now when it fits these digits into their placeholders, which contain a decimal point, the result will be correct.

Returning to the MULT= option: This option lets the programmer alter the way a picture format handles powers-of-10 conversion: the MULT= specification, a number, overrides the implied multiplier. For example, you might print values with a format such as

```
PICTURE UNITS OTHER='000,000 UNITS';
```

but to print "thousands of units," you might instead code

```
PICTURE THOU OTHER='000 THOUSAND UNITS' (MULT=.001);
```

Remember that, due to the way SAS processes a picture, the printed value will be truncated to the next lower thousand, i.e., 10001 and 10999 both will print as "10 THOUSAND UNITS", unless the PICTURE statement option ROUND is coded.

The NOEDIT option can be used to label ranges of values when the desired label contains numeric characters.

Problem: Suppose in the CHECKS. example above, you wished to print >1,000,000!!! instead of >>OVERFLOW<<.

Solution: Code

```
PICTURE CHECKS LOW-0='NEGATIVE!'
1000000-HIGH='>1,000,000!!!'
(NOEDIT)
OTHER='000,000. DOLLARS 00 CTS' (FILL='*');
```

What NOEDIT does is force the format to consider a picture as a value label, i.e., not to use numerals as placeholders for value digits.

Printing Format Catalogs

PROC FORMAT can be used to print the contents of format catalogs. To do this, the FMTLIB option can be coded on the PROC statement, e.g.,

```
PROC FORMAT LIBRARY=MYFMTS FMTLIB; RUN;
```

lists the contents of the formats and informats in the catalog MYFMTS.FOR-MATS (remember that the catalog name FORMATS is assumed if it is not specified along with the libref in the LIBRARY=option). The listing is in the order the format was stored, which is usually ascending by value/range but may not be if the format was created with the NOTSORTED option.

To illustrate FMTLIB output, Listing 11.7 shows the results of running it on a catalog containing several of the formats we illustrated earlier—VALUE formats Q28 and AGES, and PICTURE formats PHONEF and PAID.

Note that only the PROC FORMAT is needed to produce a FMTLIB listing; no INVALUE, VALUE, or PICTURE statements appear when you want to get a picture of an existing format. There are, however, a couple of statements that are used with the FMTLIB option. The SELECT statement restricts catalog processing to selected members, and not all the informats and formats in the catalog, e.g.,

```
PROC FORMAT FMTLIB LIBRARY=MYLIB.ALPHA;
  SELECT BETA GAMMA;
RUN;
```

prints the contents of only the members BETA and GAMMA out of the formats catalog MYLIB.ALPHA. A special form of the SELECT statement allows you to select a group of formats based on the first character(s) of their name. To do so, you append a colon to the first character(s). For example,

```
SELECT PIE: ;
```

selects formats PIE, PIEINSKY, PIEDPIPR, and whatever other format names start with the letters PIE. You can use this construction in a list of names. To select all formats that start with A *or* X as well as format FRED, code

```
SELECT A: X: FRED;
```

The EXCLUDE statement is the opposite of SELECT: *all* formats and informats in the catalog are printed *except* those specified on the EXCLUDE statement. If neither EXCLUDE nor SELECT are specified, all the formats and informats in the catalog are printed. Do not use both an EXCLUDE and a SELECT statement in the same PROC FORMAT step. As with SELECT, you can use the colon suffix

```
---------------------------------------------------------------------------
|        FORMAT NAME: AGES     LENGTH:    8    NUMBER OF VALUES:     4     |
|   MIN LENGTH:   1  MAX LENGTH:  40  DEFAULT LENGTH   8  FUZZ: STD        |
|-------------------------------------------------------------------------|
|START            |END              |LABEL  (VER. 6.08    02JAN93:10:55:13) |
|-----------------+-----------------+-------------------------------------|
|             18|             25|UNDER 26                                   |
|             26|             35|26-35                                      |
|             36|             50|36-50                                      |
|             51|HIGH           |OVER 50                                    |
---------------------------------------------------------------------------


---------------------------------------------------------------------------
|        FORMAT NAME: PAID     LENGTH:    9    NUMBER OF VALUES:     2     |
|   MIN LENGTH:   1  MAX LENGTH:  40  DEFAULT LENGTH   9  FUZZ: STD        |
|-------------------------------------------------------------------------|
|START            |END              |LABEL  (VER. 6.08    02JAN93:10:55:13) |
|-----------------+-----------------+-------------------------------------|
|              0|              0|**PAID**         P    F   M1              |
|              0<HIGH          |00,009.99        P    F   M100             |
---------------------------------------------------------------------------


---------------------------------------------------------------------------
|       FORMAT NAME: PHONEF   LENGTH:   14    NUMBER OF VALUES:    1       |
|   MIN LENGTH:   1  MAX LENGTH:  40  DEFAULT LENGTH  14  FUZZ: STD        |
|-------------------------------------------------------------------------|
|START            |END              |LABEL  (VER. 6.08    02JAN93:10:55:13) |
|-----------------+-----------------+-------------------------------------|
|**OTHER**        |**OTHER**        | 000) 000-0000      P(  F   M1         |
---------------------------------------------------------------------------


---------------------------------------------------------------------------
|        FORMAT NAME: Q28F     LENGTH:   11    NUMBER OF VALUES:     5     |
|   MIN LENGTH:   1  MAX LENGTH:  40  DEFAULT LENGTH  11  FUZZ: STD        |
|-------------------------------------------------------------------------|
|START            |END              |LABEL  (VER. 6.08    02JAN93:10:55:13) |
|-----------------+-----------------+-------------------------------------|
|              0|              0|(NO ANS)                                   |
|              1|              1|YES                                        |
|              2|              2|MAYBE                                      |
|              3|              3|NO                                         |
|              4|              4|REFUSED ANS                                |
---------------------------------------------------------------------------
```

Listing 11.7. Sample output from FMTLIB option of PROC FORMAT

to generalize the exclusion to all formats whose names begin with a certain set of one or more characters.*

The MAXSELEN= and MAXLABELEN= labels limit the length of the start/end values and of the labels, respectively, printed by the FMTLIB (or PAGE) option. In any case, the maximum specifiable MAXSELEN= with FMTLIB (which is the default if MAXSELEN= is not specified) is 16, and the MAXLABELEN= maximum (and default) with FMTLIB is 40; i.e., FMTLIB will print only the first 40 characters of a label even if it is really lengthier. If you need to print longer values or labels, you may create an output control dataset (see below) and print it directly, e.g., with PROC PRINT.

The PAGE option is an alternative to FMTLIB. It behaves exactly as does FMTLIB, except that, if more than one format or informat is to be printed, PAGE starts each one at the top of a new page, while FMTLIB prints them one after the other without interposing forced page breaks.

Control Datasets

Much attention is given in the *SAS Procedures* manual to format control datasets, but they don't really have much practical value for most applications. However, they can help provide comprehensive format documentation and, in some circum-

---

*The current versions of the SAS manuals neglect an important feature of the selection/exclusion process: For character formats, names are to include their dollar sign. This is true even though in the directory of the format catalog the dollar sign does not appear listed in the name. (The directory will show numeric formats with entry type FORMAT, and character formats as entrytype FORMATC, but the names will not show the dollar sign. It is, in fact, perfectly permissible to have formats of the same apparent name in the same catalog [e.g., formats ABC and $ABC can happily coexist; in the catalog, there will be two entries with the name ABC, one with type FORMAT and one with type FORMATC]. User inclusion of "$" before the format name is equivalent to the catalog's notation of entrytype FORMATC.) Suppose you have a catalog containing at minimum the numeric formats JIM, JOE, JERRY, and ALICE, and the character formats $ARLENE, $ABBY, $JOIIN, and $JACK. Then

```
SELECT JO: A:;
```

will select JOE and ALICE only, *not* JOE, $JOHN, ALICE, $ARLENE, and $ABBY. Similarly,

```
EXCLUDE $A:;
```

will exclude $ARLENE and $ABBY, but not ALICE. And the FORMAT procedure will patiently explain (in a note to the SAS log) that it cannot find any format named "ARLENE" if you were to write

```
SELECT JERRY ALICE ARLENE;
```

—because you didn't write $ARLENE. To select all the formats, you would need something like

```
SELECT $J: J: $A: A:;
```

The bottom line is that you will do well always to imagine the leading dollar sign as an integral part of a character format's name.

OBS	FMTNAME	START	END	LABEL	MIN	MAX	DEFAULT
1	AGES	18	25	UNDER 26	1	40	8
2	AGES	26	35	26-35	1	40	8
3	AGES	36	50	36-50	1	40	8
4	AGES	51 HIGH		OVER 50	1	40	8
5	PAID	0	0	**PAID**	1	40	9
6	PAID	0 HIGH		00,009.99	1	40	9
7	PHONEF	**OTHER**	**OTHER**	000) 000-0000	1	40	14
8	Q28F	0	0	(NO ANS)	1	40	11
9	Q28F	1	1	YES	1	40	11
10	Q28F	2	2	MAYBE	1	40	11
11	Q28F	3	3	NO	1	40	11
12	Q28F	4	4	REFUSED ANS	1	40	11

OBS	LENGTH	FUZZ	PREFIX	MULT	FILL	NOEDIT	TYPE	SEXCL	EEXCL	HLO
1	8	1E-12		0		0	N	N	N	
2	8	1E-12		0		0	N	N	N	
3	8	1E-12		0		0	N	N	N	
4	8	1E-12		0		0	N	N	N	H
5	9	1E-12		1		0	P	N	N	
6	9	1E-12		100		0	P	Y	N	H
7	14	1E-12	(	1		0	P	N	N	O
8	11	1E-12		0		0	N	N	N	
9	11	1E-12		0		0	N	N	N	
10	11	1E-12		0		0	N	N	N	
11	11	1E-12		0		0	N	N	N	
12	11	1E-12		0		0	N	N	N	

Listing 11.8. Sample dataset from CNTLOUT option of PROC FORMAT

stances, facilitate replication of selected formats or informats in other catalogs and even the "porting" of formats from one computer system to another.

Control datasets are created by the CNTLOUT= option used on the PROC FORMAT statement to create output control datasets. For example,

```
PROC FORMAT CNTLOUT=NEWFMTS;
```

creates a SAS dataset, NEWFMTS, which contains information on the formats and informats in the catalog WORK.FORMTAS (since in this example no LIBRARY= option was specified, the default libref is WORK, and the default format catalog name is FORMATS).

The options MAXLABELEN= and MAXSELEN= options can be used with the CNTLOUT= option, as can the SELECT and EXCLUDE statements. SELECT and EXCLUDE control which informats and formats in the catalog will contribute observations to the CNTLOUT= dataset. If neither is coded, then all contribute. MAXLABELEN= and MAXSELEN= limit the length of the labels and the start/end values as they are stored in the control dataset.

Listing 11.8 shows a control dataset based on the same formats that were listed in Listing 11.7 by the FMTLIB option. You can see for yourself how the dataset is structured: there is one observation for each value or range, for each format. The variables FMTNAME is the format name, and DEFAULT, MIN, MAX, LENGTH, and FUZZ correspond to the FORMAT statement options of the same name. PREFIX, MULT, FILL, and NOEDIT can take nonblank/nonzero values for PICTURE statements only, where they equate to the picture options of the same name.

The variable LABEL is, of course, the formatted value. START and END describe the value range; observe that the same value can appear as both START and END, indicating a single value instead of a multivalue range. SEXCL and EEXCL take values yes ('Y') or no ('N') depending on if the start or end values are excluded from the range. For example, for the range "100<–200" SEXCL='Y' and EEXCL='N'.

The TYPE variable takes values N, C, P, I, J if the observation represents respectively a numeric VALUE format, a character VALUE format, a PICTURE format (always numeric), a numeric informat, or a character informat.

The HLO variable takes on values composed of the letters H, L, O, N, R, S, F, and I, which can appear in various combinations. H indicates that the end of the value range is HIGH, L that the beginning of the range is LOW, O that the range is OTHER, N that the format has no ranges, including no OTHER range (i.e., is a null format). S in the HLO value indicates this format or informat was stored NOTSORTED. R is used for picture formats only, if the ROUND option was specified. F indicates that a format was used in lieu of a label (or, in the case of a user-defined informat, that an informat was used in lieu of an invalue). I is used to indicate that an informat was defined with an unquoted numeric range.

The CNTLIN= Option

As a review of its variables will show, a control dataset such as that created by CNTLOUT= contains all the information necessary to fully describe a format or informat. Once a CNTLOUT= dataset has been created, the formats that comprise it can be automatically and exactly recreated by specifying the dataset in the CNTLIN= option of another FORMAT step. If "CDS" is a dataset created by the CNTLOUT= option of FORMAT step, then a subsequent step

```
PROC FORMAT LIBRARY=NEWLIB CNTLIN=CDS; RUN;
```

will recreate its formats and informats exactly (in the catalog NEWLIB.FORMATS). This is how control datasets can be used to replicate formats in other libraries.

A control dataset may be modified to alter its component variables before being used with CNTLIN= (perhaps you can think of some uses for this). It is also possible, and can actually be quite useful, to use a "codebook" dataset—one that contains variables representing both input values and output labels—as a CNTLIN= dataset. All that is really required is that the dataset contain variables FMTNAME, START, and LABEL; the other variables need not be present. If a codebook dataset does not quite fit the bill, you may be able to rebuild it for use with the FORMAT procedure as a CNTLIN= dataset. In Chapter 20, we will see an alternative way—using SAS Macros—to build formats from an input dataset without having first to rebuild it to conform to CNTLIN= specifications.

part III

BASE SAS PROCEDURES

12

Procedures for Describing Data

Descriptive statistics reveal the formal characteristics of value distributions: averages, quantiles, distribution shape, frequencies, and so forth. The PLOT, FREQ, and MEANS were examined earlier in this book. An additional three procedures used primarily to generate descriptive statistics—CORR, UNIVARIATE, and TABULATE—are introduced in this chapter. We don't delve into statistical theory, and assume the reader planning to use these procedures has a prior idea of what s/he is going after by way of analysis. On the other hand, only a minimal grasp of statistics is assumed of the reader trying just to understand what the procedures are generally about.

THE CORR PROCEDURE

A correlation statistic is a measure of association between two variables. Correlations are the basis for many other statistical analyses. PROC CORR reports the correlations between pairs of variables. By default, Pearson product-moment correlations are given, though other measures of correlation can be ordered by option.* We will restrict our examples to the Pearson correlation.

---

*The statistically oriented reader should consult the SAS documentation for a description of the various technical options available with CORR and with other SAS procedures.

PROC CORR begins with the PROC statement

```
PROC CORR [options];
```

where the options may specify the input dataset (DATA=), request one of the different correlation coefficients just mentioned, suppress or alter default print-outs or call for additional printed results, specify the treatment of missing values or the denominator type used to calculate variances,* or ask that an output dataset be created.

The VAR and BY statements may be used with CORR in a manner consistent with their use in other PROCs. If no VAR statement is used, the numeric variables in the input dataset are all correlated with each other. If a BY statement is used (the dataset must of course be grouped or indexed by the BY variables), the analysis is done for each group separately.

A WITH statement may be used with PROC CORR. The WITH statement, like VAR, specifies one or more variable names. If used, then it serves as a kind of second VAR statement: Each variable in the VAR statement is correlated with each variable in the WITH statement. If no WITH statement appears, variables in the VAR statement are correlated, all with each other. For example,

```
PROC CORR;
  VAR ROCK PAPER SCISSOR MATCH;
RUN;
```

produces the 16 correlations ROCK with ROCK (all 1, of course), PAPER, SCIS-SOR, MATCH, PAPER with ROCK, PAPER, SCISSOR, MATCH, and so on. If instead we wrote

```
PROC CORR;
  VAR ROCK PAPER;
  WITH SCISSOR MATCH;
RUN;
```

we would see four correlations: ROCK with SCISSOR and MATCH, and PAPER with SCISSOR and MATCH.

FREQ or WEIGHT statements may appear. Used with PROC CORR, the FREQ statement names a single variable which represents the number of times the observation is to be counted, i.e., the number of "real" observations the current record stands for. This is similar to the FREQ statement under PROC MEANS.

---

*This option, VARDEF=, is also available with PROCs MEANS, UNIVARIATE, and TABULATE. By default, the degrees of freedom N=1 is used as the denominator for obtaining variance estimates. VARDEF=N tells SAS to use uncorrected N, VARDEF=WEIGHT specifies the sum of weights to be used, VARDEF=WDF the corrected sum of weights minus 1.

The WEIGHT statement under PROC CORR is used to compute weighted product-moment correlations, and should not be used if correlations other than the Pearson type are requested.

Printed output from PROC CORR includes, by default, the correlation coefficients and their p-values (a measure of statistical significance). The correlations are normally printed in a rectangular array, the VAR variables across and the WITH variables down, with two values (the correlation and the p-value) at each juncture. The N, mean, standard deviation, and median, minumum, and maximum of the variables are also printed by default; therefore it is sometimes wasteful to run PROC MEANS if PROC CORR is also planned. An example of printed output from PROC CORR is shown in Listing 12.1.

Output Datasets

Output datasets may be requested with an option on the PROC CORR statement. OUT= (or OUTP=) asks for an output dataset with Pearson product-moment

Correlation Analysis

4 'VAR' Variables: FACTOR1 FACTOR2 FACTOR3 CRITERON

Simple Statistics

Variable	N	Mean	Std Dev	Sum	Minimum	Maximum
FACTOR1	63012	1.5018	0.5000	94632	1.0000	2.0000
FACTOR2	63012	3.0032	1.4133	189240	1.0000	5.0000
FACTOR3	63012	2.4921	1.1128	157032	1.0000	4.0000
CRITERON	63012	3.2950	1.1897	207624	1.0000	5.0000

Pearson Correlation Coefficients / Prob > |R| under Ho: Rho=0 / N = 63012

	FACTOR1	FACTOR2	FACTOR3	CRITERON
FACTOR1	1.00000	-0.00607	0.00251	-0.00074
	0.0	0.1275	0.5291	0.8532
FACTOR2	-0.00607	1.00000	0.01630	0.84039
	0.1275	0.0	0.0001	0.0001
FACTOR3	0.00251	0.01630	1.00000	0.19804
	0.5291	0.0001	0.0	0.0001
CRITERON	-0.00074	0.84039	0.19804	1.00000
	0.8532	0.0001	0.0001	0.0

Listing 12.1. Sample output from PROC CORR

OBS	_TYPE_	_NAME_	FACTOR1	FACTOR2	FACTOR3	CRITERON
1	MEAN		1.50181	3.00324	2.49210	3.29499
2	STD		0.50000	1.41335	1.11281	1.18970
3	N		63012.00000	63012.00000	63012.00000	63012.00000
4	CORR	FACTOR1	1.00000	-0.00607	0.00251	-0.00074
5	CORR	FACTOR2	-0.00607	1.00000	0.01630	0.84039
6	CORR	FACTOR3	0.00251	0.01630	1.00000	0.19804
7	CORR	CRITERON	-0.00074	0.84039	0.19804	1.00000

Listing 12.2. An output dataset produced by PROC CORR

correlations; other correlation measures can be requested with other options. If only the output dataset is desired, the usual printed output can be suppressed with the NOPRINT option on the PROC statement. For example,

```
PROC CORR DATA=MYDATA NOPRINT OUT=CORROUT;
```

creates the dataset CORROUT, but not the usual printed output.

The output dataset produced by PROC CORR is a so-called TYPE=CORR dataset.* A TYPE=CORR dataset created by PROC CORR contains the variables named in the BY statement, if any, followed by two character variables _TYPE_ and _NAME_, followed by variables named in the VAR statement. The observations are identified by the _TYPE_ and _NAME_ variables, and the values of the BY variables if any. For each combination of BY variable values (if any), or else once, there is created one observation of _TYPE_='MEAN', one 'STD', and one 'N'; the value of the statistic identified by the variable _TYPE_ for each VAR variable appears as the value of that variable. Next come one or more correlation observations, _TYPE_='CORR'. In these observations, the correlations appear as the values of the VAR variables. Each observation represents one WITH variable (if WITH is used, otherwise each VAR variable), which is identified by the variable _NAME_. _NAME_ is left blank with _TYPE_= MEAN, STD, or N observations. Listing 12.2 gives an example of a PROC CORR output dataset (printed with PROC PRINT and based on the same dataset from which the CORR output of Listing 12.1 was generated).

THE UNIVARIATE PROCEDURE

As its name implies, PROC UNIVARIATE is used to produce univariate, or one-variable, descriptive statistics. PROC MEANS and several other procedures

---

*This is one of several "special" SAS datasets which may be used by certain statistical procedures. They are SAS datasets containing variables and observations, and could in principle be created with a DATA step. What distinguishes TYPE=CORR or other "special" statistical datasets is the particular arrangement of the data. Procedures that normally calculate correlations before doing something else (e.g., regression analysis PROCs) may skip this step if an appropriate TYPE=CORR dataset already exists.

produce univariate statistics, of course, but PROC UNIVARIATE offers some additional descriptive statistics, and a few data displays besides.*

The PROC UNIVARIATE statement can take options that specify the input SAS dataset (DATA=), suppress or alter default printout or call for additional printed results, specify the denominator type used to calculate variances, or ask that the hypothesis that the data come from a normal distribution be tested. An output dataset may be requested, but this is done with an OUTPUT statement and not on the PROC statement.

VAR, BY, and FREQ statements may be used with PROC UNIVARIATE, and their effect is the same as when used in some other procedures, including MEANS and CORR. A WEIGHT statement in PROC UNIVARIATE can be used to identify a variable that will be used to calculate weighted means and variances.

Using the same dataset used for the PROC CORR example above, and selecting (with a VAR statement) the variable CRITERON, default output from PROC UNIVARIATE is shown in Listing 12.3. The listing reveals that univariate produces a great variety of information about a variable's distribution, and that UNIVARIATE is the procedure of choice when descriptive quantiles (percentage cutoffs) are desired. Giving as it does the five highest and five lowest values, UNIVARIATE is also good for detection of suspicious extreme values, called outliers, at the high or low end of the distribution. As UNIVARIATE also can produce many of the statistics given by PROC MEANS, one usually need not run MEANS when UNIVARIATE is planned.

Output Datasets

Output datasets produced by PROC UNIVARIATE resemble those of PROC MEANS, and are created in the same way. An OUTPUT statement of the form

```
OUTPUT [OUT=dataset] <statistic=name>...;
```

provides variable names to contain the statistic(s) desired. Any of the statistics normally printed by PROC UNIVARIATE can be requested. The dataset will have one observation per unique BY group (if no BY statement, a single observation), containing the BY variables (if any) and the variables named on the OUTPUT statement, whose values are the statistics. (Review PROC MEANS, Chapter 5.)

More than one output dataset may be created by coding more than one OUTPUT statement. Each OUTPUT statement should specify a different dataset name, of course, but the statistics selected can overlap if desired.

The ID Statement

An ID statement,

```
ID variables;
```

---

*The displays that UNIVARIATE can produce are illustrated in your *SAS Procedures* manual. They include stem/leaf diagrams, box plots, and normal probability plots.

Univariate Procedure

Variable=CRITERON

Moments

N	63012	Sum Wgts	63012
Mean	3.294991	Sum	207624
Std Dev	1.189699	Variance	1.415383
Skewness	-0.04987	Kurtosis	-1.07309
USS	773304	CSS	89184.7
CV	36.10628	Std Mean	0.004739
T:Mean=0	695.2307	Pr>|T|	0.0001
Num ^= 0	63012	Num > 0	63012
M(Sign)	31506	Pr>=|M|	0.0001
Sgn Rank	9.9264E8	Pr>=|S|	0.0001

Quantiles(Def=5)

100% Max	5	99%	5
75% Q3	4	95%	5
50% Med	3	90%	5
25% Q1	2	10%	2
0% Min	1	5%	1
		1%	1
Range	4		
Q3-Q1	2		
Mode	2		

Extremes

Lowest	Obs	Highest	Obs
1(	32988)	5(	63008)
1(	32987)	5(	63009)
1(	32986)	5(	63010)
1(	32985)	5(	63011)
1(	32984)	5(	63012)

Listing 12.3. Sample output from PROC UNIVARIATE

may appear with the statements following PROC UNIVARIATE. If it does, the variables it names will appear in the output dataset(s). The value for the ID variable in the OUTPUT dataset will be that of the first observation in the BY group (or in the dataset, if no BY statement appears).

The ID statement with PROC UNIVARIATE also plays a limited role in annotating printed output. The first eight characters of the ID variable are used to identify the observations containing the five highest and five lowest values. This is helpful if you wish to use these values not for the detection of outliers, but as a quick indication of highest and lowest rankings among a group.

THE TABULATE PROCEDURE

The TABULATE procedure provides ways to summarize and display descriptive information in hierarchical tables. The ways TABULATE can group, arrange, and print tabular data are many, and the ways a user can get confused with TABULATE are many, too. For both these reasons, SAS Institute recently published a monograph devoted exclusively to PROC TABULATE* that you should study if you want to get deeply involved with what the procedure has to offer the expert user. Here, we introduce the features of the procedure as applied to its simpler applications.

Like PROC MEANS, PROC TABULATE can produce several different summary statistics describing the variables in a SAS dataset. TABULATE's specialty is producing a unique style of printed output, a kind of hierarchical crosstabulation. It is so good at this that valuable applications for the procedure can be created even if another PROC or DATA step is used to calculate the quantities and only the tabular-arrangement features of TABULATE are exploited.

TABULATE is an excellent tool for categorical display, and should be considered as an alternative to FREQ when planning a descriptive analysis of discrete (categorical, noncontinuous) variables, for while FREQ displays at most two variables' "crossings" per table, TABULATE can display many. The statistics available with TABULATE also make it a good candidate when one or more continuous variables is to be analyzed within the crossings of two or more categorical variables.

Examples: Categorical Analysis

Let's jump right into some TABULATE examples and return later to a more formal look at the procedure's statements and options. To show variations on the TABULATE theme, we'll use a dataset containing medical information on elderly patients in four study groups from a fictional study of high blood pressure. The variables included are STDYGP, SEX, RACE, BMASSGP (body mass group), BPSYST (systolic blood pressure), and BPDIAST (diastolic).

Before getting into the blood pressure analyses themselves, suppose we wish to describe the sample with reference to group membership: how many underweight white females and so forth. Now, PROC FREQ could always be used for a complete breakdown, with a statement such as

---

*SAS Guide to the Tabulate Procedure; this and other SAS System documentation are described in Chapter 22.

```
TABLES RACE*BMASSGP*SEX*STDYGP;
```

However, it would be very cumbersome indeed to review these tables once they have been generated, for FREQ can display only two variables per table. One-way frequencies are not so bad to look at (see Listing 12.4), but do not provide crosstabulations. To be sure, you could choose any two of the four variables per page (indeed, FREQ does this automatically when more than two variables are crossed in a TABLES specification), but you would still be confronted with many pages of output to digest. For example, choosing tables of STDYGP and SEX as in the TABLES statement above results in 4 (RACE) * 3 (BMASSGP) = 12 separate printed tables. The least we could get away with would be six tables to fully "see" the four variables in some fashion.

So, let's instead use PROC TABULATE, as shown in Listing 12.5. Disregard the "F=" and RTS option for now. Just observe how all four variables manage to show up in one table. (Note that N is the number in the category, corresponding to a frequency count for the category.)

What about the marginals? We can change only the TABLES statement, using the special name ALL, to produce the results shown in Listing 12.6. Note that this goes well beyond the powers of FREQ: the ALLs with FREQ would not get each and every possible marginal, but only two at a time. You'd need additional TABLES statements—resulting in even more two-way FREQ tables—to get the "higher" marginal totals.

Simpler Breakdowns

As can be seen in the listings, the ability to display everything on one page goes only so far—so far as the page dimensions! TABULATE simply continues on the next page when it runs out of length or width, just as most SAS procedures do.

For this or other reasons, the user may wish *not* to try to print everything in one table. TABULATE provides that choice: You can go to several tables, as with FREQ. But more control is available over just how the tables will be constituted.

Problem: Produce five tables, one for each study group and one for ALL study groups; also change the layout to have RACE along the rows instead of the columns.

Solution: The new TABLES statements and results appear in Listing 12.7. (To conserve space, only two of the five tables are shown.)

What if you don't want the "cells," just ALL? Leave the CLASS variable out of the TABLES statement. Or, don't even code it on the CLASS statement (unless another TABLES statement is to use it). If a variable is not named on TABLES, that variable will simply be ignored for purposes of subgrouping, just as FREQ would subgroup only those variables named on its TABLES statement.

Example: Summary Analysis

Problem: Examine the continuous variables BPSYST and BPDIAST in the context of the categorical breakdowns, showing means and standard deviations.

```
<<< PROGRAM SOURCE CODE FOLLOWS >>>

TITLE '"Blood Pressure in the Elderly" study';
PROC FORMAT;
  VALUE BFMT 1='Bottom Q' 2='Mid 2 Q' 3='Top Q';
  VALUE RFMT 3='Hispanic' 2='Black' 1='White' 9='other';
  VALUE SFMT 0='Female' 1='Male';
RUN;
PROC FREQ DATA=MEDDATA.BPSTUDY;
  TABLES BMASSGP SEX RACE STDYGP;
  FORMAT SEX SFMT. RACE RFMT. BMASSGP BFMT.;
  TITLE2 'One-Way Frequencies: Sample Demographics';
RUN;


    <<< SAS JOB OUTPUT FOLLOWS >>>

      "Blood Pressure in the Elderly" study
      One-Way Frequencies: Sample Demographics
```

BMASSGP	Frequency	Percent	Cumulative Frequency	Cumulative Percent
Bottom Q	364	24.3	364	24.3
Mid 2 Q	724	48.3	1088	72.5
Top Q	412	27.5	1500	100.0

SEX	Frequency	Percent	Cumulative Frequency	Cumulative Percent
Female	729	48.6	729	48.6
Male	771	51.4	1500	100.0

RACE	Frequency	Percent	Cumulative Frequency	Cumulative Percent
White	684	45.6	684	45.6
Black	681	45.4	1365	91.0
Hispanic	107	7.1	1472	98.1
other	28	1.9	1500	100.0

STDYGP	Frequency	Percent	Cumulative Frequency	Cumulative Percent
1	361	24.1	361	24.1
2	429	28.6	790	52.7
3	360	24.0	1150	76.7
4	350	23.3	1500	100.0

Listing 12.4. One-way frequencies of TABULATE example data

```
        <<< PROGRAM SOURCE CODE FOLLOWS >>>

PROC TABULATE DATA=MEDDATA.BPSTUDY;
  CLASS SEX STDYGP RACE BMASSGP;
  TABLES SEX*STDYGP, RACE*BMASSGP*F=4.0 /RTS=15;
  FORMAT SEX SFMT. RACE RFMT. BMASSGP BFMT.;
  LABEL BMASSGP='Body Mass group';
  TITLE2 'Cross-Tabulation of Sample Demographics';
RUN;


        <<< SAS JOB OUTPUT FOLLOWS >>>
```

"Blood Pressure in the Elderly" study
Cross-Tabulation of Sample Demographics

		RACE										
		White			Black			Hispanic			other		
		Body Mass group			Body Mass group			Body Mass group			Body Mass group		
		Bot-tom Q	Mid 2 Q	Top Q	Bot-tom Q	Mid 2 Q	Top Q	Bot-tom Q	Mid 2 Q	Top Q	Bot-tom Q	Mid 2 Q	Top Q
		N	N	N	N	N	N	N	N	N	N	N	N
SEX	STDYGP												
Female	1	20	43	19	18	40	18	3	8	1	2	2	1
	2	24	40	23	23	46	30	3	7	2	.	2	1
	3	17	40	24	21	38	33	4	9	5	.	.	.
	4	22	37	18	19	33	16	3	6	6	1	.	1
Male	1	20	37	17	20	44	32	1	10	1	2	2	.
	2	27	57	26	25	45	26	2	7	8	2	1	2
	3	18	41	22	15	30	22	3	8	6	2	1	1
	4	22	39	31	22	46	19	1	2	1	2	3	.

Listing 12.5. PROC TABULATE illustrated

```
<<< New TABLES statement, rest of source code same as Listing 12-5 >>>

TABLES (SEX ALL)*(STDYGP ALL), (RACE ALL)*(BMASSGP ALL)*F=4.0 /RTS=15;

<<< SAS JOB OUTPUT FOLLOWS >>>
```

"Blood Pressure in the Elderly" study
Cross-Tabulation of Sample Demographics

		RACE											
		White				Black				Hispanic			
		Body Mass				Body Mass				Body Mass			
		Bot-tom Q	Mid 2 Q	Top Q	ALL	Bot-tom Q	Mid 2 Q	Top Q	ALL	Bot-tom Q	Mid 2 Q	Top Q	ALL
		N	N	N	N	N	N	N	N	N	N	N	N
SEX	STDYGP												
Female	1	20	43	19	82	18	40	18	76	3	8	1	12
	2	24	40	23	87	23	46	30	99	3	7	2	12
	3	17	40	24	81	21	38	33	92	4	9	5	18
	4	22	37	18	77	19	33	16	68	3	6	6	15
	ALL	83	160	84	327	81	157	97	335	13	30	14	57
Male	STDYGP												
	1	20	37	17	74	20	44	32	96	1	10	1	12
	2	27	57	26	110	25	45	26	96	2	7	8	17
	3	18	41	22	81	15	30	22	67	3	8	6	17
	4	22	39	31	92	22	46	19	87	1	2	1	4
	ALL	87	174	96	357	82	165	99	346	7	27	16	50
ALL	STDYGP												
	1	40	80	36	156	38	84	50	172	4	18	2	24
	2	51	97	49	197	48	91	56	195	5	14	10	29
	3	35	81	46	162	36	68	55	159	7	17	11	35
	4	44	76	49	169	41	79	35	155	4	8	7	19

Listing 12.6. PROC TABULATE output with marginal frequencies

Continued

```
|    +------+----+----+----+----+----+----+----+----+----+----+----|
|    |ALL   | 170| 334| 180| 684| 163| 322| 196| 681|  20|  57|  30| 107|
-----------------------------------------------------------------------
```

"Blood Pressure in the Elderly" study
Cross-Tabulation of Sample Demographics

		RACE										
		other				ALL						
		Body Mass					Body Mass				
		Bot-tom Q	Mid 2 Q	Top Q	ALL		Bot-tom Q	Mid 2 Q	Top Q	ALL
		N	N	N	N		N	N	N	N
SEX	STDYGP									
Female	1	2	2	1	5		43	93	39	175
	2	.	2	1	3		50	95	56	201
	3	.	.	.	.		42	87	62	191
	4	1	.	1	2		45	76	41	162
	ALL	3	4	3	10		180	351	198	729
Male	STDYGP									
	1	2	2	.	4		43	93	50	186
	2	2	1	2	5		56	110	62	228
	3	2	1	1	4		38	80	51	169
	4	2	3	.	5		47	90	51	188
	ALL	8	7	3	18		184	373	214	771
ALL	STDYGP									
	1	4	4	1	9		86	186	89	361
	2	2	3	3	8		106	205	118	429
	3	2	1	1	4		80	167	113	360
	4	3	3	1	7		92	166	92	350
	ALL	11	11	6	28		364	724	412	1500

Listing 12.6. *Continued*

```
<<< New TABLES statement, rest of source code same as Listing 12-5 >>>

TABLES STDYGP ALL, (RACE ALL)*(SEX ALL), (BMASSGP ALL)*F=4.0 /RTS=15;

<<< SAS JOB OUTPUT FOLLOWS >>>
```

"Blood Pressure in the Elderly" study
Cross-Tabulation of Sample Demographics

STDYGP 1

```
-----------------------------------
|             | Body Mass   |     |
|             |-------------|     |
|             |Bot-|    |    |     |
|             |tom |Mid |Top |     |
|             | Q  |2 Q | Q  |ALL  |
|             |----+----+----+---- |
|             | N  | N  | N  | N   |
|-------------+----+----+----+-----|
|RACE  |SEX   |    |    |    |     |
|------+------|    |    |    |     |
|White |Female|  20|  43|  19|  82 |
|      |------+----+----+----+---- |
|      |Male  |  20|  37|  17|  74 |
|      |------+----+----+----+---- |
|      |ALL   |  40|  80|  36| 156 |
|------+------+----+----+----+-----|
|Black |SEX   |    |    |    |     |
|      |------|    |    |    |     |
|      |Female|  18|  40|  18|  76 |
|      |------+----+----+----+---- |
|      |Male  |  20|  44|  32|  96 |
|      |------+----+----+----+---- |
|      |ALL   |  38|  84|  50| 172 |
|------+------+----+----+----+-----|
|Hispa-|SEX   |    |    |    |     |
|nic   |------|    |    |    |     |
|      |Female|   3|   8|   1|  12 |
|      |------+----+----+----+---- |
|      |Male  |   1|  10|   1|  12 |
|      |------+----+----+----+---- |
|      |ALL   |   4|  18|   2|  24 |
|------+------+----+----+----+-----|
|other |SEX   |    |    |    |     |
|      |------|    |    |    |     |
|      |Female|   2|   2|   1|   5 |
|      |------+----+----+----+---- |
|      |Male  |   2|   2|   .|   4 |
|      |------+----+----+----+---- |
|      |ALL   |   4|   4|   1|   9 |
|------+------+----+----+----+-----|
|ALL   |SEX   |    |    |    |     |
|      |------|    |    |    |     |
|      |Female|  43|  93|  39| 175 |
|      |------|----+----+----+---- |
```

Listing 12.7. PROC TABULATE, "distributed" output

Continued

```
       |        |Male  |  43|  93|  50| 186|
       |        |------+----+----+----+----|
       |        |ALL   |  86| 186|  89| 361|
       -------------------------------------
```

<<< To save space, three pages (STDYGP 2,3,4) deleted here, last page follows >>>

"Blood Pressure in the Elderly" study
Cross-Tabulation of Sample Demographics

ALL

		Body Mass		
		Bot-tom Q	Mid 2 Q	Top Q	ALL
		N	N	N	N
RACE	SEX				
White	Female	83	160	84	327
	Male	87	174	96	357
	ALL	170	334	180	684
Black	SEX				
	Female	81	157	97	335
	Male	82	165	99	346
	ALL	163	322	196	681
Hispa-nic	SEX				
	Female	13	30	14	57
	Male	7	27	16	50
	ALL	20	57	30	107
other	SEX				
	Female	3	4	3	10
	Male	8	7	3	18
	ALL	11	11	6	28
ALL	SEX				
	Female	180	351	198	729
	Male	184	373	214	771
	ALL	364	724	412	1500

Listing 12.7. *Continued*

Solution: TABULATE can do this, using a VAR statement to specify the continuous variables. You could squeeze everything into one table, but it would take many pages. Better to turn this into several simpler tables in some fashion. For example, to get nine tables, group 1 females, group 1 males, etc., and the grand means, use two TABLES statements, as in Listing 12.8. (To save space, only the "group 1 females" and the grand means tables are shown in the listing.)

The TABLES Statement

Now that we've seen some examples of TABULATE code results, let's examine its mechanisms more closely. We'll begin with the TABLES (equivalently, TABLE) statement, the most important component of a TABULATE step.

General Syntax of the TABLES Statement

The TABLES statement under PROC TABULATE has a syntax unique in the SAS language, with special operators and elements to help the user communicate with the procedure. Elements of the TABLES statement include variable names, statistic= keywords, the ALL keyword, special operators, the F= keyword with format specifiers, and denominator specifiers, which together constitute what is called a *table specification*. The operators in a table specification include the comma, the asterisk, and the blank, which are used to indicate the table layout; the parentheses, for grouping variables separated by asterisks or blanks; and the angle brackets, which are used to set off denominator specifiers. TABLES also may include certain options, placed after a slash after the table specification. Refer to the examples presented in the listings above as we continue our discussion.

A table specification consists of one, two, or three *table expressions* separated by commas; there are thus zero, one, or two commas within a table specification. Within each table expression the other operators and keywords are used to construct a table *dimension*. Asterisks and blanks have a function similar to their role in the TABLES statement with PROC FREQ: An asterisk indicates a crossing, and a blank indicates a concatenation. Parentheses are used to group subexpressions containing these operators distributively, e.g., (A B) * C becomes A*C B*C. This is also like PROC FREQ.

But unlike FREQ, each crossing does not define a separate table, only a separate column or row structure within a *single table*; in the examples shown above, the expression "SEX*AGEGP" affected one table dimension. It is the comma operator that determines the table dimension boundary. With one comma, there are two dimensions; the expression to the left defines columns, the expression to the right defines rows. If two commas separate three expressions, then the first expression defines pages (in effect, separate tables), the second one columns, and the third one rows. If there is but a single table expression with no commas, only a single column table is built.

```
<<< PROGRAM SOURCE CODE FOLLOWS >>>


PROC TABULATE DATA=MEDDATA.BPSTUDY;
  CLASS SEX STDYGP RACE BMASSGP;
  VAR BPSYST BPDIAST;
  TABLES SEX*STDYGP, RACE*BMASSGP,
     N*F=4.0 (BPSYST BPDIAST)*(MEAN STD)*F=6.2 /RTS=15;
  TABLES BPSYST BPDIAST, N*F=4.0 (MEAN STD) *F=6.2/RTS=15;
  FORMAT SEX SFMT. RACE RFMT. BMASSGP BFMT.;
  LABEL BMASSGP='Body Mass';
  TITLE2 'Blood Pressure Averages within Sex and Study Group';
RUN;


<<< SAS JOB OUTPUT FOLLOWS >>>
```

"Blood Pressure in the Elderly" study
Blood Pressure Averages within Sex and Study Group

SEX Female
AND STDYGP 1

			BPSYST		BPDIAST	
		N	MEAN	STD	MEAN	STD
RACE	Body Mass					
White	Bottom Q	20	139.05	5.09	85.75	2.47
	Mid 2 Q	43	139.98	4.92	85.74	2.29
	Top Q	19	138.21	5.45	86.42	2.36
Black	Bottom Q	18	137.28	5.04	85.22	1.80
	Mid 2 Q	40	139.78	4.69	85.55	2.39
	Top Q	18	139.44	4.09	86.33	2.70
Hispanic	Bottom Q	3	140.67	4.16	86.67	0.58
	Mid 2 Q	8	138.38	5.10	84.75	2.96
	Top Q	1	132.00	.	85.00	.
other	Bottom Q	2	143.50	3.54	85.50	2.12
	Mid 2 Q	2	133.00	2.83	82.50	0.71
	Top Q	1	141.00	.	90.00	.

```
<<< (To save space, 7 tables (Female/groups 2-4, Male/groups 1-4) omitted here) >>>
<<< (Remaining below is the printout produced by the second TABLES statement  ) >>>
```

"Blood Pressure in the Elderly" study
Blood Pressure Averages within Sex and Study Group

	N	MEAN	STD
BPSYST	1500	138.73	4.69
BPDIAST	1500	85.76	2.48

Listing 12.8. PROC TABULATE with continuous variables

Statistic Keywords

In the example of summary analysis given above, the keywords MEAN and STD were used to obtain sample means and standard deviations. One of the confusing features of the TABLES statement is that statistic keywords are entered with a syntax similar to variables: They are crossed with variable names using an asterisk.

When VAR (analysis) variables are to be printed, the default is SUM; since we wanted other statistics, they had to be specified explicitly. (Should we have wanted SUM as well, it would have to be explicitly coded along with the other statistic names.) By default, when only CLASS (categorical) variables are to be printed, the statistic N is assumed; therefore, in the earlier examples no statistic was written. (Indeed, if any statistic except N [or PCTN] had been coded, there would have been generated a compiler error: The only valid statistic for CLASS variables is N.)

Format Specifications

Left to its own devices, PROC TABULATE will generally print all cell values with a default 12.2 format. With small or integral values, such as in our examples, this can result in a lot of blank space, and may cause a table to extend over more pages than is necessary. If a smaller format width suffices, the procedure will conserve space accordingly. Also, it is sometimes desirable to have the output formatted with a special format, perhaps a user-created format.

For this reason, TABULATE provides the ability to specify cell value formats. This may be done right on the TABLES statement with the F= keyword (which may alternatively be coded as FORMAT=), which gives a format specification. So another of the potentially confusing features of the TABLES statement is that format specifications, like statistic keywords, are coded by crossing with variables or statistics, as shown in the examples above.

The ALL Keyword

As seen in the examples, ALL provides a way to get marginal totals. When ALL is concatenated with a CLASS variable, each level (or each formatted level; see the FORMAT statement, below) of the CLASS variable is reported, followed by a report of the total (marginal) statistic across levels of the CLASS variable (when the statistic is N or SUM, the total is in fact a genuine total). ALL can appear before the variable, in which case the ALL column or row will come before the single levels. As seen in the examples, one variable's ALL can be crossed with another's when parentheses are used for grouping. This results in a "higher" level of summary.

Denominator Specifiers and PCTN/PCTSUM

TABULATE can print percentages of N's (frequencies) or SUMs. Constructing percentage denominators can be *very* confusing, but if you understand how the ALL keyword works, you can understand denominators.

A denominator specification consists of one or more of the variables in the TABLES statement (if more than one, they should be crossed with asterisks). All the variables can be CLASS variables, but a single analysis variable may be crossed with one or more CLASS variables. The denominator crossing is set off by angle brackets,* and preceded by PCTN (or PCTSUM, if that is appropriate), which term is then crossed with whatever else is in the table expression. In effect, what the denominator specification does is to replace the variables with their ALL for the purpose of creating a denominator for the percentage. The denominator is the group total (that which is "100%") on which the percentage is based.

Every crossing that exists in the TABLES statement must somehow be represented among the denominator specifications, or the compiler will be faced with an ambiguity. You can usually concatenate ALL after the denominator crossing to satisfy this requirement.

Options on the TABLES Statement

Certain options may be specified on the TABLES statement, after a slash following the table specification. The RTS= option, illustrated in our listings, helps conserve paper by shortening the space used for row labels, which by default would take one quarter the system linesize; take care that enough space remains to print row labels completely. The BOX= option is useful for tables with a page dimension; it can place text within the usually empty box at the upper left. BOX=_PAGE_ shows the page dimension in the box, if it fits, rather than on top of the table. Whether or not there is a page dimension, BOX=varname or BOX='text' places a variable name or a literal string within the box; if the string doesn't fit, it will be truncated. ROW= specifies whether all title elements in a row crossing are given space even if they are blank. ROW=FLOAT says no, don't leave blank space, while ROW=CONST (the default) leaves it blank.

For the cells, the FUZZ= option allows trivial values to be excluded: Values less than the fuzz value, which should be a numeric literal, are taken to be zero for computation and for printing. MISSTEXT='text' gives up to 20 characters of text to print when cell values are missing. Of course, a MISSTEXT value should not be longer than the format width.

The CONDENSE option asks that multiple pages of a TABLES that has three dimensions be printed on a single physical page, if there is enough room to do so. Without CONDENSE, each page is printed on a separate sheet, even if there are only a few rows.

The PROC TABULATE Statement

The PROC statement takes some optional keywords. DATA=, of course, specifies the input dataset. MISSING requests missing values to be considered valid levels

---

*This is the only use for angle brackets in SAS programming, apart from their service as comparison operators. In this book, of course, we have used angle brackets to group syntactic elements in generalized statement descriptions.

for analysis. As with certain other procedures, if the user does *not* code MISSING, then if an observation is missing *any* of the CLASS variables, it is excluded entirely from the analysis. The ORDER= option is similar to that of PROC FREQ (see Chapter 5).

The FORMCHAR= option changes the characters used to print the borders of the cells. This option, also available with PROCs FREQ and PLOT (though not discussed in Chapter 5) and with other procedures including CHART, can help you make prettier displays, or accommodate nonstandard printers. Consult your SAS manuals for details. Some tables look quite good with no borders at all, just the numbers in neat rows and columns, and you can use a blank FORMCHAR= for this. If FORMCHAR= is not used, then the default FORMCHAR= system option (see Chapter 21) controls the characters used to print cell borders.

The FORMAT= option on the PROC statement defines a default format for cell values. It replaces the system default of 12.2, but may itself be overridden if F= (or FORMAT=) is coded on a TABLES statement.

The CLASS and VAR Statements

Little need be said here, for all was implied above. CLASS defines discrete (categorical) variables. VAR defines continuous or "analysis" variables. All variables appearing in a TABLES statement must have been defined in either a CLASS or a VAR statement.

The FORMAT Statement

A FORMAT statement may be used to help group the CLASS variables into levels of the user's choosing. Normally, it will refer to a user-defined format. Distinguish the FORMAT statement from the FORMAT= option of the PROC or TABLES statement; the FORMAT= option prescribes a numeric format for the display of variable values within cells, while the FORMAT statement in PROC TABULATE should only be used for the purpose of partitioning CLASS variables into value groups.

The LABEL and KEYLABEL Statements

The LABEL statement can be used to define labels for rows or columns, replacing variable names. KEYLABEL is used for the special purpose of replacing a statistic name, e.g.,

```
KEYLABEL MEAN='AVERAGE' N='COUNT';
```

has columns in tables that show means labeled AVERAGE instead, and columns showing N's labeled COUNT instead.

More precise labeling control can be had by the technique of stating a label on the TABLES statement itself. This is done by following either a variable name or a statistic keyword with an equal sign and label text in single quotes, e.g.,

```
TABLES AGEGP*SEX,BMASSGP='BODY MASS' *
    (BPSYST='SYSTOLIC' BYDIAST='DIASTOLIC');
```

would get the same results as

```
TABLES AGEGP*SEX,BMASSGP*(BPSYST BYDIAST);
```

but column names would be different on the output. Labels on the TABLES statement override defaults that may be specified in a KEYLABEL statement.

Other Statements

A BY statement may be used with PROC TABULATE, although there is usually no reason for this given the way TABULATE creates classes. FREQ and WEIGHT statements can be used, and have the effect they do with PROC MEANS.

Challenges of PROC TABULATE

Using PROC TABULATE often requires much testing as well as planning. With a complex TABLES statement, you may find that the output is not laid out exactly as expected. There may be wasted space or too little space. Furthermore, if a column label is too long for the formatted column width, or if a row label is too long given the space allotted (by default or by RTS=), the label will be broken up with hyphens in a seemingly arbitrary fashion. For these reasons, it is recommended that you try several different layouts on a sample of your data and look at the results before running the "real" job.

When attempting to produce percentages using denominator specifications, special care must be taken that the results are what were intended. Check crucial cell values by hand or by some other computational method to see that denominators have been specified correctly.

13

Procedures for Displaying Data

The procedures discussed in this chapter share as their primary mission the display of data in layouts chosen by the user. We saw the PRINT and PLOT procedures in Chapter 5. In this chapter, we introduce three more "display procedures"—CHART, TIMEPLOT, and REPORT.

CHART and TIMEPLOT share with PLOT the purpose of providing graphic printout displays. CHART produces various kinds of bar graphs, pie graphs and so on, while TIMEPLOT presents a sequence of variable values as they change between successive observations.

REPORT shares with PRINT the purpose of laying out the values of variables directly, in basically tabular fashion, but provides a good deal more control over the form of that layout, can even perform calculations that create new variables not in the input dataset but that can be displayed in the printout, and can summarily consolidate data across observations for display as a single line value.

THE CHART PROCEDURE

CHART complements PLOT, offering additional ways to display the range of one or more variables' values with the graphic impact. CHART produces displays that are good for showing relative measurements between different categories. That is, the kinds of displays produced by CHART are generally appropriate when one variable is discrete (categorical) and others continuous. By contrast, PLOT is better suited when all the variables are continuous.

CHART can produce three different kinds of histograms (bar chart), pie charts, and star charts (values displayed as radial distances from a common center). While FREQ has the TABLES statement and PLOT the PLOT statement, there are five different chart request statements, one for each of the five possible chart types. (At first, this can make CHART seem more complicated than PLOT, but it is not really more complex, it just can do more things.) Each chart request begins with a keyword, names one or more variables to chart, and may specify one or more options after a slash, e.g.,

```
VBAR VAR1-VAR4 / MISSING TYPE=PCT REF=50;
```

If more than one chart variable appears, a separate chart is produced for each; ways to represent more than one variable in a chart, using chart request options, will become clear below.

A BY statement can be used with PROC CHART, if desired, to produce output separately for appopriately arranged indexed BY value groups.

CHART Procedure Options

The CHART procedure provides several statements that each control a different type of chart. Most of the options affecting the CHART procedure are specified on these statements. A few options may be specified on the PROC CHART statement itself.

One of the procedures PROC CHART statement can take is the common DATA= option to specify the SAS dataset input to the procedure. The FORMCHAR= option may be used to specify the printer characters to be used for producing the chart. When coded on the PROC CHART statement, it overrides the FORMCHAR= system option. Your SAS manuals, specifically your operating system *Companion*, will show you how to code the FORMCHAR= option.

The LPI= option (for "lines per inch") is also coded on the PROC statement, if desired. It specifies proportions of PIE and STAR charts so they continue to look round regardless of the lines per inch and characters per inch your printer uses. LPI should be set to (10 * lines-per-inch)/columns-per-inch. By default, LPI=6, which will handle a printer using 10 characters per inch and 6 lines per inch. To print 8 lines per inch and 12 columns per inch, specify LPI=6.6667.

Other procedure options, besides those just just discussed, are coded on the chart request statements, after a slash. Some options apply only to certain of the chart requests. Many options, including those discussed directly below, may be used on any of the five types of chart request statement. Others, that apply only to one or a few of the chart request statements, will be discussed as we proceed ͻ review these statements.

Chart Content Type

The quantities displayed in the chart may represent frequencies, sums, means, or percentages. In order that the procedure may calculate the size of chart sections (bars, slices) correctly, it must know which of these is wanted. The TYPE= option is used to specify this. When TYPE=FREQ, each section represents the frequency with which a value or range of values occurs. TYPE=CFREQ is similar, except that each section is a cumulative frequency: The frequency of each value or range plus the values or ranges that have been charted to the left. TYPE=PERCENT (abbreviated TYPE=PCT) has each section represent the percentage of observations falling into a given range. TYPE=MEAN and TYPE=SUM cause a mean or a sum to be calculated and used for the value of the section.

The variable for which the mean or the sum is calculated must be specified by the SUMVAR= option. TYPE= need not always be specified. When SUMVAR= is coded, TYPE defaults to SUM. Otherwise, the default TYPE is FREQ.

Charting Intervals

When numeric variables are being charted, PROC CHART assumes them to be continuous unless told otherwise. The DISCRETE option on the chart request stipulates that each value of a numeric variable is a categorical value. If DISCRETE is not specified, CHART will attempt to construct intervals which the chart sections will represent by assigning midpoint values.

If the chart variable is indeed continuous, you may choose midpoint intervals with the MIDPOINTS= option, instead of letting the procedure decide on its own (which may not give the results you want). MIDPOINTS= is followed by a list of values separated by blanks. For example, coding

```
VBAR AGE / MIDPOINTS=10 20 30 40 50 60 70 80;
```

requests a chart with eight bars, the first representing a range of values with a midpoint of 10, and so on. You can control the minimum and maximum value of the axis along which quantities are displayed with the AXIS= option, details of which may be found in your *SAS Procedures* manual.

Other Options

The MISSING option may be coded to specify that "missing" is considered a valid level for the chart variable(s).

The FREQ= option can be used to provide a weighting factor, most applicable when input observations represent more than one true observation. It specifies a variable name. The FREQ= variable tells how many times the current observation is to be counted.

Bar Charts (Histograms)

Many variations on the bar chart theme are possible, and CHART provides several of them, of which we can show only a few. For purposes of this presentation, the dataset that is listed in Listing 13.1* will be used in the examples.

---

*The dataset was printed in two sets of columns using the multiple-panel facility of the REPORT procedure. PROC REPORT is discussed later in this chapter.

Y E A R	Q U A R T E R	P R O D U C T	R A N D T E S T	F A C T O R 1	F A C T O R 2	Y E A R	Q U A R T E R	P R O D U C T	R A N D T E S T	F A C T O R 1	F A C T O R 2
1980	1	A	7	7	32.7	1983	1	A	8	7	12.8
1980	1	B	8	7	29.8	1983	1	B	9	6	9.1
1980	1	C	8	4	8.2	1983	1	C	4	7	39.7
1980	2	A	7	5	5.1	1983	2	A	7	4	7.4
1980	2	B	8	7	11.8	1983	2	B	3	6	13.3
1980	2	C	4	5	39.2	1983	2	C	8	4	34.7
1980	3	A	0	6	36.7	1983	3	A	4	8	31.7
1980	3	B	3	5	7.2	1983	3	B	6	7	12.1
1980	3	C	9	5	27.8	1983	3	C	4	5	37.8
1980	4	A	7	5	34.2	1983	4	A	0	3	37.0
1980	4	B	5	4	8.9	1983	4	B	0	4	38.2
1980	4	C	0	7	21.9	1983	4	C	7	3	9.4
1981	1	A	4	8	23.9	1984	1	A	4	6	10.7
1981	1	B	0	8	25.5	1984	1	B	8	6	35.1
1981	1	C	5	4	33.7	1984	1	C	8	6	16.1
1981	2	A	8	3	29.3	1984	2	A	0	5	25.9
1981	2	B	4	4	18.9	1984	2	B	4	6	23.1
1981	2	C	9	3	13.1	1984	2	C	0	7	36.0
1981	3	A	0	5	10.0	1984	3	A	5	6	34.4
1981	3	B	0	5	7.6	1984	3	B	9	4	8.4
1981	3	C	9	5	38.4	1984	3	C	1	4	25.6
1981	4	A	9	5	30.6	1984	4	A	7	8	27.2
1981	4	B	7	8	16.8	1984	4	B	9	5	19.3
1981	4	C	3	4	33.8	1984	4	C	1	7	21.0
1982	1	A	6	3	7.0	1985	1	A	5	7	28.8
1982	1	B	8	8	12.5	1985	1	B	3	4	10.2
1982	1	C	5	5	28.0	1985	1	C	7	8	37.5
1982	2	A	9	7	20.6	1985	2	A	2	6	6.0
1982	2	B	5	3	30.8	1985	2	B	8	7	37.6
1982	2	C	0	4	36.3	1985	2	C	0	3	22.2
1982	3	A	9	5	8.7	1985	3	A	9	4	30.2
1982	3	B	5	5	20.2	1985	3	B	7	8	13.0
1982	3	C	6	6	18.1	1985	3	C	2	4	10.3
1982	4	A	9	5	19.9	1985	4	A	7	5	18.7
1982	4	B	8	4	34.9	1985	4	B	6	7	26.1
1982	4	C	6	6	10.9	1985	4	C	2	6	25.5

Listing 13.1. List of dataset to be used for CHART examples

Vertical Bar Charts

Vertical bar charts, requested by the VBAR statement, show relative magnitudes between different categories as the relative lengths of vertical columns or column segments. Such charts are requested with the VBAR statement. Two simple examples, one with a discrete and one with a continuous variable, are shown in Listing 13.2. Note the use of asterisks in the body of each bar. You can specify another character instead of the asterisk with the SYMBOL= option; follow SYMBOL= with a character enclosed in single quotes, or more than one character to force overprinting (a well-darkened bar may be achieved with SYMBOL= 'AOX').

Vertical bars may be segmented or "stacked" to represent two variables: what the bar as a whole represents and another variable's portion of it. Use the SUBGROUP= option to specify the second variable. See Listing 13.3. Vertical bars may be subdivided by grouping rather than stacking. Instead of using SUBGROUP=, use GROUP= to cause this effect. See Listing 13.4.

Note how CHART has formatted the output of Listing 13.4 in order to fit the linesize, by narrowing the bar width to one character. Charts produced by PROC CHART must fit on a single page, taking into account the LINESIZE and PAGESIZE system options (described in Chapter 21). If PROC CHART determines that a vertical bar chart simply cannot fit on one page, it may decide to produce a horizontal bar chart instead, which due to its design can handle more levels than can a vertical chart using the same amount of space.

The order of bars on a chart depends normally on the values of the chart variable and subgroup variables. The user can make the order depend on calculated quantities—sums, means, frequencies, the heights of the bars themselves—by specifying the ASCENDING or DESCENDING options (Listing 13.5).

CHART will print a blank bar when the bar value is zero. If you expect several bars to be zero and don't want their chart variable values to take space on the chart, specify the NOZEROS option.

As mentioned earlier, if the chart variable is continuous and neither the DISCRETE nor the MIDPOINTS= options are coded, CHART will choose its own ranges. Generally, CHART bases its decisions on the room available on the page for the chart to print. Instead of MIDPOINTS=, the LEVELS= option can be used to specify the *number* of ranges CHART should create. CHART will then build the number of midpoints specified.

A reference line can be drawn on the response axis to separate portions of the chart at a specified point. The REF= option is used to do this. The value specified with REF= depends on the type of the chart, e.g., if TYPE=FREQ, then it should be a frequency, if TYPE=PCT a percentage, TYPE=MEAN a mean, etc.

Horizontal Bar Charts

Horizontal bar charts, requested by the HBAR statement, show bars from left to right across the page, rather than from the bottom toward the top. A single line of

```
<<< PROGRAM SOURCE CODE FOLLOWS >>>

TITLE 'First CHART Example';
PROC CHART DATA=CHART;
  VBAR RANDTEST /DISCRETE;
RUN;
TITLE 'Second CHART Example';
PROC CHART DATA=CHART;
  VBAR FACTOR2;
RUN;


<<< SAS JOB OUTPUT FOLLOWS >>>
```

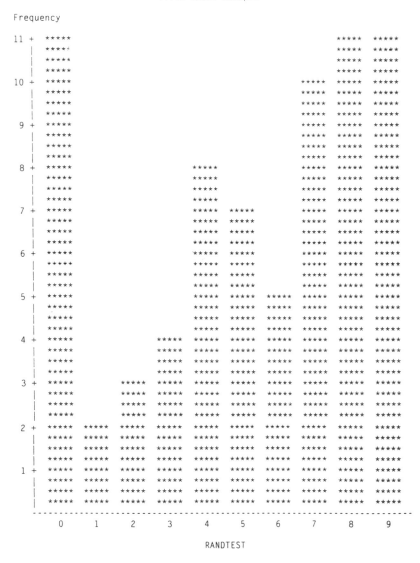

Listing 13.2. PROC CHART examples: Vertical bar charts

Continued

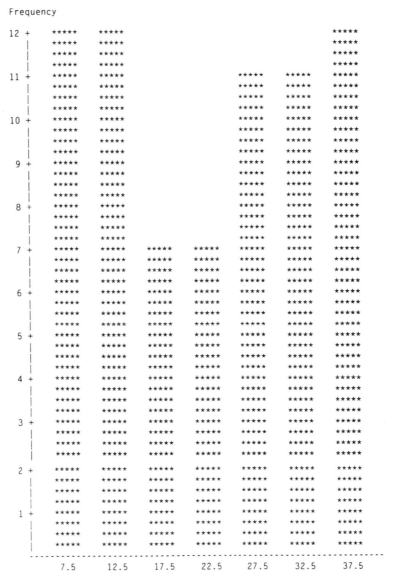

Second CHART Example

Listing 13.2. *Continued*

```
          <<< PROGRAM SOURCE CODE FOLLOWS >>>

TITLE 'A "Stacked Bar" Chart';
PROC CHART DATA=CHART;
  VBAR RANDTEST /DISCRETE SUBGROUP=PRODUCT;
RUN;


          <<< SAS JOB OUTPUT FOLLOWS >>>

                    A "Stacked Bar" Chart

Frequency


11 +  CCCCC                                             CCCCC  CCCCC
   |  CCCCC                                             CCCCC  CCCCC
   |  CCCCC                                             CCCCC  CCCCC
   |  CCCCC                                             CCCCC  CCCCC
10 +  CCCCC                                      CCCCC  CCCCC  CCCCC
   |  CCCCC                                      CCCCC  CCCCC  CCCCC
   |  CCCCC                                      CCCCC  CCCCC  CCCCC
   |  CCCCC                                      CCCCC  CCCCC  CCCCC
 9 +  CCCCC                                      CCCCC  CCCCC  CCCCC
   |  CCCCC                                      CCCCC  CCCCC  CCCCC
   |  CCCCC                                      CCCCC  CCCCC  CCCCC
   |  CCCCC                                      CCCCC  CCCCC  CCCCC
 8 +  CCCCC                  CCCCC                BBBBB  BBBBB  BBBBB
   |  CCCCC                  CCCCC                BBBBB  BBBBB  BBBBB
   |  CCCCC                  CCCCC                BBBBB  BBBBB  BBBBB
   |  CCCCC                  CCCCC                BBBBB  BBBBB  BBBBB
 7 +  BBBBB                  CCCCC  CCCCC         BBBBB  BBBBB  BBBBB
   |  BBBBB                  CCCCC  CCCCC         BBBBB  BBBBB  BBBBB
   |  BBBBB                  CCCCC  CCCCC         BBBBB  BBBBB  BBBBB
   |  BBBBB                  CCCCC  CCCCC         BBBBB  BBBBB  BBBBB
 6 +  BBBBB                  CCCCC  CCCCC         AAAAA  BBBBB  BBBBB
   |  BBBBB                  CCCCC  CCCCC         AAAAA  BBBBB  BBBBB
   |  BBBBB                  CCCCC  CCCCC         AAAAA  BBBBB  BBBBB
   |  BBBBB                  CCCCC  CCCCC         AAAAA  BBBBB  BBBBB
 5 +  BBBBB           BBBBB  BBBBB  CCCCC         AAAAA  BBBBB  AAAAA
   |  BBBBB           BBBBB  BBBBB  CCCCC         AAAAA  BBBBB  AAAAA
   |  BBBBB           BBBBB  BBBBB  CCCCC         AAAAA  BBBBB  AAAAA
   |  BBBBB           BBBBB  BBBBB  CCCCC         AAAAA  BBBBB  AAAAA
 4 +  AAAAA    CCCCC  BBBBB  BBBBB  CCCCC         AAAAA  BBBBB  AAAAA
   |  AAAAA    CCCCC  BBBBB  BBBBB  CCCCC         AAAAA  BBBBB  AAAAA
   |  AAAAA    CCCCC  BBBBB  BBBBB  CCCCC         AAAAA  BBBBB  AAAAA
   |  AAAAA    CCCCC  BBBBB  BBBBB  CCCCC         AAAAA  BBBBB  AAAAA
 3 +  AAAAA  CCCCC  BBBBB  AAAAA  BBBBB  BBBBB    AAAAA  BBBBB  AAAAA
   |  AAAAA  CCCCC  BBBBB  AAAAA  BBBBB  BBBBB    AAAAA  BBBBB  AAAAA
   |  AAAAA  CCCCC  BBBBB  AAAAA  BBBBB  BBBBB    AAAAA  BBBBB  AAAAA
   |  AAAAA  CCCCC  BBBBB  AAAAA  BBBBB  BBBBB    AAAAA  BBBBB  AAAAA
 2 +  AAAAA  CCCCC  CCCCC  BBBBB  AAAAA  AAAAA  BBBBB  AAAAA  AAAAA  AAAAA
   |  AAAAA  CCCCC  CCCCC  BBBBB  AAAAA  AAAAA  BBBBB  AAAAA  AAAAA  AAAAA
   |  AAAAA  CCCCC  CCCCC  BBBBB  AAAAA  AAAAA  BBBBB  AAAAA  AAAAA  AAAAA
   |  AAAAA  CCCCC  CCCCC  BBBBB  AAAAA  AAAAA  BBBBB  AAAAA  AAAAA  AAAAA
 1 +  AAAAA  CCCCC  AAAAA  BBBBB  AAAAA  AAAAA  AAAAA  AAAAA  AAAAA  AAAAA
   |  AAAAA  CCCCC  AAAAA  BBBBB  AAAAA  AAAAA  AAAAA  AAAAA  AAAAA  AAAAA
   |  AAAAA  CCCCC  AAAAA  BBBBB  AAAAA  AAAAA  AAAAA  AAAAA  AAAAA  AAAAA
   |  AAAAA  CCCCC  AAAAA  BBBBB  AAAAA  AAAAA  AAAAA  AAAAA  AAAAA  AAAAA
    --------------------------------------------------------------------
         0     1     2     3     4     5     6     7     8     9

                               RANDTEST


     Symbol PRODUCT    Symbol PRODUCT    Symbol PRODUCT

        A   A             B   B             C   C
```

Listing 13.3. PROC CHART, "Stacked" bars

```
    <<< PROGRAM SOURCE CODE FOLLOWS >>>

TITLE 'A Grouped Bar Chart';
PROC CHART DATA=CHART;
  VBAR RANDTEST /DISCRETE GROUP=PRODUCT;
RUN;

    <<< SAS JOB OUTPUT FOLLOWS >>>
```

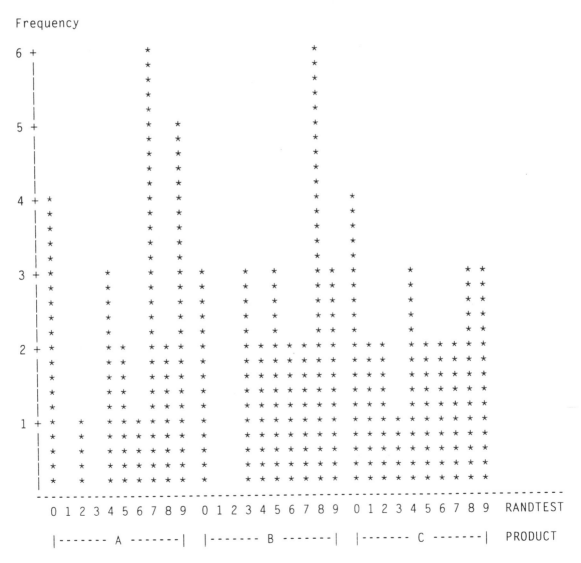

Listing 13.4. PROC CHART, Grouped bars

```
      <<< PROGRAM SOURCE CODE FOLLOWS >>>

TITLE 'Another way to look at it ...';
PROC CHART DATA=CHART;
  VBAR RANDTEST /DISCRETE GROUP=PRODUCT ASCENDING;
RUN;

      <<< SAS JOB OUTPUT FOLLOWS >>>
```

                    Another way to look at it ...

Frequency

```
6 +                         *                     *
  |                         *                     *
  |                         *                     *
  |                         *                     *
  |                         *                     *
5 +                      *  *                     *
  |                      *  *                     *
  |                      *  *                     *
  |                      *  *                     *
  |                      *  *                     *
4 +                   *  *  *                     *                           *
  |                   *  *  *                     *                           *
  |                   *  *  *                     *                           *
  |                   *  *  *                     *                           *
  |                   *  *  *                     *                           *
3 +                *  *  *  *        *  *  *  *  *              *  *  *  *
  |                *  *  *  *        *  *  *  *  *              *  *  *  *
  |                *  *  *  *        *  *  *  *  *              *  *  *  *
  |                *  *  *  *        *  *  *  *  *              *  *  *  *
  |                *  *  *  *        *  *  *  *  *              *  *  *  *
2 +          *  *  *  *  *  *     *  *  *  *  *  *  *  *     *  *  *  *  *  *  *  *  *
  |          *  *  *  *  *  *     *  *  *  *  *  *  *  *     *  *  *  *  *  *  *  *  *
  |          *  *  *  *  *  *     *  *  *  *  *  *  *  *     *  *  *  *  *  *  *  *  *
  |          *  *  *  *  *  *     *  *  *  *  *  *  *  *     *  *  *  *  *  *  *  *  *
  |          *  *  *  *  *  *     *  *  *  *  *  *  *  *     *  *  *  *  *  *  *  *  *
1 +    *  *  *  *  *  *  *  *     *  *  *  *  *  *  *  *  *  *  *  *  *  *  *  *  *  *  *  *
  |    *  *  *  *  *  *  *  *     *  *  *  *  *  *  *  *  *  *  *  *  *  *  *  *  *  *  *  *
  |    *  *  *  *  *  *  *  *     *  *  *  *  *  *  *  *  *  *  *  *  *  *  *  *  *  *  *  *
  |    *  *  *  *  *  *  *  *     *  *  *  *  *  *  *  *  *  *  *  *  *  *  *  *  *  *  *  *
  |    *  *  *  *  *  *  *  *     *  *  *  *  *  *  *  *  *  *  *  *  *  *  *  *  *  *  *  *
  ----------------------------------------------------------------------------------------
      1 3 2 6 5 8 4 0 9 7  1 2 4 6 7 0 3 5 9 8  3 1 2 5 6 7 4 8 9 0   RANDTEST

      |------- A -------|  |------- B -------|  |------- C -------|   PRODUCT
```

Listing 13.5. Vertical bars, grouped, ascending frequency display within groups

symbols, rather than a thick block of symbols, is always used, and horizontal bar charts can therefore display more bars than is usually possible with vertical charts. All the options discussed thus far—general chart options *and* VBAR options—are available to HBAR. Examples of horizontal bar charts are shown in Listings 13.6 and 13.7. As can be seen, statistics are printed to the right of the bars in horizontal bar charts. Normally, CHART will attempt to print frequencies, cumulative frequencies, percents, and cumulative percents if no SUMVAR= variable is specified. With SUMVAR= and TYPE=MEAN, frequencies and means may be printed; with SUMVAR= and TYPE=SUM, frequencies and sums may be printed. Any or all of these can be suppressed with options (available only on the HBAR statement): If any of FREQ, CFREQ, PERCENT, CPERCENT, SUM, or MEAN are coded explicitly, by implication CHART suppresses statistics *not* coded. NOSTAT suppresses them all. If an option is coded that is incompatible with the chart (for example, SUM when TYPE=MEAN), the option is simply ignored.

Block Charts

The BLOCK statement requests a special kind of bar chart which uses normal printer characters to produce the illusion of a third dimension. A block chart is an alternative to stacked or grouped bars for representing subgroups. All the general chart request options, and most of the options discussed under VBAR (excepting ASCENDING, DESCENDING, REF=), may be applied to block charts. An example of a block chart is shown in Listing 13.8.

Care must be taken not to overextend the number of blocks in any chart, since each chart must fit on one page. Your *SAS Procedures Guide* provides a table giving the maximum safe numbers of BLOCK*GROUP levels. As with VBAR, if CHART cannot satisfy a BLOCK request it may resort to an HBAR display instead.

The NOHEADER (synonym: NOHEADING) option can be used with block (and pie and star) charts to suppress the default heading that the procedure usually places on the chart.

Pie Charts

Everyone is familiar with pie charts: A circle ("100%") is fitted with two or more radii. The segments outlined by two radii and the arc they subtend are likened to slices of a pie, and their areas relative to the whole represent a percentage of the whole.

Pie charts are produced with a PIE chart request. The number of slices for the pie is determined much as the number of bars in a VBAR graph is determined. If the chart variable is continuous, therefore, the DISCRETE or MIDPOINTS= options might be used. Other options that may be used with the PIE statement are limited to those discussed under "CHART Procedure Options," above. An example pie chart is given in Listing 13.9. As you see, CHART attempts to print numeric values within the slices to provide maximum information.

As with other charts, pies are limited to a single page, taking into account PAGESIZE and LINESIZE. If the printer used does not print six lines per inch

```
      <<< PROGRAM SOURCE CODE FOLLOWS >>>

TITLE 'A Horizontal CHART Display';
PROC CHART DATA=CHART;
  HBAR FACTOR2 / GROUP=YEAR;
RUN;


      <<< SAS JOB OUTPUT FOLLOWS >>>


                      A Horizontal CHART Display

    YEAR   FACTOR2                              Cum.              Cum.
           Midpoint                      Freq   Freq   Percent   Percent
                     |
    1980     7.5     |********************    4      4     5.56      5.56
            12.5     |*****                   1      5     1.39      6.94
            17.5     |                        0      5     0.00      6.94
            22.5     |*****                   1      6     1.39      8.33
            27.5     |*********               2      8     2.78     11.11
            32.5     |*********               2     10     2.78     13.89
            37.5     |*********               2     12     2.78     16.67
                     |
    1981     7.5     |*****                   1     13     1.39     18.06
            12.5     |*********               2     15     2.78     20.83
            17.5     |*********               2     17     2.78     23.61
            22.5     |*****                   1     18     1.39     25.00
            27.5     |*********               2     20     2.78     27.78
            32.5     |***************         3     23     4.17     31.94
            37.5     |*****                   1     24     1.39     33.33
                     |
    1982     7.5     |*********               2     26     2.78     36.11
            12.5     |*********               2     28     2.78     38.89
            17.5     |*********               2     30     2.78     41.67
            22.5     |*********               2     32     2.78     44.44
            27.5     |*****                   1     33     1.39     45.83
            32.5     |*********               2     35     2.78     48.61
            37.5     |*****                   1     36     1.39     50.00
                     |
    1983     7.5     |***************         3     39     4.17     54.17
            12.5     |***************         3     42     4.17     58.33
            17.5     |                        0     42     0.00     58.33
            22.5     |                        0     42     0.00     58.33
            27.5     |                        0     42     0.00     58.33
            32.5     |*********               2     44     2.78     61.11
            37.5     |********************    4     48     5.56     66.67
                     |
    1984     7.5     |*****                   1     49     1.39     68.06
            12.5     |*****                   1     50     1.39     69.44
            17.5     |*********               2     52     2.78     72.22
            22.5     |*********               2     54     2.78     75.00
            27.5     |***************         3     57     4.17     79.17
            32.5     |*****                   1     58     1.39     80.56
            37.5     |*********               2     60     2.78     83.33
                     |
    1985     7.5     |*****                   1     61     1.39     84.72
            12.5     |***************         3     64     4.17     88.89
            17.5     |*****                   1     65     1.39     90.28
            22.5     |*****                   1     66     1.39     91.67
            27.5     |***************         3     69     4.17     95.83
            32.5     |*****                   1     70     1.39     97.22
            37.5     |*********               2     72     2.78    100.00
                     |
                     ----+----+----+----+
                         1    2    3    4

                             Frequency
```

Listing 13.6. Grouped horizontal bars

```
<<< PROGRAM SOURCE CODE FOLLOWS >>>

TITLE 'And another one (note effect of NOZEROS option)';
PROC CHART DATA=CHART;
  HBAR FACTOR1 / DISCRETE GROUP=YEAR SUBGROUP=PRODUCT NOZEROS;
RUN;


<<< SAS JOB OUTPUT FOLLOWS >>>
```

And another one (note effect of NOZEROS option)

YEAR	FACTOR1		Freq	Cum. Freq	Percent	Cum. Percent
1980	4	BBBBBCCCCC	2	2	2.78	2.78
	5	AAAAAAAAAABBBBBCCCCCCCCCC	5	7	6.94	9.72
	6	AAAAA	1	8	1.39	11.11
	7	AAAAABBBBBBBBBBBCCCCC	4	12	5.56	16.67
1981	3	AAAAACCCCC	2	14	2.78	19.44
	4	BBBBBCCCCCCCCCC	3	17	4.17	23.61
	5	AAAAAAAAAABBBBBCCCCC	4	21	5.56	29.17
	8	AAAAABBBBBBBBBB	3	24	4.17	33.33
1982	3	AAAAABBBBB	2	26	2.78	36.11
	4	BBBBBCCCCC	2	28	2.78	38.89
	5	AAAAAAAAAABBBBBCCCCC	4	32	5.56	44.44
	6	CCCCCCCCCC	2	34	2.78	47.22
	7	AAAAA	1	35	1.39	48.61
	8	BBBBB	1	36	1.39	50.00
1983	3	AAAAACCCCC	2	38	2.78	52.78
	4	AAAAABBBBBCCCCC	3	41	4.17	56.94
	5	CCCCC	1	42	1.39	58.33
	6	BBBBBBBBBB	2	44	2.78	61.11
	7	AAAAABBBBBCCCCC	3	47	4.17	65.28
	8	AAAAA	1	48	1.39	66.67
1984	4	BBBBBCCCCC	2	50	2.78	69.44
	5	AAAAABBBBB	2	52	2.78	72.22
	6	AAAAAAAAAABBBBBBBBBBCCCCC	5	57	6.94	79.17
	7	CCCCCCCCCC	2	59	2.78	81.94
	8	AAAAA	1	60	1.39	83.33
1985	3	CCCCC	1	61	1.39	84.72
	4	AAAAABBBBBCCCCC	3	64	4.17	88.89
	5	AAAAA	1	65	1.39	90.28
	6	AAAAACCCCC	2	67	2.78	93.06
	7	AAAAABBBBBBBBBB	3	70	4.17	97.22
	8	BBBBBCCCCC	2	72	2.78	100.00

```
     ----+----+----+----+----+
         1    2    3    4    5
              Frequency
```

Symbol	PRODUCT		Symbol	PRODUCT		Symbol	PRODUCT
A	A		B	B		C	C

Listing 13.7. Horizontal bars both grouped and stacked

```
<<< PROGRAM SOURCE CODE FOLLOWS >>>

TITLE 'The Famous PROC CHART "Block"-type Chart!';
PROC CHART DATA=CHART;
  BLOCK PRODUCT / TYPE=MEAN SUMVAR=RANDTEST GROUP=YEAR DISCRETE;
RUN;

    <<< SAS JOB OUTPUT FOLLOWS >>>

            The Famous PROC CHART "Block"-type Chart!

        Mean of RANDTEST by PRODUCT grouped by YEAR
```

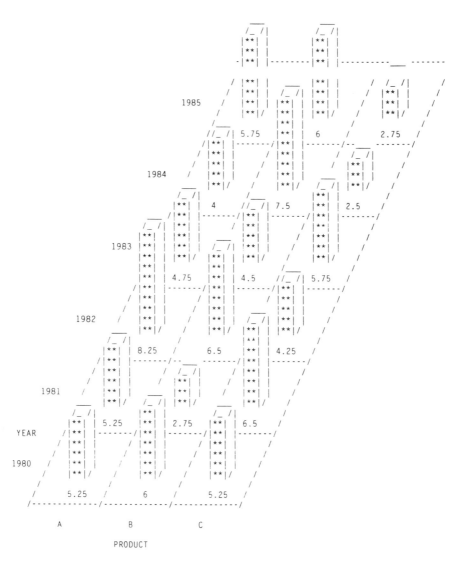

Listing 13.8. A block chart

<<< PROGRAM SOURCE CODE FOLLOWS >>>

```
TITLE ' '; * Enough of these silly titles!;
PROC CHART DATA=CHART;
  PIE QUARTER / TYPE=SUM SUMVAR=FACTOR2;
RUN;
```

<<< SAS JOB OUTPUT FOLLOWS >>>

Sum of FACTOR2 by QUARTER

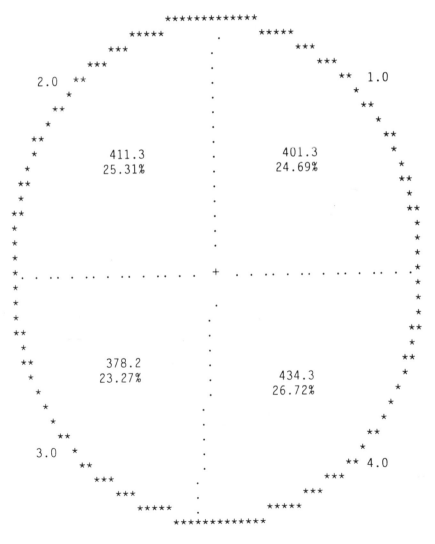

Listing 13.9. A pie chart

and ten characters per inch, the LPI= option on the PROC CHART statement may help round out the circle (because we didn't do that in our example, the pie took on an eccentric shape).

Star Charts

Less familiar than the pie is the star chart, so-called because the lengths of radial lines differ, forming a "star" rather than a circular "pie." The lengths of these radial lines are used to carry additional information that cannot be represented with a pie chart with equal radii. Normally, the center of the star represents a value of zero, though if any values to be charted are negative, the center represents the minimum. The AXIS= option can be used to alter these defaults.

An example of a star chart is presented in Listing 13.10 (which admittedly, with these data and on this book's page, doesn't look very nice). The same options that can be used with the PIE statement can be used with the STAR statement.

THE TIMEPLOT PROCEDURE

PROC TIMEPLOT is used to display an ordered sequence of observations. The displays produced are often valuable for analysis if successive observations contain variables' values at successive times. The procedure can then display how a variable's value changes over time, hence the name TIMEPLOT. However, the different values do not *have* to be measurements at different times; TIMEPLOT may be used to observe how the values of a variable change between observations for whatever reasons they change.

TIMEPLOT produces a plotting element for every single observation in the dataset. In this way it's like a "plotted PRINT," and indeed, values are normally printed as well as plotted on the output. If data are to be summarized, then the input dataset must already account for this; PROC TIMEPLOT might well be used after PROC SUMMARY. The horizontal axis of the plot represents variable values, while points on the vertical axis, one per printed line, correspond to each observation (except if a CLASS statement is used; see below). Output from PROC TIMEPLOT can easily span more than one page, and this is definitely permitted.

A BY statement can be used with TIMEPLOT, but even if a BY statement is not used, a preceding SORT may be important to produce a meaningfully ordered display: TIMEPLOT reports data in the order found in the dataset. If BY is used, it is often best to specify the UNIFORM option on the PROC TIMEPLOT statement; otherwise the horizontal scale will be determined for each BY group separately and the relative magnitudes will be less easily compared by eye. Another option that may be coded on the PROC statement is MAXDEC=, giving the maximum number of decimal places to be printed for numbers appearing in the "print" portion of the output.

```
<<< PROGRAM SOURCE CODE FOLLOWS >>>

PROC CHART DATA=CHART;
  STAR RANDTEST / DISCRETE;
RUN;

<<< SAS JOB OUTPUT FOLLOWS >>>
```

Listing 13.10. A star chart

Plot Specifications

TIMEPLOT is a vehicle for interpreting PLOT requests, and the many options that may be placed after a slash on the PLOT statement(s) give the user a good deal of freedom in designing a display tailored to particular needs.

One or more PLOT statements must be coded for PROC TIMEPLOT to do anything. The general form of the PLOT statement is

```
PLOT <<varname>|<varname=symbol>|<(varnames)=symbol>>...[/ options];
```

The elements after the PLOT keyword are called the plot specifications, and they can take one of the three indicated forms, which may be mixed within a single PLOT statement if desired.

The purpose of the "varname=symbol" specification is to specify the character used to plot the variable's value. The symbol may be a variable name, in which case the first character of the formatted value of the variable named is used as the plot character, or else it may be a single character enclosed in single quotes, e.g.,

```
PLOT APPLE='*' ORANGE='+';
```

Using a variable for the symbol allows an additional item of information to come into play: The value of a separate variable is represented as the actual character, while the plot variable is still represented by the horizontal distance of the character from an arbitrary reference point. The "(varnames)=symbol" specification is used to specify a common symbol for plotting more than one variable, which will appear together on one plot. If the simple "varname" specification is used, the default plot character is the first character of the variable name.

Using the dataset created for our PROC CHART examples, PROC TIMEPLOT is illustrated in Listing 13.11.

Some PLOT Statement Options

Most of the detailing a user can specify is done with PLOT statement options, which follow a slash after the PLOT specifications. We will discuss only some of these here; see your *SAS Procedures* manual for more details.

Overlaying Plots

Generally, each specification in a PLOT request is prepared on a separate plot. Coding the OVERLAY option causes all variables named in all specifications to be printed on the same plot (Listing 13.12). If two symbols would be overlaid in the same print position, an alternative symbol is used, as in PROC PLOT; true physical overprinting is not performed. The "collision" symbol can be specified with OVPCHAR=.

```
<<< PROGRAM SOURCE CODE FOLLOWS >>>

TITLE 'PROC TIMEPLOT Illustrated with data from Listing 13.1':
TITLE2 'Note: Values in the dataset already sorted by YEAR and QUARTER':
TITLE3 'RANDTEST is plotted; PRODUCT provides the plot symbol':
PROC TIMEPLOT DATA=CHART:
  PLOT RANDTEST=PRODUCT:
RUN:


<<< SAS JOB OUTPUT FOLLOWS >>>
```

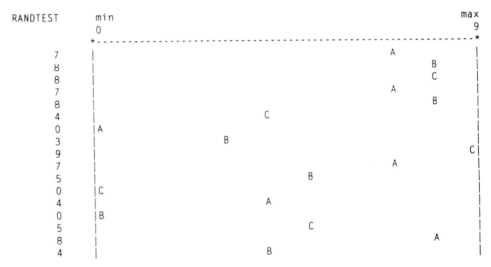

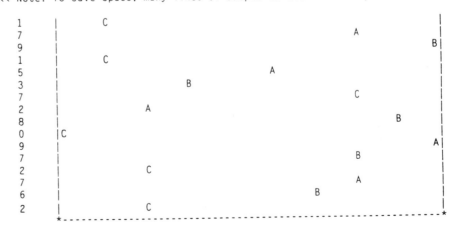

Listing 13.11. PROC TIMEPLOT illustrated

```
    <<< PROGRAM SOURCE CODE FOLLOWS >>>

TITLE2 'RANDTEST and the "FACTORs"';
PROC TIMEPLOT DATA=CHART;
  PLOT FACTOR1='1' FACTOR2='2' RANDTEST=PRODUCT /OVERLAY OVPCHAR='*';
RUN;


    <<< SAS JOB OUTPUT FOLLOWS >>>
```

PROC TIMEPLOT Illustrated with data from Listing 13.1
RANDTEST and the "FACTORs"

```
FACTOR1     FACTOR2     RANDTEST     min                                    max
                                     0                                      39.7
                                     *-------------------------------------*
    7         32.70         7        |          *                    2      |
    7         29.80         8        |       1B                  2          |
    4          8.20         8        |    1    *                             |
    5          5.10         7        |     *  A                              |
    7         11.80         8        |       1B     2                        |
    5         39.20         4        |    C1                               2|
    6         36.70         0        |A      1                          2    |
    5          7.20         3        |    B 1 2                              |
    5         27.80         9        |       1    C              2           |
    5         34.20         7        |       1 A                    2        |
    4          8.90         5        |     1B     2                          |
    7         21.90         0        |C      1              2                |
    8         23.90         4        |     A    1             2              |
    8         25.50         0        |B         1          2                 |
    4         33.70         5        |    1C                        2        |
    3         29.30         8        |    1     A                 2          |
    4         18.90         4        |     *               2                 |

    <<< Note: To save space, many lines of output deleted at this point >>>

    4         25.60         1        | C   1                   2            |
    8         27.20         7        |        A1                  2         |
    5         19.30         9        |     1    B           2               |
    7         21.00         1        | C     1            2                 |
    7         28.80         5        |      A 1                   2         |
    4         10.20         3        |    B1      2                          |
    8         37.50         7        |        C1                          2 |
    6          6.00         2        | A    *                               |
    7         37.60         8        |       1B                           2 |
    3         22.20         0        |C   1                 2               |
    4         30.20         9        |      1    A               2          |
    8         13.00         7        |       B1     2                       |
    4         10.30         2        | C  1      2                          |
    5         18.70         7        |      1 A           2                 |
    7         26.10         6        |       B1             2               |
    6         25.50         2        | C   1                2               |
                                     *-------------------------------------*
```

Listing 13.12. PROC TIMEPLOT with overlaid plots

Plots are also overlaid, in effect, if more than one variable name is used in the "(varnames)=symbol" specification. In such cases, the several variables named appear in the same plot.

Sizing and Positioning Plots

The POS= option specifies the number of print positions on a line to be used for the plot. The AXIS= option can also be used to specify the location of tic marks for the horizontal axis. Each tic position consists of one character width, unless POS= is also specified. If POS=0 is specified along with AXIS=, the plot expands to fill the space available on the page.

Reference Lines

Vertical reference lines can be drawn within a plot using the REF= option. One or more values may be specified. The special value REF=MEAN(var) can be used, in which case the mean value of the specified variable is calculated for all observations in the dataset, and used for the reference line. The reference line is normally composed of the vertical bar character; an alternative can be specified with REFCHAR=. Should a plotting variable collide with a reference line, the plot character is printed instead of the reference line character.

Some Other PLOT Options

REVERSE asks that the plot be printed with values descending from left to right, rather than with the smaller values toward the left and larger toward the right. HILOC causes the leftmost plot character on a line to be connected by hyphens with the rightmost. It is often used if several variables are being plotted on the same plot, and the SAS variables represent high and low values of the same conceptual variable: HILOC shows the range spread between the high and the low values. JOINREF makes the leftmost symbol connect to the rightmost symbol on a line, whether or not either symbol is a plot symbol or a REF symbol. It may be used, for example, to illustrate graphically the degree of positive and negative departure of values from a mean. JOINREF encompasses HILOC; if both are coded, then JOINREF controls.

The CLASS Statement with PROC TIMEPLOT

If a CLASS statement is used with PROC TIMEPLOT, it causes all observations for a given combination of class variables to be plotted on the same line, though only the last value of the plotting symbol appears in the printed section. Generally, the CLASS statement is used if a variable name is specified for the symbol, and the variable changes meaningfully inside the data. Using CLASS also makes most sense if the data are at least grouped, if not actually sorted, by CLASS variable values, for CLASS is used to plot many different values on one line, based on the CLASS variable values. Consecutive observations with the same CLASS value (or same class value combination, if more than one CLASS variable) result in a single line of output, in effect merging the plot using the value of the symbol variable to distinguish points along the single line.

When used for certain special purposes (or when used incorrectly), the symbol variable might not be different for each observation, resulting in a loss of data—only one line is printed for each CLASS group, yet if the symbol is the same, it can only be used once. The SAS log will show a warning if multiple-symbol conflict occurs.

The ID Statement

CLASS variable values are listed along with the other variables on the left (PRINT-like) part of the output. To list variables' values without merging or suppressing lines, use the ID statement instead of CLASS. Variables named in an ID statement are included in the print, but not the plot.

THE REPORT PROCEDURE

The REPORT procedure,* grandchild of the Version 5.16/18 QPRINT procedure (now obsolete), gives the SAS user a great deal of control over data presentation. In SAS sessions under the SAS Display Manager, the REPORT procedure may be invoked as an interactive development system. In such cases, a REPORT window is displayed and the user creates reports on-screen, prescribing their component data elements and modifying their layouts dynamically, using procedure sub-windows to control various features that give rise to a finished report definition.

Since in the scope of this book we don't delve into interactive procedures, we will not review interactive REPORT development techniques, nor the features (such as dynamic highlighting and "traffic lighting") that are used when developing a report meant more for on-screen viewing than for printing. We will be concerned instead with the PROC REPORT "language," sometimes called its *batch language*.† Using the batch language, a user can gain full to all REPORT procedure features, no less than when REPORT is invoked interactively under DMS. When you've learned the REPORT batch language, you may find it more efficient or easier to use than the interactive method. Or, you may find it convenient in your practice to "rough out" reports using the batch language, then fine-tune them

---

*Although it is part of the Base SAS software, primary documentation for the REPORT procedure is found not in the *SAS Procedures Guide* but in a separate publication, the *SAS Guide to the REPORT Procedure*.

†The PROC REPORT statements do not really comprise a full-fledged programming language as do, say, the statements of the SQL procedure. What they do is determine the layout and (with COMPUTE groups and embedded DATA Step Language) some of the content of the report.

interactively; some users even find the opposite approach (initial interactive development, then modification of batch code which the interactive procedure generates on command) to be useful.

Below, we will take a sample dataset and examine some variations on its display that can be produced by the REPORT procedure, describing language elements as we go along. REPORT is rich with features and options, and we cannot go over all of them here, nor all the output variations they make possible. But you will see at least some of the ways REPORT can control the appearance of your printed output. You will also see that the procedure provides much more besides layout control. For example, *without first rebuilding the input dataset* you can use REPORT to:

- Produce output in order sorted by selected columns' values, regardless of the sort status of the input dataset;
- Reduce groups of observations to summary statistics and print these summary lines instead of—or, along with—observation values;
- Print values of quasi-variables not existing in the input dataset, created using DATA Step Language syntax entirely within the REPORT procedure.

Our Sample Dataset

The data purportedly come from a summary of yearly sales figures for a certain company. The file contains in order three classification variables: REGION, geographic sales region; CATEGORY, avenue of sales, e.g., "wholesale"; YEAR; and two analysis variables: PROJECTD, sales dollars as forecast prior to the sales year; and ACTUAL, actual sales dollars cumulated after the end of the year. The file is sorted by REGION, CATEGORY, and descending YEAR. Listing 13.13 is the result of printing the dataset with the following program:

```
TITLE 'Sales Summary, Key Regions, 3-year Recap';
TITLE2 'Detail Data';
PROC PRINT NOOBS DATA=MYCO.REVENUE LABEL SPLIT='/';
  LABEL REGION='Sales/Region' CATEGORY='Category' YEAR='Year'
        PROJECTD='Projected/Sales' ACTUAL='Actual/Sales';
RUN;
```

A Simple PROC REPORT Call

Listing 13.13 could have been reproduced exactly as shown were the PROC PRINT statement above replaced by

```
PROC REPORT DATA=MYCO.REVENUE HEADSKIP;
```

and the rest of the code left exactly as is. The differences: If a variable label is available, REPORT uses it by default, while PRINT does not (it is told to do so with the LABEL option); SPLIT= was not required in this program since

```
                    Sales Summary, Key Regions, 3-year Recap
                               Detail Data

       Sales                                   Projected     Actual
       Region          Category     Year         Sales       Sales

       Northeast       Corporate    1992        2832000      3078225
       Northeast       Corporate    1991        3580000      3718121
       Northeast       Corporate    1990        3120000      3166209
       Northeast       Direct       1992        4770000      4826176
       Northeast       Direct       1991        5250000      5465593
       Northeast       Direct       1990        1224000      1378125
       Northeast       Wholesale    1992        6750000      6649193
       Northeast       Wholesale    1991        9200000      8955082
       Northeast       Wholesale    1990        8300000      8505035
       South/Central   Corporate    1992        2145000      1913527
       South/Central   Corporate    1991        2445000      2298737
       South/Central   Corporate    1990        2385000      2554576
       South/Central   Direct       1992        3825000      4022004
       South/Central   Direct       1991        3667500      3419090
       South/Central   Direct       1990        2808000      2559600
       South/Central   Wholesale    1992        5550000      5745731
       South/Central   Wholesale    1991        3420000      3208675
       South/Central   Wholesale    1990        6412500      6300068
       West            Corporate    1992        1264800      1506342
       West            Corporate    1991        1999200      2210282
       West            Corporate    1990        2142000      2359095
       West            Direct       1992        5074500      5291008
       West            Direct       1991        4437000      4402112
       West            Direct       1990        4921500      5137655
       West            Wholesale    1992        7055000      7266686
       West            Wholesale    1991        8032500      7864673
       West            Wholesale    1990        6375000      6584031
```

Listing 13.13. Sample dataset for illustration of PROC REPORT

REPORT assumes the forward slash as its default split character; REPORT does not normally produce observation numbers, so NOOBS is never used; the blank line PRINT inserts between a column heading and the first data value is not normally inserted by REPORT, so HEADSKIP was used.*

Were the LABEL statement left out of both code segments, again the PROC PRINT and PROC REPORT results would be identical except (of course) that

---

*Another difference, important only if you wish to run REPORT non-interactively but under a DMS session: you would also use the NOWINDOWS option on the PROC REPORT statement, to instruct the procedure to execute to completion and send its output to the OUTPUT window. If NOWINDOWS is not specified, DMS will instead send the results to the REPORT window and begin a report-modification subsession.

variable names, not labels, would head up the columns. On the other hand, a LABEL statement is not required to produce a report exactly the same as Listing 13.13. Instead, the PROC REPORT code could be fully expanded as follows:

```
PROC REPORT DATA=MYCO.REVENUE NOWINDOWS HEADSKIP;
COLUMN REGION CATEGORY YEAR PROJECTD ACTUAL;
DEFINE REGION / DISPLAY 'Sales/Region';
DEFINE CATEGORY / DISPLAY 'Category';
DEFINE YEAR / DISPLAY 'Year';
DEFINE PROJECTD / DISPLAY 'Projected/Sales';
DEFINE ACTUAL / DISPLAY 'Actual/Sales';
RUN;
```

The COLUMN statement can be used as can the VAR statement in PROC PRINT, to specify variables and the order in which they are to be displayed; we did not strictly need it to produce Listing 13.13 for the same reason we did not need a VAR statement in the PROC PRINT version, i.e., we wanted all dataset variables shown, in the order they exist in the dataset. In the REPORT procedure, items in the columns may include the values not only of dataset variables but of summary statistics computed across observations, or of computations based on variables or constants according to your specifications. The COLUMN statement can define these, too, as we will see; it can also be used to arrange several columns of data under a single unified subheading.

DEFINE statements, which have no analogue in PROC PRINT, may be used instead of LABEL statements to provide variable labels. DEFINE has other important purposes in REPORT applications, as we will now describe.

Usage Definitions

DEFINE statements are used within the context of a REPORT procedure call to describe how various items will contribute to or be used in the report. The DEFINE statement has the form

```
DEFINE item [ / <usage>
<<'header'>...> <options> ];
```

The order of the elements after the slash isn't usually important (although as a matter of good coding form, it is preferable to place the usage definition first, followed by column headers and any other options). The item being defined may be a variable, the result of a computation, or a summary statistic, depending on its usage definition. Several types of usage are provided. We already have seen the result of using DISPLAY: it indicates that values are to be displayed as they are. DISPLAY is the default for a character variable if its usage is not made explicit on a DEFINE statement.

Another usage type is ORDER, which serves to re-order observations, and also eliminates redundancies in row labelling. Listing 13.14 shows what happens if the program code shown above were changed only by substituting "ORDER" for

```
              Sales Summary, Key Regions, 3-year Recap
                             Detail Data
```

Category	Sales Region	Year	Projected Sales	Actual Sales
Corporate	Northeast	1992	2832000	3078225
		1991	3580000	3718121
		1990	3120000	3166209
	South/Central	1992	2145000	1913527
		1991	2445000	2298737
		1990	2385000	2554576
	West	1992	1264800	1506342
		1991	1999200	2210282
		1990	2142000	2359095
Direct	Northeast	1992	4770000	4826176
		1991	5250000	5465593
		1990	1224000	1378125
	South/Central	1992	3825000	4022004
		1991	3667500	3419090
		1990	2808000	2559600
	West	1992	5074500	5291008
		1991	4437000	4402112
		1990	4921500	5137655
Wholesale	Northeast	1992	6750000	6649193
		1991	9200000	8955082
		1990	8300000	8505035
	South/Central	1992	5550000	5745731
		1991	3420000	3208675
		1990	6412500	6300068
	West	1992	7055000	7266686
		1991	8032500	7864673
		1990	6375000	6584031

Listing 13.14. PROC REPORT using ORDER variables

"DISPLAY" in the two statements that define REGION and CATEGORY, and by switching the positions of REGION and CATEGORY in the COLUMN statement:

```
TITLE2 'Detail Data';
PROC REPORT DATA=MYCO.REVENUE NOWINDOWS HEADSKIP;
COLUMN CATEGORY REGION YEAR PROJECTD ACTUAL;
DEFINE REGION / ORDER 'Sales/Region';
DEFINE CATEGORY / ORDER 'Category';
DEFINE YEAR / DISPLAY 'Year';
DEFINE PROJECTD / DISPLAY 'Projected/Sales';
DEFINE ACTUAL / DISPLAY 'Actual/Sales';
RUN;
```

The output is displayed as if sorted by CATEGORY and then REGION. No matter what the order of the observations in the dataset, the REPORT output obeys the

```
        Sales Summary, Key Regions, 3-year Recap
           Total Sales over All Three Regions

                              Projected      Actual
        Category      Year        Sales       Sales

        Corporate     1990      7647000     8079880
                      1991      8024200     8227140
                      1992      6241800     6498094
        Direct        1990      8953500     9075380
                      1991     13354500    13286795
                      1992     13669500    14139188
        Wholesale     1990     21087500    21389134
                      1991     20652500    20028430
                      1992     19355000    19661610
```

Listing 13.15. PROC REPORT using GROUP variables

ORDER usage on the DEFINE statements in conjunction with the item ordering on the COLUMN statement.* The DESCENDING option can be used with ORDER to make the sort sequence descending instead of ascending. If in the example just listed YEAR were defined as ORDER DESCENDING instead of DISPLAY, the results would be exactly the same. They would *not* be exactly the same, however, if there were not one and only one observation per value of year, since suppression of redundant row values would also take place: Observe how the ORDER usage causes an item's value to display only when it changes from the value in the previous row.

Summarizing Data By Groups.

The GROUP usage type defines items that will be used for grouping variables. One use for grouping items is to summarize the data observations. Listing 13.15 shows the results when the following program is run:

```
TITLE 'Sales Summary, Key Regions, 3-year Recap';
TITLE2 'Total Sales over All Key Regions';
PROC REPORT DATA=MYCO.REVENUE NOWINDOWS HEADSKIP;
COLUMN CATEGORY YEAR PROJECTD ACTUAL;
DEFINE YEAR / GROUP 'Year';
DEFINE CATEGORY / GROUP  'Category';
DEFINE PROJECTD / SUM  'Projected/Sales';
DEFINE ACTUAL / SUM 'Actual/Sales';
RUN;
```

---

*Observe that the DEFINE statements do not have to be placed in any particular order: we did not change their order even though we changed the order of items on the COLUMN statement.

```
            Sales Summary, Key Regions, 3-year Recap
                Total Sales over All Three Regions
```

| | 1990 | | Year 1991 | | 1992 | |
Category	Projected Sales	Actual Sales	Projected Sales	Actual Sales	Projected Sales	Actual Sales
Corporate	7647000	8079880	8024200	8227140	6241800	6498094
Direct	8953500	9075380	13354500	13286795	13669500	14139188
Wholesale	21087500	21389134	20652500	20028430	19355000	19661610

Listing 13.16. PROC REPORT using an ACROSS variable

REGION, being left out of the program code, does not subdivide the summarization itself. Instead, the values in the PROJECTD and ACTUAL columns represent the sum over all REGIONs in each CATEGORY*YEAR group. Thus as you see, REPORT gives you the ability to prepare data summaries without your having to build a summarized dataset prior to printing.

In the program code just presented, note how both CATEGORY and YEAR were defined with GROUP usage, and PROJECTD and ACTUAL were deemed analysis variables (by coding a statistic name as the usage element*). This was necessary; in general (though there are exceptions), if there are any ORDER or DISPLAY items in a report definition, GROUP items will be "demoted" to ORDER, and no grouping will take place; a note is placed in the SAS log to advise you when this occurs.

Crosstabular Layout

REPORT gives you the ability to place some of your "columns" across instead of down the page. The ACROSS usage definition serves this purpose. To work correctly, the COLUMN statement must usually associate the across item with another item or items. The following program, whose results are shown in Listing 13.16, shows the same data as in Listing 13.15 but in crosstabular layout:

```
PROC REPORT DATA=SASUSER.REVENUE NOWINDOWS HEADSKIP;
COLUMN CATEGORY YEAR,(PROJECTD ACTUAL);
DEFINE YEAR / ACROSS 'Year';
DEFINE CATEGORY / GROUP  'Category';
DEFINE PROJECTD / SUM  'Projected/Sales';
DEFINE ACTUAL / SUM 'Actual/Sales';
RUN;
```

---

*The word ANALYSIS could also be coded for clarity, but would be redundant since a statistic name would still be required. The statistics that might be requested are those familiar from, for example, the MEANS procedure: N, NMISS, MEAN, MIN, MAX, VAR, STD, STDERR, SUM of course, and a few others.

Observe how YEAR is associated with both analysis variables in the COLUMN statement: the variables are grouped in parentheses* and tied to YEAR with a comma so that they will appear under YEAR in the output.

DEFINE Statement Options

The DEFINE statement provides numerous options to control your printed output. The ORDER= option can be used to refine the sort order used to display GROUP, ORDER, and ACROSS items. Similarly to PROC FREQ's TABLES statement option of the same name, valid ORDER= values are DATA (based on first occurences as encountered in the dataset), FORMATTED (based on the formatted values of the item), FREQ (based on item frequencies), and INTERNAL (being the same as PROC SORT would order them). If an item has a format, the default when ORDER= is not specified is FORMATTED.

The DESCENDING option was already described in our earlier discussion of the ORDER usage option. DESCENDING can also be used with the GROUP and ACROSS usage types.

Column headers and item values may be justified within the spacing given by the FORMAT= and WIDTH= options using one of the options RIGHT, LEFT, or CENTER.

If you require more space within a column than is implied by the value format, you can use the WIDTH= option to specify an exact width. Space *between* columns can be controlled with the SPACING= option, where you specify how many blank spaces should intervene between the column being defined and the column to its left in the aggregate report definition. The FLOW option causes character values as well as column heads to use the split character (or spaces, if no split character is defined) if necessary in order to keep the text within column bounds.

Sometimes, values in a column will turn out to be all zero (or missing). To suppress such a column, you can code the NOZERO option. When NOZERO is coded, a column is inserted and printed only if at least one of the item's component values is neither zero nor missing. In some circumstances, you want a column to be suppressed unconditionally; this can occur when you wish to use the values of the column only to help order the rows of the report, or you need to use the defined value only to help compute other values (using COMPUTE groups, discussed later below). In these cases, the NOPRINT option should be used to suppress the actual column printout.

Breakpoints

Let's now produce a report that shows both detailed data *and* summary statistics, meanwhile illustrating a few minor variations. The following report produces the output to be found in Listing 13.17:

---

*If only one analysis variable were to appear under the ACROSS variable, parentheses would not be necessary.

Sales Summary, Key Regions, 3-year Recap
Detail, with Yearly Summaries

Sales Region		Category	Projected	Actual
Northeast	1992	Corporate	2,832,000	3,078,225
		Direct	4,770,000	4,826,176
		Wholesale	6,750,000	6,649,193
			----------	----------
			14,352,000	14,553,594
	1991	Corporate	3,580,000	3,718,121
		Direct	5,250,000	5,465,593
		Wholesale	9,200,000	8,955,082
			----------	----------
			18,030,000	18,138,796
	1990	Corporate	3,120,000	3,166,209
		Direct	1,224,000	1,378,125
		Wholesale	8,300,000	8,505,035
			----------	----------
			12,644,000	13,049,369
----------			----------	----------
Northeast			45,026,000	45,741,759
----------			----------	----------
South/Central	1992	Corporate	2,145,000	1,913,527
		Direct	3,825,000	4,022,004
		Wholesale	5,550,000	5,745,731
			----------	----------
			11,520,000	11,681,262
	1991	Corporate	2,445,000	2,298,737
		Direct	3,667,500	3,419,090
		Wholesale	3,420,000	3,208,675
			----------	----------
			9,532,500	8,926,502
	1990	Corporate	2,385,000	2,554,576
		Direct	2,808,000	2,559,600
		Wholesale	6,412,500	6,300,068
			----------	----------
			11,605,500	11,414,244
----------			----------	----------
South/Central			32,658,000	32,022,008
----------			----------	----------

Listing 13.17. Creating breakpoint actions in PROC REPORT

Continued

```
West                1992   Corporate   1,264,800    1,506,342
                           Direct      5,074,500    5,291,008
                           Wholesale   7,055,000    7,266,686
                                       ----------   ----------
                                       13,394,300   14,064,036

                    1991   Corporate   1,999,200    2,210,282
                           Direct      4,437,000    4,402,112
                           Wholesale   8,032,500    7,864,673
                                       ----------   ----------
                                       14,468,700   14,477,067
```

```
<<< Note here the listing goes to a new page; when this occurs, the values >>>
<<< of all group variables are printed again, for reference; below, the    >>>
<<< value of REGION ("West") shows up on the first line of the new page.    >>>
```

```
                    Sales Summary, Key Regions, 3-year Recap
                       Detail, with Yearly Summaries

     Sales
     Region                     Category    Projected      Actual

     West                1990   Corporate   2,142,000    2,359,095
                                Direct      4,921,500    5,137,655
                                Wholesale   6,375,000    6,584,031
                                            ----------   ----------
                                            13,438,500   14,080,781

     -------------                          ----------   ----------
     West                                   41,301,500   42,621,884
     -------------                          ----------   ----------

                                            ==========   ==========
                                            118985500    120385651
```

Listing 13.17. *Continued*

```
TITLE 'Sales Summary, Key Regions, 3-Year Recap';
TITLE2 'Detail, with Yearly Summaries';
PROC REPORT DATA=SASUSER.REVENUE NOWINDOWS HEADSKIP;
COLUMN REGION YEAR CATEGORY PROJECTD ACTUAL;
DEFINE YEAR / GROUP DESCENDING ' ';
DEFINE CATEGORY / GROUP 'Category' RIGHT ;
DEFINE REGION/ GROUP 'Sales/Region' ;
DEFINE PROJECTD / SUM  'Projected' FORMAT=COMMA10.;
DEFINE ACTUAL / SUM 'Actual' FORMAT=COMMA10.;
BREAK AFTER YEAR / SKIP OL SUMMARIZE SUPPRESS;
BREAK AFTER REGION / SKIP OL UL SUMMARIZE;
BREAK AFTER /SKIP DOL SUMMARIZE;
RUN;
```

The BREAK statement is PROC REPORT's powerful way of controlling what happens as values of ORDER, GROUP, or ACROSS variables change. BREAK must include either 'AFTER' or 'BEFORE', and the name of an item. When AFTER is chosen, the break is written after the last item of the break variable group; when BEFORE is chosen, the break is written before the first item of the group. OL, UL, DOL, and DUL signify overline, underline, double-overline, and double-underline, respectively; SKIP instructs the procedure to place a blank line between the group and the break item. SUPPRESS instructs the procedure not to print the value (nor any over- or underlining) of the break variable. In this example, had SUPPRESS not been coded on the YEAR break definition, the value of YEAR (and of REGION, because YEAR is nested within it in the grouping order) would have printed (with overlines) on each yearly-summary line, cluttering the output. Compare the printout of the values of REGION, which are not suppressed.

The SUMMARIZE option is what causes the summary lines to appear in the first place. BREAK (and RBREAK) summaries produced by the SUMMARIZE option normally follow the usage of their component line item: here the summarized lines are totals, but if we had defined PROJECTD (or ACTUAL) with usage, say, of MEAN instead of SUM, then the YEAR, REGION, and grand-summary lines would also be means.

The RBREAK statement is PROC REPORT's way of controlling what happens at the beginning or the end of an entire report. In this example, we have included grand-total summaries at the end.* RBREAK specifies BEFORE or AFTER, but (of course) no particular item; the options available are the same as those that can be used on a BREAK statement.

The present example illustrates these other fine-tune adjustments: DESCENDING in the YEAR definition preserves the recent-year-first order of the detail data; values of CATEGORY were right-justified to associate them more eye-pleasingly with the numeric columns; formats were used to make the numbers

---

*The summary line totals printed without commas only because the width we specified (using FORMAT=) was not sufficient to hold them. This is a normal behavior of the COMMAn. format when there is insufficient width.

themselves easier to read; and for less-cluttered headings, the column title was removed entirely from YEAR and the word "Sales" from the titles for PROJECTD and ACTUAL.

Gross Layout Control: Panels and "Wrapped" Lines

If a logical report line is less than half the defined page width, the user has the option to lay out the report in vertical "panels," as if the pages were somehow narrowed and pasted together side-by-side. A telephone book provides a good illustration of the concept: Names, addresses, and phone numbers represent three "variables," but the set of columns appears more than once per physical page. Listing 13.1 at the beginning of this chapter is an example of a multiple-panel printout.

PROC REPORT allows the user to create multiple panels per page with the PANELS= option on the PROC statement. The PROC REPORT default could be expressed as PANELS=1.

PROC REPORT also allows for rows to "wrap around" when the logical report line would be *longer* than the defined page width, or more precisely, in cases where there are too many vertical columns to display alongside each other. By default in these cases, and like PROC PRINT, PROC REPORT displays one set of columns on the first page, then goes to another page to display the next set of columns of the same logical observations. The PROC REPORT statement option WRAP will force display of a row value from each logical column in sequence; if there is not enough room within the defined page width, the procedure will adjust column headers as best it can and print all row values before going to the next line and printing the next row.

Computed Values

One type of item usage we did not mention yet in our discussion is COMPUTED usage. Using "COMPUTE groups", you can calculate values to appear in report columns but which do not have to represent a particular variable from the input dataset. As a simple example, let's modify the code that created Listing 13.15 by adding a column showing the variance of the actual sales figures from those that were projected:

```
TITLE 'Sales Summary, Key Regions, 3-Year Recap';
TITLE2 'Total Sales over All Key Regions';
PROC REPORT DATA=MYCO.REVENUE NOWINDOWS HEADSKIP;
COLUMN CATEGORY YEAR PROJECTD ACTUAL VARIANCE;
DEFINE YEAR / GROUP 'Year';
DEFINE CATEGORY / GROUP 'Category' RIGHT ;
DEFINE PROJECTD / SUM  'Projected/Sales';
DEFINE ACTUAL / SUM 'Actual/Sales';
DEFINE VARIANCE / COMPUTED FORMAT=5.1 WIDTH=12 'Variance/  (%)' CENTER;
COMPUTE VARIANCE;
   VARIANCE=(ACTUAL.SUM-PROJECTED.SUM)*100/ACTUAL.SUM;
ENDCOMP;
RUN;
```

VARIANCE is not an actual dataset variable. I call it a pseudo-variable, though, because it takes on a value for each dataset observation and can be labelled, formatted, or summarized as can true variables. For purposes of this report, WIDTH= was specified so that the column would have enough room to include the item label on one line; if WIDTH= were not specified, the FORMAT= length (5) would cause the label to be chopped displeasingly into three parts printed on separate lines.

The output from this example is shown in Listing 13.18. Observe how VARIANCE appears no different from the other analysis variables, although it does not exist in any dataset but only in the aggregate REPORT definition. Its computation had to be based on "ACTUAL.SUM" and "PROJECTD.SUM" because of the usage with which these items were defined.

When an item is given the COMPUTE usage on a DEFINE statement, a COMPUTE group is expected within the REPORT code. A COMPUTE group always begins with a COMPUTE statement, which takes one of two general forms, and ends with the statement

```
ENDCOMP;
```

The first form of COMPUTE statement is used when a computed value is to appear at a breakpoint in the report:

```
COMPUTE <BEFORE>|<AFTER> [item];
```

The item, if used, is the name of an item of usage type ORDER, GROUP, or ACROSS. Like BREAKs defined with respect to an item, the COMPUTE group will be executed either right before or right after the item value changes. If no

```
             Sales Summary, Key Regions, 3-year Recap
                 Total Sales over All Three Regions

                              Projected      Actual     Variance
        Category      Year        Sales       Sales         (%)

        Corporate     1990      7647000     8079880         5.4
                      1991      8024200     8227140         2.5
                      1992      6241800     6498094         3.9
        Direct        1990      8953500     9075380         1.3
                      1991     13354500    13286795        -0.5
                      1992     13669500    14139188         3.3
        Wholesale     1990     21087500    21389134         1.4
                      1991     20652500    20028430        -3.1
                      1992     19355000    19661610         1.6
```

Listing 13.18. PROC REPORT with a computed column variable

either at the beginning or at the end of the report.

The second form of the COMPUTE statement, the form we used in the example above that generated Listing 13.18, is

```
COMPUTE item [ / length];
```

In this case, the item must appear in the COLUMN statement, for the computed value will be associated with line items and not with preceeding or succeeding summary lines. If a length is specified, it is normally of the form LENGTH=n, though it may also (or alternatively) include the word CHAR. In either case, the procedure understands the computed item to be of character type; length is not used for numeric variables, and need not be since computed items exist only for the purpose of the REPORT procedure and are not stored in any SAS dataset.

You have great freedom in using COMPUTE groups for almost anything you could do using DATA Step Language, though you do not use dataset-reading statements such as INPUT, SET, or MERGE. You can have code of any length, execute code segments conditionally or iteratively, and so on. You can also use a special statement, the LINE statement, to place computed values directly within the text of a break line. Consider this alternative to the example just given, whose results are presented in Listing 13.19:

```
             Sales Summary, Key Regions, 3-year Recap
                Total Sales over All Three Regions

                          Projected      Actual     Variance
    Category      Year       Sales        Sales        (%)

    Corporate     1990      7647000      8079880        5.4
                  1991      8024200      8227140        2.5
                  1992      6241800      6498094        3.9
              3-year Aggregate Variance is    3.91%.

    Direct        1990      8953500      9075380        1.3
                  1991     13354500     13286795       -0.5
                  1992     13669500     14139188        3.3
              3-year Aggregate Variance is    1.44%.

    Wholesale     1990     21087500     21389134        1.4
                  1991     20652500     20028430       -3.1
                  1992     19355000     19661610        1.6
              3-year Aggregate Variance is   -0.03%.
```

Listing 13.19. PROC REPORT with values computed at breakpoints

```
TITLE 'Sales Summary, Key Regions, 3-year Recap';
TITLE2 'Total Sales over All Key Regions';
PROC REPORT DATA=SASUSER.REVENUE NOWINDOWS HEADSKIP;
COLUMN CATEGORY YEAR PROJECTD ACTUAL VARIANCE;
DEFINE YEAR / GROUP 'Year';
DEFINE CATEGORY / GROUP  'Category';
DEFINE PROJECTD / SUM  'Projected/Sales';
DEFINE ACTUAL / SUM 'Actual/Sales';
DEFINE VARIANCE / COMPUTED FORMAT=5.1 WIDTH=12 'Variance/   (%)'
CENTER;
COMPUTE VARIANCE;
  VARIANCE=(ACTUAL.SUM-PROJECTD.SUM)*100/ACTUAL.SUM;
ENDCOMP;
COMPUTE AFTER CATEGORY;
  VARIANCE=(ACTUAL.SUM-PROJECTD.SUM)*100/ACTUAL.SUM;
  LINE '3-year Aggregate Variance is ' VARIANCE 6.2 '%.';
  LINE ' ';
ENDCOMP;
RUN;
```

In this example the procedure correctly computes the aggregate variance based on the sumtotal of all categories' projections and actuals within each region. It "knows" to do this since this VARIANCE followed "COMPUTE AFTER CATEGORY".

14

Utility Procedures

There are computer programs designed to help process, organize, document, translate, and arrange data so it can be kept and processed most effectively. Such programs have come collectively to be called utility programs or simply "utilities." The SAS System provides a number of utility procedures to help you work with your data files. Some of these procedures are specific to certain operating systems, others—including those discussed in this chapter—are common to the SAS System whatever its installation.*

In this chapter, we look at base SAS procedures that help manage files in SAS data libraries, namely the DATASETS procedure and several others that perform subsets of DATASETS functions. We also review the COMPARE procedure, which helps account for and document changes made to the content of SAS datasets, and the FORMS procedure, which serves the special but important purpose of displaying observations on special forms such as mailing labels.

We stretch things a bit to include them under the "utility" chapter heading, but because it was nevertheless the best available place within the larger book structure, this chapter is also home to our brief introduction to the SQL procedure and to our treatment of the TRANSPOSE procedure.

---

*Even so, there may be differences in specific usage details. Check your SAS manuals, especially the *SAS Companion* for your operating system, to see if there are notes that describe how the procedures discussed below are used in your SAS environment. You will also want to review the *SAS Companion* to see if there are other procedures, specific to your operating system, that you might want to know about and use.

SAS LIBRARY MANAGEMENT

Recall that SAS datasets and other SAS files may be stored severally in a single operating system file called a SAS library. Several utility procedures provide ways to organize SAS libraries or the SAS files stored within them.

Note: In the past, each of these utilities had to be called as a different procedure, and they are discussed as such here. With Version 6 of the SAS System, the DATASETS procedure was made to subsume the functions of several of these utilities, augmenting its original purpose but consistent with it. You can use statements submitted with PROC DATASETS to perform the same functions as the CONTENTS, COPY, and APPEND procedures.

Documenting SAS Files with PROC CONTENTS

Whenever a user creates a permanent SAS dataset, some form of documentation should be prepared. The documentation should provide sufficient means for someone to determine what information the file contains and how to get at it. PROC CONTENTS has some nice ways to supplement hand-prepared documentation. Note that the CONTENTS statement of the DATASETS procedure provides the same functions as the CONTENTS procedure.

The PROC CONTENTS statement takes the form

```
PROC CONTENTS [DATA=<dsname>|<_ALL_>] [options];
```

If DATA= is not specified, the dataset most recently created in the present job (the "last" dataset) is used. If DATA=_ALL_, then all SAS files in the library will be described, or else all SAS files of the type(s) specified by the MEMTYPE= option will be described. Valid values for MEMTYPE include DATA (dataset), CATALOG, VIEW, PROGRAM (containing a compiled-and-stored program, see Chapter 21), and ALL (all member types). If MEMTYPE= is not coded, the default for PROC CONTENTS is MEMTYPE=DATA.

Imagine a dataset created by the following statements:

```
DATA POLL.RESULTS(LABEL='Results of Poll');
  INFILE SURVEY1;
  LENGTH Q1-Q12 AGE 3;
  FORMAT AGE AGEGRP.; * A USER-DEFINED FORMAT;
  INPUT NAME $ 1-25 ADDRESS $ 26-55 SEX $ 56 AGE 57-58
    (Q1-Q12) (1.);
  SCORE1 = SUM(OF Q1-Q3) / SUM(OF Q4-Q6);
  LABEL SCORE1='Ratio of Attitude to Intention Items';
RUN;
```

Running

```
PROC CONTENTS DATA=POLL.RESULTS;
```

under the operating system gives results like those shown in Listing 14.1.* At the top part of the output, general information concerning the dataset is shown. The main CONTENTS results are presented in a table, showing in alphabetical order by variable name each variable's type and length, position in the SAS dataset vector, permanent format and informat if any, and label if any. Add the POSITION option:

```
PROC CONTENTS DATA=POLL.RESULTS POSITION;
```

and get a listing of the variables in order of their physical positions in the data vector, as well as alphabetically (Listing 14.2). This is helpful if you intend to use a double-hyphen variable list abbreviation when accessing the dataset.

On the other hand, you may only need a simple list of the variable names in the dataset. Using the option SHORT on the contents statement gives you what you need. SHORT can be combined with the POSITION option. Listing 14.3 shows the results of

```
PROC CONTENTS DATA=POLL.RESULTS SHORT POSITION;
```

With SHORT but without POSITION, the results would be the same except that the list of variables ordered by position would be omitted.

Printing the Library Directory

When you code

```
PROC CONTENTS DATA=libref._ALL_;
```

the procedure gives contents information for all SAS files of the selected member type(s) in the referenced SAS library. The entries are presented in alphabetical order in the output, preceded by a directory listing them all. If desired, the library listing can be produced without having to print the contents for all members. To print only the directory, code

```
PROC CONTENTS DATA=libref._ALL_ NODS;
```

The NODS option suppresses the printout of the datasets' contents and leaves only the library directory; see Listing 14.4. As an alternative, you can print the contents of one member but include the library directory as well, by coding the DIRECTORY option as in

```
PROC CONTENTS DATA=libref.dsname DIRECTORY;
```

---

*Specific results may vary somewhat depending on your computer operating system.

```
                          The SAS System

                       CONTENTS PROCEDURE

Data Set Name: POLL.RESULTS              Observations:          150
Member Type:   DATA                      Variables:             17
Engine:        V608                      Indexes:               0
Created:       11:23 Sunday, January 10, 1993   Observation Length:    103
Last Modified: 11:23 Sunday, January 10, 1993   Deleted Observations:  0
Protection:                              Compressed:            NO
Data Set Type:                           Sorted:                NO
Label:         Results of Poll

               -----Engine/Host Dependent Information-----

                    Data Set Page Size:          4096
                    Number of Data Set Pages:    5
                    File Format:                 607
                    First Data Page:             1
                    Max Obs per Page:            39
                    Obs in First Data Page:      16

            -----Alphabetic List of Variables and Attributes-----

  #  Variable  Type  Len  Pos  Format   Label
-----------------------------------------------------------------------------
 15  ADDRESS   Char   30   64
 13  AGE       Num     3   36  AGEGRP.
 14  NAME      Char   25   39
  1  Q1        Num     3    0
  2  Q2        Num     3    3
  3  Q3        Num     3    6
  4  Q4        Num     3    9
  5  Q5        Num     3   12
  6  Q6        Num     3   15
  7  Q7        Num     3   18
  8  Q8        Num     3   21
  9  Q9        Num     3   24
 10  Q10       Num     3   27
 11  Q11       Num     3   30
 12  Q12       Num     3   33
 17  SCORE1    Num     8   95           Ratio of Attitute to Intention Items
 16  SEX       Char    1   94
```

Listing 14.1. PROC CONTENTS sample output

```
<<< Note: The POSITION option produces a dataset heading summary and an    >>>
<<< alphabetic list of variables, followed by the positional list. To save space >>>
<<< below, the summary and alpha list (the same as Listing 14-1) were removed.  >>>
```

CONTENTS PROCEDURE

-----Variables Ordered by Position-----

#	Variable	Type	Len	Pos	Format	Label
1	Q1	Num	3	0		
2	Q2	Num	3	3		
3	Q3	Num	3	6		
4	Q4	Num	3	9		
5	Q5	Num	3	12		
6	Q6	Num	3	15		
7	Q7	Num	3	18		
8	Q8	Num	3	21		
9	Q9	Num	3	24		
10	Q10	Num	3	27		
11	Q11	Num	3	30		
12	012	Num	3	33		
13	AGE	Num	3	36	AGEGRP.	
14	NAME	Char	25	39		
15	ADDRESS	Char	30	64		
16	SEX	Char	1	94		
17	SCORE1	Num	8	95		Ratio of Attitute to Intention Items

Listing 14.2. PROC CONTENTS, POSITION option

Output Dataset

PROC CONTENTS can produce an output dataset if the OUT= option is coded on
the PROC statement. As shown in Listing 14.5, produced by the program

```
PROC CONTENTS DATA=POLL.RESULTS OUT=TEST NOPRINT;RUN;
PROC PRINT DATA=TEST; RUN;
```

the name, type, attributes, and position of each variable, the number of observations, the number of variables, and other information (some of which may be
operating system-dependent) is captured. A scheme for dataset documentation
tailored to individual needs can be built from this dataset. The NOPRINT option
on the dataset can be used, as it can with some other procedures that produce
output datasets, to suppress the default printout in cases where the output dataset
only is desired. If we did not code NOPRINT in this example, then the normal
PROC CONTENTS output would have been printed, followed by the PROC PRINT
output.

```
                          The SAS System

                       CONTENTS PROCEDURE

            -----Alphabetic List of Variables for POLL.RESULTS-----

ADDRESS    AGE      NAME      Q1       Q2       Q3       Q4       Q5
Q6         Q7       Q8        Q9       Q10      Q11      Q12      SCORE1
SEX


                   -----Variables Ordered by Position-----

Q1         Q2       Q3        Q4       Q5       Q6       Q7       Q8
Q9         Q10      Q11       Q12      AGE      NAME     ADDRESS  SEX
SCORE1
```

Listing 14.3. PROC CONTENTS, SHORT option

Deleting Datasets

You can delete SAS datasets from a library with the DELETE procedure.

```
PROC DELETE DATA=ddname.dsname; RUN;
```

removes "dsname" from library "ddname". Actually, under most operating systems the data is not actually removed, but it is expunged from the library directory and its internal pointers and the space it occupied is free to be assigned to new members.

The DELETE statement under PROC DATASETS performs the same function as the DELETE procedure (PROC DATASETS is discussed below).

```
                          The SAS System

                       CONTENTS PROCEDURE

                       -----Directory-----

              Libref:        WORK
              Engine:        V608
              Physical Name: C:\SAS\SASWORK

              #  Name     Memtype   Indexes
              ----------------------------
              1  FORMATS  CATALOG
              2  RESULTS  DATA
              3  REVENUE  DATA
```

Listing 14.4. A library directory produced by PROC CONTENTS

The SAS System

OBS	LIBNAME	MEMNAME	MEMLABEL	TYPEMEM	NAME	TYPE	LENGTH	VARNUM
1	POLL	RESULTS	Results of Poll		ADDRESS	2	30	15
2	POLL	RESULTS	Results of Poll		AGE	1	3	13
3	POLL	RESULTS	Results of Poll		NAME	2	25	14
4	POLL	RESULTS	Results of Poll		Q1	1	3	1
5	POLL	RESULTS	Results of Poll		Q2	1	3	2
6	POLL	RESULTS	Results of Poll		Q3	1	3	3
7	POLL	RESULTS	Results of Poll		Q4	1	3	4

OBS	LABEL	FORMAT	FORMATL	FORMATD	INFORMAT
1			0	0	
2		AGEGRP	0	0	
3			0	0	
4			0	0	
5			0	0	
6			0	0	
7			0	0	

OBS	INFORML	INFORMD	JUST	NPOS	NOBS	ENGINE	CRDATE	MODATE
1	0	0	0	64	150	V608	10JAN93:11:23:58	10JAN93:11:23:59
2	0	0	0	36	150	V608	10JAN93:11:23:58	10JAN93:11:23:59
3	0	0	0	39	150	V608	10JAN93:11:23:58	10JAN93:11:23:59
4	0	0	1	0	150	V608	10JAN93:11:23:58	10JAN93:11:23:59
5	0	0	1	3	150	V608	10JAN93:11:23:58	10JAN93:11:23:59
6	0	0	1	6	150	V608	10JAN93:11:23:58	10JAN93:11:23:59
7	0	0	1	9	150	V608	10JAN93:11:23:58	10JAN93:11:23:59

OBS	DELOBS	IDXUSAGE	MEMTYPE	IDXCOUNT	PROTECT	COMPRESS	REUSE	SORTED
1	0	NONE	DATA	0	- - -	NO	NO	.
2	0	NONE	DATA	0	- - -	NO	NO	.
3	0	NONE	DATA	0	- - -	NO	NO	.
4	0	NONE	DATA	0	- - -	NO	NO	.
5	0	NONE	DATA	0	- - -	NO	NO	.
6	0	NONE	DATA	0	- - -	NO	NO	.
7	0	NONE	DATA	0	- - -	NO	NO	.

Listing 14.5. An output dataset produced by PROC CONTENTS

Continued

OBS	SORTEDBY	CHARSET	COLLATE	NODUPKEY	NODUPREC
1	.			NO	NO
2	.			NO	NO
3	.			NO	NO
4	.			NO	NO
5	.			NO	NO
6	.			NO	NO
7	.			NO	NO

The SAS System

OBS	LIBNAME	MEMNAME	MEMLABEL	TYPEMEM	NAME	TYPE	LENGTH	VARNUM
8	POLL	RESULTS	Results of Poll		Q5	1	3	5
9	POLL	RESULTS	Results of Poll		Q6	1	3	6
10	POLL	RESULTS	Results of Poll		Q7	1	3	7
11	POLL	RESULTS	Results of Poll		Q8	1	3	8
12	POLL	RESULTS	Results of Poll		Q9	1	3	9
13	POLL	RESULTS	Results of Poll		Q10	1	3	10
14	POLL	RESULTS	Results of Poll		Q11	1	3	11

OBS	LABEL	FORMAT	FORMATL	FORMATD	INFORMAT
8			0	0	
9			0	0	
10			0	0	
11			0	0	
12			0	0	
13			0	0	
14			0	0	

OBS	INFORML	INFORMD	JUST	NPOS	NOBS	ENGINE	CRDATE	MODATE
8	0	0	1	12	150	V608	10JAN93:11:23:58	10JAN93:11:23:59
9	0	0	1	15	150	V608	10JAN93:11:23:58	10JAN93:11:23:59
10	0	0	1	18	150	V608	10JAN93:11:23:58	10JAN93:11:23:59
11	0	0	1	21	150	V608	10JAN93:11:23:58	10JAN93:11:23:59
12	0	0	1	24	150	V608	10JAN93:11:23:58	10JAN93:11:23:59
13	0	0	1	27	150	V608	10JAN93:11:23:58	10JAN93:11:23:59
14	0	0	1	30	150	V608	10JAN93:11:23:58	10JAN93:11:23:59

Listing 14.5. *Continued*

OBS	DELOBS	IDXUSAGE	MEMTYPE	IDXCOUNT	PROTECT	COMPRESS	REUSE	SORTED
8	0	NONE	DATA	0	---	NO	NO	.
9	0	NONE	DATA	0	---	NO	NO	.
10	0	NONE	DATA	0	---	NO	NO	.
11	0	NONE	DATA	0	---	NO	NO	.
12	0	NONE	DATA	0	---	NO	NO	.
13	0	NONE	DATA	0	---	NO	NO	.
14	0	NONE	DATA	0	---	NO	NO	.

OBS	SORTEDBY	CHARSET	COLLATE	NODUPKEY	NODUPREC
8	.			NO	NO
9	.			NO	NO
10	.			NO	NO
11	.			NO	NO
12	.			NO	NO
13	.			NO	NO
14	.			NO	NO

The SAS System

OBS	LIBNAME	MEMNAME	MEMLABEL	TYPEMEM	NAME	TYPE	LENGTH	VARNUM
15	POLL	RESULTS	Results of Poll		Q12	1	3	12
16	POLL	RESULTS	Results of Poll		SCORE1	1	8	17
17	POLL	RESULTS	Results of Poll		SEX	2	1	16

OBS	LABEL	FORMAT	FORMATL	FORMATD	INFORMAT
15			0	0	
16	Ratio of Attitute to Intention Items		0	0	
17			0	0	

OBS	INFORML	INFORMD	JUST	NPOS	NOBS	ENGINE	CRDATE	MODATE
15	0	0	1	33	150	V608	10JAN93:11:23:58	10JAN93:11:23:59
16	0	0	1	95	150	V608	10JAN93:11:23:58	10JAN93:11:23:59
17	0	0	0	94	150	V608	10JAN93:11:23:58	10JAN93:11:23:59

OBS	DELOBS	IDXUSAGE	MEMTYPE	IDXCOUNT	PROTECT	COMPRESS	REUSE	SORTED
15	0	NONE	DATA	0	---	NO	NO	.
16	0	NONE	DATA	0	---	NO	NO	.
17	0	NONE	DATA	0	---	NO	NO	.

OBS	SORTEDBY	CHARSET	COLLATE	NODUPKEY	NODUPREC
15	.			NO	NO
16	.			NO	NO
17	.			NO	NO

Listing 14.5. *Continued*

Copying Members Between Libraries with PROC COPY

PROC COPY is used to make an exact copy of a dataset from one library in another library. (As with DELETE, the same functions are available through PROC DATASETS.) The statement has the form

```
PROC COPY IN=libref OUT=libref [MEMTYPE=memtype] [MOVE];
```

MEMTYPE= specifies a member type to be affected by the procedure. The default for PROC COPY is MEMTYPE=ALL. The MOVE option requests that members be deleted from the input library after being successfully copied to the output library, as if subsequent DELETEs were performed on them.

Statements allowed under PROC COPY are SELECT or its opposite EXCLUDE, to specify datasets in the input library for selection or exclusion from processing:

```
SELECT [or, EXCLUDE] members [/ MEMTYPE=memtype];
```

If neither SELECT nor EXCLUDE appears, all the library's datasets are copied. Otherwise, only the members listed are copied. If the MEMTYPE= option appears, it overrides the MEMTYPE= specified on the COPY statement. You can, if you like, override even this, for example, as in

```
SELECT A B C(MEMTYPE=DATA) D / MEMTYPE=CATALOG;
```

which selects dataset C and catalogs A, B, and D. The member list on a SELECT or INCLUDE statement can be abbreviated in a couple of ways. A colon can be used to generalize the name:

```
SELECT DAT: ;
```

which selects all members whose names begin with the string "DAT". Datasets that are named with sequential numbers at name-end can be referenced with the hyphen abbreviation, as in

```
EXCLUDE DS1-DS3 ;
```

PROC COPY is an efficient way of gathering files from several libraries into one, of making tape backups from online datasets, etc. Not only is it the easiest (or only) method of copying non-dataset files such as catalogs and stored programs from one library to another, but when used to copy SAS data files, it is much more efficient than using a DATA step with SET: it doesn't construct a PDV and work observation by observation, it just grabs big chunks of data and replicates them from one storage location to another.

Managing SAS Library Members with PROC DATASETS

PROC DATASETS is a handy utility for managing the files in SAS libraries. All types of direct-access (disk-stored) SAS files may be processed, not just SAS

```
1   PROC DATASETS LIBRARY=WORK;
                              -----Directory-----

                          Libref:         WORK
                          Engine:         V608
                          Physical Name: C:\SAS\SASWORK

                          #  Name     Memtype   Indexes
                          ----------------------------
                          1  FORMATS  CATALOG
                          2  RESULTS  DATA
                          3  REVENUE  DATA
                          4  TEST     DATA
1                               RUN;
```

Listing 14.6. PROC DATASETS sample output in the SAS Log

datasets. (Tape and tape-format datasets may not be processed.) With DATASETS, it is possible to modify dataset variables' names or format, informat, or label attributes; to delete library members; to change or exchange the names of library members; to build indexes on SAS datasets; and as may be the user's coding preference, to perform the functions of the CONTENTS, COPY, or APPEND procedures.

A number of statements may appear with PROC DATASETS for use in requesting any of these actions. Password protection (see Chapter 21) can be specified as dataset options on most DATASETS statements to allow access to password-protected members (members of memtype CATALOG cannot be password-protected). Dataset passwords can themselves be altered with PROC DATASETS's MODIFY statement.

For illustration, a library of several temporary datasets was created (DDname WORK, DSnames EXAMPLE1 through EXAMPLE6; the contents of the datasets are not important for our purposes). The dataset directory can be displayed with

```
PROC DATASETS LIBRARY=WORK; RUN;
```

for when there are no statments requesting more action, all the procedure does is list the library members, in alphabetical order. Observe how the output of PROC DATASETS goes to the SAS log, not to the usual procedure print file (Listing 14.6; however, output from the CONTENTS statement goes to the print file, just as if PROC CONTENTS were executed).

PROC DATASETS is designed to be executed in RUN groups. That is to say, a RUN statement (RUN;) does not necessarily terminate the procedure, but does cause the statements that precede it to be executed. The procedure terminates at the next DATA or PROC statement (or if none, at the end of the source code). The distinction has practical relevance mainly in an interactive environment,* al-

---

*In a Display Manager session, SAS library contents can also be reviewed and manipulated dynamically, in the DIRECTORY window.

though applications in batch processing can be devised. To terminate the procedure definitively, use a QUIT statement (QUIT;) after the last RUN.

Deleting Members

The DELETE statement with PROC DATASETS specifies members to be deleted (i.e., removed from the library, as with PROC DELETE; more precisely, the data are not actually removed but the directory entry is unassigned and the space freed for other members). Just as KEEP can be used in a DATA step as the opposite of DROP, a SAVE statement can be used instead of DELETE, to specify members that are *not* to be deleted. If neither a DELETE nor a SAVE statement appears with the DATASETS group, no dataset deletion takes place.

Changing Member Names

The CHANGE statement may be used to rename members within a library:

```
CHANGE oldname=newname;
```

is the form. Members can also exchange names with the EXCHANGE statement. The effect of these statements is shown in Listing 14.7, as is processing by RUN groups.

The AGE statement provides a special way of renaming members that allows multiple datasets created by the same source code to coexist in the same library. Usually, when a SAS job successfully creates a SAS dataset, a preexisting dataset of the same name in the same library will be destroyed. To use the old name yet save the old dataset, the old dataset must be renamed, for example:

```
PROC DATASETS DDNAME=EXAMPLE;
  CHANGE HAPPY=HAPPY1;
RUN;
DATA EXAMPLE.HAPPY;
  [more SAS statements]
RUN;
```

But using the AGE statement rather than CHANGE allows you systematically to save several generations of data. It acts to *postpone* the destruction of a dataset by another of the same name. Consider the job

```
PROC DATASETS LIBRARY=BESTSELR;
  AGE THISWEEK WEEK2-WEEK10;
RUN;
DATA BESTSELR.THISWEEK;
  [more SAS statements]
RUN;
```

```
2   PROC DATASETS LIBRARY=WORK;
                            -----Directory-----

                          Libref:        WORK
                          Engine:        V608
                          Physical Name: C:\SAS\SASWORK

                          #  Name     Memtype  Indexes
                          ---------------------------
                          1  FORMATS  CATALOG
                          2  RESULTS  DATA
                          3  REVENUE  DATA
                          4  TEST     DATA
3    CHANGE TEST=MYTEST; EXCHANGE RESULTS=REVENUE; RUN;

NOTE: Changing the name WORK.TEST to WORK.MYTEST (memtype=DATA).
NOTE: Exchanging the names WORK.RESULTS and WORK.REVENUE (memtype=DATA).
4    EXCHANGE MYTEST=RESULTS; RUN;

NOTE: Exchanging the names WORK.MYTEST and WORK.RESULTS (memtype=DATA).
5    CHANGE MYTEST=RESULT1; RUN;

NOTE: Changing the name WORK.MYTEST to WORK.RESULT1 (memtype=DATA).
6   QUIT;

NOTE: The PROCEDURE DATASETS used 0.7 seconds.
```

Listing 14.7. PROC DATASETS: library change notations in the SAS Log

The AGE statement in PROC DATASETS causes a cascade of renames to take place, as if the statements executed were

```
DELETE WEEK10;
CHANGE WEEK9=WEEK10;
CHANGE WEEK8=WEEK9;
[more CHANGE  statements, through WEEK2=]
CHANGE THISWEEK=WEEK2;
```

That is, the last named dataset on the AGE statement is deleted, and all the other names are sequentially replaced. After DATASETS executes, the name THIS-WEEK is free for the following DATA step. Such a job could be run without alteration each week, and the ten most recent weeks' data would always be available.

Printing Member Contents

The CONTENTS statement under PROC DATASETS provides the same services as PROC CONTENTS, which we discussed above.

Copying Between Libraries

The COPY statement under PROC DATASETS can be used to copy one or more members to another library in a manner equivalent to that produced by the COPY procedure. Instead of IN= and OUT= as would be specified on a PROC COPY statement, only OUT= is specified on a COPY statement coded under PROC DATASETS, since the input library is already known (it is the one that was specified on the PROC DATASETS statement).

When a COPY statement is used with PROC DATASETS, a SELECT or EXCLUDE statement may also appear. The syntax and effects of these statements are the same as when they are used under PROC COPY.

Changing Data Attributes

A MODIFY statement may accompany PROC DATASETS in order to change whole-dataset attributes (label, type, password protection, indexes) or variable attributes (name, label, format or informat). Whole-dataset attribute changes (except for indexes) are specified on the MODIFY statement itself, which has the form

```
MODIFY member [(modifications)];
```

"member" must be a member of memtype DATA; MODIFY works only on SAS datasets. Desired modifications are specified in the form of options in parentheses. LABEL='label' provides text to become the dataset label. TYPE= (which has nothing to do with MEMTYPE) can be used to declare a dataset to be of a special SAS statistics-content dataset such as a CORR, COV, or FACTOR dataset; these topics go beyond the scope of our discussion.

Dataset passwords may be assigned or changed using the MODIFY statement (though passwords and password-setting go beyond the scope of this book). The SORTEDBY= dataset option on the modify statement establishes or changes the asserted sort order; SORTEDBY= in general is explained in Chapter 4.

Variable attributes can be changed with LABEL, FORMAT, INFORMAT, and RENAME statements during a PROC DATASETS step, provided a MODIFY statement has also been issued that identifies the dataset that is to be worked upon.

Building Dataset Indexes

Dataset indexes can be created or removed with PROC DATASETS. Dataset indexes are described generally in Chapter 21, along with the method by which they are created in the DATA Step.

In a PROC DATASETS step, a MODIFY statement must be issued to identify the dataset to be indexed. Then, one or more indexes may be assigned with an INDEX CREATE statement, or deleted with an INDEX DELETE statement. If a single variable is named, i.e.,

```
INDEX CREATE variable;
```

then a simple index is created on the variable. Composite indexes are created with the form

```
INDEX CREATE <index=(variables)>... [/ [UNIQUE] [NOMISS];
```

Composite indexes, and the UNIQUE and NOMISS options, are described in Chapter 21.

One or more indexes may be removed from a SAS dataset during PROC DATA-SETS, with the INDEX DELETE statement

```
INDEX DELETE index(es);
```

As when indexes are created, a MODIFY statement must also be included when they are deleted in order to identify what dataset to work on.

Repairing Damaged Files

The DATASETS procedure provides a means of attempting to salvage SAS files that were damaged due to physical problems during their creation, such as a disk damage or I/O error. Memtypes of DATA and CATALOG are valid (if ALL is chosen, it means DATA and CATALOG only). REPAIR does its best to make the SAS file usable, but may not completely succeed. For example, not all observations in a dataset may be recovered although the header will be restructured to make the dataset usable.

Appending to Data Files

The APPEND statement performs the same functions as the APPEND procedure, and uses the same options as on the PROC APPEND statement (DATA=, BASE=, FORCE). We cover the APPEND procedure later in this chapter.

SAS CATALOG MANAGEMENT

The CATALOG procedure allows you to manage SAS catalog entries. The PROC CATALOG statement has the general form

```
PROC CATALOG CATALOG=[libref.]catalog
[<ENTRYTYPE=entrytype> | <KILL> ];
```

KILL deletes all entries in the catalog, of all entry types, without removing the catalog itself from the SAS library. The ENTRYTYPE= option has no effect: all entries are removed, so be careful. To remove entries selectively by entry type, use a DELETE statement (see below) instead of the KILL option.

ENTRYTYPE= is analogous to the MEMTYPE= option used in library-management procedures to limit the kinds of members that are up for processing. In subsequent statements, an entry may be referred to by a single-level name, with the second level provided by ENTRYTYPE, or explicitly with a two-level "name .type" reference (four-level names are not used because the libref and catalog are already known from the required CATALOG= option; if no libref is specified, its usual default is WORK).

ENTRYTYPE= can be specified on the statements within PROC CATALOG, either following a slash, to refer to all entries named on the statement, or as a dataset option in parentheses after an entry name.* If ENTRYTYPE= is to be specified in either place on a subsequent statement, it should not be specified on the PROC CATALOG statement, for an entrytype specified on the PROC statement will hold for the entire procedure and *not* be overridden by an entrytype specified on a subsequent statement.

PROC CATALOG, like PROC DATASETS and a few other SAS procedures, is designed to be executed in RUN groups, the fact being particularly meaningful in an interactive execution environment.†

Listing the Catalog Directory

The CATALOG procedure statement CONTENTS is used to list the entries in the catalog. The CONTENTS statement has the form

```
CONTENTS [<OUT=dsname> | <FILE=fileref>];
```

If neither OUT= nor FILE= is specified, then the output goes to the standard print output file. An example of CONTENTS is shown in Listing 14.8.

If FILE= is specified, the output goes not to the print file but to the external file associated with the named fileref.

If OUT= is specified, the output goes to the named SAS dataset, which will contain one observation per catalog entry (or per catalog entry of the entry type that the user specified, if any). The dataset variables include NAME (the entry name), TYPE (the entry type), DATE (the date the entry was last modified), and DESC (the description label assigned to the entry, if any). Two other variables are also included: LIBNAME (the libref used when the CATALOG procedure was invoked) and MEMNAME (the name of the catalog). These variables will have the

---

*The syntax for using ENTRYTYPE= on a CATALOG procedure statement is similar to that used with MEMTYPE= on the SELECT or EXCLUDE statement under PROC COPY, as seen earlier in this chapter.

†In a Display Manager session, SAS catalog contents can also be reviewed and manipulated dynamically, in the CATALOG window.

```
        <<< PROGRAM SOURCE CODE FOLLOWS >>>

PROC CATALOG CATALOG=WORK.FORMATS;
   CONTENTS;
RUN; QUIT;



        <<< SAS JOB OUTPUT FOLLOWS >>>
```

```
                        The SAS System

                Contents of Catalog WORK.FORMATS

    # Name       Type      Date       Description

    1 AGEGP      FORMAT    01/10/93   FORMAT:MAXLEN=16,16,1
    2 AGEGRP     FORMAT    01/10/93   FORMAT:MAXLEN=16,16,1
```

Listing 14.8. PROC CATALOG, CONTENTS statement

same values for each entry in the catalog, showing their utility when several OUT= datasets are used together to rebuild a dataset with information on many catalogs.

Deleting Catalog Entries

The DELETE statement is used to remove entries selectively from the catalog; the SAVE statement is an alternative that specifies which entries *not* to remove from the catalog.

Copying Entries Between Catalogs

The COPY statement under PROC CATALOG is used to copy or move entries from one catalog to another. It requires the OUT= option to specify the catalog (or libref.catalog, if the catalog is in another library) where the entry or entries will be copied. Optionally, IN=[libref.]catalog may also be specified, which will override the catalog named on the PROC statement as the catalog containing entries to be copied. Using IN= is a convenience to allow manipulation of multiple catalogs in the same PROC CATALOG step.

The ENTRYTYPE= option can appear on the COPY statement, but does not override the same option on the PROC statement.

The MOVE option on the COPY statement deletes the entry(ies) in the original catalog after copying, as if a DELETE statement were submitted.

A SELECT or EXCLUDE statement may be used along with the COPY statement, to select entries for copying or exclude entries from being copied. If neither

SELECT nor EXCLUDE appears, then all members (or all members of the established entry type) will be copied or moved.

Changing Entry Descriptions

The MODIFY statement under PROC CATALOG allows you to assign or to change the descriptive label associated with a catalog entry. The DESCRIPTION= (or DESC=) option follows the entry name in parentheses, e.g.,

```
MODIFY MYENTRY (DESC='This is what MYENTRY is about');
```

Renaming Catalog Entries

Similar to the DATASETS procedure, the CATALOG procedure provides the CHANGE and EXCHANGE statements to rename catalog entries.

```
CHANGE <oldname=newname>... [/ ENTRYTYPE=entrytype];
```

changes the name of one or more entries to the new name specified, while

```
EXCHANGE <name1=name2>... [/ ENTRYTYPE=entrytype];
```

exchanges names between two entries.

APPENDING SAS DATA FILES

PROC APPEND can be used to attach the observations in one dataset to observations in another, i.e., to *append* one to the other. APPEND attempts to grab large pieces of the dataset and copy them much as does PROC COPY. It is thus much more efficient than a DATA step with a SET statement, which establishes a program data vector and reads and writes observations one by one.

The form of the PROC statement is

```
PROC APPEND BASE=dataset [options];
```

The BASE= dataset, whether permanent or temporary, is the one that is augmented by the observations in another dataset, specified by a DATA= option (or the last dataset created, if no DATA= is coded). The BASE= dataset, in other words, is the one to which you want to add records, and will usually exist by the time you run APPEND (though if it does not, APPEND creates it and simply copies the input dataset). After APPENDing, the BASE= dataset has its old observations, plus the observations from the DATA= dataset tacked on at the end. The DATA= dataset is not affected by the procedure. The BASE= becomes the "last" dataset (that is, that dataset which the next job step will use if a dataset name is not explicitly specified), though technically it is not new. An example of APPEND is illustrated, by the SAS job log, in Listing 14.9.

If there are variables in the BASE= dataset not found in the DATA= dataset, these variables become missing in observations appended to BASE= from DATA=. If there are variables in the DATA= dataset not found in the BASE= dataset, or that are lengthier or different in type, the compiler will print a message to the log and stop processing the step, unless the FORCE option is coded on the PROC statement. With FORCE, the procedure continues; if variables in DATA= are longer than BASE=, they are truncated to fit; if DATA= contains variables not found in BASE=, these will be dropped; if variable types do not agree, the BASE= type prevails and a missing value will be assigned in the new observation.

Because it works on existing datasets rather than rebuilds new ones, this procedure can only be executed on direct-access datasets, i.e., you cannot use APPEND with tape or tape-format datasets. Always proceed with caution if there is no backup of the base dataset.

DATA VERIFICATION USING PROC COMPARE

In cases where a series of changes have been made to important sets of data, it is essential to document the changes made to the data. The best way to do this is to retain all the source code and input data that created the SAS datasets in question. A useful supplement to this are results from PROC COMPARE. PROC COMPARE takes two datasets—such as a newly formed dataset and one from which it was formed before changes were made—and reports the differences between them. It has other uses besides data documentation: Whenever it is necessary to get an idea of the differences between two sets of variables, PROC COMPARE may help.

The PROC COMPARE statement usually names two datasets with its DATA= and COMPARE= options, for example:

```
PROC COMPARE DATA=MY.NEWDATA COMPARE=OLD.MYDATA;
```

We call the DATA= dataset the "base" dataset for purposes of comparison. If DATA= is omitted, the most recently created SAS dataset will be used. The

```
<<< Note: MYLIB.SASDATA started with 27 obs, NEWDATA with 15 obs >>>

12    PROC APPEND BASE=MYLIB.SASDATA DATA=NEWDATA; RUN;

NOTE: Appending WORK.NEWDATA to MYLIB.SASDATA.
NOTE: 15 observations added.
NOTE: The data set MYLIB.SASDATA has 42 observations and 5 variables.
NOTE: The PROCEDURE APPEND used 0.17 seconds.
```

Listing 14.9. PROC APPEND illustrated

COMPARE= dataset is called the "comparison" dataset. If COMPARE= is omitted, the DATA= dataset is treated as the comparison as well as the base dataset; this can be used to compare two sets of variables from the *same* dataset.

All variables are compared by name, and for comparison of a variable to take place its name must be identified. A VAR statement may be used to identify the variables to be compared. It is possible to compare variables with different names between the base and comparison datasets by using a WITH statement (this is also how different variables are compared in a single dataset). If WITH is not used, or if the variables named on WITH number less than those on VAR, then the procedure expects to use variables of the same name on the comparison dataset as on the base dataset. Examples:

```
PROC COMPARE DATA=ADATA COMPARE=BDATA;
  VAR P D Q;
  WITH X Y Z;
```

compares variables P, D, Q from ADATA with X, Y, Z from BDATA. Respectively, P is compared with X, D with Y, Q with Z. If there were no WITH statement at all, PROC COMPARE would expect that both ADATA and BDATA contained variables P, D, Q and would compare P with P, D with D, and Q with Q.

```
PROC COMPARE ...;
  VAR P D Q;
  WITH X;
```

causes COMPARE to compare P in the base dataset with X in the comparison dataset, but to assume that both datasets contain D and Q for purposes of comparison. It is, however, more clear to code a full WITH set if a WITH statement is used at all.

PROC COMPARE often is programmed with an ID statement, which names variables on the base and comparison datasets that are used to match observations for comparison. The statement

```
ID CLASS;
```

for example, when used in a PROC COMPARE group, instructs the procedure to perform comparisons only between observations that have the same value of a variable CLASS. More than one ID statement can be used to classify observations. Because of the sequential nature of the comparison operations, when ID is used the records in the datasets must be sorted or indexed by the ID variable(s).* The entire comparison sequence can also take place within BY groups, i.e., a BY statement *and* an ID statement can appear; if so, the dataset must be sorted by the BY variable(s) and then the ID variable(s). If neither ID nor BY is used, records

---

*This is a rare case in which ordered data are expected even if a BY statement is not used.

from the base and comparison datasets are compared in the order they exist in the datasets, the first with the first, the second with the second and so on.

An example illustrating PROC COMPARE and its output is given in Listing 14.10. There are many variations on the theme, and a large number of procedure options are available to the user. Options on the PROC COMPARE statement allow the user to modify or respecify the rules for numeric comparisons, to extend or suppress parts of the output, to stipulate the treatment of missing values, the content of the ouput dataset (see below) if one is requested, and otherwise control the comparison. For details, consult your *SAS Procedures* guide.

Output Datasets

PROC COMPARE will produce an output dataset if the option OUT=dsname is specified on the PROC statement. The output dataset may contain an observation for each observation found in both the base and comparison datasets after BY and ID are taken into account, i.e., an observation for each comparison attempted by the procedure. However, procedure options can be used to limit the content of the dataset, for example, only to observations that show some difference between the base and comparison datasets. As with some other procedures, when OUT= is used, the regular printed output from PROC COMPARE can be suppressed with NOPRINT.

PRINTING SPECIAL FORMS

The SAS System includes a procedure, PROC FORMS, that helps place information in several regular rectangular units on a page. Used especially for mailing labels, continuous forms of any kind can, in principle, be processed. To use PROC FORMS, you must have a sample of your continuous forms, or at least all relevant width, length, and spacing measurements at hand. More to the point, you should have measured the forms in units natural to your printer. Many printers print six lines to the inch, for example, and ten characters to the inch across. If the forms are 1 inch in length and 3 inches wide, you will inform the procedure the forms are six lines long and 30 print columns wide. This dimension information is given PROC FORMS as options on the PROC statement. If continuous forms consist of mailing labels six lines long, 24 print columns wide, three labels across with a space of two columns (1/5 inch) between them horizontally and one line (1/6 inch) between labels vertically, the statement

```
PROC FORMS WIDTH=24 LINES=6 SKIP=1 NACROSS=3 BETWEEN=2;
```

perfectly describes them.

The PROC statement having described the form dimensions, one or more LINE statements follow to describe the data to be placed within the form. The statement

The SAS System

COMPARE Procedure
Comparison of TEST.FIRST with TEST.SECOND
(Method=EXACT)

Data Set Summary

Dataset	Created	Modified	NVar	NObs
TEST.FIRST	10JAN93:13:24:09	10JAN93:13:24:09	3	127
TEST.SECOND	10JAN93:13:24:10	10JAN93:13:24:10	3	127

Variables Summary

Number of Variables in Common: 3.

Observation Summary

Observation	Base	Compare
First Obs	1	1
First Unequal	26	26
Last Unequal	104	104
Last Obs	127	127

Number of Observations in Common: 127.
Total Number of Observations Read from TEST.FIRST: 127.
Total Number of Observations Read from TEST.SECOND: 127.

Number of Observations with Some Compared Variables Unequal: 5.
Number of Observations with All Compared Variables Equal: 122.

Values Comparison Summary

Number of Variables Compared with All Observations Equal: 1.
Number of Variables Compared with Some Observations Unequal: 2.
Total Number of Values which Compare Unequal: 5.
Maximum Difference: 0.82377.

Listing 14.10. PROC COMPARE illustrated

Continued

```
                      The SAS System

                    COMPARE Procedure
        Comparison of TEST.FIRST with TEST.SECOND
                     (Method=EXACT)

                Variables with Unequal Values

          Variable  Type  Len  Ndif   MaxDif

             A       NUM    8    1     0.824
             B       NUM    8    4     0.815
```

Value Comparison Results for Variables

Obs	||	Base A	Compare A	Diff.	% Diff
86	||	0.8457	0.0219	-0.8238	-97.4100

Obs	||	Base B	Compare B	Diff.	% Diff
26	||	0.9868	1.8017	0.8148	82.5700
52	||	0.7132	1.3020	0.5889	82.5700
78	||	0.5178	0.9453	0.4275	82.5700
104	||	0.7901	1.4424	0.6524	82.5700

Listing 14.10. *Continued*

```
LINE 3 FNAME MI LNAME;
```

for example, asks that on line # 3 of the form the variables FNAME, MI, and LNAME should be written.

Example output from PROC FORMS can be viewed in *SAS Basics*, which also describes other statements and options used with the procedure.

AN INTRODUCTION TO THE *SQL* PROCEDURE

PROC SQL, introduced with SAS release 6.06, represents a significant enhancement to the SAS System. It is an implementation of the standard SQL (sometimes informally pronounced as "sequel") programming language well-conforming (with a few exceptions) to the ANSI SQL standard. By including an SQL compiler with SAS software, SAS Institute achieved two benefits. First, users of database management software such as IBM's DB2 would have the ability to structure SQL queries, to which DB2 responds, using SAS/ACCESS software (which allows users to run SAS analyses even if their data are held in another form; see Chapter 22 under "Connectivity"). Although SAS/ACCESS allows the user to use "regular" SAS statements to process database data, many database users start out more familiar with SQL than with the SAS language and procedures. Second, the SQL procedure can be used not only against files of ACCESS-supported datasets,* but against standard SAS datasets, providing capabilities that for some applications far surpass what could easily be achieve using "traditional"—non-SQL-based—SAS methods. Hence, SQL was included in the Base SAS software. PROC SQL can create SAS datasets (either as data files or SQL data views), or can be used for reporting.

A complete exposition of the SAS System SQL language implementation, or all the ways it can be used to supplement traditional SAS processing techniques, would go far beyond the scope of this book. We will illustrate here just a taste of SQL syntax and terminology, and refrain from going into particular applications. Users who are interested in exploring PROC SQL in depth will wish to study the *SAS Guide to the SQL Procedure*. Because the SAS System SQL language implementation conforms well to ANSI-standard SQL (the *Guide* lists noteworthy exceptions), most books pertaining to SQL in general are applicable to the SAS implementation.

Some Basic Definitions

Although SAS data files do not comprise a relational database, their "rectangular" layout (as a set of observations each containing a value for each of a specified set of variables) fits in with the SQL concept of a *table*. In the abstract, a table is a collection of data that can be thought of as arranged into a set of rows, each of which comprises a set of column values. There is therefore an approximate terminological equivalence, sufficient to describe PROC SQL processing, between a SAS data file and a PROC SQL table, between a SAS observation and a SQL row, and between a SAS variable and a SQL column.

With Version 6 of the SAS System a family of data structures called SAS data views (see Chapter 1; cf. Chapter 21) are available to the user. These contain not

---

*Actually, in release 6.06 of the SAS System, SQL code could not be passed directly to the database software. This caused all kinds of capacity and performance problems with some databases, such as DB2, when large tables were being processed. Starting with release 6.07, an SQL "pass-through" was included so that SAS/ACCESS could send SQL code directly to the database. Users are no longer limited to only the SAS methods, but can push the limits of their database using its internal access methods while still realizing the advantages of the SAS System for analysis and reporting.

actual data values, but descriptions sufficient to allow the correct data values to be obtained from other sources. The term *view* is used in non-SAS SQL processing as well, and for similar purposes. Usually, views are created to express some conjoining of separate tables where physical creation of a new table would be impractical. Views created by the SQL procedure are equivalent to stored query expressions statements (described below), which are retrieved and executed at runtime when the view is accessed.

The Structure of SQL Queries

A *query* is, as the term implies, a formal "question asked" of one or more tables or views. Queries are expressed with a SQL statement containing one or more *table expressions*—instances of conjoined SELECT and FROM clauses (it is a "selection from" its data sources)—and other optional clauses that control row selection, for example, or column ordering.

Consider the dataset used to illustrate the REPORT procedure in Chapter 13. Compare Listing 13.13 with the results of the step

```
TITLE 'A SQL "PRINT"';
PROC SQL;
  SELECT *
  FROM MYCO.REVENUE;
QUIT;
```

the results of which are shown in Listing 14.11. This select statement says "Select all columns (*) from the table MYCO.REVENUE," and the default is to simply list them as rows on the output. You can compare for yourself the PRINT or REPORT statement code that would produce this effect.

The example illustrates the two portions of a table expression, a SELECT clause and a FROM clause. I've titled the output 'A SQL "PRINT"' ' to emphasize the fact that quite frequently the results from a SQL query indeed look very much like those from PROC PRINT (or a simple PROC REPORT). Observe that no special statement needed to be used to cause the results to print; that is part of the query function.

As with all SAS syntax, the layout of the source code doesn't matter; we could have written

```
SELECT * FROM MYCO.REVENUE;
```

or for that matter the whole step as

```
PROC SQL; SELECT * FROM MYCO.REVENUE; QUIT;
```

but it is good form when writing SQL code to separate clauses by lines, and (in the case of queries with multiple or complex table expressions) to indent groups of lines relatively to follow the logic of the query.

A SQL "PRINT"

REGION	CATEGORY	YEAR	PROJECTD	ACTUAL
Northeast	Corporate	1992	2832000	3078225
Northeast	Corporate	1991	3580000	3718121
Northeast	Corporate	1990	3120000	3166209
Northeast	Direct	1992	4770000	4826176
Northeast	Direct	1991	5250000	5465593
Northeast	Direct	1990	1224000	1378125
Northeast	Wholesale	1992	6750000	6649193
Northeast	Wholesale	1991	9200000	8955082
Northeast	Wholesale	1990	8300000	8505035
South/Central	Corporate	1992	2145000	1913527
South/Central	Corporate	1991	2445000	2298737
South/Central	Corporate	1990	2385000	2554576
South/Central	Direct	1992	3825000	4022004
South/Central	Direct	1991	3667500	3419090
South/Central	Direct	1990	2808000	2559600
South/Central	Wholesale	1992	5550000	5745731
South/Central	Wholesale	1991	3420000	3208675
South/Central	Wholesale	1990	6412500	6300068
West	Corporate	1992	1264800	1506342
West	Corporate	1991	1999200	2210282
West	Corporate	1990	2142000	2359095
West	Direct	1992	5074500	5291008
West	Direct	1991	4437000	4402112
West	Direct	1990	4921500	5137655
West	Wholesale	1992	7055000	7266686
West	Wholesale	1991	8032500	7864673
West	Wholesale	1990	6375000	6584031

Listing 14.11. A simple SQL query

Notice that a SQL procedure is properly terminated by a QUIT statement (or the next PROC statement), not a RUN statement. The SQL procedure can carry on with additional queries. But unlike procedures that use RUN groups, where RUN serves to trigger execution and QUIT (or the next PROC) terminates the procedure, with SQL the RUN statement simply has no effect; queries are always executed immediately.

Selecting Rows and Columns

The output of the SQL query

```
SELECT YEAR, PROJECTD, ACTUAL
FROM MYCO.REVENUE
WHERE REGION='Northeast' AND CATEGORY='Direct';
```

Selecting Rows and Columns

YEAR	PROJECTD	ACTUAL
1992	4770000	4826176
1991	5250000	5465593
1990	1224000	1378125

Listing 14.12. A SQL query with a WHERE clause

is shown in Listing 14.12. Here we have limited the columns (variables) by naming specific ones in the SELECT clause, and added a WHERE clause to limit the rows (observations) chosen by the query. Observe that the whole query takes the apparent form of a single SAS statement: there is only one semicolon, at the end.

The commas separating column names are required. In most other SAS statements (such as the VAR statement that may be used with many SAS procedures other than SQL), lists of variable names are entered without columns, but SQL syntax demands them. An attempted SELECT clause written

```
SELECT YEAR PROJECTD ACTUAL
```

would fail as a syntax error. At the same time, the legitimate end of a list should *not* be followed with a comma; a query such as

```
SELECT THIS, THAT, THOSE,
FROM ABC.DEFG;
```

would also fail, because "FROM" would not be correctly recognized as the beginning of a FROM clause.

The WHERE clause consists of an expression that is evaluated per row. If the expression is true, the row is selected for processing. This action is very similar to SAS WHERE-expression processing in other contexts (i.e., WHERE= dataset options and WHERE statements).

Ordering Rows and Columns

As does the VAR statement (for example), or a COLUMN statement with PROC REPORT, a SELECT clause can be used to order as well as select variables. If we wanted the columns to print in the order PROJECTD, ACTUAL, YEAR, we would write

```
SELECT PROJECTD, ACTUAL, YEAR
```

```
                    Ordering Rows and Columns

          PROJECTD     ACTUAL      YEAR
          - - - - - - - - - - - - - - - - - - - - - - - - - - - -
          1224000     1378125      1990
          5250000     5465593      1991
          4770000     4826176      1992
```

Listing 14.13. A SQL query with an ORDER BY clause

The SQL procedure, like the REPORT procedure, can perform an implicit sorting on the rows of the report. To do so, an ORDER BY clause is written. Listing 14.13 presents the result of the query

```
SELECT PROJECTD, ACTUAL, YEAR
FROM MYCO.REVENUE
WHERE REGION='Northeast' AND CATEGORY='Direct'
ORDER BY YEAR ;
```

The keyword DESCENDING (or the abbreviation DESC) can be used after the name of an item on the ORDER statement, as it can on a BY statement (or a REPORT procedure DEFINE statement), to specify a descending sort order for that item. ASCENDING or ASC can also be used, but is not required as the default sort order is ascending.

More than one item can be specified the effect being that, as with a BY statement, items are sorted "from the left." That is,

```
ORDER BY A, B, C
```

request the same sort order as in

```
BY A B C ;
```

If more than one item is specified, they must be separated by columns. DESCENDING (DESC) and ASCENDING (ASC) along with the name it modifies are considered part of a single item, and are never separated from each other by commas, for example,

```
ORDER BY P DESC, Q
```

Computed Columns

The SQL procedure, like the REPORT procedure, has the ability to create "pseudo-variables," columns that do not exist in the input dataset but whose values are

```
YEAR   PROJECTD    ACTUAL  VARIANCE    VARPCT
- - - - - - - - - - - - - - - - - - - - - - - - - - - - - - - - - - -
1992   4770000   4826176    -56176   -1.17769
1991   5250000   5465593   -215593   -4.10653
1990   1224000   1378125   -154125   -12.5919
```

Listing 14.14. A SQL query with a computed column

derived from some sort of computation defined over each row. With the data we have been using for the SQL examples thus far, the query

```
SELECT YEAR, PROJECTD, ACTUAL,
    PROJECTD-ACTUAL AS VARIANCE,
    (PROJECTD-ACTUAL)*100/PROJECTD AS VARPCT
FROM MYCO.REVENUE
WHERE REGION='Northeast' AND CATEGORY='Direct' ;
```

produces results as seen in Listing 14.14. Note that you can use computed columns in the ORDER BY clause if you so require.

A recent enhancement to the SQL procedure allows you to save some keystrokes by using the name of a computed column elsewhere in the SELECT clause. To do so, its name is preceded by the keyword CALCULATED; the SELECT clause of the foregoing example could thus have been written

```
SELECT YEAR, PROJECTD, ACTUAL,
    PROJECTD-ACTUAL AS VARIANCE,
    CALCULATED VARIANCE *100/PROJECTD AS VARPCT
```

This usage is valid only in the same SELECT clause, or in the WHERE clause; calculation definitions cannot be "passed down" to other table expressions in the query.

In any event, as you see, the usual form of a computed item is "expression AS columnname". However, you can suppress the generation of a column name simply by leaving the AS-columnname part off, i.e., by specifying the column computation without "AS columnname". In this case, the column will be created, but it will have a blank heading.

A variant on column creation involves a CASE construct, which has a form much like the DATA Step SELECT statement. The query

```
SELECT YEAR, PROJECTD, ACTUAL,
    PROJECTD-ACTUAL AS VARIANCE,
    CASE
        WHEN ABS((CALCULATED VARIANCE)*100/PROJECTD)>=4)
            THEN  'Unacceptable'
        ELSE 'Acceptable'
    AS VARFLAG
FROM MYCO.REVENUE
WHERE REGION='Northeast' AND CATEGORY='Direct' ;
```

produces results as shown in Listing 14.15. There are two basic forms of CASE group, those with an expression after CASE and before the first WHEN, and those without an expression after CASE: in the first type the CASE expression and the WHEN expression are tested for equality, while in the second type (illustrated above) the WHEN expression is truth-evaluated "on its own." This is quite analogous to the DATA Step SELECT group, where the SELECT statement can contain an expression or not and if it does is compared for equality with the expression on a WHEN statement. Note a couple of syntactic differences between CASE expressions and DATA Step SELECT groups: The keyword ELSE is used instead of OTHERWISE for the "none of the above" action, and the word THEN must follow the WHEN expression and precede the column assignment. Note, too, that the DATA Step SELECT group is a general utility: any executable SAS statement may, potentially, follow a WHEN expression; in PROC SQL, WHEN-THEN is followed by a column assignment.

Setting Column Attributes

It was already mentioned that a computed column can be given a blank heading by eliminating "AS columnname" from its definition. You can also replace the name of a pre-existing column with another name by *adding* an "AS columnname" (in which case, the "new" name is called the column's *alias*). For example, if a table contains the column ABC, its values can be listed under the heading (alias) "XYZ" with

```
SELECT ABC AS XYZ
```

Or, you can give a column a more expressive label by using LABEL= instead of AS columnname, e.g.,

```
SELECT ABC LABEL='Values of column "ABC"'
```

As for the column values themselves, they can be formatted for output using FORMAT= and a valid SAS format (system-provided or user-defined), e.g.,

```
SELECT DATE FORMAT=MMDDYY8.
```

could be used to print a date value with the MMDDYY8. format. Both FORMAT= and LABEL= may be used together, or FORMAT= can be used after AS columnname.

YEAR	PROJECTD	ACTUAL	VARIANCE	VARFLAG
1992	4770000	4826176	-56176	Acceptable
1991	5250000	5465593	-215593	Unacceptable
1990	1224000	1378125	-154125	Unacceptable

Listing 14.15. A column computed by a CASE group

The use of LABEL= and FORMAT= is, of course, similar to usage in other SAS System DATA and PROC steps, but it is an enhancement to standard SQL, which does not provide such a mechanism.

Row Grouping by Summary Statistics

A column item specification of the form "statistic(expression)" can be used along with the GROUP BY clause to cause a summarization to take place over a set of rows. The following query produces the results shown in Listing 14.16:

```
SELECT CATEGORY LABEL='Category',
    YEAR LABEL='Year',
    SUM(PROJECTD) LABEL='Projected Sales',
    SUM(ACTUAL) LABEL='Actual Sales'
FROM MYCO.REVENUE
GROUP BY CATEGORY, YEAR ;
```

Compare Listing 14.16 and its SQL source code with Chapter 13, Listing 13.5 and its PROC REPORT code. The REPORT code gives nicer-looking output (for it can suppress reduntant row values for GROUP or ORDER variables), but the data results are the same. Many of the familiar SAS descriptive statistics besides SUM can be used to define the grouping.

Group Selection

We come now to one of the PROC SQL features that has no direct analog in other SAS processing: the selection of groups for further processing based on a condition that involves the group as a whole. This is done with the HAVING clause. As an example, let's add the clause to the immediately foregoing example (that produced Listing 14.16):

```
          Sales Summary, Key Regions, 3-year Recap
               Total Sales over All Key Regions


                                      Projected      Actual
          Category         Year          Sales        Sales
          ------------------------------------------------
          Corporate        1990        7647000      8079880
          Corporate        1991        8024200      8227140
          Corporate        1992        6241800      6498094
          Direct           1990        8953500      9075380
          Direct           1991       13354500     13286795
          Direct           1992       13669500     14139188
          Wholesale        1990       21087500     21389134
          Wholesale        1991       20652500     20028430
          Wholesale        1992       19355000     19661610
```

Listing 14.16. Row grouping with summary statistics

```
SELECT CATEGORY LABEL='Category',
YEAR LABEL='Year',
SUM(PROJECTD) LABEL='Projected Sales',
SUM(ACTUAL) LABEL='Actual Sales'
FROM MYCO.REVENUE
GROUP BY CATEGORY, YEAR ;
```

which yields Listing 14.17. Compare this with the previous listing: only those rows are included that indicate a sum greater than 10,000,000 of PROJECTD within CATEGORY and YEAR.

While in this case the HAVING expression includes a statistics column that appears in the table (SUM(PROJECTD)), it need not, but could instead contain another statistical expression to be evaluated over the grouping function. Thus, we can remove the line

```
SUM(PROJECTD) LABEL='Projected Sales',
```

from the foregoing example and get a table with the same rows as in Listing 14.17, but without the "Projected Sales" column; that is, the selection is still based on the group sum of PROJECTD, but only CATEGORY, YEAR, and ACTUAL appear in the output.

Special SQL Expressions

Besides the normal SAS operators and functions, PROC SQL permits certain expressions that take special syntactic forms not found outside the SQL procedure.

The BETWEEN-AND condition, e.g.,

```
WHERE X BETWEEN 15 AND 20
```

corresponds to the non-SQL statement

```
WHERE 15 < X < 20 ;
```

The word NOT can be used, as in

```
                               Projected     Actual
         Category      Year       Sales       Sales
         ------------------------------------------
         Direct        1991    13354500    13286795
         Direct        1992    13669500    14139188
         Wholesale     1990    21087500    21389134
         Wholesale     1991    20652500    20028430
         Wholesale     1992    19355000    19661610
```

Listing 14.17. Group selection with a HAVING clause

```
WHERE X NOT BETWEEN 15 AND 20
```

to request the inverse (in this case, all values of X not falling between 15 and 20). The CONTAINS condition is equivalent to the SAS function INDEX: use

```
WHERE A CONTAINS 'Hello'
```

as you would

```
WHERE INDEX(A,'Hello') > 0 ;
```

The IN condition looks the same as the traditional SAS IN operator:

```
WHERE VAR IN ('VALUE1','VALUE2')
```

The IS condition is used for testing missing or nonmissing: the clause

```
WHERE V1 IS NULL AND V2 IS NOT NULL
```

equates to the WHERE statement

```
WHERE V1=. AND V2 NE .;
```

PROC SQL implements the "sounds-like" (=*) and LIKE operators, which are available also in non-SQL WHERE expressions but not in non-WHERE expressions.

The EXISTS condition has no analog outside the SQL procedure. Its right-side argument is a subquery (subqueries are discussed below), and EXISTS is true if the subquery returns more than zero rows. The construction NOT EXISTS is also permitted, and is true if the subquery comes up empty.

Some Capabilities of the SQL Procedure

We won't delve into them in this book (again, the *SAS Guide to the SQL Procedure* is recommended for further study), but the SQL procedure can be used for purposes other than exploring the data in a single SAS dataset. Two of its more important uses are querying more than one table and building new tables.

Querying Multiple Tables

It is possible to bring together information from more than one table (dataset) in a single SQL query, and this is one of the areas where the SQL procedure gives "added value" to the SAS System.

When information is brought together from two or more tables to produce a result, the result is called a *join* of the several tables. In relational processing, several kinds of joins are defined. Simple SQL joins can mimic SAS merges, but provide additional control. With a MERGE, if there are similarly-named items in many datasets the values of items from datasets "to the right" are used. SQL queries allow greater control of what dataset's values will remain in the result of the query.

SQL queries can also be used to perform "fuzzy" merges, as if one could match to a range of BY values, or indeed to any relationship between values. For example, one could stipulate that a match occurs if the value of a variable in one dataset is less than the value of the variable in another dataset. One can even match on the basis of entirely different variables. And one can use subqueries as the object of a WHERE clause to constrain the observations that are able to contribute to the final result.

Creating New Tables

SAS datasets can be built and rebuilt using PROC SQL. To do so, a query is included after a variant on the CREATE phrase. The statement

```
CREATE TABLE MYLIB.MYDS AS   query ;
```

(where "query" is any valid SQL query) results in a new SAS dataset MYLIB .MYDS (remember that a SQL "table" simply means a SAS data file to the SAS System). Specifically, this new dataset will be a SAS data file, containing the data values that result from execution of the query. SAS data views can also be created by the SQL procedure, by substituting the word VIEW for TABLE in the CREATE statement.

There are ways to enter constant data in a new table, and to insert constant rows into rebuilt tables. More significantly, because of the power of SQL to query multiple tables there are dataset rebuilds that can be accomplished by joining multiple tables that would be difficult to replicate using traditional SAS processing methods.

TRANSPOSING DATASET OBSERVATIONS

It is occasionally convenient to switch rows with observations to turn the dataset "rectangle" on its side. Although this can be accomplished with DATA Step programs, there also exists a SAS procedure for this purpose. PROC TRANSPOSE can make the task quite simple, if you have an application for it. TRANSPOSE is an interesting procedure to experiment with, and it can indeed take some practice and experimentation to see if what you think is going to happen will actually happen in practice.

Let's take an example before actually reviewing the procedure's controlling statements and options. Suppose a scientist collects a single response measurement on four experimental groups of animals subjected to one of three treatments in a balanced design. Data are summarized to show the modal response for each

```
<<< PROGRAM SOURCE CODE FOLLOWS >>>

TITLE 'Experimental Data';
PROC PRINT DATA=EXPT1.RESULTS; RUN;
TITLE 'Data Transposed';
PROC TRANSPOSE DATA=EXPT1.RESULTS OUT=TRANS;
  BY GROUP; ID TREATMNT;
RUN;
PROC PRINT DATA=TRANS; RUN;

<<< SAS JOB OUTPUT FOLLOWS >>>
```

Experimental Data

OBS	GROUP	TREATMNT	RESPONSE
1	1	1	4
2	1	2	5
3	1	3	3
4	2	1	7
5	2	2	6
6	2	3	5
7	3	1	8
8	3	2	6
9	3	3	9
10	4	1	3
11	4	2	8
12	4	3	5

Data Transposed

OBS	GROUP	_NAME_	_1	_2	_3
1	1	RESPONSE	4	5	3
2	2	RESPONSE	7	6	5
3	3	RESPONSE	8	6	9
4	4	RESPONSE	3	8	5

Listing 14.18. PROC TRANSPOSE illustrated

group under each treatment, and stored in EXPT1.RESULTS. There are 12 observations, one for each group-treatment combination, sorted by GROUP and TREATMNT.

Problem: For certain statistical analyses, the responses for each group must all be given on one observation, with variables showing the value of the response variable under each treatment.

Solution: See Listing 14.18. A new variable, _NAME_, contains the name of an input dataset variable, RESPONSE. The other variables are named based on the value of TREATMNT since ID TREATMENT was requested. (Since TREATMNT was a numeric variable, the values were prefixed by underscores to create valid variable names.)

TRANSPOSE Statements and Options

Datasets

The DATA= option on the PROC statement of course names the input SAS dataset. The OUT= option on the PROC statement, names the output dataset. As with most other PROC statements, if DATA= is not used, then the dataset most recently created in the program will serve for input. If OUT= is not used, then the output dataset name will follow the "DATAn" naming convention described in Chapter 3.

Output Dataset Structure

The **VAR** statement specifies variables of the input dataset that will define the observations of the output dataset (and whose names will appear as values of the variable _ NAME_). If VAR is *not* used, the default is all the numeric variables that were not named in another output-affecting statement, such as BY or ID. In the example of Listing 14.18, there was one numeric variable, RESPONSE, left over after BY and ID had taken care of variables GROUP and TREATMNT. Therefore, only "RESPONSE" appears as a value of the output dataset variable _ NAME_.

If a BY statement is used with PROC TRANSPOSE (and as with other procedures, this can be accomplished only if the observations are correctly grouped, sorted, or indexed), then for each variable group exactly one observation per unique BY value combination will be produced in the TRANSPOSE output dataset. The BY variables appear in the output dataset, as can be seen in Listing 14.18.

Variable Names and Labels

With PROC TRANSPOSE, the **ID** statement

```
ID variable;
```

can be used to produce the names of the non-BY/non- _ NAME_ variables in the output dataset. If the ID variable is associated with a SAS format, then the formatted value is used; otherwise the literal value is used. If the result is numeric (or more precisely, if it begins with a numeral), an underscore will be placed before it to generate a valid SAS variable name; as you know, SAS variable names cannot begin with a numeral. "Problem" characters (invalid in variable names) in

Data Transposed (without ID)

OBS	GROUP	_NAME_	COL1	COL2	COL3
1	1	TREATMNT	1	2	3
2	1	RESPONSE	4	5	3
3	2	TREATMNT	1	2	3
4	2	RESPONSE	7	6	5
5	3	TREATMNT	1	2	3
6	3	RESPONSE	8	6	9
7	4	TREATMNT	1	2	3
8	4	RESPONSE	3	8	5

Listing 14.19. Another PROC TRANSPOSE illustration

the value will be converted to acceptable forms, usually also with underscores, and the value will be truncated if longer than eight characters.

If an ID statement does *not* appear, then the variables will be named xxx1, xxx2, . . ., where "xxx" is "COL" by default or else specified by the user with the PREFIX= option on the PROC statement. If in the program of Listing 14.18 the ID statement did not appear, and if PREFIX= was not used, then the last three variables would have been COL1, COL2, and COL3.

If the input dataset contains a variable that can serve as an appropriate label for the ID variable, then an IDLABEL statement could also be used.

```
IDLABEL variable;
```

causes the value of "variable" to serve as the label for the variables created by ID.

The name of the variable _ NAME_ can itself be changed to something more to the user's taste, with the PROC statement option NAME=.

If one or more input dataset variables has a variable label associated with it, then a variable _ LABEL_ appears in the output dataset, the values of which will correspond to the input label. As the NAME= option can be used to alter the default name "_ NAME_", so too the name of the variable _ LABEL_ can be changed with the LABEL= option on the PROC TRANSPOSE statement.

Caution: Lest you think it easy to second-guess PROC TRANSPOSE, look at Listing 14.19 to see what happens if the statement

```
ID TREATMNT;
```

were to be left out of the TRANSPOSE step in the example of Listing 14.18: The variables are named COL1, COL2, COL3, *and* (because the ID statement did not eliminate TREATMNT and no VAR statement was used) both TREATMNT and RESPONSE generate transposed observations.

Remember that more complex datasets could produce even more unexpected results. The moral is, of course and as always, to test your programs before relying on them.

part IV

MORE DATA STEP PROGRAMMING

15

SAS Functions

The SAS DATA Step Language provides a great many *functions*: rigidly-defined evaluations not easily expressed with elemental operators. Mathematical and statistical functions abound. Other functions manipulate character variables, and still others serve purposes not easily described as numeric or character: interpreting SAS formats and informats, or translating and evaluating date/time variables. In this chapter, we will review most of the more generally useful SAS functions in each category. Your *SAS Language* reference summarily documents all the SAS functions.

FUNCTION TERMS

A SAS function term consists of a function identifier (i.e., the function name), followed immediately by a set of parentheses which contain zero or more function *arguments*, or parameters that are passed to the function for it to work with. The numbers and types of arguments allowed depend on the function in question, but they could include constants, variables (some functions allow abbreviated variable lists), other function terms, or entire expressions. When two or more arguments are specified, they are separated by commas.

Function terms may be incorporated into larger expressions. The parentheses of a function term should help you remember that functions have the highest priority in expression evaluation, that is, they are evaluated first. Of course, expressions *within* functions must be evaluated before the function can be resolved. If

"Q=ROUND(A+B/C)", the expression A+B/C is evaluated and then the result is rounded and assigned to Q. If "Q=X+Y*ROUND(A+B/C)", the parenthesized expression is evaluated, rounded, multiplied by Y, and added to X.

NUMERIC FUNCTIONS

Those SAS functions that take numeric arguments (which may be numeric constants or variables, or expressions whose results are numeric) and return a numeric result* are called numeric functions. For our discussion we can distinguish those that are used to perform general arithmetic or mathematical operations, those that are used for rounding, those that produce statistical summaries, and those that perform bitwise operations.

Mathematical Functions

SQRT takes a single numeric argument and returns its square root: SQRT(4) returns 2. **ABS** takes a single argument and returns its absolute value: ABS(-10) returns 10. The **MOD** function is used for modular arithmetic, returning the remainder when the first of two arguments is divided by the second: MOD(28,5) returns 3.

Logarithmic functions **LOG** and **LOG10** provide the natural and the base-10 logarithms, respectively, of a single argument. **Trigonometric** and hyperbolic functions, which take a single argument, have names that correspond to their traditional mathematical names. They include SIN, COS, TAN, SINH, COSH, TANH, ARCSIN, ARCOS, ATAN.

Rounding Functions

Three SAS functions provide a way to round fractional values. The function **CEIL**, for ceiling, returns the next integer greater than or equal to the argument: CEIL(28.3) returns 29, CEIL(32) returns 32. The **FLOOR** function does the opposite, returning the next integer smaller than or equal to the argument: FLOOR(126.7) returns 126. The **INT** function returns the integer portion of the argument, i.e., truncates the value to an integer the value of the argument. If an argument is zero or positive, INT and FLOOR will return the same result. However, if an argument is negative, the results will differ: INT(-3.4) returns -3 (as would CEIL(-3.4), but FLOOR(-3.4) returns -4.

The more general rounding function is appropriately named **ROUND**, which can be used to round values to the nearest unit, which by default is 1 (yielding nearest-integer rounding). Following the traditional rule, "5 or more" rounds up, otherwise rounding is down: ROUND(23.4) returns 23, ROUND(23.5) returns 24. ROUND can take an optional second argument, specifying a roundoff unit (for

---

*The end result of a function evaluation, a value based on the nature of the function and its use in context, is said to be *returned* by the function: TAN(X) returns the tangent of X.

example, ROUND(12.345.01) yields 12.35. If left off, the second argument is assumed to be 1: ROUND(X) is the same as ROUND(X,1).

The second argument to ROUND may be a whole number instead of a fraction. To round to the nearest thousand:

```
CLOSENUF = ROUND(BIGNUMBR,1000)
```

Furthermore, the roundoff unit need not be a power of 10. One can round to the nearest half (using .5), the nearest fifth (.2), or the nearest dozen if you like (12). The "5 or more" rule is modified appropriately to "round up" values equal to or greater than the interval midpoint and "round down" others.

Statistical Functions

Many SAS procedures provide methods of calculating descriptive statistics on selected variables across a number of observations. Using functions, many descriptive statistics can be calculated across *different* variables within the *same* observations, and the result assigned to another variable. If any argument values are missing, these functions return a value based on the *non*missing arguments; missing values are *not* propagated by the statistical functions. So, even simple functions such as SUM (see below) are more than mere conveniences.

The SUM Function

SUM takes an arbitrary number of arguments and returns the sum of their nonmissing values: SUM(3,5,.,–2) returns 10 (by contrast, the result of "3+5+.+2" is missing). The SUM function, and the other statistical functions as well, has a special modified form to allow single-hyphen-abbreviated variable lists: The terms SUM(OF VAR1–VAR4) and SUM(VAR1,VAR2,VAR3,VAR4) are equivalent. SUM(VAR1–VAR4) is different: without "OF", "VAR1–VAR4" is taken to mean the result of a subtraction of VAR4 from VAR1 (expressions are normally allowed as function arguments, remember), and the compiler is happy to allow you to take the sum of a single argument if that is your peculiar taste.

The SUM function is useful in accumulating totals.

Problem: Sales bonuses are paid monthly along with workers' paychecks. A dataset contains the worker's name and bonus figures for the year in variables JAN, FEB, etc. Create a dataset that contains workers' names and quarterly and annual bonus totals.

Solution:

```
DATA BNSTOTAL;
  SET EMPLOYEE.BONUS;
  QUARTER1 = SUM(JAN,FEB,MAR);
  QUARTER2 = SUM(APR,MAY,JUN);
  QUARTER3 = SUM(JUL,AUG,SEP);
  QUARTER4 = SUM(OCT,NOV,DEC);
  YEAR = SUM(OF QUARTER1-QUARTER4);
  KEEP NAME QUARTER1 -- YEAR;
RUN;
```

The MEAN Function

MEAN returns the arithmetic average of the nonmissing arguments.

Problem: A dataset contains a series of student test scores on each of six tests. Each observation contains the student's name followed by six separate numbers; the variable names are NAME and TEST1 through TEST6. Create a dataset that contains the average score for each student.

Solution:

```
DATA TESTAVG;
  SET SCORES;
AVERAGE = MEAN(OF TEST1-TEST6);
RUN;
```

MEAN returns the mean of nonmissing values of TEST1 through TEST6, and the result is stored in AVERAGE.

Other Statistical Functions

MIN returns the minimum value: MIN(3,4,2) yields 2. MAX returns the maximum value. **RANGE** returns the range as a single number: the difference between MAX and MIN. Useful in some situations are **N**, which gives the number of arguments that are nonmissing, and its brother **NMISS**, which gives the number of arguments missing.

The statistical functions discussed above are illustrated in Listing 15.1. Other descriptive statistics that have function forms include **VAR** and **STD**, the variance and standard deviation of their respective argument lists; **STDERR**, the

```
1    DATA _NULL_;
2      A=2; B=3; C=4.5; D=18; E=20; F=-10.5; G=.;
3      SUMABCG=SUM(A,B,C,G);  * Missing does not matter here;
4      PLUSABCG=A+B+C+G;       * (but it does here);
5      MEANABD=MEAN(A,B,D);
6      MAXMANY=MAX(A,B,C,10,14,19,E); * OK to mix constants & variables;
7      MINBF=MIN(OF B--F);     * Use "OF" with abbreviated lists;
8      ALLN=N(OF A--G);  ALLNMISS=NMISS(OF A--G);
9      RANGECDE=RANGE(C,D,E);
10      PUT '---> ' _ALL_;      * right here in the log;
11    RUN;

---> A=2 B=3 C=4.5 D=18 E=20 F=-10.5 G=. SUMABCG=9.5 PLUSABCG=.
MEANABD=7.6666666667 MAXMANY=20 MINBF=-10.5 ALLN=6 ALLNMISS=1 RANGECDE=15.5
_ERROR_=0 _N_=1
NOTE: Missing values were generated as a result of performing an operation on
      missing values.
      Each place is given by: (Number of times) at (Line):(Column).
      1 at 4:17
```

Listing 15.1. Statistical functions illustrated

standard error of the mean; **SKEWNESS** and **KURTOSIS**; **USS** and **CSS**, the uncorrected and corrected sums of squares; and **CV**, the coefficient of variation. Remember that only nonmissing values are taken into account when these functions' results are calculated.

Related Functions

The SAS compiler also provides a number of statistics-related functions useful for theoretical and applied statistical research. There are random number generators, probability distribution functions returning the probability that an argument falls below a certain value, and several others. Consult *SAS Basics* for details.

Bitwise Operations

The SAS compiler supports the manipulation of numeric values by the values of their component bits. The general user will not find much of practical value in these capabilities, but the programmer familiar with other computer languages may recognize the applicability for, say, data encryption, or in certain circumstances for multiplication and division. The arguments to the bitwise functions must be numeric, non-negative, and non-missing.

The **BAND, BOR**, and **BXOR** take two arguments and return the bitwise logical AND, OR, or XOR of the arguments, respectively. The logical AND of 2 bits is '1' if and only if both their values are '1' (and is '0' otherwise), the logical OR of 2 bits is '1' if and only if either of their values is '1', and the logical XOR (exclusive or) of 2 bits is '1' if and only if exactly one, and not both, of the bits is '1'. So, for example,

```
BAND(10,12) = 8    [ BAND('1010'B,'1100'B) = '1000' ]
```

and

```
BXOR(10) = 6    [ BXOR('1010'B,'1100'B) = '0110' ]
```

The **BNOT** function takes a single argument and returns the logical NOT thereof: each bit that was a '1' becomes a '0' and vice versa. But does

```
BNOT(10) = 5    [ BNOT('1010'B) = '0101' ]    ?
```

No, it is a much greater value, in fact, the value of the largest 32-bit integer minus 10. As you know, the SAS System supports "double-precision" numerics and the value of most arguments can range from zero to the largest unsigned 32-bit integer. Or in other words, full eight-byte numerics of any bit patterns whatever can be input to the functions (the exceptions are the second arguments to the

BLSHIFT and BRSHIFT functions, which can range from 0 to 31). All those 28 zero bits to the left (not shown in the example input above since they were zero) are changed to ones by BNOT.

Bitshifting operations can be accomplished by the **BLSHIFT** and **BRSHIFT** functions. These functions shift the bits of the first argument to the left or right, respectively, by the number of positions specified in the second argument, zero-filling the "spaces" left on the right or the left. For example,

```
BLSHIFT(10,2) = 40    [ BLSHIFT('1010'B,2) = '101000' ]
```

CHARACTER FUNCTIONS

Character functions are functions that are meant to operate on character arguments. It is possible to give character functions numeric arguments, but these are treated for purposes of the function as character (e.g., number 123 is treated as the character string variable '123'). The result returned by a character function may be character or numeric, depending on the specific function.

Shortening and Alignment

SAS character variables can be as long as 200 bytes. If the variable's attributed length is longer than the specific value, character values are "padded on the right" with blanks, i.e., spaces are used to fill out the remaining length. If a character variable has a length of 10, the word "HELLO" would be stored as "HELLO".

This creates at least two kinds of problems. First, comparison operations might inadvertently fail. The second kind of problem arises when variables are to be concatenated; extra blanks can wind up in the middle. For example, if you have a dataset containing lastname, firstname, middlename, and want to print out mailing labels using a character concatenation such as

```
NAME = FIRST || MID || LAST;
```

an unfortunate result such as

```
JOHN        PAUL        JONES
```

can occur if there are trailing blanks.

The **TRIM** function is provided to avoid problems such as this. TRIM strips a character value of trailing blanks, returning a value that stops at the last non-blank character of the argument, having a length equal to the length of the argument up to the last nonblank character. The TRIM function does not touch leading or intervening blanks, only trailing blanks. That is to say, blanks at the beginning or in the middle of the argument are preserved; only the blanks after the last nonblank character are removed. TRIM is often useful in conjunction with character concatenation (illustrated below at Listing 15.2), or when a comparison test can fail if trailing blanks are not removed (an example is shown under our discussion below of the INDEX function).

The **TRIMN** function is similar to TRIM with one exception. When TRIM is passed a blank value, it returns a single blank: TRIM(' ') = ' '. If a null string (a string of zero length) is required when the input value is blank, use TRIMN instead. Suppose you have a dataset that includes three variables FIRST, MIDDLE, and LAST, character values containing first, middle, and last names, where MIDDLE is blank (character missing) if there is no middle name. To create a full name, being the concatenation of the two or three names separated by single blanks, use

```
FULLNAME=TRIM(FIRST)||' '||TRIMN(MIDDLE)||' '||TRIMN(LAST);
```

You could use TRIMN(FIRST) and TRIMN(LAST) if you wish, but you *must* use TRIMN(MIDDLE) and not TRIM(MIDDLE) if you want to avoid having two blanks between the first and last name when the middle name is absent.

Two other functions deal with the realignment of leading and trailing blanks. **RIGHT** slides the nonblank portion of its single argument to the right, effectively moving trailing blanks left.

If WORD='HELLO ':

```
1          *** STRING FUNCTIONS TRIM, LEFT, RIGHT ***;
2          DATA _NULL_;
3          A='PRUNES'; B='ARE';C='GOOD'; D='FOR' ; E='YOU';
4          LENGTH CVAR $ 25;
5          CVAR=A;  PUT CVAR=;
6          CVAR=A||' '||B; PUT CVAR=;
7          RVAR=E||D||RIGHT(CVAR); PUT RVAR=;
8          X=RIGHT(CVAR);
9          RVAR2=E||D||X; PUT RVAR2=;
10         Y=LEFT(X);
11         LVAR=E||D||Y; PUT LVAR=;
12         NEWVAR=CVAR||' '||C||' '||D||' '||E; PUT NEWVAR=;
13         TVAR=TRIM(CVAR)||' '||C||' '||D||' '||E; PUT TVAR=;
```

```
CVAR=PRUNES
CVAR=PRUNES ARE
RVAR=YOUFOR                    PRUNES ARE
RVAR2=YOUFOR                   PRUNES ARE
LVAR=YOUFORPRUNES ARE
NEWVAR=PRUNES ARE                    GOOD FOR YOU
TVAR=PRUNES ARE GOOD FOR YOU
```

Listing 15.2. Character functions that remove or realign blanks

```
RGHTWORD = RIGHT(WORD);
```

results in RGHTWORD having the value '   HELLO'. **LEFT** has the opposite effect. Blanks that are found to the left of any other character, called leading blanks, are effectively placed at the end as the nonblank portion of the argument is shifted left. In our example, LEFT(RGHTWORD) becomes 'HELLO   ' again.

Unlike TRIM, RIGHT and LEFT do not remove blanks, they just shift the position of the nonblank center of the argument one way or another. RIGHT is of limited usefulness in most practical circumstances, but LEFT is frequently helpful in conjunction with TRIM, as in TRIM(LEFT(X)), in order to purge both leading and trailing blanks for comparison or concatenation. Examples of these three functions are shown in Listing 15.2.

Length

LENGTH returns a numeric value, the number of bytes in the character expression given in its single argument, exclusive of trailing blanks. More precisely, LENGTH returns the position of the last nonblank character in the argument. Taking the previous examples, LENGTH(WORD) returns the numeric value 5, but LENGTH(RGHTWORD) returns 10. Among other uses, LENGTH may help moderate the effect of other character functions.

You cannot use LENGTH to check for a missing (blank) value, for if there are zero nonblank characters, LENGTH returns 1, not 0 as you might think.

String and Character Search

Several SAS functions examine the value of a character variable or expression, and retrieve information about character substrings within it.

String Search

INDEX finds the position of a specific character substring within another. IN-DEX takes two arguments, the first the string and the second the substring to find. The position of a substring is where it begins, counting characters from the left; if the substring is not found, the position is defined to be zero. For example, INDEX('ABCDE','DE') returns 4, since 'DE' begins in the fourth position of 'ABCDE'. INDEX('ABCDE','EFG') returns 0, since the second argument is not found anywhere in the first. This latter feature of INDEX can prove very useful.

Problem: You have an external dataset containing a list of names, addresses, and occupations. The information was just typed in directly, without regard to columns, and looks like this:

```
JOHN A HUGHES, 3443 SILVER STREET, PITTSFIELD, MACHINIST
SUSAN W WAGSTAFF, 129-B 16TH AVENUE, SPRING VALLEY, WELDER
PETER OZECHOVSKI, L-5 COLONY, EXOSPHERE, CHEMICAL ENGINEER
```

Produce a subset of this list containing records only for the teaching profession.

Solution: It is not necessary to assign the occupation to a character variable, which in a free-form list with variable lengths and numbers of words would be quite difficult. Instead:

```
DATA TEACHERS;
INFILE MAINLIST;
INPUT WHOLTHNG $CHAR80.;
IF INDEX(WHOLTHNG,'TEACHER') > 0;
RUN;
```

The INDEX function takes trailing blanks seriously:

```
INDEX('ABCDEFG','ABC ')
```

returns 0, not 1. This can become a practical problem if the second argument is a character variable and not a constant: if the length of the current value of the variable is less than the total length of the variable, the value as "padded on the right" with blanks is compared. In these cases, the TRIM( ) function can come in handy. Thus for illustration, a variant solution to the previous problem:

```
DATA TEACHERS;
LENGTH OCCUPATN $15; RETAIN OCCUPATION 'TEACHER';
INFILE MAINLIST;
INPUT WHOLTHNG $CHAR80.;
IF INDEX(WHOLTHNG,OCCUPATN) > 0; * WRONG;
IF INDEX(WHOLTHNG,TRIM(OCCUPATN)) > 0; * RIGHT;
RUN;
```

The **INDEXW** function performs the same task as INDEX, but does not recognize strings not beginning at a word boundary. Generally, "words" in the SAS System are separated by special characters or blanks, while a consecutive combination of letters, numerals, and underscores constitute a "word."* Thus

```
INDEX('ISHTAR','TAR')
```

returns a value of 4, but

```
INDEXW('ISHTAR','TAR')
```

returns 0.

---

*A SAS "word" of this type is also known as a "token," especially when discussing the SAS Macro Language as we do in Chapter 19.

Character Search

INDEX and INDEXW look for groups of characters considered as a unit, i.e., for character strings. Other character functions look at individual characters within strings. **INDEXC** searches for particular characters, and **VERIFY** searches for "error" characters based on a specified set of valid ones.

INDEXC takes two or more arguments. It returns the position in argument1 of the first character found that matches *any* character in *any* of the subsequent arguments. For example,

INDEXC('ROOSEVELT','FRANKLIN','DELANO') returns 1, because the first character in ROOSEVELT was found in one of the following arguments. INDEXC('TRUMAN','HARRY S') returns 2. If none of the characters in any of the second or subsequent arguments is found in the first argument, then the function returns zero, e.g., if FRUIT1='FIG' and FRUIT2='PRUNE', then INDEXC (FRUIT1,FRUIT2) returns 0. The INDEXC function has a variety of uses. One common application is to "proofread" data entry for errors.

Problem: From a lengthy dataset of names you want to purge as many errors as possible. To start, look at any names with nonalphabetic characters.
Solution:

```
DATA BADNAMES; * NAMES WITH NONALPHA CHARACTERS;
SET MYDATA.LIST;
IF INDEXC(NAME,'0123456789!@#$%^&*()-+''' "<>,.?:;') > 0;
RUN;
PROC PRINT DATA=BADNAMES; RUN;
```

Note, by the way, the two consecutive apostrophes in the character constant, which the compiler interprets as a single apostrophe and not as the ending quote for the string. If the constant string were delimited with double quotes, a single apostrophe could appear, but there would have to be two consecutive double quotes.

Problem: As another example of this use for INDEXC, suppose you know that each address must have a number. Produce a list of addresses with no numbers.
Solution:

```
DATA BADADDR; * ADDRESSES WITHOUT NUMBERS;
  SET MYDATA.LIST;
  IF INDEXC(ADDRESS,'0123456789') = 0;
RUN;
PROC PRINT DATA=BADADDR; RUN;
```

The VERIFY function returns the position of the first character in argument1 that is *not* found in any subsequent argument, or zero if all characters in argument1 have a match in the subsequent argument(s). It verifies that the first argument contains only characters found in the second or subsequent arguments. (Don't get confused by the fact that VERIFY returns 0 (false) if the characters are all "verified," nonzero if not. Just be mindful of that fact.) So, another solution to the BADNAMES problem is:

```
DATA BADNAMES; * NAMES WITH ILLEGAL CHARACTERS BY
MISTAKE;
SET MYDATA.LIST;
IF VERIFY(NAME,' ABCDEFGHIJKLMNOPQRSTUVWXYZ') > 0;
RUN;
```

Note that the blank space must be included in the string (here, we have placed it before the A); otherwise, the spaces within the names would cause them all to fail verification.

The SCAN Function

SCAN returns the nth word from argument1, where *n* is specified in argument2. SCAN('HOW ARE YOU?',2) returns ARE, because 'ARE' is the second word in 'HOW ARE YOU?'. The function determines where a "word" begins and ends by looking for special delimiting characters, that is to say, characters which are not taken to be part of any word but stand for a separation between words. Unlike, say, the INDEXW function, SCAN lets the user determine what characters will or will not be treated as delimiters by using a literal string of them as a third argument. The characters thus specified will not be treated as part of any word, but as showing where one word ends or another begins. Thus SCAN ('H1E1L1P',3,'1') returns 'L'. If a third parameter is not given, then by default the delimiter list includes those characters that the SAS System uses for determining a word: the blank, the period and comma, the left and right parentheses, the solid and broken vertical lines, the dollar sign, the ampersand, and certain other special symbols. If you do use a third argument, the default list is canceled and you must specify all the delimiters that may be needed. Leading delimiters (delimiter characters appearing before the first word) are ignored, and consecutive delimiters (delimiters appearing next to each other) are treated as one delimiter. So

```
SCAN('   HOW   ARE   YOU?',2)
```

also returns 'ARE'. If a word at a later ordinal position than the number of words in the first argument is called for, the result is character missing, i.e., blank: SCAN('A-B-C-D',7,'-') returns blank, since there is no seventh word.

Problem: Suppose that in the list of employees in an earlier example the names are always typed in order first, middle initial, last, although sometimes there is no middle initial. Select those whose last name is JONES.

Solution:

```
DATA JONESES;
  INFILE MAINLIST;
  INPUT WHOLTHNG $CHAR80.;
  IF (LENGTH(SCAN(WHOLTHNG,2)) = 1 AND SCAN(WHOLTHNG,3) = 'JONES,')
      OR SCAN(WHOLTHNG,2) = 'JONES,';
```

Follow the subsetting IF statement. It contains two phrases, separated by OR. (The first phrase is parenthesized for clarity, although AND is of higher precedence than OR anyway.) First, the second word of WHOLTHNG is obtained. If it is exactly one character in length, therefore a middle initial (assumption), the third word must be the surname. If that word is 'JONES', the IF condition is true and the record is selected. If the second word is not a middle initial (one character long), the phrase after the OR is examined: If the second word (in this case assumed the surname) is 'JONES', the condition is true and the record is selected.

Another example of SCAN: Observe that in the list of persons and occupations, the name, address, and occupation are separated by commas. Assume this is consistent throughout the dataset, and there are no other commas except between these logical items.

Problem: Create a SAS dataset containing name, address, and occupation as separate variables.

Solution:

```
DATA JOBS;
  INFILE MAINLIST;
  INPUT WHOLTHNG $CHAR80.; DROP WHOLTHNG;
  LENGTH NAME ADDRESS OCCUPATN $ 30; * CHOOSE SAFE MAX. LENGTH;
  NAME = SCAN(WHOLTHNG,1,',');
  ADDRESS = SCAN(WHOLTHNG,2,',');
  OCCUPATN = SCAN(WHOLTHNG,3,',');
RUN;
```

String and Character Manipulation

Several character functions work upon characters or strings to change them around. The function **UPCASE**, useful in interactive SAS and some other applications, replaces each lowercase character in its single argument with its uppercase equivalent, e.g., UPCASE('Abcde')='ABCDE'. **LOWCASE** does the opposite. **REVERSE** returns its argument with the characters reversed in order: REVERSE('HI THERE!') returns '!EREHT IH'.

The **TRANSLATE** function replaces the occurrence of specified characters with replacement characters. TRANSLATE takes at least three arguments. The first argument is the string in which characters are to be replaced, the second contains the characters to use for replacement, and the third the characters to be replaced. For example, TRANSLATE('MOTHER','B','M') returns BOTHER; in words, this function term says "In the string 'MOTHER', replace with the character B all occurrences of the character M." If additional arguments are supplied, they must come in pairs: replacements and then characters to replace:

```
TRANSLATE('MOTHER','F','M','A','O')
```

returns 'FATHER'.

The **TRANWRD** function is like TRANSLATE except that it operates on strings of characters instead of individual characters. Only one set of replacements is used. For example,

```
TRANWRD('FATHER','HER','HEAD')
```

returns 'FATHEAD'.

TRANWRD, like some other string-processing functions, is sensitive to trailing blanks, so you may need to use TRIM (or TRIMN) if the second or third argument to TRANWRD is a character variable.

The **COMPRESS** and **COMPBL** functions may be used to "squeeze out" unwanted characters from a character string. COMPRESS takes two arguments, the first a character variable or string and the second a list of characters to remove from it. Thus

```
COMPRESS('MERRY','ER')
```

returns 'MY' due to the removal of occurrences of characters E and R. If a second argument is not specified, then by default the blank is removed: COMPRESS ('A B C') is the same as COMPRESS('A B C',' ') and yields 'ABC'. COMPBL, which takes one argument, is similar to COMPRESS with no second argument, except that rather than squeezing out all blanks, COMPBL leaves exactly one blank where it found one or more blanks:

```
COMPBL('ONE        BLANK')
```

yields 'ONE BLANK', where

```
COMPRESS('ONE        BLANK')
```

would return 'ONEBLANK'.

The **QUOTE** and **DEQUOTE** functions add and remove, respectively, quotation marks from around a character value. QUOTE adds double quote marks at the beginning and the end of the value. DEQUOTE strips outer quotation marks, whether single or double.

The SUBSTR Functions

The function name SUBSTR is used for two distinct purposes. In both cases, "SUBSTR" means "substring" (a contiguous group of characters from within a character string, less than or equal to the length of the character string).

The first use of SUBSTR is as a search function, where it returns a substring of specified position and length. The first argument is the input character string, the second the position in the string the desired substring starts, and the third the length of the desired substring. SUBSTR('QRSTUV',3,2) returns ST. The third argument may be omitted; if so, it is understood that the user desires the remaining portion of argument 1, beginning at the position of argument 2:

```
SUBSTR('QRSTUV',3)
```

returns STUV.

The second use of SUBSTR produces an action different from all other SAS functions. Other function terms, including the first use of SUBSTR, appear to the right of assignment statements, either alone or in expressions. The second use of SUBSTR is invoked by the SAS compiler when it finds the term appearing on the *left* of a special assignment-like statement. This usage causes the portion of a string variable named as argument 1 to take on the value of a substring identified on the right. Replacement begins at the position given by argument 2, and continues through the position specified by argument 3. The SAS statements

```
CVAR = 'THIS ONE';
SUBSTR(CVAR,3,2) = 'AT';
```

result in a value for CVAR of 'THAT ONE'. If the third argument is omitted, the first argument is replaced to its end. In this cases, if the substring is too long to fit from the specified position to the end of the alloted variable length, only the characters up to the length allowed will be used, while if it is shorter than the available length, the remainder of the variable is filled with blanks:

```
CVAR 'THIS ONE';
SUBSTR(CVAR,3) = 'AT';
```

gives CVAR the value 'THAT   '. In using the SUBSTR function to the left of the assignment operator, argument1 must be a character variable, i.e., it cannot be a constant, an expression, or a numeric variable, for the action is to insert a substring directly into an existing variable's PDV storage location.

Some more examples of both kinds of SUBSTR function are shown in Listing 15.3.

```
1          *** EXAMPLES OF THE SUBSTR FUNCTION ***;
2          DATA _NULL_;
3          A='ABCDEFGHIJKLMNOP';
4          B=SUBSTR(A,5,3);* FROM 5TH POSITION FOR 3 CHARACTERS;
5          C=SUBSTR(A,5);  * FROM 5TH POSITION TO END;
6          PUT A=; PUT B=; PUT C=;
7          SUBSTR(A,3,5)='SUBSTITUTES 1ST 5 OF THIS';
8          PUT A=;
9          SUBSTR(A,10)='X'; *SUBSTITUTES TO END, IN THIS CASE SHORTENS;
10         PUT A=;
11         RUN;
```

```
A=ABCDEFGHIJKLMNOP
B=EFG
C=EFGHIJKLMNOP
A=ABSUBSTHIJKLMNOP
A=ABSUBSTHIX
```

Listing 15.3. The SUBSTR function

DATE/TIME FUNCTIONS

Date/time functions work with SAS date/time values (discussed in Chapter 8).* Depending on the particular function, the arguments may be numeric or date/time, and the values returned may be numeric, date/time, or character. The date/time *formats* convert values for the purpose of writing them; the *functions* return values that can be used for any purpose, such as assignment or comparison. These SAS functions provide the user with powerful ways to handle peculiarities of calendar and clock.

Conversion to SAS Date/Time Values

Several functions serve to construct SAS date, time, and datetime values, by returning a numeric value corresponding to the correct SAS date/time value. This is valuable in converting external input to SAS date values when an informat will not work (such as when month, day, and year are located in separated fields), or when separate parts of a date/time value have already been stored in separate variables (e.g., YEAR, MONTH, etc.)

The function **MDY** takes three numeric arguments and returns a SAS date value as if the three were month, day, and year. If A = 3, B = 5, and C = 12, MDY(A,B,C) returns the SAS date equivalent of March 5, 1912. The function will not accept an invalid month or day (i.e., a month greater than 12, a day greater than the number of days in the indicated month), in which case it returns a missing value. The third parameter, unless it gives a full four digits, is interpreted in the 1900s.

DATEJUL makes a SAS date value out of a Julian date, which is a date of the form "yyddd": "yy" is the year, and "ddd" the sequence number of the day of the year: December 31 is the 365th day of non-leap years, and so on. For example, DATEJUL(78015) returns the SAS date value for January 15, 1978. Julian dates have some applications in data processing, although SAS datetime values make it possible to deal effectively with dates without resorting to Julian style.

For business purposes, you can use **YYQ** to create a SAS date value from a year and quarter; the first day of the quarter is returned: YYQ(75,2) results in the date value representing April 1, 1975.

The **HMS** function creates a SAS time value from up to three parameters representing hour, minute, and second, while with **DHMS**, a SAS datetime value can be created: The first argument to DHMS is a SAS date, and up to three more arguments can be given to represent the hour, minute, and second. For example, if THEDAY=MDY(3,15,80), then DHMS(THEDAY,15,30) returns the datetime value representing March 15, 1980, 3:30 PM. Or, if no date has yet been created, DHMS(MDY(3,15,80),15,30) does the job. HMS returns a SAS time value, DHMS a SAS datetime value.

---

*In this book we use the term "date/time" generically, to mean "date, time, or datetime," the three kinds of SAS date and time values.

Current Date and Time

Three functions use the computer system clock to get the current date/time information. The functions take a null argument (i.e., an empty set of parentheses). **DATE**, which also may be written TODAY, results in the SAS date value for the current day. **TIME** returns the current time as a SAS time value, and similarly, **DATETIME** returns the SAS datetime value for the current moment, the moment the statement executes.

These functions might be used in an ongoing data-gathering system.

Problem: A company collects a great deal of information each day, and each evening these data are read and used to update a master dataset. The date of the latest update must be recorded for each record.

Solution: Create a variable (here called LASTDATE) by assignment:

```
LASTDATE = TODAY();
```

and add this to the rebuilt dataset.

Used in conjunction with other date/time functions, you can calculate durations relative to the current moment. In Chapter 8 we illustrated the calculation of current age from birthdate and today's date,

```
AGE = (TODAYDT - BRTHDT) / 365.25;
```

but we didn't know how the date values got there. Here's one way, given month of birth in BMO, day in BDA, year in BYR:

```
TODAYDT=TODAY();  BRTHDT=MDY(BMO,BDA,BYR);
```

In practice, if the two additional variables are not themselves needed:

```
AGE = (TODAY() - MDY(BMO,BDA,BYR)) / 365.25;
```

Conversion from SAS Date/Time Values

SAS provides a number of handy functions for turning SAS date/time values back into values we humans can more easily understand. Functions that so operate on SAS date values include **DAY** (day of month), **WEEKDAY** (day of week), **MONTH**, **QTR** (calendar quarter), **YEAR**, and **JULDATE** (Julian date). These functions return their respective results as ordinary numeric values. Suppose the date value representing February 3, 1986 is stored in the variable SOMEDATE. Then DAY(SOMEDATE) returns 3, WEEKDAY(SOMEDATE) returns MONDAY, MONTH(SOMEDATE) returns 2, QTR(SOMEDATE) returns 1, YEAR(SOME-DATE) returns 1986, and JULDATE(SOMEDATE) returns 86034. Corresponding to these date-converting functions are the time functions **HOUR**, **MINUTE**, and **SECOND**, which take as their single argument either a time or a datetime value.

These functions can help create data processing subgroups.

Problem: Retrieve financial records for the first quarter of the current calendar year, given the date in a variable RECDATE.
Solution:

```
IF YEAR(RECDATE)=YEAR(TODAY()) AND QTR(RECDATE)=1;
```

As for the time-converting functions, these have applications in the analysis of realtime systems, such as computer systems or utility-delivery systems (hour-by-hour and minute-by-minute usage, etc.).

Conversion Between SAS Date/Time Values

DATEPART returns the "date part" of the datetime value as a date value. **TIMEPART** returns the "time part" of a datetime value as a time value. Curiously, there is no simple reverse conversion from a date and a time value to a datetime value. It would be useful to have a function that did this. For now, you have to work around this using other functions.

Counting or Incrementing Time Intervals

SAS provides two functions to deal directly with date or time intervals. The first of these, **INTCK**, can help in certain data processing tasks involving calculation of time spent or time between. INTCK takes three arguments. The first is an interval, the second a "from" value, the third a "to" value. Here is an illustration: INTCK('DAY','25NOV87'D,'30NOV87'D) returns 5. The first argument must be a constant from the specific list shown in Table 15.1, or a character variable containing a value from the list. The "DT" prefix can be used in front of any of the date intervals (not the time intervals) to indicate datetime rather than data calculations. A numeral, or a period and a numeral, may follow the value to indicate a multiple or an offset shift. An interval name suffixed by a numeral serves to multiply the basic interval by that numeral. Thus "WEEK3" specifies an interval of three weeks, "DAY15" one of 15 days, etc. A period and numeral indicates that the standard beginning of the interval be shifted accordingly. The offset suffix has a meaning specific to each interval, as noted also in Table 15.1. For YEAR (for example) it is a month, and thus the date for "YEAR" generally corresponds to January 1, but "YEAR.5" to May 1.

To be very exact, be very careful: INTCK counts from fixed interval beginnings. Unless the interval name is specifically suffixed with a period and numeral, a week, for example, starts each Sunday, a year on January 1, a day at midnight. Furthermore, INTCK always returns an integer value, and partial intervals are not considered, so, for example,

```
INTCK('YEAR','01JAN50','31DEC50')
```

results in a value of 0, while

TABLE 15.1. DATE/TIME INTERVALS USED WITH THE INTCK AND INTNX FUNCTIONS

Name	Type*	Meaning Without Increment	Increments**
DAY	D	each day	days
HOUR	T	each hour	hours
MINUTE	T	each minute	minutes
MONTH	D	the first day of each quarter	months
QTR	D	the first day of each quarter	months
SECOND	T	each second	seconds
SEMIMONTH	D	the first and sixteenth of each month	semimonths
SEMIYEAR	D	the first of January and of July	months
TENDAY	D	approximate ten-day intervals in month: 1–10, 11–20, 21–end (28/9, 30, or 31)	tendays
WEEK	D	each Sunday	days
WEEKDAY	D	days, with weekends treated as part of the preceding weekday. Default weekends are Saturday and Sunday.	days
WEEKDAYnW	D	overrides default weekends, where n is any combination of numerals 1–7, e.g., WEEKDAY1W = Sunday and WEEKDAY671W = Friday, Saturday, Sunday.	days
YEAR	D	The first of January	months

*In this Table, type "D" means Date or Datetime, "T" means Time. If type then in use, it is understood to mean a date value, unless prefixed with "DT" (e.g., DTDAY), in which case it means a datetime value.

**The increments by which an offset is calculated when the interval name is followed by a period and a numeral; see text for explanation.

```
INTCK('YEAR','31DEC50','01JAN51')
```

returns 1.

   INTNX, like INTCK, takes three arguments, the first being an interval specification, from the same valid list permitted INTCK, and with the same caution about specifying datetime versus date intervals as may be appropriate to the second argument, which is a date, time, or datetime value. Unlike INTCK, the third argument is not a comparison date/time value but rather a number, the number of intervals by which the second argument is to be incremented. For example, if THISDAY = '30AUG88'D, the statement

```
THATDAY = INTNX('YEAR',THISDAY,1);
```

results in THATDAY taking a value corresponding to August 30, 1989.

FORMATTING FUNCTIONS

The PUT Function

   The PUT function produces as its result a character value, being that which results from applying a SAS format (system or user-defined). PUT takes two arguments. The first is a constant, variable, or expression, and the second must be a SAS format identifier, including its period or w.d extension. If DAYVAL is the SAS date value for November 16, 1962, then PUT(DAYVAL,MMDDYY8.) returns the string 11/16/62. A character string is returned because the result of formatting a value is a character string. The format itself must agree in implicit type with the variable, i.e., use character formats with character values, numeric formats with numeric values, just as usual; review Chapter 11.

As you continue to use SAS for different data processing problems, you'll come to find a good friend in the PUT function. One of the nice things it does is allow conditional choices (such as selecting records) to be made on the basis of formatted values, including user-formatted values.

Problem: You work for a retail outlet that uses the SAS System for inventory. A SAS format, INAME, has been created with PROC FORMAT that associates a great many numeric codes, variable ICODE, with a verbal description of a stock item. The OTHER= option of the VALUE statement was used, so that items that have not been given a verbal description print as UNASSIGNED. Produce a list of items that have not yet been given a description, so this data may be added to the FORMAT procedure and the format be updated.

Solution:

```
DATA NONAME;
  SET ...;
  IF PUT(ICODE,INAME.)='UNASSIGNED';
RUN;
PROC PRINT; RUN;
```

The INPUT Function

The brother of PUT is INPUT, which takes two arguments, the first of which is a constant, variable, or expression, the second a valid SAS informat. For example, if X='$27,685', coding

```
Y = INPUT(X,COMMA6.)
```

results in a Y value of 27685. The result of an INPUT call takes the type of the informat, so here a character value (and one with non-numeric components) is smoothly converted to a numeric value. But as *SAS Basics* cautions, you should not go the other way and convert numeric to character using the INPUT function, or you may get an unexpected result: The compiler first does a BEST12. conversion before the ultimate character conversion, and the result may not look as intended.

Format Specification at Runtime

The PUT and INPUT functions require literal specification of a format as the second argument. But what if you do not know until runtime what format you want to use? The **PUTC**, **PUTN**, **INPUTC**, and **INPUTN** functions allow the second argument to be a character expression that yields the name of a format. The expression can be a constant or a variable, and all these functions ask of you is that you know whether a character or a numeric format will be required: PUTN and INPUTN expect the name to be that of a numeric format, PUTC and INPUTC expect the name to be of a character format. Thus, PUT(X,DOLLAR.), PUTN(X, 'DOLLAR'), and

```
V='DOLLAR'; PUTN(X,V);
```

are equivalent.

A third and fourth function argument are optional. These must evaluate to integers, and can serve as the "w" and "d" of the function, e.g., INPUTC(X, $CHAR15.), INPUTC(X,'CHAR',15), and

```
A='CHAR'; B=15; INPUTC(X,A,B);
```

are equivalent.

16

Flow of Control

Generally, the order in which a computer program takes actions corresponds to the order of executable statements in source code, from first to last. But there often are reasons actions must be taken in an order very different from the order in which statements are written down in the source code. You may need to skip pieces of code under certain circumstances, or repeat pieces of code several times, or get instructions from another place within the source code.

The SAS DATA Step Language, like most other programming languages, provides a number of ways to direct the computer to take conditional, repetitive, or "out-of-sequence" action. The order in which computer actions are taken, as opposed to the order in which source statements physically occur, is called the program's *flow of control*. Statements which force flow of control to depart from "first statement to last" are discussed in this chapter.

CONDITIONAL CHOICE OF ACTION

To take a conditional choice of action means to execute a certain statement or group of statements if and only if certain conditions are satisfied. The SAS DATA Step Language provides two statement constructs that allow the user to specify conditional choice: the IF-THEN-ELSE group (and its special case, the subsetting IF) and the SELECT group.

IF-THEN-ELSE (Review)

As described in Chapter 3, the IF-THEN-ELSE group consists of an IF-THEN statement and an optional ELSE statement. The IF-THEN statement consists of the keyword IF, followed by a SAS expression yielding a logical truth value, then the keyword THEN followed either by an executable SAS statement or just the terminal semicolon (a "null" statement). If the expression following IF evaluates as "true" (nonmissing, nonzero), the statement following THEN, if present, is executed; otherwise it is skipped and control passes to the statement immediately following, or if the statement following THEN was a form of the DO statement or a SELECT statement (see below), to the statement immediately following the END of the DO or SELECT group. An either-or choice of action is specified by immediately following the IF-THEN statement (or the END, if THEN specifies DO or SELECT) with an ELSE statement: the keyword ELSE followed by an executable statement or the null statement. The statement following ELSE will be executed only when the expression following IF in the preceding IF-THEN statement evaluates as "false" (zero or missing).

The subsetting IF statement is akin to the IF-THEN statement, except without the THEN clause (the subsetting IF statement terminates with a semicolon immediately after the logical expression following IF). When the logical expression following IF evaluates true, execution continues with the next statement. Otherwise, the remaining statements in the step are skipped for the current iteration, and the next iteration of the DATA step begins; the current observation is not added to the dataset being created.

IF-THEN-ELSE provides a way to specify two mutually exclusive choices of action. As we saw in Chapter 5, because IF statements are themselves executable statements that can follow ELSE, it is possible to specify a set of more than two mutually exclusive choices using a series of ELSE IFs:

```
IF APPLES >= 109 THEN PRICE = 'OUT OF CONTROL';
ELSE IF 89 <= APPLES < 109 THEN PRICE = 'EXPENSIVE';
ELSE IF 69 <= APPLES < 89 THEN PRICE = 'OK';
ELSE IF APPLES > . THEN PRICE = 'GOOD';
```

A statement that should execute if none of the IF clauses evaluate true may be coded as a simple ELSE statement, following the last ELSE IF:

```
ELSE PRICE='UNKNOWN';
```

The SELECT Statement Group

There is another way to specify a set of mutually exclusive choices, which produces results similar to a series of ELSE IFs. This is the SELECT group, which consists of a SELECT statement, followed by one or more WHEN statements, an optional OTHERWISE statement, and END. The outlook on the prices of apples can be expressed with the following:

```
SELECT;
WHEN (APPLES >= 109) PRICE = 'OUT OF CONTROL';
WHEN (89 <= APPLES < 109) PRICE = 'EXPENSIVE';
WHEN (69 <= APPLES < 89) PRICE = 'OK';
WHEN (APPLES > .) PRICE = 'GOOD';
OTHERWISE PRICE = 'UNKNOWN';
END;
```

There is nothing SELECT-WHEN-OTHERWISE can accomplish for you that cannot be done by IF-ELSE groups. But in cases where many contingent choices present themselves, a SELECT group can apprear more orderly. Users familiar with structured languages may prefer the SELECT construct.

There are several things to learn about the SELECT group. In the first place, notice that the WHEN statement, generally of the form

```
WHEN (<expression>,....) statement;
```

is similar to IF-THEN: The WHEN statement causes the statement after the parenthesized expression to be executed if the expression evaluates true, just like an IF-THEN statement. (If more than one expresion is included, the statement executes if any of them is true.) Furthermore, the rules of SELECT group processing dictate that (1) WHEN conditions will be evaluated in the order coded, and as soon as one of them is true, the remaining WHEN statements are not evaluated; and (2) if and only if no WHEN condition is true, the statement following the keyword OTHERWISE is executed. Thus the first WHEN statement is like an IF-THEN statement, the second and subsequent WHEN statements like ELSE-IF-THEN statements, and the OTHERWISE statement like a final ELSE statement. The operation of the SELECT statement is illustrated in Figure 16.1.

One difference between IF-THEN/ELSE-IF and SELECT is that while a final ELSE statement need not be present, if a SELECT group ends without an OTHERWISE statement *and* no WHEN condition was found true, the DATA step will terminate with an error. This may be what you want, but if not you can still use SELECT and, if you desire no OTHERWISE condition, avoid the error by coding "OTHERWISE;", i.e., the keyword OTHERWISE followed by the null statement.

Another difference between the SELECT group and multiple ELSE-IF statements lies in the interaction of the SELECT and WHEN statements. A parenthesized expression may follow SELECT, in which case the logical truth value determined at each WHEN is not that of the WHEN expression itself, but that of the *equation of the SELECT expression with the WHEN expression*. Thus the following code sections both result in Y having a value of 42:

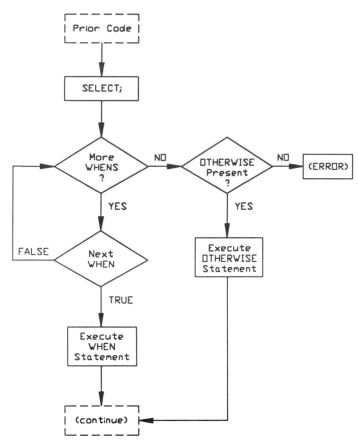

Figure 16.1. Flow of control, SELECT statement. (See text for explanation.)

```
[1]     X = 2;
        SELECT;
          WHEN (X=1) Y=23;
          WHEN (X=2) Y=42;
          WHEN (X=3) Y=0;
          OTHERWISE Y=.;
        END;
[2]     X = 2;
        SELECT (X);
          WHEN (1) Y=23;
          WHEN (2) Y=42;
          WHEN (3) Y=0;
          OTHERWISE Y=.;
        END;
```

In the second segment, at the first WHEN the equation "X = 1" is tested, and so forth. This use of the SELECT group—a variable name as the SELECT expression and a series of constants as the WHEN expressions—is similar to constructs found in some other programming languages, and some users may prefer it when appropriate to the task at hand.

To implement a "null" choice, i.e., to do nothing, you can code a null statement following the expression:

```
WHEN (expression) ;
```

A LEAVE statement (discussed later in this chapter in the context of DO groups) may also be used, but a null statement is sufficient to accomplish the same purpose.

REPEATED ACTION

The SAS DATA Step compiler automatically takes care of one crucial repetitive process: input and output of data. A SAS DATA step, when reading an input file, normally tends to repeat itself once for each observation in the file. But there are some computations which you may wish to repeat for *each* observation being processed. In other words, you may wish to repeat a series of executable statements a number of times within a single DATA step iteration.

DO Groups

Repetitive sequences are so important a mechanism in data processing that common to all but the most rudimentary procedural programming languages we find formal ways for specifying that a sequence of actions is to repeat more than once. In many languages some form of DO group is used. In the SAS DATA Step Language, repeated action can be achieved by several forms of DO groups.

We encountered the simplest form of DO group earlier in this book: a sequence of statements beginning with "DO;" and terminating with "END;". In these early examples, DO was used as a conditional choice: DO the group of statements IF so-and-so; i.e., "IF . . . THEN DO; . . . END;". This is the simplest instance of repeated execution: Execute the following statements once. A simple DO;—END; may also be used within SELECT groups.

There are other kinds of DO groups, which begin with other kinds of DO statements, to handle the case of many executions: execute a set of statements zero or more times. Whereas the unconditional DO statement "DO;" depends for conditional execution on other statements, these other forms of DO statement carry their selection guidelines with them. Still, they *may* be initiated as an IF-THEN or SELECT consequence.

Iterative DO Groups

There are occasions when it is necessary to carry out actions for several specific values of a certain variable. The variable may be of intrinsic interest to a problem, or it may be a temporary variable used simply for counting. An example of the latter is illustrated by the following code, which prints a very noticeable error message:

```
IF VALUE > 100 OR VALUE < 51 THEN
DO I = 1 TO 25;
PUT 'VALUE OUT OF RANGE!! >>> ' VALUE;
END;
```

This message will get noticed, for it is printed 25 times.

This kind of DO statement we call the iterative DO, generally

```
DO index = <start [TO stop [BY increment]]>,...;
```

where "index" is a SAS variable (which DO will create if it doesn't already exist in the PDV) and "start", "stop", and "increment" may be constants, variables, or expressions. There may be more than one "start [-stop [-increment]]" group, and if so they must be separated by commas; each such group is called a *clause* of the iterative DO. Alternatively, or conjointly, a list of values separated by commas may be given instead of TO. Numeric values, constant or expression-resolved, need not be integers. These are some valid iterative DO statements:

```
DO VAR7 = 1 TO 10;
DO CI = Q, R, XVAL, 6, 29;
DO X = 5 TO 37;
DO A = 7;
DO DVAL = 1,3,217,29.8,4;
DO TREE = A TO R BY 2.5;
DO FINAL = 3, Z+6, 10 TO 20, P, 31.4 TO 60 BY 3;
DO VEGGIE = 'CARROT','POTATO','EGGPLANT','CUCUMBER';
```

(The last one shows that you can DO a character variable. Only the list-of-values method can be used with character variables, of course.) A generalized flowchart for the iterative DO is given in Figure 16.2.

Problem: A SAS dataset has records with variables M, Q, and RATE, indicating that an amount of money M is deposited for Q calendar quarters in an account yielding RATE percent annual interest calculated quarterly. For example, M=1000, Q=8, and RATE=6.9 would mean "$1,000 deposited for 2 years (8 quarters) in an account paying 6.9% interest." No further deposits are made, but the interest is allowed to remain in the account. For each observation, what is the total at the end of the Q'th quarter?

Solution: Using an iterative DO group, code:

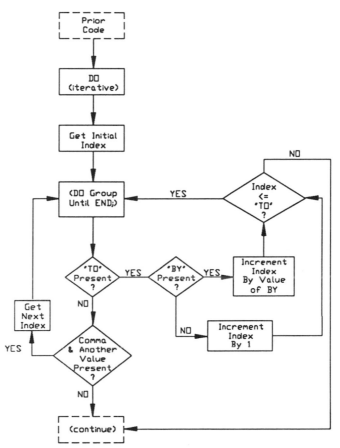

Figure 16.2. Flow of control, iterative DO group. Whether the statements of the group execute or not depend on the value of the index variable, which is altered systematically after each iteration.

```
DATA MORMONEY;
  SET OUR.MONEY;
  BUCKS = M;
  QRATE=RATE/4; * DIVIDE RATE BY 4 FOR QUARTERLY INTEREST;
  DO QUARTER = 1 TO Q;
    BUCKS = BUCKS + QRATE * BUCKS;
  END;
  DROP QUARTER QRATE; * CONSERVE SPACE, NOT NEEDED IN DATASET;
RUN;
```

The DO group executes once for each quarter. The calculation is repeated Q times, each time increasing the value of BUCKS, and only after Q iterations is the DO group exited. That is, "BUCKS=BUCKS+QRATE*BUCKS;" is executed Q times in a row for each observation in OUR.MONEY, and only thereafter is an observation written to EARNINGS. The executing step does not get "to the bottom," where an observation is written, until after the DO has completed. There will be exactly one observation in MORMONEY for each observation in OUR.MONEY (see Listing 16.1).

Problem: How much money would be in the account at the end of each quarter, not just at the end of the year?

Solution: Create a dataset as follows:

```
DATA QTRMONEY;
  SET OUR.MONEY;
  BUCKS = M;
  QRATE=RATE/4;
  DO QUARTER = 1 TO Q;
    BUCKS = BUCKS + QRATE * BUCKS;
    OUTPUT;
  END;
  * DO NOT DROP QUARTER, WILL BE USED;
  DROP Q QRATE; * ON THE OTHER HAND, WE DO NOT NEED Q;
RUN;
```

This dataset QTRMONEY has **Q** observations for each observation from OUR.MONEY, because OUTPUT appears within the DO group. Now, each observation in QTRMONEY gives a value for BUCKS that corresponds to one quarter. We can display this dataset with

```
PROC PRINT DATA=QTRMONEY;
  BY M RATE NOTSORTED;
  ID QUARTER;
  VAR BUCKS;
RUN;
```

Sample Dataset 'OUR.MONEY'

OBS	M	Q	RATE
1	25000	6	0.086
2	42000	12	0.091
3	1500	18	0.102

Result 'MORMONEY'

OBS	M	Q	RATE	BUCKS
1	25000	6	0.086	28403.39
2	42000	12	0.091	55015.26
3	1500	18	0.102	2360.12

Listing 16.1. Example iterative DO group

the result of which is shown in Listing 16.2.

Expression-Conditional DO Groups

A simple DO can be conditioned on the value of an expression following IF or SELECT WHEN. It is possible to place an expression right inside a DO statement, with quite different effects. There are two forms of the DO statement that allow this: DO WHILE and DO UNTIL. The DO WHILE statement takes the form

```
DO WHILE (expression);
```

where "expression" is a valid SAS expression yielding a true/false value. If the expression is true (nonzero, nonmissing), the group of statements immediately following, up until the required END statement, will be executed. If the expression is false, the statements will be skipped. Then the WHILE expression is evaluated again and the process repeats. See Figure 16.3.

The DO UNTIL statement is similar to DO WHILE, except that the expression is tested *after* the process. That is to say, the DO group statements are performed, and then the expression is evaluated to see if the statements should be performed again; see Figure 16.4. When DO UNTIL is used, the statements in the DO group will be executed at least once no matter what the value of the expression. Be careful when using DO WHILE or DO UNTIL that the test expression eventually terminates the repetition, or that the group is terminated by some other means. Don't allow the execution to go on forever.

Situations that may call for an expression-conditional DO group often involve conditional SETting or INPUTting (when the natural process of DATA step iteration must be changed or augmented), problems where the conditional expression is determined by input data (i.e., a value retrieved by INPUT or SET during the course of the DO group is tested in the WHILE or UNTIL expression), or those occasional applications where a repetitive computational procedure must be programmed at an elementary level.

Hybrid Iterative/Conditional-Expression Form

Some SAS implementations allow a form of the SAS DO statement that combines the logic of iterative and conditional-expression execution. Such a statement looks like an iterative DO clause with a WIIILE or UNTIL appended, e.g.,

```
DO I=2 TO 10 BY 2 WHILE(VAR1 > 100);
```

This statement behaves as follows: First WHILE is evaluated; if it is true (i.e., if VAR1>100), then the DO group may continue. However, when I has exceeded the value of 10, it will not execute even if WHILE is true. In other words, WHILE is necessary for the DO to be executed, but the iterative DO condition must still be satisfied.

```
                    Result 'QTRMONEY'

--------------------------- M=25000 RATE=0.086 ---------------------------

            QUARTER        BUCKS

                1        25537.50
                2        26086.56
                3        26647.42
                4        27220.34
                5        27805.57
                6        28403.39


--------------------------- M=42000 RATE=0.091 ---------------------------

            QUARTER        BUCKS

                1        42955.50
                2        43932.74
                3        44932.21
                4        45954.42
                5        46999.88
                6        48069.13
                7        49162.70
                8        50281.15
                9        51425.05
               10        52594.97
               11        53791.50
               12        55015.26


--------------------------- M=1500 RATE=0.102 ---------------------------

            QUARTER        BUCKS

                1         1538.25
                2         1577.48
                3         1617.70
                4         1658.95
                5         1701.26
                6         1744.64
                7         1789.13
                8         1834.75
                9         1881.53
               10         1929.51
               11         1978.72
               12         2029.17
               13         2080.92
               14         2133.98
               15         2188.40
               16         2244.20
               17         2301.43
               18         2360.12
```

Listing 16.2. A DO group with OUTPUT

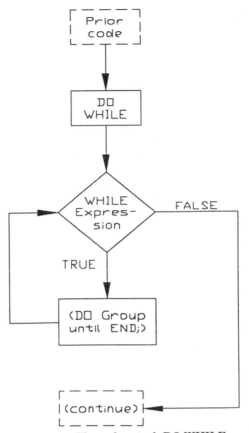

Figure 16.3. Flow of control, DO WHILE group.

Nested DO groups

Problem: For lexical analysis, a dataset named TEST is to be created from an input file of free text by sampling every 20th line. Observations in TEST will have one variable, LINE. The analysis program will be run on many different input files, and regardless of the length of the input file, TEST should be restricted to a maximum of 100 lines for each run. For any run, the input text file has a record length of 80 and is found in fileref TINPUT.

Solution:

```
DATA TEST;
  INFILE TINPUT;
  DO I = 1 TO 100;
    DO O = 1 TO 20;
      INPUT LINE $CHAR80.;
    END;
    OUTPUT;
  END;
  DROP I O;
  STOP;
RUN;
```

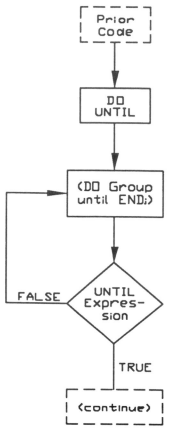

Figure 16.4. Flow of control, DO UNTIL group. Compare Figure 16.3.

This program illustrates the use of *nested* DO groups, that is, DO groups that are placed within, "nested" within, other DO groups. Just like any other executable statements within an iterative DO group, a subordinate nested DO group is executed once for each value of its parent's index variable.

Take a close look at this example; a specific flowchart is shown in Figure 16.5. The first time through the DATA step, the value of I is set to 1 and the outer group begins to execute. Then O is set to 1 and the inner group begins to execute. The inner group continues to execute until its DO is complete, which is to say 20 times. Each time, it retrieves a fresh record from TINPUT. Only after the 20th iteration does the step continue past the inner group's END to the OUTPUT statement. The 20th line is output to TEST, and the outer DO group has completed its first iteration. Now I gets the value 2, the second group begins again with a fresh start at O = 1, goes 20 times, and another observation is output. I gets the value 3, and the process continues. If TINPUT has 2,000 or fewer lines, the step terminates naturally after the last line is read, because INPUT stops DATA step execution after end-of-file, no matter where in the DO we happen to be. However, to limit TEST to 100 observations when TINPUT has more than 2,000 records, the STOP

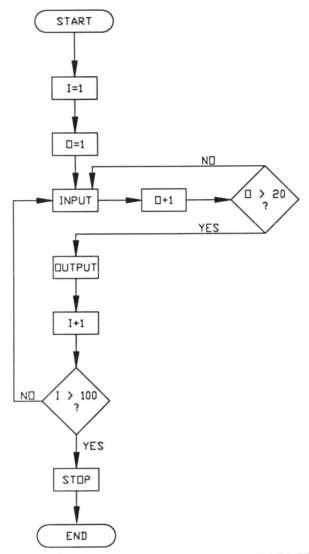

Figure 16.5. Logic of the nested DO groups in the "DATA TEST; . . ." example (see text).

statement is necessary. If it were not there, the DATA step would simply return "to the top" for another iteration *after* the outer DO completed its task, and the results would be just as if the outer DO statement and its END were simply omitted from the source code.

Each END statement in a set of nested groups closes the DO that most closely precedes it. The SAS compiler cares only that there be one and only one END statement for each DO statement, and will use each END to close the last-opened DO. It is good form, however, to show appropriate indentation in your source code.

Not only does the program become more human-understandable, but it helps prevent unclosed ("hanging") DO groups, i.e., DO without END. Be cautioned that it is a *very common error* in SAS programming to forget one or more END statements. Whether or not DO groups are nested, if there is not one END for each DO you will at least get a warning message on the log that a "hanging DO" occurred. If any executable statements follow the place where END should have been, the "hanging DO" will cause *wrong results*. In some cases, a "hanging DO" will confuse the compiler enough that the step will halt in error.

Skipping the Current Iteration

The CONTINUE statement stops processing of the current iteration of a DO group. CONTINUE may be placed at any point within the DO group, and is often used to execute all or a portion of the code during an iteration depending on a truth condition. In a program like this:

```
DO [any iterative or expression-conditional type];
   [some code...]
   IF V<=0 THEN CONTINUE;
   [more code]
END;
```

Breaking Out of a DO Group

It is permissible to exit a DO group "prematurely." There are a number of ways to do this, and generally, you would do so upon the evaluation of a condition (e.g., in an IF-THEN statement).

The LEAVE statement can be used within a DO group in order to break out of the group and continue with the next statement after END. The difference between CONTINUE and LEAVE is that CONTINUE skips the rest of the DO group but (if the group is an interative type) continues again from its beginning. LEAVE, on the other hand, terminates the DO group; no more DO iterations are done. In a program like this:

```
DO [any iterative or expression-conditional type];
   [some code...]
   IF V<=0 THEN LEAVE;
   [more code]
END;
[still more code]
```

as soon as the IF-THEN statement executes when V is negative, the DO terminates completely and execution continues with "still more code."

An iterative or expression-conditional DO group can also be ended by altering its conditions of repeated execution within the statements of the group itself. Condition-expression DO groups use this method as a matter of course: Sometime during the DO group execution a variable appearing in the WHILE or UNTIL expression is altered, which causes the expression to be false upon its next evaluation. Similarly, an iterative DO group can be escaped by altering the index variable within the group, setting it to its upper bound (or even out of bound). For example, the following code breaks a DO group when a certain variable X is found to have a value of 3:

```
DO I = 1 TO 50;
  [SAS statements]
  IF X=3 THEN I = 50;
  [SAS statements]
END;
```

This DO group completes execution when X is 3, but doesn't execute after that.

Finally, you can exit a DO group using a RETURN statement to go "to the top" of the step code and begin with another observation. Or, you could use a GOTO statement that points to a label outside the DO group. Both RETURN and GOTO are discussed later in this chapter.

Infinite Loops

Avoid the infinite loop: the DO group that never stops. Here's one in the abstract:

```
DO UNTIL X = 3;
  [SAS statements that never cause X to be 3]
END;
```

Array Processing

Arrays in the SAS DATA Step Language bear superficial resemblance to arrays in other computer languages. But except for the so-called "temporary" arrays we will discuss later below, SAS arrays neither declare data structures nor allocate storage. Arrays in SAS are used strictly as a shorthand, a way of processing many variables with few statements. In the SAS DATA Step Language (and again, except for "temporary" arrays), an "array" boils down simply to an *ordered list of variable names*. An array has meaning only during the processing of the DATA step in which it is declared (using the ARRAY statement, see below); array declarations are not saved with SAS datasets.

Arrays in SAS are often used in conjunction with DO groups, to carry out action repeatedly on a sequence of variables. By being made the objects of an array declaration, variables gain pseudonyms (array "locations") which, because of their ordinal arrangement, are especially suitable for repetitive processing.

Declaring an Array

You assign a set of variables their array pseudonyms by means of the ARRAY statement. There are two primary forms of ARRAY statement, one which declares an "explicitly subscripted" and one an "implictly subscripted" array. Implicitly subscripted arrays, which we will get to later in this section, are an obsolescent form. You should get in the habit of using the preferred explicitly subscripted arrays. An explicitly subscripted array is declared with the ARRAY statement, which has the general form

```
ARRAY arrayname {<<< n > |<n1:n2>>,...>|<*>}
[$] [length] [variables[(values)]];
```

For the moment, let's consider the most typical case of the generalized ARRAY statement,

```
ARRAY arrayname {n} variables;
```

and return later to the other variations.

ARRAY serves to tell the SAS System you may wish to refer to its element variables by pseudonyms. For example,

```
ARRAY EX {3} CREDIT TIME CUE;
```

sets up an array named "EX" containing three elements (with respect to the array, the variable names are called its elements), being the variables CREDIT, TIME, and CUE. Like other nonexecutable statements, ARRAY affects the program data vector if it is the statement on which a variable is first named. But otherwise, nothing happens to variables simply because they are named in an ARRAY statement. They can always be referred to by their own rightful names, and a variable can be named in more than one ARRAY statement.

Having been declared in an array, each variable can be referred to by a subscripted array reference, that is, the array name followed by a set of braces containing a positive integer (or an expression that evaluates to a positive integer). The integer must fall within the range defined in the ARRAY statement, and the elements named in the ARRAY statement correspond to that range in the order defined. By default, the lower bound of the range is 1 and the upper bound the cardinal number of elements, and the first variable named on the ARRAY statement is element 1. Thus given the ARRAY example above that set up the array EX, the variable CREDIT has a pseudonym, EX{1}, TIME the pseudonym EX{2}, and CUE can be referred to by EX{3}. One then could write, for example,

```
EX{3} = 5;
```

to set the value of CUE to 5, or (and this kind of usage is more typical in array processing)

```
DO I=1 TO 3;
  EX{I} = 0;
END;
```

to set the values of CREDIT, TIME, and CUE all to zero.

The explicitly subscripted ARRAY statement is written with the number of array elements specified in curly braces* immediately after the array name, although you can simply write an asterisk instead of an integer, i.e., {*}, and SAS will count the elements for you.

```
ARRAY FRUIT {6} APPLE ORANGE PEAR PLUM NECTRINE KIWI;
```

and

```
ARRAY FRUIT {*} APPLE ORANGE PEAR PLUM NECTRINE KIWI;
```

both create the identical six-element array, and FRUIT{3} refers to the variable PEAR in either case.

The name of an array must follow the syntax rules for SAS variable names: it must begin with a letter or underscore, followed by zero or more letters, numerals, or underscores to a maximum length of eight characters. An array name must not match the name of any variable in the program data vector, whether created by the DATA step or brought in from another dataset (e.g., with SET or MERGE).

The type of variables in the same array must agree. That is, the elements of any given array must be all numeric or all character. If desired, to incorporate all PDV variables of a type into an array, the shorthand keywords _NUMERIC_ or _CHARACTER_ (discussed in Chapter 2) may be used in lieu of a variable list.

Using Arrays

Array processing comes in most useful in cases where a computing process is to be performed repetitively on many variables.

Suppose raw data are stored in an external file with spaces between values and single periods to indicate missing values. The variables will be named ID, AGE, GRADE, SCORE1-SCORE5, and SCALE. Later it is realized that for some analyses SCORE1-SCORE5 and SCALE should be treated as true zero if missing, not as missing values. A DATA statement to recode these missings to zeroes could accomplish this with a series of IFs:

```
DATA NEW.RESULTS;
  INFILE OUR.INPUT;
  INPUT ID AGE GRADE SCORE1-SCORE5 SCALE;
  IF SCORE1=. THEN SCORE1=0;
  IF SCORE2=. THEN SCORE2=0;
  IF SCORE3=. THEN SCORE3=0;
  IF SCORE4=. THEN SCORE4=0;
  IF SCORE5=. THEN SCORE5=0;
  IF SCALE=. THEN SCALE=0;
RUN;
```

---

*To accommodate keyboards or monitors that don't have braces, square brackets or parentheses may be used instead. Because of the possible use of parentheses as subscript brackets, you should not choose as the name of your array one that matches the name of any SAS function; if you do, then that function will not be available for use within the same DATA step.

Problem: But what if there were 100 SCOREs and 50 SCALEs?
  Solution:

```
DATA NEW.RESULTS;
  INFILE OUR.INPUT;
  INPUT ID AGE GRADE SCORE1-SCORE100 SCALE1-SCALE50;
  ARRAY SS {150} SCORE1-SCORE100 SCALE1-SCALE50;
  DO I=1 TO 150;
    IF SS{I}=. THEN SS{I}=0;
  END;
  DROP I;
RUN;
```

150 IF statements have been replaced by a single IF statement within a DO group that is to execute 150 times. At the first execution, I=1 and SS{I} is SS{1} which is a reference to the variable SCORE1, and it goes on until S{150}, a reference to the variable SCALE50.

There are many possible variations on what you can do with array processing. You may, for example, declare more than one array and process matching observations. If you have the prices of ten items in one set of variables arranged in an array PRICES, and variables representing quantities sold of the same ten items in an array SOLD, you could declare a third array, GROSS, of ten variables and write

```
DO I=1 TO 10;
  GROSS{I} = PRICES{I} * SOLD{I};
END;
```

and maybe add a variable to represent the total gross:

```
DO I=1 TO 10;
  GROSS{I} = PRICES{I} * SOLD{I};
  TOTAL + GROSS{I};
END;
```

Whenever you have a large number of variables that need to be treated by some repetitive process, you should stop to consider whether arranging them in arrays would facilitate the task.

Variations on Array Declaration

The explicit ARRAY statement supports variations that give you more expressive power in designing your applications.

Initializing Variables. A set of values can be placed in parentheses following the variable list. The statement

```
ARRAY ZOO {*} PARROTS OCELOTS RMADILOS (23,42,19);
```

assigns the value 23 to PARROTS, 42 to OCELOTS, 19 to RMADILOS. Elements are assigned values in order, and if there are not enough values to go around then ARRAY does not do anything to the remaining elements:

```
ARRAY ZOO {*} PARROTS OCELOTS RMADILOS (23,42);
```

causes no assignment of value to RMADILOS.

Implied Variables. It is permissible to leave off the list of variable names when creating an array, in which case variable names will be constructed from the array name suffixed by consecutive integers beginning with 1. That is, for example,

```
ARRAY MINE {5} ;
```

creates an array whose five elements are variables MINE1, MINE2, MINE3, MINE4, MINE5. If these variables do not already exist in the program data vector, they will be created. The type and the length of ARRAY-created variables can be controlled by the ARRAY statement. This is where the "$" and the length specifications come in. By default, new variables will be numeric, length 8. This would be the case in the example just shown. If instead we coded

```
ARRAY MINE {5} $ ;
```

we would also create variables MINE1-MINE5 if they did not exist, but they would be created as character variables. A length, if specified, must be an integer literal and a valid SAS length (1 to 8 for numerics, 1 to 200 for character variables). For example,

```
ARRAY MINE {5} 4;
```

would create numeric variables MINE1-MINE5 (if they did not already exist in the PDV) and assign them a SAS length of 4 instead of the default 8.

It should be obvious that the "{*}" subscript specification should not be used if variables are to be named implicitly by the ARRAY statement.

Multidimensional Arrays. An array may be declared to have more than one dimension. Dimensions are separated by commas in the array declaration, e.g.,

```
ARRAY TWO {2,2} A B C D;
```

The order of reference is "row-major." Here, the 2x2 array TWO has variables A=TWO{1,1}, B=TWO{1,2}, C=TWO{2,1}, D=TWO{2,2}; generally, dimensions to the right cycle fastest. Multidimensional arrays are offered as a convenience for referring to variables that logically fall into a multirow, "tabular" conception.

Multidimensional arrays can be declared without variable names if the variables are to be created. If so, they are created with the array name suffixed with sequential numbers from 1 to the total number of elements implied by the dimensions.

The DIM Function. The DIM function returns an integer corresponding to the number of elements in an array dimension. In the example just given,

```
DO I=1 TO DIM(R);
```

could have been written instead of

```
DO I=1 TO 50;
```

The DIM function helps you write more general code: SAS code that can be used in different situations with small modification. If you write a DATA statement with several DO statements that can be used with a variety of different element lists, using DIM helps you avoid having to rewrite the DO statements each time. In conjunction with the asterisk convention for element counting in ARRAY, i.e.,

```
ARRAY EXAMPLE {*} variables;
```

only the variable list may need to be changed between the different programs.

The DIM function can be used with multidimensional arrays, but it only gives one of the dimensions. The DIM function's most general form is

```
DIM(array,dimension);
```

which can alternatively be written

```
DIMdimension(array);
```

That is, the expressions DIM(X,3) and DIM3(X) are equivalent.* Both evaluate to the number of elements of the third dimension of array X. If a dimension is not given (in either position), it defaults to 1. Thus DIM(R), DIM(R,1), DIM1(R) are equivalent.

Altering the Default Subscript Range. An array dimension need not begin with 1; it can begin with any integer. To begin an array with an integer other than 1 you name the lower and upper bounds of the dimension range explicitly, separated by a colon:

```
ARRAY MYARRAY {6:8} A B C;
```

declares a three-element array consisting of variables A, B, and C. However, the appropriate array references for these variables are not MYARRAY{1}, MYARRAY{2}, and MYARRAY{3} but MYARRAY{6}, MYARRAY{7}, and MYARRAY{8}.

---

*This whimsical syntactic variation is peculiar to the DIM function and its close relatives HBOUND and LBOUND (which are discussed below). Don't try it with other SAS functions.

Altering the lower boundary of an array can be a convenience when you are dealing with variables that have a "natural" numbering. For example, if you have variables that have data for years 1991 through 1995, you might want to array them with a range of 91:95. You may specify any or all dimensions of a multidimensional array using the lower:upper syntax.

If you are comfortable with using zero as a lower bound (such that a ten-element array, say, would begin with element 0 and go through element 9), you can implement this with the "n1:n2" syntax and realize a savings in execution time. The SAS compiler, which itself is written in the C language, internally converts array subscripts to the zero base natural to that language. If you stipulate a zero base yourself, e.g.,

```
ARRAY Z {0:9} VAR1-VAR10;
```

the compiler does not have to perform a subtraction calculation on the subscripts you use. Of course, you must be careful to refer to the correct variable: the first variable is element zero, the last of n elements is number $n-1$.

As with any ARRAY statement, variables can be created implicitly by not naming them on the statement. However, they are still created with the array name suffixed with sequential numbers from 1 to the total number of elements implied by the dimensions. For example,

```
ARRAY A {11-20};
```

creates variables A1-A10, not A11-A20. A{11} would be used to reference variable A1, and so on. To create variable names that match the array references, you would have to name them explicitly:

```
ARRAY A {11-20} A11-A20;
```

The HBOUND and LBOUND Functions. The HBOUND and LBOUND functions are related to the DIM function, but allow for the possibility of a range starting with an integer other than 1. They thus provide an even more general way than does DIM of constructing iterative DO statements. HBOUND (for "high bound") and LBOUND ("low bound") give the high and low range boundaries of an array dimension; DIM, giving the cardinal number of elements in the dimension, only implies the array bounds if the lower bound is 1 (the default). Put another way,

```
DO I = 1 TO DIM(A);
```

yields the same result as

```
DO I = LBOUND(A) TO HBOUND(A);
```

if (and only if) A is an array whose first dimension subscript range begins with 1.

The general forms for these functions are the same as for DIM: Two arguments, the first an array name, the second an integer indicating the array dimension (which can instead be written in front of the parentheses, and which if absent defaults to 1).

Implicitly Subscripted Arrays

The implicitly subscripted ARRAY statement does not declare the number of elements in the array, and elements are not referenced directly by number. Rather, a special *index variable* is used to get at a specific element. The index variable on an implicit ARRAY statement is coded within parentheses (not braces), where the element count would be in an explicit ARRAY. If not dropped, the index variable *will* be added to dataset(s) being built by the step. The statement

```
ARRAY DEMOGR (D) AGE SEX EDUCATN INCOME;
```

defines an array named DEMOGR consisting of four elements AGE through INCOME as shown. AGE is element 1, INCOME element 4. D is the index variable.

The value of the index variable at the time the array name is used in an executable statement determines which of the variables named on the ARRAY statement will be called upon. In the current example, the statements

```
D=3; DEMOGR=7;
```

result in the variable EDUCATN being assigned the value 7, because EDUCATN is the third variable, D is made "3," and D is the index variable of the array DEMOGR. The assignment "DEMOGR=7;" does not mention D—the subscript is *implicit*.

Be sure to understand that whenever the name of an implicitly subscripted array is used, the variable referred to will be that variable whose ordinal position in the array definition corresponds to the current value of the index variable. In the example, DEMOGR is not a variable; it is an array name. If the array EXPLDMOG were defined

```
ARRAY EXPLDMOG {*} AGE SEX EDUCATN INCOME;
```

then an equivalent SAS statement affecting EDUCATN would be

```
EXPLDMOG{3} = 7;
```

Here are two more statement groups that produce identical results:

```
DO D=1 TO 4; DEMOGR=0; END;
```

and

```
DO D=1 TO 4; EXPLDMOG{D}=0; END;
```

Each sets the values of AGE, SEX, EDUCATN, and INCOME to zero. With DEMOGR the index variable is cycled by an iterative DO through its four valid values, and the single statement in the DO group (DEMOGR=0;) is executed four times: for the first element (AGE), the second (SEX), and the others. The explicit array construction also cycles a variable through four values, using it each time as an explicit subscript.

An implicitly subscripted array may be defined without an index variable, but an index variable still exists: the default _I_. If DEMOGR were defined

```
ARRAY DEMOGR AGE SEX EDUCATN INCOME;
```

then the DO group illustrated would be

```
DO _I_=1 TO 4; DEMOGR=0; END;
```

There is one difference: As mentioned above, when an index variable is specified, that variable is added to the dataset being built unless it is dropped. However, _I_ is not added to any dataset being built.

The DO OVER Statement. There is a special DO statement that may be used only with an implicitly subscripted array name. Its function is similar to the DIM function with explicitly subscripted arrays: It allows an iterative DO covering all elements of an array to be coded without specifying the number of elements in the array. Whether the index variable is _I_ or some other variable does not matter; the index variable is not named in the DO OVER statement, which has the form

```
DO OVER arrayname;
```

Again with array DEMOGR as the example:

```
DO OVER DEMOGR; DEMOGR=0; END;
```

The DO OVER statement says, in effect, to execute the DO group once for each variable in the array.

DO OVER can be used with multiple arrays that have the same number of elements and the same index variable. Just use any of the array names so that DO OVER can get its index dimension.

"Temporary" Arrays

Under certain circumstances, you may find it helpful to arrange a set of constant values into an array. As an example, suppose a sample of products have been tested in an attempt to assess conformance with quality control standards. A dataset TESTS contains descriptive information about the products and also the variables TEST1 through TEST5, representing the results of five tests. Now, the passing value is stipulated for each test. Suppose for the five tests, the passing values are 15, 18, 18, 20, and 12. Then the following step could be written to select only those sample members that fail one or more tests:

```
DATA FAILS;
  SET TESTS;
  ARRAY TESTS {5};
  ARRAY T {5} (15,18,18,20,12);
  DO I=1 TO 5;
    IF TESTS{I} < T{I} THEN DO; OUTPUT; RETURN; END;
  END;
RUN;
```

TESTS arrays the five variables TEST1 to TEST5, and T arrays five new variables T1 through T5 (implicit variable naming has been used for both arrays, but that is beside the point here).

In this case, it would be more efficient to make T a temporary array. All arrays are temporary, of course; they exist only for the duration of the DATA step. The designation "temporary array" has a special meaning: the elements of the array are *not* SAS variables, and they can *only* be referred to by their array designations. A temporary array is produced by replacing the variable name list with the word _TEMPORARY_. In the present example, the array T could have been declared as a temporary array:

```
ARRAY T {5} _TEMPORARY_ (15,18,18,20,12);
```

and the rest of the program left as is. Variables T1 through T5 are *not* created, but neither are they needed since the only purpose of the array was to contain a set of constants.

Temporary arrays are the exception to the rule that an array is but an alternative way of referring to specific variables. A temporary array is in fact an internal data structure that is defined by its ARRAY statement. It exists separately from the program data vector. Indeed, it is this fact that makes temporary arrays attractive when they can be used: it takes less computer resources to deal with temporary arrays than with arrays composed of variables. When you make reference to an array element that is a SAS variable, at execution the system must first look up the variable name and then go to the PDV to locate the value. When you reference an element of a temporary array, the value is located directly.

The values of temporary array elements do not have to be constants, nor do they need to be initialized on the ARRAY statement. You can assign values to them dynamically during the DATA step. If you do not initialize them, then before assignment they are missing. However, the values of a temporary array are not reset to missing at each iteration. No RETAIN statement is necessary; temporary array elements are not part of the PDV and are not affected by step iteration.

TRANSFER OF CONTROL

There are statements that allow control to pass anywhere within the DATA step—even "backward," straight out of a DO group, etc.

The RETURN statement provides a means to skip execution of statements following it in the DATA step. The Data Step Language also provides two statements that provide limitless transfer of control anywhere in a DATA step the user wishes. These are GOTO and LINK. Both transfer control immediately to another section of the program, which is identified by a statement label.*

The RETURN Statement

The RETURN statement consists simply of the keyword:

```
RETURN;
```

Except when used with LINK, RETURN causes SAS to write an observation immediately to the output dataset (*except* if OUTPUT is present elsewhere), and return "to the top" of the step for the next iteration.

```
DATA;
  [SAS statements]
RETURN;
  [more SAS statements]
RUN;
```

causes "more SAS statements" to be skipped. As you might suspect, RETURN is usually executed as a consequence of a condition evaluation (IF-THEN or SELECT).

The GOTO Statement

The GOTO statement takes the form

```
GOTO label;
```

where "label" is a valid statement label located elsewhere within the DATA step source code. Transfer of control by GOTO can be used as a sort of negative DO, a "Don't DO." Consider the following code fragment:

```
DATA;
  [some statements]
  IF condition THEN DO;
    [some more statements]
  END;
  [still more statements]
RUN;
```

---

*Statement labels were introduced in Chapter 7, with the EOF= option of the INFILE statement (EOF= effects a transfer-of-control operation in its own right). To review, a statement label consists of any valid SAS name followed immediately by a colon. The line of code

```
PASS2: SET C.DATAX;
```

consists of a label, PASS2, and a SET statement. It identifies a place in the source code that may be used for transfer of control.

The same effect can be achieved with a GOTO:

```
DATA;
  [some statements]
  IF NOT(condition) THEN GOTO THERE;
  [some more statements]
THERE:
  [still more statements]
RUN;
```

As an example, consider

```
DATA;
SET A;
IF VAR1 < 3 THEN DO;
CASE = 'YES';
COUNT + 1;
END;
MERGE B;
RUN;
```

and the equivalent

```
DATA;
SET A;
IF VAR1 >= 3 THEN GOTO SKIPCASE;
CASE = 'YES';
COUNT + 1;
SKIPCASE:
MERGE B;
RUN;
```

This use of GOTO is, like the choice between DROP or KEEP, a matter of personal convenience. GOTO is shunned by many modern programmers because of the chaos it can introduce to a complex program written in the typical third-generation computer language. But in the normally much shorter and simpler DATA Step programs, GOTO may freely be used in the manner just illustrated.

There are also those instances where GOTO is decidedly useful, in other programming languages as well as the SAS DATA Step Language. One of these cases is when there is a need to break out of a repetitive control structure.

Problem: Imagine that three datasets ANALY1, ANALY2, ANALY3 each contain a variable SCALE. The total number of observations in the input datasets are not known beforehand. Create a second dataset, SAMPPOS, that contains up to 50 observations, but not more, from each of the three datasets. Only positive values of SCALE are to be included.

Solution: The following DATA step examines the input datasets in turn:

```
DATA SAMPPOS;
RETAIN COUNT 0; DROP COUNT;
DO WHILE (COUNT <= 50);
SET ANALY1 END=FINISH1;
IF SCALE > 0 THEN DO;
COUNT + 1;
OUTPUT;
END;
IF FINISH1 THEN GOTO TWO;
END;
TWO:
COUNT = 0; * RESET THE COUNTER;
DO WHILE (COUNT <= 50);
SET ANALY2 END=FINISH2;
IF SCALE > 0 THEN DO;
COUNT + 1;
OUTPUT;
END;
IF FINISH2 THEN GOTO THREE;
END;
THREE:
COUNT = 0; * RESET THE COUNTER;
DO WHILE (COUNT <= 50);
SET ANALY3 END=FINISH3;
IF SCALE > 0 THEN DO;
COUNT + 1;
OUTPUT;
END;
IF FINISH3 THEN GOTO DONE;
END;
DONE:
STOP;
RUN;
```

By using a "counter" variable in a DO expression, the number of observations written to SAMPPOS from any of the input datasets is restricted to a maximum (in this case 50). If a positive value of SCALE is encountered, the simple inner DO is executed, writing an observation and incrementing the counter. When 50 positive observations from ANALY1 have been written, the first iterative DO is completed, and the step moves on (to reset the counter and begin the next iterative DO, or after the last DO to STOP). If ANALY1 or ANALY2 have less than 50 positive observations, however, the next SET in the DO group will want to terminate the DATA step, which in this case would be premature. Therefore, the END= option is used, and if the last observation has been read the GOTO statement will be executed. Transfer out of the DO group is achieved, the same SET is not executed again, and the program continues with the next group.

The statement

```
IF FINISH3 THEN GOTO DONE;
```

is not strictly necessary in this particular program, since SET can this time be allowed to terminate the step if there are less than 50 positive observations in ANALY3. It is good form, however, to make the logic of the program explicit. The STOP statement is necessary in case ANALY3 has 50 or more statements, so that the DO does not begin again.

The RETURN Statement with GOTO

A RETURN can help keep a GOTO group isolated from other statements when building a dataset. In some cases, it may be better to use GOTOs than DO groups to isolate a section of code. Consider, for example, the following code segment, hypothetically to be executed in lieu of all other program statements at several different points in a SAS program. It uses RETURN to skip any following statements:

```
DATA;
  [some SAS statements]
  IF condition1 THEN DO;
    HELP = YES;
    ALERT + 1;
    PUT 'WARNING!' ALERT= _N_= ', CONTACT DATA SECURITY';
    RETURN;
  END;
  [some more SAS statements #1];
  IF condition2 THEN DO;
    HELP = YES;
    ALERT + 1;
    PUT 'WARNING!' ALERT= _N_= ', CONTACT DATA SECURITY';
    RETURN;
  END;
  [some more SAS statements #2];
  IF condition3 THEN DO;
    HELP = YES;
    ALERT + 1;
    PUT 'WARNING!' ALERT= _N_= ', CONTACT DATA SECURITY';
    RETURN;
  END;
  [some more SAS statements #3];
  IF condition4 THEN DO;
    HELP = YES;
    ALERT + 1;
    PUT 'WARNING!' ALERT= _N_= ', CONTACT DATA SECURITY';
    RETURN;
  END;
  [some more SAS statements #4];
RUN;
```

As you can see, if any of the IF conditions are satisfied, an identical DO group performs its function, which includes returning to the top of the step for the next observation. In such a case, it would be easier and clearer to code the following:

```
DATA;
  [some SAS statements]
  IF condition1 THEN GOTO SKIP;
  [some more SAS statements #1];
  IF condition2 THEN GOTO SKIP;
  [some more SAS statements #2];
  IF condition3 THEN GOTO SKIP;
  [some more SAS statements #3];
  IF condition4 THEN GOTO SKIP;
  [some more SAS statements #4];
  RETURN;
SKIP:
  HELP = YES;
  ALERT + 1;
  PUT 'WARNING!' ALERT= _N_= ', CONTACT DATA SECURITY';
RUN;
```

The RETURN is absolutely necessary to segregate the special-case code segment from the remaining code. Were it not there, then the three "alert" statements would be executed for every iteration of the step, even if none of the IF conditions were satisfied.

LINK and RETURN

The LINK statement takes the form

```
LINK label;
```

where "label" is a valid statement label located elsewhere within the DATA step source code. Like its close cousin GOTO, LINK immediately transfers control to the first executable statement following the named statement label. LINK differs from GOTO in the way it makes the compiler treat the first RETURN statement following the statement label. RETURN usually transfers control back "to the top" of the DATA step. GOTO does not alter this behavior. RETURN following LINK execution, however, transfers control back to the first statement after the LINK (see Figure 16.6). Using LINK, it is possible to write DATA step subroutines.* While a DO group is useful to execute a group of statements only at one point in a program, LINK makes it easier if the same group of statements must be executed at several different points.

---

*For example, LINK- RETURN is quite similar to BASIC's GOSUB-RETURN.

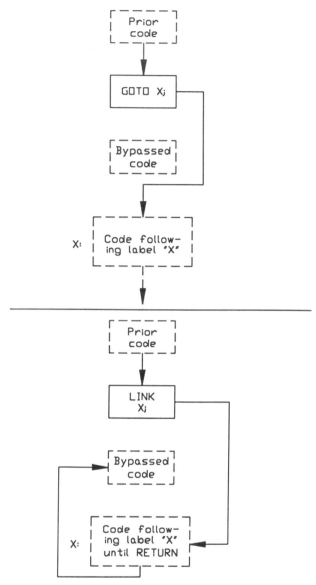

Figure 16.6. The difference between GOTO and LINK. GOTO transfers control and is done; a RETURN would return for the next step iteration. LINK must always have a subsequent RETURN, which sends control back to the statement immediately following LINK.

LINKs can be nested, that is, a secondary LINK statement can be placed after the label but before the RETURN of another LINK. It is perfectly permissible to have DO groups within LINKed statements, and it is even allowed to have a LINK within a DO group.

Note that a statement label, even if named on LINK, doesn't by itself effect flow of control. You can avoid inadvertently executing a LINK group twice by coding an unconditional RETURN before it, e.g.,

```
DATA A;
  SET SOMEDATA;
  IF X=42 THEN LINK FORTYTWO;
  ELSE FOREST=PINE;
  RETURN;
FORTYTWO:
 FOREST=OAK;
  RETURN;
RUN;
```

If the first RETURN statement were not present, FOREST would always equal OAK at the end of each iteration, whether or not X=42.

17

Custom Output

SAS procedures are the main methods used to produce the actual output from the SAS System. But there are times when procedures just can't give exactly what output is needed, no matter how cleverly they are used. Sometimes an external, non-SAS file needs to be written; SAS procedures are not, as a rule, equipped to do this.

At times like these, programming statements of the SAS DATA Step Language can be used to create precisely designed output. Because the user specifies the form of the output precisely, rather than relying on a procedure to do so, we call the results *custom output*; when the output is to be printed, the term *custom report* is sometimes used.

The designers of the SAS System provided two statements, FILE and PUT, that are used for producing custom output. In this chapter, we cover the FILE and PUT statements, after which we describe how to create external files. We then discuss some techniques for producing custom reports.

THE FILE STATEMENT

FILE identifies an external file to which PUT statements will write, just as INFILE specifies an external file from which INPUT gets data. Like INFILE, FILE is an executable statement; PUT statements write to the last-executed FILE reference. The FILE statement has the form

```
FILE [<fileref>|<'file'>|<LOG>|<PRINT>|<PUNCH>]
[typeoption] [options];
```

If a fileref is specified, it must have been previously assigned either within the SAS program by a FILENAME statement, or prior to the SAS program with a method appropriate to the operating system. The fileref may point to an aggregate storage location (such as a PDS, under the MVS operating system), in which case the desired member is specified in parentheses after the fileref. A literal file name can be specified within single quotes in lieu of a fileref.

Three special keywords may be used instead, to direct output to the SAS log, to the standard print file, and to the standard punch file. FILE PRINT is used to direct output to the SAS standard output file, i.e., the place where PROC output goes. This is often done when custom reports are being produced. FILE PUNCH directs output to the standard punch file, not often used nowadays as punched cards are rare. FILE LOG directs output to the SAS log. If no FILE statement has yet been executed during the DATA step, PUT writes to the SAS log by default (as INPUT reads from CARDS if no INFILE statement was executed).

"Typeoption" asks the compiler to create a special operating system file. The types available are operating-system specific. See the *SAS Companion* for your operating system for details.

There are many FILE statement options. Some of these are most helpful for controlling action on the printed page, and are discussed later in this chapter. Others are used for such purposes as designating print versus non-print files, or determining action to be taken when output would exceed the allowable line length; these are discussed immediately below. Still others are operating-system specific; browse your *SAS Companion* to learn about these.

Print versus Non-Print Files

Computer systems have standard methods to control line and page ejects sent to printer output devices, based on codes embedded in the file itself. Files that contain such information we call print files, and those that do not are nonprint files. The special filerefs LOG and PRINT cause SAS to prepare print file output by default (the SAS log output is a printable file). Other filerefs cause SAS to prepare nonprint output by default.

You can override the default by specifying the PRINT or the NOPRINT options. The PRINT option forces output to be prepared with page and line control, and NOPRINT forces output to be prepared without this information.

Action on Line Overrun

As the INFILE statement provides options to control events when an attempt is made to read past the end of a line (review Chapter 8), so the FILE statement allows you to control what happens if a PUT statement attempts to construct a line longer than the maximum line size. The default action is FLOWOVER: the offending data item, and all items after it on the PUT statement (and if the PUT ends with @ or @@, on the next PUT statement), are written to the next output line. More lines are written as needed to accommodate overflow items, and a message on the SAS log indicates whether flowover action happened during the step.

If DROPOVER is coded, then the offending item and all items after it on the PUT statement are simply not written out. A new line is not begun. The step proceeds normally, but SAS issues a message on the log stating that data was lost. If you want to consider an attempt to PUT past the end of a line an error and halt the DATA step, use the STOPOVER option instead.

WRITING EXTERNAL FILES

PUT Statement Review

We first discussed PUT with reference to the SAS log (Chapter 6), showing how the PUT statement could be used to write comments to the log. PUT is also used to write external files or custom reports; a preceding FILE is used to command the lines to be PUT to the external file or on the PRINT file, instead of the SAS log. The PUT statement looks very much like the INPUT statement. As with INPUT, the "null" PUT statement "PUT;" causes the current line to be written to the output file, even if the line is blank. Otherwise, PUT specification(s) determine the content of the current line.

As FILE is to INFILE, so PUT is to INPUT—only more so. There is little we need to say about PUT, because the PUT specifications and their actions follow the same rules we studied when discussing INPUT in Chapters 3 and 8. Free-format (list-style) output is achieved by naming a variable with neither column(s) nor a format identifier, column output by following a variable name with a column number or "first-last" numbers, and formatted output by following a name with a SAS format. SAS formats are followed closely: For example, if a decimal specifier is nonzero, a decimal point will be output, if $DOLLARw.n is used, a dollar sign will be output, etc. The column pointer behaves the same as on INPUT: if a list-style PUT specification has been executed, the column pointer advances one column past the value, and otherwise advances to the column immediately after the value. The column pointer operators + and @, and the line pointer operators / and #, are available with PUT and function just as they do in the INPUT statement. As with INPUT, the trailing @ or @@ may be used to hold the current line until it is released by a subsequent PUT (@ and @@) or at the end of the DATA step iteration (@). Formats and pointer control expressions can be grouped in parentheses following a variable list in parentheses, just as in the INPUT statement. There is even an analogue to named input, as we saw in Chapter 8: The PUT Statement.

```
PUT VAR3=;
```

writes "VAR3=" and then the value of VAR3.

The PUT specifications _INFILE_ and _ALL_ do not have an analogous construction in the INPUT statement. As shown in Chapter 6,

```
PUT _INFILE_;
```

causes the current input buffer to be written, and

```
PUT _ALL_;
```

writes the variables in the current program data vector, including special SAS variables, in named style (i.e., name=value). Another specification available with PUT that has no analogue with INPUT is _PAGE_. "PUT _PAGE_;" causes the pointer to advance to the first line of a new output page. This is normally used when preparing custom reports, not when writing an external data file.

Information in SAS datasets is written to external files using FILE and PUT in a SAS DATA step. All the data-handling features of the DATA step are available in the process. These powerful tools can also be used to manipulate data from one external dataset to another without ever passing through a SAS dataset.

Examples: External Files from SAS Datasets

There is nothing mysterious about writing external files from SAS datasets. When reading from an external file to a dataset, you think of ways to get the data using INPUT statements, based on the construction of the file. To create an external file, simply turn that process around: Based on what you want your file to look like, construct PUT statements. The art is in getting the needed data all together. This is done with the same DATA step statements as are used for dataset building.

Write Selected Variables

Suppose a business keeps its records and produces the majority of its reports using the SAS System. However, some reports are produced instead by specialized accounting software that cannot read SAS datasets. The software expects input data, in fixed fields, consisting of standard letters and numerals.

Problem: The character variables NAME (25 characters max), ADDRESS (35 max), CITY (25 max), and STATE (2), and the numeric variables ZIP, BAL, TRANS, MFACTOR, and CFACTOR are needed. It is known that ZIP will have five numerals, BAL and TRANS are monetary values less than $1 million, and MFACTOR and CFACTOR are integers with values less than 1,000.

Solution:

```
DATA _NULL_;
  SET FINANCE.ACCOUNTS;
  FILE OUTFILE; * ASSUMES OUTFILE DEFINED EARLIER IN JOB;
  PUT NAME $CHAR25. ADDRESS $CHAR35. CITY $CHAR25. STATE $2.
      ZIP 5. (BAL TRANS) (Z9.2) (MFACTOR CFACTOR) (Z3.);
RUN;
```

The leading zero format, Zn.w, is used as a safety: many non-SAS software packages cannot handle blanks in numeric fields.

Note the use of the special SAS dataset name _NULL_ to avoid building an unnecessary SAS dataset. When a DATA step begins with

```
DATA _NULL_;
```

the SAS compiler creates a program data vector, executes DATA step statements, but does not output an observation at the end of each DATA step iteration. No dataset is created. This saves computer resources in cases where the DATA Step Language is used strictly to produce custom output. In general, DATA _NULL_ allows you to use the DATA Step Language as a prorgramming language without having to build an unnecessary SAS dataset.

Write Only Selected Records

Suppose market research survey data are contained in a SAS library with libref MKTSVY1. Dataset RESPNDNT contains names and addresses of survey respondents, with variables NAME, ADDRESS, CITY, STATE, and ZIP as in the previous example. Dataset DEMOGR contains age, sex, income, and other demographic variables, and dataset TSURV1 the results of a mail survey, with "yes" answers coded as 1, "no" as 0. The variable ID contains the respondent's unique identification number. Each dataset is sorted by ID, and there is one and only one record for each respondent in each dataset.

Problem: To prepare for a telephone interview, a sample of respondents is chosen as a pilot group. A subcontractor is to take the names and addresses and obtain telephone numbers, but needs an external dataset to do so. Needed for the pilot are phone numbers of female respondents aged 20–39 who answer "yes" to survey questions 5 and 7 and live in ZIP code prefix areas 116, 275, and 945.

Solution:

```
DATA _NULL_;
FILE SAMPLE1; * DEFINED EARLIER IN JOB;
MERGE MKTSVY1.RESPNDNT MKTSVY1.DEMOGR MKTSVY1.TSURV1;
BY ID;
ZIPAREA=INT(ZIP/100);
IF (ZIPAREA=116 OR ZIPAREA=275 OR ZIPAREA=945)
AND SEX='F' AND 20<=AGE<=39 AND Q5=1 AND Q7=1
THEN PUT NAME $CHAR25. ADDRESS $CHAR35. CITY $CHAR25.
STATE $2. ZIP 5.;
RUN;
```

Take Alternative Action

Suppose a certain software program can only process standard files, not SAS datasets. The first record in the file must contain the number of variables and the field width of each variable. It also demands that if separate analyses are to be produced for record subgroups, each such group must be preceded by one record containing the phrase "GROUP=groupid," where "groupid" is any number or name the user chooses (the program will use that name in the output). After this record come the records to be analyzed. Variables must occupy consecutive fields, with leading zeroes required. If a variable is missing, its field must be filled with X's. A SAS dataset contains integer variables VAR1 through VAR6, none of which will ever take more than seven column places. The subgrouping desired is by the variable CATEGORY, whose value will also be used for the group name. Data are sorted BY CATEGORY.

Problem: Create the external file.

Solution: Using special automatic variables _N_, FIRST.by and LAST.by:

```
DATA _NULL_;
  FILE OUT;
  IF _N_=1 THEN PUT '6,7';
  SET OUR.INDATA;
  BY CATEGORY;
  IF FIRST.CATEGORY THEN PUT 'GROUP=' LEFT(CATEGORY);
  ARRAY A {*} VAR1-VAR6;
  DO I=1 TO DIM(A);
    IF A{I}=. THEN PUT 'XXXXXXX' @;
    ELSE PUT A{I} Z7. @;
  END;
  PUT;
RUN;
```

Note the use of a null PUT statement to release the line for writing at the end of the DO group.

Examples: External Files from Other External Files

It may seem odd at first, but there are times when the SAS System can be just the ticket for transforming one external file into another without the data ever seeing the inside of a SAS dataset. INFILE and INPUT read the input records, then FILE and PUT are used to write the output records. The examples below show only a few of the many ways the SAS DATA Step Language might be used purely as a programming language to manipulate external data. Often, the special PUT specification _INFILE_ will come in handy to copy entire records from one file to another.

Subset a File

Problem: Records in an external dataset have a sex code, "M" or "F," in column 18. Select only the "M" records for another dataset.

Solution:

```
DATA _NULL_;
  INFILE ALL;
  FILE MALES;
  INPUT SEX $ 18;
  IF SEX='M' THEN PUT _INFILE_;
RUN;
```

By the way, the FILE statement could have come before INFILE, or after INPUT. So long as the FILE statement comes *somewhere* before the PUT statement, and so long as no other FILE statement comes between, it is all right. The same holds for INFILE and INPUT.

Copy Portions of Records

Problem: Only the first 60 columns of a much longer record are needed for a certain external dataset.

Solution: The best thing to do is use the LINESIZE option on the INFILE statement:

```
DATA _NULL_;
  FILE PART;
  INFILE WHOLE LS=60;
  INPUT;
  PUT _INFILE_;
RUN;
```

You can go the other way and cut off the first 60 columns, putting only the rest (from column 61 on), with the START=var option of the INFILE statement:

```
DATA _NULL_;
  FILE LASTPART;
  INFILE WHOLE START=S;
  INPUT;
  S=61;
  PUT _INFILE_;
RUN;
```

Make Duplicate Records

Imagine a dataset contains the weight in grams of several hundred eggplants sampled from a field treated with an experimental fertilizer. Many of the measurements are the same, and to conserve space only one record per unique weight is written. Columns 1–4 contain the weight, and columns 5–7 the number of eggplants of that weight.

Problem: For a certain software package to use the data, the data should be written out so that each record contains the weight of a single fruit.

Solution:

```
DATA _NULL_;
  INFILE FERTLZR;
  FILE USEDATA;
  INPUT WEIGHT 1-4 NUM 5-7;
  DO I=1 TO NUM;
    PUT WEIGHT Z3.;
  END;
RUN;
```

"Proofread" Data

Suppose a data file with 80-byte records is supposed to contain only numeric information—no alphabetics, special characters, or blanks—but that data entry mistakes may have been made.

Problem: Pass only all-numeric records to a "clean" dataset, and list records that have illegal characters for further investigation, including their locations in the file in the listing.

Solution: Here is our first example of two different FILES:

```
DATA _NULL_;
  INFILE INDATA;
  INPUT ALL $CHAR80.;
  IF VERIFY(ALL,'0123456789')=0 THEN DO;
    FILE GOODFILE;
    PUT _INFILE_ ;
  END;
  ELSE DO;
    FILE LOG;
    PUT _N_ ': ' _INFILE_ ;
  END;
RUN;
```

The implicit record number is placed before a colon and a space, and the record written to the log, whenever an invalid character is discovered. We use a SAS variable rather than _INFILE_ so that the VERIFY function can operate: _INFILE_ is not a variable and cannot be an argument to the function. (Note that the chosen name "ALL" is not the same as the special SAS name _ALL_ and is perfectly valid here.) But for convenience, and to save the program from having to format ALL for output, we can still use _INFILE_ as the object of the PUT statement.

Add Sequence Numbers

Problem: An external file is to be sent on punched cards to another, old-fashioned computer installation. Sequence numbers should be placed in columns 72–80 in case the cards are ever dropped. We assume that there is nothing of consequence after column 71.

Solution:

```
DATA _NULL_;
  INFILE STUFF;
  FILE PUNCH;
  PUT _INFILE_ @72 _N_ Z8.; * WARNING: OVERWRITE AFTER COL 71;
RUN;
```

Select Records by Sequence

Let a public health agency's file contain confidential information about birth defects. The information is maintained on three consecutive records. The first contains the mother's name and social security number, the next two the birth defect information and other incidental information (such as infant sex, birth weight, etc.).

Problem: For research purposes, copies of the file must be made for distribution with the first record of each set of three removed to preserve confidentiality.
Solution:

```
DATA _NULL_;
  INFILE BRTHDFCT;
  FILE BDCOPY;
  INPUT;
  IF MOD(_N_,3)=1 THEN DELETE;
  PUT _INFILE_;
RUN;
```

Delete Portions of Record

Problem: A similar public health file contains name and social security number in columns 31–65 of a single record with a record length of 180. To maintain confidentiality, a single record is to be written without this information.
Solution:

```
DATA _NULL_;
  INFILE BRTHDFCT;
  INPUT FIRST $CHAR30. @66 LAST $CHAR115.;
  FILE COPY;
  PUT FIRST $CHAR30. LAST $CHAR115.;
RUN;
```

"Mask" Portions of Records

Problem: The same public health file is to be copied. While the sensitive information in columns 30–65 must be suppressed, to keep confusion to a minimum the other information should appear in the same columns of the new record. That is, what was in columns 66–180 should not be moved 35 positions left.
Solution: Overwrite the output buffer:

```
DATA _NULL_;
  INFILE BRTHDFCT;
  FILE MASKCOPY;
  INPUT;
  PUT _INFILE_ @31 'XXXXXXXXXXXXXXXXXXXXXXXXXXXXXXXXXXXX';
RUN;
```

A variation includes a sequence number in lieu of personal data, and shows the use of the "*n**" specifier with a PUT character constant:

```
DATA _NULL_;
  INFILE BRTHDFCT;
  FILE MASKCOPY;
  INPUT;
  PUT _INFILE_ @36 30*'X' @31 _N_ Z5.;
RUN;
```

Merge External Data

Let three different external files, FILE1, FILE2, and FILE3, each contain an identifying number in columns 1–6, and different kinds of information in columns 7–30. The files are sorted in order of columns 1–6, and all have the same number of records and the same ID numbers.

Problem: A new external file is to be built with records that contain all the information in the three files, in order.

Solution: Here is an elegant use of the SAS language to handle non-SAS data:

```
DATA _NULL_;
  FILE NEWFILE;
  INFILE FILE1;
  INPUT ID 1-6 PART1 $CHAR24.;
  INFILE FILE2;
  INPUT PART2 $CHAR24.;
  INFILE FILE3;
  INPUT PART3 $CHAR24.;
  PUT ID 1-6 (PART1-PART3) ($CHAR24.);
RUN;
```

Selective Merge

In the final example, we let SAS datasets intervene, for there are those times when going from external file to external file is just too complex. Imagine that three files similar to those in the last example are to be merged. The records are sorted by ID values in columns 1–6, but the IDs within the three files may be different.

Problem: Write an external dataset that contains the data available for IDs that appear in the third file, but not for IDs that do not appear in the third file.

Solution:

```
DATA F1;
  INFILE FILE1;
  INPUT ID 1-6 PART1 $CHAR24.;
RUN;
DATA F2;
  INFILE FILE2;
  INPUT ID 1-6 PART2 $CHAR24.;
RUN;
DATA F3;
  INFILE FILE3;
  INPUT ID 1-6 PART3 $CHAR24.;
RUN;
DATA _NULL_;
  MERGE FILE1 FILE2 FILE3(IN=IN3);
  BY ID; IF IN3;
  FILE NEWFILE;
  PUT ID 1-6 (PART1-PART3) ($CHAR24.);
RUN;
```

CUSTOM REPORTS

FILE Statement Options Used Primarily for Printable Output

Several FILE statement options are designed primarily or exclusively in order to give users fine control over the layout of custom output. Let's review some here, and then see how they can be used in the examples to follow.

Setting Maximum Line and Page Sizes

The maximum line size is the longest line, in characters, that SAS will allow to be written to the output file. By default, the maximum line size for PUNCH is 80, for LOG, PRINT, and other print files some standard system default, and for external files the record length defined to the SAS System. You can override the default with the LINESIZE= option, which may be abbreviated LS=. A SAS DATA step will not write a line of greater length than the specified line size; exactly what will happen to such a line is controlled by other options (see "line overrun," in our discussion of the FILE statement earlier in this chapter).

Page size applies to print files only, and is the number of lines SAS will write before causing a page-eject action. The system default can be overridden on the FILE statement with the PAGESIZE= option, which may be abbreviated PS=.

Setting the Output Buffer Size

Normally, the PUT statement has access to one line, and when that line is filled it is written to the output file. In another direct analogy to INPUT, if any PUT statement in the DATA step uses the linepointer control #, then a number of lines corresponding to the highest number following any # is retained in memory and PUT statements can move freely back and forth between these lines until PUT releases the buffer for writing (i.e., when a PUT ends without a trailing @ or @@).

You can override these defaults by specifying the number of lines to be available to the linepointer with the N= option. While a particular value may be specified after N=, the most typical use for this option is in handling print files with the special "N=PAGESIZE," which may be abbreviated "N=PS" (if the output file is a print file, *only* N=1 or N=PS are valid). Coding the N=PS option allows the line pointer to roam freely among the lines on an output page before the page is written to the print file. This is valuable in creating many kinds of special reports, because it provides "full page access," as we will see later in this chapter.

Determining Remaining Page Lines

Also useful in handling custom reports is the LINESLEFT=variable option, which may be abbreviated LL=. Specifying LL=variable on the FILE statement creates a SAS variable that contains the number of lines remaining on the current page, i.e., pagesize minus current-line-number. As we will soon illustrate, this variable can be used in comparison operations to determine whether it is prudent to continue writing on the same page or if a new page should be started.

Determining the Current Pointer Location

COLUMN=varname creates a variable whose value at any time is the column at which the PUT statement column pointer sits. LINE=varname creates a variable whose value is that of the current PUT statement line pointer.

Suppressing Title Printing

When creating custom reports with fileref PRINT, the title line(s) defined by default ("The SAS System") or by any current TITLE statements can be omitted from the output pages with the NOTITLES option. To resume printing titles, a subsequent FILE PRINT statement may specify the option TITLES.

Note that FOOTNOTEs do *not* print on pages constructed with FILE statements in any case.

Defining a Custom Page Heading

When creating custom reports, you can specify a sequence of statements you wish executed each time PUT advances to a new page, whether due to a _PAGE_ specification or simply the fact that the next line trips past the current pagesize. The code is placed following a statement label defined in the HEADER= option on the FILE statement, and is terminated by a RETURN statement. HEADER=label causes a LINK-type action whenever a new page is begun. The option is called HEADER because it is normally used to specify one or more PUT statements that write a consistent page heading, as we will see in examples to follow.

Examples: Custom Output

A Simple Report

Let a SAS dataset, BILLS, represent a customer database maintained by a retail store. BILLS contains information on customers whose accounts are one or more months overdue: CUSTNUM, customer ID number; BALANCE, amount due; MONTHS, months overdue.

Problem: Produce a listing of overdue accounts, by months overdue, highlighting customers who (1) owe over $400 or (2) owe over $200 and are more than one month past due. Arrange the listing by customer number within months.

Solution: This may be accomplished with some data manipulation and the PRINT procedure, but let's see how a list could be produced with DATA and PUT. Listing 17.1 shows one approach. The input dataset is sorted by MONTHS and CUSTNUM within MONTHS. DATA _NULL_ is begun, and the sorted dataset is SET. At each new month, a new page and heading are produced, along with a

```
<<< PROGRAM SOURCE CODE FOLLOWS >>>

PROC PRINT DATA=BILLS; TITLE 'Bills In Arrears'; RUN;
PROC SORT DATA=BILLS; BY MONTHS CUSTNUM; RUN;
DATA _NULL_;
  FILE PRINT;
  SET BILLS; BY MONTHS;
  IF FIRST.MONTHS THEN
    PUT / '    :::: Months in arrears: ' MONTHS '::::' /;
  PUT 'Customer number: ' CUSTNUM @30 BALANCE DOLLAR8.2 @;
  IF BALANCE >= 400 OR (BALANCE>=200 AND MONTHS >1) THEN
    PUT @50 '*** IMMEDIATE FOLLOWUP! ***';
  ELSE PUT;
  IF LAST.MONTHS THEN PUT _PAGE_;
RUN;

<<< SAS JOB OUTPUT FOLLOWS >>>
```

Bills In Arrears

OBS	CUSTNUM	BALANCE	MONTHS
1	28	236.06	1
2	42	21.63	1
3	45	410.88	1
4	50	11.52	3
5	65	331.27	3
6	68	31.74	4
7	69	293.98	1
8	71	237.68	1
9	77	96.08	4
10	89	111.62	3
11	90	270.04	1
12	91	411.43	3
13	93	12.06	2
14	105	381.94	3
15	107	45.67	3
16	108	115.52	1
17	113	234.21	3
18	116	186.93	4
19	123	6.48	1
20	126	127.48	3
21	129	58.58	2
22	130	298.55	1
23	132	447.37	3
24	134	168.73	1
25	145	223.42	2
26	157	117.02	1

Listing 17.1. "FILE PRINT" example

notation showing the months overdue. Then each account is shown; if over $400 or over $200 and more than a month overdue, a notation is printed.

Using Page Headers

Let's make the report of Listing 17.1 a little fancier, in order to illustrate the use of HEADER=.

The program shown in Listing 17.2 begins with the sorted BILLS dataset of the previous problem. The FILE statement contains HEADER=, identifying a label (in this case "H") which will be linked whenever a new page is begun. By using NOTITLES, the usual SAS title line is suppressed, leaving free the design of a particular title with the header link. Our variable PAGE (not to be confused with the special PUT directive _PAGE_) is created in order to place a page number on the output, which won't appear automatically since NOTITLES was used. PAGE is started with a value of 1 by RETAIN, then after each page is begun, the number is incremented for the subsequent page. The conjunctive condition "IF _N_>1," avoids an empty page at the beginning. Incidentally, note how the easiest way to code the cosmetic underlines is one time using the "*" abbreviation, to call for a row of 68 equals signs to simulate a double underline, and another time simply lining up explicit hyphens (for single underlines) under the words where they are to appear, so spaces need not be hand-counted.

The LINESLEFT= Option

Should the BILLS dataset of the above examples have had more observations, such that more than a pageful fell in any one month, then that month or months would span more than one output page. The program was designed so each new page would show the correct page number, and the correct MONTHS value. But suppose you wanted to annotate each page that has a continuation, by placing the notice "CONTINUED" at the bottom. There are a couple of ways to do this, one of them using the LINESLEFT= (LL=) option. In a variation of the previous program, a FILE statement with the LL= option:

```
FILE PRINT NOTITLES HEADER=H LL=L;
```

creates a variable, L, that tells how many print lines are left on the page. Then you could write after the ELSE PUT a statement such as

```
IF L=4 THEN PUT // @50 '(CONTINUED)' _PAGE_;
```

to skip a couple of lines and put "(CONTINUED)" in the lower right. For an even fancier solution, you might instead code these lines:

```
IF L=4 THEN DO;
  CONT='(CONTINUED)';
  PUT // @50 CONT _PAGE_;
END;
```

```
   <<< PROGRAM SOURCE CODE FOLLOWS >>>

DATA _NULL_;
  RETAIN PAGE 1; * PREPARE PAGE NUMBERS;
  FILE PRINT NOTITLES HEADER=H;
  SET BILLS;  BY MONTHS;
  IF _N_>1 AND FIRST.MONTHS THEN PUT _PAGE_;
    PUT @6 CUSTNUM @29 BALANCE DOLLAR8.2 @;
  IF BALANCE >= 400 OR (BALANCE>=200 AND MONTHS >1) THEN
    PUT @52 '****';
  ELSE PUT;
  RETURN;
H: PUT 'Customers in arrears ' MONTHS ' months'  @60 'PAGE ' PAGE 2.
    / 68*'='   //
      'Customer Number' @30 'Balance' @50 'Followup' /
      '----------------' @30 '-------' @50 '--------' /  ;
    PAGE+1; *INCREMENT PAGE NUMBER FOR NEXT TIME;
    RETURN;
RUN;

   <<< SAS JOB OUTPUT FOLLOWS >>>
```

```
Customers in arrears 1  months                              PAGE  1
====================================================================

Customer Number                Balance            Followup
----------------               -------            --------

      28                      $236.06
      42                       $21.63
      45                      $410.88              ****
      69                      $293.98
      71                      $237.68
      90                      $270.04
     108                      $115.52
     123                        $6.48
     130                      $298.55
     134                      $168.73
     157                      $117.02
```

Listing 17.2. FILE PRINT with HEADER=

Continued

and change the first statement after the label H to begin

```
PUT 'CUSTOMERS IN ARREARS ' MONTHS CONT @60 'PAGE '
PAGE 2.
```

adding within the header (but after the PUT statement) the statement

```
Customers in arrears 2  months                                    PAGE   2
============================================================================

Customer Number                  Balance              Followup
- - - - - - - - - - - - - - -    - - - - - - -        - - - - - - - -

      93                         $12.06
     129                         $58.58
     145                        $223.42                 ★★★★


Customers in arrears 3  months                                    PAGE   3
============================================================================

Customer Number                  Balance              Followup
- - - - - - - - - - - - - - -    - - - - - - -        - - - - - - - -

      50                         $11.52
      65                        $331.27                 ★★★★
      89                        $111.62
      91                        $411.43                 ★★★★
     105                        $381.94                 ★★★★
     107                         $45.67
     113                        $234.21                 ★★★★
     126                        $127.48
     132                        $447.37                 ★★★★


Customers in arrears 4  months                                    PAGE   4
============================================================================

Customer Number                  Balance              Followup
- - - - - - - - - - - - - - -    - - - - - - -        - - - - - - - -

      68                         $31.74
      77                         $96.08
     116                        $186.93
```

Listing 17.2. *Continued*

```
CONT=' ';
```

so that "(CONTINUED)" appears in the title line of the "continued" months but
does not appear at the head of pages that were not triggered by the L=4 condition.

More than One Report

By using more than one FILE statement specifying different print files, it is easy
to write more than one custom report in the same DATA step. Listing 17.3 shows

```
DATA _NULL_;
  RETAIN PAGE 1; * PREPARE PAGE NUMBERS;
  FILE PRINT NOTITLES HEADER=H LINESLEFT=L;
  SET BILLS;  BY MONTHS;
  IF _N_>1 AND FIRST.MONTHS THEN PUT _PAGE_;
  PUT @6 CUSTNUM @29 BALANCE DOLLAR8.2 @;
  IF BALANCE >= 400 OR (BALANCE>=200 AND MONTHS >1) THEN
    PUT @52 '****';
  ELSE PUT;
  IF L=4 THEN DO;
    CONT='(continued)';
    PUT // @50 CONT;
  END;
  IF BALANCE >= 400 OR (BALANCE>=200 AND MONTHS >1) THEN DO;
    FILE PRINT1 NOTITLES HEADER=H1 PRINT;
    * ("PRINT" option used since fileref "PRINT1" does not imply it);
    PUT CUSTNUM @30 BALANCE @43 MONTHS;
  END;
  RETURN;
H: PUT 'Customers in arrears ' MONTHS ' months' CONT @60 'PAGE '
       PAGE 2. / 68*'='   //
       'Customer Number' @30 'Balance' @50 'Followup' /
       '---------------' @30 '-------' @50 '--------' /  ;
   PAGE+1; *INCREMENT PAGE NUMBER FOR NEXT TIME;
   CONT=' ';
   RETURN;
H1: PUT 'Customers In Arrears Needing IMMEDIATE FOLLOWUP!' //
        'Customer Number' @30 'Balance' @40 'Months' /
        '---------------' @30 '-------' @40 '--------' /  ;
    RETURN;
RUN;
```

Listing 17.3. FILE PRINT with two output files (source code only)

the source code of a program that could be used to produce the report we have just discussed (showing our example code in context), and a second report showing which customers need "immediate action." Note that our fileref "PRINT1" must have been defined earlier in the job (e.g., with a FILENAME statement, or else in external job control), because it is not a standard print file.

Custom Reports and Output Datasets

There is no reason why you cannot produce one or more external files and a printout in the same DATA step. Just use FILE statements appropriately, directing output to PRINT or to another, nonprint dataset instead of another print file. Always be careful that the correct FILE statement executes at the right time (i.e., before you attempt to PUT something there).

Likewise, there is nothing to prevent creating one or more SAS datasets while creating PRINT output or one or more print or nonprint datasets. Just use one or more SAS dataset names on the DATA statement (with OUTPUT statements if required for selectivity if building more than one dataset) and proceed. You can do all the complex SETting, MERGEing, and whatever else is required in the DATA step whether or not an external dataset is also being created. After all, FILE and PUT are but two of many statements available for DATA step programming; they do not conflict with other DATA step manipulations.

Full Page Access with the N=PS Option

Problem: Employee's names are stored in the variables LAST and FIRST, each with a length of 12, their room number in ROOM and four-digit phone extensions in EXT. Print a concise phone listing.

Solution: This can be done without full page access. At least 50 lines per page will be available, even after you print your headings, and you could divide the input dataset into separate 50-item datasets, MERGE two of them at a time until they're done, placing values from one into one set of variables and others into another, and PUTting first the one set of variables and then the other. That is, if you had two datasets, one with the first 25 names and one with the second 25, you could produce the first page with

```
MERGE ONE(RENAME=(LAST=LAST1 FIRST=FIRST1 ROOM=ROOM1 EXT=EXT1))
TWO(RENAME=(LAST=LAST2 FIRST=FIRST2 ROOM=ROOM2 EXT=EXT2));
FILE PRINT HEADER=HDR;
PUT LAST1 FIRST1 @27 ROOM1 2. +2 PHONE1 4. @41
LAST2 FIRST2 @67 ROOM2 2. +2 PHONE2 4. ;
```

The trick is to create the multiple datasets in the first place. This is not hard, but it can get quite messy, especially if it involves many records, many pages, or production of many columns per page. Of course, for this kind of application there is no reason nowadays to bother with the merge strategy *nor* with full page access, thanks to the panels facility of the REPORT procedure. Before this was invented,* however, the best way was to use N=PS and PUT statements and the solution is still a good one for illustrating N=PS. It is shown in Listing 17.4. This approach is good for many other listings besides phone books, when the combined length of variables is short, and may accomplish things that would be hard to do with precision, even using PROC REPORT. The form illustrated—nested DO groups, lines within columns, SET and pointer control—is standard procedure.

---

*More precisely, before the Version 5.16/18 QPRINT procedure with its MULTIPLE option, itself now obsolete with REPORT.

```
<<< PROGRAM SOURCE CODE FOLLOWS >>>

TITLE 'EMPLOYEE LOCATOR';
TITLE2 '----------------------------------------';
DATA _NULL_;
  FILE PRINT N=PS HEADER=HEAD;
  DO COL=1,43;
    COL2=COL+26; * LINE UP THE ROOMS, PHONES NICELY;
    DO LIN=6 TO 55;
      SET PERSONS END=LASTONE; * PERSONS IS SORTED BY LAST,FIRST;
      PUT #LIN @COL LAST FIRST @COL2 ROOM 3. +2 PHONE 4.;
    END;
  END;
  IF NOT(LASTONE) THEN PUT _PAGE_;
  RETURN;
HEAD:
PUT '    NAME' @27 'ROOM/PHONE' @48 'NAME' @69 'ROOM/PHONE' /
    25*'='    @27    '==========' @43 25*'=' @69 '=========='   ;
  RETURN;
RUN;
```

```
<<< SAS JOB OUTPUT FOLLOWS >>>
```

```
                        EMPLOYEE LOCATOR                        1
           ----------------------------------------

    NAME                    ROOM/PHONE        NAME                    ROOM/PHONE
========================= ==========      ========================= ==========

AGABAO JULIA              578  1171       ETHRIDGE FRANCES          755  1113
AMBULIA OSCAR             180  1195       FAIRCHILD MARY            288  1123
ANDERSON EARL             176  1032       FERGUSON JEAN             608  1007

    <<< 44 LINES OMITTED HERE >>>

EILERS PERRY              631  1138       KEMPER FRED               475  1084
EPSTEIN VIRGIE            240  1030       KILLEBREW MARY            648  1093
ESCHMANN WILLIE           542  1074       KING DELLA                193  1173




                        EMPLOYEE LOCATOR                        2
           ----------------------------------------

    NAME                    ROOM/PHONE        NAME                    ROOM/PHONE
========================= ==========      ========================= ==========

KLUGH ALICE               332  1047       ROTHENBERG JOHN           634  1193
KNOWLES CATHERINE         318  1123       RUTSCH MARY               148  1089
KNOX ELOISE               300  1194       SAYE ANGELINA             140  1141

    <<< 44 LINES OMITTED HERE >>>

ROSA SAMUEL               111  1119       YOUNG ANNA                212  1129
ROSS GERALDINE            257  1132       YUH PEGGY                 133  1081
ROSHONG LUCINDA           196  1127       YOUNG KING                130  1001
```

Listing 17.4. FILE PRINT with N=PS

18

A SAS-Based Business System

To conclude our examination of DATA Step programming, let's construct a complete SAS-based business system including inventory management and invoicing. In the real world, perhaps not all of these functions would be handled entirely within the SAS System; or perhaps more procedure output might be used for the reporting function where here we have concentrated on illustrating custom reporting. But see what can be done if you put your creativity to using the SAS System—especially its DATA Step Language—to provide a complete data processing solution.

DESIGNING OUR SAS-BASED SYSTEM

For illustrative purposes, let's create a fictional business, to which we will apply our data processing effort.

Jiminy's Crickets is a family business with four product lines: their staple "Somethin' Fishy," wholesale bait crickets; "Cheepers Creepers," pet crickets (as in Japan, little cages and all); "Gryllidae Series 101," purebred crickets for scientific research; and the latest, somewhat faltering enterprise, "Les Criquettes!" gourmet fried crickets (regular, no-salt, and barbeque).

To move from paper-and-pencil to computer-based accounting, Jiminy's has contracted with us to write a business data processing system, and for its flexibility and power we have, naturally, chosen to implement it using the SAS System.

Data Processing Goals

The principles of file organization, reporting, and transaction processing that will be illustrated in the following pages could be applied to create a very elaborate system, with a detailed accounting structure and completely automated processes for inventory, billing, and so on. But to stay within the scope of this presentation, we must set more modest goals. Accordingly, we will be satisfied with planning only a few of the important functions of a small business data processing system, and not attempt a formal accounting structure. We will keep individual reports simple. We will not get into forecasting or projections, nor operations analysis, nor graphic data displays, even though these are strong selling points for using the SAS System, because we have not covered the SAS add-on products tailored for these tasks. And we will not implement elaborate data integrity and error-checking schemes, although SAS software is more than equal to the task.

Reporting Objectives

We will produce one document for internal use, and three paper instruments for doing business. We will also keep records on cash flow and on sales.

The internal document will be a sales summary, per product line, reported quarterly. The paper instruments will be:

1. Invoices, daily. To keep the illustration simple, postulate that Jiminy's fills orders daily, never runs out of stock, and all customers have good credit. The "invoice" process then can fully subsume customer order processing: invoices go out with shipments.
2. Billing statements for customers, monthly.
3. Jiminy's orders to replenish inventory, weekly, to be based on actual decrease of stock during the week. Simplifying postulates: (a) it has been pre-decided how much is sufficient to have on hand of any item; (b) the process is run on the same day each week, so we can confidently use the past seven days' data each time.

Required Input Data

There are two data sources, which are also the two endpoints. From the customers will come order and money data, and to customers will go invoices (along with items). From vendors will come invoices (along with stock items), and to vendors will go Jiminy's own orders.

The data required for the system include a number of elements that satisfy our reporting requirements and several other elements that are needed to prepare or organize the data (e.g., various ID numbers). Table 18.1 summarizes the data elements that will be used in our example application. Their purposes will become clear as we develop the implementation below.

File Design

Considering the output needed and the sources of input, we decide to keep eight principal files. Their association with the logical data elements is given in Table

TABLE 18.1. DATA ELEMENTS USED IN "JIMORDS" EXAMPLE

Item	Definition
CASHIN	Money amount received from a customer
CINDATE	Date of receipt of money from a customer
CORDATE	Date of customer order
CUSTADDR	Address of customer
CUSTID	Unique id number of customer
CUSTNAME	Name of customer
CUSTPO	Customer purchase order number on order to Jiminy's
INVDATE	Date of Jiminy's invoice to customer
JDESCRIP	Description of Jiminy's product
JIMPO	Jiminy's purchase order number on order to vendor
JINVENT	Jiminy's internal inventory stock number
JINVOICE	Jiminy's invoice number for billing
JQUANT	Quantity of items ordered by customer of Jiminy's
JSTOCK	Jiminy's inventory stock number of ordered item
NPER	Number of vendor items needed to each Jiminy item (inventory)
OCOUNT	Quantity per unit order (dozen, gross, each, etc.)
ONHAND	Quantity of stock items known on hand
PCLASS	Product class code (there are four product classes)
PRICE	Jiminy's price to customers of item
REQUIRED	Quantity of stock items required to be on hand
SALSPRSN	Name of salesperson completing customer order
SUBTOT	Total amount due Jiminy's on invoice
VDESCRIP	Description of vendor's product
VENDADDR	Address of vendor
VENDID	Unique id number of vendor
VENDNAME	Name of vendor
VOCOUNT	Vendor's quantity per unit order
VORDATE	Date of Jiminy's order
VPRICE	Price to Jiminy's of vendor stock item
VQUANT	Quantity of items ordered by Jiminy's of vendor
VSTOCK	Vendor's inventory stock number of ordered item

18.2. (There will also be an additional file, CBALDUE, to hold running monetary balances, transaction files of raw data, and small miscellaneous data stores.)

One of the system files, CASHIN, functions as a cash journal. CASHIN shows money arriving from customers, and will serve as the repository for payments that are reported on customers' statements. We presume the file is updated on a timely basis.

Information on businesses with whom Jiminy's deals—names and addresses—is to be archived in CUSTMERS and VENDORS. CUSTMERS (customers) buy from Jiminy's, VENDORS sell to Jiminy's. They are identified by the key variables CUSTID and VENDID, respectively. Two files keep records of orders—CUSTORDS orders from Jiminy's customers, JIMORDS orders to Jiminy's vendors—and serve as the basis for actual invoicing and ordering.

We will keep information on Jiminy's stock, keyed by the identification number JSTOCK, in a dataset called PRODUCTS, and in INVENT keep tabs on the supplies needed to make, handle, or distribute the products. ISTOCK will store information linking Jiminy's stock items to inventory items; this separate file is

TABLE 18.2. DATA ELEMENTS AND DATA FILES IN "JIMORDS" EXAMPLE

Item	JIMORDS	CUSTORDS	PRODUCTS	CUSTMERS	VENDORS	CASHIN	ISTOCK	INVENT
CASHIN						X		
CINDATE						X		
CORDATE		X						
CUSTADDR[a]				X				
CUSTID		X		X		X		
CUSTNAME				X				
CUSTPO		X						
INVDATE		X						
JDESCRIP			X					
JIMPO	X							
JINVENT							X	X
JINVOICE		X						
JQUANT		X						
JSTOCK		X	X				X	
NPER							X	
OCOUNT			X					
ONHAND								X
PCLASS			X					
PRICE			X					
REQUIRED								X
SALSPRSN		X						
SUBTOT		X						
VDESCRIP								X
VENDADDR[a]					X			
VENDID	X				X			X
VENDNAME					X			
VOCOUNT								X
VORDATE	X							
VPRICE								X
VQUANT	X							
VSTOCK	X							X

[a] In the data files the address is broken into several variables.

called for because supply inventory and product stock have a "many-to-many" relationship, i.e., more than one supply can be required for a stock product and more than one product may use the same supply.

SYSTEM IMPLEMENTATION

Initialize Permanent Files

The principal data files described above, plus the file CBALDUE that will be used strictly as a convenience in preparing billings and orders, are initialized by the job shown in Listing 18.1. These datasets will have *zero* observations—there are no assignment nor data-reading statements in the DATA steps—but will have variables with attributes as shown (in other words, the SAS compiler writes a dataset

```
* PERMANENT FILE SETUP -RUN THIS JOB ONCE INITIALLY;
***** JIMORDS: JIMINY''S ORDERS OF STOCK FROM VENDORS*****;
DATA JIMORDS.JIMORDS(LABEL=ORDERS TO REPLENISH INVENTORY);
ATTRIB VENDID    LABEL='OUR VENDOR ID          ' LENGTH=4;
ATTRIB VSTOCK    LABEL='VENDOR STOCK #          ' LENGTH=$12;
ATTRIB JIMPO     LABEL='OUR PURCHASE ORDER #    ' LENGTH=4;
ATTRIB VQUANT    LABEL='QUANTITY ORDERED        ' LENGTH=3;
ATTRIB VORDATE   LABEL='VENDOR ORDER DATE       ' INFORMAT=MMDDYY6.;
RUN;


***** CUSTORDS: CUSTOMER ORDERS OF MERCHANDISE FROM JIMINY''S *****;
DATA CUSTORDS.CUSTORDS(LABEL=ORDERS FROM CUSTOMERS);
ATTRIB JSTOCK    LABEL='OUR PRODUCT STOCK #     ' LENGTH=4;
ATTRIB CUSTID    LABEL='OUR CUSTOMER ID         ' LENGTH=4;
ATTRIB SALSPRSN  LABEL='SALESPERSON             ' LENGTH=$15;
ATTRIB CORDATE   LABEL='CUSTOMER ORDER DATE     ' INFORMAT=MMDDYY6.;
ATTRIB JINVOICE  LABEL='OUR INVOICE NUMBER      ' LENGTH=4;
ATTRIB INVDATE   LABEL='INVOICE/SHIPPING DATE   ' INFORMAT=MMDDYY6.;
ATTRIB JQUANT    LABEL='QUANTITY ORDERED        ' LENGTH=3;
ATTRIB CUSTPO    LABEL='CUSTOMER PO #           ' LENGTH=$12;
ATTRIB SUBTOT    LABEL='ITEM PRICE * QUANTITY   ' LENGTH=4;
RUN;


***** PRODUCTS: OUR PRODUCT LINE *****;
DATA PRODUCTS.PRODUCTS(LABEL=OUR PRODUCT LINE);
ATTRIB PCLASS    LABEL='OUR PRODUCT CLASS       ' LENGTH=$1;
     * C = SOMETHIN'' FISHY;
     * P = CHEEPERS CREEPERS;
     * G = GRYLLIDAE SERIES 101;
     * Q = LES CRIQUETTES!;
ATTRIB JSTOCK    LABEL='OUR PRODUCT STOCK #     ' LENGTH=4;
ATTRIB JDESCRIP  LABEL='OUR PRODUCT DESCRIPTION ' LENGTH=$20;
ATTRIB PRICE     LABEL='OUR STANDARD PRICE      ' LENGTH=4;
ATTRIB OCOUNT    LABEL='QUANTITY PER UNIT ORDER ' LENGTH=4;
RUN;


***** VENDORS: OUR VENDORS *****;
DATA VENDORS.VENDORS(LABEL='OUR VENDORS');
ATTRIB VENDID    LABEL='OUR VENDOR ID           ' LENGTH=4;
ATTRIB VENDNAME  LABEL='VENDOR NAME             ' LENGTH=$30;
AIIRIB VENDADR1  LABEL='VENDOR ADDRESS: STREET  ' LENGTH=$30;
ATTRIB VENDCITY  LABEL='VENDOR ADDRESS: CITY    ' LENGTH=$20;
ATTRIB VENDSTAT  LABEL='VENDOR ADDRESS: STATE   ' LENGTH=$2;
ATTRIB VENDZIP   LABEL='VENDOR ADDRESS: ZIP     ' LENGTH=4;
RUN;
```

Listing 18.1. File setup source code, "Jiminy's" example

Continued

```
***** CUSTMERS: OUR CUSTOMERS *****;
DATA CUSTMERS.CUSTMERS(LABEL='OUR CUSTOMERS');
ATTRIB CUSTID   LABEL='OUR CUSTOMER ID          ' LENGTH=4;
ATTRIB CUSTNAME LABEL='CUSTOMER NAME             ' LENGTH=$30;
ATTRIB CUSTADR1 LABEL='CUSTOMER ADDRESS: STREET' LENGTH=$30;
ATTRIB CUSTCITY LABEL='CUSTOMER ADDRESS: CITY  ' LENGTH=$20;
ATTRIB CUSTSTAT LABEL='CUSTOMER ADDRESS: STATE ' LENGTH=$2;
ATTRIB CUSTZIP  LABEL='CUSTOMER ADDRESS: ZIP   ' LENGTH=4;
RUN;

***** CASHIN: MONEY RECEIVED IN PAYMENT FROM CUSTOMERS *****;
DATA CASHIN.CASHIN(LABEL=CASH IN: PAYMENT RECEIVED);
ATTRIB CASHIN   LABEL='CASH IN: AMOUNT           ' LENGTH=4;
ATTRIB CINDATE  LABEL='CASH IN DATE              ' INFORMAT=MMDDYY6.;
ATTRIB CUSTID   LABEL='OUR CUSTOMER ID           ' LENGTH=4;
RUN;

***** CBALDUE: BALANCE DUE FOR CUSTOMERS (FOR PERIODIC STATEMENT)****;
DATA CBALDUE.CBALDUE(LABEL='BALANCE DUE FOR CUSTOMERS');
ATTRIB CUSTID   LABEL='OUR CUSTOMER ID           ' LENGTH=4;
ATTRIB BALDUE   LABEL='BALANCE FROM LAST STMT    ' LENGTH=4;
ATTRIB CBALDATE LABEL='DATE OF LAST STMT         ' INFORMAT=MMDDYY6;
RUN;

***** INVENT: INVENTORY OF PRODUCTS AND SUPPLIES *****;
DATA INVENT.INVENT(LABEL='PRODUCT/SUPPLY INVENTORY');
ATTRIB JINVENT  LABEL='OUR INVENTORY ID NUMBER ' LENGTH=4;
ATTRIB ONHAND   LABEL='QUANTITY ON HAND        ' LENGTH=4;
ATTRIB REQUIRED LABEL='QUANTITY REQUIRED       ' LENGTH=4;
ATTRIB VENDID   LABEL='PREFERRED VENDOR ID     ' LENGTH=4;
ATTRIB VSTOCK   LABEL='VENDOR STOCK #          ' LENGTH=$12;
ATTRIB VDESCRIP LABEL='VENDOR STOCK DESCRIPTION' LENGTH=$20;
ATTRIB VOCOUNT  LABEL='QUANTITY PER UNIT ORDER ' LENGTH=4;
ATTRIB VPRICE   LABEL='VENDOR PRICE PER UNIT   ' LENGTH=4;
RUN;

***** ISTOCK: PRODUCT/SUPPLY <-> JSTOCK CONGRUENCE  ***;
DATA ISTOCK.ISTOCK(LABEL='PRODUCT/SUPPLY <-> JSTOCK');
ATTRIB JINVENT  LABEL='OUR INVENTORY ID NUMBER ' LENGTH=4;
ATTRIB JSTOCK   LABEL='OUR PRODUCT STOCK #     ' LENGTH=4;
ATTRIB NPER     LABEL='NUMBER JINVENT PER JSTOCK' LENGTH=3;
RUN;
```

Listing 18.1. *Continued*

header, but closes the dataset without writing any observations). The reason to create the datasets "blank" is simply to keep the update process apart from the initialization process. This initialization module (or sequence of modules: no reason why they have to be run together) has a single, run-once task. Attribute statements are used to lay out the variables.* Each variable is stored in a reasonably conservative length, and the variables and the datasets are labeled. It was advisable with few exceptions to have one dataset per library, because of the updating that must go on. Note the choice of a libref that mimics its dataset name; this makes things easier to remember.

Keeping Current

By contrasting the processes of recording monetary transactions with those designed to keep customer and vendor information accurate, two different methods of applying transactions to permanent data files will be illustrated.

One of these methods, which we apply below to cash transactions, can be used in any kind of transactions process that requires continual reference to a historical series of events. The technique necessitates only a simple chronological record, showing each transaction. In our example, we will use a simple APPEND to maintain such a record on a daily basis.

The other approach to be illustrated involves more stable information, that nevertheless must occasionally be changed. This suggests using UPDATE on a periodic basis, as we illustrate in another example.

Cash Transactions

Cash transactions, which will be represented in the file CASHIN (money received from customers), are discrete, temporal events that it makes sense to record chronologically. This way, subsequent sorting can be held to a minumum. We might prepare a simple external file containing customer ID number and monetary amount (call it RECEIPTS), and assuming as we do that cash is recorded daily, this simple APPEND job will suffice:

```
** CASH RECEIVED **;
DATA CASHIN;
  LENGTH CASHIN 4 CINDATE 8 CUSTID 4;
  INFILE RECEIPTS;
  INPUT CUSTID 1-8 CASHIN 11-18;
  CINDATE=TODAY();
RUN;
PROC SORT; BY CUSTID; RUN;
PROC APPEND BASE=CASHIN.CASHIN DATE=CASHIN; RUN;
```

---

*In a few instances, some logical variables have been expanded to several. For example, CUSTADDR, customer address in our conceptual model, becomes four variables showing street address, city, state, zip.

Notice the LENGTH statement in the example program. The lengths are the same that were defined for the permanent file at initialization. Were they different, the append would fail. Dataset [WORK.]CASHIN is a new dataset, and does not automatically know about the attributes of the permanent dataset CASHIN.CASHIN with which it is to mingle; it must be told.

Business Connections

Vendor and customer records differ from cash transactions in two fundamental ways, as far as data processing is concerned. First, they are repositories of information identifying persons or companies with whom we have ongoing relationships. The information (name and address) is to be linked by ID numbers (VENDID or CUSTID) at different times for different purposes, and it is best to store information in order by ID number. Second, while orders are placed, filled, and finished, business contacts go on and on. If a customer or vendor moves, it is improper to define a new VENDID and create a new observation; the current observation should be changed.

Accordingly, adding vendors can most parsimoniously be treated as an update operation. Information can be added whether new or changed, in the same process. This is done with UPDATE:

```
** ADD VENDORS **;I
DATA VENDORS;
LENGTH VENDID 4 VENDNAME VENDADR1 $30 VENDCITY $20 VENDSTAT $2
       VENDZIP 4;
INFILE VENDTRAN;
INPUT VENDID 1-8 VENDNAME 11-40 / VENDADR1 1-30 VENDCITY 31-50
       VENDSTAT 51-52 VENDZIP 53-57;
RUN;
PROC SORT; BY VENDID;
DATA M; UPDATE VENDORS.VENDORS VENDORS; BY VENDID; RUN;
DATA VENDORS.VENDORS; SET M; RUN;
```

Note that with this UPDATE strategy, we need to create a temporary dataset and then replace the permanent one with it.

For CUSTMERS, we will do approximately the same thing, but will also take the opportunity to initialize a record in the CBALDUE dataset, needed for the billing statement report. Customers will be sorted by CUSTID. See the discussion on billing statements below.

Customer Orders/Invoice Process

This process shows how two closely related activities can be implemented together. We have postulated that Jiminy's fills each order as it is processed, and because we have to print invoices, it seems inoffensive to couple these two modules—"Order Entry" and "Print Invoices"—together as one. They can easily be separated if Jiminy's changes its way of doing business. They take input from a simple file of easily entered data.

The source code, and example output (an invoice) is shown in Listing 18.2. The first DATA step creates a dataset, CORDS, conforming to the CUSTORDS data vector. It takes its input from raw data, which contains an additional data field for a variable (to be DROPped) that signifies whether the record begins a new order; if so, a different INPUT strategy is needed. With this setup, CUSTID, CORDATE, CUSTPO, and SALSPRSN must be entered only once per order sheet; for the remaining line items only the JSTOCK and JQUANT are needed.* The RETAIN statement ensures that the other values are kept from the first line item. Note that we do not yet have an invoice number; this we will get presently.

The data to this point are now sorted by JSTOCK to prepare to get item descriptions and prices from the PRODUCTS file. We will also get OCOUNT, which tells the units in which Jiminy's requires orders to be made (e.g., each, dozen, gross), and upon which the price is based.

Now the temporary dataset—customer orders combined with product information—is sorted BY CUSTID in preparation for invoicing. Dataset CORDS3 is created to bring in customer name/address information from CUSTMERS. A macro processor strategy is employed to communicate information from one dataset to another: We initialize (external to this program) a small dataset, INVNUM, containing a single observation with a lone variable (JINVOICE). Its mission is to hold last-used invoice number. With the DATA _NULL_ step, that number is retrieved and placed in a global macro variable, INV.

Next we take care of a little bit of business that will help format the invoices nicely in the units column (for DATA CUSTORDS is also the step wherein invoices are printed), and begin to build the final CUSTORDS transaction dataset. The KEEP statement leaves CUSTORDS with only those variables that are wanted for adding to the archive file, yet all the information we just took the trouble to get can still be used for invoices. The variable INVDATE is set to today's date, and the value &INV is retrieved from the symbol table, placed in a DATA step variable JINV. (We do not use JINVOICE for this purpose because of attribute conflicts. Below we will set JINVOICE, whose attributes [numeric, length 4] were created way back in DATA CORDS, to JINV, which being a macro variable was character; character-to-numeric conversion is done.)

At the first record of each invoice, which will be FIRST.CUSTID because we have sorted by CUSTID, we create an invoice number by incrementing the last used number by one. Now we can start a new invoice with PUT _PAGE_; the header will use the invoice number, invoice date, and customer information. The total amount of the invoice (TOTDUE) should, of course, be zero at its beginning. We need to do this explicitly, for TOTDUE is RETAINed so we can print a bottom line amount.

The price of the line item is the price of the stock item times the quantity of units ordered, and is stored in SUBTOT; thus the detail line can be printed.

---

*Review Listing 18.1 and Table 18.1 for definitions of these variables. The sample invoice was produced from the records corresponding to the three data lines (spacing approximate):

```
126239 121988 6219-JC22    10039    15    BABBITT
100032 20
100122 1
```

```
***** ORDER ENTRY *****;
DATA CORDS;
LENGTH JSTOCK CUSTID 4 SALSPRSN $15 CORDATE 8 JINVOICE 4 INVDATE
8
       JQUANT 3 CUSTPO $12 SUBTOT 4;
INFORMAT CORDATE MMDDYY6.;
INFILE CUSTTRAN;
  INPUT CNUM 1 @;  DROP CNUM; *ONLY USED FOR I/O CONTROL: 1=FIRST
ITEM;
  RETAIN;  * KEEP VALUES FROM CNUM=1;
  IF CNUM=1 THEN
  INPUT CUSTID 2-9 @12 CORDATE  CUSTPO 19-30 JSTOCK 32-39 JQUANT
42-45
       SALSPRSN 47-61;
  ELSE INPUT JSTOCK 2-9 JQUANT 12-15;
RUN;
***** BUILD TEMPORARY DATASET WITH ALL INVOICE INFORMATION *****;
PROC SORT DATA=CORDS; BY JSTOCK; RUN;
DATA CORDS2; * ADDS STOCK DESCRIPTIONS FOR INVOICES;
  MERGE CORDS(IN=INC)
        PRODUCTS.PRODUCTS(KEEP=JSTOCK JDESCRIP PRICE OCOUNT);
  BY JSTOCK; IF INC;
RUN;
PROC SORT DATA=CORDS2; BY CUSTID;
DATA CORDS3; * ADDS CUSTOMER INFORMATION FOR INVOICES;
  MERGE CORDS2(IN=INC) CUSTMERS.CUSTMERS;
  BY CUSTID; IF INC;
RUN;
***** GET INVOICE NUMBER, PRINT INVOICES *****;
DATA _NULL_; * GET LAST INVOICE NUMBER;
  SET CUSTORDS.INVNUM;
  CALL SYMPUT('INV',JINVOICE);
RUN;
PROC FORMAT; * FORMAT FOR COMMON UNIT AMOUNTS (OCOUNT);
  VALUE OCFRM 1=' EACH' 12='DOZEN' 144='GROSS' 1000='THOUS';
RUN;
DATA CUSTORDS; * FINAL TEMPORARY DATASET;
  SET CORDS3 END=LAST;
  BY CUSTID;
  KEEP JSTOCK--SUBTOT;
  INVDATE=TODAY();
  IF _N_=1 THEN JINV=&INV; *GET OLD INVOICE NUMBER;
  RETAIN JINV TOTDUE ;
  FILE PRINT NOTITLES HEADER=H;
  IF FIRST.CUSTID THEN DO;
    JINV+1; *CREATE NEW INVOICE NUMBER;
    PUT _PAGE_; *START NEW INVOICE;
    TOTDUE=0;   *TOTAL DUE BEGINS AT ZERO;
  END;
  JINVOICE=JINV;
  SUBTOT=PRICE*JQUANT;
  TOTDUE + SUBTOT;
  PUT @1 JSTOCK @10 JDESCRIP @31 JQUANT @36 OCOUNT OCFRM.
      @41 PRICE 8.2 @51 SUBTOT 10.2;
```

Listing 18.2. Example program to enter orders and print invoices

Continued

```
   IF LAST.CUSTID THEN
     PUT @50 11*'=' / @51 TOTDUE DOLLAR10.2 /////
      'PLEASE ADD TAX IF APPLICABLE';
   IF LAST THEN CALL SYMPUT('INV',JINVOICE);
 RETURN;
 H:
   PUT 'JIMINY''S CRICKETS - I N V O I C E - NUMBER: ' JINV
      'DATE: ' INVDATE MMDDYY8. ////
      'TO: ' @10 CUSTNAME / @10 CUSTADR1 / @10
      @10 CUSTCITY +4 CUSTSTAT+2 CUSTZIP /
      @50 'REF YOUR PO # ' CUSTPO /
      @50 '          DATED ' CORDATE MMDDYY8. ////
 'STOCK    ITEM                   #  UNIT    @       AMOUNT  ' /
 '======== ==================== ==== ==== ======== ===========' //;
 RUN;
 PROC APPEND BASE=CUSTORDS.CUSTORDS DATA=CUSTORDS; RUN;
 DATA CUSTORDS.INVNUM; JINVOICE=&INV; RUN; *UPDATE INVNUM;

 <<< SAS JOB OUTPUT FOLLOWS >>>

 JIMINY'S CRICKETS - I N V O I C E - NUMBER: 10878 DATE: 12/19/88

 TO:       YE OLDE TACQUEL SHOPPE
           126 BAY BRIDGE ALLEY
           ST FRANCIS    CA   91919
                                         REF YOUR PO # 6219-JC22

                                         DATED 12/14/88

 STOCK    ITEM                   #  UNIT    @       AMOUNT
 ======== ==================== ==== ==== ======== ===========

 100032   GIANT BONKERS          20 THOUS  10.00      200.00
 100039   CRICKIT CONTAINERS     15 GROSS  12.00      180.00
 100122   LITTLE SQUIRMERS        1 THOUS   7.00        7.00
                                                  ===========
                                                     $387.00

 PLEASE ADD TAX IF APPLICABLE
```

Listing 18.2. *Continued*

Meanwhile, the running total is incremented by the value of SUBTOT. At the last line item per customer for that day's process, the total due is printed and the invoice terminates.

IF LAST refers back to the SET statement; if we have just processed the last transaction of the day, we must replace the latest invoice number. This we happen to do after APPENDing the customer orders to the archive file, with a DATA step that overwrites CUSTORDS.INVNUM.

Observe that CUSTORDS stores orders line by line. This way, all ordering information down to the stock item is preserved. Invoice totals can be reconstructed if desired; we'll do just that in the monthly billing statements process, next discussed. SALSPRSN, not used for these customer communications, will be used later when the internal sales report is produced.

Billing Statements

The amount due each month is based on orders and payments for the month and on any carry-over from before, that is, if $100 was owed at the end of the last billing period, the current billing period begins with a $100 debt. Carry-over will be kept in the dataset CBALDUE that exists only for this purpose. Observations in CBALDUE can be added as new customers are added, and new customers are added in a manner identical to the way new vendors are added, because customers also have IDs, names, addresses. A program that takes care of both these tasks follows. New balances are initialized to zero, and the opportunity is taken to check that the same customer was not mistakenly entered twice (if duplicates are found, they can be corrected later and the datasets rewritten):

```
** ADD CUSTOMERS **;
DATA CUSTMERS;
LENGTH CUSTID 4 CUSTNAME CUSTADR1 $30 CUSTCITY $20
       CUSTSTAT $2 CUSTZIP 4;
INFILE CUSTTRAN;
INPUT CUSTID 1-8 CUSTNAME 11-40
      / CUSTADR1 1-30 CUSTCITY 31-50
CUSTSTAT 51-52 CUSTZIP 53-57;
RUN;
PROC SORT; BY CUSTID;
DATA M; UPDATE CUSTMERS.CUSTMERS CUSTMERS; BY CUSTID; RUN;
DATA CUSTMERS.CUSTMERS; SET M; RUN;
** ADD ZERO BALANCE **;
DATA C;
SET CBALDUE.CBALDUE(IN=INCC) CUSTMERS(KEEP=CUSTID IN=INC);
BY CUSTID;
IF INC THEN DO; * NEW ACCOUNTS;
BALDUE=0; * NEW ACCOUNTS START WITH ZERO BALANCE;
CBALDATE=TODAY();
END;
IF INCC AND INC THEN PUT '==>DUPLICATE! ' CUSTID;
RUN;
DATA CBALDUE.CBALDUE; SET C; RUN;
```

The billing routine itself, with example output, is shown in Listing 18.3. Records from CUSTORDS are selected that were dated within the just past month; notice how a January billing requires different treatment. The data are next summarized to one invoice per observation (DATA CORDM), because the monthly statement should not go into the details of each invoice. In DATA CASHM are the cash received records for the month.

Now TRANS is built by interleaving the order records, which will become debits, and the cash receipts, which are credits. It is now apparent why the RENAME to "DATE" was done in earlier steps. DEB is a flag that will be used later to distinguish debits from credits. DATA ALL is required because of the logic to be taken later, and DATA USE serves but to merge customer information (name, address) so the billings can be printed.

```
***** MONTHLY STATEMENTS TO CUSTOMERS *****;
DATA CORDS; * REPORTING MONTH (=MONTH JUST ENDED);
  T=TODAY(); * GET TODAY''S DATE;
  SET CUSTORDS.CUSTORDS;
  IF (YEAR(T)=YEAR(INVDATE) AND  MONTH(T)=MONTH(INVDATE)+1)
  OR (YEAR(T)=YEAR(INVDATE)+1 AND MONTH(T)=1
      AND MONTH(INVDATE)=12);
  KEEP CUSTID SUBTOT JINVOICE CUSTPO INVDATE T;
  RENAME INVDATE=DATE;
RUN;
PROC SORT; BY JINVOICE; RUN;
DATA CORDM; * SUMMARIZE TO ONE ENTRY PER INVOICE;
  SET CORDS;
  BY JINVOICE;
  RETAIN INVTOT;
  IF FIRST.JINVOICE THEN INVTOT=SUBTOT;
  ELSE INVTOT + SUBTOT;
  IF LAST.JINVOICE THEN OUTPUT;
  DROP SUBTOT;
RUN;
PROC SORT; BY CUSTID DATE; RUN;
DATA CASHM;
  T=TODAY(); * GET TODAY''S DATE;
  SET CASHIN.CASHIN;
  IF (YEAR(T)=YEAR(CINDATE) AND  MONTH(T)=MONTH(CINDATE)+1)
  OR (YEAR(T)=YEAR(CINDATE)+1 AND MONTH(T)=1
      AND MONTH(CINDATE)=12);
  RENAME CINDATE=DATE;
RUN;
PROC SORT; BY CUSTID DATE; RUN;
DATA TRANS;
  SET CORDM(IN=INCO) CASHM;
  BY CUSTID DATE;
  IF INCO THEN DEB=1; *DEBIT, OTHERWISE (DEB=.) CREDIT;
RUN;
DATA ALL; SET CBALDUE.CBALDUE TRANS; BY CUSTID;
  IF T=. THEN T=TODAY(); * GET DATE (CBALDUE RECORDS);
RUN;
DATA USE; MERGE ALL(IN=INA) CUSTMERS.CUSTMERS;
  BY CUSTID; IF INA;
RUN;
DATA MLAST;
  SET USE;
  BY CUSTID;
RETAIN RUNNING 0;*RUNNING BALANCE;
FILE PRINT NOTITLES HEADER=H;
IF FIRST.CUSTID THEN DO; * FIRST RECORD IS FROM CBALDUE;
  PUT _PAGE_; *START NEW INVOICE;
  IF LAST.CUSTID THEN DO; * FIRST AND LAST = NO ACTION;
    PUT /// 'NO ACTIVITY ON ACCOUNT THIS MONTH'
        /// 'LAST ACTIVITY: ' CBALDATE MMDDYY8.
    /// '      CLOSING BALANCE=' BALDUE  DOLLAR8.2;
    RETURN;
  END;
  RUNNING=BALDUE;
  RETURN; * THAT''S ALL FOR THE CBALDUE RECORD;
```

Listing 18.3. Example monthly billings program

Continued

```
  END;
   IF DEB THEN LINK LINE1; *DEBITS;
   ELSE LINK LINE2; *CREDITS;
   IF LAST.CUSTID THEN DO;
     OUTPUT; KEEP RUNNING CUSTID; *NEED FINAL SUMMARY TOTAL ONLY;
     PUT // '-------------------------------' //
            '                CLOSING BALANCE=' RUNNING DOLLAR8.2;
      IF RUNNING<0 THEN PUT '== THIS IS A >>CREDIT<< TO YOUR ACCOUNT';
   END;
RETURN;
LINE1: * DEBITS, FROM INVOICE;
  RUNNING + INVTOT;
  PUT DATE MMDDYY8. @15 'X' @18 CUSTPO @31 JINVOICE
     @41 INVTOT 7.2 @51 RUNNING 7.2;
RETURN;
LINE2: * CREDITS, FROM CASH IN;
  CASHIN = 0-CASHIN; * REPORT AS NEGATIVE DEBIT;
  RUNNING + CASHIN;
  PUT DATE MMDDYY8. @12 'X' @18 'THANK YOU'
     @40 CASHIN 8.2 @51 RUNNING 7.2;
RETURN;
H:
  PUT 'JIMINY''S CRICKETS - STATEMENT DATED ' T MMDDYY8.
      ' COVERING PRIOR MONTH' //
      'TO: ' @10 CUSTNAME / @10 CUSTADR1 / @10
      @10 CUSTCITY +4 CUSTSTAT+2 CUSTZIP //
'DATE    CRE DEB YOUR PO #   OUR INV.  AMOUNT    BALANCE   ' /
'======== === === ============ ======== ======== ===========' //
DATE MMDDYY8. @18 'CARRY OVER' @51 BALDUE  7.2;
RETURN;
RUN;
DATA UP; * UPDATE CBALDUE;
  UPDATE CBALDUE.CBALDUE MLAST(RENAME=(RUNNING=BALDUE)); BY CUSTID;
RUN;
PROC PRINT; TITLE 'UP';
DATA CBALDUE.CBALDUE; SET UP; RUN;

<<< SAS JOB OUTPUT FOLLOWS >>>

JIMINY'S CRICKETS - STATEMENT DATED 01/04/89 COVERING
PRIOR MONTH

 TO:     VIVISEC INC
         192 MAIMEM ROAD
         BLUDLUSZT    MI   33333
DATE    CRE DEB YOUR PO #   OUR INV.  AMOUNT   BALANCE
======== === === ============ ======== ======== ===========
                 CARRY OVER                       0.00


NO ACTIVITY ON ACCOUNT THIS MONTH

LAST ACTIVITY: 02/17/88

        CLOSING BALANCE=   $0.00
```

Listing 18.3. *Continued*

```
<<< NEW PAGE >>>

JIMINY'S CRICKETS - STATEMENT DATED 01/04/89 COVERING PRIOR MONTH

TO:      YE OLDE TACQUEL SHOPPE
         126 BAY BRIDGE ALLEY
         ST FRANCIS    CA   91919

DATE      CRE DEB YOUR PO #      OUR INV.  AMOUNT   BALANCE
========  === === ============   ========  ======== ===========
                  CARRY OVER                           0.00

12/09/88      X   6220-JB03      10820      340.00    340.00
12/19/88      X   6219-JC22      10878      387.00    727.00
12/21/88      X   6219-JC35      10910      545.00   1272.00
12/21/88  X       THANK YOU                -1000.00   272.00


- - - - - - - - - - - - - - - - - - - - - - - - - - - -

         CLOSING BALANCE= $272.00

<<< NEW PAGE >>>

JIMINY'S CRICKETS - STATEMENT DATED 01/04/89 COVERING PRIOR MONTH

TO:      THE FLOUNDERING PERCH
         62-B PIER 39
         WATERCRESS    AL   11111

DATE      CRE DEB YOUR PO #      OUR INV.  AMOUNT   BALANCE
========  === === ============   ========  ======== ===========

                  CARRY OVER                          227.50

12/19/88  X       THANK YOU                 -250.00   -22.50
- - - - - - - - - - - - - - - - - - - - - - - - - - -

         CLOSING BALANCE=  $-22.50
== THIS IS A >>CREDIT<< TO YOUR ACCOUNT
```

Listing 18.3. *Continued*

DATA MLAST retains a RUNNING balance, and will be used to print the statements.*

A DO group is executed IF FIRST.CUSTID, and the purpose of DATA ALL is revealed: by interleaving TRANS after CBALDUE, ALL contains a first observation for each customer that can be used to initialize RUNNING, to prepare the carry-over value for the header routine, and to determine if there was any activity for that customer during the prior billing period. (If the CBALDUE record is the

---

*In this example, as with the invoices, a fully computer-generated form is produced. Alternatively, preprinted forms could be used, provided the custom report takes into account layout in positioning output fields. PROC FORMS could also be used.

only record for a given CUSTID, then there were no orders nor cash payments during the billing period.) Each subsequent observation for a customer ID, if any, must be either a debit (DEB=1) or else a credit. The events are handled by separate routines, LINE1 or LINE2, as the appropriate LINK is executed. When the last observation has been processed, an output observation is written and the closing balance is reported. The output observation contains the closing balance, and is used to recreate CBALDUE. One observation per CUSTID is written to MLAST, but only when CUSTID was associated with at least one credit or debit transaction during the billing period. To rebuild CBALDUE, we therefore use UPDATE.

Inventory Upkeep

In the simple scheme we have adopted to replenish stock, we stipulate a certain amount of items needed on hand and a number required. "Inventory" includes all items needed for the business (supplies, stock items, materials), but we assume for this illustration that each item can be associated with one or more of Jiminy's products (dataset ISTOCK), so that it can be determined, as each of a given product sold, just how inventory has been depleted.

Each item in the inventory has been given a code number, which along with an ID number of the preferred vendor is stored in the INVENT dataset. The vendor's price and stock information is also stored there, to give the possibility of auto-mated purchase orders. (Vendor information would be updated when a preferred vendor changes, by a process not illustrated here.) We also store two variables crucial to keeping up stock on hand: REQUIRED, how many of the item Jiminy's determines is sufficient to keep on hand for any week, and ONHAND, how many items were on hand at the end of the preceding week.*

The program itself—absent the details of purchase order preparation—is illus-trated in Listing 18.4. Let's look at how ordering may be done, and how to update the dataset with which orders are tracked. Listing 18.5 shows several of the datasets produced by the program, so you can follow along.

As we assume the process is run on the same day each week, we can choose the data for reporting as shown: the previous seven days of customer orders (dataset WEEK). This is combined with PRODUCTS to find out how many of Jiminy's were actually depleted (dataset WEEKGONE), because some items are measured in multiple units (dozen, gross, etc.). The count is then totaled over each stock item with PROC SUMMARY.

Dataset ISTOCK (itself kept up by simple processes not illustrated here) con-nects inventory items with products. It contains three variables: JSTOCK, prod-uct stock number, JINVENT, inventory item number, and NPER, which tells how many inventory items are depleted per stock item sold. A DATA step creates a

---

*ONHAND will be modified downward by the program to be described. ONHAND is modified upward, presumably, when Jiminy's receives shipments from vendors. This pro-cess is not illustrated.

```
*** PURCHASE ORDERS TO REPLENISH INVENTORY ***;
DATA WEEK;
  SET CUSTORDS.CUSTORDS;
  IF 0 < TODAY()-INVDATE < 8;
  KEEP JSTOCK JQUANT;
RUN;
PROC SORT; BY JSTOCK; RUN;
DATA WEEKGONE;  * GET ABSOLUTE AMOUNT ITEMS USED;
  MERGE WEEK(IN=INW) PRODUCTS.PRODUCTS(KEEP=JSTOCK OCOUNT);
  BY JSTOCK;
  IF INW;
  QUANT=JQUANT*OCOUNT;
  KEEP JSTOCK QUANT;
RUN;
PROC SUMMARY NWAY DATA=WEEKGONE; * GET TOTAL ORDERED PER JSTOCK;
  CLASS JSTOCK;
  VAR QUANT;
  OUTPUT OUT=WEEKSUM SUM=;
RUN;
DATA USED;                      * CALCULATE INVENTORY ITEMS USED PER JSTOCK;
  MERGE WEEKSUM(IN=INWEEK KEEP=JSTOCK QUANT) ISTOCK.ISTOCK;
  BY JSTOCK; IF INWEEK;
  RETAIN USED 0;
  IF FIRST.JSTOCK THEN USED=0;
  USED=USED+QUANT*NPER;
  IF LAST.JSTOCK THEN OUTPUT;
  KEEP JINVENT USED;
RUN;
PROC SORT; BY JINVENT;
PROC SUMMARY NWAY DATA=USED; * GET TOTAL USED PER JINVENT;
  CLASS JINVENT;
  VAR USED;
  OUTPUT OUT=USEDSUM SUM=;
RUN;
DATA REINVENT(DROP=ORDER) ORDER;
  MERGE INVENT.INVENT USED(KEEP=JINVENT USED IN=U);
  BY JINVENT;
  DROP USED;
  IF U THEN ONHAND=ONHAND-USED;
  OUTPUT REINVENT;
  IF ONHAND < REQUIRED THEN DO;
     ORDER=CEIL(((REQUIRED-ONHAND)+.3*REQUIRED)/VOCOUNT);
     OUTPUT ORDER;
  END;
RUN;
DATA INVENT.INVENT; SET REINVENT; RUN; * SERVES TO UPDATE ONHAND;
```

Listing 18.4. Example inventory/order program source code

```
                              WEEKGONE                                        1

                   OBS      JSTOCK      QUANT

                    1       100032      20000
                    2       100039       2160
                    3       100122       1000
                    4       100122       1000
                    5       100122       1000


                              WEEKSUM                                         2

           OBS      JSTOCK     _TYPE_      _FREQ_      QUANT

            1       100032        1           1       20000
            2       100039        1           1        2160
            3       100122        1           3        3000


                           ISTOCK.ISTOCK                                      3

              OBS     JINVENT      JSTOCK      NPER

               1       18869       100032       2
               2      100039       100039       1
               3       18868       100122       2
               4       12246       101922       1
               5       18869       116298       4


                                USED                                         4

                   OBS     JINVENT      USED

                    1       18868       6000
                    2       18869      40000
                    3      100039       2160


                           INVENT.INVENT                                     5
```

OBS	JINVENT	ONHAND	REQUIRED	VENDID	VSTOCK	VDESCRIP	VOCOUNT	VPRICE
1	12246	200	150	1223	10026	DELUXE INSECT CAGE	12	26.95
2	18868	45500	35000	1286	262R	REG BAGS PINT CAPAC.	1000	4.50
3	18869	42250	40000	1286	262H	HVY DTY BAGS QT CAP	1000	8.50
4	100039	2575	1800	1016	355-J6A	INSECT BOXES, SMALL	144	6.95

Listing 18.5. Datasets illustrating example inventory/order program

Continued

REINVENT   6

OBS	JINVENT	ONHAND	REQUIRED	VENDID	VSTOCK	VDESCRIP	VCOUNT	VPRICE
1	12246	200	150	1223	10026	DELUXE INSECT CAGE	12	26.95
2	18868	39500	35000	1286	262R	REG BAGS PINT CAPAC.	1000	4.50
3	18869	2250	40000	1286	262H	HVY DTY BAGS QT CAP	1000	8.50
4	100039	415	1800	1016	355-J6A	INSECT BOXES, SMALL	144	6.95

ORDER   7

OBS	JINVENT	ONHAND	REQUIRED	VENDID	VSTOCK	VDESCRIP	VCOUNT	VPRICE	ORDER
1	18869	2250	40000	1286	262H	HVY DTY BAGS QT CAP	1000	8.50	50
2	100039	415	1800	1016	355-J6A	INSECT BOXES, SMALL	144	6.95	14

Listing 18.5. *Continued*

dataset, USED, which takes the weekly summary and calculates the inventory depletion. When this is summarized by JINVENT (dataset USEDSUM), we know how much of each inventory item was depleted. Now that the depletion is known, the inventory information can be updated and the orders placed. Dataset REINVENT mirrors the original INVENT, except that if any of the item were used, the variable ONHAND is decreased by that amount. If the amount on hand falls below the amount stipulated as required, an observation of the dataset ORDER is built. (This implementation presumes the general policy is that when an order is placed, it shall be for such an amount that would raise the amount on hand to 30% over the amount required. The variable ORDER is computed accordingly.) The final DATA step shown simply rewrites INVENT with the REINVENT dataset, which is the same except for ONHAND.

Now what remains is to produce purchase orders, and to update the permanent dataset JIMORDS. This kind of thing was shown above, in the invoice process, and will not be illustrated again.

Quarterly Sales Summary

The simple descriptive and display procedures remain a highly effective way to obtain crucial business data. In this last example, some easy PROC PRINT and PROC SUMMARY steps are used to produce sales reports for internal use. Listing 18.6 shows the program used to produce the sales summaries, and Listing 18.7 discloses the output of the program.

Calls to SYMPUT are used simply to prepare for the reports' titles; later in the program listing, TITLE2 calls upon the symbolic variables. The PUT function is used because without it, QTR(TODAY( )) and YEAR(TODAY( )) would be written in BEST12. format, leaving spaces in the title:

```
FOR          1988, QUARTER          2
```

instead of

```
FOR 1988, QUARTER 2
```

One PROC SUMMARY creates all the data we need, and the single output dataset serves for three different reports. (The ID statement in PROC SUMMARY was necessary so that JDESCRIP would be kept in the output dataset SSUM.) For the printed output, PROC PRINT's SUM statement does nicely to reconstruct subtotals. Judiciously we subset the summary dataset and use PRINT to display the data, and get a full sales picture thereby. Subtotals are printed by the procedure, and the grand total is printed under double lines at the end of each step's output. The labels placed on the BY lines come from the original initialization of the files.

```
   *** SALES SUMMARIES ***;
 PROC SORT DATA=CUSTORDS.CUSTORDS OUT=CUSTORDS; BY JSTOCK; RUN;
 DATA SALES;
   CALL SYMPUT('QUARTER',PUT(QTR(TODAY()),1.));  * GET DATE FOR USE
:
   CALL SYMPUT('YEAR',PUT(YEAR(TODAY()),4.));       *    IN TITLES.   ;
   MERGE CUSTORDS PRODUCTS.PRODUCTS;
   BY JSTOCK;
   IF (YEAR(TODAY())=YEAR(INVDATE) AND QTR(TODAY())=QTR(INVDATE)+1)
   OR (YEAR(TODAY())=YEAR(INVDATE)+1 AND QTR(TODAY())=1
      AND QTR(INVDATE)=4);
   KEEP JSTOCK SALSPRSN PCLASS JDESCRIP SUBTOT;
 RUN;
 PROC SUMMARY;
   CLASS PCLASS SALSPRSN JSTOCK;
   ID JDESCRIP;
   VAR SUBTOT;
   OUTPUT OUT=SSUM SUM=SALES;
 RUN;
 PROC FORMAT; VALUE $PCF
     'C'='SOMETHIN'' FISHY' 'P'='CHEEPERS CREEPERS'
     'G'='GRYLLIDAE 101'  'Q'='LES CRIQUETTES';
 RUN;
 DATA PCLASS;
   SET SSUM;
   IF _TYPE_='110'B;
 RUN;
 PROC PRINT DATA=PCLASS; BY PCLASS;
   ID SALSPRSN;
   FORMAT PCLASS $PCF.;
   VAR SALES;
   SUM SALES;
   TITLE 'SALES SUMMARY PER SALESPERSON, PER PRODUCT CLASS';
   TITLE2 "FOR &YEAR, QUARTER &QUARTER";
 RUN;
 DATA PSALE;
   SET SSUM;
   IF _TYPE_='101'B;
 RUN;
 PROC PRINT DATA=PSALE; BY PCLASS;
   ID JSTOCK JDESCRIP;
   FORMAT PCLASS $PCF.;
   VAR SALES;
   SUM SALES;
   TITLE 'SALES SUMMARY WITHIN PRODUCT CLASS';
   TITLE2 "FOR &YEAR, QUARTER &QUARTER";
  RUN;
 DATA PSUMRY;
   SET SSUM;
   IF _TYPE_='111'B;
 RUN;
 PROC PRINT DATA=PSUMRY; BY PCLASS SALSPRSN;
   ID JSTOCK JDESCRIP;
   FORMAT PCLASS $PCF.;
   VAR SALES;
   SUM SALES;
   TITLE 'DETAILED SALES SUMMARY';
   TITLE2 "FOR &YEAR, QUARTER &QUARTER";
  RUN;
```

Listing 18.6. A program to produce sales summaries

```
              SALES SUMMARY PER SALESPERSON, PER PRODUCT CLASS 1
                        FOR 1988, QUARTER 2

-------------------- OUR PRODUCT CLASS=SOMETHIN' FISHY --------------------

                        SALSPRSN        SALES

                        BABBITT         57240
                        BINDER          44100
                        GRANDIS         29385
                        ZIGLAR           8955
                        -------        ------
                        PCLASS         139680


-------------------- OUR PRODUCT CLASS=GRYLLIDAE 101 ---------------------

                        SALSPRSN        SALES

                        BINDER          50895
                        GRANDIS         33975
                        SHWARZ          76320
                        -------        ------
                        PCLASS         161190


-------------------- OUR PRODUCT CLASS=CHEEPERS CREEPERS --------------------

                        SALSPRSN        SALES

                        BINDER          22815
                        GRANDIS         15210
                        ZIGLAR          34200
                        -------        -----
                        PCLASS          72225


-------------------- OUR PRODUCT CLASS=LES CRIQUETTES --------------------

                        SALSPRSN        SALES

                        BINDER            423
                        CONNELLI          633
                        GRANDIS           279
                        -------        ------
                        PCLASS           1335
                                       ======
                                       374430
```

Listing 18.7. Output from sales summaries program

Continued

```
                  SALES SUMMARY WITHIN PRODUCT CLASS 2
                         FOR 1988, QUARTER 2

-------------------- OUR PRODUCT CLASS=SOMETHIN' FISHY ---------------------

        JSTOCK          JDESCRIP                 SALES

        100032      GIANT BONKERS                18990
        100039      CRICKIT CONTAINERS           17100
        100122      LITTLE SQUIRMERS             84735
        100309      CRICKET FLIES                18855
        ----------                               ------
        PCLASS                                   139680


-------------------- OUR PRODUCT CLASS=GRYLLIDAE 101 -----------------------

        JSTOCK          JDESCRIP                 SALES

        100593      BREEDING FML #AR-6B          25245
        100600      CRICKET EGGS #BX-2           22815
        100683      CAGE LINERS                  113130
        ----------                               ------
        PCLASS                                   161190


------------------- OUR PRODUCT CLASS=CHEEPERS CREEPERS --------------------

        JSTOCK          JDESCRIP            SALES

        100219      WHISTLERS               38025
        100226      CRICKET CHOW            34200
        ----------                          -----
        PCLASS                              72225


--------------------- OUR PRODUCT CLASS=LES CRIQUETTES ---------------------

        JSTOCK          JDESCRIP            SALES

        100406      LES CRIQ! REG             843
        100413      LES CRIQ! BARBQ            75
        100496      LES CRIQ! NOSALT          417
        ----------                          ------
        PCLASS                              1335
                                            ======
                                            374430
```

Listing 18.7. *Continued*

```
                        DETAILED SALES SUMMARY
                         FOR 1988, QUARTER 2

     <<< DATA DELETED TO SAVE SPACE >>>

   ------------ OUR PRODUCT CLASS=GRYLLIDAE 101 SALESPERSON=BINDER-------------

                 JSTOCK              JDESCRIP          SALES

                 100593       BREEDING FML #AR-6B      7965
                 100600       CRICKET EGGS #BX-2       7200
                 100683       CAGE LINERS             35730
                 ------------                          -----
                 SALSPRSN                             50895

   ------------ OUR PRODUCT CLASS=GRYLLIDAE 101 SALESPERSON=GRANDIS-------------

                 JSTOCK              JDESCRIP          SALES

                 100593       BREEDING FML #AR-6B      5310
                 100600       CRICKET EGGS #BX-2       4815

100683     CAGE LINERS            23850
                 ------------                          -----
                 SALSPRSN                             33975


   ------------ OUR PRODUCT CLASS=GRYLLIDAE 101 SALESPERSON=SHWARZ -------------

                 JSTOCK              JDESCRIP          SALES

                 100593       BREEDING FML #AR-6B     11970
                 100600       CRICKET EGGS #BX-2      10800
                 100683       CAGE LINERS             53550
                 ------------                          ------
                 SALSPRSN                             76320
                 PCLASS                              161190

     <<< DATA DELETED TO SAVE SPACE >>>
```

Listing 18.7. *Continued*

part V

THE SAS MACRO LANGUAGE

19

SAS Macros: Basic Concepts and Methods

In this chapter and the next we review all of the basic features of the SAS Macro facility and many of its advanced features as well. What you should attempt to achieve in studying these two chapters is a comprehensive appreciation of what macro processing is all about* and—for those of you who have already struggled with the Macro Language to frustration—a deeper understanding of what you've been doing and trying to do.

This chapter begins with an intuitive view of what SAS macros are about and why they are used. It continues with a look at the macro facility and how it fits in with the SAS System. The two pillars of the macro facility—macro variables and macros themselves— are described. The chapter continues with a concise tutorial in the elements of Macro Language programming: macro expressions and statements, macro variable assignment, flow of control, and user interaction. Finally, we look at how the execution of a program with macros affects the SAS log.

MACROS: REASONS WHY

When I was a boy in New York City, the buses and subways were filled with advertisements that read as follows: "If u cn rd ths u cn gt a gd jb n gd pa!"

---

*To achieve the breadth of coverage planned for these chapters in the context of this book we must get by without extensive examples. Readers wishing a fleshier treatment of some of the topics reviewed in Part V should consult the *SAS Guide to Macro Processing*.

"Speedwriting" (does it still exist?) was a compromise between the idea of short-hand and the familiar Latin alphabet. Let's shorten things even more by agreeing that, just for now, the symbol GDJBPA will stand for the phrase "get a good job and good pay," and FURDT for "If you can read this." Now we can communicate the same Speedwriting slogan in even shorter length, as follows: "FURDT you can GDJBPA!"

This scheme may not sell as a substitute for written English, but consider another language, the language of the SAS System. Suppose that from a dataset, MASTER.DATA, subsets are occasionally to be printed. Sometimes all records with the varible DATE equal to the current year are needed, sometimes records with the variable SEX = 'F,' and so on, but always the same, simple PRINT. For example,

```
DATA;
   SET MASTER.DATA;
   IF AGE>25;
RUN;
PROC PRINT; RUN;
```

on one occasion,

```
DATA;
   SET MASTER.DATA;
   IF SEX='M';
RUN;
PROC PRINT; RUN;
```

on another occasion, etc.

Let's agree, for the moment, that the symbol DST will stand for

```
DATA;
   SET MASTER.DATA;
   IF
```

and the symbol PRT for

```
; RUN;
PROC PRINT; RUN;
```

Now, the lines

```
DST AGE>>25 PRT
```

and

```
DST SEX='M' PRT
```

accomplish the same two tasks.

Now, suppose the situation is this.

Problem: You work for a nationwide company, divided into 28 sales regions, data for each of which are maintained in similar SAS datasets in libraries REGION1, REGION2, . . ., REGION28. A report of gross sales over each product line is to be produced, covering each region separately. Model source code for Region 1 is shown in Listing 19.1.

Of course, you could copy this whole code section 27 times, changing "REGION1" to the appropriate region in the TITLE and PROC statements. This is easily done with modern full-screen editors.

Solution: But what if there were a magic word, SMRYPRT, standing for the 22 lines of code from the CLASS statement in PROC SUMMARY through the end of the DATA _NULL_ step?

```
TITLE 'SALES REPORT FOR REGION1';
PROC SUMMARY DATA=REGION1.SALES;
SMRYPRT
```

and Region 1 is accounted for. Then just copy these three lines 28 times, with small changes (to REGION2, REGION3, etc.), and the code will be much more concise.

```
PROC SUMMARY DATA=REGION1.SALES;
   CLASS PRODUCT;
   VAR SALES;
   OUTPUT OUT=USE SUM=;
 RUN;
 PROC SORT DATA=USE; BY DESCENDING _TYPE_; * PLACE GRAND TOTAL LAST;
 TITLE 'SALES REPORT FOR REGION1';
 DATA _NULL_;
   SET USE;
   FILE PRINT N=PS HEADER=H;
   DO COL=1 TO 101 BY 25;
     DO ROW=3 TO 52;
     IF NOT(LAST) THEN PUT #ROW @COL PRODUCT $10. +2 SALES COMMA9.2;
     END;
   END;
   IF LAST THEN PUT #55 @1 125*'=' //
     'REGIONAL SUMMARY OF SALES: ALL PRODUCTS --- '
     SALES DOLLAR14.2;
   PUT _PAGE_;
   RETURN;
 H: PUT 5*' PRODUCT    TOTAL $      ' /
       5*'---------- ---------      ' //;
 RETURN;
 RUN;
```

Listing 19.1. Sample source code to illustrate macros (see text)

Code Reduction

What has just been demonstrated is *code reduction*, the most elemental use of a SAS macro: A little symbol is made to stand for a lot of code. SAS macros are the mechanisms used to get the SAS System to take one sequence of code and have it stand for another.

The earliest version of the SAS System "macro" concept was a simple tool to do just code reduction. The old-fashioned macros were implemented with the MACRO "statement," which is not a SAS statement in the usual sense. It ends with a percent sign (%), not a semicolon, for it may *include* semicolons. Its general form is:

```
MACRO macname text %
```

The macro name "macname" was any valid SAS name, the text any SAS code segment of whatever length, so long as it did not include an unquoted percent sign.

```
MACRO DST DATA;
  SET MASTER.DATA;
  IF %
```

and

```
MACRO PRT ; RUN;
  PROC PRINT; RUN;%
```

were how we might get the SAS System to interpret the symbols illustrated earlier. Or, for the "28 regions" example:

```
MACRO SMRYPRT
[code the last 22 lines of Listing 19.1 here]
%
```

These old-style macros, part of SAS history, should not be used today. In the present-day Macro Language, our original example becomes:

```
%MACRO DST;
    DATA;
  SET MASTER.DATA;
  IF
%MEND;
```

and

```
%MACRO PRT;
  ; RUN;
  PROC PRINT; RUN;
%MEND;
```

A %MACRO statement, which *does* end with a semicolon, signifies the beginning, and a %MEND statement, rather than a lone percent sign, signifies the end of the macro. There is another difference: When you write the shorthand name in your program, you use a percent sign in front of it, e.g.,

```
%DST SEX='F' %PRT
```

A Better Taste of the Macro Language

The modern SAS Macro Language does much more than simple code reduction. For example, one can use the SAS Macro Language to generate code selectively, conditionally, or iteratively. In the "SMRYPRT" example given above, three lines had to be copied 28 times, with the region number changed. Here's how to write the code *one* time and get all 28 regional reports. First, change the program in Listing 19.1 a little: Wherever "REGION1" appears, replace with "REGION&X" (REGION-ampersand-X). Next, change the single quotes in the TITLE statement to double quotes. Then:

```
%MACRO SMRYPRT;
   %DO X=1 %TO 28;
[Listing 19.1 here, but with REGION&X and doublequoted titles]
   %END;
%MEND SMRYPRT;
%SMRYPRT
```

and the job is done.

THE SAS MACRO FACILITY

In computer science, a *macro* generally means a temporary, shorthand convention allowing a certain sequence of characters in source code that will stand for another, "real" sequence of source code. Going from the concise macro representation back to the longer, "usual" code is called *expanding* the macro. Usually the component of a language translator that first sets up the shorthand convention and then intercepts and expands the shorthand coded in a program is called the macro *preprocessor*, because the shorthand is taken care of before the "real" translation begins.

Sometimes preprocessing entails a good deal more than simple expansion, for "short-hands" can be designed to signify more than just condensed code. The SAS System macro preprocessor is one of the most advanced of any modern computer language. It allows iterative code generation (as seen in the final example of the last section), conditional code generation, passing of parameters to the macro in source code, passing of values to and from the macro processor from the DATA Step Language (and hence to/from SAS datasets), and user interaction during on-line sessions. We use the more general term *code generation*, rather than just code expansion, to better denote what the SAS preprocessor is all about.

The Macro Preprocessor in the SAS System

Before you study the Macro Language itself, it is essential to understand some things about the preprocessor, macro variables, and macro preparation. Let's first consider what happens to your source code when the SAS System gets hold of it.

When a SAS program commences, the source code is read into a temporary data structure called the *input stack*, and an internal utility called the *wordscanner* begins to break the code into *tokens*, the smallest units of meaning in a computer language (as morphemes are in natural language). SAS tokens include alphabetic words, numbers, punctuation, etc. These tokens are placed in a data structure called the "word queue," from which they are retrieved and resolved by various means into SAS statements. See Figure 19.1.

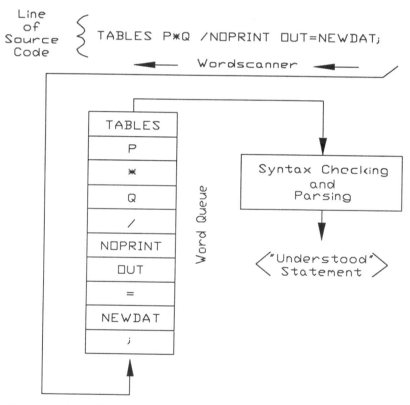

Figure 19.1. A SAS statement is born. Source code is broken into tokens (morphemes) by the "wordscanner" functions. The tokens enter a queue from which they are retrieved in order and translated into machine instructions by the appropriate component of the SAS System (such as the DATA Step compiler or a procedure parser).

There are basically four classes of tokens of meaning to the wordscanner: names,* numbers, character literals (i.e., string constants), and special characters (i.e., characters not alphabetic, numeric, or the underscore). The wordscanner recognizes the end of a token when either a blank space or the beginning of another token is encountered. The statement

```
TABLES (A B)*C /NOPERCENT;
```

is comprised of 10 tokens: the names TABLES, A, B, C, and NOPERCENT, and the special characters (,), *, /, and ;. The statement

```
A=B+123/(16*Y);
```

consists of 12 tokens: the names A, B, and Y, the numbers 123 and 16, and seven special characters. Literals (i.e., strings enclosed in quotes; review Chapter 2) are treated as single tokens. The statement

```
TITLE 'SOME FUN, HEY?';
```

is composed of but three tokens, the name TITLE, the character literal 'SOME FUN, HEY?', and the special character ";".

Now, as has been said, the object of all this is so the SAS System can pass the tokens to the word queue for constructing statements SAS can understand. However, when the token % (percent sign) or the token & (ampersand) is encountered, and is followed immediately by a name (e.g., %ABC or &XYZ), and provided the macro facility is active (via the MACRO system option, see later in this chapter), statement-building is temporarily suspended as the macro preprocessor is called into action. There are several actions the macro preprocessor may take, depending on which of these "macro trigger" tokens was coded, what name follows it, and also on the history of the program's execution prior to that point. Assuming no errors have been made, the macro facility may send generated code back through the wordscanner. Indeed, if the generated code itself contains more ampersands or percent signs, the macro processor might be called into play more than once. Generation of code for passage back through the wordscanner is one of two primary operating modes of the macro preprocessor, and is illustrated in Figure 19.2.

The other primary operating mode of the preprocessor is to *prepare* to generate code, not actually to do so. The distinction will become clear as we discuss macro variables and macro definition. In either case, the preprocessor is essentially a *string processing utility*: It deals with input and output of character strings. The

*A "name" to the SAS parser is different from a "name" to the wordscanner. When we speak of a "name" in discussing tokenization, this may refer to a keyword, a function name, etc., not only a dataset or variable name, and it might be more than eight characters long. Relative to the wordscanner, a "name" is simply a token string that begins with an alphabetic or an underscore, and continues as long as there are consecutive letters, numerals, and underscores (or in other words, until a blank or a special character is encountered).

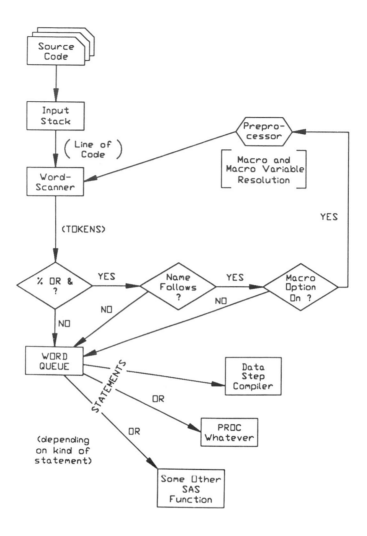

Figure 19.2. Code generation in abstract. If the & or the % token is encountered by the wordscanner, and is followed immediately (no spaces) by a name, the macro preprocessor takes over. The preprocessor generates more code for input to the process.

DATA and PROC steps deal in entities such as datasets and observations; the macro preprocessor deals in sequences of characters.

Macro Variables

A variable, to the DATA or PROC step, refers to a data structure within the program data vector or a SAS dataset. The variable takes on a value (numeric or character, depending on its type) based on the program that creates it. A *macro variable* is another entity entirely. Macro variables, like SAS variables, have names and values. But a macro variable value, which is always a character string

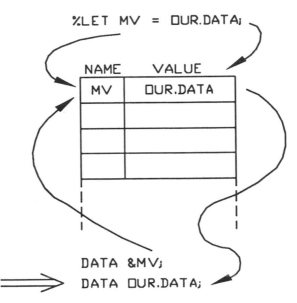

Figure 19.3. The symbol table is an abstract data structure that associates macro variables (symbols) with values, which are always character strings. Symbols are added to the symbol table in several ways; use of the %LET statement is illustrated. Values are retrieved from the table when a symbol appears after an ampersand in executing code. Here "DATA &MV;" becomes "DATA OUR.DATA;"

(there is no other type), can include almost any text, and depending on the operating system and certain SAS system options, may be of great length, even many thousands of characters. Macro variable values are stored neither in SAS datasets nor in the program data vector, but in an internal data structure called the *symbol table*.* The name of a macro variable serves as a symbol standing for its value, hence the term "symbol table." See Figure 19.3.

A macro variable is indicated in SAS code by the & trigger: When in the course of a SAS job the token & is followed by a valid macro variable name (these obey the rules of SAS variable names, i.e., they must be one to eight characters long, begin with an underscore or a letter, and contain only letters, numerals, or underscores†), this constitutes a *macro variable reference*. A macro variable reference can appear virtually anywhere in SAS code—within a DATA step, within a PROC step, between steps, inside or outside a macro definition. This is because

---

*For convenience in this chapter's discussion we simplify things. Actually we are talking about the *global symbol table*. In Chapter 20, we will see during a SAS job there can exist several symbol tables of different scope.

†Do not create any macro variable with a name that begins with the letters SYS. As discussed in Chapter 20, SAS reserves SYS as the first three letters of certain special variables.

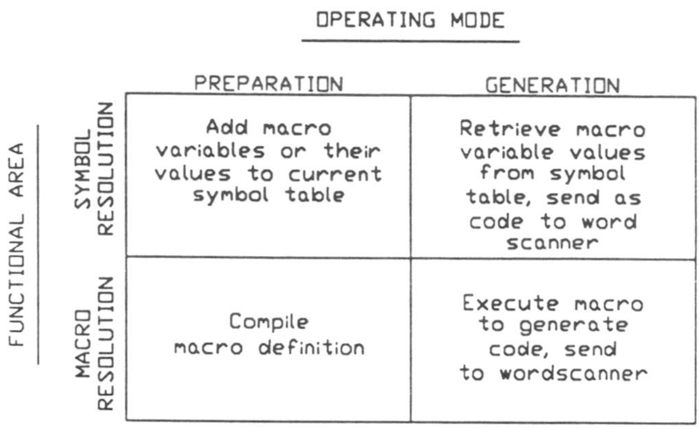

OPERATING MODE

		PREPARATION	GENERATION
FUNCTIONAL AREA	SYMBOL RESOLUTION	Add macro variables or their values to current symbol table	Retrieve macro variable values from symbol table, send as code to word scanner
	MACRO RESOLUTION	Compile macro definition	Execute macro to generate code, send to wordscanner

Figure 19.4. The four responsibilities of the macro preprocessor.

macro variables are handled by the preprocessor, not by any PROC or DATA step.

Macro variables can be put to good use even when not associated with macros per se, i.e., when coded outside a macro definition. Indeed, macros and macro variables are two separate domains: As the macro preprocessor has two modes of operation (code generation or preparation for code generation), so it works in two functional areas, symbol resolution or macro resolution (Figure 19.4).

Symbol Preparation

An entry in the macro symbol table exists only if the symbol is one of the standard macro variables automatically created by the SAS System, or if your program has created it. If you use a macro variable reference that does not exist, the reference cannot be resolved. It doesn't have a "missing value"; it simply doesn't exist. The macro variable *reference* will emerge literally (and the SAS log will note a warning). For example, if a macro variable XYZ has already been defined as the string MALE, the code segment

```
DATA; SET MAIN; IF SEX="&XYZ";
```

will, after resolution by the macro processor, appear to SAS as

```
DATA; SET MAIN; IF SEX="MALE";
```

If XYZ has *not* yet been added to the symbol table, the result seen by the compiler will remain

```
DATA; SET MAIN; IF SEX="&XYZ";
```

An Important Aside: Double Quotes and Macro Resolution. A SAS literal may be bounded by either single or double quotes. The difference matters only as follows: If a literal is bounded by double quotes, the macro processor may be called into action if any macro triggers appear within the literal. If a literal is bounded by single quotes, the macro processor will not be called to look at it. Thus in the example above, had the user coded

```
DATA; SET MAIN; IF SEX='&XYZ';
```

this exact code would go straight through to the DATA step compiler *whether or not* a macro variable XYZ were currently defined. Note that a double-quoted literal is still passed on as a single token when the macro processor is done with it.

Back to Symbol Preparation. A variable may be added to the symbol table in one of several ways. One way is with the macro variable assignment statement %LET. The %LET statement takes the form

```
%LET macvarname=[macro_expression];
```

If the macro expression* is absent, e.g.,

```
%LET MVAR=;
```

the macro variable will be created, but it will have a null value. This is not the same as having no variable at all. The code

```
%LET SAMPLE=OTHER.DATASET;
DATA ONE; SET &SAMPLE; RUN;
%LET SAMPLE=;
DATA TWO; SET &SAMPLE; RUN;
```

will result in SAS receiving (after preprocessing)

```
DATA ONE; SET OTHER.DATASET; RUN;
DATA TWO; SET ; RUN;
```

But the code

```
DATA ONE; SET &SAMPLE; RUN;
%LET SAMPLE=;
DATA TWO; SET &SAMPLE; RUN;
```

assuming no prior %LET statement or other creation of the symbol SAMPLE during the job, will result in SAS receiving

---

*Macro expressions, which may include regular SAS code, are described later in this chapter.

```
DATA ONE; SET &SAMPLE; RUN;
DATA TWO; SET ; RUN;
```

because there is no symbol with the name SAMPLE until the %LET is encountered. (Of course, running this job will generate an error because "&SAMPLE" is
not a valid SAS dataset name.)

Other ways macro variables may be created include the variable reference
environment statements %GLOBAL and %LOCAL, a call to the SYMPUT function from a DATA step, and passage of parameters from macro definition arguments when the macro is executed. We'll discuss reference environments and
SYMPUT in Chapter 20, macro definition and execution below.

Macro Preparation

Macro preparation begins when the preprocessor receives a %MACRO statement
from the word queue. The %MACRO statement takes the form

```
%MACRO macroname [(<parameter>,...)] [/ options];
```

If this statement comes through the word queue to the preprocessor, a macro will
be *compiled*, i.e., prepared for the task of code generation. Once a macro has been
compiled, it may be used at any later point in the program.*

Rules for forming macro names are like those for variable or dataset names†:
alphanumeric/underscore, first character not a numeral, eight or fewer characters. The name should not be the same as any macro statement keyword or the
name of any macro function, and there are a few other "reserved" words besides.
The preprocessor is less forgiving than the DATA compiler when it comes to
assigning names that are homonymous with any Macro Language keyword, and
an attempt to create a macro named with any of these words will cause a macro
compilation error.

After the %MACRO statement triggers macro preparation, the preprocessor
continues to receive and compile code until a %MEND statement is received, at
which point the macro is stored for later use. The %MEND statement is coded

```
%MEND [macroname];
```

and its sole purpose is to indicate to the preprocessor that code intended as part of
a macro is complete. The macro name, not required, is nevertheless recommended,
as it will make it easier to understand the source code. If used, it must match the
name of the macro as coded in the closest preceding %MACRO statement; a

---

*A macro can also be compiled in an earlier program and stored, for future use, in a
SAS catalog maintained for that purpose. See Chapter 21, under "Precompilation."

†Under some operating systems, additional restrictions may apply. Consult the *SAS
Companion* for your operating system.

%MEND always completes the closest preceding %MACRO. Between the %MACRO and %MEND statements may come two kinds of text: regular SAS code and special Macro Language statements.

Macro Parameters

The parameters, or arguments, of a macro are used to identify macro variables that may be given values by the program as the macro is called to be executed. Both *positional* and *keyword* parameters are allowed. Examples:

```
%MACRO TASTY(CAKE,PIE,COOKIE);
```

defines three macro variables, CAKE, PIE, and COOKIE, as positional parameters.

```
%MACRO G(X1=,X3=TRACKS,X5=LRECL,X7=);
```

defines four macro variables, X1, X3, X5, and X7, as keyword parameters, giving X3 and X5 nonnull default values of "TRACKS" and "LRECL", respectively.

```
%MACRO TRY(PNAME,RNAME,VAL=5);
```

defines three macro variables, the first two positional and the third keyword, the third taking the nonnull default value "5." If both positional and keyword arguments are given, all keyword arguments must follow all positional arguments, e.g.,

```
%MACRO WRONG(NO=,NEVER);
```

is incorrect. How the parameters of a macro definition are used we will see later on. Note that a macro does not have to have parameters; many do not.

MACRO Statement Options

There are three options that may appear after a slash on the %MACRO statement. The STMT option specifies that the macro may be invoked with the general %-name invocation or statement-style invocation. The CMD option specifies the macro may be invoked under interactive SAS with the general %-name invocation or full-screen command-style invocation. We will be concerned in this book only with %-name invocation. The remaining option that may appear is PARMBUFF (abbreviation: PBUFF), which causes macro calls to write the system variable SYSPBUFF; this is described in Chapter 20.

What Happens During Macro Preparation?

Basically, three things:

Symbol Prepreparation. The name of the macro itself, as well as the names of any variables named as parameters to the macro, are stored for use when the macro is invoked (executed). The intended macro variables will not enter the symbol table as such until the macro executes.

Statement Translation. Most Macro Language statements, if any are present (and a macro may have none), are translated into a compiled form. That is, the macro preprocessor prepares to generate code beyond mere expansion of constant text or symbol substitution. Compiled macros can be stored for later use using the methods described in Chapter 21, or may be used just for the current job.

Text Storage. Constant text is stored as literal strings within the compiled macro code for use when the macro is executed. Constant text includes "regular" SAS code, the %TSO or %CMS statements, macro function terms [except %STR or %NRSTR functions (see Chapter 20), whose *results* are stored], macro expressions, macro variable references, and nested macro definitions (i.e., %MACRO/ %MEND groups wholly contained within an "outer" macro). These are stored directly rather than being evaluated, for evaluation is (except for %STR and %NRSTR) an execution-time, not a compile-time activity. The distinction will become clear as we proceed with our discussion.

Code Generation

Variable Resolution

When an ordinary macro variable reference (i.e., a single ampersand followed by a name) is encountered in open code,* if the variable currently exists in an active symbol table, its value is substituted for the reference by the macro processor. If the variable does not currently exist the variable reference as it is literally (ampersand + variable name) is passed through directly. It behooves the user to know just when a macro variable exists and when it does not, in order to avoid inadvertently using a variable reference when there is no variable to resolve. This will be discussed further in Chapter 20.

For purposes of this chapter, it is sufficient that you know that any variable defined in a %LET statement coded outside any macro definition remains defined (which is to say it exists) throughout the remainder of the program, and that any variable defined by %LET within a macro, or named as a parameter on %MACRO, remains defined at least whenever the macro in question is executing.

Macro Execution

A macro executes at the point it is invoked, that is, at that point when the wordscanner receives its name after a percent sign. For example, if a macro POP has been defined with

---

*Open code is any code outside a macro definition, in regular SAS code (whether or not the SAS code was generated from an executed macro).

```
%MACRO POP; [SAS code ...] %MEND;
```

it can be executed with

```
%POP
```

As with macro variable references, macro invocations can be placed anywhere within a SAS program, though using a macro reference when the macro has not yet been defined is an error. A macro is defined throughout a job if it comes in from a compiled macro catalog or from an autocall source member (the autocall facility is described in Chapter 21), or from the point within the job that the macro code is placed, if it is defined within the job.

Of course, you are responsible for using macro invocations correctly. Given

```
%MACRO POP; GOES THE WEASEL %MEND;
```

the SAS code generated by %POP is

```
GOES THE WEASEL
```

Then

```
PROC PRINT; VAR %POP;
```

could be valid, but

```
PROC PRINT; %POP;
```

will never be valid: the procedure parser will complain with a "statement not valid" error and halt compilation, because there is no GOES statement in the PRINT procedure.

Macro Processing and SAS Job Flow

Macro processing transcends step boundaries. Because a macro can "stand for" virtually any sequence of SAS code, including DATA and PROC statements, you can do things such as control the flow of entire program segments, not just DATA step segments. It is this feature of the Macro Language—the ability to control execution logic within a step *or* across any number of DATA or PROC steps—that is the single most important capability of the macro facility, because without (and sometimes even with) great programming contortions this kind of trans-step guidance would otherwise not be possible.

Step-by-Step Execution Still Holds

Just because a macro may be defined to include more than one step does not mean a SAS job no longer consists of a series of one or more job steps. Remember that macro processing ultimately results in SAS code, and that the code is passed on dynamically as the macro runs. Keep in mind that if the generated SAS code includes a step boundary, macro execution is suspended while the step is executed; when the SAS step has run to completion, macro execution continues from the point it was suspended.

MACRO PROGRAMMING

Since macros and macro variables are simply mechanisms whereby one set of code is made to stand for another, macro programming is simply *the art of preparing and using SAS macros and macro variables to make SAS programming easier.* You cannot be a good macro user unless you are already a competent SAS user, because all macros do is stand for SAS code.

Yet even so, there seems to be nothing that mystifies new SAS users more than the Macro Language. Why is this? The simple reason that Macro Language programming confounds new users is, I think, that it makes SAS code "invisible." So besides appearing exotic, with its % statements and all, its effects appear like magic. Usually the SAS System and the user speak the same language: What you write is what you expect SAS software to receive. With macros, you write something down and send it to the computer, but the preprocessor transforms it into something else before the SAS System really gets down to business.

Still, as with any other SAS facility, to master macros the secret of success is simply to *understand how things work.* So let us begin.

Macro Language Statements: In General

The term "SAS Macro Language" refers to a rather small set of statements that are used to prepare macros or macro variables. They differ from the usual SAS statements in their use of the special prefix token "%."* (Three of these statements—%MACRO, %MEND, and %LET—have already been introduced above.) The statements of the Macro Language, like regular SAS statements, begin with an identifying keyword (%-prefixed) and end with a semicolon. Macro Language statements may be grouped into several functional areas, e.g., assignment, flow of control, user communications, and operating system communications. They may further be classified as macro-dependent or macro-independent: macro-dependent Macro Language statements may only appear inside a macro definition, i.e., between a %MACRO statement and its %MEND, while macro-independent Macro Language statements may appear either inside or outside macro definitions. Do

---

*A small number of SAS statements begin with a keyword preceded by the % token, yet are not to be strictly considered part of the Macro Language. The %INCLUDE statement, which specifies either a file reference or (in interactive SAS) a set of prior program lines from which secondary SAS source code is to be taken, is a prime example.

not be confused by the simple fact that some statements called "Macro Language" may appear outside a macro definition. A list of Macro Language statements appears in Table 19.1; as you see, there are not really all that many of them.

Macro Functions

The SAS Macro Language has its own set of built-in functions which return results that are used in Macro Language statements. Several macro functions will be discussed below and in Chapter 20.

Macro Expressions

Many Macro Language statements may contain expressions. In an analogy to regular SAS expressions, Macro Language expressions are used for assignments, for conditional evaluation, e.g., in %IF-%THEN statements, or as arguments to macro functions. Macro Language expressions may be built of macro variables, macro function terms, operators, and constant text. The operators that may be used include the comparison operators $=$, $>$, $<$, $>=$, $<=$, and $=$, or their mnemonic equivalents EQ, GT, LT, GE, LE, and NE. In addition, in circumstances where an arithmetic rather than a string result might be achieved (because all operands resolve to integer numerals, see below), arithmetic operators may appear.

An expression is evaluated based on its complete resolution, i.e., on what it turns out to be after any macro variables or macros within it are taken care of. If

TABLE 19.1. STATEMENTS OF THE SAS MACRO LANGUAGE

Functional Group	Statement	I[a]	Function
Macro Boundary	%MACRO	N	Indicates the beginning of a macro definition
	%MEND	N	Indicates the end of a macro definition
Flow of Control	%DO	N	Begins a conditional sequence. Varieties: simple %DO, %DO %UNTIL, %DO %WHILE, iterative %DO
	%END	N	Ends a conditional sequence begun by %DO
	%IF–%THEN	N	Tests and acts on condition true
	%ELSE	N	Following %IF–%THEN, acts on condition false
	%GOTO	N	Transfer control absolutely to label location
Assignment	%LET	Y	Assigns value to macro variable
Reference Environment[b]	%GLOBAL	Y	Names macro variable to global environment
	%LOCAL		Names macro variable to local environment
Communication	%*	N	Macro comment statement
	%PUT	Y	Write message to SAS log
	%INPUT	Y	Accept line of input from interactive user
Operating System	%CMS	Y	Execute CMS command
	%TSO	Y	Execute TSO command
Macro invocation	%macname	Y	Execute macro "macname," if compiled

[a] Macro-independence: If Y, statement can be coded outside a macro definition (in open circle).
[b] Macro variable reference environments are discussed in Chapter 20.

all the resolved operands are integer numerals (i.e., consist only of the digits 0 to 9), then the expression will normally be evaluated numerically rather than by character comparison; if comparison operators are also included, then this also will be based on the numeric comparison. The order of evaluation is similar to that used in SAS DATA Step expressions. As in the DATA Step, the result of a comparison operation is either 0 (false) or 1 (true).

Macro expressions that contain nonintegral operands evaluate based on the *character values* of their operands. In this case, *only* comparison operators are allowed. The evaluation of "equals," "less than," or "greater than" is based on the same criterion on which sorting would be based. On IBM systems using the EBCDIC coding convention, by default

```
Z < 7
```

is true, and you will find on most systems that

```
2.0 > 2
```

is also true. '2.0' is *not* an integer numeral, and is therefore treated as a character string, and the string '2.0' sorts after '2_'.

We will take a look at macro expression evaluation during our discussion of the %EVAL function later in this chapter.

Text Within Macros

As noted earlier, between %MACRO and %MEND may be placed not only Macro Language statements but also regular SAS code. Regular SAS code may also appear *within* certain Macro Language statements, such as after the %THEN of an %IF-%THEN statement or as a constant part of an expression.

Coding and Using Simple Macros

By "simple" macro, I mean one that does little more than expand code and perhaps resolve one or more macro variables, in other words, macros that use only the %MACRO, %MEND, and possibly %LET statements. Such macros are not difficult either to understand or to code and can be put to good use by anyone who uses the SAS System regularly. You should consider using macros (1) whenever some segment of code must be used repeatedly in a program, and (2) whenever some segment of code must be changed very slightly and reused. Use macros if it increases coding efficiency, which may be true if the repetitive code is lengthy. The first "SMRYPRT" example given earlier in this chapter was a good example; following is another, showing the use of the %LET statement.

Imagine you are a sociologist studying vacation patterns. You have asked people to fill out a questionnaire listing their popular vacation spots, and to indicate the start and end dates they may have visited each one during the past few years. The data are contained in a dataset VACDATA, having four variables:

ID, an identification number for the questionnaire respondent; SPOT, the vacation spot, represented by a code number; BEGDATE, a SAS date value giving the beginning of the stay; and ENDDATE, a SAS date value giving the end of the stay. One observation is created for each vacation spot mentioned, so there may be more than one observation per ID.

Your attention turns first not to the individual respondents, but to the distribution of vacation time itself, over the course of a year, and to use PROC TIMEPLOT to plot the distribution of vacation days (Julian numbers 1 to 365 will do) over the course of calendar year 1992. You need input for TIMEPLOT, and decide to write a DATA step with a fairly straightforward algorithm:

```
For each vacation period (there is one period per
observation)
    determine the days in the period falling in 1992
    for each day in 1992
      add one to a counter
Plot the results
```

Your chosen implementation follows:*

```
DATA ;
  RETAIN DAY1-DAY365 0;
  SET OURSTUDY.VACDATA END=FINI;
  BD=JULDATE(BEGDATE); ED=JULDATE(ENDDATE);
  IF 92001<=BD<=92365 OR 92001<=ED<=92365;<R> * GET 1992 ONLY;
  IF 92001>BD THEN FIRST=1; ELSE FIRST=BD-92000;
  IF 92365<ED THEN LAST=365; ELSE LAST=ED-92000;
  ARRAY DATES {365} DAY1-DAY365;
  DO X=FIRST TO LAST;
    DATES{X} + 1;
  END;
  IF FINI THEN OUTPUT; * OUTPUT ONLY AT LAST OBS, GET TOTALS;
RUN;
PROC TRANSPOSE NAME=DAY; RUN;
PROC TIMEPLOT;
  PLOT COL1='*'/JOINREF REF=0 REFCHAR='>';
  ID DAY;
  TITLE 'VACATION DAYS REPORTED IN 1992';
RUN;
```

Problem: Using macro variables for variations, generalize the program to plot the days for *any chosen year*.

---

*So not to lead us off the present subject, output is not illustrated; as an exercise, see if you can picture what the output would look like, then create some sample data and run a job to see if your prediction was correct.

Solution: The year is represented by a constant string throughout the program, so use a macro variable to change the code as follows:

```
DATA :
  RETAIN DAY1-DAY365 0;
  SET OURSTUDY.VACDATA END=FINI;
  BD=JULDATE(BEGDATE); ED=JULDATE(ENDDATE);
  IF &Y.001<=BD<=&Y.365 OR &Y.001<=ED<=&Y.365;
  IF &Y.001>BD THEN FIRST=1; ELSE FIRST=BD-&Y.000;
  IF &Y.365<ED THEN LAST=365; ELSE LAST=ED-&Y.000;
  ARRAY DATES {365} DAY1-DAY365;
  DO X=FIRST TO LAST;
    DATES{X} + 1;
  END;
  IF FINI THEN OUTPUT; * OUTPUT ONLY AT LAST OBS, GET TOTALS;
RUN;
PROC TRANSPOSE NAME=DAY; RUN;
PROC TIMEPLOT;
  PLOT COL1='*'/JOINREF REF=0 REFCHAR='>';
  ID DAY;
  TITLE "VACATION DAYS REPORTED IN 19&Y";
RUN;
```

"92" is no longer "hard-coded," which would necessitate numerous changes if ever another year were desired. Now, you could code the macro assignment statement

```
%LET Y=92;
```

prior to this DATA Step code and run the program. Next time, should it be desired that vacation days for another year be plotted, only the %LET statement need be changed.

An Aside: The Null Name Terminator

Before we proceed further . . . did you notice that instead of &Y001 (to replace 92001), &Y.001 was used? In other words, a period was placed after the variable name. Why? Because what follows immediately is a numeral. Since a macro variable may contain numerals, the macro processor will think you are referring to a macro variable Y001, not Y, when it sees &Y001. The single period is used as a *null terminator* for a macro name precisely in instances such as this. You may always use a period after a variable name, although it is strictly necessary only if the name is followed immediately by a letter, a numeral, an underscore, or a literal period. Thus in the TITLE statement, a period after &Y was not necessary, because the name was followed by a special character (the double quote mark), which cannot itself be part of a macro variable name. Whenever a macro name is followed by a period, the macro preprocessor will understand the period to signify that the name has just ended; the correct name, in this case Y and *not* Y001 (or

Y365), will be looked up in the symbol table. A period *could* have been used in the TITLE statement; it just was not needed, because a blank or a special character performs the same signification.

What about legitimate periods in text? For example, suppose the libname OURSTUDY, used in this example, were to change between programs. It is desired to have a macro variable, LIB, represent this. For the present example, the %LET statement

```
%LET LIB=OURSTUDY;
```

would set the variable to the correct ddname, and should be coded prior to using &LIB in the text. But even then,

```
SET &LIB.VACDATA;
```

would result in an error: After macro resolution, the compiler would see

```
SET OURSTUDYVACDATA;
```

and complain. The solution is to code the SET statement as

```
SET &LIB..VACDATA;
```

The first period only is taken as the null macro name terminator, and the second period remains to be passed through as constant text.

Back to Vacation Days

The results of the example program, given

```
%LET Y=92;
```

is identical to the nonmacro example. It is not yet a macro, but is still a valid use of macro statements and variables.* The program as it stands can cover any vacation year with a change only to the %LET statement. If instead it is desired to run several years within the *same* job, it is better to make it a macro. Here is a simple way to "recycle" code in the same program. Proceed by coding

```
%MACRO VDAYS;
```

before the DATA statement, and

---

*Remember that macro variable references may be used anywhere in a program, not just within a macro, so long as the symbol has been defined, and that %LET is one of those Macro Language statements that can be used outside a macro definition.

```
%MEND VDAYS;
```

after the last RUN. Do *not* put the %LET statement inside the macro, but use %LET statements after the macro definition and call the macro as you wish:

```
%LET Y=90;
%VDAYS
%LET Y=91;
%VDAYS
%LET Y=92;
%VDAYS
```

yields three duplicates of the program in sequence; the year is different each time.

If another variable is used, which need not change each time, you may just have to assign it once, because macro variables created outside a macro definition by %LET keep their values unless and until changed. So, if you are getting data from 1986, 1987, and 1988 all from OURSTUDY.VACDATA, and you used &LIB..VACDATA in your macro, just code

```
%LET LIB=OURSTUDY;
```

once, before the first invocation of %VDAYS.

Subsetting Observations by Macro

Problem: Write a variation of the VDAYS macro to study the vacation days of any particular vacation spot.

Solution: Include an IF or WHERE statement after SET, e.g.,

```
SET etc. ;
  WHERE SPOT=&SPOT;
  BD=JULDATE  etc. ;
```

Then prior to invocation, use another %LET statement:

```
%LET SPOT=123;
%LET Y=92;
%VDAYS
```

(You needn't choose the name SPOT for your macro variable, but there's no reason not to: The macro variable SPOT is entirely different from the dataset variable SPOT, and this usage causes SAS no problem at all.)

Even more generally, you could write the VDAYS macro to select by SPOT *or not*, as you wish. One way is to code only a macro reference followed by a semicolon after the SET statement, instead of the IF statement:

```
SET etc. ;
  &CHOOSE
  BD=JULDATE  etc. ;
```

Now, you can write something like

```
%LET Y=92;
%LET CHOOSE=;
%VDAYS
%LET CHOOSE=IF SPOT=421;
%VDAYS
%LET CHOOSE=IF SPOT<<2000;
%VDAYS
```

the first time getting all SPOTs, the second time getting SPOT 421, the third time getting all those SPOTs whose code number is less than 2,000, and so on. In the first invocation, the innocent null statement (i.e., a lone semicolon) is passed to the compiler. This is not because &CHOOSE is one semicolon, but because &CHOOSE is nothing (the semicolon in the %LET statement is the terminus of the %LET statement and not part of the variable). The semicolon in the SAS code is due to the semicolon following the invocation of &CHOOSE in the macro. But the first %LET statement is required: Recall that a null macro variable is not the same as a nonexisting macro variable. If %VDAYS were executed before CHOOSE is declared, SAS would fail to find CHOOSE in the symbol table and the reference &CHOOSE would be passed straight through to the compiler, which upon seeing the line

```
&CHOOSE;
```

would complain about the invalid statement and not be able to continue.

As you see, a macro variable can include just about any SAS code. There is no reason why CHOOSE cannot equal

```
IF SPOT<2000
```

or almost anything else. In fact, there are ways (you will see) to include even semicolons (or even ampersands and percent signs) inside a macro variable.

Listing 19.2 shows the actions of another simple macro, for you to examine.

Parameter Assignment

When a macro is defined with parameters, macro variables are assigned values each time the macro is executed, by values passed to the macro at invocation. Suppose the %MACRO statement of the vacation days example shown above (with SET &DD..VACDATA) had been coded

```
        <<< PROGRAM SOURCE CODE FOLLOWS >>>

%MACRO EASY;   %* NOTE: THIS IS A MACRO COMMENT STATEMENT!;
%********************** E A S Y ***************************;
%*   EXAMPLE MACRO TO SELECT A PRE-EXISTING SAS DATASET,      :
%*   AND RUN YOUR CHOICE OF PROCEDURES ON IT,                 :
%*   WITH UP TO 2 PROCEDURE MODIFYING STATEMENTS              :
%*      MUST USE %LET TO SET VARIABLES:                       :
%*             INDAT= INPUT DATASET                           :
%*             PROC = DESIRED PROCEDURE                       :
%*             X1   = ANY PROCEDURE MODIFYING STATEMENT       :
%*             X2   = ANOTHER PROCEDURE MODIFYING STATEMENT   :
%*   X1, X2 MAY BE NULL, INDAT & PROC MUST NOT BE NULL        :
%***********************************************************;
PROC &PROC DATA=&INDAT;
&X1;
&X2;
TITLE "DATASET: &INDAT  -  PROCEDURE: &PROC";
TITLE2 "MODIFIERS: &X1; &X2;";
RUN;
%MEND EASY;
%LET PROC=PRINT N;
%LET INDAT=TEST;
%LET X1 = VAR V1 V2;
%LET X2 = ID NAME;
%EASY

        <<< SAS JOB OUTPUT FOLLOWS >>>


               DATASET: TEST  -  PROCEDURE: PRINT N
                 MODIFIERS: VAR V1 V2; ID NAME;

                    NAME      V1      V2

                    BILLY     21      280
                    JOEY      25      195
                    FREDDY    31      180
                    JERRY     29      190

                         N = 4
```

Listing 19.2. A simple macro

```
%MACRO VDAYS(Y,DD);
```

Now instead of using %LET statements, the call

```
%VDAYS(92,OURSTUDY)
```

would suffice. When the macro preprocessor receives this invocation, the very first thing it does is to assign the values 92 and OURSTUDY, respectively, to the symbols Y and DD.

Macro variables defined as parameters by %MACRO are created and exist only while the macro is executing (they are *local* to the macro; see "Macro Variable Reference Environments", Chapter 20). Prior executions of the macro, or external %LET statements appearing to name the same variable, etc., do not matter. Were the statement

```
%MACRO VDAYS(Y,DD);
```

used to begin the macro definition, care would have to be taken *not* to code something like

```
%LET DD=OURSTUDY;
%LET Y=92;
  %VDAYS
```

for the result would be an error: Y and DD, *at VDAYS execution*, would exist but be null,* resulting in statements such as

```
SET .VACDATA;
```

and

```
IF 001<=BD<=365 OR 001<=ED<=365;
```

being passed to the SAS compiler. There *are* times you want a parameter to be null, such as in certain macro flow-of-control applications (see below), but this example is not of one of those times.

Passing a Null Positional Parameter. In the case of positional parameters such as those in this example, if you *do* want a parameter to be null upon macro execution (i.e., at invocation), you can do as we have just shown and code the invocation with no variable list, although it is better practice to code the name with an empty variable list, i.e.,

```
%MYMACRO()
```

You can pass some but not all values (leaving the remainder null) when the parameters are positional. Given a macro that begins with

```
%MACRO FUN(JOY,RAPTURE,HAPPY);
```

the invocation

---

*If a symbol of the same name exists in both the global and local environments, the local one is used; again, this will be explained further in Chapter 20.

```
%FUN(SKIING,READING,SWIMMING)
```

results in the macro variables having the values JOY=SKIING, RAPTURE= READING, HAPPY=SWIMMING, while the invocation

```
%FUN(CLIMBING)
```

results in JOY=CLIMBING, with RAPTURE and HAPPY null. In some cases, you may require a "placeholder" comma. The invocation

```
%FUN(,,EATING)
```

gives null values of JOY and RAPTURE, with HAPPY=EATING.

Another illustration is provided in Listing 19.3. Since each passed value is separated by a comma, a null value (i.e., nothing) followed by a comma lets a value pass null. Since positional parameters start out null at invocation, unless a nonnull value is passed, it is not necessary to use placeholders if you wish all values to be null, or if you wish only values "to the right" of all else (as in "%FUN(CLIMBING)") to be null.

Using Keyword Parameters. Keyword parameters are used primarily to set up nonnull defaults for macro execution. Suppose the VDAYS macro were instituted beginning with

```
%MACRO VDAYS(Y=92,DD=OURSTUDY);
```

In this case, an invocation such as

```
%VDAYS()
```

would not fail, because the starting values of the macro variables would have valid nonnull defaults. As with positional parameters, you can change some keyword parameters and leave others alone. The invocation

```
%VDAYS(Y=91)
```

would cause the default value of Y=92 to be replaced with 91, but the default value of DD, OURSTUDY, would be unchanged.

A %MACRO statement can use a keyword parameter yet preserve a null default by setting a null default. Coding

```
%MACRO TEST(FACTOR1=,FACTOR2=,TRIAL=TEST,USER=,KEY=ALPHA);
```

sets up a macro which, upon execution, creates five symbolic variables, three of which default to null and two (TRIAL and KEY) to the nonnull values shown. Any or all of these can be named on invocation, in order that any or all of them be changed. So the invocation

```
%TEST(FACTOR2=BENZENE,TRIAL=PRELIM,USER=DR. JONES)·
```

```
<<< PROGRAM SOURCE CODE FOLLOWS >>>

%MACRO PUTIT(ONE,TWO,THREE,FOUR);
PUT "::ONE=&ONE:TWO=&TWO:THREE=&THREE:FOUR=&FOUR::";
%MEND PUTIT;
DATA _NULL_; FILE PRINT;
PUT 'Invoking with all four variables';
%PUTIT(A,B,C,D);
PUT ' (but remember, a comma, not a blank, separates parameters:)';
%PUTIT(A B C D); * <-- this is ONE parameter (the first one) ;
PUT 'Invoking with first, second, fourth parameters';
%PUTIT(ALPHA,BETA,,DELTA);
PUT 'Invoking with second parameter only';
%PUTIT(,SECOND);
PUT 'Invoking with third parameter only';
%PUTIT(,,THIRD);
PUT 'Invoking with no parameters';
%PUTIT();
PUT '%LET statement has no effect on values of passed parameters:';
%LET ONE='UNO'; %LET THREE='TRES';
%PUTIT();
RUN;


<<< SAS JOB OUTPUT FOLLOWS >>>

Invoking with all four variables
::ONE=A:TWO=B:THREE=C:FOUR=D::
 (but remember, a comma, not a blank, separates parameters:)
::ONE=A B C D:TWO=:THREE=:FOUR=::
Invoking with first, second, fourth parameters
::ONE=ALPHA:TWO=BETA:THREE=:FOUR=DELTA::
Invoking with second parameter only
::ONE=:TWO=SECOND:THREE=:FOUR=::
Invoking with third parameter only
::ONE=:TWO=:THREE=THIRD:FOUR=::
Invoking with no parameters
::ONE=:TWO=:THREE=:FOUR=::
%LET statement has no effect on values of passed parameters:
::ONE=:TWO=:THREE=:FOUR=::
```

Listing 19.3. Macro invocation parameters

starts the macro with FACTOR1 null, KEY=ALPHA, and the other values as shown. A null value may be used to override a nonnull value, e.g.,

```
%TEST(TRIAL=,USER=USERID)
```

invokes the macro with a null value for TRIAL.

Keyword parameters may be coded in any order on invocation, not only in the order shown on the %MACRO statement, and neither is there any need for "placeholders." The following invocation runs the same TEST as above:

```
%TEST(TRIAL=PRELIM,USER=DR. JONES,FACTOR2=BENZENE)
```

The reason this is allowed is that keyword parameters must be invoked with their keyword names (and an equal sign). The keyword unambiguously references the correct symbol. Positional parameters rely on their positions, hence the name, and do not have any other way of telling the preprocessor which variables they are meant for.

Remember that macro variable values created by parameter passing (keyword or position) exist only for the duration of macro execution; each time the macro is invoked it starts afresh, as it were. If you next execute the TEST macro with

```
%TEST(KEY=BETA)
```

the value of TRIAL will be TEST, and FACTOR1, FACTOR2, and USER will be null.

Mixing Keyword and Positional Parameters. As mentioned earlier in this chapter, you can code both positional and keyword parameters on a %MACRO statement, but all positional parameters must come before all keyword parameters. Upon invocation, the positional parameters must all be accounted for, in their correct order and with any necessary placeholders, before any keyword parameters (in any order) are used.

Internal Documentation

Two statements are available to document the SAS job log: the macro comment and the %PUT.

The Macro Comment Statement

A macro comment is a statement of the form

```
%* [anything] ;
```

It looks like a SAS statement-style comment but with "%*" instead of "*" at the head. It can only be used inside a macro definition, and only appears in the log inside the macro definition: when the macro is executed, it will not show. In contrast, should a regular SAS comment be used, then each time the macro is executed, the comment will pass through to the SAS log. In other words, the macro

```
%MACRO DONOTHNG;
%*THIS MACRO DOES NOTHING;
%MEND;
```

and the macro

```
%MACRO DONTHNG2;
*THIS MACRO DOES NOTHING;
%MEND;
```

differ in that the invocation

```
%DONOTHNG
```

really does nothing, but the invocation

```
%DONTHNG2
```

will leave the SAS log with the comment statement

```
*THIS MACRO DOES NOTHING;
```

each time it is used.

A good habit to develop, when you code complicated macros, is to give each a "heading" with macro comments, briefly describing what the macro is for, what its variables represent, and perhaps how it is used.

The %PUT Statement

The %PUT statement is used to write text to the SAS log. The %PUT statement may be used inside or outside a macro definition. It can be used to annotate the log relative to a point of macro execution, especially if the macro execution display options (discussed later in this chapter) are turned off:

```
%MACRO WHATEVR;
%PUT MACRO WHATEVR NOW COMMENCING EXECUTION ...;
[body of macro]
%MEND;
```

Note that the text following the Macro Language %PUT statement does not have to be quoted (and should not be, unless you want to see the quote marks printed).

Flow of Control

The Macro Language provides several statements that direct the program to execute segments of code conditionally or iteratively. These statements include the %IF-%THEN-%ELSE group, the %GOTO statement, and several forms of the %DO-%END group. The way these statements operate are analogous to their namesakes in the DATA Step Language, but they are not valid outside a macro definition; any attempt to use them outside will result in a compile-time error.

The %IF-%THEN and %ELSE Statements; Simple %DO Groups

As the IF-THEN statement can select a SAS statement within a DATA step, depending on the evaluation of a condition, so the %IF-%THEN statement can select a segment of SAS code upon a condition. The form of the statement is

```
%IF macro-expression %THEN [code];
```

where the "code" is either constant text, a macro function, or a macro statement. If the code following %THEN is lengthy, or contains semicolons (though there is a way around this), it is often best to encase it within a simple %DO-%END group, much as a simple DO-END group holds multiple statements for conditional execution in the DATA step. The simple %DO and the %END statements can surround any code in a macro, including other macro statements and constant text.

Problem: An analyst needs to construct data subsets from time to time, and select one of several standard reports describing the subset. The reports are based on different DATA and PROC strategies.

Solution:

```
%MACRO
R(LIB1=IN,LIB2=OUT,DS1=STANDARD,DS2=STANDARD,SEL=,RPT=F);
%************************ R *********************************;
%* MACRO TO RUN ANY OF THREE TYPES OF REPORTS ON A DATASET    ;
%*    WHICH MAY BE A SELECTION FROM ANOTHER DATASET.          ;
%*      VARIABLES: LIB1=INPUT LIBNAME (USE "WORK" FOR TEMP. DS)  ;
%*                 LIB2=OUTPUT LIBNAME (DITTO)                  ;
%*                 DS1=INPUT SAS DATASET NAME                 ;
%*                 DS2=OUTPUT SAS DATASET NAME                ;
%*                 SEL=SELECTION CRITERIA (SUBSETTING IF CLAUSE) ;
%*                 RPT= F=FREQ,P=PRINT,S=CUSTOM,OTHER=NOTHING   ;
%*      REQUIRED: LIB1,DS1,RPT(USUALLY)                       ;
%************************************************************;
%IF &SEL NE %THEN %DO;
DATA &LIB2..&DS2;
  SET &LIB1..&DS1;
  IF &SEL;
  %LET CURRENT=&LIB2..&DS2;
RUN;
%END;
%ELSE %LET CURRENT=&LIB1..&DS1;
%IF &RPT=F %THEN %DO;
PROC FREQ DATA=&CURRENT;
  [etc etc etc]
RUN;
%END;
%ELSE %IF &RPT=P %THEN %DO;
PROC PRINT DATA=&CURRENT;
  [etc etc etc]
RUN;
%END;
%ELSE %IF &RPT=S %THEN %DO;
DATA _NULL_; SET &CURRENT;
  [code for custom report]
RUN;
%END;
%MEND R;
```

Let's begin to analyze this macro with a look at the first %IF:

```
%IF &SEL NE %THEN %DO;
```

What does this mean? It looks like an error, but it is not; it means, "If the current value referenced by the symbol SEL is not null (If &SEL NE nothing), then do the following." The preprocessor has no trouble with this, because the first nonblank after the NE operator is the %THEN keyword, implying nothing after the NE, and because *the Macro Language is a string processing language*, it compares the value of SEL to the null string (which happens, in this example, to be the %MACRO statement default).

Why do this? Well, suppose the analyst wants a report based on the entire input dataset, and does not want to create a subset. An entire, unnecessary DATA step is avoided by this method. (What if the user does want a selection for analysis, but doesn't want to store it permanently? Just use the value of WORK for the variable LIB2.) If a new dataset is required, the remainder of the job will report on the old dataset, i.e., on &LIB2..&DS2, hence the %LET statement. But if &SEL is null on invocation, the %ELSE statement executes and has the remainder of the job report on the old, un-rebuilt dataset. For example,

```
%R(LIB1=DEPT6,DS1=SALARY,RPT=S)
```

causes only the following code to be emitted by the preprocessor:

```
DATA _NULL_; SET DEPT6.SALARY;
  [code for custom report]
RUN;
```

The reason this particular code gets generated (moving on to the remainder of this example macro) is that the macro enables one of three alternative processes: one that begins with PROC FREQ, one with PROC PRINT, and one with DATA _NULL_. Each of these processes is bound within a simple %DO group. (For other applications, note that any number of steps, in any variation, can be bound within the %DO group.) Upon invocation, the user passes a parameter, RPT, for which the macro handles three distinct alternatives: the single-character strings F, P, or S. The default is set by the %MACRO statement to be F. What if a null value, or a value other than F, P, or S, is given to RPT? In this macro, nothing happens, apart from the creation of the dataset if &SEL is not null. Therefore, this macro could be used to create the subset &DD2..&DS2 without reporting anything afterward. For example,

```
%R(DS1=QUARTER1,DS2=QTR1M,SEL=SEX = 'MALE',RPT=)
```

creates a dataset from IN.QUARTER1, selecting IF SEX='MALE', output to OUT.QTR1M, and cascades right through the %ELSE %IFs to %MEND. Here is all the SAS System would see after the macro preprocessor is done with its business:

```
DATA OUT.QTR1M;
  SET IN.QUARTER1;
  IF SEX = 'MALE';
RUN;
```

Execution Logic. The logic of %IF-THEN and %ELSE is identical to that of their namesakes in the DATA Step Language, and nothing more need be said. As you can see, multiple conditions can be implemented with %ELSE-%IFs, just as in the DATA step.*

%DO Is Not Necessary. Lest the reader be left with the wrong impression from the examples just discussed, let's reiterate that any macro statement or expression, or constant text, may follow %THEN in the %IF-%THEN statement. Thanks to functions we will discuss in Chapter 20, such as %STR, quite lengthy segments of SAS code may be conditioned on an %IF without using %DO groups.

%DO Statements of the Macro Language

The Macro Language allows several forms of %DO statement. Each begins a group that ends with the %END statement. The simple %DO statement,

```
%DO;
```

we have just seen. The Macro Language also has its own forms of iterative %DO, %DO-%WHILE, and %DO-%UNTIL.

%DO-%WHILE and %DO-%UNTIL Statements. The Macro Language supports a control mechanism like that provided by the DATA Step Language DO-WHILE and DO-UNTIL statements. The statement form

```
%DO %WHILE(macroexpression);
```

causes a series of statements to be executed if "macroexpression" is true, and executed again until the expression becomes false, and

```
%DO %UNTIL(macroexpression);
```

causes a series of statements to be executed, and executed again until the expression becomes false. A %DO-%UNTIL group executes at least once; a %DO-%WHILE group may not execute at all. Review Chapter 17 to distinguish the two; the logic is the same for the DATA and Macro forms.

Iterative %DO Groups. The iterative %DO statement takes the form

```
%DO index=start %TO stop [%BY increment];
```

---

*Because the Macro Language provides no analogue to the SELECT statement, this is the only way to implement multiple alternatives.

but unlike the DATA step DO statement, "index" is a macro variable name (coded *without* an ampersand).

The Macro Language iterative %DO is less flexible than its DATA Step analogue. The start, stop, and (if used) increment values must be integers, or macro expressions that evaluate to integers.* For example,

```
%DO Q=1 %TO 17;
```

is legal, but

```
%DO Q=1.5 %TO 5.5;
```

is not. Multiple clauses are not allowed, neither another start-%TO-stop specification nor a %WHILE or %UNTIL group, and there is no way to pass a value list in lieu of a "start-%TO- stop" construct, i.e., you *cannot* code anything like

```
%DO MVAR=1,7,12;
```

or for that matter, anything like

```
%DO MVAR=ABC,DEF,G;
```

An illustrative use for the iterative %DO group was shown in the introductory section of this chapter, where 28 different reports were generated from a single macro invocation. Here's a variation, assuming we want a very general macro that handles N regions:

```
%MACRO SMRYPRT(N);
  %DO X=1 %TO &N;
[you'd code Listing 19.1, all 24 lines but with REGION&X, here]
  %END;
%MEND SMRYPRT;
```

This would be invoked, of course, with a call such as

```
%SMRYPRT(28)
```

The index variable need not be so closely bound to the data; it may be simply a counter, used to force a specific number of executions of some segment of SAS code.

---

*What little arithmetic the macro processor does (see the discussion of %EVAL below) extends only to integers. But none of this changes the fact that the variable used is a macro variable (if the variable doesn't exist, %DO will create it), and its values character strings. The preprocessor places to and obtains from the symbol table only character values; the internal algorithms used when %DO is executed treats these values *as if* they were integers.

Problem: Generate a varying number of similar random subsets, with replacement, from a master dataset:

```
%MACRO
DORAN(COUNT,DS=MASTER.DATA,SEED=12345,CRITER=.5);
  %DO I=1 TO &COUNT;
  DATA RAND&I;
    SET &DS;
    IF RANUNI(&SEED) > &CRITER;
  RUN;
  %END;
%MEND DORAN;
```

Then the invocation

```
%DORAN(8)
```

would create eight datasets RAND1, RAND2, . . . , RAND8, each with about half the observations of MASTER.DATA randomly selected.

The %GOTO Statement

The %GOTO statement, like its namesake in the DATA Step Language, directs macro execution to another point in the macro. That point is indicated by a macro label, which looks like a DATA Step label (i.e., a name followed by a colon) except it is preceded by a percent sign.* On the %GOTO statement, the percent sign is *not* coded. If it is appropriate, a macro expression or macro invocation that results in a label may be coded instead of a constant.

Problem: A macro is to be invoked with a positional parameter. If the parameter is null, do not execute the macro but report the fact to the SAS log.

Solution: Tack on a "null check" at the beginning of the macro:

```
%MACRO SOMETHNG(X);
%IF &X= %THEN %DO;
   %PUT NOTE: NULL VALUE ENTERED FOR X, SKIPPING MACRO LOGIC.;
   %GOTO BAD;
%END;
[the "real" macro code ...]
%BAD: %*;
%MEND SOMETHNG;
```

Now, should the invocation

---

*Like macro names, labels should only be chosen that are not identical to any Macro Language keyword, and neither should a label be allowed to conflict with the name of any macro used in the program.

```
%SOMETHNG()
```

be encountered, nothing except the note to the log makes it through. Note that to get the label %BAD to point to the end of the macro, it is actually made to point to a macro comment statement immediately prior to %MEND, not to %MEND itself. %MEND is not part of the true body of the macro, and cannot take a label.

There is no such thing as a "%LINK" or a "%RETURN" statement in the SAS Macro Language. %GOTO is the only way to transfer control to an arbitrary location, and there you stay (unless, of course, you use another %GOTO).

Macro Functions

There are a number of functions available in the Macro Language. Macro functions help produce effects that otherwise would be difficult or impossible to achieve. Each function has a keyword name, always used with a percent sign prefix, followed by parentheses containing the argument(s) to the function. Arguments to macro functions may be constant strings, or they may be macro expressions that resolve to strings.* As with regular SAS functions, any evaluation that needs to be performed within the parentheses is done before the function itself is evaluated. You may use macro functions in macro statements allowed outside as well as inside macro definitions, keeping in mind that like macro variables, they will be evaluated during the preprocessing phase.

The Macro Language functions can be grouped under four headings: compile-time quoting, runtime quoting, expression evaluation, and string manipulation. The quoting functions will be covered in Chapter 20, the other categories below.

Expression Evaluation: The %EVAL Function

The macro preprocessor has some limited arithmetic and logic calculation abilities, which it applies under certain well-specified circumstances. One of these circumstances is the appearance of an %EVAL function,

```
%EVAL(expression)
```

The macro expression that is an argument to %EVAL normally will consist only of integer strings (i.e., numerals with no decimal points); expressions consisting of integer strings joined by arithmetic or logical/comparison operators; or symbolic variables or macros that resolve to such strings or expressions. Character operations (i.e., concatenation) are not allowed.

Exceptions to the Rule. Though %EVAL is usually associated with integer arithmetic, you can also use the %EVAL function to generate a logical truth value (1 or

---

*Some functions are specifically designed to input a string that *looks* like a macro expression (i.e., has & or % in it, or appears with symbolic or mnemonic operators) yet have it treated as a text string without resolution.

0, meaning true or false, respectively) with character operands, provided one and only one operator, which must be a comparison operator (=, >, <, etc.), appears. In such cases, %EVAL resorts to string comparison. The results may not always be what one would expect on a casual glance, e.g., "1.0=1.00" is 0 (character comparison, strings 1.0 and 1.00 not equal, logical false), yet "1=1+0" is 1 (all integral operands, therefore numeric evaluation).

A string (constant or as resolved) that contains nonnumeric characters in it, in the presence of any operators except comparison operators, or a nonintegral string in the presence of no operators, will cause the %EVAL function to fail in error. Examples of good and of bad %EVAL calls are shown in Listing 19.4. It is possible, using quoting functions (see Chapter 20), to compare strings that include symbols usually used as arithmetic or logical operators.

Implicit Evaluation. In most circumstances where a macro expression may be coded, such as the %IF clause of an %IF-%THEN statement, the %WHILE expression of a %DO-%WHILE, or an argument to a macro function, an implied %EVAL will be performed. Consider the code

```
%IF &X=&Y %THEN [something];
```

If &X has the value 1 and &Y the value 1.0, the expression is false, yet if &X is 3-2 and &Y is 5-4, the expression is true. There is a more insidious danger that arises in this kind of case, for if &X or &Y contains an arithmetic or logical operator, including mnemonic operators (AND, OR, etc.) which the user may innocently have meant to be part of a literal string, an implicit %EVAL will be performed.

In cases where implicit evaluation must be avoided, quote the expression. When the problem code is part of the macro definition itself, generally use the %STR function. If as in the &X=&Y case the code may be a result of symbolic evaluation, i.e., something you "cannot see," generally use the %QUOTE function. These quoting functions are discussed in Chapter 20.

```
1    %LET A= %EVAL(1+2);
2    %LET B= %EVAL(&A-7);
3    %LET C= %EVAL(&B-1.0);
ERROR: A character operand was found in the %EVAL function or %IF condition
       where a numeric operand is required. The condition was: -4-1.0
4    %LET D= %EVAL(&B>1.0);
5    %LET E= %EVAL(3<1.0);
6    %LET F= %EVAL(&A+&E);
7    %LET G= %EVAL(&A/&B);
8    %LET H= %EVAL(&A);
9    %LET I= %EVAL(1.0);
ERROR: A character operand was found in the %EVAL function or %IF condition
       where a numeric operand is required. The condition was: 1.0
10   %PUT ::A=&A:B=&B:C=&C:D=&D:E=&E:F=&F:G=&G:H=&H:I=&I:::;
::A=3:B=-4:C=:D=0:E=0:F=3:G=0:H=3:I=::
```

Listing 19.4. Uses and abuses of %EVAL

String Manipulation

Several SAS Macro Language functions are concerned with string manipulation. Two of them, **%LENGTH** and **%INDEX**, return an integer string based on a calculation. The remainder return a string based directly on the input argument. Each of the functions has an analogue in functions of the SAS DATA Step Language (Chapter 15). Their arguments can be constant strings or macro expressions.

%LENGTH(arg) returns the length, in characters, of its (resolved) argument. Given

```
%LET ABC=SANTA CLAUS;
%LET DEF=IS COMING TO TOWN;
```

then %LENGTH(&ABC) returns 11, %LENGTH(&ABC &DEF!) returns 30.

%INDEX(arg1,arg2) returns the starting position of the first instance of arg2 within arg1; if arg2 is not found within arg1, it returns zero. Given

```
%LET NAUGHTY=I SAW MOMMY KISSING SANTA CLAUS;
%LET NICE=KISSING;
```

then %INDEX(&NAUGHTY,&NICE) returns 13. There is no analog to the INDEXC function in the Macro Language.

%UPCASE(arg) returns its argument with all lowercase alphabetics changed to uppercase. It is useful particularly in interactive systems where the macro must test a value entered by a user who may be using lowercase at his or her terminal (the %INPUT statement will be discussed later in this chapter):

```
%PUT WOULD YOU LIKE TO CONTINUE (Y/N)?;
%INPUT CHOICE;
%IF %UPCASE(CHOICE)=Y %THEN ...;
```

%SUBSTR(arg1,arg2[,arg3]) returns that part of arg1 that begins in position arg2 and continues for a length of arg3. If arg3 is not specified, that part of arg1 that begins at arg2 and goes through the end is returned. Here's a roundabout way to state your menu preference

```
%LET THANKS=THANKS FOR A JOB WELL DONE, IT WAS A
RARE PRIVILEGE;
%LET DINNER1=STEAK; %LET DINNER2=ROAST BEEF;
%PUT I LIKE MY &DINNER1 %SUBSTR(&THANKS,18,9).;
%PUT AND MY &DINNER2 %SUBSTR(&THANKS,38,4)!;
```

%SCAN(arg1,arg2[,delims]) looks for the arg2'th "word" in arg1, using the delimiter character(s) specified or a default list (including the blank and many special characters). arg2 must be an integer or a macro expression that evaluates to an integer. The default delimiter list and the logic of the function, are the same as those for the DATA step SCAN function; see Chapter 15.

These last three functions, %UPCASE, %SUBSTR, and %SCAN, return an unquoted result; the significance of special characters is not removed. The remaining three string manipulation functions are %QUPCASE, %QSUBSTR, and %QSCAN, which function identically except that they return a quoted result. Macro quoting is discussed in Chapter 20.

User Interaction

Two statements allow SAS macros to communicate with a user in interactive applications.* One of these, the **%PUT** statement, has already been introduced. It can be used to send messages to the user via the interactive log:

```
%PUT %STR(    TANFASTIC TANNING SALONS MANAGEMENT INFO
SYSTEM);
%PUT %STR(---------------------------------------------------);
%PUT %STR(CHOOSE ONE OF THE FOLLOWING OPTIONS:);
%PUT %STR(              1. ENTER DATA);
%PUT %STR(              2. QUARTERLY REPORTS);
%PUT %STR(              3. SALES SUMMARY);
%PUT %STR(              4. PROJECTIONS);
%INPUT OPTN;
```

In this example, SAS sends a menu to the user. The %STR function (see Chapter 20) is used to make the lines on the screen look nice by preserving leading blanks.

The user sees the menu in the SAS log, which appears at his or her terminal. After the last line of the menu, the %INPUT statement in this example asks for a value to a macro variable OPTN; presumably, the macro goes on to decide what to do if the strings 1, 2, 3, or 4, or something else entirely is entered. The %INPUT statement has the general form

```
%INPUT [<macvar>...];
```

i.e., zero, one, or many variables may be named. %INPUT is used only in interactive sessions. Its job is to wait for the user to enter something at the terminal, and to deal with what is entered. In the Tanfastic Tanning example, the SAS System will wait patiently after showing the %PUT statements on the log, until the user hits the "enter" key (presumably, after having typed something).

The **%INPUT** statement, which may be used inside or outside a macro definition, counts the words in what the user enters, using only the blank (or multiple blanks) as its delimiter. That is to say, the line entry

```
APPLE ORANGE  PEAR   CUCUMBER ARMENIAN-MUSKMELON
```

---

*There are other ways to communicate with the user interactively, involving Display Manager features and other methods beyond the scope of this book.

is considered five words. An exception is created by quotation:

```
APPLE 'ORANGE   PEAR    CUCUMBER ARMENIAN-MUSKMELON'
```

is just two words. Each word is assigned to each variable named on the %INPUT statement, in turn. As with other quote-marked text in macro usage (and see our discussion of the %STR function in Chapter 20), the quotes become part of the value if used, so that

```
'FRENCH TOAST' SYRUP
```

in response to

```
%INPUT BREKFAST TOPPING;
```

yields a value of 'FRENCH TOAST', *quotes included*, for &BREKFAST.* If there are more macro variables named than words entered on the line following %IN-PUT, then the trailing variables will be assigned null values, e.g.,

```
%INPUT P Q R S;
```

followed by only two words leaves &R and &S both null. On the other hand, if there are more words in the line entered than macro variables named on the %INPUT statement, the rest of the line gets assigned to the automatic macro variable SYSBUFFR. If %INPUT is coded without any variable named, the entire line gets assigned to SYSBUFFR. Each time %INPUT executes, &SYSBUFFR is replaced. So, for example, if the user enters the line

```
THE QUICK BROWN FOX
```

in response to

```
%INPUT V1 V2;
```

the value &SYSBUFFR is BROWN FOX. If entered in response to

```
%INPUT;
```

&SYSBUFFR is THE QUICK BROWN FOX, and if entered in response to

```
%INPUT P Q R S;
```

then &SYSBUFFR is null.

---

*You could use macro functions to get rid of the quotes:
%LET BREKFAST=%SUBSTR(&BREKFAST,2,%LENGTH(&BREKFAST)-2);

Operating System Calls

Some operating systems are capable of having the SAS System call on commands or command procedures native to the system. Under such systems, the %SYSEXEC statement can be used to pass commands through to the system. The statement consists of the word %SYSEXEC, followed by a literal command to the operating system or else a macro expression that resolves to an operating system command. For example, the statement

```
%TSO LISTC L(SYS2.SAS);
```

passes the command "LISTC L(SYS2.SAS)" to the operating system.

MACRO ERRORS; MACROS AND THE SAS LOG

Macro Errors

As you know, compile-time and runtime errors and warnings may be generated by the SAS System and appear in your SAS job log, helping you to debug your programs. Similarly, the macro preprocessor reports macro compilation or execution errors and warnings to the SAS log. A buggy macro may generate a number of errors of either or both kinds, first as the preprocessor complains (upon macro compilation or upon execution) and then, whether or not the preprocessor has a problem, as the SAS System has a bad time with the generated code. The SAS log shown in Listing 19.5 gives an example of a macro resulting in errors of both kinds. Macro errors usually print without an associated error number, and can thus be picked apart quickly from other SAS errors, which normally show an error number in the log.

Debugging

In the listing, it would appear easy to determine what caused the errors. The compile-time errors are noted, and we can figure out what happened. Let's do so and fix the macro.

The first macro error is associated with two %ELSE statements (the error underlines the word after the %ELSE). "Used without %IF" . . . well, the problem is the semicolon. A double semicolon was used, correctly, to let a single semicolon through with the INPUT statement. But this separated the %ELSE from the %IF statement, which is supposed to precede it immediately. We could use %DO groups, or remove the %ELSE; let's choose the latter. We note that the last %ELSE (line 13) gives no error, so we catch the single semicolon in line 12 that *is* an error; let's double it.

Next there is a macro error in line 11, and careful inspection leads us to see that we used THEN instead of %THEN. So we fix it. The next error is "invalid symbolic name." It's *not supposed* to be a symbolic name, it's an input specification . . .

```
1     %MACRO BADBOY(INP); %*** A MACRO WITH ERRORS ***;
2     %** IT IS SUPPOSED TO CREATE FOUR DATASETS,
3         EACH WITH A SUBSET OF VARIABLES FROM AN INPUT FILE,
4         AND THEN PRINT THEM;
5     %DO I=1 %TO 4;
6        DATA DS&I; INFILE &IN;
7        %IF &I=1 %THEN INPUT (V1-V4) (2.);;
8        %ELSE %IF I=2 THEN INPUT @9 (X1-X5) (1.);;
ERROR: There is no matching %IF statement for the %ELSE. A dummy macro will
       be compiled.
9        %ELSE %IF &I=3 %THEN INPUT @20 ID 5. TRACK_NO 3.;
ERROR: There is no matching %IF statement for the %ELSE. A dummy macro will
       be compiled.
10       %ELSE %IF &I=4 %THEN %INPUT @30 VALID $1. NEWVAL 3.;
ERROR: There is no matching %IF statement for the %ELSE. A dummy macro will
       be compiled.
11    %END;
12    RUN;
13    %PROC PRINT; TITLE "DS&I";
14    RUN;
15    %MEND BADBOY;
16    %BADBOY('TEST19');

      180
WARNING: Apparent invocation of macro BADBOY not resolved.

ERROR 180-322: Statement is not valid or it is used out of proper order.
```

Listing 19.5. A buggy macro

oh yes, we foolishly wrote %INPUT instead of INPUT. So we fix this. The warning that BADBOY is not a macro name is a corollary of the other errors: If a macro fails compilation, it will not exist. This in turn caused a line to drop through the preprocessor to the SAS compiler (for the preprocessor could not resolve the macro reference), resulting in the complaint about an invalid statement (there is no %BADBOY statement in the SAS System).

So we resubmit the job, and—we get Listing 19.6! Now a different class of errors has emerged, because unlike the example in Listing 19.5, %BADBOY succeeded in getting compiled and executed. What we see now are the errors "inside" the macro. Well, it appears first of all* that the macro variable INP (look at the MACRO statement) was misspecified in the body of the macro as IN (look at the

---

*Compared with older versions of the SAS System, such as Version 5.18 and before, we are fortunate that *anything* is apparent. It used to be that without using system options MPRINT or MACROGEN (MPRINT is discussed below, MACROGEN a related Version 5 option that has no effect in Version 6) the error lines would print alone, without the input line that caused them. Now, if there is an error, by default the system will print the offending line along with a note that reminds you the line came from the invoked macro.

```
33    %MACRO BADBOY(INP); %*** A MACRO WITH ERRORS ***;
34    %** IT IS SUPPOSED TO CREATE FOUR DATASETS,
35         EACH WITH A SUBSET OF VARIABLES FROM AN INPUT FILE,
36         AND THEN PRINT THEM;
37    %DO I=1 %TO 4;
38      DATA DS&I; INFILE &IN;
39      %IF &I=1 %THEN INPUT (V1-V4) (2.);;
40      %IF I=2 %THEN INPUT @9 (X1-X5) (1.);;
41      %IF &I=3 %THEN INPUT @20 ID 5. TRACK_NO 3.;;
42      %IF &I=4 %THEN INPUT @30 VALID $1. NEWVAL 3.;;
43    %END;
44    RUN;
45    %PROC PRINT; TITLE "DS&I";
46    RUN;
47    %MEND BADBOY;
48    %BADBOY('TEST19');
WARNING: Apparent symbolic reference IN not resolved.
WARNING: Apparent symbolic reference IN not resolved.
NOTE: Line generated by the invoked macro "BADBOY".
48    DATA DS&I; INFILE &IN;
                              -
                             200
ERROR 200-322: The symbol is not recognized.


NOTE: The SAS System stopped processing this step because of errors.
WARNING: The data set WORK.DS1 may be incomplete.  When this step was stopped
         there were 0 observations and 4 variables.
WARNING: Data set WORK.DS1 was not replaced because this step was stopped.
NOTE: The DATA statement used 0.48 seconds.
```

Listing 19.6. A buggy macro (example continued)

Continued

INFILE statement). And, we carelessly typed "%PROC" when we meant to type "PROC" (probably because we were hitting "%" so much to type the rest of the macro, it just kind of happened).

Program Logic Errors Not Revealed

All right, let's fix the recently discovered errors, and re-run to yield the SAS log shown in Listing 19.7. There are no error messages, but a reading of the log does show a rather serious mistake: though the program "works," there is only one printout, not four!* It appears we mistakenly ended the interative %DO after the

---

*Only the log is shown in the listing; look at the log notes. And actually, the title of that lone printout (were we to see it) would not be "DS4", but "DS5"! Do you know why? Think about it.

```
WARNING: Apparent symbolic reference IN not resolved.
WARNING: Apparent symbolic reference IN not resolved.
NOTE: Line generated by the invoked macro "BADBOY".
48      DATA DS&I; INFILE &IN;
                          -
                         200
ERROR 200-322: The symbol is not recognized.


NOTE: The SAS System stopped processing this step because of errors.
WARNING: The data set WORK.DS2 may be incomplete.  When this step was stopped
         there were 0 observations and 0 variables.
WARNING: Data set WORK.DS2 was not replaced because this step was stopped.
NOTE: The DATA statement used 0.44 seconds.


   <<< The same thing happens two more times: warnings, unrecognized symbol &IN,    >>>
   <<< and notes about datasets (DS3 and DS4). These were eleted here to save space.  >>>


WARNING: Apparent invocation of macro PROC not resolved.
NOTE: Line generated by the invoked macro "BADBOY".
48        %PROC PRINT;
            -
           180

ERROR 180-322: Statement is not valid or it is used out of proper order.

NOTE: Line generated by the invoked macro "BADBOY".
48                    TITLE "DS&I"; RUN;
```

Listing 19.6. *Continued*

INPUT routines instead of after the PRINT/RUN. We also see (inspecting the log closely) that the second dataset did not read anything with INPUT. How could that be? Aha, a missing ampersand at line 11; of course "I=2" is false.

Such an error would not be revealed by mechanical means, not even with the options discussed below (which, because they would cause a more verbose log listing, would only serve to confuse the issue at hand). Only careful attention to program logic—and to the output of programs, including log notes—can uncover and resolve them.

System Options Affecting Log Display

There are three SAS system options* that may be used to write macro execution

---

*Instructions on the use of SAS system options in general, and descriptions of many specific options (including some relevant to macro processing), may be found in Chapter 21.

results to the log. The MPRINT and SYMBOLGEN options may be used to document the execution of the program more fully, as well as to help in macro debugging; the MLOGIC option is used only for debugging.

MPRINT causes the completely resolved source code to hit the log. What you see with MPRINT is, basically, what the SAS parser "sees." The macro we have been using for our examples of macro errors, with the newly discovered errors fixed, is shown and executed without MPRINT in Listing 19.8, and executed again with the MPRINT option on in Listing 19.9. Finally, Listing 19.10 shows the effect of combining the system options MPRINT and NONOTES. This provides a concise view of macro expansion and could be useful in the debugging stages, however the better log documentation for production applications is given when NOTES is left on.

SYMBOLGEN displays the values of macro variables in the SAS log, making clear the variables and their values in the expanded code listing. It is usually used along with MPRINT to provide complete program documentation (MPRINT will not show the values of macro variables that appear external to macro execution).

```
97    %MACRO BETRBOY(INP); %*** A MACRO WITH ERRORS (ALMOST) ALL FIXED! ***;
98    %** THIS MACRO IS SUPPOSED TO CREATE FOUR DATASETS,
99        EACH WITH A SUBSET OF VARIABLES FROM AN INPUT FILE,
100       AND THEN PRINT THEM;
101   %DO I=1 %TO 4;
102     DATA DS&I; INFILE &INP;
103     %IF &I=1 %THEN INPUT (V1-V4) (2.);;
104     %IF I=2 %THEN INPUT @9 (X1-X5) (1.);;
105     %IF &I=3 %THEN INPUT @20 ID 5. TRACK_NO 3.;;
106     %IF &I=4 %THEN INPUT @30 VALID $1. NEWVAL 3.;;
107   %END;
108   RUN;
109   PROC PRINT; TITLE "DS&I";
110   RUN;
111   %MEND BETRBOY;
112   %BETRBOY('TEST19.DAT');

NOTE: The infile 'TEST19.DAT' is:
      FILENAME=C:\SAS\MASAS2\TEST19.DAT,
      RECFM=V,LRECL=132

NOTE: 16 records were read from the infile 'TEST19.DAT'.
      The minimum record length was 69.
      The maximum record length was 69.
NOTE: The data set WORK.DS1 has 16 observations and 4 variables.
NOTE: The DATA statement used 0.28 seconds.
```

Listing 19.7. Macro errors fixed, but logic errors remain (example continued)

Continued

```
NOTE: The infile 'TEST19.DAT' is:
      FILENAME=C:\SAS\MASAS2\TEST19.DAT,
      RECFM=V,LRECL=132

NOTE: 0 records were read from the infile 'TEST19.DAT'.
NOTE: The data set WORK.DS2 has 1 observations and 0 variables.
NOTE: The DATA statement used 0.33 seconds.


NOTE: The infile 'TEST19.DAT' is:
      FILENAME=C:\SAS\MASAS2\TEST19.DAT,
      RECFM=V,LRECL=132

NOTE: 16 records were read from the infile 'TEST19.DAT'.
      The minimum record length was 69.
      The maximum record length was 69.
NOTE: The data set WORK.DS3 has 16 observations and 2 variables.
NOTE: The DATA statement used 0.44 seconds.


NOTE: The infile 'TEST19.DAT' is:
      FILENAME=C:\SAS\MASAS2\TEST19.DAT,
      RECFM=V,LRECL=132



NOTE: 16 records were read from the infile 'TEST19.DAT'.
      The minimum record length was 69.
      The maximum record length was 69.
NOTE: The data set WORK.DS4 has 16 observations and 2 variables.
NOTE: The DATA statement used 0.44 seconds.


NOTE: The PROCEDURE PRINT used 0.11 seconds.
```

Listing 19.7. *Continued*

The MLOGIC option, not illustrated here, is used in debugging the more perplexing macro problems. It shows each point at which the macro processor makes a decision, i.e., each and every %DO execution, %IF execution, etc., displaying the values of the macro variables at the time. MLOGIC can generate very lengthy listings, but these may be needed to trace out just what the macro processor is doing during the execution of a macro.

```
113  %MACRO BESTBOY(INP); %*** A MACRO WITH ERRORS ALL FIXED! ***;
114  %** THIS MACRO CREATES FOUR DATASETS,
115      EACH WITH A SUBSET OF VARIABLES FROM AN INPUT FILE,
116      AND THEN PRINTS THEM;
117  %DO I=1 %TO 4;
118    DATA DS&I; INFILE &INP;
119    %IF &I=1 %THEN INPUT (V1-V4) (2.);;
120    %IF &I=2 %THEN INPUT @9 (X1-X5) (1.);;
121    %IF &I=3 %THEN INPUT @20 ID 5. TRACK_NO 3.;;
122    %IF &I=4 %THEN INPUT @30 VALID $1. NEWVAL 3.;;
123  RUN;
124  PROC PRINT; TITLE "DS&I";
125  RUN;
126  %END;
127  %MEND BESTBOY;
128  %BESTBOY('TEST19.DAT');
```

```
NOTE: The infile 'TEST19.DAT' is:
      FILENAME=C:\SAS\MASAS2\TEST19.DAT,
      RECFM=V,LRECL=132

NOTE: 16 records were read from the infile 'TEST19.DAT'.
      The minimum record length was 69.
      The maximum record length was 69.
NOTE: The data set WORK.DS1 has 16 observations and 4 variables.
NOTE: The DATA statement used 0.22 seconds.




NOTE: The PROCEDURE PRINT used 0.05 seconds.




NOTE: The infile 'TEST19.DAT' is:
      FILENAME=C:\SAS\MASAS2\TEST19.DAT,
      RECFM=V,LRECL=132

NOTE: 16 records were read from the infile 'TEST19.DAT'.
      The minimum record length was 69.
      The maximum record length was 69.
NOTE: The data set WORK.DS2 has 16 observations and 5 variables.
NOTE: The DATA statement used 0.5 seconds.


NOTE: The PROCEDURE PRINT used 0.11 seconds.
```

Listing 19.8. The macro fully fixed (example continued)

Continued

```
NOTE: The infile 'TEST19.DAT' is:
      FILENAME=C:\SAS\MASAS2\TEST19.DAT,
      RECFM=V,LRECL=132

NOTE: 16 records were read from the infile 'TEST19.DAT'.
      The minimum record length was 69.
      The maximum record length was 69.
NOTE: The data set WORK.DS3 has 16 observations and 2 variables.
NOTE: The DATA statement used 0.5 seconds.



NOTE: The PROCEDURE PRINT used 0.11 seconds.



NOTE: The infile 'TEST19.DAT' is:
      FILENAME=C:\SAS\MASAS2\TEST19.DAT,
      RECFM=V,LRECL=132

NOTE: 16 records were read from the infile 'TEST19.DAT'.
      The minimum record length was 69.
      The maximum record length was 69.
NOTE: The data set WORK.DS4 has 16 observations and 2 variables.
NOTE: The DATA statement used 0.44 seconds.


NOTE: The PROCEDURE PRINT used 0.11 seconds.
```

Listing 19.8. *Continued*

```
129  OPTIONS MPRINT;
130  %BESTBOY('TEST19.DAT');
MPRINT(BESTBOY):    DATA DS1;
MPRINT(BESTBOY):    INFILE 'TEST19.DAT';
MPRINT(BESTBOY):    INPUT (V1-V4) (2.);
MPRINT(BESTBOY):    ;
MPRINT(BESTBOY):    ;
MPRINT(BESTBOY):    RUN;
```

```
NOTE: The infile 'TEST19.DAT' is:
      FILENAME=C:\SAS\MASAS2\TEST19.DAT,
      RECFM=V,LRECL=132
```

```
NOTE: 16 records were read from the infile 'TEST19.DAT'.
      The minimum record length was 69.
      The maximum record length was 69.
NOTE: The data set WORK.DS1 has 16 observations and 4 variables.
NOTE: The DATA statement used 0.38 seconds.
```

```
MPRINT(BESTBOY):    PROC PRINT;
MPRINT(BESTBOY):    TITLE "DS1";
MPRINT(BESTBOY):    RUN;
```

```
NOTE: The PROCEDURE PRINT used 0.17 seconds.
```

```
MPRINT(BESTBOY):    DATA DS2;
MPRINT(BESTBOY):    INFILE 'TEST19.DAT';
MPRINT(BESTBOY):    ;
MPRINT(BESTBOY):    INPUT @9 (X1-X5) (1.);
MPRINT(BESTBOY):    ;
MPRINT(BESTBOY):    RUN;
```

```
NOTE: The infile 'TEST19.DAT' is:
      FILENAME=C:\SAS\MASAS2\TEST19.DAT,
      RECFM=V,LRECL=132
```

```
NOTE: 16 records were read from the infile 'TEST19.DAT'.
      The minimum record length was 69.
      The maximum record length was 69.
NOTE: The data set WORK.DS2 has 16 observations and 5 variables.
NOTE: The DATA statement used 0.66 seconds.
```

```
MPRINT(BESTBOY):    PROC PRINT;
MPRINT(BESTBOY):    TITLE "DS2";
MPRINT(BESTBOY):    RUN;
```

```
NOTE: The PROCEDURE PRINT used 0.11 seconds.
```

Listing 19.9. The MPRINT option

Continued

```
MPRINT(BESTBOY):    DATA DS3;
MPRINT(BESTBOY):    INFILE 'TEST19.DAT';
MPRINT(BESTBOY):    ;
MPRINT(BESTBOY):    INPUT @20 ID 5. TRACK_NO 3.;
MPRINT(BESTBOY):    ;
MPRINT(BESTBOY):    RUN;
```

```
NOTE: The infile 'TEST19.DAT' is:
      FILENAME=C:\SAS\MASAS2\TEST19.DAT,
      RECFM=V,LRECL=132
```

```
NOTE: 16 records were read from the infile 'TEST19.DAT'.
      The minimum record length was 69.
      The maximum record length was 69.
NOTE: The data set WORK.DS3 has 16 observations and 2 variables.
NOTE: The DATA statement used 0.48 seconds.
```

```
MPRINT(BESTBOY):    PROC PRINT;
MPRINT(BESTBOY):    TITLE "DS3";
MPRINT(BESTBOY):    RUN;
```

```
NOTE: The PROCEDURE PRINT used 0.16 seconds.
```

```
MPRINT(BESTBOY):    DATA DS4;
MPRINT(BESTBOY):    INFILE 'TEST19.DAT';
MPRINT(BESTBOY):    ;
MPRINT(BESTBOY):    ;
MPRINT(BESTBOY):    INPUT @30 VALID $1. NEWVAL 3.;
MPRINT(BESTBOY):    RUN;
```

```
NOTE: The infile 'TEST19.DAT' is:
      FILENAME=C:\SAS\MASAS2\TEST19.DAT,
      RECFM=V,LRECL=132
```

```
NOTE: 16 records were read from the infile 'TEST19.DAT'.
      The minimum record length was 69.
      The maximum record length was 69.
NOTE: The data set WORK.DS4 has 16 observations and 2 variables.
NOTE: The DATA statement used 0.48 seconds.
```

```
MPRINT(BESTBOY):    PROC PRINT;
MPRINT(BESTBOY):    TITLE "DS4";
MPRINT(BESTBOY):    RUN;
```

```
NOTE: The PROCEDURE PRINT used 0.16 seconds.
```

Listing 19.9. *Continued*

```
131   OPTIONS NONOTES;
132   %BESTBOY('TEST19.DAT');
MPRINT(BESTBOY):    DATA DS1;
MPRINT(BESTBOY):    INFILE 'TEST19.DAT';
MPRINT(BESTBOY):    INPUT (V1-V4) (2.);
MPRINT(BESTBOY):    ;
MPRINT(BESTBOY):    ;
MPRINT(BESTBOY):    RUN;
MPRINT(BESTBOY):    PROC PRINT;
MPRINT(BESTBOY):    TITLE "DS1";
MPRINT(BESTBOY):    RUN;
MPRINT(BESTBOY):    DATA DS2;
MPRINT(BESTBOY):    INFILE 'TEST19.DAT';
MPRINT(BESTBOY):    ;
MPRINT(BESTBOY):    INPUT @9 (X1-X5) (1.);
MPRINT(BESTBOY):    ;
MPRINT(BESTBOY):    RUN;
MPRINT(BESTBOY):    PROC PRINT;
MPRINT(BESTBOY):    TITLE "DS2";
MPRINT(BESTBOY):    RUN;
MPRINT(BESTBOY):    DATA DS3;
MPRINT(BESTBOY):    INFILE 'TEST19.DAT';
MPRINT(BESTBOY):    ;
MPRINT(BESTBOY):    INPUT @20 ID 5. TRACK_NO 3.;
MPRINT(BESTBOY):    ;
MPRINT(BESTBOY):    RUN;
MPRINT(BESTBOY):    PROC PRINT;
MPRINT(BESTBOY):    TITLE "DS3";
MPRINT(BESTBOY):    RUN;
MPRINT(BESTBOY):    DATA DS4;
MPRINT(BESTBOY):    INFILE 'TEST19.DAT';
MPRINT(BESTBOY):    ;
MPRINT(BESTBOY):    ;
MPRINT(BESTBOY):    INPUT @30 VALID $1. NEWVAL 3.;
MPRINT(BESTBOY):    RUN;
MPRINT(BESTBOY):    PROC PRINT;
MPRINT(BESTBOY):    TITLE "DS4";
MPRINT(BESTBOY):    RUN;
```

Listing 19.10. MPRINT with NONOTES

20

More Macro Processing Features

In this chapter we review still more features of the macro facility, including macro variable resolution, Macro Language quoting, and macro/DATA step intercommunication.

MACRO VARIABLE RESOLUTION

Concatenated References

Macro variable references may be concatenated:

```
%LET A=TOONER; %LET B=VILLE; %LET C=TROLLEY;
%PUT &A&B &C;
```

will write

```
TOONERVILLE TROLLEY
```

So long as each variable is defined, any number of macro references may follow each other. This is because the preprocessor perceives a macro reference name to end at any blank or special character—including an ampersand. "&A&B" is unambiguously &A followed by &B.

If a number, letter, or underscore is to follow the reference, the situation is more complicated:

```
%PUT STATION=&A&B &CSTOP;
```

will not cause the preprocessor to write

```
TOONERVILLE TROLLEYSTOP
```

as intended, but to write

```
TOONERVILLE &CSTOP
```

and complain about not finding the symbol CSTOP in the active tables. The solution has already been revealed, in Chapter 19: Use a period as a separator, as in

```
%PUT STATION=&A&B &C.STOP;
```

A period after the name in a macro variable reference is interpreted to signify the end of the reference, as another special character or a blank would do, but unlike a blank or other special character it generates not even itself; i.e., the preprocessor does not let such a period escape into open code. To place a period after a macro reference, code two of them:

```
%PUT &A&B &C..STOP;
```

gives

```
TOONERVILLE TROLLEY.STOP
```

and so, for that matter, would

```
%PUT &A.&B. &C..STOP;
```

Indirect Variable Reference

The macro processor attempts to resolve all open code macro references before passing code through to the "regular" SAS System. It does so by going through the code and, if a macro "trigger" is found, resolving the reference and putting it back through the wordscanner. In resolving references, the macro preprocessor works systematically, left to right. It also happens that the preprocessor is designed to detect two ampersands in a row, and resolve these to one ampersand. This makes for some interesting possibilities.*

---

*The present discussion does not generalize to the macro trigger %. You cannot expect triple or double percent signs to work as triple or double ampersands do. Extra percent signs will generally be passed through to open code. It is macro variable resolution under consideration here.

One of these possibilities is your option to store the symbolic name of one macro variable as the value of another macro variable, and be able to retrieve the first variable's value by reference through the second variable:

```
%LET DOG=POMERANIAN;
%LET PET=DOG;
%PUT I LIKE MY &PET;
%PUT IT IS A &&&PET;
```

results in the lines

```
I LIKE MY DOG
IT IS A POMERANIAN
```

being written to the SAS log. The reference &&&PET is an *indirect* reference to the value POMERANIAN: the value of PET is the name of a symbol which in turn contains the value that is finally retrieved.

Figure 20.1 reveals the mechanism of the second %PUT, which is based on the

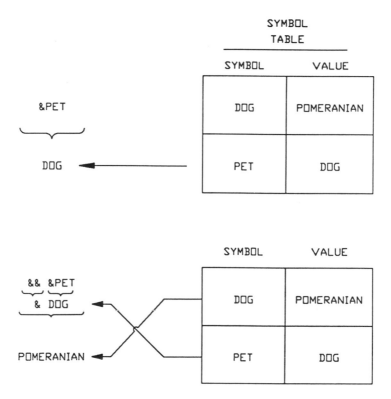

Figure 20.1. Indirect reference with macro variables. PET contains DOG, but DOG is also a symbol that can be resolved. Typical indirect reference situations involve three ampersands.

facts that (1) symbolic resolution takes place left to right, (2) two ampersands in a row resolve to one, and (3) if any macro references remain, they continue to pass through the preprocessor for symbolic resolution. So, on first pass, && goes to &, &PET goes to DOG, and &DOG remains to pass back through the wordscanner. &DOG being a symbolic reference, the preprocessor looks for it in the symbol table, returns POMERANIAN, and is done with its business.

Different numbers of ampersands produce different results. In this case, two and four produce DOG, five and six POMERANIAN, seven &POMERANIAN (and a complaint from the preprocessor, under the option SERROR [see Chapter 21], that there is no symbol "POMERANIAN"). See Figure 20.2.

As another, somewhat different example of indirect reference, suppose we establish the following:

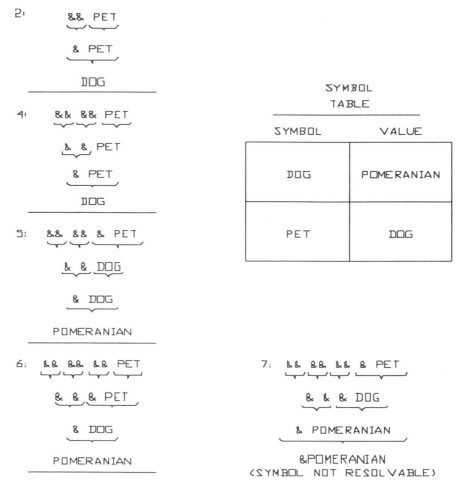

Figure 20.2. Indirect reference with other than three ampersands. Two ampersands act as one, while other numbers of ampersands give various results.

```
%LET APPLES=GOOD FRUIT;
%LET APPLAUSE=OUR REWARD;
%LET APPROVAL=OUR SATISFACTION;
%LET X=AP;
```

What will the following %PUT statement write?

```
%PUT &X.PLAUSE FOR EATING &X.PLES IS &X.PROVAL;
```

It writes

```
APPLAUSE FOR EATING APPLES IS APPROVAL
```

But if we code

```
%PUT &&&X.PLAUSE FOR EATING &&&X.PLES IS &&&X.PROVAL;
```

we get

```
OUR REWARD FOR EATING GOOD FRUIT IS OUR SATISFACTION
```

If you sketch out what happens, you can see why. The reference &X.PLAUSE takes but a single pass by the preprocessor. &X, which is detached from PLAUSE by the concatenation period, is resolved to AP, and PLAUSE passes through directly. However, &&&X.PLAUSE takes two scans. The first results in &AP-PLAUSE, because the first two ampersands resolve to one, and &X.PLAUSE resolves to APPLAUSE. The second scan, of &APPLAUSE, retrieves OUR RE-WARD.

Indirect reference may be useful in complex situations where the name of a symbol will not be known until execution, e.g., as a result of a RESOLVE function, discussed later. It is possible to achieve "indirect indirect" references, for instance if we had set up a third variable

```
%LET ANIMAL=PET;
```

Delayed Variable Reference

In the second example of indirect reference given above, a macro variable name was broken into pieces, one of which (AP) was stored in another macro variable (X). But what if the *second* part of the variable, not the first, was stored:

```
%LET PARTING=IS SUCH SWEET SORROW;
%LET BOING=A LONELY SOUND;
%LET X=ING;
```

If we code

```
%PUT BO&X PART&X;
```

we'll simply get

```
BOING PARTING
```

But if we code

```
%PUT &BO&X &PART&X;
```

we will get

```
&BOING &PARTING
```

and complaints from the system (under the option SERROR) that symbolic references (PART and BO) could not be found in the symbol table. If the preprocessor were to act upon &PARTING, it would give us no trouble, but it has reacted to &PART. We would like to keep the preprocessor's hands off these symbols *until* we've suffixed the resolved value of X to them, or in other words, we want to *delay* the preprocessor's action for one pass.

Again, multiple ampersands come to the rescue. This time, we use only two, in front of the references like so:

```
%PUT &&BO&X &&PART&X;
```

and produce

```
A LONELY SOUND IS SUCH SWEET SORROW
```

for on the first pass two ampersands resolve to one, &X is resolved, and a second pass remains to be correctly resolved. This is not difficult to understand; just draw a picture like before (see Figure 20.3).

Using dual ampersands in the pattern &&VAR1&VAR2 to achieve delayed resolution often comes in handy in macro programming. Good examples include those occasions when a varying number of macro variables has to be created using a call to SYMPUT, and then retrieved one by one in an iterative loop. Just such an example will be given when we discuss SYMPUT later in this chapter.

MACRO VARIABLE REFERENCE ENVIRONMENTS

Imagine yourself in a room within a room. Each room is lined with one-way mirrors so people inside can see outside, but not the other way. Your friend Alice is in the room with you. Jane is in the room just outside yours, Bill in another room that is inside yours, and Joe is outside all rooms, getting some fresh air. Figure 20.4 depicts the situation. Now, who can see whom? You and Alice can see

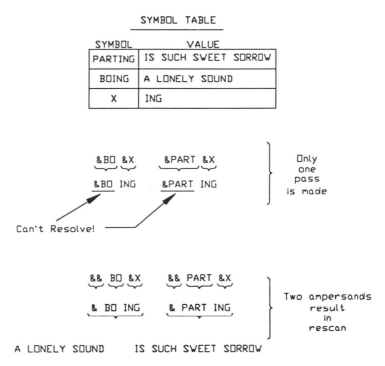

Figure 20.3. Delayed reference with macro variables. Multiple amper-sands are resolved on successive rescans of the code; if an ampersand drops away, the token is changed.

Jane, but Jane can't see either of you. No one sees Bill, though he can see everybody, and everybody can see Joe, though he can't see anybody.

Understanding variable reference environments is just as easy. You just have to remain aware of what "rooms" your macro variables are in, and when they exist (these peculiar "rooms" may appear and disappear from time to time).

The Global Environment

When a SAS job commences (under the default option MACRO, which "turns on" the macro facility; see Chapter 21), the outermost place to be—outside all "rooms"—is created. Variables that come into existence outside any macro defini-tion go into this "global" area: into the *global symbol table*. Another way to say this is that these variables *exist in the global reference environment*. Variables that exist in the global environment include those created by %LET statements outside any macro definition, the system variables which we discuss in the next section (except SYSPBUFF), variables created by %GLOBAL statements inside any macro when the macro first executes, and, in the majority of instances, variables created by a call to the SYMPUT routine.

Macro variables created in the global environment remain in existence through-out the course of your job.

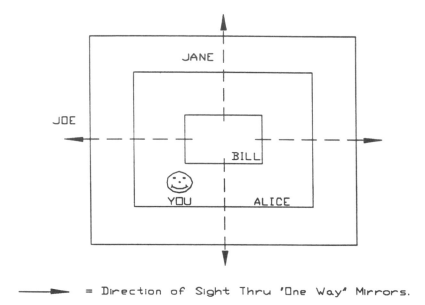

= Direction of Sight Thru 'One Way' Mirrors.

Figure 20.4. "Rooms within rooms," an analogy to macro variable reference environments. See text for explanation.

Local Environments

When a macro executes, it builds itself its own "room." More properly, it creates a *local symbol table*, in which variables may be created and said to exist in the macro's *local reference environment*. If another macro is invoked within the definition of a macro, then the subsidiary macro, while it executes, creates a room within a room: a more "inner" environment. Macro variables are created in the local environment of a macro only when the macro is executing, and then only under any of these specific circumstances:

1. If the macro definition contains a statement that can create a macro variable, e.g., %LET, %DO or %INPUT (but not %GLOBAL), *and* the variable named does *not* already exist in any outer environment (including the global environment and the local environment of a macro, if any, within which the present macro is executing), then a variable is created in the local environment. If the named variable exists in an outer environment, a local variable is not created, but rather the value of the named variable in the nearest outer environment it exists is replaced. However, if a variable is named in a %LOCAL statement, then even if it has the same name as a variable in an outer environment, it is created in the local symbol table.

   Stated another way, and perhaps more clearly, variables named in Macro Language statements are created locally, *except*:
   (a) If a variable-creating statement other than %LOCAL or %GLO-BAL is contained in the macro definition but the same symbol

name already exists in any outer environment, then the variable in the nearest outer environment is replaced and a local variable is not created.

(b) If a variable is named in a %GLOBAL statement, it is created in the global symbol table, and a local variable is not created.

(c) If a variable is named in a %LOCAL statement, it is created in the local environment.

2. Variables named as positional or keyword parameters become local to the executing macro, just like %LOCAL variables, whether another variable has the same name or not.

3. A call to SYMPUT, if executed from within an executing macro, creates a macro variable in the local environment, *if* the environment is not empty at the time SYMPUT is called. A local environment is empty if it has no macro variables created within it by any Macro Language statement *and* there is no %GOTO statement in the macro definition that uses a macro expression to get its label.

Even when the same name is used, macros in different reference environments are entirely different. When referenced by a macro, the "nearest" variable—if a local one exists, then that one, or else the first variable found proceeding "out" toward the global environment—is used. When referenced outside a macro, i.e., in open SAS code, then only the global environment is available, of course.

A local environment disappears after its macro completes execution. Only the global environment stays in existence throughout the SAS job. During its execution, any macro can "see" any variable in its own local environment, any variable in a more "outer" environment, and any variable in the global environment. It cannot "see" any variable in a more "inner" environment. And again: if the same variable name exists in more than one environment, the "nearest" one is used.

An Illustration

The foregoing discussion may have left you confused, so to "bring it home" let's turn you and your friends from Figure 20.4 into a bit of SAS source code. The SAS job log is shown in Listing 20.1. JOE is a global variable, and exists throughout the course of the job. Macro SHOW1 contains a call to macro SHOW2, which in turn calls SHOW3. The program itself contains a single invocation, to SHOW1.*

When SHOW1 begins to execute and reaches %LET, its local variable JANE exists. This macro can "see" JANE, and also JOE, but no other variables. When SHOW2 reaches its %LETs, ALICE and YOU come into being, and four variables can be "seen" for the duration of SHOW2. SHOW3 is brought in, and for a time there are five variables in existence. When SHOW3 completes, BILL goes away, and so on.

---

*The log gives the results of the macro (%PUTs) before the invocation, as expected, but I do not know why the %LET statement before the invocation is so peculiarly printed in the midst of the %PUT results. This also happened on the next listing. "Unresolved reference" warnings were deleted, for clarity, from this and the next listing.

```
1     %MACRO SHOW1;
2     %******************** S H O W 1, 2, ... ****************;
3     %*    ILLUSTRATES REFERENCE ENVIRONMENTS            ;
4     %*     BY CALLING SUBSIDIARY MACROS, EACH OF WHICH   ;
5     %*     MAY CREATE AND DISPLAY VARIABLES.             ;
6     %*********************************************************;
7     %PUT SHOW1 NOW EXECUTING;
8     %LET JANE=PRESENT!;
9     %PUT JOE:&JOE JANE:&JANE YOU:&YOU ALICE:&ALICE BILL:&BILL;
10    %SHOW2
11    %PUT JOE:&JOE JANE:&JANE YOU:&YOU ALICE:&ALICE BILL:&BILL;
12    %PUT SHOW1 FINISHED;
13    %MEND SHOW1;
14    %MACRO SHOW2;
15    %PUT SHOW2  NOW EXECUTING;
16    %LET ALICE=PRESENT!;
17    %LET YOU=PRESENT!;
18    %PUT JOE:&JOE JANE:&JANE YOU:&YOU ALICE:&ALICE BILL:&BILL;
19    %SHOW3
20    %PUT JOE:&JOE JANE:&JANE YOU:&YOU ALICE:&ALICE BILL:&BILL;
21    %PUT SHOW2 FINISHED;
22    %MEND SHOW2;
23    %MACRO SHOW3;
24    %PUT SHOW3 NOW EXECUTING;
25    %LET BILL=PRESENT!;
26    %PUT JOE:&JOE JANE:&JANE YOU:&YOU ALICE:&ALICE BILL:&BILL;
27    %PUT SHOW3 FINISHED;
28    %MEND SHOW3;
29    %SHOW1
SHOW1 NOW EXECUTING
WARNING: Apparent symbolic reference JOE not resolved.
WARNING: Apparent symbolic reference YOU not resolved.
WARNING: Apparent symbolic reference ALICE not resolved.
WARNING: Apparent symbolic reference BILL not resolved.
JOE:&JOE JANE:PRESENT! YOU:&YOU ALICE:&ALICE BILL:&BILL
SHOW2  NOW EXECUTING
WARNING: Apparent symbolic reference JOE not resolved.
WARNING: Apparent symbolic reference BILL not resolved.
JOE:&JOE JANE:PRESENT! YOU:PRESENT! ALICE:PRESENT! BILL:&BILL
SHOW3 NOW EXECUTING
WARNING: Apparent symbolic reference JOE not resolved.
JOE:&JOE JANE:PRESENT! YOU:PRESENT! ALICE:PRESENT! BILL:PRESENT!
SHOW3 FINISHED
WARNING: Apparent symbolic reference JOE not resolved.
WARNING: Apparent symbolic reference BILL not resolved.
JOE:&JOE JANE:PRESENT! YOU:PRESENT! ALICE:PRESENT! BILL:&BILL
SHOW2 FINISHED
WARNING: Apparent symbolic reference JOE not resolved.
WARNING: Apparent symbolic reference YOU not resolved.
WARNING: Apparent symbolic reference ALICE not resolved.
WARNING: Apparent symbolic reference BILL not resolved.
JOE:&JOE JANE:PRESENT! YOU:&YOU ALICE:&ALICE BILL:&BILL
SHOW1 FINISHED
```

Listing 20.1. Macro Variable reference environments

The effects of the %GLOBAL and %LOCAL statements are shown in Listing 20.2. You can see that JOE does not come into existence until the %GLOBAL statement in SHOWIT2. SHOWIT3 contains a %LOCAL statement, creating an entirely different JOE in its local environment; its %PUT statement reveals that it is this local JOE who shows up until after SHOWIT3 is complete, at which point SHOWIT2 and SHOWIT1 still "see" the global JOE.

AUTOMATIC "SYSTEM" MACRO VARIABLES

The macro preprocessor provides a number of automatic variables. These symbols are always available, and are treated as part of the global environment. The names of SAS System automatic macro variables begin with the letters SYS (for SYStem, we suppose); avoid naming your own variables with this prefix. The values of some can be changed by your program, but others cannot; all can be read and used by your program. Table 20.1 gives the names and content of several useful system variables.

MACRO QUOTING AND QUOTING FUNCTIONS

Macro Quoting: In General

To pass a string of characters unencumbered by SAS System attempts at translation, you encase the characters in quotes. This becomes what is called a character literal. The macro preprocessor also has ways to pass a string of characters through without the preprocessor attempting to translate them. This is not done with quote marks, however, but with several macro functions that exist precisely for this purpose.

Macro quoting is a difficult subject. The rules of quoting are consistent, but idiosyncratic. Each function has its own rules, and when you combine them, it may be difficult to follow what's going on, and when. Study carefully, and experiment.

Macro Language or Text?

Items that may require macro quoting are those that might either be part of a macro statement or part of intended text. Take the semicolon, for example. Suppose you want to place the string

```
PROC PRINT; VAR X;
```

in a macro variable. You couldn't very well write

```
30
31    %MACRO SHOWIT1;
32    %******************** S H O W I T 1. 2. ... ************;
33    %*    ILLUSTRATES REFERENCE ENVIRONMENTS          :
34    %*    BY CALLING SUBSIDIARY MACROS, EACH OF WHICH   :
35    %*    MAY CREATE AND DISPLAY VARIABLES.            :
36    %**********************************************************;
37    %PUT SHOWIT1 NOW EXECUTING;
38    %LET JANE=PRESENT!;
39    %PUT JOE:&JOE JANE:&JANE YOU:&YOU ALICE:&ALICE BILL:&BILL;
40    %SHOWIT2
41    %PUT JOE:&JOE JANE:&JANE YOU:&YOU ALICE:&ALICE BILL:&BILL;
42    %PUT SHOWIT1 FINISHED;
43    %MEND SHOWIT1;
44    %MACRO SHOWIT2;
45    %PUT SHOWIT2 NOW EXECUTING;
46    %LET ALICE=PRESENT!;
47    %LET YOU=PRESENT!;
48    %GLOBAL JOE;
49    %LET JOE=GLOBAL!;
50    %PUT JOE:&JOE JANE:&JANE YOU:&YOU ALICE:&ALICE BILL:&BILL;
51    %SHOWIT3
52    %PUT JOE:&JOE JANE:&JANE YOU:&YOU ALICE:&ALICE BILL:&BILL;
53    %PUT SHOWIT2 FINISHED;
54    %MEND SHOWIT2;
55    %MACRO SHOWIT3;
56    %PUT SHOWIT3 NOW EXECUTING;
57    %LET BILL=PRESENT!;
58    %LOCAL JOE;
59    %LET JOE=LOCAL!;
60    %PUT JOE:&JOE JANE:&JANE YOU:&YOU ALICE:&ALICE BILL:&BILL;
61    %PUT SHOWIT3 FINISHED;
62    %MEND SHOWIT3;
63    %SHOWIT1
SHOWIT1 NOW EXECUTING
WARNING: Apparent symbolic reference JOE not resolved.
WARNING: Apparent symbolic reference YOU not resolved.
WARNING: Apparent symbolic reference ALICE not resolved.
WARNING: Apparent symbolic reference BILL not resolved.
JOE:&JOE JANE:PRESENT! YOU:&YOU ALICE:&ALICE BILL:&BILL
SHOWIT2 NOW EXECUTING
WARNING: Apparent symbolic reference BILL not resolved.
JOE:GLOBAL! JANE:PRESENT! YOU:PRESENT! ALICE:PRESENT! BILL:&BILL
SHOWIT3 NOW EXECUTING
JOE:LOCAL! JANE:PRESENT! YOU:PRESENT! ALICE:PRESENT! BILL:PRESENT!
SHOWIT3 FINISHED
WARNING: Apparent symbolic reference BILL not resolved.
JOE:GLOBAL! JANE:PRESENT! YOU:PRESENT! ALICE:PRESENT! BILL:&BILL
SHOWIT2 FINISHED
WARNING: Apparent symbolic reference YOU not resolved.
WARNING: Apparent symbolic reference ALICE not resolved.
WARNING: Apparent symbolic reference BILL not resolved.
JOE:GLOBAL! JANE:PRESENT! YOU:&YOU ALICE:&ALICE BILL:&BILL
SHOWIT1 FINISHED
```

Listing 20.2. %GLOBAL and %LOCAL statements

TABLE 20.1. SELECTED SYSTEM MACRO VARIABLES

Variable	W[a]	Contains	Example
SYSDATE		Current date in DATE6. or DATE7. format	If today is June 16, 1989 then &SYSDATE=16JUN89
SYSDAY		Current day of week	If today is Friday, then &SYSDAY=FRIDAY
SYSTIME		Current time, HH:MM	If it is 2:45 PM, then &SYSTIME=14:45
SYSLAST	Y	Most recently-created SAS dataset as libname.dsname	MYLIB.MYDATA
SYSLIBRC	Y	Return code from last LIBNAME statement; if non-zero, then LIBNAME did not execute correctly	
SYSERR		The return code from a SAS procedure. If nonzero, then a user interrupt, warning, or error occurred	
SYSPBUFF	Y	The only system variable local to the macro invoking it, exists only if PARMBUFF option coded on MACRO statement, contains the parameter string, including any parentheses or commas.	If %MACRO IT(A,B)/PARMBUFF; then subsequent invocation %IT(ONE,TWO) yields &PARMBUFF=(ONE,TWO)

[a]W: If you can write to as well as read this variable, a Y shows in this column. If no Y appears, a program can access but cannot change the variable.

```
%LET MVAR=PROC PRINT; VAR X;;
```

or MVAR would have the value "PROC PRINT" because the *first* semicolon would be taken as the end of the %LET statement, not as part of a string ("VAR X;;" would pass through as regular SAS code).

What's Wrong With Quote Marks? In a SAS program without macros, there is nothing that requires quotation marks. That is to say, no SAS statement makes use of quote marks for its syntax. It was therefore easy for the designers of the SAS System to make a rule that when quote marks appear, they are meant to bind character literals, and that if a real quote mark is needed, one just must code two in a row.

In the macro facility, however, each character is as important as any other. The Macro Language exists precisely to allow users to represent one set of code with another set of code. The preprocessor cannot judge that you really don't mean a quote mark when you write one, or that you really mean a single one when you write two. Thus, you could write the statement

```
%LET MVAR='PROC PRINT; VAR X;';
```

and achieve a result, but the result would be that MVAR would contain

```
'PROC PRINT; VAR X;'
```

and not

```
PROC PRINT; VAR X;
```

as intended. The quotes on the right side of the %LET assignment do serve to prevent the the inner semicolons from being tokenized, but when the assignment actually takes place the entire string, including the quotes, is taken for the value of the symbol.

What Do Macro Quoting Functions Accomplish?

The term "remove the significance" of a token is sometimes used to describe what macro quoting does. In regular SAS quoting, the quote marks remove the significance of tokens between them, i.e., the text of a literal is but one undifferentiated token and is not syntactically interpreted. Analogously, the macro quoting functions remove the significance from code that could otherwise be construed as part of the Macro Language. Besides semicolons and quote marks, troublesome items can include the macro preprocessor triggers & and % themselves, and the evaluation operators (including their mnemonic forms such as EQ, LE, OR, etc.). Quoting functions can ensure that the code is treated as constant text, not as a macro statement or part thereof, and they do this without using quote marks. Several different functions are provided in order that even the most peculiar situations may be correctly handled.

Compile-Time and Runtime Quoting

As described in Chapter 19, most macro function terms are stored directly as text within the compiled macro, because most macro functions are meant to operate at runtime, i.e., at macro invocation. Macro quoting functions are no exception: Most of them are intended to handle the state of affairs that exists when the macro is actually invoked.

Two of the macro quoting functions, however, are designed to be applied as the macro is being prepared, i.e., at macro compile-time. It is said in SAS circles that you should use a compile-time function when you can see what you are quoting, and a runtime function when you cannot see what you are quoting. You can "see" the code you are writing in a macro definition; you cannot "see" what the result of a particular symbol resolution or macro call will be when the macro executes.

Compile-Time Quoting

Two functions are used for compile-time quoting: %STR and %NRSTR. These were the first of the macro quoting functions to be invented when the macro facility was first developed, and remain the most important ones for general macro use.

The %STR Function

Problem: Resolve the PROC PRINT situation illustrated earlier.
Solution:

```
%LET MVAR=%STR(PROC PRINT; VAR X;);
```

Here, the %STR function is used to remove the significance of the semicolons as far as the preprocessor is concerned. The preprocessor looks at the string

```
PROC PRINT; VAR X;
```

as a single entity, to be assigned to MVAR. The same result could be achieved in this case by coding

```
%LET MVAR=PROC PRINT%STR(;) VAR X%STR(;);
```

or

```
%LET MVAR=PROC PRINT%STR(; VAR X;);
```

because quoting functions only change characters that they are designed for. In this example, only the semicolon is a candidate for quoting, and whether we enquote with %STR the whole phrase or only parts with semicolons makes no difference: the nonsemicolon text is stored identically in any case.

%STR is also used to remove the significance from operators which otherwise would be taken as a sign for automatic expression evaluation in an explicit or implicit %EVAL function. For example, the statement

```
%IF &X=&P+&Q %THEN [something];
```

tests an expression, $\&X = \&P + \&Q$. Normally, an expression such as this would be used when the values of X, P, and Q are all integers and you want to test that the value of &X is equal to the sum of the values of &P and &Q. But perhaps you mean to see if the value of the variable X is actually the literal string formed by placing a plus sign between the values of &P and &Q. To explain the difference, first,

```
%LET X=5; %LET P=2; %LET Q=3;
```

In this case, the %IF expression is true. But

```
%LET X=%STR(2+3);
```

and the expression is *not* true, because the character value "2+3" is not the same as the sum of "2" and "3". The statement

```
%IF %STR(&X)=%STR(&P+&Q) %THEN [something];
```

causes the plus sign not to be taken as an operator, but as another character, on both sides of the equation, and with X being "2+3", P being "2", and Q being "3", the expression evaluates true.

You could *not* use

```
%IF %STR(&X)=%STR(&P)+%STR(&Q) %THEN [something];
```

in this case. Again, the question is: Would the quoting function act upon this bit of text, or would it leave it alone? %STR quotes operators (including mnemonic operators), and therefore placing an operator inside %STR is not the same as placing it outside. For the same reason, you could not use

```
%IF %STR(&X=&P+&Q) %THEN [something];
```

because placing the equal sign comparison operator within %STR is different from placing it outside. Were you to try this variation, you would in fact get an error: the preprocessor would find no comparison operator, because the "=" is quoted, and therefore no comparison to be evaluated.

Using %STR to Preserve Blanks. %STR not only quotes semicolons and operators, but also may embrace leading blanks that otherwise would be ignored:

```
%MACRO DEMO(A,B);
%PUT                                    &A;
%PUT                                       &B;
%PUT %STR(                                    &A);
%PUT %STR(                                       &B);
%MEND DEMO;
%DEMO(HELLO,THERE);
```

results in the SAS log receiving

```
HELLO
THERE

                              HELLO
                                 THERE
```

With the first two %PUT statements, SAS assumes that the user is just exercising the right to use as many spaces as desired to enter source code. In the next two %PUT statements, the ambiguity disappears: It is clear that the blanks are meant as part of the value by the way %STR is specified.

The %NRSTR Function

As you know, the macro preprocessor, upon resolving a macro or symbol reference, sends the resulting code back through the system so that any resulting macro tokens can also be intercepted. "Rescanning" refers to the way the macro preprocessor passes again and again through a piece of code until all ampersands and percent signs have been disposed of. Carefully planned rescanning can help in the processing of macro variable references, as seen earlier in this chapter.

Several of the quoting functions have "NR" counterparts, standing for "no rescan." %NRSTR is the no-rescan counterpart of the %STR function. It differs from %STR in that it quotes ampersands and percent signs, allowing them to pass literally through and become part of the macro variable or SAS code that the function is producing, as in

```
%LET SPONSOR=%NRSTR(M&M CANDIES);
```

%STR looks for and resolves macro and macro variable references in its argument, %NRSTR doesn't.

Quoting "Problem" Characters

Suppose you wish to pass a character literal containing a single (i.e., unmatched) quotation mark, such as

```
LUIGI'S PIZZA PALACE
```

You cannot write

```
%LET VAR=LUIGI'S PIZZA PALACE;
```

because the single quote will be interpreted as the beginning of a literal, and the job will fail in error because the apparent quotation is never closed. And as it happens, neither

```
%STR(LUIGI'S PIZZA PALACE);
```

nor

```
%NRSTR(LUIGI'S PIZZA PALACE);
```

will solve the problem: the quote mark is still taken as such, and the job will fail. The problem is illustrated in Listing 20.3.

The SAS System does provide a way out of this: What you need to do is *quote the quote*, which is accomplished in this circumstance by placing a percent sign immediately before it. Inside a %STR or %NRSTR function, a percent sign immediately followed by a single or a double quote removes the meaning of the quote mark as the beginning of a literal. In other words, code

```
%STR(LUIGI%'S PIZZA PALACE)
```

to solve the present problem. Immediately upon the preprocessor's encountering this character combination within a %STR argument, the quote mark is changed to something that *looks like* a quote mark, but is not taken to be one by the SAS wordscanner. The "%" will not be printed, but an apostrophe will. As you need to quote single unmatched quotemarks (single or double) so you may need to quote unmatched parentheses, which you do also with a percent sign:

```
64     %MACRO APPOSTS;
65     DATA A;
66     LENGTH PROMO $ 40;
67     PROMO="ONLY THE BEST AT &PLACE!";
68     RUN;
69     PROC PRINT; RUN;
70     %MEND APPOSTS;
71     *** INVOKE WITH TWO APOSTROPHES, THEY REMAIN;;
72     %LET PLACE=LUIGI''S PIZZA PALACE;
73     %APPOSTS
```

NOTE: The data set WORK.A has 1 observations and 1 variables.
NOTE: The DATA statement used 1.14 seconds.

NOTE: The PROCEDURE PRINT used 0.39 seconds.

```
74     *** INVOKE WITH TWO APOSTROPHES IN %STR, THEY STILL REMAIN;;
75     %LET PLACE=%STR(LUIGI''S PIZZA PALACE);
76     %APPOSTS
```

NOTE: The data set WORK.A has 1 observations and 1 variables.
NOTE: The DATA statement used 0.16 seconds.

NOTE: The PROCEDURE PRINT used 0.05 seconds.

```
77     *** INVOKE WITH ONE APOSTROPHE IN %STR, BIG MESS;;
78     %LET PLACE=%STR(LUIGI'S PIZZA PALACE);
79     %APPOSTS
```
WARNING: The current word or quoted string has become more than 200
         characters long. You may have unbalanced quotation marks.
```
80     *** AS YOU CAN SEE, THIS CREATES A BIG PROBLEM.  THE LITERAL
81     DOES NOT END (OR SO IT APPEARS TO THE %STR FUNCTION).
82     THE PROBLEM IS THE SAME AS IT WOULD BE IN REGULAR
83     SAS CODE
84     IF QUOTE MARKS DO NOT BALANCE OUT;
```

    <<< SAS JOB OUTPUT FOLLOWS; "The SAS System" is the default SAS page title >>>

                            The SAS System

              OBS   PROMO

           1   ONLY THE BEST AT LUIGI''S PIZZA PALACE!

    <<< 2nd OUTPUT PAGE >>>

                            The SAS System

              OBS   PROMO

           1   ONLY THE BEST AT LUIGI''S PIZZA PALACE!

Listing 20.3. Failure to depict a single quote mark

```
%PUT %STR(PARENTHESES: ());
```

writes

```
PARENTHESES: ()
```

because the parentheses are "closed," matched within the function's parentheses. But to write

```
REVERSED PARENTHESES: )(
```

code

```
%PUT %STR(REVERSED PARENTHESES: %)%();
```

for, clearly,

```
%PUT %STR(REVERSED PARENTHESES: )();
```

is certainly an error.

In the same way, you can quote the macro triggers themselves. Both are quoted with a prefixed percent sign:

```
%LET AMPER=%STR(%&VAR YIELDS THE VALUE OF "VAR");
%LET MACR=%STR(%%MACR CALLS FOR THE MACRO "MACR");
%PUT &AMPER; %PUT &MACR;
```

results in

```
&VAR YIELDS THE VALUE OF "VAR"
%MACR CALLS FOR THE MACRO "MACR"
```

Runtime Quoting

The quoting functions described below all work at runtime, that is, as the macro is executed, not when it is compiled. The function terms are stored as text when the macro is compiled and perform their work when it is invoked.

%QUOTE

The %QUOTE function is the runtime equivalent of %STR. It removes the meaning from the semicolon and from arithmetic and logical operators, which otherwise might cause subtle havoc. Suppose you want a state abbreviation in a comparison:

```
%IF STATE=&STATE %THEN %DO;
```

What if the state were Oregon? The resolved statement

```
%IF STATE=OR %THEN %DO;
```

will cause the macro to fail, because "OR" is the name of an operator. But using %QUOTE, as follows:

```
%IF STATE=%QUOTE(&STATE) %THEN %DO;
```

if the value of &STATE contains any operators, including the mnemonic (alphabetic) operators, they will not be syntactically interpreted by the preprocessor, but allowed to pass literally. Another situation is illustrated in Listing 20.4, which shows what can happen when an innocent-looking variable list is misinterpreted by the macro preprocessor as an attempted implicit evaluation.

Unmatched parentheses, quote marks, or macro triggers can be quoted inside a %QUOTE function using the percent sign, the same as in the %STR function.

%BQUOTE

The %BQUOTE (Blind Quote) function can be used when an unmatched quotation mark or parenthesis may be part of the resolved value of a macro expression. %BQUOTE will quote these special characters, much as if they arrived preceded by a percent sign in a %STR or %QUOTE function.

%NRQUOTE and %NRBQUOTE

These functions allow a single attempt at resolution of macro triggers within the resolved values of their arguments. They are not analogous to %NRSTR, because macro and macro variable resolution will be attempted on their arguments. After the function is completed, however, the result is quoted. Therefore, for example, if a reference cannot be resolved the function will issue a warning message, but its result can be used by another macro statement without another attempt at resolution. If this seems confusing, don't worry; these functions are used only rarely in Macro Language programming.

%SUPERQ

%SUPERQ takes as its argument the name of a macro variable (without an ampersand), returning its apparent value without any attempt to resolve any operators, macro triggers, or quote marks within it.

Unquoting

Items quoted by macro functions are automatically unquoted when they emerge into open code, i.e., when the tokens cross the boundary from macro processing back to regular SAS code. Consequently, the SAS user seldom needs to restore the

```
1    %MACRO VPROC(PROC,VLIST);
2    %*********************** V P R O C ****************************;
3    %*   SIMPLEMINDED MACRO TO RUN A PROC  WITH A VARIABLE LIST   ;
4    %*   DOES NOT CARE IF AN ABBREVIATED VARIABLE LIST IS GIVEN   ;
5    %**************************************************************;
6    PROC &PROC;
7    %IF %QUOTE(&VLIST) NE %THEN %STR(VAR &VLIST;);
8    RUN;
9    %MEND VPROC;
10   %MACRO VPOOF(PROC,VLIST);
11   %*********************** V P O O F ****************************;
12   %*   SIMPLEMINDED MACRO TO RUN A PROC  WITH A VARIABLE LIST   ;
13   %*   BLOWS UP IF AN ABBREVIATED VARIABLE LIST IS GIVEN        ;
14   %**************************************************************;
15   PROC &PROC;
16   %IF &VLIST NE %THEN %STR(VAR &VLIST;);
17   RUN;
18   %MEND VPOOF;
19   OPTIONS MPRINT;
20   DATA DUMB;
21   ARRAY X {*} X1-X10;
22   DO I=1 TO 10; X{I}=42; END;
23   RUN;

NOTE: The data set WORK.DUMB has 1 observations and 11 variables.
NOTE: The DATA statement used 1.14 seconds.


24   %VPROC(PRINT,X1 X2 X3)
MPRINT(VPROC):   PROC PRINT;
MPRINT(VPROC):   VAR X1 X2 X3;
MPRINT(VPROC):   RUN;

NOTE: The PROCEDURE PRINT used 0.48 seconds.


25   %VPOOF(PRINT,X1 X2 X3)
MPRINT(VPOOF):   PROC PRINT;
MPRINT(VPOOF):   VAR X1 X2 X3;
MPRINT(VPOOF):   RUN;

NOTE: The PROCEDURE PRINT used 0.17 seconds.


26   %VPROC(PRINT,X1-X10)
MPRINT(VPROC):   PROC PRINT;
MPRINT(VPROC):   VAR X1-X10;
MPRINT(VPROC):   RUN;

NOTE: The PROCEDURE PRINT used 0.16 seconds.


27   %VPOOF(PRINT,X1-X10)
MPRINT(VPOOF):   PROC PRINT;
ERROR: A character operand was found in the %EVAL function or %IF condition
       where a numeric operand is required. The condition was: &VLIST NE
ERROR: The macro will stop executing.
```

Listing 20.4. Failing to %QUOTE when necessary

```
1     %MACRO EEVAL;  %*MACRO TO EVALUATE EXPRESSIONS;
2     %ITER: %PUT PLEASE ENTER YOUR INTEGER EXPRESSION;
3     %INPUT;
4     %LET EXP=%QUOTE(&SYSBUFFR);
5     %IF &EXP EQ %THEN %GOTO %ITER;
6     %PUT &EXP = %EVAL(%UNQUOTE(&EXP));
7     %MEND;
8     %EEVAL
PLEASE ENTER YOUR INTEGER EXPRESSION
1+2+3-4 = 2
```

<<< NOTE ABOVE: "1+2+3-4" WAS ENTERED; " =2" WAS PROVIDED BY SAS >>>

Listing 20.5. Using %UNQUOTE to enable a desired %EVAL

apparent meaning of any tokens that may have been changed to quoted form by macro functions. But there are some cases where the user must explicitly cause unquoting, and for this the %UNQUOTE function was invented. %UNQUOTE immediately undoes the quoting caused by any macro function.

One case in which an explicit %UNQUOTE is required is when a quoted result must later be used in unquoted form within the same macro. In this case, the automatic unquoting done when text passes through to open code has not yet taken place. Listing 20.5 provides an illustration. Macro EEVAL first determines if the user has entered something in response to %INPUT; if not, he or she is prompted again. The %QUOTE prevents the implicit %EVAL of the %IF statement from blowing up. But if the user has indeed entered something,* another %EVAL is to be performed; the string must first be unquoted so its special characters have their usual significance.

INFORMATION EXCHANGE WITH THE DATA STEP

One can actually communicate from one DATA step to another, or from a DATA step to another part of the SAS System, with the symbol table the intermediary. SAS Version 5.15 (and later subversions) handles this with two CALL routines (SYMPUT and EXECUTE) and two special functions (SYMGET and RESOLVE). All are executed from the DATA step. SYMPUT and SYMGET are described in *SAS Basics*, the other two in later documentation.

The SYMPUT Routine

By far, the most useful of the four routines is SYMPUT. A call to SYMPUT has the form

---

*The string 1+2+3−4 was entered for this example.

```
CALL SYMPUT(arg1,arg2);
```

where "arg1" is either a literal string (enclosed in quotes), a character variable, or a character expression. The string, or the value of the variable or of the expression, must be a valid macro variable name. "arg2" may be a literal string (enclosed in quotes), a numeric or character variable, or a numeric or character expression.

SYMPUT places the value of arg2 into the macro variable named by arg1; if that variable does not yet exist in the symbol table, SYMPUT creates it. The reference environment used by SYMPUT is that local environment that exists when the DATA step executes (i.e., at RUN;), provided the environment is not empty at the time; if it is empty, then the nearest outer environment is used, which in most circumstances will be the global environment. (If a macro that contains a call to SYMPUT also contains all the macro variable references to the variable written by SYMPUT, then the difference is moot.)

One manner in which SYMPUT may be used is illustrated in Listing 20.6.* The problem is to split an input dataset into two or three groups, depending on either the median or the interquartile range. Then statistics could be run on the separate groups. The result is achieved by running PROC UNIVARIATE, placing in UNIVARIATE's output dataset (it will have one member, since no BY variable was used) either the median, or the first and third quartile cutoffs. Next, SYMPUT is used in a DATA _NULL_ step to place the appropriate value(s) into macro variable(s); in this case, the macro variable is named the same as the DATA step variable, though this is not at all necessary. Note the quotes around the macro variable name, because SYMPUT is being given the name as a literal. Finally, a DATA step creates the temporary datasets of interest. PROC PRINT illustrates one of them; in a real application, of course, other steps would follow the invocation of this macro. Study the listing until you are sure you understand it.

Another example of SYMPUT is given in Listing 20.7, which shows a macro that makes a SAS format out of a SAS dataset (based on an idea from the SAS Institute macro course). You might wish to use this macro in your own work, in those cases where PROC FORMAT with CNTLIN= is not practical.

Look carefully at the SYMPUT calls. The macro variable name is made up of a concatenation of the constant FMT with the value of a macro variable I, which is created in an iterative %DO. "arg2" is a little messy, especially where the character formats are concerned, because of the way double quotes have been used in both a concatenation within SYMPUT and in the text stored in the macro variables; two double quotes resolve to one, etc. Later, &I is used with a delayed variable reference to get the values back out.

---

*A failsafe way to include internal documentation is also shown in the listing: The condition "%IF 0" is always false; hence, everything in the %DO group following it is passed over by the preprocessor.

```
1    %MACRO SPLIT(DSN,VAR,GROUPS=2);
2    %IF 0 %THEN %DO; %*** DOCUMENTATION ***;
3    ***************************************************************
4    SPLIT A DATASET INTO TWO OR THREE GROUPS FOR PURPOSES OF
5    STATISTICAL ANALYSES.  IF &GROUPS=2, THEN THERE ARE
6    TWO DATASETS CREATED, ONE WITH SUBJECTS BELOW THE MEDIAN
7    AND ONE WITH SUBJECTS AT OR ABOVE THE MEDIAN OF A CRITERION
8    VARIABLE, &VAR.  IF &GROUPS=3, THEN THERE ARE THREE GROUPS,
9    LOWER QUARTILE, MIDDLE 2 QUARTILES, UPPER QUARTILE.
10   OTHER VALUES OF &GROUPS ARE INVALID
11   DATASETS ARE NAMED "LOW" AND "HIGH" (GROUPS=2)
12   OR "LOW", "MID", AND "HIGH" (GROUPS=3)
13   THIS VERSION CREATES ONLY TEMPORARY ANALYSIS DATASETS
14
15   ***************************************************************
16   %END;  %*** END DOCUMENTATION ***;
17   %IF &VAR= OR &DSN= %THEN %DO;
18   %PUT CANNOT HAVE A BLANK VALUE FOR VAR OR FOR DSN!;
19   %GOTO EXIT;
20   %END;
21   %IF &GROUPS NE 2 AND &GROUPS NE 3 %THEN %DO;
22   %PUT VALUE OF GROUPS MUST BE EITHER 2 OR 3!;
23   %GOTO EXIT;
24   %END;
25   PROC UNIVARIATE NOPRINT DATA=&DSN;
26   VAR &VAR;
27   OUTPUT OUT=___TEMP
28   %IF &GROUPS=2 %THEN MEDIAN=M;
29   %ELSE   Q1=Q1 Q3=Q3;
30   ;
31   RUN;
32   DATA _NULL_; SET ___TEMP;
33   %IF &GROUPS=2 %THEN CALL SYMPUT('M',M) %STR(;);
34   %ELSE %DO;
35   CALL SYMPUT('Q1',Q1);
36   CALL SYMPUT('Q3',Q3);
37   %END;
38   RUN;
39   %IF &GROUPS=2 %THEN %DO;
40   DATA LOW; SET &DSN;
41   IF &VAR < &M;
42   RUN;
43   DATA HIGH; SET &DSN;
44   IF &VAR >= &M;
45   RUN;
46   %END;
47   %ELSE %DO;
48   DATA LOW; SET &DSN;
```

Listing 20.6. A macro illustrating CALL SYMPUT

Continued

```
49    IF &VAR < &Q1;
50    RUN;
51    DATA MID; SET &DSN;
52    IF &Q1<= &VAR < &Q3;
53    RUN;
54    DATA HIGH; SET &DSN;
55    IF &VAR >= &Q3;
56    RUN;
57    %END;
58    %EXIT: %*DO NOTHING;
59    %MEND SPLIT;
60    DATA TESTSPLT;
61    DO I=1 TO 20;
62    OUTPUT;
63    END;
64    RUN;
```

NOTE: The data set WORK.TESTSPLT has 20 observations and 1 variables.
NOTE: The DATA statement used 1.2 seconds.


```
65    %SPLIT(TESTSPLT,I)
```

NOTE: The data set WORK.___TEMP has 1 observations and 1 variables.
NOTE: The PROCEDURE UNIVARIATE used 0.6 seconds.

NOTE: Numeric values have been converted to character
      values at the places given by: (Line):(Column).
      65:18
NOTE: The DATA statement used 0.28 seconds.

NOTE: The data set WORK.LOW has 10 observations and 1 variables.
NOTE: The DATA statement used 0.17 seconds.

NOTE: The data set WORK.HIGH has 10 observations and 1 variables.
NOTE: The DATA statement used 0.38 seconds.


```
66    PROC PRINT DATA=LOW; TITLE 'LOW, GROUPS=2 (default)'; RUN;
```

NOTE: The PROCEDURE PRINT used 0.44 seconds.

Listing 20.6. *Continued*

```
67   %SPLIT(TESTSPLT,I,GROUPS=3)

NOTE: The data set WORK.___TEMP has 1 observations and 2 variables.
NOTE: The PROCEDURE UNIVARIATE used 0.22 seconds.


NOTE: Numeric values have been converted to character
      values at the places given by: (Line):(Column).
      67:19   67:41
NOTE: The DATA statement used 0.22 seconds.


NOTE: The data set WORK.LOW has 5 observations and 1 variables.
NOTE: The DATA statement used 0.22 seconds.


NOTE: The data set WORK.MID has 10 observations and 1 variables.
NOTE: The DATA statement used 0.2 seconds.


NOTE: The data set WORK.HIGH has 5 observations and 1 variables.
NOTE: The DATA statement used 0.22 seconds.


68   PROC PRINT DATA=LOW; TITLE 'LOW, GROUPS=3'; RUN;

NOTE: The PROCEDURE PRINT used 0.11 seconds.


69   * Just to show what happens with an invalid GROUPS value: ;
70   %SPLIT(TESTSPLT,I,GROUPS=7)
VALUE OF GROUPS MUST BE EITHER 2 OR 3!
```

Listing 20.6. *Continued*

By using iterative %DO groups in the manner shown, this macro can handle any reasonable number of observations in the input dataset. Listing 20.8 shows the macro in action.

The SYMGET Function

In the examples just given, it was possible to retrieve the values created by SYMPUT with macro variable references. Macro SPLIT made use of constant macro variable names (M, Q1, Q3); macro MAKEFMT used a systematically ordered series of names, FMT1, FMT2, FMT3, etc., made the subject of a delayed reference (&&FMT&I). If instead the names of values are not known in advance,

```
<<< SAS JOB OUTPUT FOLLOWS >>>
```

LOW, GROUPS=2 (default)

OBS	I
1	1
2	2
3	3
4	4
5	5
6	6
7	7
8	8
9	9
10	10

LOW, GROUPS=3

OBS	I
1	1
2	2
3	3
4	4
5	5

Listing 20.6. *Continued*

or do not follow so regular a formula, but can only be known at DATA step execution time, then one cannot use a simple macro reference. This occurs, for example, if the macro variable names are stored as values in a SAS dataset or an external file. Consider the macro definition

```
%MACRO SUBSTVAL(DSOUT,INFILE,A=,B=,C=,D=,E=);
%*********************S U B S T V A L************;
%*    SUBSTITUTE CHARACTER VALUES IN A DATASET    ;
%*************************************************;
DATA &DSOUT;
  INFILE &INFILE;
  INPUT MACNAME $ @@;
  LENGTH CVAL $20;
  CVAL=SYMGET(MACNAME);
RUN;
%MEND;
```

Now let the external file with fileref ABSTRACT contain the records

```
%MACRO MAKEFMT(NAME=,DD=,FROM=,VALUE=,LABEL=,OTHER=);
%IF 0 %THEN %DO; %*** DOCUMENTATION ***;
**********************************************************************
*  MACRO MAKEFMT : CREATE A SAS FORMAT FROM A SAS DATA FILE          *
EXAMPLE FOR NUMERIC FORMAT:
'    %MAKEFMT(NAME=FMTNAME,FROM=DSN,VALUE=VAR,LABEL=CHARVAR,OTHER=BAD) '
EXAMPLE FOR CHARACTER FORMAT:
'    %MAKEFMT(NAME=$ANYFMT,FROM=DS,VALUE=V1,LABEL=V2,DD=SASLIB)        '
  WHERE
      NAME    = FORMAT NAME
      FROM    = INPUT SAS DATASET NAME
      VALUE   = VARIABLE GIVING RAW VALUES TO BE FORMATTED
      LABEL   = VARIABLE GIVING FORMAT LABELS TO BE ASSOCIATED WITH VALUES
      DD      = OUTPUT SAS FORMAT LIBRARY DD (OPTIONAL)
      OTHER   = LABEL FOR "OTHER" VALUES (OPTIONAL)
REQUIRED: NAME, FROM, VALUE, LABEL.
NOTE!: 'VALUE/LABEL CHARACTERS &,",%, AND ' WILL BE CHANGED TO BLANKS!
**********************************************************************
%END; %*** END DOCUMENTATION ***;
%PUT %STR(Macro MAKEFMT: From MASTERING THE SAS SYSTEM by Jay A. Jaffe);
%IF %SUBSTR(&NAME,1,1)=%STR($) %THEN %LET TYPE=$;
%ELSE %LET TYPE=%STR();
DATA _NULL_;
  SET &FROM END=LASTREC;
  CI=LEFT(PUT(_N_,5.));
  &LABEL=TRANSLATE(&LABEL,'    ','"''%&');
%IF &TYPE=%STR($) %THEN
  %DO;
    &VALUE=TRANSLATE(&VALUE,'    ','"''%&');
    CALL SYMPUT('FMT'|| CI,""""||&VALUE||"""" = """||&LABEL||"""");
  %END;
%ELSE
    CALL SYMPUT('FMT'|| CI,&VALUE||" = """||&LABEL||"""") %STR(;);
    IF LASTREC THEN CALL SYMPUT('ENTRIES',LEFT(PUT(_N_,5.)));
  RUN;
 %IF &DD=%STR() %THEN
  PROC FORMAT %STR(;);
 %ELSE
  PROC FORMAT DDNAME=&DD %STR(;);
   VALUE &NAME
 %DO I=1 %TO &ENTRIES;
   &&FMT&I
 %END;
 %IF &OTHER NE %STR() %THEN
   OTHER = "&OTHER" ;
  ;
  RUN;
%PUT %STR(Done! Thank you for using macro MAKEFMT!);
%MEND MAKEFMT;
```

Listing 20.7. A macro that writes a PROC FORMAT step

```
177   DATA TEST;
178   INPUT ITEM FORMAT $;
179   LIST;
180   CARDS;

RULE:----+----1----+----2----+----3----+----4----+----5----+----6----+----7---
181   18 PEASE
182   19 PORRIDGE
183   29 HOT
184   30 PEASE
185   38 PORRIDGE
186   90 COLD
NOTE: The data set WORK.TEST has 6 observations and 2 variables.
NOTE: The DATA statement used 0.17 seconds.


187   RUN;
188   OPTIONS MPRINT;
189   %MAKEFMT(FROM=TEST,NAME=NEWFORM,VALUE=ITEM,LABEL=FORMAT,OTHER=????)
Macro MAKEFMT: From MASTERING THE SAS SYSTEM by Jay A. Jaffe
MPRINT(MAKEFMT):    DATA _NULL_;
MPRINT(MAKEFMT):    SET TEST END=LASTREC;
MPRINT(MAKEFMT):    CI=LEFT(PUT(_N_,5.));
MPRINT(MAKEFMT):    FORMAT=TRANSLATE(FORMAT,' ','"''%&');
MPRINT(MAKEFMT):    CALL SYMPUT('FMT'|| CI,ITEM||" = """||FORMAT||"""") ;
MPRINT(MAKEFMT):    IF LASTREC THEN CALL SYMPUT('ENTRIES',LEFT(PUT(_N_,5.)));
MPRINT(MAKEFMT):    RUN;

NOTE: Numeric values have been converted to character
      values at the places given by: (Line):(Column).
      189:1
NOTE: The DATA statement used 0.16 seconds.


MPRINT(MAKEFMT):    PROC FORMAT ;
MPRINT(MAKEFMT):    VALUE NEWFORM 18 = "PEASE    " 19 = "PORRIDGE" 29 = "HOT
 " 30 = "PEASE    " 38 = "PORRIDGE" 90 = "COLD     " OTHER = "????" ;
WARNING: Format NEWFORM is already on the library.
NOTE: Format NEWFORM has been output.
MPRINT(MAKEFMT):    RUN;

NOTE: The PROCEDURE FORMAT used 0.44 seconds.


Done! Thank you for using macro MAKEFMT!
190   DATA TESTIT;
191     INPUT NUMBER @@ ;
192     LIST;
193     CARDS;
```

Listing 20.8. The %MAKEFMT macro illustrated

Continued

```
RULE:----+----1----+----2----+----3----+----4----+----5----+----6----+----7---
194  1 2 18 19 30 59 69 90 100
NOTE: SAS went to a new line when INPUT statement reached past the end of a
      line.
NOTE: The data set WORK.TESTIT has 9 observations and 1 variables.
NOTE: The DATA statement used 0.38 seconds.

195  RUN;
196  PROC PRINT;
197    FORMAT NUMBER NEWFORM.;
198    TITLE 'Our New Format is Illustrated';
199  RUN;

NOTE: The PROCEDURE PRINT used 0.22 seconds.


     <<< SAS JOB OUTPUT FOLLOWS >>>

              Our New Format is Illustrated

              OBS      NUMBER

               1       ????
               2       ????
               3       PEASE
               4       PORRIDGE
               5       PEASE
               6       ????
               7       ????
               8       COLD
               9       ????
```

Listing 20.8. *Continued*

```
A B B B A C D D E
E D C C C B B E
```

The call

```
%SUBSTVAL(SASDS,ABSTRACT,A=FIRST,
          B=SECOND,D=FOURTH,C=THIRD)
```

then produces the dataset whose PRINTed output is shown in Listing 20.9. One might use a similar program to create, for example, a list of teams in an amateur sports league, where the order of playoffs remains the same but the specific teams change from season to season.

```
Dataset SASDS, created by %SUBSTVAL based on data file ABSTRACT

          OBS     MACNAME      CVAL

           1        A         FIRST
           2        B         SECOND
           3        B         SECOND
           4        B         SECOND
           5        A         FIRST
           6        C         THIRD
           7        D         FOURTH
           8        D         FOURTH
           9        E
          10        E
          11        D         FOURTH
          12        C         THIRD
          13        C         THIRD
          14        C         THIRD
          15        B         SECOND
          16        B         SECOND
          17        E
```

Listing 20.9. Output from SYMGET( ) function example

SYMGET is not part of the Macro Language, but a DATA Step function; syntactically, it can be used whenever a SAS function term can normally be used. Its argument must be a macro variable name in quotes, a SAS character variable whose value is a macro variable name (as in our example), or a character expression that resolves to a macro variable name. If the argument does not resolve to a macro variable name that exists in any active reference environment, the function will complain of an illegal argument and return a missing value. (In our example, this did not happen: &E was null, not nonexistent.) The length of the returned value of SYMGET, unless you specify otherwise, is the maximum character variable length of 200. Therefore, it is usually wise to supply a new LENGTH statement before assigning a variable using SYMGET, stating the maximum reasonable length expected.

The RESOLVE Function

RESOLVE, like SYMGET, is a DATA Step function. It returns a character value (of length 200 unless shortened). But where SYMGET expects the name of an existing macro variable as its argument, RESOLVE expects its argument to be, more generally, any macro expression: either a literal macro expression (in which case it must be enclosed in quotes), a SAS character variable whose value is a macro expression, or a character expression that resolves to a macro expression. RESOLVE thus differs from SYMGET in the wider variety of arguments it can accept.

RESOLVE also differs from SYMGET in that if a macro reference cannot be resolved, it will be passed through literally, as the macro preprocessor would. That is to say,

```
%LET X=HELLO;
DATA; Y=RESOLVE('&X'); RUN;
```

gives Y a value of HELLO, but if the %LET statement were not present and X not defined, Y would have the literal value &X.

RESOLVE also differs in this important way from SYMGET: If a macro variable value itself contains a macro variable reference, RESOLVE will resolve the reference, but SYMGET will not:

```
%LET X=%STR(HI &THERE);
%LET THERE=BUDDY;
DATA; LENGTH SYMGOT RESOLVED $10;
  SYMGOT=SYMGET('X');
  RESOLVED=RESOLVE('&X');
RUN;
```

yields a dataset with SYMGOT='HI &THERE ' and RESOLVED='HI BUDDY '.

The EXECUTE Routine

A DATA Step CALL routine, EXECUTE takes a single argument representing a macro expression. The same rules apply to the argument as they do to the argument of the RESOLVE function: it must be a macro expression enclosed in quotes, a SAS character variable whose value is a macro expression, or a character expression that resolves to a macro expression. But while the result of RESOLVE is a character string, the result of CALL EXECUTE is submission of SAS code for execution. If the argument resolves to a macro invocation, then the macro is executed immediately, wherever in the calling DATA step one might be. If, however, this macro execution results in the generation of executable SAS statements, or if the argument to EXECUTE otherwise resolves to executable SAS statements, these execute *after* the calling DATA step is completed.

EXECUTE can have a variety of uses. One application is when you may or may not wish to execute a piece of SAS code, or a macro, but cannot know what to do until a data value is retrieved. Consider Listing 20.10. Macro PRTINVAL prints the invalid records only if there were any invalid records in the first place.

You should always be sure to end a DATA step that uses CALL EXECUTE with a RUN statement.

```
1    %MACRO PRTINVAL;
2    %*** USED WITH MACRO MAKEDS ***;
3    PROC PRINT DATA=____NVLD;
4    TITLE "INVALID DATA, CAN'T ADD TO &OUT, RUN OF &SYSDATE";
5    RUN;
6    %MEND;
7    %MACRO MAKEDS(OUT,IN,VAR,LO,HI);
8    %IF 0 %THEN %DO; %*** DOCUMENTATION ***;
9    ******************************************************
10   MAKE A DATASET FROM ANOTHER, SELECTING
11   VARIABLES ON THE BASIS OF LOW AND HIGH CUTOFFS
12   PRINT CONTROL LISTING OF OBSERVATIONS WITH
13   VARIABLES THAT FAIL CUTOFFS.
14     5 REQUIRED POSITIONAL PARAMETERS:
15       OUTPUT DATASET NAME
16       INPUT DATASET NAME
17       VARIABLE NAME (MUST BE NUMERIC)
18       LOW CUTOFF  (MUST RESOLVE TO NUMBER)
19       HIGH CUTOFF (DITTO)
20   MACRO PRTINVAL MUST ALREADY BE COMPILED
21   ******************************************************
22   %END; %*** END DOCUMENTATION;
23   DATA &OUT ____NVLD;
24   %* WE USE A BIZARRE NAME FOR THE CONSTANT DATASET, THAT
25   NO ONE WOULD CHOOSE FOR THEIR OUTPUT DATASET;
26   SET &IN END=LAST;
27   RETAIN ____NVLD 0;
28   DROP ____NVLD;
29   IF &LO<=&VAR<=&HI THEN OUTPUT &OUT;
30   ELSE DO;
31   ____NVLD=1;
32   OUTPUT ____NVLD;
33   END;
34   IF LAST AND ____NVLD THEN CALL EXECUTE('%PRTINVAL');
35   ELSE IF LAST THEN PUT "ALL OK FOR &OUT ON &SYSDATE";
36   RUN;
37   %MEND;
38   DATA TEST; DO I=1 TO 10; OUTPUT; END; RUN;
```

NOTE: The data set WORK.TEST has 10 observations and 1 variables.
NOTE: The DATA statement used 1.1 seconds.

```
39   %MAKEDS(TEST1,TEST,I,1,10)
```

Listing 20.10. CALL EXECUTE illustrated

Continued

```
ALL OK FOR TEST1 ON 17JAN93
NOTE: The data set WORK.TEST1 has 10 observations and 1 variables.
NOTE: The data set WORK.____NVLD has 0 observations and 1 variables.
NOTE: The DATA statement used 0.44 seconds.


40    %MAKEDS(TEST2,TEST,I,3,7)

NOTE: The data set WORK.TEST2 has 5 observations and 1 variables.
NOTE: The data set WORK.____NVLD has 5 observations and 1 variables.
NOTE: The DATA statement used 0.38 seconds.


NOTE: CALL EXECUTE generated line.
1   +PROC PRINT DATA=____NVLD; TITLE "INVALID DATA, CAN'T ADD TO TEST2, RUN
OF 17JAN93"; RUN;

NOTE: The PROCEDURE PRINT used 0.44 seconds.


   <<< SAS JOB OUTPUT FOLLOWS >>>

            INVALID DATA, CAN'T ADD TO TEST2, RUN OF 17JAN93

                   OBS        I

                    1         1
                    2         2
                    3         8
                    4         9
                    5        10
```

Listing 20.10. *Continued*

part VI

USING THE SAS SYSTEM

21

Base SAS Features

Many software systems contain service features designed to make using the software on the whole easier, faster, or better in some way. Certainly, the SAS System is no exception, and the Base SAS software is as rich in service features as it is in its languages and procedures. In this chapter, I describe some of the more important services the Base SAS software offers for your advantage.*

We begin with an overview of some the more generally useful SAS system options, including those that help control the appearance of printed output, that determine the contents of the SAS log, or that help you handle error conditions in the ways you think best. We then look at how you can configure the SAS System—to set up your jobs and sessions so they start off right.

We continue with a look at some of the ways you might choose to store your datasets for maximum effectiveness, and the tradeoffs associated with these decisions. In this regard we consider DATA Step views, compressed data files, and indexed datasets.

Finally, we look at how you can precompile and store executable code for DATA Step programs and for SAS macros, and how precompilation can save computer time for repetitively-run applications.

---

*To keep within the scope of the book as a whole, which does not attempt to train you in the Display Manager System, I reluctantly refrain from discussing any of the DMS-related features and options.

SAS SYSTEM OPTIONS

There are processing options that appear within certain SAS statements and whose effects have limited scope, and there are those that have a broader effect on processing of the job as a whole. These latter might be called global options, because they affect the SAS program from their point of specification forward across steps, but the proper SAS jargon is *system options*.

The user can specify SAS system options with an OPTIONS statement, which consists simply of its name OPTIONS followed by one or more valid option specifications of the user's choice. OPTIONS is a global statement that may appear almost anywhere in your program source code. System options may also be set at SAS invocation, by a parameter passed with job control or in a configuration file as we discuss later in this chapter. Some system options can *only* be specified at invocation, and cannot be re-set with an OPTIONS statement.

Some options can be specified both on OPTIONS and on other SAS statements (usually, as dataset options). In these cases, the effect is that the options specified on other statements temporarily override the system option in effect, for the purpose of that particular job step.

Several SAS options have been discussed elsewhere throughout this book. Of the many other SAS system options, some of the more generally useful are noted below. You would do well to browse the SAS documentation, especially the *SAS Language Guide* and the *SAS Companion* for your operating system, to become aware of other system options that might help you in your work.

Options for the SAS Log

You can suppress the printing of source code with the **NOSOURCE** option, and the printing of %INCLUDEd source with **NOSOURCE2**. The latter is useful if a standard, unchanging segment of code is to be included in many programs and you don't want to clutter the log. The former can be used for programs that run on a regular basis without change, for which the log is needed only for historical documentation and not for primary documentation or for debugging.

NONOTES can be used to suppress messages that begin with "NOTE:". Warnings and errors are not affected. However, "NOTE:" messages contain important information about SAS dataset creation and it is not recommended that you routinely withhold them from view.

The **FULLSTIMER** (or **FULLSTATS**) option controls whether certain processing statistics, such as CPU or I/O resources (specifics are operating-system dependent), are printed in SAS log notes.*

---

*The **STIMER** option helps control whether these statistics are collected by the system; it takes some computer resource overhead to maintain the performance statistics and in some cases, such as when DATA Step views are executed, performance can be severely downgraded unless NOSTIMER is used.

The **LOG**= and **ALTLOG**= system options, which may be specified only in a system invocation or in a configuration file, allow you to specify an alternative destination (file or output device; the values allowed depend on your operating system) for the SAS log, or for an additional (alternative) copy of the log. If LOG= is not specified, the SAS log goes to its standard output destination; if ALTLOG= is not specified, no copy of the log is made.

Options for Printable Output

LINESIZE= and **PAGESIZE**=, which may be abbreviated LS= and PS=, respectively, determine how many characters per line and how many lines per page will be used for the log and standard print output. Normal computer-paper-sized output takes a default line size of 132 and a page size of 60. Most listings in this book were run with LS=79, which enabled me to prepare them in 8 1/2-inch draft. The numbers include only the printable portion; hence a 66-line physical page can get about three lines top and bottom for border when PS=60 is used.*

CENTER insists that print output be centered on the page; this is the default. If NOCENTER is specified as a system option, then output lines are left-justified. (Spacing within lines is preserved, so NOCENTER does not harm columnar procedure output.) **OVP** specifies whether overprinting will be allowed. SAS error messages stand out because they are overprinted, for example, and certain plot and custom output requires it. NOOVP is useful if your printer does not support overprinting, or if you will be examining the log online (overprint becomes three identical lines on your terminal screen).

DATE causes the date and time of job execution to appear in the first title line of each output page, at the right-hand side; NODATE suppresses this behavior. **NUMBER** causes the sequential page number to appear in printable output, also to the right of the first title line; NONUMBER suppresses the page number. Normally, SAS keeps a running page counter so that the page number increments continually throughout the job, even if more than one DATA or PROC step produces printable output. The **PAGENO**= option can be used to set or reset the page number so (for example) output from separate procedures can be separately numbered; the value specified with PAGENO= should be an integer constant.

Some procedures, such as PROC PRINT, print the BY variable information in separator lines above the BY group, if the procedure was called with a BY statement. The **NOBYLINE** option can be used to suppress this, and also causes a page eject between BY groups. It is often used in conjunction with TITLE statements that specify #BYVAR, #BYVAL, or #BYLINE.

As you know, the system numeric missing value normally prints as a period. You can alter the character used to indicate numeric missing values with the

---

*The bottom of the page is ejected by a formfeed, handled by the printer hardware. The top of the physical page can be set manually by positioning the top of form a few inches below the physical paper perforation. The SAS system option SKIP= can be used to have SAS skip a number of lines at the top of each page.

MISSING= option. Specify a single character, within single quotes. A popular character is the blank:

```
OPTIONS MISSING=' ';
```

makes some output look nicer.

FORMCHAR= specifies the box/border characters used by procedures such as FREQ, TABULATE, PLOT, and CHART. This option takes a special syntax:

```
OPTIONS FORMCHAR(printdevice)='characters';
```

To have FORMCHAR= apply to the standard output device, use STANDARD as the "printdevice." FORMCHAR= is useful primarily for printers that do not have certain characters. For example, if the vertical bar is not present, it cannot be used to compose a vertical separator; perhaps an exclamation point will have to be used instead. FORMCHAR= is also useful to achieve special effects: Specifying all blanks can sometimes produce cleaner FREQ or TABULATE output. Consult your SAS manuals if you are thinking of altering the default FORMCHAR= option.

The **PRINT**= and **ALTPRINT**= system options, which may be specified only in a system invocation or in a configuration file, allow you to specify an alternative destination (file or output device; the values allowed depend on your operating system) for the SAS standard print output (i.e., where PROC and FILE PRINT output goes), or for an additional (alternative) copy of this output. These options are directly analogous to LOG= and ALTLOG=. If PRINT= is not specified, the SAS log goes to its standard output destination; if ALTPRINT= is not specified, no copy of the print file is made.

Source Code Preprocessing

Though we did not do so in this book, it is possible to use lowercase characters in data lines read with INPUT or in character literals enclosed in quotes. Other input to the SAS System (source code not in quotes, for example) is automatically converted to uppercase. If you set the **CAPS** option on, *all* input, including data lines and literals, have their lowercase letters changed to uppercase.

The **CHARCODE** option is for those whose terminals do not have the vertical bar, underscore, or brackets. These symbols may be substituted with a two-character sequence if CHARCODE is toggled on. The first character is a question mark. The substitutions allowed are: ?- (hyphen) for the underscore, ?/ for the vertical bar, ?(and ?) for the brackets. In addition, the logical "not" sign can be represented with ?=.

Source code input to the SAS System, at least on IBM systems, must come in records with a fixed length of 80 columns ("card image"). If columns 73–80 of the first source record contain numerals, SAS assumes that the entire file is sequence-numbered and ignores these columns. Under some circumstances, data can be lost at the end of lines if CARDS is used (if the system believes numerals at the right are line numbers when in fact they are not). Under other circumstances, if only part of an input file is numbered, an "Error: Statement Not Valid" can occur as the system tries to interpret a line number as part of a SAS statement. The options **S**= and **S2**= allow you to specify explicitly just how lengthy the logical input lines are. For example, specifying S=72 says, "I don't care what is in columns 73–80, ignore them" and avoids the syntax error. S=80 can then be used before CARDS if needed. S2 is for %INCLUDEd files.

Related is the **CARDIMAGE** option, which asserts that source and instream data are in fact to be treated as if they were arriving on 80-column "cards"; with CARDIMAGE in effect, tokens can be split between lines, but literals spanning more than one line may be expanded as if they continued to the end of each line before the last. If NOCARDIMAGE is in effect, then the last nonblank is taken as the last character in the physical line and literals split between lines are not expanded; but tokens may not be split between lines. CARDIMAGE normally gives better results when used with IBM mainframe systems, NOCARDIMAGE with other systems.

Limiting Observations Processed

The SAS dataset options OBS= and FIRSTOBS= have system option analogues. **OBS**= specifies the last observation to be processed in SAS datasets and **FIRST-OBS**= the first observation. Dataset options override the system options, and in the case of OBS= and FIRSTOBS=, the dataset options should be used to avoid problems. It is easy to set the system option OBS= to some small value to print a test sample of a new dataset, then forget to turn it back to OBS=MAX (which is how to specify that all dataset observations should be processed) and go on to create other datasets—each of which then has only a handful of observations. If you use an OPTIONS statement with FIRSTOBS= or OBS=, *all* subsequent INFILE, SET, MERGE, and UPDATE statements in the program are affected unless the options are reset or overriden with dataset options.

OBS= is most useful as a system option in the case OBS=0, which is used to test SAS syntax before submitting a program. As you know, the compiler may do this for you upon finding an error in your program. With OBS=0 you can eliminate the syntax errors before your "real" job and delete the OPTIONS statement after debugging.

Options for Error Handling

INVALIDDATA–'character' is used to assign a missing value to a variable when an INPUT value cannot be interpreted; see Chapter 8. By default, the system missing value (.) is assigned, but with INVALIDDATA= you can specify the underscore or a single letter A–Z to indicate that "missing due to invalid data" be given a special missing value.

ERRORS= specifies the number of observations for which complete error messages will be printed if a runtime problem causes a data error. Default is ERRORS=20. These error messages can be quite lengthy, since the program data vector is printed with all variables named. Other compiler actions, such as setting problem variables missing, still take place regardless of the ERRORS= value.

The option **NODSNFERR** can be useful in certain circumstances. It causes the normal "Dataset Not Found" error not to occur. Most installations generally have the DSNFERR option set on, and if you attempt to SET or MERGE a dataset that does not exist, the step terminates with this error. Under NODSNFERR, the step proceeds, acting as if the null dataset _NULL_ had instead been specified. When a _NULL_ dataset is passed for input to a SET, MERGE, UPDATE, or MODIFY statement, the **NOVNFERR** option may be set in order that this not generate "variable not found" errors, only warnings.

NOFMTERR can be used to continue processing a step even if a requested SAS format cannot be found. For example, trying to print a variable with a certain user-defined format, but not having that format available (either by an earlier PROC FORMAT or in a format library), generally causes an error. Under NOFM-TERR, processing continues with a default format (usually, w. or $w.).

The options **DKRICOND**= and **DKROCOND**= control the action the system takes when it discovers various irregularities (such as a program reference to a nonexistent variable) during the processing of input and output datasets, respectively. Valid values for the options are the literals ERROR, WARN, and NOWARN. DKRxCOND=ERROR causes the system to treat the occurrence as an error, setting the error flag and producing an error note on the SAS log. WARN does not set the error flag, but produces a warning note on the SAS log. NOWARN allows the occurrence to pass without even producing a warning.

Options Affecting the Macro Facility

The MACRO option, which can only be specified at SAS System invocation or configuration, determines whether the macro preprocessor will be available to your job at all. Specifying NOMACRO may save a little memory; however any attempt to use macro variables, macro calls, or macro statements will cause an error since the SAS System will not be able to recognize them.

The **IMPLMAC** and **CMDMAC** options control, respectively, whether statement-style and command-style macro invocations will be understood by the system. You can save processing time by using NOIMPLMAC and (in your display manager sessions) NOCMDMAC, if they are not needed.

Two options, **MERROR** and **SERROR**, determine whether the macro facility will issue warnings when it looks for a macro or a macro variable, respectively, but cannot find one. These options are usually on by default, and I suggest leaving them that way. They generally indicate programmer intervention is needed.

Other options concerning the macro facility include MPRINT, SYMBOLGEN, and MLOGIC, described in Chapter 19, and several options that have to do with "autocall" or with precompiled macros. These options will be discussed in context, later in this chapter.

Information Transfer from the Host Environment

It is possible to pass information from the SAS invocation itself to the SAS job. This may be done either by using the automatic macro variable &SYSPARM, or the DATA Step function SYSPARM( ). The value of &SYSPARM, and equivalently the value returned by SYSPARM( ), is set by using the SAS system option of the same name, SYSPARM=. An OPTIONS statement can set it:

```
OPTIONS SYSPARM='VALUE';
```

but it finds more practical use when set as an option upon SAS invocation, e.g., under OS/MVS Batch:

```
// EXEC SAS,OPTIONS='SYSPARM=''''ABC'''''
```

(the extra quotes are needed because the value of SYSPARM is single-quoted within an options string that must itself be single-quoted). In this example, the value of the macro variable SYSPARM, and also the value returned by the DATA Step function SYSPARM( ), is the literal 'ABC'.

SAS System Options: Determining Installation Defaults

Each SAS System option has a default value. To find out what the defaults are at your installation, you can code

```
PROC OPTIONS; RUN;
```

which prints a complete listing. PROC OPTIONS lists the SAS system options in effect at the time it executes; therefore to examine the defaults, execute it before setting any of the system options yourself. OPTIONS output is written to the SAS log. Along with each option setting is printed a one-line description of the option, and the resulting listing can take more than a page; if you wish, you can use the SHORT option on the PROC statement and the settings of the options will be given in rows, without descriptions, taking up only a few lines. In either case, the list will be divided into three parts: "session options" that could in principle be reset with an OPTIONS statement, "configuration options" that can be set only at invocation or in a configuration file (configuration files will be discussed shortly below), and "host options", that are specific to the operating system under which the SAS program or session is running. Options in the first two categories are available on all host systems supporting the version of the SAS System you are running; options in the host category may include some that are and some that are not re-settable with an OPTIONS statement.

If you like, you can use the SAS system option VERBOSE, specified at invocation or in a configuration file, to briefly list the settings of the SAS system options at the beginning of the SAS log. Only the invocation and configuration options will be listed.

CONFIGURING THE SAS SYSTEM

The SAS System provides several mechanisms that you can use to make your program or session go more smoothly right from the start. These include the ability to pass options to the system at invocation or in configuration files, to automatically call in a standard sequence of source code before going on to your program proper, to provide "autocall" macro definitions, and to specify catalog search sequences for permanent user-defined formats.

The rational and general methods used to accomplish each of these purposes is described below; you should consult the *SAS Companion* for your operating system to determine exactly how to implement them.

Passing Options at Invocation and by Configuration

You can pass one or more system options to the SAS System when it is invoked, that is to say, when the SAS supervisor is called as an executable application. The methods used to pass options at invocation will vary depending on your operating system. For example, under MVS batch you may pass an enquoted string of valid SAS options as an OPTIONS= parameter on the EXEC statement; a string of options can likewise be passed in an OPTIONS( ) parameter to the TSO SAS CLIST. One interesting invocation option is INITSTMT=, which passes one or more SAS statements to execute before the source file (but after any AUTOEXEC= file; see below) is read.

The number of parameters that may be passed by OPTIONS= is subject to operating system constraints, such as the length of the options specification string. But you can bundle any number of system options together in what is called a *configuration file*, and pass them as a group on invocation. The option CONFIG= (which, of course and unlike other invocation options, can be specified only by OPTIONS= and not in a configuration file) allocates the file reference. The configuration file itself is nothing more than a standard, editable operating system file that contains system option specifications. If some SAS System defaults displease you, you can develop a configuration file of overriding options, and specify only the CONFIG= option on invocation. You can, naturally, build separate configuration files for batch and for interactive work, or for whatever reason you might want easy access to multiple configurations. Under some operating systems, both a system-wide default and a user-specified configuration file can both be used, such that the user can override selected installation defaults while leaving others intact.

Autoexec Files

SAS code can be placed in a standard, editable file called an *autoexec file*. Then if an AUTOEXEC= option is used to allocate the file reference, these statements will be the very first executed, before both INITSTMT= code (if any) and the source input.* Like configuration files, multiple autoexec files can be kept to help you easily bring up different SAS System initializations.

Autocall Macros

While you can always %INCLUDE macro source code within your program, you need not do so explicitly if you take advantage of the macro "autocall" feature. If the MAUTOSOURCE system option is specified, then when the SAS System encounters a macro call while processing your program and the macro has not been defined in the code prior to the call, the system will search one or more aggregate storage locations for a member corresponding to the macro name. These locations, collectively referred to as the *autocall library*, can be specified as file-names or filerefs with the SASAUTOS= system option (or alternatively, in some cases, by non-SAS means specific to your operating system). The member, when found, should contain the macro source code.

The autocall feature is attractive because you can build libraries of macros that are useful to more than one program. While typically each member of an autocall library will contain a single macro definition, you may wish to store very closely related macros in a single library member, subject to the restriction that the member name must also be the name of one of the macros within the member. If you store more than one macro definition in an autocall member, then that member-name macro must be the first of these macros to be invoked in the calling program, whereupon all the macros within the member will be compiled.

When you use autocall, the MRECALL option comes into play. If MRECALL is in effect, then the autocall library may be searched multiple times in the same job even if a macro name could not be located earlier in the job. If NOMRECALL is specified, only one search is done. MRECALL should be used only in unusual circumstances such as where your job must deallocate and reallocate different autocall libraries for some reason. In most circumstances, NOMRECALL should be used in order to save processing time.

The Base SAS Autocall Library.

Base SAS software is shipped with a small library of macros that will become the default autocall library at most installations; you may wish to concatenate your own autocall library (if you have one) along with the Base SAS library under a common file reference.

Many of the macros found in the Base SAS library behave as if they were Macro Language functions.† These include the following string handlers, the arguments to which may be any macro expression. %**LEFT**(ARG) left-justifies its argument

---

*Another invocation option, SYSIN=, is used to tell the SAS System where to look for the source input file.

†Indeed, the %SUPERQ function in SAS Version 6 did not exist in Version 5, which did, however, have an autocall macro of the same name that provided similar functionality.

by removing leading blanks, and **%TRIM**(ARG) removes trailing blanks. **%CM-PRESS**(ARG) compresses multiple blanks within its argument into a single blank, and removes leading and trailing blanks. Even if ARG was quoted, these functions return an unquoted result. Use %QLEFT, %QTRIM, or %QCMPRESS to get a quoted result. **%VERIFY**(ARG1,ARG2) returns the position of the first character in ARG1 that was not found in ARG2. You may find these and other Base SAS autocall macros worthy of inspection as examples of SAS macro definitions.

Format Catalogs

User-defined formats and informats produced by the FORMAT procedure are stored in SAS catalogs as entry types FORMAT and INFMT (numeric formats/informats), and FORMATC and INFMTC (character formats/informats). The FMT-SEARCH= option specifies a libref or libref.catalog (or a series of these, concatenated in paretheses) that specifies where the formats are to be found; if no catalog name is specified, the catalog FORMATS is sought in the specified library.

Version 5 Formats.

SAS Version 6 can use and create Version 5 user formats (and informats) under those operating systems that supported Version 5. These are stored in external files (under MVS, in load libraries), not in SAS catalogs. The file reference SASLIB (specified in the SASLIB= option at invocation option) is normally used to allocate the Version 5 format library.

DATA STEP VIEWS

It is possible to create SAS dataset views that map to external data files. While PROC SQL views (Chapter 14) ultimately depend on SAS datasets, and SAS/Access views on specific database structures, input data views are not constrained to any particular form of data, so long as that data can be treated as logical records that could be read, in principle, by an INPUT statement.

To create and store a DATA Step view, the DATA step is coded as usual, but with the DATA statement option VIEW= (after a forward slash), i.e.,

```
DATA dsname / VIEW=libref.viewname;
  program code
RUN;
```

Note the RUN statement, which should be used to end a view definition. The program will be compiled, but not execute. Instead, a view definition based on program specifications will be stored in the referenced SAS library (or if none, the WORK library) as the type VIEW member "viewname".

Input DATA Step views may be based on SAS datasets or data views, as well as on external data. That is to say, whether INPUT or SET (or MERGE, etc.) is used to retrieve the data does not matter as far as the view logic is concerned, so long as the files or libraries are appropriately allocated. Thus, you have an alternative to the SQL procedure for creating dataset-based views: you can use the DATA Step Language.

Caution: Source code for a view is *not* saved with the view. If you need the source code (and even if you don't plan to use it again, you may want it for documentation), save it separately. Source code is *not* stored along with your DATA Step view, nor can it be discovered or recovered from the view. Save your source code either in an editable file standard to your operating system, or, if you prefer and if you normally work in the Display Manager environment, you can save it from the DMS Program Window to a catalog of your choosing with the SAVE primary command (it will be stored as type SOURCE; remember that the views themselves are not saved in SAS catalogs, but in library files of type VIEW).

Once you have created an input DATA Step view, you use it as you do any SAS data view, i.e., by referring to it in your source code just as if you were referring to a SAS dataset. The difference is that the data for your view are retrieved "on the fly" from the input data sources described by the view, whether these be in SAS dataset or external file form.

It is not always easy to know whether using a view versus using a dataset will save computer resources, since the data management tasks the SAS System uses with views are so different from those used with datasets. Certainly, permanent storage can be saved if you use an input view, since you do not need to store an additional data file. But it can be more expensive to use a view; not only will the time to interpret the data usually be lengthier (after all, the SAS System is optimized to read SAS datasets directly, without additional realtime translation), but in some cases SAS will actually go ahead and build a kind of temporary dataset anyway, for use until the step is done. If you are considering using views for a production application, run some tests with the STIMER and FULLSTIMER options on, sometimes with views and sometimes with datasets.

COMPRESSED DATA FILES

When a SAS data file is created, whether as an output file from some procedure or as the result of a DATA step, its observations can be stored in "compressed" form. Compressed datasets are so-called because they take up less storage room than noncompressed datasets.

To build a compressed dataset, you simply specify the dataset option COMPRESS=YES. COMPRESS= can also be specified as a SAS System option. As with other options that can be used both as system and as dataset options, the setting of the COMPRESS= dataset option overrides that of the system option with respect to the dataset with which it is associated. In any case, the COMPRESS= option has effect only when the dataset is created, and whether it is compressed or not becomes a permanent characteristic of the dataset. You cannot compress or "un-compress" an existing dataset; you would have to re-build a new dataset, with SET in a DATA step, to alter whether the observations are compressed or not.

Compressing datasets saves storage space; the amount saved will be noted, for your information, on the SAS log. Greater savings are generally found with character variables than with numeric variables. File compression can decrease data access time somewhat, since fewer input/output actions may be needed. However, processing time can be increased both at dataset creation and when the dataset is later used, since it takes computing effort to compress the observations in the first place and then to un-compress them for reading when the dataset is referenced.

Since compressed observations are not of equal length, the SAS System cannot simply calculate a file offset in order to reach a compressed dataset observation directly. You cannot, therefore, use the POINT= option on the SET or MODIFY statements to read a compressed dataset by random access. Furthermore, although they can be used, the FIRSTOBS= (and even the OBS=) dataset options operate more slowly, since the dataset has to be processed observation by observation.

To decide whether to compress a SAS dataset (and it should be obvious that only permanent SAS datasets should ever be compressed), consider both how large the dataset will be and how frequently it will be referenced. Large datasets kept mainly for archival or occasional-use purposes are the best candidates for compression. Depending on the amount of space saved and the relative cost of space and of processing time at your installation, you may wish to compress large datasets even if they are used relatively frequently. If the costs are nontrivial, you should do some testing to determine whether the space saving outweighs the increase in processing time.

INDEXED DATASETS

SAS datasets may be "indexed" by one or more variables. Observations in an indexed dataset can, in some circumstances, be located by the SAS System based on the value(s) of the index variable(s); the index is a system of relations between index variable values and observation location. Both compressed and uncompressed datasets may be indexed. Indexes can make it possible to use BY statements with unsorted input datasets, and can also speed up WHERE processing. The *SAS Language* manual provides a full explanation of when indexes are used by the SAS System (the System, not the user, determines when an index will be used), and what will constitute an appropriate index for a given BY or WHERE process.

A SAS index may be based on one variable, in which case it is called a *simple* index, or on more than one variable, in which case it is called a *composite* index. Indexes have names, but this is simply to enable index creation and deletion; the variable names, not the index name, are used in BY or WHERE statements. In the case of simple indexes, the name should be the same as that of the variable; in the case of composite indexes, the name should not be the same as any variable.

A dataset index need not be created by a DATA step. Indexes can be added to a PROC SQL data view using the SQL procedure CREATE INDEX statement or dropped with DROP INDEX. Indexes can be added to or removed from a SAS dataset with the DATASETS procedure, using the INDEX CREATE and INDEX DELETE statements within a MODIFY statement group.

You can create an index on a SAS dataset in the DATA step, using the INDEX= dataset option used on the DATA statement. Some examples of such DATA statements:

- a simple index for the dataset CUSTOMER based on variable ZIP-CODE:

```
DATA CUSTOMER(INDEX=(ZIPCODE));
```

- two simple indexes:

```
DATA CUSTOMER(INDEX=(ZIPCODE LASTNAME));
```

- one simple and one composite index:

```
DATA COLORS(INDEX=(WARMTH WHEEL=(HUE SATURATN)));
```

In the last example, the indexes created are WARMTH, a variable, and WHEEL, a composite index based on the variables HUE and SATURATN.

It is tempting to go ahead and create dataset indexes if there is some reason to believe certain variables might be used for BY or WHERE processing. But indexes cost computer resources to create and to maintain. Furthermore, it is not always a straightforward matter to determine whether an index will be used for a particular task, or how much computer time will be saved (for some tasks, index use can actually take more time).

Generally speaking, it is good to create indexes for large datasets from which small subsets are often to be selected by WHERE processing, provided the distribution of the index variables is more or less random or uniform. In most other situations, it may not be worthwhile to create an index, and the only way to know if indexing is justified may be to benchmark data extraction on indexed and nonindexed versions of the same logical dataset. In all cases indexes should be created sparingly, and with a known objective for each one.

PRECOMPILATION

Compiling and Storing DATA Language Programs

As we have emphasized before, the course of a SAS program proceeds in steps that are executed one after the other in sequence. A PROC step calls upon the services of a "packaged" executable program, giving the program the information it needs to complete the PROC request according to the user's wishes. A DATA step, on the other hand, contains programming language code that must first be compiled into an executable form before actual execution.

Each DATA compilation costs computer resources, mainly CPU time. Actually, many DATA Step programs are simple and cheap to compile. But some lengthy, complicated programs can be more costly. Prior to SAS Version 6, a DATA Step program had to be compiled immediately prior to each execution. Now, it is possible to compile program code to executable form, store it in a SAS library, and then execute the program at a later time, even in another job. Of course, there are no savings for "one-shot" programs, but for programs that will be run many times, the savings can be substantial. There is little reason not to precompile in these cases. It is not the same as with data views, where the relative costs may be hard to assess: a DATA step program will execute in exactly the same way whether or not it has been precompiled.

To create and store a compiled program, the DATA step is coded with a syntax similar to that used to create an input DATA Step view:

```
DATA dsname / PGM=libref.pgmname;
  program code
RUN;
```

Note the RUN statement used to end the stored program definition. The program will be compiled, but will not immediately execute. Instead, the executable code will be stored in the referenced SAS library (or if none, the WORK library) as the type PGM member "pgmname". And although the PGM= DATA statement option seems similar to the VIEW= option, stored DATA Step programs and input dataset views are very different entities, used for very different purposes.

To execute a stored program, the form of DATA step

```
DATA PGM=libref.pgmname;
  <REDIRECT statement(s)>
RUN;
```

is used. RUN with no operands must end the step. Optional REDIRECT statements can be used to override the names of datasets and external files that had been encoded in the original program source. Redirection allows you the ability to code and compile a generalized program and yet be able to use it on "real" datasets without having to rename them. For example:

```
DATA SOMEDATA / PGM=MYLIB.SP1;
  INFILE X; INPUT X Y Z;
    more statements
RUN;
```

then at execution:

```
LIBNAME GOOD 'MY.REAL.SASOUTPT';
FILENAME X 'MY.INPUT.DATA';
DATA PGM=MYLIB.SP1;
  REDIRECT SOMEDATA=GOOD.OUTDATA;
  REDIRECT X=MY.INFILE;
RUN;
```

You can use SET, MERGE, UPDATE, or MODIFY in your program and redirect input the same way (after using LIBNAME instead of FILENAME, of course), but *Caution:* Although the names may differ, redirected input SAS datasets must correspond in terms of variable type attributes specified in the code, or else you will get errors, which depending on circumstances may cause the step to halt or go ahead and produce an output dataset, but one that is not laid out exactly as you would expect.

Note that although you need not force your datasets to have the same names as those in the stored program, you must know the dataset names used in the stored program in order to code your REDIRECT statement. This brings up another note of caution: As with DATA Step views, you must decisively *save your program source code* if you want ever to refer to it again. Source code is *not* stored along with a compiled program, nor can it be discovered or recovered from the compiled code.

Compiling and Storing SAS Macros

Complex SAS macros can take surprising amounts of CPU time to compile. With SAS Version 6.07, the ability to pre-compile and store SAS macro code was made available. As with compiled DATA Step programs, you would typically do this for code that was meant to be executed more than once. You need to specify the SAS system options MSTORE (to allow you to store compiled macros) and SASM STORE= (to specify a libref that will contain the stored macro catalog; WORK is *not* allowed) in order to store—or to use— compiled macros.

A macro to be compiled and stored is coded in the same way as any other macro, except that the option STORE is placed on the %MACRO statement, after a forward slash, as in

```
%MACRO SAVEME / STORE;
  macro source code
%MEND;
```

Macros compiled with /STORE will be saved to a catalog named SASMACR in the referenced library. You can list the members of this catalog using PROC CATA-LOG or the DMS Catalog Window, but you cannot use these catalog facilities to copy or to rename stored compiled macros, as you can with most other catalog entry types.

To use stored compiled macros, you also must specify MSTORE and SASM STORE=. Then, when the SAS supervisor intercepts an apparent macro call, it will search first the macros already compiled in the current program (if any), then the SASMACR catalog in the SASMSTORE= library,* and finally the autocall library (if MAUTOSOURCE and SASAUTOS= have also been specified), until the named macro is found.

Although the compiled macro facility does not substitute for the autocall facility, it might be profitable to compile and store your autocall libraries, including even the Base SAS standard autocall library. Indeed, the Base SAS autocall library is shipped with a macro COMPSTOR to do this very thing, i.e., to compile and store many of the Base SAS autocall macros. You may wish to examine the code for COMPSTOR and create something similar for use with your own macro libraries.

The same caution applies with regard to stored compiled macros as to stored DATA Step programs or views: *save your source code.* Macro source code is not stored along with the compiled macro nor can it be regenerated from it.

---

*At this writing, only one SASMSTORE= library may be referenced at a time, and the catalog name within it must be SASMACR. We can hope that future releases of the SAS System will implement an option similar to the FMTSEARCH= option to allow different catalog names and, more importantly, concatenated library reference for macro invocations.

22

SAS User Resources

In this final chapter of *Mastering the SAS System*, I wish to address three topics. First, I provide a concise explanation of SAS software documentation, some of which you may want to keep near at hand in order to make full use of the Base SAS Software. Next, I draw your attention to some ways you can get help with or additional information about SAS programming and the SAS System. Finally, I offer capsule descriptions of many of the add-on program products that are available for license, some of which may in fact be licensed and available at your installation.

SAS SOFTWARE DOCUMENTATION

SAS Institute publishes an extensive series of reasonably-priced reference documents covering its software. You will find that most (not all) SAS documentation is published perfect-bound, 8.5x11-inch format. Normally, you will order these from SAS Institute as bookstores generally do not carry them. You can call or write the book sales department at SAS Institute and it will happily send you its current publications catalog. Keep in mind that the publications are described below as they exist now, as I write; who knows but that six months or a year hence, re-arranged or re-styled documentation may be issued for certain products.

General Types of SAS Manuals

It will be helpful if we make a distinction between "primary" and "secondary" documentation: Primary documentation tells you what you must know in order to make full use of a SAS software product (including the Base software), describing all its features. In other words, primary documentation is the reference material for the software. If you are using a SAS product without having available its primary documentation, you operate at a disadvantage. Secondary documentation gives you guidance in the use of a product, assuming you have primary documentation available to look up the details. The term "secondary" does not mean inferior or less important. Good secondary guides can help you learn the ins and outs of a software product and "bring you up to speed" faster than if you have only the primary reference manuals to study. *Mastering the SAS System* can itself be considered a secondary document, designed to support your use of the Base SAS software.

It has been the habit of the SAS Institute to issue manuals with the titles containing the name of the software product followed by one of the phrases "Usage," "Reference," or "Usage and Reference."* When both are brought together, it usually means the total number of pages was small enough to justify printing a single manual to document the product,† and in such cases, the manual will normally be divided into two main Parts (you guessed it: Usage and Reference). **Reference** manuals (or parts) contain primary documentation **Usage** manuals' (or parts') secondary documentation. Documentation for some SAS products do not share this convention. For example, some SAS products have a "User's Guide" that, like "Usage and Reference," contains primary and secondary documentation. SAS/ETS software has a User's Guide, and also an "Applications Guide" which serves as additional secondary documentation. The Base SAS software manuals are also exceptions to the general naming pattern; Base SAS documentation is discussed below.

In any case, virtually all SAS manuals' titles will include the major SAS version number, and (because manuals may be issued in updated editions to cover subversion developments) an edition number. Sometimes, subcomponents of certain products are documented (primary and secondary) under separate cover. (The REPORT procedure in the Base Software is an example we discuss below.) The SAS publications catalog does a good job of laying out the manuals available for each software product under the product's heading, and catalog descriptions will help you get the right manual editions for your SAS software version.

An important class of publication that many SAS users unfortunately ignore is the operating system "Companion," usually entitled *SAS Companion for the [xxx]*

---

*For some products, including the Base SAS software, a smaller, spiral-bound "Syntax" guide is available, providing a handy summary recapitulation of language and procedure elements. The Syntax guides are designed for quick reference by users experienced with the software, and are not meant to replace other manuals.

†In some cases, on the other hand, a manual may be too large to print in one book, and will be issued in more than one volume. In such cases, as in a multi-volume dictionary or encyclopedia, one volume just takes up where the other left off in sequence and all volumes are required. When you order such manuals from SAS Institute, as when you buy your dictionary, this is automatically taken care of: they are bundled and priced together.

Operating System. While the SAS System is designed to be similar between different operating systems, and SAS source code to work under various operating systems, it is also designed to take advantage of (or in some cases, accommodate) the differences between systems. "Companion" manuals provide primary documentation that is to be used along with other, general SAS documentation.

Another important class of publication that many SAS users also unwittingly ignore are the "Changes and Enhancements" manuals. These are usually published as a so-called "Technical Report," with the words "Changes and Enhancements" along with a version/subversion number (such as "Release x.xx") in the title along with the product name, and a unique report number (for example, SAS Technical Report P-229 is *SAS/STAT Software: Changes and Enhancements, Release 6.07*). The reason for these manuals is that it not always practical or cost-effective for SAS Institute to publish an entirely new edition of a manual when a sub-version is released; Changes and Enhancements describe the additional or different features of the new software release. They are primary documentation that should be used along with other reference manuals.*

Documentation for the Base SAS Software

Primary documentation for the Base SAS software is divided into two principal reference manuals. *SAS Language: Reference* fully documents the DATA Step Language (hence the name), as well as the Display Manager system, global SAS features and options, and the nature of SAS files and the SAS approach to data processing. The *SAS Procedures Guide* documents the procedures that belong with the Base software, with the exception of the REPORT procedure and with only an overview of the SQL procedure. The REPORT procedure is well-documented in the *SAS Guide to the REPORT Procedure, Usage and Reference*, while PROC SQL is documented in *SAS Guide to the SQL Procedure: Usage and Reference*. Remember also that the *SAS Companion* for your operating system is an essential part of your Base SAS documentation.

At this writing, these manuals are in early editions and cover SAS release 6.06, now obsolescent. Users of Release 6.07 will want to acquire Technical Report P-222: Changes and Enhancements to the Base SAS Software, as well as the Changes and Enhancements report (if any) for their operating system *Companion*. I should mention that TR P-222 updates not only the two Base SAS reference guides, but also the SQL and REPORT guides. Users of Version 6.08 may wish to acquire TR P-242 (*SAS Software Changes and Enhancements, Release 6.08*) in addition to TR P-222 to fully complete their documentation, although with respect to the Base SAS software 6.08 adds very little over 6.07 and only a small number of pages in the 6.08 report concern the Base software.

---

*Recent versions of the SAS Publications Catalog have been confusing on this matter; catalog copy may state that a manual covers versions 6.06 and 6.07, when the manual in fact covers only 6.06. Usually, however, later in the copy it is revealed that if you want complete documentation through 6.07, you must also order a certain Changes and Enhancements report.

Two general Base SAS usage guides, *SAS Language and Procedures: Usage* and *SAS Language and Procedures: Usage 2*, are available. Advertised as being for beginning and advanced users, respectively, these books do not neatly fall on one or the other side of the line although the topics in the second one are on the whole meant for the more sophisticated user. These task-oriented secondary references exemplify a variety of useful SAS techniques, and for the serious SAS student can be a good enhancement to the material presented in the primary manuals and in *Mastering the SAS System*. Another, brief usage guide, *SAS Programming Tips: A Guide to Efficient SAS Programming*, may be of interest to "power" users who enjoy "tips and tricks" presentations.

There are also several usage guides that concern portions of the Base SAS software. The *SAS Guide to TABULATE Processing* is recommended for those who want to use PROC TABULATE to its fullest. For those wishing to master the SAS Macro Language, the *SAS Guide to Macro Processing* can supplement the material presented in Part V of *Mastering the SAS System*. The edition of the Macro Language guide current at the time of this book's writing (Version 6, 2nd Edition) must be supplemented with information found in TR P-222 (the Changes and Enhancements for the Base SAS software); there were no substantive changes to the TABULATE procedure from Versions 6.06 to 6.07.

SAS Institute Periodicals

SAS Communications

A quarterly magazine, this publication announces new SAS program products, often includes articles about how the SAS System is being used at various sites to particular ends, provides a few technical tips, and generally helps keep you up on what's happening with the SAS System. No level of SAS expertise is assumed of the reader. Write SAS Institute and ask to be placed on the mailing list; at this writing, there is still no cost for this service.

Observations

Also published quarterly, this publication is meant for intermediate/advanced SAS programmers. It provides articles of a technical nature that may help deepen your understanding of particular aspects of SAS data structures or programming methods. I find about one out of every five or so articles to be of interest; because at this writing the volumes have been slim (it has only been in publication since late 1991), that means about one article per issue. *Observations* is not free; contact the SAS Institute's book sales department to subscribe.

SUGI Proceedings

Each year, the SAS User's Group International hosts a several-day convention (the name notwithstanding, conventions thus far all have been held in the United States). Papers presented at these conventions are published in the annual *SUGI Proceedings*, which can be ordered through the SAS Institute's book sales department.

Each volume tends to be more voluminous than the largest SAS manuals, running even to 1,000 or more 8.5x11 pages. Some of the articles are concise tutorials on some new feature of SAS software. Most articles are concerned with some narrow aspect of application, and are often case-studies. Some articles are appropriate for beginners, while others assume considerable SAS programming knowledge.

I usually find about 70% of the articles in the *Proceedings* not worth the bother to skim, but that is only because the titles indicate matter that doesn't interest me. Some of the other articles give me some new bits of information or implementation ideas, and a few are real gems. Your own reactions depend on your areas of interest and level of expertise.

GETTING HELP WITH THE SAS SYSTEM

If no one has yet told you, let me: Each SAS installation site has appointed an individual in its employ to serve as the "SAS Software Consultant." S/he is your official contact point for all SAS problems, and is authorized to contact SAS Institute's technical support division for problems that s/he cannot resolve. Make it your business to find out who is assigned as the SAS Software Consultant at your site.

Sadly, some sites do not assign a SAS Software Consultant who is equal to the task. Some simply assign the role to the same person who serves as the SAS Software Representative, who installs and maintains the SAS System on the computer. This may be a systems programmer qualified to fix problems with the installation, but who does not necessarily know much about SAS software. In mainframe shops especially, where COBOL reigns, the SAS System is often considered but another of many applications packages and the normal procedure is for users to fend for themselves with problems of software use.

The SAS Sample Library

You may not know it, but your SAS installation should have, if not accessible on line at least on tape, a collection of sample programs illustrating SAS applications. You can examine the source code of these programs, then submit them and see what happens. The samples are not really supported by SAS Institute, and some don't work well. Nevertheless, they may help you as you study the various SAS procedures. Ask your SAS Software Consultant how to locate the sample library.

The SAS Usage Notes Database

It is generally best to direct your technical problem questions to your SAS Software Consultant, who is supposed to know how to use the usage notes and who is authorized to call SAS Institute for further assistance. However, advanced users who wish to forge ahead in problem resolution may wish to consult the latest version of the SAS "Usage Notes" themselves. Distributed with each install tape, including maintenance tapes, as an FSP-browsable dataset, Usage Notes describe unresolved problems, outstanding bugs, and other technical advisory notices.

If you wish to peruse this database, ask your SAS Software Consultant about how to access the Usage Notes. There will also be technical report documentation for your version of SAS software that provides a guide to the Usage Notes, as well as to the sample library.

SAS "ADD-ON" PROGRAM PRODUCTS

This book is about the Base SAS software, the heart of the SAS System. But here in this final chapter, I would like to draw your attention to some of the others that might be available in your SAS software environment (ask your SAS Software Consultant), without explaining how they work. By the time you read this, perhaps more products will have been added to the greater SAS System; and, not all the SAS add-ons available even now are included in this discussion.

Of the products that are listed below, SAS/INSIGHT®, SAS/EIS®, and SAS/ LAB® were introduced with Version 6.08 of the SAS System; the others are available under Version 6.07 as well. Nct all products may be available under all operating systems. If you contact the SAS Institute software sales department, they will be more than happy to discuss (and send product literature concerning) any of the available SAS add-on products.

Remember: The Base SAS software is required before these add-on products can be installed. And to use any of them effectively, you must already be familiar with the concepts and techniques of Base SAS data processing.

Statistical Analysis

Several SAS Institute program products deliver procedures that are used for advanced statistical analysis. Among these are SAS/STAT, SAS/ETS, SAS/OR, and SAS/QC. Another product, SAS/IML, provides the ability to perform matrix mathematics at an elementary level (and also offers graphical and dataset-building capabilities based on matrix manipulation). And two products released with Version 6.08, SAS/LAB and SAS/INSIGHT, provide bases for dynamic interactive/ exploratory analysis in an interactive environment.

SAS/STAT® software provides an extensive array of procedures designed for statistical analysis.* There are many procedures for multivariate and regression analysis, analysis of variance, categorical analysis, discriminant analysis, survival

---

*In prior versions of the SAS System, many procedures were included with the Base SAS software, but beginning with Version 6 they are licensed separately in the SAS/STAT product.

analysis, and multidimensional scaling. All procedures are well-documented (the manuals are thick, even compared to most other SAS manuals), with the sophisticated user in mind; options and computational algorithms are explained in detail, and references to technical literature supplement the descriptions.

SAS/ETS® software is used for advanced applications in econometric forecasting and modeling. It contains procedures for handling time-series data, including multivariate as well as univariate time series. There are also procedures that solve and estimate parameters of systems of simultaneous equations, such as occur in investigations of theoretical models in econometrics, finance, and natural science. Both linear and nonlinear models are supported. SAS/ETS also contains a couple of display procedures designed specifically to report financial data.

SAS/OR® software is used for operations research and management of tangible resources. A knowledge of operations research will be very helpful if you want to use the procedures. Project planning, including critical path modeling and optimal resource allocation, are facilitated by the SAS/OR procedures. SAS/OR also contains a display procedure to produce Gantt charts.

SAS/QC® software may also interest project managers; it consists of several statistical and display procedures for quality control, with procedures designed optimally to analyze within-product variations.

SAS/IML® software (the name originally standing for "Interactive Matrix Language") can be used by the mathematically inclined to program special calculations that are not yet available in SAS procedures and are difficult or impossible to achieve with the DATA Step Language. SAS/IML even has direct data creation and manipulation abilities; with it, you can create and manipulate SAS dataset-like structures in a direct manner, bypassing the DATA step, in a way no other SAS facility allows. Such applications are not for beginners, but users sophisticated both in the SAS System and in matrix manipulation may discover ways to save time and resources with IML applications.

SAS/INSIGHT® software is an analytical toolbox that offers a dynamic interactive environment for analyzing data. With it, SAS datasets can be manipulated and their contents displayed in various graphical ways, with or without additional statistical summarization. Meant for users familiar with other "point-and-click" applications, it offers the advantage of having the power of SAS analytic tools behind it.

SAS/LAB® software provides an entry interface to SAS data analysis with features that help guide data analysis and manage data. It may prove attractive especially to those without a strong statistical background, as it is designed to help the user select and prepare appropriate statistical analyses, as well as to help manage SAS data and even to save and organize output.

SAS/Assist®

The SAS/Assist product can be used by SAS beginners to "get into" the SAS System and produce results. Through a series of menus and data-entry screens, SAS/Assist leads the user through defining data to analyzing and presenting it. SAS/Assist takes the responses the user provides and constructs SAS program code from them. Since no generic system can provide enough control over data processing tasks to satisfy all requirements, it is important for the user who wishes to master the SAS System to study SAS data management and programming techniques. However, SAS/Assist can help produce quick results when those are needed, and some application developers might find it efficient in certain cases to start a new project with SAS/Assist and then modify the source code it produces, instead of beginning each program from scratch.

SAS/GRAPH®

SAS/GRAPH is a complete set of tools for producing graphic data displays. SAS/GRAPH was one of the earliest of the add-on products to be released (1980). It has enjoyed great popularity and gone through several major enhancements. SAS/GRAPH has procedures to create displays including several kinds of charts, several kinds of plots, geographic maps, and a number of three-dimensional kinds of displays. A complete annotation facility is available to produce titles and legends that can be overlaid on plots produced by the basic graphic procedures. Once created, graphs can be stored for re-display or re-printing. Data is input to SAS/GRAPH procedures, as to any other procedures, from SAS datasets built for the purpose.

To use SAS/GRAPH, you need access to one of the many different graphics devices supported, which include various graphics-capable terminals, hardcopy plotter and slide devices, and certain printers. SAS/GRAPH can be used for hardcopy without a graphics terminal, but the development/debugging cycle will be torturously drawn out as you work "blind" from hardcopy trials.

Interactive Applications Development

SAS/FSP® software was invented to give developers a way of building applications that take advantage of the capabilities of full-screen interactive sessions. SAS/FSP consists of several procedures: FSVIEW, FSBROWSE, FSEDIT, FSLIST, and FSLETTER.

PROC **FSVIEW** is used to browse a SAS dataset in full-screen mode. Screens of SAS observations can be scrolled left-right and up-down, and when used in end-user applications, screen attributes (e.g., color) can be used to accentuate selected display fields. Like PROC PRINT, data are displayed one observation per line, variables arranged horizontally.

PROC **FSBROWSE** allows you to browse a SAS dataset *observation by observation*. Each screen shows a different observation, with the fields on the screen representing different variables in the observation. You can create screens of your own design, and display data fields within them. A series of commands can be used to search for particular values of variables and otherwise move about within the dataset in systematic fashion.

PROC **FSEDIT** is the same as PROC FSBROWSE, except there are commands to add and delete observations, and values of variables may be changed and saved. PROC FSEDIT will be preferred over PROC EDITOR by most users who undertake direct interactive dataset editing.

PROC **FSLIST** is used to browse *external* files, such as an OS dataset. Because most operating systems with datasets browsable by FSLIST have their own ways of displaying data, FSLIST is useful mainly as a convenience for users who need to take a quick look at an external file without having to terminate and then reinvoke a SAS session.

PROC **FSLETTER** is designed for the special purpose of producing, cataloging, altering, and "merge-printing" form letters. Designers of SAS-intensive business systems may wish to use FSLETTER instead of wordprocessing systems for repetitive correspondence. PROC FSLETTER may also be applied to "personalized" text in other contexts, such as questionnaires and individualized reports, where the data are SAS-based.

SAS/AF® software provides the BUILD procedure, which enables a developer to create menu-driven interactive applications, AF applications can be built that access other SAS System resources, as well as provide help screens and tutorial sequences. Application end-users see a series of menus and related screens. Behind the scenes, the AF programmer may have created an application of great power or sophistication, using various SAS System resources. SAS/Assist, for example, is itself a SAS/AF application.

Both the SAS/FSP product and the SAS/AF product come with a programming language component called *Screen Control Language*, SCL for short. Using SCL, developers can create routines that work together with FSP or AF procedures to produce sophisticated applications. If you wish to use FSP (or AF) to its fullest, you should get the separately-published documentation for Screen Control Language as well as the product documentation.

SAS/EIS® software offers the promise of "executive information systems" from within the SAS System. It facilitates the development of applications that include familiar EIS user facilities such as "drill-down," what-if analyses, variance reporting, and graphic quantity displays to be developed around SAS data. An EIS application is embedded as a SAS/Assist subcomponent.

Connectivity

SAS/Access® family of products provides SAS programs the ability to read and write data from non-SAS application systems. For example, SAS/Access-DB2 software, which interacts with IBM's mainframe database manager DB2, provides methods for creating and querying DB2 tables, for converting DB2 tables to SAS data files, and for passing SQL queries to DB2. Several other SAS/Access products are available, depending on your operating system.

SAS/Connect® software provides intersystem connectivity for SAS users: ways to communicate between a SAS session running on one computer and one on another (host) computer. Using SAS/Connect, a user may access data or programs on a remote system, or upload and download programs or data.

SAS/SHARE® software offers a way for multiple users to have shared write access to SAS data libraries. A systems administrator implements the software with different methods and levels of access to preserve data integrity, after which end users can access shared datasets for updating as well as reading.

Index

\# line pointer control, 46

$, to designate character value, 38

@ column pointer control, 45

(tilde), as format modifier, 43

&, as a list input specifier, 38

\+ column pointer control, 45

@, trailing
  INPUT statement, 36, 57–9
  PUT statement, 408, 416

/ line pointer control, 46

:, as format modifier, 43

=* operator (WHERE expressions), 123, 347

? INPUT specifier, 155

? operator (WHERE expressions), 122

?? INPUT specifier, 155

@@, trailing
  INPUT statement, 36, 59–60
  PUT statement, 408, 416

ABS function, 356

access descriptor, 9

access engines, 5

AGE statement, PROC DATASETS, 326

ALL, 409

ALTLOG= system option, 539

ALTPRINT= system option, 540

APPEND procedure, 332–3

arguments, function, 355

array processing, 389f

ARRAY statement, 389–91, 396

arrays, declaring, 389–91, 392–98

arrays, explicitly subscripted, 390
  DIM function, 394
  HBOUND function, 395
  LBOUND function, 395
  subscript ranges, 394

arrays, implicitly subscripted, 390, 396–7
  DO OVER statement, 397

arrays, initial values, 392–3

arrays, multidimensional, 393

arrays, temporary, 397–8

arrays, using, 391

$ASCII format, 232

$ASCII informat, 159

Assignment statement, 15, 55–6

ATTRIB statement, 64–5

attributes, of variables, 60–65
  altering, 76
  set at DATA Step compile, 65

attributes, variable
  altered for PROC step, 97

autocall macros, 545

autoexec file, 544

AUTOEXEC= invocation option, 544

BAND function, 359

bar charts, 281–9

Base SAS, Base SAS Software
  see Base software
Base software, 4–6
batch execution, 10
batch language
  PROC REPORT, 300
BEST format, 229
BETWEEN-AND operator (WHERE expressions), 122,
  347
BINARY format, 230
$BINARY format, 233
BINARY informat, 158
bit-test comparisons, 183
BITS informat, 158
bitwise operations, functions for, 359
block charts, 289
BNOT function, 359
BOR function, 359
%BQUOTE macro function, 520
BREAK statement, PROC REPORT, 310
breakpoints, PROC REPORT output, 307–11
BXOR function, 359
BY groups
  and SAS procedures, 113f
  FIRST.by and LAST.by variables, 192
  missing, with MERGE, 192
  several, with MERGE, 192
  with UPDATE, 216
BY statement, 68, 86
  placement in DATA step, 92
  with MERGE, 90, 192f
  with MODIFY, 220
  with PROC CORR, 260
  with PROC SUMMARY, 185
  with PROC TABULATE, 278
  with PROC TRANSPOSE, 350
  with PROC UNIVARIATE, 263
  with SET, 88
  with UPDATE, 214
BY variables
  in titles, 114
#BYLINE keyword in TITLE statement, 114, 539
BYLINE system option, 539
#BYVAL keyword in TITLE statement, 114, 539
#BYVAR keyword in TITLE statement, 114, 539
BZ informat, 157

CAPS system option, 540
CARDIMAGE system option, 541
CARDS statement, 33–5
CARDS4 statement, 35
CASE construct, PROC SQL query, 343
CATALOG procedure, 329–32
catalogs, SAS

  see SAS catalogs
CEIL function, 356
CENTER system option, 94, 539
CHANGE statement, PROC CATALOG, 332
CHANGE statement, PROC DATASETS, 326
$CHAR format, 232
character formats, 231–3
character functions, 360–68
character search, functions for, 364–3
CHARCODE system option, 540
CHART procedure, 279–94
  options, 280
CLASS statement, PROC SUMMARY, 177f
  and the _TYPE_ variable, 179, 180
CLASS statement, PROC TABULATE, 277
CLASS statement, PROC TIMEPLOT, 299–300
CMDMAC system option, 542
CNTLIN= option, PROC FORMAT, 256
CNTLOUT= option, PROC FORMAT, 255
code generation, 464f
code reduction, 454
column attributes, PROC SQL, 344
column input, 36–8
  blanks in, 37
  decimal places in, 37
column pointer, 44
  control of, INPUT statement, 45
COLUMN statement, PROC REPORT, 303
COLUMN= option, FILE statement, 417
combining observations, 189f
  with multiple SET statements, 208f
COMMA format, 230
COMMA informat, 159
comma-delimited input, 41
comment statement, 26
comments, Macro Language, 478
comments, SAS, 26–7, 134
  delimited, 26
  statement-style, 26
COMPARE procedure, 333–5
  output dataset, 335
COMPBL function, 367
compiled DATA Step programs, 549–51
compiled macros, 551–2
%COMPRESS autocall macro, 546
COMPRESS function, 367
COMPRESS= dataset option, 547
compressed SAS files, 547
COMPSTOR autocall macro, 552
COMPUTE groups, PROC REPORT, 311–14
COMPUTE statement, PROC REPORT, 312
COMPUTED usage, PROC REPORT, 311
computed values, PROC REPORT, 311–14
concatenating datasets
  with PROC APPEND, 332

concatenating SAS datasets, 78
conditional action, 375–9
CONFIG= invocation option, 544
configuration file, 544
CONTENTS procedure, 316–19
  output dataset, 319
CONTENTS statement, PROC CATALOG, 330
CONTENTS statement, PROC DATASETS, 327
CONTINUE statement
  in DO group, 388
control datasets with PROC FORMAT, 254–6
control, transfer of, 398–405
COPY procedure, 324
COPY statement, PROC CATALOG, 331
COPY statement, PROC DATASETS, 328
CORR procedure, 259–62
  output datasets, 262
  output statistics, 261–2
CREATE TABLE, PROC SQL, 348
crosstabulation
  via PROC REPORT, 306
custom output, 406f
custom reports, 416f
  and output datasets, 422
  full-page access, 423

DATA statement, 30f
  multiple datasets, 51
  naming datasets on, 31
DATA Step
  and Macro Language, 522f
DATA step, 11
  iteration, 47–8, 51
Data Step Language, 5
DATA Step programs, compiled, 549–51
DATA Step view, 8
DATA Step views, 546
data verification, 333
DATA= statement option, 95
DATALINES statement, 34
dataset indexes
  building with PROC DATASETS, 328
dataset options, 74–6
  on DATA statement, 75
datasets, SAS
  see SAS datasets
DATASETS procedure, 324–29
  LIBRARY= option, 325
  RUN groups, 325
DATE format, 235
DATE function, 370
DATE informat, 161
DATE system option, 539
date/time constants, 161

date/time formats, 233–7
date/time functions, 161, 369–72
date/time informats, 160
date/time intervals, 371
date/time values
  arithmetic with, 160
date/time values, converting, 370
date/time values, creating, 369
DATEJUL function, 369
DATEPART function, 371
DATETIME format, 236
DATETIME function, 370
DATETIME informat, 161
DAY format, 235
DAY function, 370
DDMMYY format, 234
DDMMYY informat, 161
DDname, 32
debugging
  macros, 490
DEFINE statement, PROC REPORT, 303
  options, 307
DELETE procedure, 320
DELETE statement, 49
DELETE statement, PROC CATALOG, 331
DELETE statement, PROC DATASETS, 326
delimiter, list input, 40
DELIMITER= option (INFILE stmt), 40
DEQUOTE function, 367
DESCENDING option, PROC SUMMARY, 186
descriptive statistics
  PROC CORR, 261–2
DHMS function, 369
DIM function, 394
direct access to observations, 168f
Display Manager System (DMS), 10
DISPLAY usage, PROC REPORT definition, 304
dividing observations, 188–9
DKRICOND= system option, 542
DKROCOND= system option, 542
DO groups, 379–89
  breaking out of, 388
  expression-conditional, 383
  implicitly subscripted arrays, 397
  infinite, 389
  iterative, 380–84
  nested, 385–8
%DO groups, Macro Language, 482–4
DO OVER statement, 397
DO statement, 379
DOLLAR format, 231
DOWNAME format, 235
DROP statement, 53–5, 73
  with MERGE, 82
DROP= dataset option

DROP= dataset option (*continued*)
   on DATA statement, 75
   with MERGE, 82
   with SET, 74
DROPOVER option, FILE statement, 408
DSD= option (INFILE stmt), 41

E format, 229
E informat, 158
$EBCDIC format, 232
$EBCDIC informat, 159
ELSE statement, 52
END statement, DO group, 379, 387
END statement, SELECT group, 377
end-of-file, detecting with INFILE, 148
end-of-volume, detecting with INFILE, 149
END= option, INFILE statement, 148
END= option, SET statement, 174–5
EOF= option, INFILE statement, 150
EOV= option, INFILE statement, 149
error notes, in SAS log, 130
errors, macro, 490
errors, SAS, 28–9
   compile-time, 28
   logic, 29
   Macro Language, 28
   run-time, 29
ERRORS= system option, 155, 542
ERROR, 68, 153, 155
%EVAL macro function, 468, 485, 486
EXCHANGE statement, PROC CATALOG, 332
EXCLUDE statement
   with PROC FORMAT, 252
EXCLUDE statement, PROC COPY, 324
executable statements, 17
EXECUTE routine, 532–4
EXISTS operator (SQL WHERE expressions), 347
explicitly subscripted arrays, 390
expression-conditional DO groups, 383
expressions, Macro Language, 467
expressions, SAS, 23–4
external files, 33, 408f

FILE statement, 406–8, 416
FILENAME statement, 35
fileref, 35
FIRST.by variables
   with MERGE, 192, 201
FIRSTOBS= option, 147
FIRSTOBS= system option, 541
FLOOR function, 356
flow of control, 375f
   at input end-of-file, 150
   conditional action, 375–9
   repeated action, 379f
FLOWOVER option, FILE statement, 407
FLOWOVER option, INFILE statement, 153
FMTLIB option, PROC FORMAT, 252
FMTSEARCH= system option, 546
FOOTNOTEn statement, 96
footnotes, 96
format catalogs, 248
format identifiers, 20
format libraries, 243
format modifiers
   on INPUT statement, 42–3
FORMAT procedure, 242f
FORMAT statement, PROC DATASETS, 328
FORMAT statement, PROC TABULATE, 277
format, of variables, 64
formats, SAS
   see SAS formats
   see also user-defined formats
   see also under individual format names
formats, user-defined
   see user-defined formats
formatted input, 42
formatted values, 226
formatting functions, 372–4
FORMCHAR= system option, 540
FORMS procedure, 335–7
forms, printing, 335
FRACT format, 230
FREQ procedure, 102–110
   MISSING option, 107
   missing values, 139
   MISSPRINT option, 107
   NOFREQ option, 107
   ORDER= option, 109
   OUT= option, 110
   output datasets, 110
   TABLES statement, 102
   WEIGHT statement, 109
FREQ statement, PROC CORR, 260
FREQ statement, PROC MEANS, 112
FREQ statement, PROC SUMMARY, 186
FREQ statement, PROC UNIVARIATE, 263
FREQ variable, PROC SUMMARY output, 177
FROM clause, PROC SQL query, 339
FSBROWSE procedure, 560
FSEDIT procedure, 560
FSLETTER procedure, 561
FSLIST procedure, 561
FSVIEW procedure, 560
full-page access, 423
FULLSTATS system option, 538
FULLSTIMER system option, 538
function term, 355

function terms, 22–3
functions, Macro Language, 467, 485
functions, SAS
   see SAS functions
   see also under individual function names

GOTO statement, 399–402
%GOTO statement, 484
GROUP BY, PROC SQL query, 345
GROUP usage, PROC REPORT definition, 305–6

HAVING clause, PROC SQL query, 345
HBOUND function, 395
HEADER= option, FILE statement, 417, 419
HEX format, 230
$HEX format, 233
HEX informat, 158
HHMM format, 236
HMS function, 369
HOUR format, 236
HOUR function, 370

IB informat, 158
ID statement, PROC PRINT, 99–100
ID statement, PROC SUMMARY, 186
ID statement, PROC TIMEPLOT, 300
ID statement, PROC TRANSPOSE, 350
ID statement, PROC UNIVARIATE, 263–5
IDLABEL statement, PROC TRANSPOSE, 351
%IF and %IF-%THEN, 468
IF statement (subsetting), 48–9, 73, 167, 376
   contrasted with WHERE, 167
%IF-%THEN-%ELSE group, 479
IF-THEN statement, 52
IF-THEN-ELSE group, 52, 376
implicitly subscripted arrays, 390
IMPLMAC system option, 542
in-stream data, 33
IN= dataset option
   IN= variables, 192
   with MERGE, 84, 90, 192
   with SET, 79–81
IN= variables
   with MERGE, 201, 204
INDEX CREATE statement, PROC DATASETS, 328
INDEX DELETE statement, PROC DATASETS, 328
INDEX function, 362
%INDEX macro function, 487
INDEXC function, 364
indexed datasets, 174
indexed SAS datasets, 548–9
INDEXW function, 363

INFILE statement, 35–6
   end-of-file processing, 148
   end-of-volume processing, 149
   options and variations, 146f
   selecting records, 146
INFILE, 126
infinite DO groups, 389
INFORMAT statement, 64, 157
INFORMAT statement, PROC DATASETS, 328
informat, of variables, 64
information notes, in SAS log, 129
informats, SAS
   see SAS informats
   see also user-defined informats
   see also under individual informat names
informats, user-defined
   see user-defined informats
INITSTMT= invocation option, 544
input buffer, 44
INPUT function, 373
input specifications, 36
input stack, 456
INPUT statement, 36, 47
   column and line pointers, 43–46
   grouped specifications, 153–5
   holding records for repeated INPUT, 57–60
   invalid data, 155
   releasing a held line, 60
   trailing @, 57–9
   trailing @@, 59–60
%INPUT statement, 488
input, column, 36–8
input, comma-delimited, 41
input, formatted, 42
input, list, 38–41
INPUTC function, 374
INPUTN function, 374
INT function, 173, 356
INTCK function, 371
interactive execution, 10
interleaving SAS datasets, 88
INTNX function, 372
invalid data, 143
   in input data, 155
INVALIDDATA= system option, 541
INVALUE statement, PROC FORMAT, 163–5
invalues, in PROC FORMAT, 164
IS NULL operator, (SQL WHERE expressions, 347
iterative DO groups, 380–84

JULDATE function, 370

KEEP statement, 53–5, 73
   with MERGE, 82

KEEP= dataset option, 189
  on DATA statement, 75
  with MERGE, 82
  with SET, 74
KEY= option, MODIFY statement, 217
KEY= option, SET statement, 174
KEYLABEL statement, PROC TABULATE, 277
KURTOSIS function, 359

LABEL statement, 63
  with PROC REPORT, 303
LABEL statement, PROC DATASETS, 328
LABEL statement, PROC TABULATE, 277
labels, of variables, 63
LAST.by variables
  with MERGE, 192, 201
LBOUND function, 395
  LEAVE statement
  in DO group, 388
in SELECT group, 379
%LEFT autocall macro, 545
LEFT function, 362
LENGTH function, 362
%LENGTH macro function, 487
LENGTH statement, 62–3
length, of variables, 61–2
%LET statement, 461
libname, 10
LIBNAME statement, 32–3
LIBRARY= option, PROC FORMAT, 243, 252
libref, 31
LIKE operator (WHERE expressions), 123
line pointer, 44
  control of, INPUT statement, 46
LINE= option, FILE statement, 417
LINESIZE= option, FILE statement, 416
LINESIZE= option, INFILE statement, 148
LINESIZE= system option, 539
LINESLEFT= option, FILE statement, 416, 419
LINK statement, 403–5
list input, 38–41
  field delimiter, 40
  variable order, 39
LIST statement, 126
literals, 20
LL= option, FILE statement, 416, 419
LOG function, 356
LOG10 function, 356
LOG= system option, 539
LOWCASE function, 366
LS= option, FILE statement, 416
LS= system option, 539

macro debugging, 490

macro errors, 490
macro execution, 464f
Macro facility, 5
macro facility, 455f
  as string processor, 457
Macro Language
  statements, 466
  %DO groups, 482–4
  and DATA Step, 522f
  comments, 478
  expressions, 467
  functions, 467, 485
  quoting, 511f
  unquoting, 520–22
macro parameters, 463, 473–8
macro programming, 466f
%MACRO statement, 462
  options, 463
macro variables, 458f
  automatic (system), 511
  concatenated reference, 501
  delayed reference, 505
  indirect reference, 502–5
  reference environments, 506–11
  resolution of, 464, 501
macros
  and SAS job flow, 465
  autocall, 545
  for code reduction, 454
macros, compiled, 551–2
match-merge, 192
mathematical functions, 356
MAUTOSOURCE system option, 545
MAX function, 358
MAXID option, PROC SUMMARY, 186
MDY function, 369
MEAN function, 358
MEANS procedure, 110–113
  and PROC SUMMARY, 111
  FREQ statement, 112
  statistics, 111
  WEIGHT statement, 112
  see also SUMMARY procedure
%MEND statement, 462
MERGE statement, 47, 81f
  match-merge, 192
MERROR system option, 542
MIN function, 358
MINID option, PROC SUMMARY, 187
MINUTE function, 370
MISSING option
  PROC FREQ, 140
MISSING system option, 139
missing values, 137f
  and PROC SUMMARY, 180

and SAS procedures, 139f
by assignment, 139
character type, 144
comparison of, 142
generated by DATA step, 143
in input data, 138, 151–2
operations on, 144
PROC FREQ, 139
propagation of, 144
special, 141–2
MISSING= system option, 540
MISSOVER option, INFILE statement, 152
MLOGIC system option, 495
MMDDYY format, 234
MMDDYY informat, 161
MMSS format, 236
MOD function, 356
MODIFY processing, 217f
    distinguished from SET, MERGE, UPDATE, 217
MODIFY statement, 217
    BY processing, 220
MODIFY statement, PROC DATASETS, 328
modifying datasets in-place, 217f
MONNAME format, 235
MONTH format, 235
MONTH function, 370
MONYY format, 235
MONYY informat, 161
MPRINT system option, 494
MRECALL system option, 545
MSTORE system option, 551
multidimensional arrays, 393
multiple engine architecture, 5
MVS, 32

N function, 358
N= option, FILE statement, 416, 423
N=PS, FILE statement, 423
named input, 156
names, reserved, 18
names, SAS, 18
NAME variable, PROC CORR output, 262
NAME variable, PROC TRANSPOSE output, 350
nested DO groups, 385–8
    END statement in, 387
NMISS function, 358
NO-prefixed SAS system options
    generally see "positive"-form entry, for example see
        NOTES, not NONOTES
NOBS= option, MODIFY statement, 217
NOBS= option, SET statement, 172
NOBYLINE system option, 116
NODSNFERR system option, 542
NOFMTERR system option, 542

nonexecutable statements, 17
nonprintable characters, 159
NOTES system option, 494
NOTITLES option, FILE statement, 417
NOVNFERR system option, 542
%NRBQUOTE macro function, 520
%NRQUOTE macro function, 520
%NRSTR macro function, 516
NUMBER system option, 539
numeric formats, 227–31
numeric functions, 356–60
_N_, 68

OBS= option, 147
OBS= system option, 541
OBS=0, 541
observations, 6
    combining, with MERGE, 81
OCTAL format, 230
$OCTAL format, 233
OCTAL informat, 158
one-to-one merge, 190–1
operators, 20–22
    comparison, 21
    logical, 21
    numeric, 21
options
    see SAS system options
    see dataset options
    see statement options
    see also under individual option names
options, procedure-specific
    see under individual procedure names
OPTIONS procedure, 543
OPTIONS statement, 32
OPTIONS= invocation option, 544
ORDER BY, PROC SQL query, 342
ORDER usage, PROC REPORT definition, 304
OTHERWISE statement, SELECT group, 377
output dataset, PROC COMPARE, 335
output dataset, PROC CONTENTS, 319
output datasets
    CORR procedure, 262
    UNIVARIATE procedure, 263
OUTPUT statement
    with MODIFY, 221–5
OUTPUT statement, DATA step, 50–51, 97–8
OUTPUT statement, PROC SUMMARY, 184–5
output, custom, 406f
OVP system option, 539

PAGE statement, 133
PAGEBY statement, PROC PRINT, 115

PAGENO= system option, 539
PAGESIZE= option, FILE statement, 416
PAGESIZE= system option, 539
PAGE, 417
panels, PROC REPORT output, 311
parameters, macro, 463, 473–8
PD informat, 158
PDV, 67, 78
  during step iteration, 69
PERCENT format, 230
PERCENT informat, 158, 159
PGM= option, DATA statement, 546
PIB informat, 158
PICTURE statement, PROC FORMAT, 248–52
pie charts, 289–94
PK informat, 158
  PLOT procedure, 101–2
PLOT statement, 102
PLOT statement, PROC PLOT, 102
PLOT statement, PROC TIMEPLOT, 296–9
POINT= option, MODIFY statement, 217
POINT= option, SET statement, 170, 173
preprocessor, macro
  see Macro Facility
print files, 407
PRINT option, PROC SUMMARY, 176
PRINT procedure, 94, 98–101, 115f
  ID statement, 99–100
  LABEL option, 101
  NOOBS option, 99
  PAGEBY statement, 115
  ROUND option, 101
  SUM statement, 101
  UNIFORM option, 101
PRINT= system option, 540
PROC REPORT
  breakpoints, 307–11
PROC statement, 95
PROC step, 11
procedure options
  see under individual procedure names
procedures, SAS
  see SAS procedures
  see also under individual procedure names
program data vector
  see PDV
PS= option, FILE statement, 416
PS= system option, 539
PUT function, 372
PUT statement, 416
  trailing @, 408, 416
  trailing @@, 408, 416
  writing to the SAS log, 130
%PUT statement, 479, 488
PUT _ALL_, 409

PUT _INFILE_, 126
PUT _PAGE_, 417
PUTC function, 374
PUTN function, 374

%QCMPRESS autocall macro, 546
%QLEFT autocall macro, 546
QPRINT procedure, 300
%QSCAN macro function, 488
%QSUBSTR macro function, 488
QTR function, 370
%QTRIM autocall macro, 546
$QUOTE format, 233
QUOTE function, 367
$QUOTE informat, 159
%QUOTE macro function, 519
quoting, Macro Language, 511f
%QUPCASE macro function, 488

random selection, 172–4
RANGE function, 358
RANUNI function, 173
RB informat, 158
RBREAK statement, PROC REPORT, 310
REDIRECT statement, 550
REMOVE statement
  with MODIFY, 221–3
RENAME statement, 74
RENAME statement, PROC DATASETS, 328
RENAME= dataset option
  on DATA statement, 75
  with SET, 74
repeated action, 379f
REPLACE statement
  with MODIFY, 221–3
REPORT procedure, 300–14
  and PROC PRINT, 302
  computed values, 311
  output panels, 311
  PROC SQL compared, 345
  usage definitions, 303
reports, custom, 416f
  and output datasets, 422
  full-page access, 423
RESOLVE function, 531–2
RETAIN statement, 69
RETURN statement, 399
  with GOTO, 402
  with LINK, 403
RIGHT function, 361
ROMAN format, 231
ROUND function, 356
rounding functions, 356

RUN groups, 28
  PROC DATASETS, 325
RUN statement, 27–8

S2= system option, 541
S= system option, 541
SAME AND operator (WHERE expressions), 123
SAS catalog, 9
SAS catalogs
  changing member names in, 332
  copying members of, 331
  deleting members of, 331
  listing directory of, 330
  management of, 329f
SAS code
  style guidelines, 24–8
SAS comments
  see comments, SAS
SAS data file, 7
SAS data files
  compressed files, 547
SAS data view, 7–8, 8
  types of, 8
SAS dataset, 6
  naming on statements, 31
  observations, 6
  variables, 6
SAS dataset variables
  see variables
SAS dataset observations
  see observations
SAS dataset options
  see dataset options
  see also under individual option names
SAS datasets
  combining observations of, 189f
  concatenating with SET, 78–9
  creating more than one, 84f
  direct access to, 168f
  dividing observations of, 188–9
  indexed, 174
  indexed datasets, 548–9
  interleaving, 88
  modifying in-place, 217f
  not changed by rebuilding, 66
  repairing damage to, 329
  transposing, 348–51
SAS documentation, 553–7
SAS errors
  see errors, SAS
SAS files, 9
  SAS dataset, 6
SAS formats, 64
  character, 231–3

character formats, 226
data conversion, 230
date/time, 233–7
financial, 230–31
numeric, 227–31
numeric formats, 226
see also user-defined formats
see also under individual format names
SAS functions, 355f
  date/time, 369–72
  for formatting, 372–4
  mathematical, 356
  numeric functions, 356–60
  rounding, 356
  statistical, 357–9
  trigonometric, 356
  see also under individual function names
SAS functions, character, 360–68
SAS informats, 64, 157f
  character, 159
  for data conversion, 158
  for dates and times, 160
  for financial notation, 159
  numeric 157–9
  see also user-defined formats
  see also under individual informat names
SAS job, 11–13
SAS libraries
  changing attributes in, 328
  changing member names in, 326
  copying members of, 324, 328
  deleting members of, 320, 326
  listing contents of, 316, 327
  listing directory of, 316
  management of, 316f
SAS library, 9–10
SAS log, 124f
  components of, 126–130
  error notes in, 130
  information notes in, 129
  macro expansions in, 130
  user notes in, 130f
  warning notes in, 129
SAS macro facility
  see macro facility
SAS observations
  see observations
SAS procedure options
  see under individual procedures
SAS procedures, 5
  see also under individual procedure names
SAS sample library, 557
SAS software consultant, 557
SAS statement options
  see statement options

SAS statement options (*continued*)
  see also under individual option names
SAS statements, 14–24, 15, 17, 18, 20, 25
  executable vs nonexecutable, 17
  expressions in, 23–4
  format identifiers in, 20
  function terms in, 22–3
  literals in, 20
  modifiers, 17–18
  names in, 18
  naming datasets on, 27
  operators in, 20–22
  spacing, 15, 25
  statement domain, 17
  statement labels, 20
  syntax used in this book, 15–16
  see also under individual statment names
SAS supervisor, 4
SAS system
  configuration, 544
SAS system options, 538–43
  see also under individual option names note: "toggle"
    options are normally indexed under their positive
    form: for example, look for NOTES, not NONOTES.
SAS variables
  see variables
SAS usage notes, 557
SAS/Access software, 561
SAS/AF software, 561
SAS/Assist software, 559
SAS/Connect software, 561
SAS/EIS software, 561
SAS/ETS software, 559
SAS/FSP software, 560
SAS/Graph software, 560
SAS/IML software, 559
SAS/INSIGHT software, 559
SAS/LAB software, 559
SAS/OR software, 559
SAS/QC software, 559
SAS/SHARE software, 561
SAS/STAT software, 558
SASAUTOS= invocation option, 545
SASLIB= invocation option, 546
SASMACR catalog, 552
SASMSTORE= system option, 551
SAVE statement, PROC CATALOG, 331
SCAN function, 365
%SCAN macro function, 487
SECOND function, 370
SELECT clause, PROC SQL query, 339
  setting column attributes, 344
SELECT group, 376–9
SELECT statement, 377
  with PROC FORMAT, 252

SELECT statement, PROC COPY, 324
semicolon, 14
  as statement delimiter, 14
SERROR system option, 542
SET statement, 47, 70f
  multiple SET statements, 208f
SKEWNESS function, 359
SKIP statement, 133
SORT procedure, 86
SORTEDBY= dataset option, 86
  PROC DATASETS, 328
sorting dataset observations, 86
SOURCE and SOURCE2 system options, 538
special missing values, 141
  in input data, 142
SQL procedure, 337f
  computed values, 342–3
  creating new tables, 348
  ordering rows, 341–2
  PROC REPORT compared, 345
  query on multiple tables, 347
  query, defined, 339
  row grouping, 345
  row selection, 345
  selecting rows, 340
SQRT function, 356
SSN format, 231
star charts, 294
statement labels, 20
statements, Macro Language, 466
statements, SAS
  see SAS statements
  see also under individual statement names
statistical functions, 357–9
STD function, 358
STDERR function, 358
STIMER system option, 538
STOP statement, 386
STOPOVER option, INFILE statement, 153, 408
STORE option, %MACRO statement, 551
stored program, 9
%STR macro function, 488, 514–16
string processing
  using macro facility, 457
string search, functions for, 362–3
SUBSTR function, 367–8
%SUBSTR macro function, 487
SUM function, 357
Sum statement, 69
SUM statement, PROC PRINT, 101
SUM usage, PROC REPORT definition, 306
SUMMARY procedure, 176f
  and PROC MEANS, 176
  missing values, 180
%SUPERQ macro function, 520

symbol table, 508
symbol table, macro facility, 459
SYMBOLGEN system option, 494
SYMGET function, 526–31
SYMPUT routine, 522–6
SYSBUFFR macro variable, 489
%SYSEXEC statement, 490
SYSIN= invocation option, 545
SYSPARM function, 543
SYSPARM macro variable, 543
system options
    see SAS system options
    see also under individual option names

TABLES statement, PROC FREQ, 102
TABLES statement, PROC TABULATE, 273–6
TABULATE procedure, 265–78
    as alternative to FREQ, 109
    examples, 265–73
    options, 276
temporary arrays, 397–8
TEMPORARY, 398
time
    see date/time
TIME format, 236
TIME function, 370
TIME informat, 161
TIMEPART function, 371
TIMEPLOT procedure, 294–300
TITLE statement, 94
    null, 95
TITLEn statement, 96
titles, 96
    suppressing at PUT, 417
TOD format, 237
tokens, 456
transfer of control, 398–405
TRANSLATE function, 366
TRANSPOSE procedure, 348–51
TRANWRD function, 366
trigonometric functions, 356
%TRIM autocall macro, 546
TRIM function, 360
TRIMN function, 361
TRUNCOVER option, INFILE statement, 152
type, of variables, 60
    conversion of, 61
TYPE variable, PROC CORR output, 262
TYPE variable, PROC SUMMARY output, 177f
    and the CLASS statement, 179, 180
    bit-test comparisons, 183

UNIVARIATE procedure, 262–5

output datasets, 263
unquoting, Macro Language, 520–22
$UPCASE format, 232
UPCASE function, 366
$UPCASE informat, 159
%UPCASE macro function, 487
UPDATE statement, 47, 214f
    distinguished from MERGE, 214f
updating observations, 214f
user-defined formats, 237f
    format libraries, 243
    uses for, 237–42
user-defined informats, 161f
    created with FORMAT procedure, 162
    FORMAT procedure, 162f
    types, 162
    vs SAS informats, 162
USER= system option, 32

value grouping, 242
value labeling, 239–41
VALUE statement, PROC FORMAT, 244–8
values, formatted, 226
VAR function, 358
VAR statement, 95–6
    with PROC TRANSPOSE, 350
VAR statement, PROC CORR, 260
VAR statement, PROC TABULATE, 277
VAR statement, PROC UNIVARIATE, 263
variable
    dropping or keeping, 73
variable attributes, 60
    altered for PROC step, 97
    altering, 76
    set at DATA Step compile, 65
variable labels, 63
variable length, 61–2
variable lists, 19
variable type, 60
    conversion of, 61
variables, 6
    adding with SET, 71
    altering values, 72
    automatic variables, 68
    renaming, 74
    reordering, 76
    selection using DROP, KEEP, 53–5
    variable lists, 19
variables, format of, 64
variables, informat of, 64
variables, macro
    see macro variables
$VARYING format, 232
$VARYING informat, 159

VERBOSE system option, 125, 543
%VERIFY autocall macro, 546
VERIFY function, 364
views
    DATA Step views, 546

$w. format, 232
w.d format, 227
w.d informat, 157
warning notes, in SAS log, 129
WEEKDATE format, 235
WEEKDATX format, 236
WEEKDAY format, 235
WEEKDAY function, 370
WEIGHT statement, PROC CORR, 260
WEIGHT statement, PROC FREQ, 109
WEIGHT statement, PROC MEANS, 112
WEIGHT statement, PROC UNIVARIATE, 263
WHEN expression
    in SELECT group, 377
WHEN statement, SELECT group, 377
WHERE clause, PROC SQL query, 341
WHERE expressions
    joining with SAME AND, 123
    special operators, 122–123
    to select observations, 119f

WHERE processing (DATA step)
    efficiency of, 167
WHERE statement, 119
    contrasted with subsetting IF, 167
WHERE= dataset option, 119, 167
WITH statement, PROC CORR, 260
word queue, 456
WORDDATE format, 235
WORDDATX format, 236
WORDF format, 231
WORDS format, 231
wordscanner, 456
WORK= system option, 32

YEAR format, 235
YEAR function, 370
YYMMDD format, 235
YYMMDD informat, 161
YYQ format, 235
YYQ function, 369
YYQ informat, 161

Z format, 229
ZD informat, 158